PEARSON

# Literature

GRADE 7

PEARSON

HOBOKEN, NEW JERSEY • BOSTON, MASSACHUSETTS
CHANDLER, ARIZONA • GLENVIEW, ILLINOIS

**COVER:** Mikhail P./Shutterstock.com

Acknowledgements appear in the back of this book, and constitute an extension of this copyright page.

ISBN-13: 978-0-13-331981-1
ISBN-10: 0-13-331981-4
5 17

PEARSON

# Literature

GRADE 7

PEARSON

HOBOKEN, NEW JERSEY • BOSTON, MASSACHUSETTS
CHANDLER, ARIZONA • GLENVIEW, ILLINOIS

# Contributing Authors

*The contributing authors guided the direction and philosophy of* Pearson Literature. *They helped to build the pedagogical integrity of the program by contributing content expertise, knowledge of learning standards, and support for the shifts in instruction that are necessary for college and career readiness. Their knowledge, combined with classroom and professional experience, ensures that* Pearson Literature *is relevant for both teachers and students.*

**William G. Brozo, Ph.D.,** is a Professor of Literacy in the Graduate School of Education at George Mason University in Fairfax, Virginia. He earned his bachelor's degree from the University of North Carolina and his master's and doctorate from the University of South Carolina. He has taught reading and language arts in the Carolinas and is the author of numerous articles on literacy development for children and young adults. His books include *To Be a Boy, To Be a Reader: Engaging Teen and Preteen Boys in Active Literacy; Readers, Teachers, Learners: Expanding Literacy Across the Content Areas; Content Literacy for Today's Adolescents: Honoring Diversity and Building Competence; Supporting Content Area Literacy with Technology* (Pearson); and *Setting the Pace: A Speed, Comprehension, and Study Skills Program*. His newest book is *RTI and the Adolescent Reader: Responsive Literacy Instruction in Secondary Schools*. As an international consultant, Dr. Brozo has provided technical support to teachers from the Balkans to the Middle East, and he is currently a member of a European Union research grant team developing curriculum and providing adolescent literacy professional development for teachers across Europe.

**Diane Fettrow** spent the majority of her teaching career in Broward County, Florida, teaching high school English courses and serving as department chair. She also worked as an adjunct instructor at Broward College, Nova Southeastern University, and Florida Atlantic University. After she left the classroom, she served as Secondary Language Arts Curriculum Supervisor for several years, working with more than 50 of the district's high schools, centers, and charter schools. During her time as curriculum supervisor, she served on numerous local and state committees; she also served as Florida's K–12 ELA content representative to the PARCC Model Content Frameworks Rapid Response Feedback Group and the PARCC K–12 and Upper Education Engagement Group. Currently she presents workshops on the Common Core State Standards and is working with Pearson on aligning materials to the CCSS.

**Kelly Gallagher** is a full-time English teacher at Magnolia High School in Anaheim, California, where he has taught for twenty-seven years. He is the former co-director of the South Basin Writing Project at California State University, Long Beach, and the author of *Reading Reasons: Motivational Mini-Lessons for Middle and High School; Deeper Reading: Comprehending Challenging Texts, 4–12; Teaching Adolescent Writers;* and *Readicide: How Schools Are Killing Reading and What You Can Do About It*. He is also a principal author of *Prentice Hall Writing Coach* (Pearson, 2012). Kelly's latest book is *Write Like This* (Stenhouse). Follow Kelly on Twitter @KellyGToGo, and visit him at www.kellygallagher.org.

**Elfrieda "Freddy' Hiebert, Ph.D.,** is President and CEO of TextProject, a nonprofit organization that provides resources to support higher reading levels. She is also a research associate at the University of California, Santa Cruz. Dr. Hiebert received her Ph.D. in Educational Psychology from the University of Wisconsin-Madison. She has worked in the field of early reading acquisition for 45 years, first as a teacher's aide and teacher of primary-level students in California and, subsequently, as a teacher educator and researcher at the universities of Kentucky, Colorado-Boulder, Michigan, and California-Berkeley. Her research addresses how fluency, vocabulary, and knowledge can be fostered through appropriate texts. Professor Hiebert's research has been published in numerous scholarly journals, and she has authored or edited nine books. Professor Hiebert's model of accessible texts for beginning and struggling readers—TExT—has been used to develop numerous reading programs that are widely used in schools. Dr. Hiebert is the 2008 recipient of the William S. Gray Citation of Merit, awarded by the International Reading Association; is a member of the Reading Hall of Fame; and has chaired a group of early childhood literacy experts who served in an advisory capacity to the CCSS writers.

**Donald J. Leu, Ph.D.,** is the John and Maria Neag Endowed Chair in Literacy and Technology and holds a joint appointment in Curriculum and Instruction and Educational Psychology in the Neag School of Education at the University of Connecticut. Don is an international authority on literacy education, especially the new skills and strategies required to read, write, and learn with Internet technologies and the best instructional practices that prepare students for these new literacies. He is a member of the Reading Hall of Fame, a Past President of the National Reading Conference, and a former member of the Board of Directors of the International Reading Association. Don is a Principal Investigator on a number of federal research grants, and his work has been funded by the U.S. Department of Education, the National Science Foundation, and the Bill and Melinda Gates Foundation, among others. He recently edited the *Handbook of Research on New Literacies* (Erlbaum, 2008).

**Ernest Morrell, Ph.D.,** is a professor of English Education at Teachers College, Columbia University, and the president-elect of the National Council of Teachers of English (NCTE). He is also the Director of Teachers College's Harlem-based Institute for Urban and Minority Education (IUME). Dr. Morrell was an award-winning high school English teacher in California, and he now works with teachers and schools across the country to infuse multicultural literature, youth popular culture, and media production into standards-based literacy curricula and after-school programs. He is the author of nearly 100 articles and book chapters as well as five books, including *Critical Media Pedagogy: Achievement, Production, and Justice in City Schools* and *Linking Literacy and Popular Culture*. In his spare time he coaches youth sports and writes poems and plays.

**Karen Wixson, Ph.D.,** is Dean of the School of Education at the University of North Carolina, Greensboro. She has published widely in the areas of literacy curriculum, instruction, and assessment. Dr. Wixson has been an advisor to the National Research Council and helped develop the National Assessment of Educational Progress (NAEP) reading tests. She is a former member of the IRA Board of Directors and co-chair of the IRA Commission on RTI. Recently, Dr. Wixson served on the English Language Arts Work Team that was part of the Common Core State Standards Initiative.

**Grant Wiggins, Ed.D.,** is the President of Authentic Education in Hopewell, New Jersey. He earned his Ed.D. from Harvard University and his B.A. from St. John's College in Annapolis. Grant consults with schools, districts, and state education departments on a variety of reform matters; organizes conferences and workshops; and develops print materials and Web resources on curricular change. He is perhaps best known for being the co-author, with Jay McTighe, of *Understanding by Design* and *The Understanding by Design Handbook,* the award-winning and highly successful materials on curriculum published by ASCD.

## INTRODUCTORY UNIT: STUDENT WORKSHOPS

# UNIT 1 Does every conflict have a winner?

PART 1
## SETTING EXPECTATIONS



PART 2
## TEXT ANALYSIS GUIDED EXPLORATION

### DIFFERENT PERSPECTIVES

## PART 3
## TEXT SET DEVELOPING INSIGHT

### COMPETITION



## PART 4
## DEMONSTRATING INDEPENDENCE

### DIGITAL ASSETS KEY

These digital resources, as well as audio and the Online Writer's Notebook, can be found at **pearsonrealize.com.**

- Interactive Whiteboard Activities
- Virtual Tour
- Close Reading Notebook
- Video
- Close Reading Tool for Annotating Texts
- Grammar Tutorials
- Online Text Set

# UNIT 1 Unit at a Glance

## READ

**Text Analysis**
- Plot
- Character and Point of View
- Conflict and Resolution
- Theme
- Comparing Characters
- Conflict
- Structure
- Persuasive Techniques
- Rhetorical Devices

**Comprehension**
- Make Predictions
- Make Inferences

**Language Study**
- Latin suffix *-tion*
- Latin root *-spir-*
- Latin prefix *mal-*
- Latin suffix *-ious*

**Conventions**
- Common, Proper, and Possessive Nouns
- Personal and Possessive Pronouns
- Adjectives and Adverbs
- Comparison of Adjectives and Adverbs

**Language Study Workshop**
- Using a Dictionary and Thesaurus

## DISCUSS

**Presentation of Ideas**
- News Story

**Comprehension and Collaboration**
- Informal Debate

**Responding to Text**
- Group Discussion
- Partner Discussion
- Debate
- Panel Discussion

**Speaking and Listening Workshop**
- Delivering an Oral Summary

## RESEARCH

**Research and Technology**
- Outline
- Poster

**Investigate the Topic: Competition**
- Healthy and Unhealthy Competition
- Mind and Body
- Coaching and Competition
- A Model of Character

## WRITE

**Writing to Sources**
- Informative Article
- Journal Entry
- Anecdote
- Letter to the Author
- Explanatory Essay
- Analytical Essay
- Fictional Narrative
- Argument
- Informative Essay
- Personal Narrative
- Argumentative Essay

**Writing Process Workshop**
- Narration: Autobiographical Narrative
  - Voice: Finding Your Voice
  - Conventions: Checking Pronoun-Antecedent Agreement

## UNIT VOCABULARY

Academic Vocabulary appears in *blue*.

**Introducing the Big Question** *attitude, challenge, communication, competition, compromise, conflict, danger, desire, disagreement, misunderstanding, obstacle, opposition, outcome, resolution, struggle, understanding*

**Rikki-tikki-tavi** *revived, immensely, veranda, mourning, consolation, cunningly*

**Two Kinds *from* The Joy Luck Club** *reproach, conspired, devastated, nonchalantly, expectations, sentimental*

**The Third Wish** *verge, dabbling, presumptuous, rash, remote, malicious*

**Ribbons** *sensitive, meek, coax, laborious, exertion, furrowed*

**The Night the Bed Fell; Stolen Day** *ominous, perilous, culprit, solemn, assumption, common, discover, perspective*

**Amigo Brothers** *devastating, perpetual, evading, effective, literally, communication*

**Get More From Competition** *maximize, optimal, deteriorates, attitude, sufficient, resolution*

**Forget Fun, Embrace Enjoyment** *advocacy, trivialness, endeavors, perceive, explain, cite*

**Video Game Competitiveness, Not Violence, Spurs Aggression, Study Suggests** *aggressive, spur, blunt, experiment, insight*

**Win Some, Lose Some** *aversion, imposters, emerged, attitude, convince*

**Orlando Magic** *illustrate, debate*

# UNIT 2 What should we learn?

PART 1
## SETTING EXPECTATIONS



PART 2
## TEXT ANALYSIS GUIDED EXPLORATION

EXPLORING IDEAS

## PART 3
## TEXT SET DEVELOPING INSIGHT

### MOTIVATION



## PART 4
## DEMONSTRATING INDEPENDENCE

**DIGITAL ASSETS KEY**

These digital resources, as well as audio and the Online Writer's Notebook, can be found at **pearsonrealize.com.**

- Interactive Whiteboard Activities
- Virtual Tour
- Close Reading Notebook
- Video
- Close Reading Tool for Annotating Texts
- Grammar Tutorials
- Online Text Set

# UNIT 2 Unit at a Glance

## READ

**Text Analysis**
- Expository Essay
- Reflective Essay
- Persuasive Essay
- Word Choice, or Diction
- Comparing Fiction and Nonfiction
- Autobiography
- Expository Writing
- Characters
- Biography
- Folk Tales

**Comprehension**
- Main Idea
- Classifying Fact and Opinion

**Language Study**
- Old English suffix *-ness*
- Latin root *-just-*
- Latin root *-leg-*
- Latin root *-sol-*

**Conventions**
- Action Verbs and Linking Verbs
- The Principal Parts of Verbs
- Conjunctions and Interjections
- Simple and Compound Subjects and Predicates

**Language Study Workshop**
- Word Origins

## DISCUSS

**Presentation of Ideas**
- Oral Summary
- Response

**Comprehension and Collaboration**
- Public Service Announcement (PSA)

**Responding to Text**
- Group Discussion
- Partner Discussion
- Small Group Discussion

**Speaking and Listening Workshop**
- Evaluating a Persuasive Presentation

## RESEARCH

**Research and Technology**
- Help-Wanted Ad

**Investigate the Topic: Motivation**
- Goals and Motivation
- Money and Grades
- Klondike Gold Rush
- Snow Crystals
- Tricksters in Folk Tales
- Abraham Maslow

## WRITE

**Writing to Sources**
- Analogy
- Outline
- Persuasive Letter
- Adaptation
- Explanatory Essay
- Persuasive Essay
- Argument
- Fictional Narrative
- Informative Essay
- Folk Tale
- Autobiographical Narrative
- Informative Text

**Writing Process Workshop**
- Argument: Argumentative Essay
  - Conventions: Revising for Correct Verb Tense
  - Sentence Fluency: Revising to Combine Sentences Using Conjunctions

## UNIT VOCABULARY

Academic Vocabulary appears in *blue*.

**Introducing the Big Question** *analyze, curiosity, discover, evaluate, examine, experiment, explore, facts, information, inquire, interview, investigate, knowledge, question, understand*

**Life Without Gravity** *manned, spines, feeble, blander, globules, readapted*

**I Am a Native of North America** *distinct, communal, justifies, promote, hoarding, integration*

**All Together Now** *legislation, tolerant, culminated, fundamental, equality, optimist*

**Rattlesnake Hunt** *adequate, desolate, forage, translucent, arid, mortality*

***from* Barrio Boy; A Day's Wait** *reassuring, contraption, formidable, epidemic, flushed, evidently, adaptation, culture, diversity, tradition*

**No Gumption** *gumption, crucial, aptitude, identify, insight, purpose*

**Intrinsic Motivation Doesn't Exist, Researcher Says** *psychologists, tout, fosters, perceptions, investigate, acknowledge*

**The Cremation of Sam McGee** *cremated, whimper, loathed, images, contribute, outcome*

**A Special Gift—The Legacy of "Snowflake" Bentley** *hexagons, evaporated, negatives, observe, focus, inquiry*

**All Stories Are Anansi's** *dispute, opinion, acknowledge, communicate, contribute, tradition*

**Maslow's Theory of Motivation and Human Needs** *diagram, explain, theory*

# UNIT 3 What is the best way to communicate?

PART 1

## SETTING EXPECTATIONS



PART 2

## TEXT ANALYSIS GUIDED EXPLORATION

### SOUNDS AND IMAGES

**DIGITAL ASSETS KEY**

These digital resources, as well as audio and the Online Writer's Notebook, can be found at **pearsonrealize.com.**

- Interactive Whiteboard Activities
- Virtual Tour
- Close Reading Notebook
- Video
- Close Reading Tool for Annotating Texts
- Grammar Tutorials
- Online Text Set

# UNIT 3 Unit at a Glance

## READ

**Text Analysis**
- Forms of Poetry
- Figurative Language
- Sound Devices
- Comparing Imagery
- Repetition
- Structure
- Diction
- Primary Sources
- Irony
- Author's Viewpoint

**Comprehension**
- Draw Conclusions
- Paraphrase

**Language Study**
- Latin root *-lum-*
- Suffix *-er*
- Old English suffix *-less*
- Old English prefix *un-*

**Conventions**
- Sentence Functions and End Marks
- Independent and Dependent Clauses
- Sentence Structures
- Subject-Verb Agreement

**Language Study Workshop**
- Words With Multiple Meanings

## DISCUSS

**Presentation of Ideas**
- Presentation
- Poetry Reading

**Responding to Text**
- Group Discussion
- Partner Discussion
- Debate

**Speaking and Listening Workshop**
- Evaluating Media Messages and Advertisements

## RESEARCH

**Research and Technology**
- Scientific Explanation
- Survey

**Investigate the Topic: Heroes and Outlaws**
- Heroes and Outlaws in Literature
- Civilization's Heroes
- Outlaws After the Civil War
- Cowboys and Settlers
- Police Heroes
- The Underground Railroad
- Abolitionist Leader

## WRITE

**Writing to Sources**
- Lyric Poem, Concrete Poem, or Haiku
- Metaphor
- Paraphrase
- Poem
- Recommendation
- Character Analysis
- Persuasive Letter
- Argument
- Fictional Narrative
- Expository Essay

**Writing Process Workshop**
- Explanatory Text: Comparison-and-Contrast Essay
  - Ideas: Developing Your Ideas
  - Sentence Fluency: Revising Sentence Structures to Clarify Relationships

## UNIT VOCABULARY

Academic Vocabulary appears in *blue*.

**Introducing the Big Question** *communicate, contribute, enrich, entertain, express, inform, learn, listen, media, produce, react, speak, teach, technology, transmit*

**Poetry Collection 1** *translates, luminous, minnow, swerve, utter, fragrant*

**Poetry Collection 2** *fascinated, granite, crystal, haunches*

**Poetry Collection 3** *groves, fathom, withered, curdled, sputters, smattering*

**Poetry Collection 4** *downy, coveted, envying, incessantly, uncommonly, supple*

**Miracles; in Just—** *exquisite, distinct, appreciate, insight, perceive, unique*

**The Highwayman** *torrent, bound, strove, contrast, identify, opposing*

**Carnegie Hero Fund Commission** *commemorated, prompted, eligible, explain, definition, characteristic*

**The Myth of the Outlaw** *nondescript, repulsive, commissioned, attitude, reflect, viewpoint*

**The Real Story of a Cowboy's Life** *discipline, gauge, emphatic, challenge, attitude, evaluate*

**After Twenty Years** *spectators, intricate, simultaneously, communicate, contradiction, contribute*

**Harriet Tubman** *subjected, feigned, conferred, media, solve, reactions*

**Wanted: Harriet Tubman, Abolitionist** *convincing, facts, conclude*

# UNIT 4 Do others see us more clearly than we see ourselves?

## PART 1
## SETTING EXPECTATIONS



## PART 2
## TEXT ANALYSIS GUIDED EXPLORATION

### DRAMATIC TRANSFORMATIONS

PART 3
## TEXT SET DEVELOPING INSIGHT

### LEADERS AND FOLLOWERS



PART 4
## DEMONSTRATING INDEPENDENCE

**DIGITAL ASSETS KEY**

These digital resources, as well as audio and the Online Writer's Notebook, can be found at **pearsonrealize.com.**

- Interactive Whiteboard Activities
- Virtual Tour
- Close Reading Notebook
- Video
- Close Reading Tool for Annotating Texts
- Grammar Tutorials
- Online Text Set

# UNIT 4 Unit at a Glance

## READ

**Text Analysis**
- Dialogue
- Stage Directions
- Characters' Motives
- Setting
- Main Idea
- Tone
- Author's Argument
- Expository Writing

**Comprehension**
- Purpose for Reading
- Analyze Point of View

**Language Study**
- Latin root *-grat-*
- Latin prefix *inter-*

**Conventions**
- Prepositions and Prepositional Phrases
- Appositives and Appositive Phrases

**Language Study Workshop**
- Connotation and Denotation

## DISCUSS

**Presentation of Ideas**
- Dramatic Monologue

**Responding to Text**
- Panel Discussion
- Partner Discussion
- Debate
- Group Discussion

**Speaking and Listening Workshop**
- Conducting an Interview

## RESEARCH

**Research and Technology**
- Costume Plans

**Investigate the Topic: Leaders and Followers**
- Crowds and Their Actions
- Bullying
- McCarthyism
- Mass Hysteria
- Herd Mentality
- Wisdom of the Crowd
- Memorial to a Leader

## WRITE

**Writing to Sources**
- Letter
- Tribute
- Editorial
- Argumentative Essay
- News Report
- Argument
- Expository Essay
- Autobiographical Narrative

**Writing Process Workshop**
- Argument: Review of a Short Story
  - Word Choice: Finding the Perfect Word
  - Sentence Fluency: Revising Sentences Using Participles

## UNIT VOCABULARY

Academic Vocabulary appears in *blue*.

**Introducing the Big Question** *appearance, appreciate, assumption, bias, characteristic, define, focus, identify, ignore, image, perception, perspective, reaction, reflect, reveal*

**A Christmas Carol: Scrooge and Marley, Act I** *implored, morose, destitute, void, conveyed, gratitude*

**A Christmas Carol: Scrooge and Marley, Act II** *astonish, compulsion, severe, meager, audible, intercedes*

**Zoos: Joys or Jails?; Kid Territory: Why Do We Need Zoos?** *habitats, vulnerable, resources*

**The Monsters Are Due on Maple Street** *flustered, persistently, defiant, affect, identify, convince*

**All Summer in a Day** *slackening, vital, resilient, environment, awareness, incident*

**Joseph R. McCarthy** *unscrupulous, furor, riveted, evaluations, debate, investigations*

**The Salem Witch Trials of 1692** *accusations, successive, disbanded, established, determination, formal, simultaneously*

**Herd Mentality? The Freakonomics of Boarding a Bus** *investment, muster, succumb, behavior, contribute, assumptions*

**Follow the Leader: Democracy in Herd Mentality** *pertinent, explicit, inherent, transmitting, complex, refute*

**Martin Luther King, Jr., Memorial** *understand, materials, significance*

# UNIT 5 Community or individual—which is more important?

## PART 1
## SETTING EXPECTATIONS



## PART 2
## TEXT ANALYSIS GUIDED EXPLORATION

### EXPLAINING THE WORLD

PART 3

## TEXT SET DEVELOPING INSIGHT

### BECOMING AMERICAN



PART 4

## DEMONSTRATING INDEPENDENCE

**DIGITAL ASSETS KEY**

These digital resources, as well as audio and the Online Writer's Notebook, can be found at **pearsonrealize.com.**

- Interactive Whiteboard Activities
- Virtual Tour
- Close Reading Notebook
- Video
- Close Reading Tool for Annotating Texts
- Grammar Tutorials
- Online Text Set

# UNIT 5 Unit at a Glance

## READ

**Text Analysis**
- Myth
- Legend and Fact
- Cultural Context
- Folk Tales
- Comparing Universal Themes
- Symbolism
- Narrative Poem
- Narration
- Direct Quotation
- Dialogue
- Idiom

**Comprehension**
- Cause and Effect
- Compare and Contrast

**Language Study**
- Latin root *-dom-*
- Latin prefix *uni-*
- Latin suffix *-ity*
- Greek root *-myst-*

**Conventions**
- Infinitive Phrases and Gerund Phrases
- Punctuation Marks
- Commas
- Capitalization

**Language Study Workshop**
- Figurative Language

## DISCUSS

**Presentation of Ideas**
- Persuasive Speech
- Television News Report

**Comprehension and Collaboration**
- Debate
- Retelling

**Responding to Text**
- Group Discussion
- Partner Discussion
- Debate
- Write and Discuss

**Speaking and Listening Workshop**
- Research Presentation

## RESEARCH

**Investigate the Topic: Becoming American**
- Politics and Becoming American
- Help in "Becoming American"
- American Literature
- The Chinese Exclusion Act
- "The New Colossus"
- Urban "Melting Pots"
- Immigration to the United States

## WRITE

**Writing to Sources**
- Myth
- Description
- Plot Summary
- Review
- Comparison-and-Contrast Essay
- Autobiographical Narrative
- Expository Essay
- Explanatory Essay
- Problem-and-Solution Essay
- Short Story
- Informative Essay

**Writing Process Workshop**
- Explanatory Text: Cause-and-Effect Essay
  - Organization: Organize Logically
  - Conventions: Revising Incorrect Use of Commas

## UNIT VOCABULARY

Academic Vocabulary appears in *blue*.

**Introducing the Big Question** *common, community, culture, custom, diversity, duty, environment, ethnicity, family, group, individual, team, tradition, unify, unique*

**Demeter and Persephone** *defies, monarch, dominions, intervene, realm, abode*

**Popocatepetl and Ixtlaccihuatl** *shortsightedness, routed, decreed, relished, unanimous, feebleness*

**Sun and Moon in a Box** *regretted, reliable, curiosity, pestering, relented, cunning*

**The People Could Fly** *shed, scorned, hoed, croon, mystery, shuffle*

**The Voyage; To the Top of Everest** *impervious, inflicted, designated, saturation, attitude, challenge, environment, outcome*

**My First Free Summer** *vowed, summoned, contradiction, explain, perspective, strategy*

**How I learned English** *notions, transfixed, writhing, relationship, outcome, explain*

**mk** *adequate, deceive, ignorant, communicate, predict, process*

**Byron Yee: Discovering a Paper Son** *decipher, interrogations, scrutiny, discover, enhance, cites*

***from* Grandpa and the Statue** *subscribed, peeved, swindle, characterize, debate, discover*

**Melting Pot** *fluent, bigots, dolefully, community, attitude, compose*

**United States Immigration Statistics** *legal, approximately, individual*

# INTRODUCTORY UNIT

## WORKSHOPS

- BUILDING ACADEMIC VOCABULARY
- WRITING AN OBJECTIVE SUMMARY
- COMPREHENDING COMPLEX TEXTS
- ANALYZING ARGUMENTS
- CONDUCTING RESEARCH

## BUILDING ACADEMIC VOCABULARY

Academic vocabulary is the language you encounter in textbooks and on standardized tests and other assessments. Understanding these words and using them in your classroom discussions and writing will help you communicate your ideas clearly and effectively.

There are two basic types of academic vocabulary: general and domain-specific. **General academic vocabulary** includes words that are not specific to any single course of study. For example, the general academic vocabulary word *analyze* is used in language arts, math, social studies, art, and so on.

**Domain-specific academic vocabulary** includes words that are usually encountered in the study of a specific discipline. For example, the words *factor* and *remainder* are most often used in mathematics classrooms and texts.

### General Academic Vocabulary

| Word | Definition | Related Words | Word in Context |
|---|---|---|---|
| analyze (AN uh lyz) *v.* | break down into parts and examine carefully | analytical analysis | Our assignment is to **analyze** the story's ending. |
| appreciate (uh PREE shee ayt) *v.* | recognize the value of; be thankful for | appreciative appreciating | Once I read Frost's poem, I learned to **appreciate** his use of symbols. |
| assumption (uh SUMP shuhn) *n.* | belief or acceptance that something is true | assume assuming | The **assumption** in the essay is well supported by facts. |
| attitude (AT uh tood) *n.* | mental state involving beliefs, feelings, and values | | The writer's **attitude** toward his subject was respectful and full of admiration. |
| awareness (uh WAYR nihs) *n.* | knowledge gained from one's own perceptions or from information | aware unaware | It is important to develop an **awareness** of the writer's message. |
| bias (BY uhs) *n.* | tendency to see things from a slanted or prejudiced viewpoint | biased unbiased | You must consider if an advertisement contains **bias** or tries to mislead the reader. |
| challenge (CHAL uhnj) *v.* | act of calling into question; dare | challenging challenged | Ted invited me to **challenge** him to a debate. |

**Ordinary Language:** I **like** poems with strong rhymes and rhythms.

**Academic Language:** I **appreciate** poems with strong rhymes and rhythms.

| Word | Definition | Related Words | Word in Context |
|---|---|---|---|
| characteristic (kar ihk tuh RIHS tihk) *n.* | trait; feature | character characteristically | One **characteristic** of poetry is figurative language. |
| common (KOM uhn) *adj.* | ordinary; expected | commonality uncommon | It is **common** for an essay to contain humor. |
| communicate (kuh MYOO nuh kayt) *v.* | share thoughts or feelings, usually in words | communication communicating | It is important to be able to **communicate** thoughts and feelings in writing. |
| communication (kuh myoo nuh KAY shuhn) *n.* | activity of sharing information or speaking | communicate communicated | There seemed to be a lack of **communication** between the mother and daughter. |
| community (kuh MYOO nuh tee) *n.* | group of people who share an interest or who live near each other | commune | Local newspapers serve the **community** where the paper is published. |
| conclude (kuhn KLOOD) *v.* | bring to a close; end | concluding conclusion | The writer was able to **conclude** the essay with a positive memory. |
| contribute (kuhn TRIHB yoot) *v.* | add to; enrich | contribution contributing | Editorials **contribute** to a public discussion about an issue. |
| convince (kuhn VIHNS) *v.* | persuade; cause to accept a point of view | convincing convinced | It is important to **convince** readers of the character's dream. |
| culture (KUL chuhr) *n.* | collected customs of a group or community | cultural culturally | Folk tales reveal the values of a **culture** and teach a lesson. |
| debate (dih BAYT) *v.* | argue in an attempt to convince | debated debating | The two students tried to **debate** whether or not the new Web site was helpful. |
| define (dih FYN) *v.* | determine the nature of or give the meaning of | defined definition | I was able to **define** the story's plot quickly. |
| discover (dihs KUV uhr) *v.* | find or explore | discovering discovery | The reader tries to **discover** the reasons for the character's behavior. |
| diversity (duh VUR suh tee) *n.* | variety, as of groups or cultures | diverse diversify | Reading works from different writers provides **diversity.** |
| environment (ehn VY ruhn muhnt) *n.* | surroundings; the natural world | environs environmentally | The essay described the beautiful **environment** where the writer lived. |

**Ordinary Language:** In this essay, I will **tell the meaning** of key terms.

**Academic Language:** In this essay, I will **define** key terms.

| Word | Definition | Related Words | Word in Context |
|---|---|---|---|
| evaluate<br>(ih VAL yoo ayt) *v.* | judge; determine the value or quality of | evaluated<br>evaluation | The girl was unable to **evaluate** her friend's work without bias. |
| examine<br>(ehg ZAM uhn) *v.* | study in depth; look at closely | examining<br>examination | In order to **examine** the evidence, it was necessary to research the subject. |
| explain<br>(ehk SPLAYN) *v.* | make plain or clear | explaining<br>explanation | I will **explain** three key factors in the story's success. |
| explore<br>(ehk SPLAWR) *v.* | investigate; look into | explored<br>exploration | I wrote a research report to **explore** my ideas. |
| facts<br>(fakts) *n.* | accepted truths or reality | factual<br>nonfactual | I supported my statement with **facts** and details. |
| focus<br>(FOH kuhs) *n.* | central point or topic of investigation | focused<br>focusing | The **focus** of the essay was to provide information about water safety. |
| generate<br>(JEHN uhr ayt) *v.* | create | generated<br>generating | Before researching, I tried to **generate** a list of topics to explore. |
| identify<br>(Y DEHN tuh fy) *v.* | recognize as being; name | identification<br>identity | How do you **identify** the meaning of this poem? |
| ignore<br>(ihg NAWR) *v.* | refuse to notice; disregard | ignored<br>ignoring | If we **ignore** the message, we miss the purpose of the writing. |
| image<br>(IHM ihj) *n.* | picture; representation | imagery<br>imaging | The **image** in the book helped me to visualize the story. |
| individual<br>(ihn duh VIHJ oo uhl) *n.* | single person or thing | individuality<br>individualism | The story is told from the perspective of one **individual.** |
| inform<br>(ihn FAWRM) *v.* | tell; give information about | information<br>informative | The purpose of the research paper was to **inform** the reader about whales. |
| inquire<br>(ihn KWYR) *v.* | ask in order to learn about | inquiring<br>inquired | We were assigned to **inquire** about weather patterns and present our findings. |
| insight<br>(IHN syt) *n.* | ability to see the truth; understanding | insightful<br>insightfully | My teacher shared her **insight** about the characters with us. |

| Word | Definition | Related Words | Word in Context |
|---|---|---|---|
| investigate<br>(ihn VEHS tuh gayt)<br>*v.* | examine thoroughly | investigated<br>investigation | As a team, we were able to **investigate** each aspect of the problem. |
| media<br>(MEE dee uh) *n.* | collected sources of information, including newspapers, television, and the Internet | | The **media** are an everyday source of information and entertainment for the public. |
| opposition<br>(op uh ZIHSH uhn) *n.* | state of being against | oppose<br>opposing | The villain in the story provided **opposition** to the hero's happiness. |
| outcome<br>(OWT kuhm) *n.* | way something turns out | | We found the **outcome** of the problem to be a favorable solution. |
| perceive<br>(puhr SEEV) *v.* | be aware of; see | perceived<br>perception | I was able to **perceive** Jenny's character through her actions and words. |
| perception<br>(puhr SEHP shuhn) *n.* | act of becoming aware of through one or more of the senses | perceive<br>perceptive | My **perception** of the character changed over the course of the story. |
| perspective<br>(puhr SPEHK tihv) *n.* | point of view | | I did not agree with the writer's **perspective.** |
| produce<br>(pruh DOOS) *v.* | make; create | produced<br>producing | In order to **produce** a new show, the writing team must provide a script. |
| reaction<br>(ree AK shuhn) *n.* | response to an influence, action, or statement | react<br>reactor | I had a strong **reaction** to the claims made in the commercial. |
| reflect<br>(rih FLEHKT) *v.* | think about; consider | reflected<br>reflection | In order to **reflect** on what had been said, I took some quiet time. |
| resolution<br>(rehz uh LOO shuhn)<br>*n.* | end of a conflict in which one or both parties is satisfied | resolve<br>resolving | The **resolution** of the story helped me to see how a compromise can help many people. |
| team<br>(teem) *n.* | group united in a common goal | team *v.* | Our **team** prepared a report, and each member presented a part of it. |

| Word | Definition | Related Words | Word in Context |
|---|---|---|---|
| technology (tehk NOL uh jee) *n.* | practical application of science to business or industry | technological technologically | At one time, the computer was considered a new **technology.** |
| tradition (truh DIHSH uhn) *n.* | custom, as of a social group or culture | traditional traditionally | A **tradition** is often handed down to a new generation though storytelling. |
| transmit (trans MIHT) *v.* | send or give out | transmitted transmission | We were able to **transmit** our message over the school's radio station. |
| understanding (uhn duhr STAN dihng) *n.* | agreement; end of conflict | understand understandable | The students came to an **understanding** of how best to organize the club. |
| unify (YOO nuh fy) *v.* | bring together as one | unified unifying | It is important to **unify** details so that they support the central idea. |
| unique (yoo NEEK) *adj.* | one of a kind | uniqueness uniquely | Each writer has a **unique** way of telling a story. |

## Practice

Examples of various kinds of domain-specific academic vocabulary appear in the charts below. Some chart rows are not filled in. In your notebook, look up the definitions of the remaining words, provide one or two related words, and use each word in context.

### Social Studies: Domain-Specific Academic Vocabulary

| Word | Definition | Related Words | Word in Context |
|---|---|---|---|
| communism (KOM yuh nihz uhm) *n.* | economic and social system where the land and all products of industry belong to the government as a whole | commune communist | **Communism** failed in Eastern Europe. |
| dissent (dih SEHNT) *n.* | difference of feeling or opinion | dissention dissenter | There was much **dissent** and disagreement in the government. |
| neutrality (noo TRAL uh tee) *n.* | state of being neutral, or not taking sides in a conflict | neutral | Switzerland kept its **neutrality** during World War II. |
| segregation (sehg ruh GAY shuhn) *n.* | separation of people because of race, color, or gender | segregate segregated | The civil rights movement helped to end **segregation** in the South. |
| socialism (SOH shuh lihz uhm) *n.* | theory or system of organization in which major sources of production are owned or controlled by the community or government | social socialist | **Socialism** stresses the community rather than the individual. |
| adaptation (ad uhp TAY shuhn) *n.* | | | |
| emigration (ehm uh GRAY shuhn) *n.* | | | |
| colonization (KOL uh nih ZAY shuhn) *n.* | | | |
| nobility (noh BIHL uh tee) *n.* | | | |
| urbanization (UR buh nih ZAY shuhn) *n.* | | | |

## Mathematics: Domain-Specific Academic Vocabulary

| Word | Definition | Related Words | Word in Context |
|---|---|---|---|
| negative number (NEHG uh tihv NUM buhr) *n.* | number below zero on a number line; indicated by a minus sign | positive number | The number –4 is a **negative number,** while 4 is a positive number. |
| odds (odz) *n.* | probability that something will happen | odd<br>oddity | What are the **odds** that I will win the lottery? |
| proportion (pruh PAWR shuhn) *n.* | statement of the equality of two ratios, or the mathematical relationship of a part to the whole | proportionate<br>proportional | The teacher said that the **proportion** should be written as 4/2 = 10/5. |
| range (RAYNJ) *n.* | difference between the largest and smallest values in a group of numbers | range *v.*<br>ranging | Find the **range** in the following number set: 2, 3, 4, 5, and 6. |
| ratio (RAY shee oh) *n.* | proportionate relationship between two numbers | | The **ratio** of 5 to 2 is written as 5:2. |
| minimum (MIHN uh muhm) *n.* | | | |
| property (PROP uhr tee) *n.* | | | |
| rate (rayt) *n.* | | | |
| reliability (rih LY uh bihl uh tee) *n.* | | | |
| sequence (SEE kwuhns) *n.* | | | |

## Science: Domain-Specific Academic Vocabulary

| Word | Definition | Related Words | Word in Context |
|---|---|---|---|
| hypothesis (hy POTH uh sihs) *n.* | something not proved but assumed to be true for the purpose of further study or argument | hypothesize<br>hypothetical | The **hypothesis** that the earth was flat was later proven to be false. |
| erosion (ih ROH zhuhn) *n.* | process by which the surface of the earth is worn away by the action of water and other natural events | erode<br>eroded | The hurricane caused beach **erosion.** |
| metamorphic (meht uh MAWR fihk) *adj.* | changing in form or structure | metamorphosis | **Metamorphic** rock is formed by heat and pressure within the earth. |
| solubility (sol yuh BIHL uh tee) *n.* | ability of a substance to dissolve | soluble<br>insoluble | We tested the **solubility** of salt in a science lab. |
| synthesize (SIHN thuh syz) *v.* | form by combining parts or elements | synthetic<br>synthesis | Scientists **synthesize** compounds by combining two or more substances. |

## Science: Domain-Specific Academic Vocabulary *(continued)*

| Word | Definition | Related Words | Word in Context |
|---|---|---|---|
| energy<br>(EHN uhr jee) *n.* | | | |
| evidence<br>(EHV uh duns) *n.* | | | |
| gene<br>(jeen) *n.* | | | |
| heredity<br>(huh REHD ih tee) *n.* | | | |
| substance<br>(SUB stuhns) *n.* | | | |

## Art: Domain-Specific Academic Vocabulary

| Word | Definition | Related Words | Word in Context |
|---|---|---|---|
| intensity<br>(ihn TEHN suh tee) *n.* | quality of a color's brightness and purity | intense<br>intensify | The **intensity** of the red paint was stronger than the artist wanted. |
| linear<br>(LIHN ee uhr) *adj.* | having to do with a line | line<br>nonlinear | The sculpture of the building was **linear** and rigid. |
| saturation<br>(sach uh RAY shuhn) *n.* | degree of purity of a color | saturate<br>saturated | The **saturation** of the pink paint gave the room a lively feel. |
| texture<br>(TEHKS chuhr) *n.* | way things feel, or look as if they might feel, when touched | textured | The carpet had a thick and fluffy **texture.** |
| unity<br>(YOO nuh tee) *n.* | look and feel of wholeness in a work of art | unite<br>unified | The mural had good balance and **unity.** |
| definition<br>(dehf uh NIHSH uhn) *n.* | | | |
| form<br>(fawrm) *n.* | | | |
| motion<br>(MOH shuhn) *n.* | | | |
| space<br>(spays) *n.* | | | |
| value<br>(VAL yoo) *n.* | | | |

## Technology: Domain-Specific Academic Vocabulary

| Word | Definition | Related Words | Word in Context |
|---|---|---|---|
| database<br>(DAY tuh bays) *n.* | collection of related information stored in a computerized format | data | The library has a **database** of all its books. |
| digital<br>(DIHJ ih tuhl) *adj.* | available in an electronic format | digit<br>digitize | I have a **digital** version of that book on my computer. |
| login<br>(LOG ihn) *n.* | information related to an electronic account name and its password | logging in | I use my **login** to access my account on a secure Web site. |
| network<br>(NEHT wuhrk) *n.* | group of computers connected together to share information | network *v.*<br>networking | The Internet is the largest **network** in the world. |
| platform<br>(PLAT fawrm) *n.* | group of compatible computers that can share software | platform *adj.* | PC is the computer **platform** used in our school. |
| bookmark<br>(BO͝OK mahrk) *n.* | | | |
| copy<br>(KOP ee) *n.*, v. | | | |
| download<br>(DOWN lohd) *v.* | | | |
| input<br>(IHN po͝ot) *n.*, v. | | | |
| output<br>(OWT po͝ot) *n.*, v. | | | |

## Increasing Your Word Knowledge

Increase your word knowledge and chances of success by taking an active role in developing your vocabulary. Here are some tips for you.

To own a word, follow these steps:

| Steps to Follow | Model |
|---|---|
| 1. Learn to identify the word and its basic meaning. | The word *examine* means "to look at closely." |
| 2. Take note of the word's spelling. | *Examine* begins and ends with an *e*. |
| 3. Practice pronouncing the word so that you can use it in conversation. | The *e* on the end of the word is silent. Its second syllable gets the most stress. |
| 4. Visualize the word and illustrate its key meaning. | When I think of the word *examine*, I visualize a doctor checking a patient's health. |
| 5. Learn the various forms of the word and its related words. | *Examination* and *exam* are forms of the word *examine*. |
| 6. Compare the word with similar words. | *Examine*, *peruse*, and *study* are synonyms. |
| 7. Contrast the word with similar words. | *Examine* suggests a more detailed study than *read* or *look* at. |
| 8. Use the word in various contexts. | "I'd like to *examine* the footprints more closely." "I will *examine* the use of imagery in this poem." |

## Building Your Speaking Vocabulary

Language gives us the ability to express ourselves. The more words you know, the better able you will be to get your points across. There are two main aspects of language: reading and speaking. Using the steps above will help you to acquire a rich vocabulary. Follow these steps to help you learn to use this rich vocabulary in discussions, speeches, and conversations.

| Steps to Follow | Tip |
|---|---|
| 1. Practice pronouncing the word. | Become familiar with pronunciation guides, which will help you to sound out unfamiliar words. Listening to audiobooks as you read the text will help you learn pronunciations of words. |
| 2. Learn word forms. | Dictionaries often list forms of words following the main word entry. Practice saying word families aloud: "generate," "generated," "generation," "regenerate," "generator." |
| 3. Translate your thoughts. | Restate your own thoughts and ideas in a variety of ways, to inject formality or to change your tone, for example. |
| 4. Hold discussions. | With a classmate, practice using academic vocabulary words in discussions about the text. Choose one term to practice at a time, and see how many statements you can create using that term. |
| 5. Tape-record yourself. | Analyze your word choices by listening to yourself objectively. Note where your word choice could be strengthened or changed. |

## WRITING AN OBJECTIVE SUMMARY

The ability to write objective summaries is key to success in college and in many careers. Writing an effective objective summary involves recording the key ideas of a text while demonstrating your understanding.

### What is an Objective Summary?

An effective objective summary is a concise, complete, accurate, and objective overview of a text. The following are key characteristics of an objective summary:

- A good summary focuses on the main theme, or central idea, of a text and specific, relevant details that support that theme, or central idea. Unnecessary supporting details are left out.
- An effective summary is usually brief. However, the writer must be careful not to misrepresent the text by leaving out key elements.
- A successful summary accurately captures the essence of the longer text it is describing.
- An effective summary remains objective—the writer refrains from inserting his or her own opinions, reactions, or personal connections into the summary.

### What to Avoid in an Objective Summary

- An objective summary is not a collection of sentences or paragraphs copied from the original source.
- It is not a long recounting of every event, detail, or point in the original text.
- A good summary does not include evaluative words or comments, such as the reader's overall opinion of or reaction to the piece. An objective summary is not the reader's interpretation or critical analysis of the work.

INFORMATIONAL TEXT

## Model Objective Summary

Review the elements of an effective objective summary, which are pointed out in the sidenotes that appear next to the summary. Then, write an objective summary of a selection you recently read. Review your summary, and delete any unnecessary details, personal opinions, or evaluations of the text.

### Summary of "Mowgli's Brothers"

"Mowgli's Brothers" is one of the stories in *The Jungle Book*, written by Rudyard Kipling. The setting of the story is a jungle in India, and the ~~enchanting~~ story tells the tale of Mowgli, a young boy who is raised by wolves.

One night Mother and Father Wolf woke from their rest to find Tabaqui, a jackal, at the mouth of their cave, begging for food. No one in the jungle liked Tabaqui. However, the wolves gave him a bone to eat in spite of the fact that he upset Mother Wolf ~~by complimenting her on her four young cubs. The wolves thought it was unlucky to compliment children to their faces~~. Tabaqui further upset the wolves by bringing the news that Shere Khan, a tiger, was moving into their hunting grounds.

After Tabaqui left, Father Wolf set out on his hunt. He heard Shere Khan's roar and then saw him rolling around on the ground. The tiger had landed in a woodcutter's fire while trying to catch his prey.

Soon after that, something approached the wolves' cave. Father Wolf was ready to pounce until he saw what it was—a smiling, happy baby boy. Father Wolf gently picked up the man's cub and brought him to Mother Wolf. The man's cub was not at all afraid, and he snuggled right up with the wolf cubs.

Before long, Shere Khan stuck his big head into the cave. He wanted the man's cub, which had been his prey. The wolves wouldn't give him up, which angered the tiger. But Mother Wolf was even angrier. She said, "The man's cub is mine... He shall not be killed. He shall live to run with the Pack and to hunt with the Pack; and in the end. . .he shall hunt thee."

Mother Wolf named the man's cub Mowgli, and he was brought before the Wolf Pack for approval. With the help of Baloo the bear and Bagheera the black panther, Mowgli was accepted into the Pack. Shere Khan slinked away into the night, roaring his disapproval.

A one-sentence synopsis, or brief overview, highlighting the theme, or central idea, of the story can be an effective start to a summary.

The adjective *enchanting* indicates an opinion and should not be included in an objective summary.

Unnecessary details should be eliminated.

Transition words and phrases show chronological order and enable readers to easily follow the order of events.

If actual sentences from the story are used to show the essence of a text, they must be placed within quotation marks.

## COMPREHENDING COMPLEX TEXTS

Over the course of your school years, you will be required to read increasingly complex texts as preparation for college and a career. A complex text is a text that contains challenging vocabulary; long, complex sentences; figurative language; multiple levels of meaning; or unfamiliar settings and situations.

The selections in this textbook provide you with a range of readings, from short stories to autobiographies, poetry, drama, myths, and even science and social studies texts. Some of these texts will fall within your comfort zone; others will most likely be more challenging.

### Strategy 1: **Multidraft Reading**

Most successful readers know that to fully understand a text, you must reread it several times. Get in the habit of reading a text or portions of a text two to three times in order to ensure that you get the most out of your reading experience. To fully understand a text, try this multidraft reading strategy:

#### 1st Reading

On your first reading, look for the basics. If, for example, you are reading a story, look for who does what to whom, what conflicts arise, and how conflicts are resolved. If the text is nonfiction, look for the main ideas and the ways they are presented. If you are reading a lyric poem, read first to get a sense of who the speaker is. Also take note of the poem's setting and main focus.

#### 2nd Reading

During your second reading of a text, focus on the artistry or the effectiveness of the writing. Look for text structures and think about why the author chose those organizational patterns. Then, examine the author's creative uses of language and the effects of that language. For example, has the author used metaphor, simile, or hyperbole? If so, what effect did that use of figurative language create?

#### 3rd Reading

After your third reading, compare and contrast the text with other similar selections you have read. For example, if you read a haiku, think of other haiku you have read and ways the poems are alike or different. Evaluate the text's overall effectiveness and its central idea, or theme.

## Independent Practice

As you read this poem, practice the multidraft reading strategy by completing a chart like the one below. Use a separate piece of paper.

### "Prayers of Steel" by Carl Sandburg

Lay me on an anvil, O God.
Beat me and hammer me into a crowbar.
Let me pry loose old walls;
Let me lift and loosen old foundations.

Lay me on an anvil, O God.
Beat me and hammer me into a steel spike.
Drive me into the girders that hold a skyscraper together.
Take red-hot rivets and fasten me into the central girders.
Let me be the great nail holding a skyscraper through blue
    nights into white stars.

**Multidraft Reading Chart**

| | My Understanding |
|---|---|
| **1st Reading** Look for key ideas and details that unlock basic meaning. | |
| **2nd Reading** Read for deeper meanings. Look for ways in which the author used text structures and language to create effects. | |
| **3rd Reading** Read to integrate your knowledge and ideas. Connect the text to others of its kind and to your own experience. | |

## Strategy 2: **Close Read the Text**

To comprehend a complex text, perform a close reading—a careful analysis of the words, phrases, and sentences within the text. As you close read, use the following tips to comprehend the text:

### Tips for Close Reading

1. **Break down long sentences** into parts. Look for the subject of the sentence and its verb. Then, identify which parts of the sentence modify, or give more information about, the subject.

2. **Reread difficult passages** to confirm that you understand their meaning.

3. **Look for context clues,** such as
   - **a.** restatement of an idea. For example, in this sentence, "defeated" restates the verb *vanquished.*

     The army **vanquished,** or defeated, its enemy.
   - **b.** definition of sophisticated words. In this sentence, the underlined information defines the word *girder.*

     A **girder's** long beam provides support for the floor above.
   - **c.** examples of concepts and topics. In the following passage, the underlined text provides an example of the adjective *voracious.*

     Eating his entire dinner, two apples, and a banana finally satisfied Rob's **voracious** appetite.
   - **d.** contrasts of ideas and topics. The following sentence points out a difference between Lori and Ellen.

     Lori was **vivacious,** unlike her shy, quiet sister Ellen.

4. **Identify pronoun antecedents.** If long sentences or passages contain pronouns, reread the text to make sure you know to whom or what the pronouns refer. In the following passage, the underlined pronouns all have the antecedent *freedom.*

   **Freedom** is precious. Through it we prosper. In its absence we doubt, quake, rage, and suffer; it is just as necessary to life as is the air we breathe. For, without it, we surely perish.

5. **Look for conjunctions,** such as *and, or,* and *yet,* to help understand relationships between ideas.

6. **Paraphrase,** or restate in your own words, passages of difficult text in order to check your understanding. Remember that a paraphrase is a word-for-word restatement of an original text; it is not a summary.

INFORMATIONAL TEXT

## Close Reading Model

As you read this document, take note of the sidenotes that model ways to unlock meaning in the text.

### *from* "Speech to the Constitutional Convention" by Benjamin Franklin

To the People of the State of New York:

I confess that I do not entirely approve of this Constitution at present; but, sir, I am not sure I shall never approve of it, for, having lived long, I have experienced many instances of being obliged, by better information or fuller consideration, to change opinions even on important subjects, which I once thought right, but found to be otherwise. It is therefore that, the older I grow, the more apt I am to doubt my own judgment of others. Most men, indeed, as well as most sects in religion think themselves in possession of all truth, and that wherever others differ with them, it is so far error. . . . .

Break down this long sentence into parts. The text highlighted in yellow conveys the basic meaning of the sentence. The text highlighted in blue provides additional information.

In these sentiments, sir, I agree to this Constitution with all its faults—if they are such—because I think a general government necessary for us, and there is no form of government but what may be a blessing to the people if well administered; and I believe, further, that this is likely to be well administered for a course of years, and can only end in despotism, as other forms have done before it, when the people shall become so corrupted as to need a despotic government, being incapable of any other. I doubt, too, whether any other convention we can obtain may be able to make a better Constitution; for, when you assemble a number of men, to have the advantage of their joint wisdom, you inevitably assemble with those men all their prejudices, their passions, their errors of opinion, their local interests, and their selfish views. From such an assembly can a perfect production be expected?

Look for antecedents. In this sentence, the noun *faults* is replaced by the pronoun *they*. The conjunction *because*, highlighted in blue, indicates a cause-and-effect relationship.

Search for context clues. The words in blue are context clues that help you figure out the meaning of the word that appears in yellow.

It therefore astonishes me, sir, to find this system approaching so near to perfection as it does. . . .

## Strategy 3: **Ask Questions**

Be an attentive reader by asking questions as you read. Throughout this textbook, we have provided questions for you following each selection. These questions are sorted into three basic categories that build in sophistication and lead you to a deeper understanding of the texts you read.

Here is an example from this text:

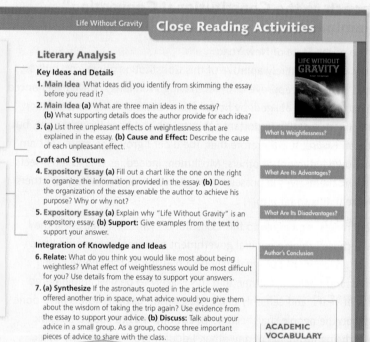

Life Without Gravity **Close Reading Activities**

### Literary Analysis

**Key Ideas and Details**

1. **Main Idea** What ideas did you identify from skimming the essay before you read it?
2. **Main Idea (a)** What are three main ideas in the essay? **(b)** What supporting details does the author provide for each idea?
3. **(a)** List three unpleasant effects of weightlessness that are explained in the essay. **(b) Cause and Effect:** Describe the cause of each unpleasant effect.

**Craft and Structure**

4. **Expository Essay (a)** Fill out a chart like the one on the right to organize the information provided in the essay. **(b)** Does the organization of the essay enable the author to achieve his purpose? Why or why not?
5. **Expository Essay (a)** Explain why "Life Without Gravity" is an expository essay. **(b) Support:** Give examples from the text to support your answer.

**Integration of Knowledge and Ideas**

6. **Relate:** What do you think you would like most about being weightless? What effect of weightlessness would be most difficult for you? Use details from the essay to support your answers.
7. **(a) Synthesize** If the astronauts quoted in the article were offered another trip in space, what advice would you give them about the wisdom of taking the trip again? Use evidence from the essay to support your advice. **(b) Discuss:** Talk about your advice in a small group. As a group, choose three important pieces of advice to share with the class.

LIFE WITHOUT GRAVITY

What Is Weightlessness?

What Are Its Advantages?

What Are Its Disadvantages?

Author's Conclusion

ACADEMIC VOCABULARY

Some questions are about **Key Ideas and Details** in the text. To answer these questions, you will need to locate and cite explicit information in the text or draw inferences from what you have read.

Some questions are about **Craft and Structure** in the text. To answer these questions, you will need to analyze how the author developed and structured the text. You will also look for ways in which the author artfully used language and how those word choices impacted the meaning and tone of the work.

Some questions are about the **Integration of Knowledge and Ideas** in the text. These questions ask you to evaluate a text in many different ways, such as comparing texts, looking at arguments in the text, and many other methods of analyzing a text's ideas.

### Preparing to Read Complex Texts

**Attentive Reading** As you read on your own, ask yourself questions like these to enrich your reading experience.

**When reading narratives, ask yourself...**

Comprehension: **Key Ideas and Details**

- Can I clearly picture the setting of the story? Which details help me do so?
- Can I picture the characters clearly in my mind? Why or why not?
- Do the characters speak and act like real people? Why or why not?
- Which characters do I like? Why? Which characters do I dislike? Why?
- Do I understand why the characters act as they do? Why or why not?
- What does the story mean to me? Does it express a meaning or an insight I find important and true?

Text Analysis: **Craft and Structure**

- Does the story grab my attention right from the beginning? Why or why not?
- Do I want to keep reading? Why or why not?
- Can I follow the sequence of events in the story? Am I confused at any point? If so, what information would make the sequence clearer?
- Do the characters change as the story progresses? If so, do their changes seem believable?

As you read independently, ask similar types of questions to ensure that you fully enjoy and comprehend texts you read for school and for pleasure. We have provided sets of questions for you on the Independent Reading pages at the end of each unit.

INFORMATIONAL TEXT

## Model

Following is an example of a complex text. The sidenotes show sample questions that an attentive reader might ask while reading.

### *from* "Owning Books" by William Lyon Phelps

in a radio broadcast on April 6, 1933:

The habit of reading is one of the greatest resources of mankind; and we enjoy reading books that belong to us much more than if they are borrowed. . . your own books belong to you; you treat them with that affectionate intimacy that annihilates formality. Books are for use, not for show; you should own no book that you are afraid to mark up, or afraid to place on the table wide open and face down. A good reason for marking favorite passages in books is that this practice enables you to remember more easily the significant sayings, to refer to them quickly, and then in later years, it is like visiting a forest where you once blazed a trail. You have the pleasure of going over the old ground, and recalling both the intellectual scenery and your own earlier self.

**Sample questions:**

**Key Ideas and Details** Does the first sentence state facts or express an opinion? Who is meant by *we* and *us*?

**Craft and Structure** What parallel structures does the writer use in this passage? What effect does that use have on readers?

**Integration of Knowledge and Ideas** To what extent do you agree with the author's viewpoint? Explain.

INFORMATIONAL TEXT

## Independent Practice

Write three to five questions you might ask yourself as you read this passage from a speech delivered by Theodore Roosevelt at the Grand Canyon in 1903.

### *from* "Speech at the Grand Canyon" by Theodore Roosevelt

. . . In the Grand Canyon, Arizona has a natural wonder which, so far as I know, is, in kind, absolutely unparalleled throughout the rest of the world. I want to ask you to do one thing in connection with it, in your own interest and in the interest of the country—to keep this great wonder of nature as it now is. I was delighted to learn of the wisdom of the Santa Fe railroad people in deciding not to build their hotel on the brink of the canyon. I hope you will not have a building of any kind, not a summer cottage, a hotel, or anything else, to mar the wonderful grandeur, the sublimity, the great loneliness and beauty of the canyon. Leave it as it is. You cannot improve on it. The ages have been at work on it, and man can only mar it. What you can do is to keep it for your children, your children's children and for all who come after you, as one of the great sights which every American, if he can travel at all, should see. . . .

## ANALYZING ARGUMENTS

The ability to evaluate an argument, as well as to make one, is an important skill for success in college and in the workplace.

### What Is an Argument?

Chances are, you have used the word *argument* to refer to a disagreement between people. This type of argument involves trading opinions and evidence in a conversational way, with both sides contributing to the discussion. A formal argument, however, presents one side of a controversial or debatable issue. Through this type of argument, the writer logically supports a particular belief, conclusion, or point of view. A good argument is supported with reasoning and evidence.

### Purposes of Argument

There are three main purposes for writing a formal argument:

- to change the reader's mind about an issue
- to convince the reader to accept what is written
- to motivate the reader to take action, based on what is written

| Elements of an Argument |
| --- |
| **Claim** (assertion)—what the writer is trying to prove<br>Example: *Sports programs should be funded by private individuals, not schools.* |
| **Grounds** (evidence)—the support used to convince the reader<br>Example: *Because students who participate in sports get the benefits of that activity, the students should do fund-raising to pay for the use of equipment and training.* |
| **Justification**—the link between the grounds and the claim; why the grounds are credible<br>Example: *For example, participants in sports often get college scholarships—money that is paid to them. Since those students benefit personally from the sports experience, they should help fund the cost of the sports activities.* |

### Evaluating Claims

When reading or listening to an argument, critically assess the claims that are made. Analyze the argument to identify claims that are based on fact or that can be proved true. Also evaluate evidence that supports the claims. If there is little or no reasoning or evidence provided to support the claims, the argument may not be sound or valid.

INFORMATIONAL TEXT

# Model Argument

## *from* "Speech Supporting Women's Suffrage" by Robert L. Owen

Women compose one-half of the human race. . . A full half of the work of the world is done by women. A careful study of the matter has demonstrated the vital fact that these working women receive a smaller wage for equal work than men do, and that the smaller wage and harder conditions imposed on the woman worker are due to the lack of the ballot. . . . Equal pay for equal work is the first great reason justifying this change of governmental policy.

There are other reasons which are persuasive: First, women, take it all in all, are the equals of men in intelligence, and no man has the hardihood to assert the contrary. . . .

Every evil prophecy against granting the suffrage has failed. The public men of Colorado, Wyoming, Utah, and Idaho give it a cordial support.

The testimony is universal:

First, it has not made women mannish; they. . .are better able to protect themselves and their children because of the ballot.

Second, they have not become office-seekers. . . It [suffrage] has made women broader and greatly increased the understanding of the community at large of the problems of good government. . . .

It has not absolutely regenerated society, but it has improved it. It has raised the . . .moral standard of the suffrage, because there are more criminal men than criminal women. . . .

The great doctrine of the American Republic that "all governments derive their just powers from the consent of the governed" justifies the plea on one-half of the people, the women, to exercise the suffrage. The doctrine of the American Revolutionary War that taxation without representation is unendurable justifies women in exercising the suffrage.

**Claim:** Smaller wages and poor working conditions for women are caused by the fact that women cannot vote.

**Grounds:** Equal pay should be given for equal work.

**Grounds:** Women are just as intelligent as men.

An opposing argument is acknowledged and refuted.

**Justification:** Women should have the right to vote because government derives its powers from the consent of the governed, and women are half of the governed population. Also, taxation without representation is against U.S. principles. If women are to be taxed, they should have a vote.

A strong conclusion does more than simply restate the claim.

## THE ART OF ARGUMENT: RHETORICAL DEVICES AND PERSUASIVE TECHNIQUES

### Rhetorical Devices

Rhetoric is the art of using language in order to make a point or to persuade listeners. Rhetorical devices such as the ones listed below are accepted elements of argument. Their use does not weaken an argument. Rather, the use of rhetorical devices is regarded as a key part of an effective argument.

| Rhetorical Devices | Examples |
|---|---|
| **Repetition** The repeated use of words, phrases, or sentences | It is not **fair** to expect this treatment. Nor is it **fair** to pay for this decision. |
| **Parallelism** The repeated use of similar grammatical structures | Good students learn to read, to question, and to respond. |
| **Rhetorical Question** Calls attention to the issue by implying an obvious answer | Shouldn't consumers get what they pay for? |
| **Sound Device** The use of alliteration, assonance, rhyme, or rhythm | The invention is both **p**ractical and **p**rofitable. |
| **Simile and Metaphor** Compares two seemingly unlike things or asserting that one thing *is* another | **Teachers** are like sparks igniting the curiosity of their students. |

### Persuasive Techniques

Persuasive techniques are often found in advertisements and in other forms of informal persuasion. Although techniques like the ones below are sometimes found in informal arguments, they should be avoided in formal arguments.

| Persuasive Techniques | Examples |
|---|---|
| **Bandwagon Approach/Anti-Bandwagon Approach** Appeals to a person's desire to belong; encourages or celebrates individuality | Anyone with any sense will vote for Richard Rock. Vote your conscience; an election is not a popularity contest. |
| **Emotional Appeal** Evokes people's fear, anger, or desire | Without working smoke detectors, your family is in danger. |
| **Endorsement/Testimony** Employs a well-known person to promote a product or idea | "I use this toothpaste, and it brightens my movie-star smile." |
| **Loaded Language** The use of words that are charged with emotion | The heroic firefighters bravely battled the raging inferno. |
| **Hyperbole** Exaggeration to make a point | Our candidate does the work of ten people. |

INFORMATIONAL TEXT

## Model Speech

The excerpted speech below includes examples of rhetorical devices and persuasive techniques.

### *from* "Inaugural Address" by Dwight D. Eisenhower

My fellow citizens:

. . . Since this century's beginning, a time of tempest has seemed to come upon the continents of the earth. Masses of Asia have awakened to strike off shackles of the past. Great nations of Europe have fought their bloodiest wars. Thrones have toppled and their vast empires have disappeared. New nations have been born.

The use of alliteration makes these phrases memorable.

For our own country, it has been a time of recurring trial. We have grown in power and in responsibility. We have passed through the anxieties of depression and of war to a summit unmatched in man's history. Seeking to secure peace in the world, we have had to fight through the forests of the Argonne, to the shores of Iwo Jima, and to the cold mountains of Korea. . .

Eisenhower uses parallelism and repetition to emphasize his main points.

How far have we come in man's long pilgrimage from darkness toward light? Are we nearing the light—a day of freedom and of peace for all mankind? Or are the shadows of another night closing in upon us?. . .

Rhetorical questions call attention to the speaker's point.

. . . we know that the virtues most cherished by free people—love of truth, pride of work, devotion to country—all are treasures equally precious in the lives of the most humble and of the most exalted. The men who mine coal and fire furnaces and balance ledgers and turn lathes and pick cotton and heal the sick and plant corn—all serve as proudly, and as profitably, for America as the statesmen who draft treaties and the legislators who enact laws.

Additional examples of parallel structure enable the audience to follow Eisenhower's ideas and to be moved by his words.

. . . We must be willing, individually and as a Nation, to accept whatever sacrifices may be required of us. A people that values its privileges above its principles soon loses both.

Sound devices, such as alliteration, are a way to emphasize a phrase.

These basic precepts are not lofty abstractions, far removed from matters of daily living. . . Patriotism means equipped forces and a prepared citizenry. Moral stamina means more energy and more productivity. . .Love of liberty means the guarding of every resource that makes freedom possible. . .

No person, no home, no community can be beyond the reach of this call. We are summoned to act in wisdom and in conscience, to work with industry, to teach with persuasion, to preach with conviction, to weigh our every deed with care and with compassion. For this truth must be clear before us: whatever America hopes to bring to pass in the world must first come to pass in the heart of America.

The parallelism created by repeated grammatical structures gives the speech rhythm.

## COMPOSING AN ARGUMENT

### Choosing a Topic

You should choose a topic that matters to people—and to you. Brainstorm topics you would like to write about, and then choose the topic that most interests you.

Once you have chosen a topic, check to be sure you can make an arguable claim. Ask yourself:

1. What am I trying to prove? What ideas do I need to get across?
2. Are there people that would disagree with my claim? What alternate, or opposing, opinions might they have?
3. Do I have evidence to support my claim? Is my evidence sufficient or relevant?

If you are able to put into words what you want to prove and answered "yes" to numbers 2 and 3, you have an arguable claim.

### Introducing the Claim and Establishing Its Significance

Before you begin writing, think about your audience and what they probably know about the topic. Then, provide only as much background information as necessary. Remember that you are not writing a summary of the issue—you are crafting an argument. Once you have provided context for your argument, clearly state your claim, or thesis. A written argument's claim often, but not always, appears in the first paragraph.

### Developing Your Claim with Reasoning and Evidence

Now that you have made your claim, you must support it with evidence, or grounds. A good argument should have at least three solid pieces of evidence to support the claim. Evidence can range from personal experience to researched data or expert opinion. Knowing your audience's knowledge level, concerns, values, and possible biases can help you decide what kind of evidence will have the strongest impact. Make sure your evidence is up to date and comes from a credible source. Don't forget to credit your sources and address the opposing counterclaim.

### Writing a Concluding Statement or Section

Restate your claim in the conclusion of your argument, and synthesize, or pull together, the evidence you have provided. Make your conclusion strong enough to be memorable to the reader; leave him or her with something to think about.

## Practice

Complete an outline like the one below to help you plan your own argument.

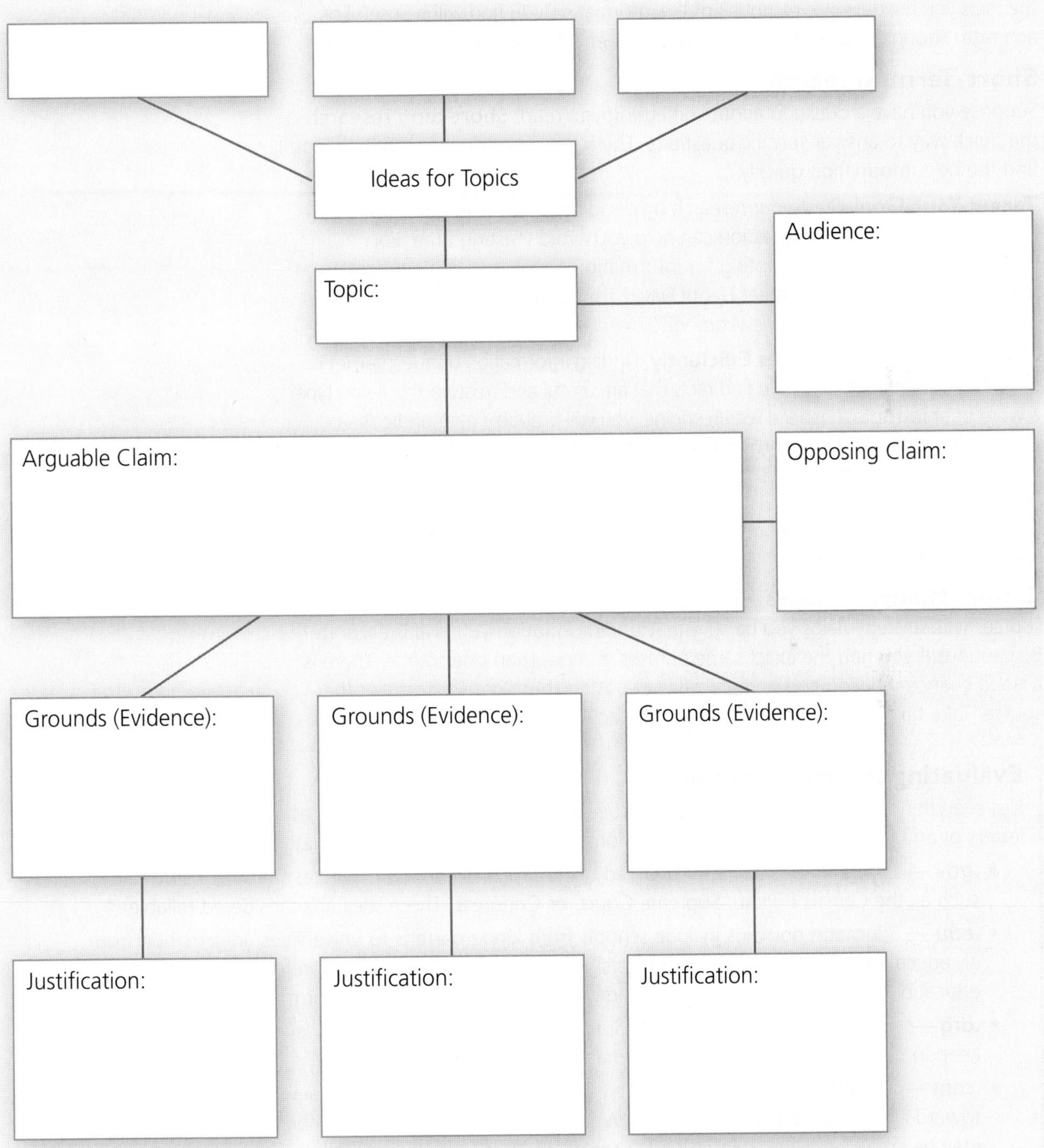

## CONDUCTING RESEARCH

Research is an organized search for information. Do you want to answer a question or explore a topic? Books, the Internet, or other reference sources will likely have the facts you need. However, not all of the information you find will be useful or accurate. Strong research skills are the key to an effective search for information.

### Short-Term Research

Suppose you have a question about something you read. **Short-term research** is the quick way to answer specific questions. The following strategies can help you find the best information quickly.

**Target Your Goal** Start your research by deciding exactly what information you need. Writing a focus question can help you avoid wasting time. For example, instead of simply hunting for information about Louisa May Alcott, you might ask "How did Alcott meet Henry David Thoreau?" or "How was Louisa May Alcott similar to Jo in *Little Women?*"

**Use Online Search Engines Efficiently** Finding information on the Internet is easy. But it can be a challenge to find facts that are useful and trustworthy. If you type a word or phrase into a general search engine, you will probably get hundreds—or thousands—of results. However, those results may not lead you to the facts you need. Scan search results before you click on one of them. The first result is not always the most relevant. Read the text and think about the source before making a choice as to which result is best. Open the page in a new window or tab so that you can return easily to your search results.

**Consult Multiple Sources** Always confirm information in more than one source. This strategy helps you be sure that the information you find is accurate. Be cautious if you find the exact same phrases in more than one source. There is a good chance that someone simply cut-and-pasted these details from another source. Take time to evaluate each source to decide if it is trustworthy.

### Evaluating Internet Domains

Not everything you read on the Internet is true, so you have to evaluate sources carefully. The last three letters of an Internet URL identify the site's domain, which can help you evaluate information on the site.

- **.gov** — Government sites are sponsored by a branch of the United States federal government, such as the Census Bureau, Supreme Court, or Congress. These sites are considered reliable.
- **.edu** — Education domains include schools from kindergartens to universities. Information from an educational research center or university department is likely to be carefully checked. However, education domains can also include student pages that are not edited or monitored.
- **.org** — Organizations are nonprofit groups and usually maintain a high level of credibility. But, keep in mind that some organizations may reflect strong biases.
- **.com** — Commercial sites exist to make a profit, so the information presented may be biased toward a particular product or service. When viewing these sites, remember that the company may be providing information to encourage sales or to promote a positive image.

## Long-Term Research

If you want to explore a topic in depth, **long-term research** allows you to carry out a detailed, comprehensive investigation. Whether your final goal is a formal research report or a media presentation, you will need to consult multiple sources for information. An organized research plan will help you gather and synthesize information from multiple sources.

As the flowchart on this page shows, long-term research is a flexible process. You will regularly adjust your approach based on what you learn about the topic in the research process. Throughout your research, you may need to adjust your approach to refocus your thesis, gather more information, or reflect on what you have learned.

## The Research Process

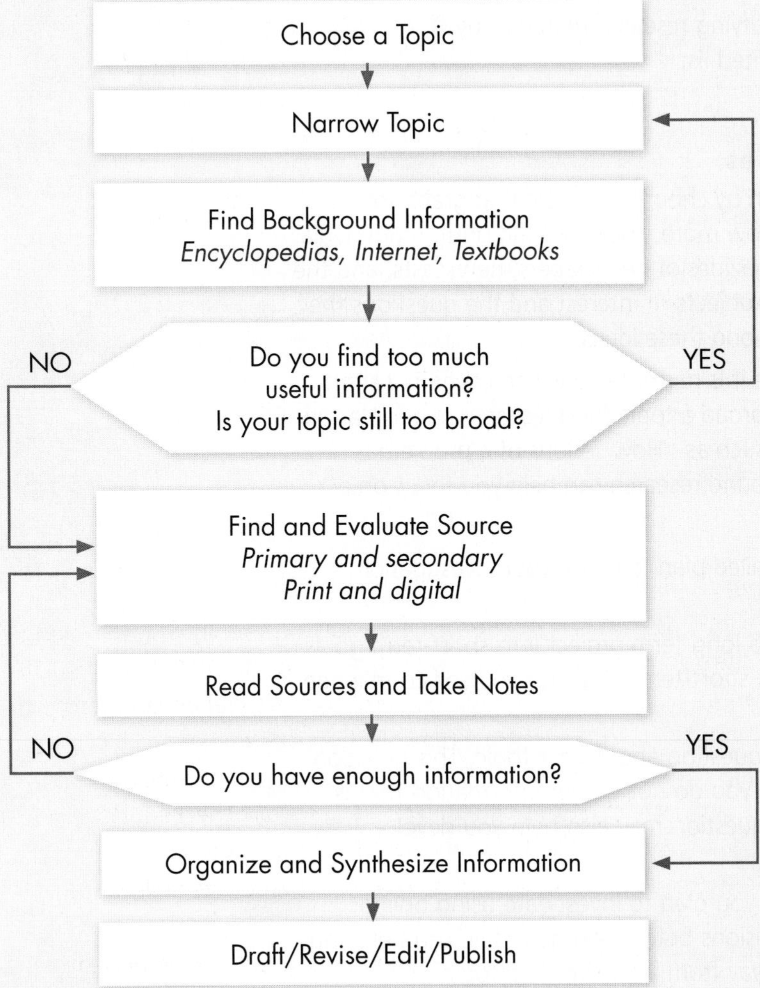


Refer to the Research Process Workshop (pages lxxii–lxxix) for more details about the steps in this flowchart.

## RESEARCH PROCESS WORKSHOP

### Research Writing: Research Report

A **research report** analyzes information gathered from reference materials, observations, interviews, or other sources to present a clear and accurate picture of a topic or answer to a question.

### Elements of a Research Report

- an overall focused topic or main idea to be analyzed
- relevant and tightly drawn questions on the topic
- a thesis statement with a clear and accurate perspective
- a clear organization and smooth transitions
- appropriate facts and relevant details to support main point
- visuals or media to support key ideas
- accurate, complete citations identifying research materials by means of footnotes or a Works Cited list
- a strong concluding statement

### Prewriting/Planning Strategies

**Choose and narrow a topic.** Begin by choosing a topic that grabs your attention and makes you curious to know more. Look through print, multimedia, and digital sources, such as recent magazines or newspapers, newscasts, and the Internet. List current events, issues, or subjects of interest and the questions they spark in you. Select your topic from among these ideas.

After you choose your topic, make sure it is narrow enough to cover in a short report. For example, "illiteracy" is too broad a topic for a research paper. Narrow the topic by asking focused questions such as "How serious of a problem is illiteracy in the United States?" Background research can help you focus on a more specific topic.

**Create a research plan.** Use a detailed plan to guide your investigation. Your plan may include these parts:

- **Set Short-Term Goals** Breaking a long-term project into short-term goals can prevent last-minute stress. Set short-term goals for yourself to manage your workload efficiently.
- **Research Question** Compose a question about your topic. This question will help you stay on track so that you do not gather information that is too broad for your purpose. This question may also help you develop your thesis statement.
- **Search Terms** Write down terms you plan to investigate using online search engines. Making these decisions before you go online can help you avoid digressions that take you away from your specified topic.
- **Source List** As you research, create a list of sources you will consult. Add sources to your list as you discover them. Place a check next to sources you have located and then underline sources you have explored thoroughly.

## Gathering Details Through Research

**Use multiple sources.** An effective research project combines information from several sources. It is important not to rely too heavily on a single source. The creativity and originality of your research depends on how you combine ideas from many places. Plan to include a variety of these types of resources:

- **Primary and Secondary Resources** Use both primary sources (firsthand or original accounts, such as interview transcripts and newspaper articles) and secondary sources (accounts that are not original, such as encyclopedia entries or an online library catalog) in your research.
- **Print and Digital Resources** The Internet allows fast access to data, but print resources are often edited more carefully. Plan to include both print and digital resources in order to guarantee that your work is accurate.
- **Media Resources** You can find valuable information in media resources such as documentaries, television programs, podcasts, and museum exhibitions. Public lectures by experts also offer an opportunity to hear an expert's thoughts on a topic.
- **Original Research** Depending on your topic, you may wish to conduct original research to include among your sources. For example, you might interview experts or eyewitnesses or conduct a survey to analyze opinions in your own community.

**Notecard**

**Education**
Papp, p.5

Only the upper classes could read.

Most of the common people in Shakespeare's time could not read.

**Take clear notes on sources.** Listed below are different strategies you may use to take notes:

- Use index cards to create **notecards** and **source cards**. Write one note per card and note the source of the information and the page number on which it is found.
- Photocopy articles and copyright pages from print sources; then, highlight relevant information.
- Print articles from the Internet or copy them directly into a folder on your computer. Remember to record the Web addresses of printouts from online sources.

**Source Card**

Papp, Joseph
and Kirkland, Elizabeth

**Shakespeare Alive!**

New York: Bantam Books, 1988

You will use these notes to help you properly cite your sources in your report.

**Credit your sources.** Copying from sources without citing them is **plagiarism**, an act that has serious academic and legal consequences. Without giving credit to a source, you are stealing another person's words. It is important to use ethical practices when conducting research.

Whether you are paraphrasing, summarizing, or using a direct quotation, you must credit the source. You can give credit by writing a *Works Cited list*, a list of the print and nonprint sources you have used.

Review pages lxxx–lxxxi to see the appropriate format for citing sources in a Works Cited list.

## Drafting Strategies

**Develop a main idea or thesis.** Review your prewriting notes to determine the overall focus of your report. Then, write a sentence that expresses your main idea. This sentence is called a **thesis statement**. As you draft, refer to your thesis statement to help keep your report focused.
**Example:** *Whales are among the most intelligent mammals on Earth.*

**Pose relevant questions.** When you research, you may come up with more questions about your topic. The questions you ask yourself should be relevant to your thesis and tightly drawn. This means you should not stray too far from the perspective you convey in your report.

**Make an outline.** Group your prewriting notes by category. Use Roman numerals (I, II, III) to number your most important points. Under each Roman numeral, use capital letters (A, B, C) for the supporting details. Use your outline as a guide for developing your draft by turning your outline notes into complete sentences. As you outline, review the data you have collected.

- Refer to the notes you made on index cards in the prewriting and researching stage.
- Confirm that the supporting details you include directly relate to the thesis statement.
- Delete any irrelevant information or research you have gathered.

**Include visuals to support key ideas.** Using charts or other visual aids allows you to present detailed information that might otherwise interrupt the flow of your report. In your writing, introduce the visual and explain its purpose. Direct readers to reference these aids as needed. To create visual aids, carry out these steps:

- Use databases and spreadsheets to organize, manage, and prepare information for your report.
- Clarify your charts, graphs, and tables by using headings and adding appropriate spacing.
- Vary the color and design of your visual aids as you display different types of information.

**PLAN YOUR CITATIONS**

As you draft, remember to use quotation marks around any words that you pick-up directly from a source. You should also give credit for ideas or facts that are unique to one source.

### Revising Strategies

**Analyze your organization.** Look over your draft and analyze your organization to see if it matches your outline. Stop at the end of each paragraph and refer to your outline. Follow these steps:

1. Mark each paragraph with the Roman numeral and capital letter from your outline and write a key word or phrase to identify the subject of the paragraph.
2. If all the paragraphs with the same Roman numeral are not next to each other, decide whether the change is an improvement. If it is not, correct it.

**Check your facts.** Read through your draft to verify that the facts, statistics, and quotations you cite are accurate. Don't rely on your memory—refer to the original source material as you work. With the exception of direct quotations, be sure you have written the information in your own words.

**Vary sentence length.** To add interest to your writing, vary the length of your sentences. Underline or highlight sentences in your draft in alternating colors so you can easily see differences in length. Then, review your color coding. Combine short, choppy sentences or break up longer sentences if there are too many of either.

**Model: Revising to Vary Sentence Length**

Basketball has been played in various forms for hundreds of years. The modern sport was introduced in 1891. An instructor at a YMCA was looking to keep his students active during the long New England winters.

The basketball hoop was made from a peach basket ~~. The basket had~~ with a closed bottom. Soon, the players realized that if they removed the bottom, the game could be played quicker.

**Review.** Ask a classmate, your teacher, or another adult to read your report to determine if the organization of your draft is clear. If your reader finds areas that require transitions, consider revising your draft by adding a word, phrase, or sentence that shows the connection between your paragraphs. Use transitions such as *at first, finally*, or *as a result* to show relationships between ideas.

Ask the reader for feedback as to whether or not you have supported your thesis statement adequately. Revise your report as needed based on your reviewer's comments.

## EDITING AND PROOFREADING

During the editing process, you will focus on giving credit to the sources you used. You will also look for mistakes in formatting, grammar, and spelling in your work.

**Focus on citations.** Cite the sources for quotations, factual information, and any ideas that are not your own. Some word-processing programs have features that allow you to create footnotes and endnotes. If you are using MLA style, citations should appear in parentheses directly after the information cited. Include the author's last name and the relevant page number.

**Example:** *In the last 50 years, one third of tropical rainforests have been destroyed (Warburton 455).*

**Create a reference list.** Following the format your teacher assigns, create a Works Cited list of the information you used to write your research report. (For more information, see Citing Sources, pp. lxxx–lxxxi).

**Focus on format.** Present your research formally by including the following formatting features: an appropriate title page, pagination, spacing and margins, and citations. Make sure you have used the assigned system for crediting sources in your paper and for listing them at the end.

**Proofread.** Carefully reread your draft and correct spelling and grammar errors. Check to be sure that you have used quotation marks correctly and that each opening quotation mark has a corresponding closing quotation mark.

### Publishing and Presenting

In addition to submitting your research report to your teacher, you might decide to use one of these strategies to share your findings with classmates.

**Give an oral report.** Use your research report as the basis for an oral presentation on your topic. Keep your audience in mind and revise accordingly as you prepare your presentation.

**Create a multimedia presentation.** Computer software makes it easy to combine text and images in an engaging way. You might record yourself reading your finished report and then add appropriate images to be viewed during playback. Or you can create a more elaborate presentation that integrates text, images, sound, and video.

**Organize a panel discussion.** If several of your classmates have written about a similar topic, plan a discussion to compare and contrast your findings. Speakers can summarize their research before opening the panel to questions from the class.

## MODEL: RESEARCH PAPER

This model research paper shows how one student developed a thesis statement by analyzing information. Notice how the writer integrates facts and details and uses parentheses to give credit for ideas taken from research sources. The Works Cited list at the end of the report gives more details about the works she used in her research.

**Hatching Chirpers:** Laura Agajanian, Santa Clara, CA

### Hatching Chirpers

A hen's egg is an amazing thing. Sitting in the nest, it seems as if it is an inanimate, or lifeless, object, but it contains everything that is needed to make a chick. In order for the chick to grow inside the egg, however, the right external conditions are needed. Under normal circumstances, these conditions are provided by the hen. They can also be reproduced and regulated in an incubator. My investigation was to discover whether the hen or the incubator would more efficiently and effectively provide the right external conditions. My hypothesis is that an incubator can provide the right external conditions more effectively and efficiently. Let's find out.

In the first paragraph, Laura identifies her main topic, the question she is investigating. In this science report, she provides a hypothesis—a proposition that the research will prove or disprove. This statement gives her perspective or viewpoint on the topic.

A chicken egg should take about twenty-one days to incubate, or take form. During that time, the eggs must be kept warm. The ideal temperature is between 99 and 100 degrees Fahrenheit. In addition, the eggs must be rotated, or turned, every eight to twelve hours. If they remain in one position for longer than that, the chick can become stuck to one side of the egg and may not form properly (Johnson 14–16).

Accurate facts and details gathered through the formal research process are presented. Since these are specific statistics that a reader might want to check, the writer gives the source.

Usually, the temperature and the turning are handled by the hen that sits on the nest. She regulates the temperature of the eggs by getting off the nest or standing above the eggs if the eggs begin to get too warm. When they have had some time to cool, she gets back on the nest. The hen turns the eggs by poking at them with her beak until each egg rolls a little to one side, eventually turning from its original position (Scott).

The report is organized to give balanced information about both methods being investigated—natural hatching and incubation.

An incubator performs these same functions. The temperature inside the incubator is measured and regulated by a thermostat that tells the heater when to turn on and when to turn off. In this way, the temperature of the eggs is kept at a constant 99 degrees. The eggs sit on a device that rolls them every eight hours. This device is controlled by an electronic timer. It is dependable because it is automatic and does not require a person to push a button for the eggs to turn. It is more efficient than a hen, because all the eggs get turned equally and consistently (Little Giant 2–6).

Based on the fact that conditions in the incubator are more consistent and controlled, I concluded that an incubator sets the ideal conditions more efficiently, and I hypothesized that it would hatch eggs more effectively. To test my hypothesis, I observed four hens sitting on a total of twenty-four eggs and placed twenty-four eggs in an incubator. Each egg was marked with a small x so that I could observe how frequently and completely each egg was turned. Chart A shows specific observations over a twenty-five-day period.

Detailed information that would interrupt the flow of the report is presented in a separate chart for readers to reference as needed.

## Chart A

| Day | Incubator Observations | Nest Observations |
|---|---|---|
| **Day 1** | **6:45 AM:** After placing the turner in the incubator, I put the 24 eggs on the turner. The temperature leveled off at 100 degrees. The eggs have warmed up quickly.<br>**5:33 PM:** The turner is working efficiently—eggs are tilted appropriately. | **7:10 AM:** After placing the 24 eggs on the nests in the cage, I put food and water in the cage. Then, I placed the hens in the cage.<br>**6:01 PM:** All hens are on the eggs. |
| **Day 5** | X marks on the eggs show that eggs have made a complete turn. | X marks on the eggs show that the eggs were not turned completely since I last checked. |
| **Day 10** | The turner seems to be tilting the eggs efficiently—X marks show a complete turn. | X marks show that 18 eggs were turned, but 6 were not. |
| **Day 15** | The temperature of the eggs is at a steady 100 degrees. Ideal temperature is 100–101 degrees (Hamre). | Two hens have moved off the nest for a brief time. Temperature of the eggs right now is 97 degrees. |
| **Day 25** | The incubator has hatched 13 out of the 24 eggs. | The hens have hatched 10 out of the 24 eggs. |

In general, the incubator eggs received much more consistent attention to their condition. The machine did not need to stop to eat or exercise, as the hens did. The marks on the eggs showed that the eggs under the hens did not always get completely turned. Sometimes, some of the eggs were turned and some were not. In addition, the hens sometimes left the nest for as long as an hour. When the temperature of the eggs was measured after a hen had been gone a long time, the egg temperature was sometimes as low as 97 degrees.

After twenty-five days, the hens had hatched ten out of the twenty-four eggs, and the incubator had hatched thirteen. The difference between the two numbers is not great enough to say that one way of incubating is more effective than the other. The incubator is definitely more efficient at delivering ideal conditions than the hens were. However, since the increased efficiency does not result in a higher number of hatches, maybe "ideal" conditions are not required for a successful hatch.

Laura concludes by explaining whether the research did or did not support her original hypothesis.

**Works Cited**


Hamre, Melvin L. "Hatching and Brooding Small Numbers of Chicks." *University of Minnesota Extension,* 2013. Web. 3 December 2015.

Johnson, Sylvia A. *Inside an Egg.* Minneapolis: Lerner Publications Company, 1982. Print.

*Little Giant Instruction Manual for Still Air Incubator and Automatic Egg Turner.* Miller Mfg. Co., So. St. Paul, MN, 1998. Print.

Scott, Wyatt. Personal Interview. 1 Dec. 2015.


In her "Works Cited" list, Laura provides information on the sources she cites, or notes, in her research report.

## CITING SOURCES AND PREPARING MANUSCRIPT

### Proofreading and Preparing Manuscript

Before preparing a final copy, proofread your manuscript. The chart shows the standard symbols for marking corrections to be made.

| Proofreading Symbols | |
|---|---|
| Insert | ∧ |
| delete | [delete mark] |
| close space | ⁀‿ |
| new paragraph | ¶ |
| add comma | ∧ with comma |
| add period | ⊙ |
| transpose (switch) | ∩∪ |
| change to cap | a̳ |
| change to lowercase | A with slash |

- Choose a standard, easy-to-read font.
- Type or print on one side of unlined 8 1/2" × 11" paper.
- Set the margins for the side, top, and bottom of your paper at approximately one inch. Most word-processing programs have a default setting that is appropriate.
- Double-space the document.
- Indent the first line of each paragraph.
- Number the pages in the upper right corner.

Follow your teacher's directions for formatting formal research papers. Most papers will have the following features:

- Title Page
- Table of Contents or Outline
- Works Cited List

### Avoiding Plagiarism

Whether you are presenting a formal research paper or an opinion paper on a current event, you must be careful to give credit for any ideas or opinions that are not your own. Presenting someone else's ideas, research, or opinion as your own—even if you have phrased it in different words—is *plagiarism*, the equivalent of academic stealing, or fraud.

Do not use the ideas or research of others in place of your own. Read from several sources to draw your own conclusions and form your own opinions. Incorporate the ideas and research of others to support your points. Credit the source of the following types of support:

- Statistics
- Direct quotations
- Indirectly quoted statements of opinions
- Conclusions presented by an expert
- Facts available in only one or two sources

### Crediting Sources

When you credit a source, you acknowledge where you found your information and you give your readers the details necessary for locating the source themselves. Within the body of the paper, you provide a short citation, a footnote number linked to a footnote, or an endnote number linked to an endnote reference. These brief references show the page numbers on which you found the information. Prepare a reference list at the end of the paper to provide full bibliographic information on your sources. These are two common types of reference lists:

- A bibliography provides a listing of all the resources you consulted during your research.
- A Works Cited list indicates the works you have referenced in your paper.

The chart on the next page shows the Modern Language Association format for crediting sources. This is the most common format for papers written in the content areas in middle school and high school. Unless instructed otherwise by your teacher, use this format for crediting sources.

## MLA Style for Listing Sources

| | |
|---|---|
| **Book with one author** | Pyles, Thomas. *The Origins and Development of the English Language.* 2nd ed. New York: Harcourt, 1971. Print. |
| **Book with two or three authors** | McCrum, Robert, William Cran, and Robert MacNeil. *The Story of English.* New York: Penguin, 1987. Print. |
| **Book with an editor** | Truth, Sojourner. *Narrative of Sojourner Truth.* Ed. Margaret Washington. New York: Vintage, 1993. Print. |
| **Book with more than three authors or editors** | Donald, Robert B., et al. *Writing Clear Essays.* Upper Saddle River: Prentice, 1996. Print. |
| **Single work in an anthology** | Hawthorne, Nathaniel. "Young Goodman Brown." *Literature: An Introduction to Reading and Writing.* Ed. Edgar V. Roberts and H. E. Jacobs. Upper Saddle River: Prentice, 1998. 376–385. Print. [Indicate pages for the entire selection.] |
| **Introduction to a work in a published edition** | Washington, Margaret. Introduction. *Narrative of Sojourner Truth.* By Sojourner Truth. Ed. Washington. New York: Vintage, 1993. v–xi. Print. |
| **Signed article from an encyclopedia** | Askeland, Donald R. "Welding." *World Book Encyclopedia.* 1991 ed. Print. |
| **Signed article in a weekly magazine** | Wallace, Charles. "A Vodacious Deal." *Time* 14 Feb. 2000: 63. Print. |
| **Signed article in a monthly magazine** | Gustaitis, Joseph. "The Sticky History of Chewing Gum." *American History* Oct. 1998: 30–38. Print. |
| **Newspaper** | Thurow, Roger. "South Africans Who Fought for Sanctions Now Scrap for Investors." *Wall Street Journal* 11 Feb. 2000: A1+. Print. [For a multipage article that does not appear on consecutive pages, write only the first page number on which it appears, followed by the plus sign.] |
| **Unsigned editorial or story** | "Selective Silence." Editorial. *Wall Street Journal* 11 Feb. 2000: A14. Print. [If the editorial or story is signed, begin with the author's name.] |
| **Signed pamphlet or brochure** | [Treat the pamphlet as though it were a book.] |
| **Work from a library subscription service** | Ertman, Earl L. "Nefertiti's Eyes." *Archaeology* Mar.–Apr. 2008: 28–32. *Kids Search.* EBSCO. New York Public Library. Web. 18 June 2008 [Indicate the date you accessed the information.] |
| **Filmstrips, slide programs, videocassettes, DVDs, and other audiovisual media** | *The Diary of Anne Frank.* Dir. George Stevens. Perf. Millie Perkins, Shelley Winters, Joseph Schildkraut, Lou Jacobi, and Richard Beymer. 1959. Twentieth Century Fox, 2004. DVD. |
| **CD-ROM (with multiple publishers)** | Simms, James, ed. *Romeo and Juliet.* By William Shakespeare. Oxford: Attica Cybernetics; London: BBC Education; London: Harper, 1995. CD-ROM. |
| **Radio or television program transcript** | "Washington's Crossing of the Delaware." *Weekend Edition Sunday.* Natl. Public Radio. WNYC, New York. 23 Dec. 2003. Television transcript. |
| **Internet Web page** | "Fun Facts About Gum." NACGM site. 1999. National Association of Chewing Gum Manufacturers. Web. 19 Dec. 1999 [Indicate the date you accessed the information.] |
| **Personal interview** | Smith, Jane. Personal interview. 10 Feb. 2000. |

All examples follow the style given in the *MLA Handbook for Writers of Research Papers*, seventh edition, by Joseph Gibaldi.

# UNIT 1

# Does every conflict have a winner?

## UNIT PATHWAY

**PART 1**
**SETTING EXPECTATIONS**

- INTRODUCING THE BIG QUESTION
- CLOSE READING WORKSHOP

**PART 2**
**TEXT ANALYSIS**
GUIDED EXPLORATION

DIFFERENT PERSPECTIVES

**PART 3**
**TEXT SET**
DEVELOPING INSIGHT

COMPETITION

**PART 4**
**DEMONSTRATING INDEPENDENCE**

- INDEPENDENT READING
- ONLINE TEXT SET

## CLOSE READING TOOL

Use this tool to practice the close reading strategies you learn.

## STUDENT eTEXT

Bring learning to life with audio, video, and interactive tools.

## ONLINE WRITER'S NOTEBOOK

Easily capture notes and complete assignments online.

Find all Digital Resources at **pearsonrealize.com.**

## Does every conflict have a winner?

A conflict is a struggle between opposing forces. A conflict can be as small as a disagreement between friends about what movie to see. On the other hand, it can be as large as a civil war. When you struggle with a decision, you have a conflict within yourself. There are many kinds of conflict. Some can be dangerous. Others, like a sports competition, can be exciting. When a conflict is worked out, it is resolved. Different kinds of conflicts are resolved in different ways.

## Exploring the Big Question

**Collaboration: One-on-One Discussion** Start thinking about the Big Question by making a list of different conflicts you have experienced or heard about. Describe one specific example of each of the following types of conflict.

- An argument or disagreement between friends
- A misunderstanding between two people
- A competition between teams or in a contest
- A struggle to make a decision
- A struggle to overcome a challenge or an obstacle

Share your examples with a partner. Talk about the cause of each conflict and the way the conflict worked out. As you exchange ideas, build upon each other's comments. You may want to use the conflict-related words on the next page in the course of your discussion.

**Connecting to the Literature** Each reading in this unit will give you additional insight into the Big Question. After you read each text, pause to consider ways in which the characters handled conflict.

## Vocabulary

**Acquire and Use Academic Vocabulary** The term "academic vocabulary" refers to words you typically encounter in scholarly and literary texts and in technical and business writing. Review the definitions of these academic vocabulary words.

**attitude** (at´ ə to͞od´) *n.* person's opinions and feelings about someone or something

**challenge** (chal´ənj) *n.* something that tests your skills and abilities

**communication** (kə myo͞o´ni kā´shən) *n.* process of sharing information or expressing thoughts and feelings

**conflict** (kän´ flikt´) *n.* struggle between opposing forces

**opposition** (äp´ə zish´ən) *n.* person, group, or force that tries to prevent you from accomplishing something

**outcome** (out´kum´) *n.* way a situation turns out; result or consequence

**resolution** (rez´ə lo͞o´shən) *n.* working out of a problem or conflict

**understanding** (un´dər stan´ diŋ) *n.* agreement

**Gather Vocabulary Knowledge** Additional words related to conflict are listed below. Categorize the words by deciding whether you know each one well, know it a little bit, or do not know it at all.

| | | |
|---|---|---|
| **competition** | **desire** | **obstacle** |
| **compromise** | **disagreement** | **struggle** |
| **danger** | **misunderstanding** | |

Then, do the following:

1. Work with a partner to say each word and explain what you think each word means.
2. Consult a print or online dictionary to confirm each word's pronunciation and meaning.
3. Then, use at least four of the words in a brief paragraph about a conflict you experienced or heard about.
4. Take turns reading your paragraphs aloud.

# Close Reading Workshop

In this workshop you will learn an approach to reading that will deepen your understanding of literature and will help you better appreciate the author's craft. The workshop includes models for close reading, discussion, research, and writing. After you have reviewed the strategies and models, practice your skills with the Independent Practice selection.

## CLOSE READING: SHORT STORY

In Part 2 of this unit you will focus on reading various short stories. Use these strategies as you read the texts.

### Comprehension: Key Ideas and Details

- Read first to unlock basic meaning.
- Use context clues to help you determine the meanings of unfamiliar words. Consult a dictionary, if necessary.
- Identify unfamiliar details that you might need to clarify through research.
- Distinguish between what is stated directly and what must be inferred.

**Ask yourself questions such as these:**

- Who are the main characters?
- What conflict drives the main events?
- What is the story's setting?

### Text Analysis: Craft and Structure

- Think about the genre of the work and how the author presents ideas.
- Analyze the author's choice of words and the impact of those words.
- Note how the setting, characters, and events work together to build suspense and establish theme.

**Ask yourself questions such as these:**

- From whose point of view, or perspective, is the story told? How does this perspective influence what the reader does and does not know?
- What do I learn about the characters from the story's dialogue and narration?

### Connections: Integration of Knowledge and Ideas

- Look for relationships among key ideas. Identify causes and effects and comparisons and contrasts.
- Look for key ideas, symbolic images, or repetition. Then, connect ideas to identify the theme of the story.
- Compare and contrast this work with other works you have read.

**Ask yourself questions such as these:**

- How has this work increased my knowledge of a subject or an author?
- What lessons have I learned that I can apply to my life?

## Read

As you read this short story, take note of the annotations that model ways to closely read the text.

### Reading Model

### "The Dinner Party" by Mona Gardner

The country is India. A colonial official[1] and his wife are giving a large dinner party. They are seated with their guests—army officers, and government attachés with their wives, and a visiting American naturalist—in their spacious dining room. It has a bare marble floor, open rafters, and wide glass doors opening onto a veranda.

A spirited discussion springs up between a young girl who insists that women have outgrown the jumping-on-a-chair-at-the-sight-of-a-mouse era and a colonel who says that they haven't.[2]

"A woman's unfailing reaction in any crisis," the colonel says, "is to scream. And while a man may feel like it, he has that ounce more of nerve control than a woman has. And that last ounce more is what counts."

The American does not join in the argument but watches the other guests. As he looks, he sees a strange expression come over the face of the hostess. She is staring straight ahead, her muscles contracting slightly.[3] With a slight gesture, she summons the native boy standing behind her chair and whispers to him. The boy's eyes widen, and he quickly leaves the room.

Of the guests, none except the American notices this or sees the boy place a bowl of milk on the veranda just outside the open doors.

The American comes to with a start. In India, milk in a bowl means only one thing—bait for a snake. He realizes there must be a cobra in the room. He looks up at the rafters—the likeliest place—but they are bare. Three corners of the room are empty, and in the fourth the servants are waiting to serve the next course. There is only one place left—under the table.[4]

**Key Ideas and Details**

**1** An Internet search will reveal that India was part of the British Empire until 1947. The "colonial official" is British.

**Craft and Structure**

**2** In this passage, a small argument breaks out between a young girl and a colonel, who believes that women lack self-control. Characters' beliefs may be clues to theme.

**Craft and Structure**

**3** The narrator's point of view is limited to what the American notices. By leaving the cause of the hostess's expression unknown, the author creates suspense.

**Craft and Structure**

**4** The dashes in this passage help convey the sense that the American's thoughts are racing as he takes in details and comes to conclusions about the snake.

His first impulse is to jump back and warn the others, but he knows the commotion would frighten the cobra into striking.[5] He speaks quickly, the tone of his voice so arresting that it sobers everyone.

"I want to know just what control everyone at this table has. I will count to three hundred—that's five minutes—and not one of you is to move a muscle. Those who move will forfeit fifty rupees. Ready!"

The twenty people sit like stone images while he counts. He is saying "two hundred and eighty" when, out of the corner of his eye, he sees the cobra emerge and make for the bowl of milk. Screams ring out as he jumps to slam the veranda doors safely shut.[6]

"You were right, Colonel!" the host exclaims. "A man has just shown us an example of perfect control."[7]

"Just a minute," the American says, turning to his hostess. "Mrs. Wynnes, how did you know the cobra was in the room?"

A faint smile lights up the woman's face as she replies, "Because it was crawling across my foot."[8]

**Integration of Knowledge and Ideas**

**5** Again, the idea of self-control surfaces as the American fights off panic.

**Craft and Structure**

**6** The climax occurs as the snake leaves and the dinner guests scream in fear.

**Integration of Knowledge and Ideas**

**7** The host's statement recalls the argument from the beginning of the story: self-control is a male trait. So far, the story seems to prove the colonel right.

**Craft and Structure**

**8** The hostess's remark shows that she has more self-control than any other character. This twist reveals the theme: Courage and self-control are not specific to a gender.

## Discuss

Sharing your own ideas and listening to the ideas of others can deepen your understanding of a text and help you look at a topic in a whole new way. As you participate in collaborative discussions, work to have a genuine exchange in which classmates build upon one another's ideas. Support your points with evidence and ask meaningful questions.

### Discussion Model

**Student 1:** The author makes sure that we know the setting of the story. In the first sentence, she says: "The country is India." That makes sense, since you'd never have a cobra at a dinner party in Great Britain.

**Student 2:** I think it's about more than just the snake. The author describes a "spacious dining room," " bare marble floor," and "wide glass doors opening onto a veranda." So the story is not only set in India, it seems like the characters are rich people in India.

**Student 3:** I agree. I wonder how Gardner's ideas about women fit into this setting. The women only get one sentence of dialogue, and the men don't seem to respect them since they don't think women have "nerve control." Is the setting important because women were not equal in colonial India?

## Research

Targeted research can clarify unfamiliar details and shed light on various aspects of a text. Consider questions that arise in your mind as you read, and use those questions as the basis for research.

### Research Model

**Questions:** *What was life like for British women in colonial India?*

**Key Words for Internet Search:** British women and colonial India

**Result:** Women in World History: British Empire, George Mason University

**What I Learned:** British women who went to India with their husbands mostly stayed at home and lived in luxury, but had few rights. Some women worked at jobs outside the home, such as teaching local women or participating in missionary work.

## Write

Writing about a text will deepen your understanding of it and will also allow you to share your ideas more formally with others. The following model essay analyzes the role that characters, setting, and plot have in establishing theme and cites evidence to support the main ideas.

### Writing Model: Argument

### Real Courage

"The Dinner Party," by Mona Gardner, appears on first reading to be a simple story with a surprise ending. Upon closer reading, however, it is clear that Gardner carefully crafted this story in order to develop a powerful theme: That both women and men are capable of great bravery and self-control. Plot events, character development, and the story's setting all work together to reveal this theme.

The writer presents the essay's thesis in the first paragraph, preparing readers for the claims and evidence that will follow.

As the story begins, a "spirited discussion" takes place between a young woman and a colonel. The two disagree about whether or not women are capable of self-control. This minor conflict sets the stage for the story events that are to come.

The story is told from a third-person limited point of view. The narrator focuses on the observations of an American naturalist, sharing with us his viewpoint of the action taking place at a small dinner party. Suspense builds as the narrator watches his hostess's "strange expression," contracting muscles, and whispered instructions to a servant. As more of the American's observations are revealed, the reader realizes the seriousness of the situation: There is a deadly snake in the room full of guests. The American, a man, controls his feelings of panic and manages to trick the guests into sitting still until the snake is successfully removed from the room.

The writer identifies elements of the author's craft and explains their significance in the story.

Following these tense events, the host of the party makes a comment about the self-control exhibited by the American, saying, "A man has just shown us an example of perfect control." It becomes apparent, however, that although the American did show bravery and control, it is the hostess herself who exhibited the most self-control. She had been aware the entire time of the snake's presence because it was resting on her foot, and she quietly took the first steps to having it removed.

Direct quotations from the story support claims.

The story's theme is made all the more powerful when you consider the story's setting of colonial India. British women in colonial India were not granted the rights and respect of British males. In fact, British women were typically regarded as fragile and needing protection. Given this context, the story's theme takes on even more power.

Evidence from research can also be used to support claims, as in this example about the story's setting.

As you read the following story, apply the close reading strategies you have learned. You may need to read the short story multiple times in order to grasp key ideas and details, appreciate its craft and structure, and integrate knowledge and ideas.

# "The Treasure of Lemon Brown"

by Walter Dean Myers

The dark sky, filled with angry, swirling clouds, reflected Greg Ridley's mood as he sat on the stoop of his building. His father's voice came to him again, first reading the letter the principal had sent to the house, then lecturing endlessly about his poor efforts in math.

"I had to leave school when I was thirteen," his father had said, "that's a year younger than you are now. If I'd had half the chances that you have, I'd . . ."

Greg had sat in the small, pale green kitchen listening, knowing the lecture would end with his father saying he couldn't play ball with the Scorpions. He had asked his father the week before, and his father had said it depended on his next report card. It wasn't often the Scorpions took on new players, especially fourteen-year-olds, and this was a chance of a lifetime for Greg. He hadn't been allowed to play high school ball, which he had really wanted to do, but playing for the Community Center team was the next best thing. Report cards were due in a week, and Greg had been hoping for the best. But the principal had ended the suspense early when she sent that letter saying Greg would probably fail math if he didn't spend more time studying.

"And you want to play *basketball*?" His father's brows knitted over deep brown eyes. "That must be some kind of a joke. Now you just get into your room and hit those books."

That had been two nights before. His father's words, like the distant thunder that now echoed through the streets of Harlem, still rumbled softly in his ears.

It was beginning to cool. Gusts of wind made bits of paper dance between the parked cars. There was a flash of nearby lightning, and soon large drops of rain splashed onto his jeans. He stood to go upstairs, thought of the lecture that probably awaited him if he did anything except shut himself in his room with his math book, and started walking down the street instead. Down the block there was an old tenement that had

### Meet the Author

Best-selling author **Walter Dean Myers** (b. 1937) writes about what he calls "the most difficult period of my life, the teen years." He dropped out of high school and joined the army when he was 17, but he did not give up on writing. He is a three-time finalist for the National Book Award. Myers bases much of his work on his childhood experiences growing up in Harlem.

**CLOSE READING TOOL**

Read and respond to this selection online using the **Close Reading Tool.**

**Vocabulary ▶**

**impromptu** (im prämp'tōō) *adj.* unscheduled; unplanned

**ajar** (ə jär') *adj.* slightly open

**tentatively** (ten' tə tiv lē) *adj.* hesitantly; with uncertainty

been abandoned for some months. Some of the guys had held an **impromptu** checker tournament there the week before, and Greg had noticed that the door, once boarded over, had been slightly **ajar**.

Pulling his collar up as high as he could, he checked for traffic and made a dash across the street. He reached the house just as another flash of lightning changed the night to day for an instant, then returned the graffiti-scarred building to the grim shadows. He vaulted over the outer stairs and pushed **tentatively** on the door. It was open, and he let himself in.

The inside of the building was dark except for the dim light that filtered through the dirty windows from the streetlamps. There was a room a few feet from the door, and from where he stood at the entrance, Greg could see a squarish patch of light on the floor. He entered the room, frowning at the musty smell. It was a large room that might have been someone's parlor at one time. Squinting, Greg could see an old table on its side against one wall, what looked like a pile of rags or a torn mattress in the corner, and a couch, with one side broken, in front of the window.

He went to the couch. The side that wasn't broken was comfortable enough, though a little creaky. From the spot he could see the blinking neon sign over the bodega on the corner. He sat awhile, watching the sign blink first green then red, allowing his mind to drift to the Scorpions, then to his father. His father had been a postal worker for all Greg's life, and was proud of it, often telling Greg how hard he had worked to pass the test. Greg had heard the story too many times to be interested now.

For a moment Greg thought he heard something that sounded like a scraping against the wall. He listened carefully, but it was gone.

Outside the wind had picked up, sending the rain against the window with a force that shook the glass in its frame. A car passed, its tires hissing over the wet street and its red taillights glowing in the darkness.

Greg thought he heard the noise again. His stomach tightened as he held himself still and listened intently. There weren't any more scraping noises, but he was sure he had heard something in the darkness—something breathing!

He tried to figure out just where the breathing was coming from; he knew it was in the room with him. Slowly he stood, tensing. As he turned, a flash of lightning lit up the room, frightening him with its sudden brilliance. He saw nothing, just the overturned table, the pile of rags and an old newspaper on the floor. Could he have been imagining the sounds? He continued listening, but heard nothing and thought that it might have just been rats. Still, he thought, as soon as the rain let up he would leave. He went to the window and was about to look when he heard a voice behind him.

"Don't try nothin' 'cause I got a razor here sharp enough to cut a week into nine days!"

Greg, except for an involuntary tremor in his knees, stood stock still. The voice was high and brittle, like dry twigs being broken, surely not one he had ever heard before. There was a shuffling sound as the person who had been speaking moved a step closer. Greg turned, holding his breath, his eyes straining to see in the dark room.

The upper part of the figure before him was still in darkness. The lower half was in the dim rectangle of light that fell unevenly from the window. There were two feet, in cracked, dirty shoes from which rose legs that were wrapped in rags.

"Who are you?" Greg hardly recognized his own voice.

"I'm Lemon Brown," came the answer. "Who're you?"

"Greg Ridley."

"What you doing here?" The figure shuffled forward again, and Greg took a small step backward.

"It's raining," Greg said.

"I can see that," the figure said.

The person who called himself Lemon Brown peered forward, and Greg could see him clearly. He was an old man.

His black, heavily wrinkled face was surrounded by a halo of crinkly white hair and whiskers that seemed to separate his head from the layers of dirty coats piled on his smallish frame. His pants were bagged to the knee, where they were met with rags that went down to the old shoes. The rags were held on with strings, and there was a rope around his middle. Greg relaxed. He had seen the man before, picking through the trash on the corner and pulling clothes out of a Salvation Army box. There was no sign of the razor that could "cut a week into nine days."

"What are you doing here?" Greg asked.

"This is where I'm staying," Lemon Brown said. "What you here for?"

"Told you it was raining out," Greg said, leaning against the back of the couch until he felt it give slightly.

"Ain't you got no home?"

"I got a home," Greg answered.

"You ain't one of them bad boys looking for my treasure, is you?" Lemon Brown cocked his head to one side and squinted one eye. "Because I told you I got me a razor."

"I'm not looking for your treasure," Greg answered, smiling. "If you have one."

"What you mean, if I have one," Lemon Brown said. "Every man got a treasure. You don't know that, you must be a fool!"

"Sure," Greg said as he sat on the sofa and put one leg over the back. "What do you have, gold coins?"

"Don't worry none about what I got," Lemon Brown said. "You know who I am?"

"You told me your name was orange or lemon or something like that."

"Lemon Brown," the old man said, pulling back his shoulders as he did so, "they used to call me Sweet Lemon Brown."

"Sweet Lemon?" Greg asked.

"Yessir. Sweet Lemon Brown. They used to say I sung the blues so sweet that if I sang at a funeral, the dead would commence to rocking with the beat. Used to travel all over Mississippi and as far as Monroe, Louisiana, and east on over to Macon, Georgia. You mean you ain't never heard of Sweet Lemon Brown?"

"Afraid not," Greg said. "What . . . what happened to you?"

"Hard times, boy. Hard times always after a poor man. One day I got tired, sat down to rest a spell and felt a tap on my shoulder. Hard times caught up with me."

"Sorry about that."

"What you doing here? How come you didn't go on home when the rain come? Rain don't bother you young folks none."

"Just didn't." Greg looked away.

"I used to have a knotty-headed boy just like you." Lemon Brown had half walked, half shuffled back to the corner and sat down against the wall. "Had them big eyes like you got, I used to call them moon eyes. Look into them moon eyes and see anything you want."

"How come you gave up singing the blues?" Greg asked.

"Didn't give it up," Lemon Brown said. "You don't give up the blues; they give you up. After a while you do good for yourself, and it ain't nothing but foolishness singing about how hard you got it. Ain't that right?"

"I guess so."

"What's that noise?" Lemon Brown asked, suddenly sitting upright.

Greg listened, and he heard a noise outside. He looked at Lemon Brown and saw the old man pointing toward the window.

Greg went to the window and saw three men, neighborhood thugs, on the stoop. One was carrying a length of pipe. Greg looked back toward Lemon Brown, who moved quietly across the room to the window. The old man looked out, then beckoned frantically for Greg to follow him. For a moment Greg couldn't move. Then he found himself following Lemon Brown into the hallway and up darkened stairs. Greg followed as closely as he could. They reached the top of the stairs, and Greg felt Lemon Brown's hand first lying on his shoulder, then probing down his arm until he finally took Greg's hand into his own as they crouched in the darkness.

"They's bad men," Lemon Brown whispered. His breath was warm against Greg's skin.

"Hey! Rag man!" A voice called. "We know you in here. What you got up under them rags? You got any money?"

Silence.

"We don't want to have to come in and hurt you, old man, but we don't mind if we have to."

Lemon Brown squeezed Greg's hand in his own hard, gnarled fist.

There was a banging downstairs and a light as the men entered. They banged around noisily, calling for the rag man.

"We heard you talking about your treasure." The voice was slurred.

"We just want to see it, that's all."

"You sure he's here?" One voice seemed to come from the room with the sofa.

"Yeah, he stays here every night."

"There's another room over there; I'm going to take a look. You got that flashlight?"

"Yeah, here, take the pipe too."

Greg opened his mouth to quiet the sound of his breath as he sucked it in uneasily. A beam of light hit the wall a few feet opposite him, then went out.

"Ain't nobody in that room," a voice said. "You think he gone or something?"

"I don't know," came the answer. "All I know is that I heard him talking about some kind of treasure. You know they found that shopping bag lady with that money in her bags."

"Yeah. You think he's upstairs?"

"Hey, old man, are you up there?"

Silence.

"Watch my back, I'm going up."

There was a footstep on the stairs, and the beam from the flashlight danced crazily along the peeling wallpaper. Greg held his breath. There was another step and a loud crashing noise as the man banged the pipe against the wooden banister. Greg could feel his temples throb as the man slowly neared them. Greg thought about the pipe, wondering what he would do when the man reached them—what he *could* do.

Then Lemon Brown released his hand and moved toward the top of the stairs. Greg looked around and saw stairs going up to the next floor. He tried waving to Lemon Brown, hoping the old man would see him in the dim light and follow him to the next floor. Maybe, Greg thought, the man wouldn't follow them up there. Suddenly, though, Lemon Brown stood at the top of the stairs, both arms raised high above his head.

"There he is!" A voice cried from below.

"Throw down your money, old man, so I won't have to bash your head in!"

Lemon Brown didn't move. Greg felt himself near panic. The steps came closer, and still Lemon Brown didn't move. He was an eerie sight, a bundle of rags standing at the top of the stairs, his shadow on the wall looming over him. Maybe, the thought came to Greg, the scene could be even eerier.

Greg wet his lips, put his hands to his mouth and tried to make a sound. Nothing came out. He swallowed hard, wet his lips once more and howled as evenly as he could.

*"What's that?"*

As Greg howled, the light moved away from Lemon Brown, but not before Greg saw him hurl his body down the stairs at the men who had come to take his treasure. There was a crashing noise, and then footsteps. A rush of warm air came in as the downstairs door opened, then there was only an ominous silence.

Greg stood on the landing. He listened, and after a while there was another sound on the staircase.

"Mr. Brown?" he called.

"Yeah, it's me," came the answer. "I got their flashlight."

Greg exhaled in relief as Lemon Brown made his way slowly back up the stairs.

"You OK?"

"Few bumps and bruises," Lemon Brown said.

"I think I'd better be going," Greg said, his breath returning to normal. "You'd better leave, too, before they come back."

"They may hang around outside for a while," Lemon Brown said, "but they ain't getting their nerve up to come in here again. Not with crazy old rag men and howling spooks. Best you stay a while till the coast is clear. I'm heading out west tomorrow, out to East St. Louis."

"They were talking about treasures," Greg said. "You *really* have a treasure?"

"What I tell you? Didn't I tell you every man got a treasure?" Lemon Brown said. "You want to see mine?"

"If you want to show it to me," Greg shrugged.

"Let's look out the window first, see what them scoundrels be doing," Lemon Brown said.

They followed the oval beam of the flashlight into one of the rooms and looked out the window. They saw the men who had tried to take the treasure sitting on the curb near the corner. One of them had his pants leg up, looking at his knee.

"You sure you're not hurt?" Greg asked Lemon Brown.

"Nothing that ain't been hurt before," Lemon Brown said. "When you get as old as me all you say when something hurts is, 'Howdy, Mr. Pain, sees you back again.' Then when Mr. Pain see he can't worry you none, he go on mess with somebody else."

Greg smiled.

"Here, you hold this." Lemon Brown gave Greg the flashlight.

He sat on the floor near Greg and carefully untied the strings that held the rags on his right leg. When he took the rags away, Greg saw a piece of plastic. The old man carefully took off the plastic and unfolded it. He revealed some yellowed newspaper clippings and a battered harmonica.

"There it be," he said, nodding his head. "There it be."

Greg looked at the old man, saw the distant look in his eye, then turned to the clippings. They told of Sweet Lemon Brown, a blues singer and harmonica player who was appearing at different theaters in the South. One of the clippings said he had been the hit of the show, although not the headliner. All of the clippings were reviews of shows Lemon Brown had been in more than 50 years ago. Greg looked at the harmonica. It was dented badly on one side, with the reed holes on one end nearly closed.

"I used to travel around and make money for to feed my wife and Jesse—that's my boy's name. Used to feed them good, too. Then his mama died, and he stayed with his mama's sister. He growed up to be a man, and when the war come he saw fit to go off and fight in it. I didn't have nothing to give him except these things that told him who I was, and what he come from. If you know your pappy did something, you know you can do something too.

"Anyway, he went off to war, and I went off still playing and singing. 'Course by then I wasn't as much as I used to be, not without somebody to make it worth the while. You know what I mean?"

"Yeah," Greg nodded, not quite really knowing.

"I traveled around, and one time I come home, and there was this letter saying Jesse got killed in the war. Broke my heart, it truly did.

"They sent back what he had with him over there, and what it was is this old mouth fiddle and these clippings. Him carrying it around with him like that told me it meant something to him. That was my treasure, and when I give it to him he treated it just like that, a treasure. Ain't that something?"

"Yeah, I guess so," Greg said.

"You *guess* so?" Lemon Brown's voice rose an octave as he started to put his treasure back into the plastic. "Well, you got to guess 'cause you sure don't know nothing. Don't know enough to get home when it's raining."

"I guess . . . I mean, you're right."

"You OK for a youngster," the old man said as he tied the strings around his leg, "better than those scalawags what come here looking for my treasure. That's for sure."

"You really think that treasure of yours was worth fighting for?" Greg asked. "Against a pipe?"

"What else a man got 'cepting what he can pass on to his son, or his daughter, if she be his oldest?" Lemon Brown said. "For a big-headed boy you sure do ask the foolishest questions."

Lemon Brown got up after patting his rags in place and looked out the window again.

"Looks like they're gone. You get on out of here and get yourself home. I'll be watching from the window so you'll be all right."

Lemon Brown went down the stairs behind Greg. When they reached the front door the old man looked out first, saw the street was clear and told Greg to scoot on home.

"You sure you'll be OK?" Greg asked.

"Now didn't I tell you I was going to East St. Louis in the morning?" Lemon Brown asked. "Don't that sound OK to you?"

"Sure it does," Greg said. "Sure it does. And you take care of that treasure of yours."

"That I'll do," Lemon said, the wrinkles about his eyes suggesting a smile. "That I'll do."

The night had warmed and the rain had stopped, leaving puddles at the curbs. Greg didn't even want to think how late it was. He thought ahead of what his father would say and wondered if he should tell him about Lemon Brown. He thought about it until he reached his stoop, and decided against it. Lemon Brown would be OK, Greg thought, with his memories and his treasure.

Greg pushed the button over the bell marked Ridley, thought of the lecture he knew his father would give him, and smiled.

# Close Reading Activities

## Read

### Comprehension: **Key Ideas and Details**

1. **(a)** Who are the main characters in "The Treasure of Lemon Brown"? **(b) Analyze:** What is one thing you learn about each main character from his actions? Cite specific details in your answer.
2. **(a)** Where does the story take place? **(b) Synthesize:** How does the setting help advance the plot?
3. **Summarize:** Write a brief, objective summary of the story, citing story details.

### Text Analysis: **Craft and Structure**

4. **(a) Generalize:** What do you learn about Lemon Brown through the way he talks? **(b) Evaluate:** Using details from the text, explain how the author's use of dialogue strengthens his characterization.
5. **(a)** Describe two key conflicts in the story. **(b) Interpret:** How are these key conflicts resolved?
6. **(a) Deduce:** At the story's end, what has Greg learned that causes him to smile? **(b) Predict:** How will Greg's relationship with his father change in the future? Cite evidence to support your prediction.
7. **(a) Interpret:** What is the story's theme? **(b) Support:** Which story elements provide the most significant clues to its theme?

### Connections: **Integration of Knowledge and Ideas**

#### Discuss

Conduct a **small-group discussion** about the setting of the story and how it contributes to the story's *mood,* or the feeling it creates in the reader. Discuss the ways in which the setting reflects Greg's personal dilemma.

#### Research

Walter Dean Myers was appointed Ambassador for Young People's Literature. Briefly research some of the work he has done in this role, considering the following:

**a.** the messages he shares with his audiences

**b.** the ways he inspires young authors

Take notes as you perform your research. Then, write a brief **explanation** of the work Walter Dean Myers does in this role and his influence on young adult readers. In your explanation, explain the message in "The Treasure of Lemon Brown," and tell why that message is inspirational.

#### Write

In this story, Walter Dean Myers plays with the meaning of the word "treasure." Think about the typical ideas associated with treasures and whether or not Myers uses the traditional definition in his story. Write an **essay** in which you discuss the value of Lemon Brown's treasure and why it is important to him. Cite details from the story to support your analysis.

**Does every conflict have a winner?**

How do Greg and his father become "winners" as a result of Greg's experience with Lemon Brown? Explain your answer.

"It takes a **thousand voices** to tell a **single story**."

**—Native American proverb**

PART 2

## TEXT ANALYSIS GUIDED EXPLORATION

# DIFFERENT PERSPECTIVES

As you read the stories in this section, notice each character's unique point of view. Then, consider how characters' perspectives change as they gain new knowledge, face challenging situations, and interact with others. The quotation on the opposite page will help you start thinking about the ways in which considering others' perspectives can broaden our view of the world.

◀ **CRITICAL VIEWING** How does this image reflect the meaning of the quotation on the opposite page?

### READINGS IN PART 2

**SHORT STORY**
**Rikki-tikki-tavi**
Rudyard Kipling (p. 26)

EXEMPLAR TEXT

**SHORT STORY**
**Two Kinds from *The Joy Luck Club***
Amy Tan (p. 48)

**SHORT STORY**
**The Third Wish**
Joan Aiken (p. 70)

**SHORT STORY**
**Ribbons**
Laurence Yep (p. 82)

**CLOSE READING TOOL**

Use the **Close Reading Tool** to practice the strategies you learn in this unit.

## Elements of a Short Story

A short story is a brief work of fiction. No two stories are identical, but they all share some common elements.

A **short story** takes readers on a quick, focused journey. Authors use the following elements of fiction to make the trip interesting.

**Characters** are the people or animals that take part in a story's action. They are driven by **motivation,** their reasons for acting as they do.

**Conflict** is the central problem or struggle that the characters face. A short story typically has one central conflict.

**Plot** is the sequence of events in a story. Events are often presented in chronological order, though they may be told out of sequence.

**Setting** is the time and place of a story. The setting can create a **mood,** or atmosphere.

**Point of view** is the perspective from which a story is told.

**Theme** is the central message expressed in a story. A theme is a general truth or observation about life or human nature.

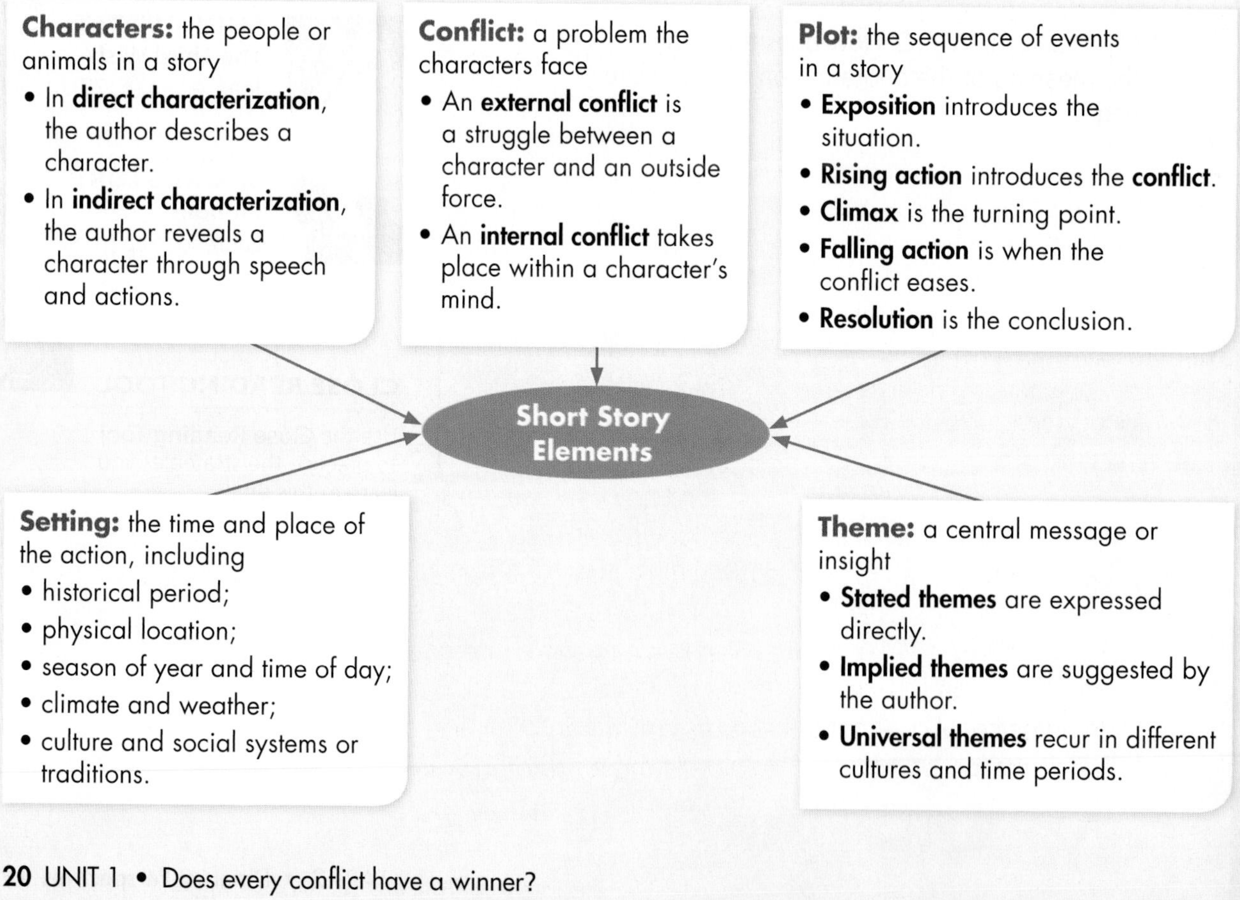

**Characters:** the people or animals in a story

- In **direct characterization**, the author describes a character.
- In **indirect characterization**, the author reveals a character through speech and actions.

**Conflict:** a problem the characters face

- An **external conflict** is a struggle between a character and an outside force.
- An **internal conflict** takes place within a character's mind.

**Plot:** the sequence of events in a story

- **Exposition** introduces the situation.
- **Rising action** introduces the **conflict**.
- **Climax** is the turning point.
- **Falling action** is when the conflict eases.
- **Resolution** is the conclusion.

**Short Story Elements**

**Setting:** the time and place of the action, including

- historical period;
- physical location;
- season of year and time of day;
- climate and weather;
- culture and social systems or traditions.

**Theme:** a central message or insight

- **Stated themes** are expressed directly.
- **Implied themes** are suggested by the author.
- **Universal themes** recur in different cultures and time periods.

## Point of View

The perspective from which a short story is told, or narrated, affects the kinds of information readers receive. When a story is told from the **first-person** point of view, the narrator is a character in the story. Readers learn only what that character knows, thinks, or feels.

When a story is told from the **third-person** point of view, the narrator is not a character, but a voice outside the story. A third-person narrator may be either **omniscient** or **limited**. An omniscient narrator is able to relate the inner thoughts and feelings of all the characters. A narrator with a limited point of view reveals the thoughts and feelings of only one character.

**Example: Points of View**

**First Person**
I could hear the footsteps, but I couldn't see a thing. Where was the light switch?

**Third-Person Omniscient**
Ted heard someone approaching, but in the darkness, he had no idea it was a burglar.

Another difference among types of narrators is that some narrators are objective, while others are subjective. An **objective narrator** is a neutral observer who reports on story events without adding personal comments. A **subjective narrator,** however, participates in the story and offers opinions about what takes place. This type of narrator can influence the way readers understand events and characters.

Some subjective narrators are unreliable, which means that readers cannot trust everything they say. For example, a story might be narrated from the perspective of a small child who is too young to understand certain story events. In this case, readers may have to piece together clues to fully grasp what is happening in the story.

**Comparing Narrators**

| Objective | Subjective |
|---|---|
| At the news conference, Max responded to each question in a careful, measured tone. It was over in less than ten minutes. | Like every good politician, Max knew how to hide his feelings. In front of the camera, he became a slick advertisement for himself. |

A narrator is a filter through which readers get information. However, the narrator does not reflect the only point of view in a story. Each character has his or her perspective as well. Two characters in a story may have very different perspectives on the same event. Readers can make inferences about a character's point of view based on the information and details the narrator provides.

## Analyzing How Elements Interact

The interaction of key story elements reveals the **theme** of a story.

In the best short stories, story elements interact to convey a meaningful **theme,** or insight about life or human nature.

**Inferring a Theme** Most authors do not simply state a story's theme. Instead, they develop it over the course of the story through elements such as character, conflict, and plot. Readers must infer, or figure out, the theme by analyzing story clues and thinking about how they add up to a central message or insight.

**Characters and Theme** To determine the theme of a story, notice the words, thoughts, and actions of the characters. Characters' **motivations,** or reasons for doing what they do, may also contribute to the theme. Note the **dialogue,** or what the characters say, as well as the narrator's observations and descriptions.

| Narrator's Observations | Theme |
|---|---|
| Dee grinned at me as she left the stage. My shy, timid friend was standing tall and proud. | A friend can help you overcome fears and develop your potential. |
| **Dialogue** | |
| "I made it!" Dee shouted to Carla in the hall. "Thanks for talking me into trying out for the play!" | |

**Conflict and Theme** Most stories focus on a **conflict,** or struggle between opposing forces. When the conflict is **external,** a character struggles with an outside force. When the conflict is **internal,** a character struggles with himself or herself. A story's central conflict often ties directly to its theme. Look at these examples:

| External Conflict | Possible Theme |
|---|---|
| Character versus a force of nature | Humans should not underestimate the power of nature. |
| Character versus society | Individuals must carve out their own paths in life. |
| **Internal Conflict** | **Possible Theme** |
| Character versus his or her fears | People may be stronger than they realize. |
| Character facing a difficult decision | People should trust their instincts. |

The ways that characters respond to a story's conflict can provide clues to the story's theme. In particular, pay attention to how the main character changes during the story and what he or she may have learned by the end.

**Plot and Theme** Events in the plot help develop a story's theme. The **exposition** and **rising action** develop the focus of the story. The **climax,** or turning point, often reveals a shift that points to an underlying message. As the story winds down to its **resolution,** that message becomes clearer.

Remember that story events may not flow in chronological order. An author may interrupt the sequence of events with a **flashback**—a scene from the past—or by **foreshadowing,** giving clues that hint at events to come. Such devices can move the story along while conveying the author's message.

**Point of View and Theme** A story may be told from the point of view of a character in the story or of an outside narrator. The narrator's point of view is crucial to the message of the story because readers know only what the narrator knows or chooses to tell. Use point of view to help you determine theme. Consider who is telling the story and what message the narrator seems to think is important.

**Setting and Theme** The place and time in which a story occurs can affect everything from the characters' motivations to the central conflict. Therefore, setting may have a strong influence on a story's message. In some cases, the setting is so important that the events of the story could not take place in any other time or location.

**Symbols and Theme** A **symbol** is a person, a place, or an object that represents something else. A dove, for example, is often a symbol for peace. Authors may use symbols to highlight or emphasize key concepts. As you read, pay attention to objects that seem to represent important ideas. Understanding the deeper meaning of a symbol can help you determine a story's theme.

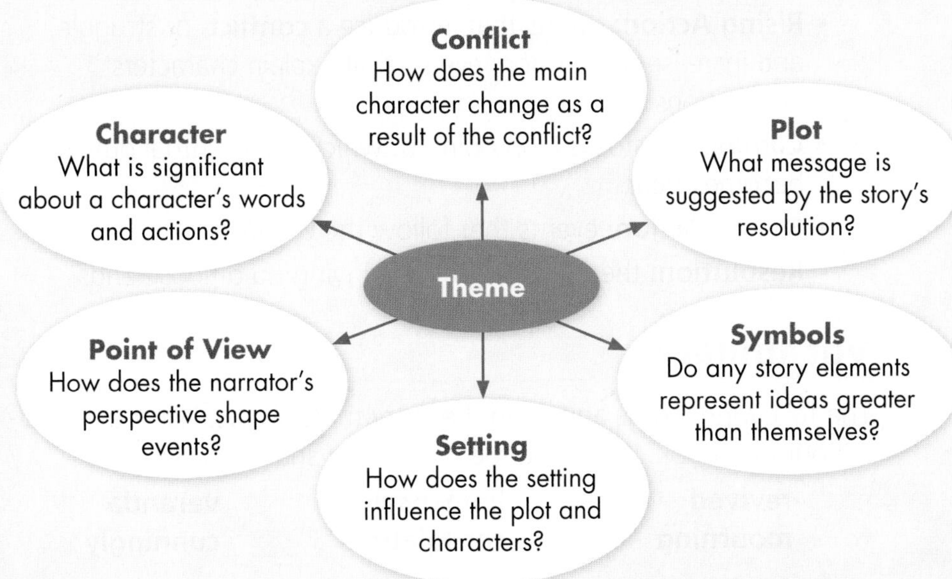
Theme
Conflict
How does the main character change as a result of the conflict?
Plot
What message is suggested by the story's resolution?
Symbols
Do any story elements represent ideas greater than themselves?
Setting
How does the setting influence the plot and characters?
Point of View
How does the narrator's perspective shape events?
Character
What is significant about a character's words and actions?

# Building Knowledge

Meet the Author

**Rudyard Kipling** (1865–1936) was born in Bombay, India, to English parents. Although he moved to England when he was five, Kipling remained attached to the land of his birth. In 1882, he returned to India and began writing the stories that would make him famous. His many popular books of stories and poems include *The Jungle Book* and *Kim*. In 1907, Kipling became the first English writer to win the Nobel Prize in Literature.

## Does every conflict have a winner?

Think about the Big Question as you read "Rikki-tikki-tavi." Take notes on how characters triumph or suffer as a result of conflicts.

## CLOSE READING FOCUS

### Key Ideas and Details: **Make Predictions**

**Predicting** means making an intelligent judgment about what will happen next in a story based on text details. You can also use prior knowledge to make predictions. For example, if a character sees dark clouds, you can predict that a storm is coming. That is because your prior knowledge tells you that dark clouds often mean stormy weather.

As you read, use details from the story and your prior knowledge to make predictions about what characters will do.

### Craft and Structure: **Plot**

**Plot** is the related sequence of events in a story. Each event moves the story forward. Some plot events hint at what might happen next. Such events create **foreshadowing.** A plot has the following elements:

- **Exposition:** introduction of the setting, the characters, and the basic situation
- **Rising Action:** events that introduce a **conflict,** or struggle, and increase the tension; events that explain characters' past actions
- **Climax:** the story's high point, at which the eventual outcome becomes clear
- **Falling Action:** events that follow the climax
- **Resolution:** the final outcome and tying up of loose ends

## Vocabulary

The following words appear in the story that follows. List the words in your notebook. Underline the words that share a suffix.

| | | |
|---|---|---|
| **revived** | **immensely** | **veranda** |
| **mourning** | **consolation** | **cunningly** |

## CLOSE READING MODEL

The passage below is from Rudyard Kipling's short story "Rikki-tikki-tavi." The notes to the right of the passage show ways in which you can use close reading skills to make predictions and analyze plot.

### *from* "Rikki-tikki-tavi"

Then Rikki-tikki went out into the garden to see what was to be seen. It was a large garden, only half cultivated, with bushes as big as summerhouses of Marshal Niel roses, lime and orange trees, clumps of bamboos, and thickets of high grass.[1]

Rikki-tikki licked his lips. "This is splendid hunting-ground," he said, and his tail grew bottlebrushy at the thought of it,[2] and he scuttled up and down the garden, snuffing here and there till he heard very sorrowful voices in a thorn-bush.

It was Darzee, the tailorbird, and his wife. They had made a beautiful nest by pulling two big leaves together and stitching them up the edges with fibers, and had filled the hollow with cotton and downy fluff. The nest swayed to and fro, as they sat on the rim and cried.[3]

"What is the matter?" asked Rikki-tikki.

"We are very miserable," said Darzee. "One of our babies fell out of the nest yesterday, and Nag ate him."[4]

**Plot**

**1** Kipling describes the garden in great detail. Because he is introducing the setting, you know that this is the exposition stage of the plot. You can expect to learn more about the characters and the basic situation soon.

**Make Predictions**

**2** Rikki-tikki is excited that the garden is "splendid hunting-ground." His tail grows large and bushy with excitement. These details reveal that he is a hunter who has confidence in his skills. You may predict that he will have a chance to use those skills before long.

**Plot**

**3** New characters, Darzee and his wife, are introduced here. You might ask yourself, "What earlier event made these birds unhappy?"

**Make Predictions**

**4** Even without knowing who or what Nag is, you may predict that the conflict in the story will involve this character.

# Rikki-tikki-tavi

## Rudyard Kipling

This is the story of the great war that Rikki-tikki-tavi fought, single-handed, through the bathrooms of the big bungalow in Segowlee cantonment.[1] Darzee, the tailorbird bird, helped him, and Chuchundra (cho͞o chun´ drə) the muskrat, who never comes out into the middle of the floor, but always creeps round by the wall, gave him advice; but Rikki-tikki did the real fighting.

He was a mongoose, rather like a little cat in his fur and his tail, but quite like a weasel in his head and his habits. His eyes and the end of his restless nose were pink; he could scratch himself anywhere he pleased, with any leg, front or back, that he chose to use; he could fluff up his tail till it looked like a bottle brush, and his war cry as he scuttled through the long grass, was: *"Rikk-tikk-tikki-tikki-tchk!"*

One day, a high summer flood washed him out of the burrow where he lived with his father and mother, and carried him, kicking and clucking,

---

1. **Segowlee cantonment** (sē gou´ lē kan tän´ mənt) *n.* living quarters for British troops in Segowlee, India.

down a roadside ditch. He found a little wisp of grass floating there, and clung to it till he lost his senses. When he **revived**, he was lying in the hot sun on the middle of a garden path, very draggled[2] indeed, and a small boy was saying: "Here's a dead mongoose. Let's have a funeral."

"No," said his mother; "let's take him in and dry him. Perhaps he isn't really dead."

They took him into the house, and a big man picked him up between his finger and thumb and said he was not dead but half choked; so they wrapped him in cotton wool, and warmed him, and he opened his eyes and sneezed.

"Now," said the big man (he was an Englishman who had just moved into the bungalow); "don't frighten him, and we'll see what he'll do."

It is the hardest thing in the world to frighten a mongoose, because he is eaten up from nose to tail with curiosity. The motto of all the mongoose family is, "Run and find out"; and Rikki-tikki was a true mongoose. He looked at the cotton wool, decided that it was not good to eat, ran all round the table, sat up and put his fur in order, scratched himself, and jumped on the small boy's shoulder.

"Don't be frightened, Teddy," said his father. "That's his way of making friends."

"Ouch! He's tickling under my chin," said Teddy.

Rikki-tikki looked down between the boy's collar and neck, snuffed at his ear, and climbed down to the floor, where he sat rubbing his nose.

"Good gracious," said Teddy's mother, "and that's a wild creature! I suppose he's so tame because we've been kind to him."

"All mongooses are like that," said her husband. "If Teddy

**◀ Vocabulary**
**revived** (ri vīvd′)
*v.* came back to life or consciousness

**Plot**
What important details about the mongoose are revealed in the exposition on the previous page?

**Comprehension**
Who is Rikki-tikki-tavi, and how does he meet Teddy?

---

2. **draggled** (drag′ əld) *adj.* wet and dirty.

doesn't pick him up by the tail, or try to put him in a cage, he'll run in and out of the house all day long. Let's give him something to eat."

They gave him a little piece of raw meat. Rikki-tikki liked it **immensely**, and when it was finished he went out into the **veranda** and sat in the sunshine and fluffed up his fur to make it dry to the roots. Then he felt better.

**Vocabulary ▶**
**immensely** (i mens´ lē) *adv.* a great deal; very much
**veranda** (və ran´də) *n.* an open porch, usually with a roof

"There are more things to find out about in this house," he said to himself, "than all my family could find out in all their lives. I shall certainly stay and find out."

He spent all that day roaming over the house. He nearly drowned himself in the bathtubs, put his nose into the ink on a writing table, and burned it on the end of the big man's cigar, for he climbed up in the big man's lap to see how writing was done. At nightfall he ran into Teddy's nursery to watch how kerosene lamps were lighted, and when Teddy went to bed Rikki-tikki climbed up too; but he was a restless companion, because he had to get up and attend to every noise all through the night, and find out what made it. Teddy's mother and father came in, the last thing, to look at their boy, and Rikki-tikki was awake on the pillow. "I don't like that," said Teddy's mother; "he may bite the child." "He'll do no such thing," said the father. "Teddy's safer with that little beast than if he had a bloodhound to watch him. If a snake came into the nursery now—"

**Make Predictions**
Based on the parents' thoughts about Rikki, what do you predict will happen in the story?

But Teddy's mother wouldn't think of anything so awful.

Early in the morning Rikki-tikki came to early breakfast in the veranda riding on Teddy's shoulder, and they gave him banana and some boiled egg; and he sat on all their laps one after the other, because every well-brought-up mongoose always hopes to be a house mongoose some day and have rooms to run about in, and Rikki-tikki's mother (she used to live in the General's house at Segowlee) had carefully told Rikki what to do if ever he came across Englishmen.

Then Rikki-tikki went out into the garden to see what was to be seen. It was a large garden, only half cultivated, with bushes as big as summer houses of Marshal Niel roses, lime and orange trees, clumps of bamboos, and thickets of high grass. Rikki-tikki licked his lips. "This is a splendid hunting ground," he said, and his tail grew bottlebrushy at the thought of it, and he scuttled up and down the garden, snuffing here and there till he heard very sorrowful voices in a thornbush.

It was Darzee, the tailorbird, and his wife. They had made a beautiful nest by pulling two big leaves together and stitching them up the edges with fibers, and had filled the hollow with cotton and downy fluff. The nest swayed to and fro, as they sat on the rim and cried.

"What is the matter?" asked Rikki-tikki.

"We are very miserable," said Darzee. "One of our babies fell out of the nest yesterday and Nag ate him."

"H'm!" said Rikki-tikki, "that is very sad—but I am a stranger here. Who is Nag?"

Darzee and his wife only cowered down in the nest without answering, for from the thick grass at the foot of the bush there came a low hiss—a horrid cold sound that made Rikki-tikki jump back two clear feet. Then inch by inch out of the grass rose up the head and spread hood of Nag, the big black cobra, and he was five feet long from tongue to tail. When he had lifted one third of himself clear of the ground, he stayed balancing to and fro exactly as a dandelion tuft balances in the wind, and he looked at Rikki-tikki with the wicked snake's eyes that never change their expression, whatever the snake may be thinking of. ●

"Who is Nag?" he said. "*I* am Nag. The great god Brahm[3] put his mark upon all our people when the first cobra spread his hood to keep the sun off Brahm as he slept. Look, and be afraid!"

He spread out his hood more than ever, and Rikki-tikki saw the spectacle mark on the back of it that looks exactly like the eye part of a hook-and-eye fastening. He was afraid for the minute; but it is impossible for a mongoose to stay frightened for any length of time, and though Rikki-tikki had never met a live cobra

Rikki-tikki licked his lips. "This is a splendid hunting ground," he said . . .

**Comprehension**
How do Teddy's parent's feel about Rikki-tikki-tavi's staying at their house?

3. **Brahm** (bräm) short for Brahma, the name of the chief god in the Hindu religion.

before, his mother had fed him on dead ones, and he knew that all a grown mongoose's business in life was to fight and eat snakes. Nag knew that too, and at the bottom of his cold heart he was afraid.

"Well," said Rikki-tikki, and his tail began to fluff up again, "marks or no marks, do you think it is right for you to eat fledglings out of a nest?"

Nag was thinking to himself, and watching the least little movement in the grass behind Rikki-tikki. He knew that mongooses in the garden meant death sooner or later for him and his family; but he wanted to get Rikki-tikki off his guard. So he dropped his head a little, and put it on one side.

"Let us talk," he said. "You eat eggs. Why should not I eat birds?"

"Behind you! Look behind you!" sang Darzee.

Rikki-tikki knew better than to waste time in staring. He jumped up in the air as high as he could go, and just under him whizzed by the head of Nagaina (nə gī́nə), Nag's wicked wife. She had crept up behind him as he was talking, to make an end of him; and he heard her savage hiss as the stroke missed. He came down almost across her back, and if he had been an old mongoose he would have known that then was the time to break her back with one bite; but he was afraid of the terrible lashing return stroke of the cobra. He bit, indeed, but did not bite long enough, and he jumped clear of the whisking tail, leaving Nagaina torn and angry.

"Wicked, wicked Darzee!" said Nag, lashing up high as he could reach toward the nest in the thornbush; but Darzee had built it out of reach of snakes; and it only swayed to and fro.

**Plot**
What details intensify the conflict here?

**▼ Critical Viewing**
Based on this photograph, which animal would you expect to win a match to the death—the cobra or the mongoose? Why?

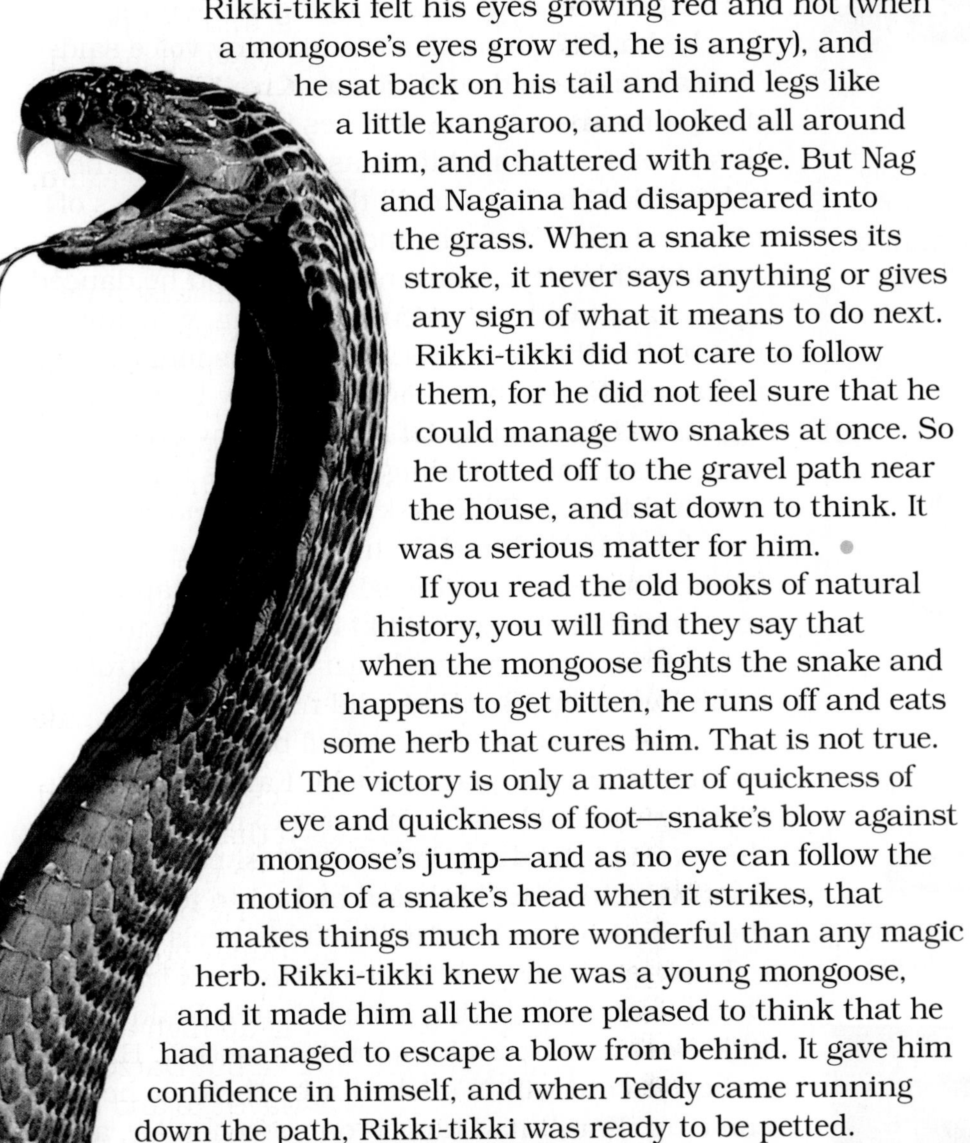

Rikki-tikki felt his eyes growing red and hot (when a mongoose's eyes grow red, he is angry), and he sat back on his tail and hind legs like a little kangaroo, and looked all around him, and chattered with rage. But Nag and Nagaina had disappeared into the grass. When a snake misses its stroke, it never says anything or gives any sign of what it means to do next. Rikki-tikki did not care to follow them, for he did not feel sure that he could manage two snakes at once. So he trotted off to the gravel path near the house, and sat down to think. It was a serious matter for him. •

If you read the old books of natural history, you will find they say that when the mongoose fights the snake and happens to get bitten, he runs off and eats some herb that cures him. That is not true. The victory is only a matter of quickness of eye and quickness of foot—snake's blow against mongoose's jump—and as no eye can follow the motion of a snake's head when it strikes, that makes things much more wonderful than any magic herb. Rikki-tikki knew he was a young mongoose, and it made him all the more pleased to think that he had managed to escape a blow from behind. It gave him confidence in himself, and when Teddy came running down the path, Rikki-tikki was ready to be petted.

**Make Predictions**
What do you predict will be the outcome of the conflict? What prior knowledge helps you make that prediction?

**Comprehension**
Who is Nagaina, and what does she do to Rikki-tikki-tavi?

## LITERATURE IN CONTEXT

### Science Connection

**Cobra Fact and Fiction**

Although the snakes in this story have fictional abilities and characteristics, many of their qualities are accurately based on those of real animals.

- Cobras do have spectacle-shaped markings on their hood, as shown in the picture below.
- Cobras are known to enter houses, just as Nag and Nagaina do in the story.
- A female cobra is extremely dangerous and vicious after laying eggs.
- Unlike the snakes in the story, however, real cobras do not travel in pairs or work together to hatch their eggs.

**Connect to the Literature**

What fictional characteristics and qualities does Kipling give to the cobras in this story?

But just as Teddy was stooping, something flinched a little in the dust, and a tiny voice said: "Be careful. I am death!" It was Karait (kə rīt′), the dusty brown snakeling that lies for choice on the dusty earth; and his bite is as dangerous as the cobra's. But he is so small that nobody thinks of him, and so he does the more harm to people. •

Rikki-tikki's eyes grew red again, and he danced up to Karait with the peculiar rocking, swaying motion that he had inherited from his family. It looks very funny, but it is so perfectly balanced a gait that you can fly off from it at any angle you please; and in dealing with snakes this is an advantage. If Rikki-tikki had only known, he was doing a much more dangerous thing than fighting Nag, for Karait is so small, and can turn so quickly, that unless Rikki bit him close to the back of the head, he would get the return stroke in his eye or lip. But Rikki did not know: his eyes were all red, and he rocked back and forth, looking for a good place to hold. Karait struck out. Rikki jumped sideways and tried to run in, but the wicked little dusty gray head lashed within a fraction of his shoulder, and he had to jump over the body, and the head followed his heels close.

Teddy shouted to the house: "Oh, look here! Our mongoose is killing a snake"; and Rikki-tikki heard a scream from Teddy's mother. His father ran out with a stick, but by the time he came up, Karait had lunged out once too far, and Rikki-tikki had sprung, jumped on the snake's back, dropped his head far between his fore legs, bitten as high up the back as he could get hold, and rolled away. That bite paralyzed Karait, and Rikki-tikki was just going to eat him up from the tail, after the custom of his family at dinner, when he remembered that a full meal makes a slow mongoose, and if he wanted all his strength and quickness ready, he must keep himself thin.

He went away for a dust bath under the castor-oil bushes, while Teddy's father beat the dead Karait. "What is the use of that?" thought Rikki-tikki. "I have settled it all"; and then Teddy's mother picked him up from the dust and hugged him, crying that he had saved Teddy from death, and Teddy's father said that he was a providence,[4] and Teddy looked on with big scared eyes. Rikki-tikki was rather amused at all the fuss, which, of course, he did not understand. Teddy's mother might just as well have petted Teddy for playing in the dust. Rikki was thoroughly enjoying himself.

**Plot**
What details in this paragraph show that the tension is over?

That night, at dinner, walking to and fro among the wineglasses on the table, he could have stuffed himself three times over with nice things; but he remembered Nag and Nagaina, and though it was very pleasant to be patted and petted by Teddy's mother, and to sit on Teddy's shoulder, his eyes would get red from time to time, and he would go off into his long war cry of "*Rikk-tikk-tikki-tikki-tchk!*"

Teddy carried him off to bed, and insisted on Rikki-tikki sleeping under his chin. Rikki-tikki was too well bred to bite or scratch, but as soon as Teddy was asleep he went off for his nightly walk round the house, and in the dark he ran up against Chuchundra the muskrat, creeping round by the wall. Chuchundra is a brokenhearted little beast. He whimpers and cheeps all the night, trying to make up his mind to run into the middle of the room, but he never gets there.

Chuchundra is a brokenhearted little beast.

"Don't kill me," said Chuchundra, almost weeping. "Rikki-tikki don't kill me."

"Do you think a snake-killer kills muskrats?" said Rikki-tikki scornfully.

"Those who kill snakes get killed by snakes," said Chuchundra, more sorrowfully than ever. "And how am I to be sure that Nag won't mistake me for you some dark night?"

"There's not the least danger," said Rikki-tikki; "but Nag is in the garden, and I know you don't go there."

**Comprehension**
What happens when Rikki meets Karait?

---

**4. a providence** (präv´ ə dəns) *n.* a godsend; a valuable gift.

"My cousin Chua, the rat, told me—" said Chuchundra, and then he stopped.

"Told you what?"

"H'sh! Nag is everywhere, Rikki-tikki. You should have talked to Chua in the garden."

"I didn't—so you must tell me. Quick, Chuchundra, or I'll bite you!"

Chuchundra sat down and cried till the tears rolled off his whiskers. "I am a very poor man," he sobbed. "I never had spirit enough to run out into the middle of the room. H'sh! I mustn't tell you anything. Can't you *hear,* Rikki-tikki?"

Rikki-tikki listened. The house was as still as still, but he thought he could just catch the faintest *scratch-scratch* in the world—a noise as faint as that of a wasp walking on a windowpane—the dry scratch of a snake's scales on brickwork.

"That's Nag or Nagaina," he said to himself; "and he is crawling into the bathroom sluice.[5] You're right, Chuchundra; I should have talked to Chua."

He stole off to Teddy's bathroom, but there was nothing there, and then to Teddy's mother's bathroom. At the bottom of the smooth plaster wall there was a brick pulled out to make a sluice for the bath water, and as Rikki-tikki stole in by the masonry curb where the bath is put, he heard Nag and Nagaina whispering together outside in the moonlight.

"When the house is emptied of people," said Nagaina to her husband, "*he* will have to go away, and then the garden will be our own again. Go in quietly, and remember that the big man who killed Karait is the first one to bite. Then come out and tell me, and we will hunt for Rikki-tikki together."

**Plot**
What details add to the conflict as Rikki overhears this conversation?

"But are you sure that there is anything to be gained by killing the people?" said Nag.

"Everything. When there were no people in the bungalow, did we have any mongoose in the garden? So long as the bungalow is empty, we are king and queen of the garden; and remember that as soon as our eggs in the melon bed hatch (as they may tomorrow), our children will need room and quiet."

---

5. **sluice** (slo͞os) *n.* drain.

"I had not thought of that," said Nag. "I will go, but there is no need that we should hunt for Rikki-tikki afterward. I will kill the big man and his wife, and the child if I can, and come away quietly. Then the bungalow will be empty, and Rikki-tikki will go."

Rikki-tikki tingled all over with rage and hatred at this, and then Nag's head came through the sluice, and his five feet of cold body followed it. Angry as he was, Rikki-tikki was very frightened as he saw the size of the big cobra. Nag coiled himself up, raised his head, and looked into the bathroom in the dark, and Rikki could see his eyes glitter.

"Now, if I kill him here, Nagaina will know;—and if I fight him on the open floor, the odds are in his favor. What am I to do?" said Rikki-tikki-tavi.

Nag waved to and fro, and then Rikki-tikki heard him drinking from the biggest water jar that was used to fill the bath. "That is good," said the snake. "Now, when Karait was killed, the big man had a stick. He may have that stick still, but when he comes in to bathe in the morning he will not have a stick. I shall wait here till he comes. Nagaina—do you hear me?—I shall wait here in the cool till daytime."

There was no answer from outside, so Rikki-tikki knew Nagaina had gone away. Nag coiled himself down, coil by coil, round the bulge at the bottom of the water jar, and Rikki-tikki stayed still as death. After an hour he began to move, muscle by muscle, toward the jar. Nag was asleep, and Rikki-tikki looked at his big back, wondering which would be the best place for a good hold. "If I don't break his back at the first jump," said Rikki, "he can still fight; and if he fights—O Rikki!" He looked at the thickness of the neck below the hood, but that was too much for him; and a bite near the tail would only make Nag savage.

"It must be the head," he said at last; "the head above the hood; and, when I am once there, I must not let go."

Then he jumped. The head was lying a little clear of the water jar, under the curve of it; and, as his teeth met, Rikki braced his back against the bulge of the red earthenware to hold down the head. This gave him just one second's purchase,[6] and he made the most of it. Then he was battered

**Comprehension**
Where are Nag and Nagaina, and what are they planning?

**6. purchase** (pʉr′ chəs) *n.* firm hold.

to and fro as a rat is shaken by a dog—to and fro on the floor, up and down, and round in great circles: but his eyes were red, and he held on as the body cart-whipped over the floor, upsetting the tin dipper and the soap dish and the fleshbrush, and banged against the tin side of the bath. As he held he closed his jaws tighter and tighter, for he made sure he would be banged to death, and, for the honor of his family, he preferred to be found with his teeth locked. He was dizzy, aching, and felt shaken to pieces when something went off like a thunderclap just behind him; a hot wind knocked him senseless and red fire singed his fur. The big man had been wakened by the noise, and had fired both barrels of a shotgun into Nag just behind the hood.

**▲ Critical Viewing**
What role does Darzee, the tailor-bird, play in the conflict between Rikki-tikki-tavi and the cobras?

**Plot**
Why is the death of Nag part of the rising action rather than the resolution?

Rikki-tikki held on with his eyes shut, for now he was quite sure he was dead; but the head did not move, and the big man picked him up and said: "It's the mongoose again, Alice; the little chap has saved *our* lives now." Then Teddy's mother came in with a very white face, and saw what was left of Nag, and Rikki-tikki dragged himself to Teddy's bedroom and spent half the rest of the night shaking himself tenderly to find out whether he really was broken into forty pieces, as he fancied.

When morning came he was very stiff, but well pleased with his doings. "Now I have Nagaina to settle with, and she will be worse than five Nags, and there's no knowing when the eggs she spoke of will hatch. Goodness! I must go and see Darzee," he said.

Without waiting for breakfast, Rikki-tikki ran to the thornbush where Darzee was singing a song of triumph at the top of his voice. The news of Nag's death was all over the garden, for the sweeper had thrown the body on the rubbish heap.

"Oh, you stupid tuft of feathers!" said Rikki-tikki angrily. "Is this the time to sing?"

"Nag is dead—is dead—is dead!" sang Darzee. "The valiant Rikki-tikki caught him by the head and held fast. The big man brought the bang-stick and Nag fell in two pieces! He will never eat my babies again."

"All that's true enough; but where's Nagaina?" said Rikki-tikki, looking carefully round him.

"Nagaina came to the bathroom sluice and called for Nag," Darzee went on; "and Nag came out on the end of a stick—the sweeper picked him up on the end of a stick and threw him upon the rubbish heap. Let us sing about the great, the red-eyed Rikki-tikki!" and Darzee filled his throat and sang.

"If I could get up to your nest, I'd roll all your babies out!" said Rikki-tikki. "You don't know when to do the right thing at the right time. You're safe enough in your nest there, but it's war for me down here. Stop singing a minute, Darzee."

"For the great, the beautiful Rikki-tikki's sake, I will stop," said Darzee. "What is it, O Killer of the terrible Nag!"

"Where is Nagaina, for the third time?"

"On the rubbish heap by the stables, **mourning** for Nag. Great is Rikki-tikki with the white teeth."

"Bother my white teeth! Have you ever heard where she keeps her eggs?"

"In the melon bed, on the end nearest the wall, where the sun strikes nearly all day. She had them there weeks ago."

"And you never thought it worthwhile to tell me? The end nearest the wall, you said?"

"Rikki-tikki, you are not going to eat her eggs?"

"Not eat exactly; no. Darzee, if you have a grain of sense you will fly off to the stables and pretend that your wing is broken, and let Nagaina chase you away to this bush! I must get to the melon bed, and if I went there now she'd see me."

Darzee was a featherbrained little fellow who could never hold more than one idea at a time in his head; and just because he knew that Nagaina's children were born in eggs like his own, he didn't think at first that it was fair to kill them. But his wife was a sensible bird, and she knew that cobra's eggs meant young cobras later on; so she flew off from the nest, and left Darzee to keep the babies warm, and continue his song about the death of Nag. Darzee was very like a man in some ways.

She fluttered in front of Nagaina by the rubbish heap, and cried out, "Oh, my wing is broken! The boy in the house threw a stone at me and broke it." Then she fluttered more desperately than ever.

Nagaina lifted up her head and hissed, "You warned Rikki-tikki when I would have killed him. Indeed and truly, you've chosen a bad place to be lame in." And she moved toward

◂ **Vocabulary**
**mourning** (môr′niŋ)
*adj.* expressing grief, especially after someone dies

**Make Predictions**
What do you think Rikki is going to do with Nagaina's eggs? What details in the story make you think so?

**Comprehension**
What prevents Rikki from celebrating Nag's death?

**Vocabulary ▶**
**consolation** (kän′ sə lā′ shən) *n.* something that comforts a disappointed person

**cunningly** (kun′ iŋ lē) *adv.* cleverly

**Plot**
Do you think this scene is the climax or part of the rising action? Why?

Darzee's wife, slipping along over the dust.

"The boy broke it with a stone!" shrieked Darzee's wife.

"Well! It may be some **consolation** to you when you're dead to know that I shall settle accounts with the boy. My husband lies on the rubbish heap this morning, but before night the boy in the house will lie very still. What is the use of running away? I am sure to catch you. Little fool, look at me!"

Darzee's wife knew better than to do *that, for* a bird who looks at a snake's eyes gets so frightened that she cannot move. Darzee's wife fluttered on, piping sorrowfully, and never leaving the ground, and Nagaina quickened her pace.

Rikki-tikki heard them going up the path from the stables, and he raced for the end of the melon patch near the wall. There, in the warm litter about the melons, very **cunningly** hidden, he found twenty-five eggs, about the size of a bantam's eggs,[7] but with whitish skin instead of shell.

"I was not a day too soon," he said; for he could see the baby cobras curled up inside the skin, and he knew that the minute they were hatched they could each kill a man or a mongoose. He bit off the tops of the eggs as fast as he could, taking care to crush the young cobras, and turned over the litter from time to time to see whether he had missed any. At last there were only three eggs left, and Rikki-tikki began to chuckle to himself, when he heard Darzee's wife screaming:

"Rikki-tikki, I led Nagaina toward the house, and she has gone into the veranda, and—oh, come quickly—she means killing!"

Rikki-tikki smashed two eggs, and tumbled backward down the melon bed with the third egg in his mouth, and scuttled to the veranda as hard as he could put foot to the ground. Teddy and his mother and father were there at early breakfast; but Rikki-tikki saw that they were not eating anything. They sat stone-still, and their faces were white. Nagaina was coiled up on the matting by Teddy's chair, within easy striking distance of Teddy's bare leg, and she was swaying to and fro singing a song of triumph.

"Son of the big man that killed Nag," she hissed, "stay still. I am not ready yet. Wait a little. Keep very still, all you three. If you move I strike, and if you do not move I strike, Oh, foolish

7. **bantam's** (ban′ təmz) **eggs** *n.* eggs of a small chicken.

people, who killed my Nag!"

Teddy's eyes were fixed on his father, and all his father could do was to whisper, "Sit still, Teddy. You mustn't move. Teddy, keep still."

Then Rikki-tikki came up and cried: "Turn round, Nagaina; turn and fight!"

"All in good time," said she, without moving her eyes. "I will settle my account with *you* presently. Look at your friends, Rikki-tikki. They are still and white; they are afraid. They dare not move, and if you come a step nearer I strike."

"Look at your eggs," said Rikki-tikki, "in the melon bed near the wall. Go and look, Nagaina."

The big snake turned half round, and saw the egg on the veranda. "Ah-h! Give it to me," she said.

Rikki-tikki put his paws one on each side of the egg, and his eyes were blood-red. "What price for a snake's egg? For a young cobra? For a young king cobra? For the last—the very last of the brood? The ants are eating all the others down by the melon bed."

Nagaina spun clear round, forgetting everything for the sake of the one egg; and Rikki-tikki saw Teddy's father shoot out a big hand, catch Teddy by the shoulder, and drag him across the little table with the teacups, safe and out of reach of Nagaina.

"Tricked! Tricked! Tricked! *Rikk-tck-tck!*" chuckled Rikki-tikki."The boy is safe, and it was I—I—I that caught Nag by the hood last night in the bathroom." Then he began to jump up and down, all four feet together, his head close to the floor. "He threw me to and fro, but he could not shake me off. He was dead before the big man blew him in two. I did it. *Rikki-tikki-tck-tck!* Come then, Nagaina. Come and fight with me. You shall not be a widow long."

Nagaina saw that she had lost her chance of killing Teddy, and the egg lay between Rikki-tikki's paws. "Give me the egg, Rikki-tikki. Give me the last of my eggs, and I will go away and never come back," she said, lowering her hood.

"Yes, you will go away, and you will never come back; for you will go to the rubbish heap with Nag. Fight, widow! The big man has gone for his gun! Fight!"

Rikki-tikki was bounding all round Nagaina, keeping just out of reach of her stroke, his little eyes like hot coals.

**Spiral Review**
**SETTING** How would a fight with Nagaina in an open space like the veranda be different from Rikki-tikki's fight with Nag?

**Plot**
What details increase the tension in the story at this point?

**Comprehension**
What does Rikki bring with him to the veranda?

Nagaina gathered herself together, and flung out at him. Rikki-tikki jumped up and backward. Again and again and again she struck, and each time her head came with a whack on the matting of the veranda and she gathered herself together like a watchspring. Then Rikki-tikki danced in a circle to get behind her, and Nagaina spun round to keep her head to his head, so that the rustle of her tail on the matting sounded like dry leaves blown along by the wind. ●

He had forgotten the egg. It still lay on the veranda, and Nagaina came nearer and nearer to it, till at last, while Rikki-tikki was drawing breath, she caught it in her mouth, turned to the veranda steps, and flew like an arrow down the path, with Rikki-tikki behind her. When the cobra runs for her life, she goes like a whiplash flicked across a horse's neck.

**Spiral Review**
**SETTING** How does the setting of the cobra's hole introduce uncertainty into the plot?

Rikki-tikki knew that he must catch her, or all the trouble would begin again. She headed straight for the long grass by the thornbush, and as he was running Rikki-tikki heard Darzee still singing his foolish little song of triumph. But Darzee's wife was wiser. She flew off her nest as Nagaina came along, and flapped her wings about Nagaina's head. If Darzee had helped they might have turned her; but Nagaina only lowered her hood and went on. Still, the instant's delay brought Rikki-tikki up to her, and as she plunged into the rat hole where she and Nag used to live, his little white teeth were clenched on her tail, and he went down with her—and very few mongooses, however wise and old they may be, care to follow a cobra into its hole. It was dark in the hole; and Rikki-tikki never knew when it might open out and give Nagaina room to turn and strike at him. He held on savagely, and struck out his feet to act as brakes on the dark slope of the hot, moist earth.

**Plot**
How does Darzee's comment in this passage add to the tension?

Then the grass by the mouth of the hole stopped waving, and Darzee said: "It is all over with Rikki-tikki! We must sing his death song. Valiant Rikki-tikki is dead! For Nagaina will surely kill him underground."

So he sang a very mournful song that he made up all on the spur of the minute, and just as he got to the most touching part the grass quivered again, and Rikki-tikki, covered with dirt, dragged himself out of the hole leg by leg, licking his whiskers. Darzee stopped with a little shout. Rikki-tikki shook some of the dust out of his fur and sneezed. "It is all over," he said. "The widow will never come out again." And the red ants that live between the grass stems heard him, and began to troop down one after another to see if he had spoken the truth.

Rikki-tikki curled himself up in the grass and slept where he was—slept and slept till it was late in the afternoon, for he had done a hard day's work.

"Now," he said, when he awoke, "I will go back to the house. Tell the Coppersmith, Darzee, and he will tell the garden that Nagaina is dead."

The Coppersmith is a bird who makes a noise exactly like the beating of a little hammer on a copper pot; and the reason he is always making it is because he is the town crier to every Indian garden, and tells all the news to everybody who cares to listen. As Rikki-tikki went up the path, he heard his "attention" notes like a tiny dinner gong; and then the steady *"Ding-dong-tock!* Nag is dead—*dong!* Nagaina is dead! *Ding-dong-tock!"* That set all the birds in the garden singing, and the frogs croaking; for Nag and Nagaina used to eat frogs as well as little birds.

When Rikki got to the house, Teddy and Teddy's mother and Teddy's father came out and almost cried over him; and that night he ate all that was given him till he could eat no more, and went

**Plot**
What part of the plot does Rikki's comment illustrate?

**Comprehension**
What happens when Nagaina goes down the snake hole?

to bed Teddy's shoulder, where Teddy's mother saw him when she came to look late at night.

"He saved our lives and Teddy's life," she said to her husband. "Just think, he saved all our lives."

Rikki-tikki woke up with a jump, for all the mongooses are light sleepers.

"Oh, it's you," said he. "What are you bothering for? All the cobras are dead; and if they weren't, I'm here."

Rikki-tikki had a right to be proud of himself; but he did not grow too proud, and he kept that garden as a mongoose should keep it, with tooth and jump and spring and bite, till never a cobra dared show its head inside the walls.

## Language Study

**Vocabulary** The words listed below appear in "Rikki-tikki-tavi." Answer each question below. Then, explain your response.

**revived** **immensely** **veranda** **mourning** **cunningly**

1. Is someone who has just been *revived* ready to run a race?
2. If you like someone *immensely,* how do you feel about him or her?
3. When you sit on a *veranda,* are you inside the house?
4. Would a *mourning* widow be likely to smile?
5. If you are *cunningly* disguised, can you be recognized?

**WORD STUDY**

The **Latin suffix** ***-tion*** is an ending that turns a verb into a noun meaning "the thing that is."

In this story, Nagaina suggests that Teddy's death will be a **consolation**, or something that is consoling, or comforting, for Darzee's wife.

### Word Study

**Part A** Explain how the **Latin suffix** ***-tion*** contributes to the meanings of the words *infection, creation,* and *restoration.* Consult a dictionary if necessary.

**Part B** Use the context of the sentences and your knowledge of the Latin suffix *-tion* to explain your answer to each question.

1. If a painting is an *imitation,* is it the original?
2. If someone offers a *suggestion,* is he being helpful?

## Literary Analysis

### Key Ideas and Details

1. **(a)** How does Rikki feel about the cobras? How do the cobras feel about Rikki? **(b) Compare:** Using details from the story, compare Rikki's and the cobras' personalities.
2. **(a)** What is the relationship between Nag and Nagaina? **(b) Analyze:** What does Nagaina do to make matters worse for Nag and herself? **(c) Draw Conclusions:** In what way does this plan make Nagaina a villain?
3. **Make Predictions** What information in the early part of the story might have led you to predict that Rikki would defeat the cobras?
4. **Make Predictions (a)** What is another prediction you made as you read this story? **(b)** Use a graphic organizer like the one on the right to show how you made your prediction.

Story Details

\+

My Prior Knowledge

=

Prediction

### Craft and Structure

5. **Plot (a)** Identify two plot events that increase the tension between Rikki and Nag. **(b)** How do Rikki's and Nag's attitudes toward Teddy's family differ? Cite details to support your response.
6. **Plot (a)** Identify two or three events that move the plot toward the climax, when Rikki and Nagaina battle. **(b)** What textual evidence supports the idea that Rikki is a hero?

### Integration of Knowledge and Ideas

7. **(a) Analyze:** What role does Darzee play in the story? **(b) Compare and Contrast:** Whose approach to life, Darzee's or Rikki's, is more effective? Explain your answer, citing evidence from the text.
8. **(a) Analyze:** "Rikki-tikki-tavi" is among the most widely read short stories ever written. Why do you think it is so popular? Use details from the story to support your position. **(b) Evaluate:** Do you think the story deserves this standing? Explain.

9. THE BIG ? **Does every conflict have a winner?** With a small group, discuss the following questions: **(a)** In what way are Nagaina's eggs innocent victims of the conflict? **(b)** How do Teddy and his family suffer? **(c)** What does this story suggest about how conflict in the natural world relates to human conflict?

**ACADEMIC VOCABULARY**

As you write and speak about "Rikki-tikki-tavi," use the words related to conflict that you explored on page 3 of this textbook.

## Conventions: **Common, Proper, and Possessive Nouns**

A **common noun** names a person, place, or thing. A **proper noun** names a specific person, place, or thing. A **possessive noun** shows ownership.

**Common nouns** are not capitalized unless they begin a sentence or are in a title. **Proper nouns** are always capitalized.

- Examples of common nouns include *singer, city,* and *boy.*
- Examples of proper nouns include *Abraham Lincoln, London,* and *Selena.*

**Possessive nouns** show ownership. They are formed in different ways for plural and singular nouns. Study the chart below.

| Type of Noun | Rule | Example |
|---|---|---|
| **Singular:** player | Add apostrophe -s. | The player's bat |
| **Singular ending in *-s*:** Lucas | Add apostrophe -s. | Lucas's room |
| **Plural that ends in *-s*:** bees | Add apostrophe. | The bees' buzzing |
| **Plural not ending in *-s*:** children | Add apostrophe -s. | The children's toys |

### Practice A

Underline the nouns in each sentence. Then, label each as a common or proper noun. Finally, identify which ones are possessive.

1. Teddy found Rikki-tikki-tavi in the middle of a path.
2. Teddy's mother took the mongoose inside.
3. The animal jumped onto the boy's shoulders.
4. Darzee and his wife cried for their baby.

**Reading Application** In "Rikki-tikki-tavi," find a sentence containing a common noun, a sentence containing a proper noun, and a sentence containing a possessive noun.

### Practice B

Complete each sentence with a noun, using the form in parentheses.

1. It was (singular possessive) idea to destroy the cobras' eggs.
2. The female cobra, (proper), wanted the last egg.
3. Teddy's (common) told his son not to be afraid.
4. The muskrat's name is (proper).

**Writing Application** Choose one of the scenes of conflict in the story. Write three sentences about it, using at least one common, proper, or possessive noun in each.

## Writing to Sources

**Informative Text** In "Rikki-tikki-tavi," a mongoose and two cobras interact in ways that are natural to the two species. Write an **informative article** that explains this interaction.

An informative article teaches readers about a topic and contains these elements:

- an introduction, a body, and a conclusion
- details that tell *when, how much, how often,* and *to what extent*
- a formal style that contains no slang or incomplete sentences
- terms specific to your topic, such as *den, venom,* and *predator*

As you write, support your ideas with specific details from the story. Cite passages precisely, weaving them smoothly into your article.

**Grammar Application** As you write, use common, proper, and possessive nouns correctly.

## Speaking and Listening

**Comprehension and Collaboration** With a partner, engage in an **informal debate** based on "Rikki-tikki-tavi." Each of you should choose an opposing viewpoint to present, defending the actions of either the mongoose or the cobras in the story. As you prepare your arguments, reread parts of the story to examine the characters' actions.

Follow these steps to complete the assignment:

- Support your ideas with valid arguments based on credible research and on story details.
- Respect your partner's time to talk. Do not interrupt. Listen carefully.
- As you listen to your partner, take note of his or her argument. When it is your turn to talk, do one of three things: (1) Explain why your partner's argument is not sufficiently supported. (2) Explain why the evidence offered contradicts your partner's argument. (3) Explain why one of your partner's arguments is illogical or inconsistent.

# Building Knowledge

Meet the Author

If **Amy Tan's** mother had gotten her way, Tan (b. 1952) would have two professions—doctor and concert pianist. Although Tan showed early promise in music, at thirty-seven she became a successful fiction writer instead. Tan has written many books—most for adults, and some for children. Writing is sometimes tough, Tan admits, but she keeps this in mind: "A story should be a gift." That thought propels Tan to keep creating memorable characters and events.

## Does every conflict have a winner?

Think about the Big Question as you read "Two Kinds." Take notes about the conflicts that arise between the main characters.

## CLOSE READING FOCUS

### Key Ideas and Details: **Make Predictions**

A **prediction** is an informed judgment about what will happen. Use details in the text to make predictions as you read. Then, read ahead to verify predictions—to check whether your predictions are correct.

- As you read, ask yourself if new details support your predictions. If they do not, revise your predictions based on the new information.
- If the predictions you make turn out to be wrong, reread to look for details you might have missed.

### Craft and Structure: **Character and Point of View**

A **character** is a person or animal in a literary work.

- A **character's motives** are the emotions or goals that drive him or her to act in a certain way.
- **Character traits** are the individual qualities that make each character unique. You can identify character traits by noticing how characters think, act, and speak.

A character's **point of view** is his or her unique perspective.

- When a story is told from the **first-person point of view,** the narrator is a character who participates in the action and uses the first-person pronoun *I*.
- When a story is told from the **third-person point of view,** the narrator is not a character in the story. He or she uses third-person pronouns such as *he* and *she* to refer to the characters.

## Vocabulary

The following words are critical to the meaning of the story that follows. Copy the words into your notebook. As you read, record each word's definition.

| | | |
|---|---|---|
| **reproach** | **conspired** | **devastated** |
| **nonchalantly** | **expectations** | **sentimental** |

Two Kinds
from
The Joy Luck Club
Amy Tan


## CLOSE READING MODEL

The passage below is from Amy Tan's story "Two Kinds." The annotations to the right of the passage show ways in which you can use close reading skills to make predictions and analyze character and point of view.

### *from* "Two Kinds"

And after seeing my mother's disappointed face once again, something inside of me began to die. I hated the tests, the raised hopes and failed expectations.[1] Before going to bed that night, I looked in the mirror above the bathroom sink and when I saw only my face staring back—and that it would always be this ordinary face—I began to cry. Such a sad, ugly girl! I made high-pitched noises like a crazed animal, trying to scratch out the face in the mirror.

And then I saw what seemed to be the prodigy side of me—because I had never seen that face before. I looked at my reflection, blinking so I could see more clearly. The girl staring back at me was angry, powerful.[2] This girl and I were the same. I had new thoughts, willful thoughts, or rather thoughts filled with lots of won'ts. I won't let her change me, I promised myself. I won't be what I'm not.[3]

So now on nights when my mother presented her tests, I performed listlessly, my head propped on one arm. I pretended to be bored. And I was.[4] I got so bored I started counting the bellows of the foghorns out on the bay while my mother drilled me in other areas.

**Character and Point of View**

**1** The narrator uses the first-person pronouns *my, me,* and *I* and shares her innermost thoughts and emotions. These details reveal that the story is written in the first-person point of view.

**Character and Point of View**

**2** As the narrator gains new insights into her own personality, she reveals new character traits. Despite her feelings of failure and frustration, she realizes that she is "powerful."

**Make Predictions**

**3** The narrator promises to be true to herself. Since a *promise* implies commitment, you may predict that she is determined to resist her mother's attempts to change her.

**Make Predictions**

**4** The narrator describes her performance as *listless,* or lacking energy and effort. Her obvious boredom might lead you to predict that the mother will become frustrated and give up on the "tests."

# Two Kinc

*from*
**The Joy Luck Club**

**Amy T**

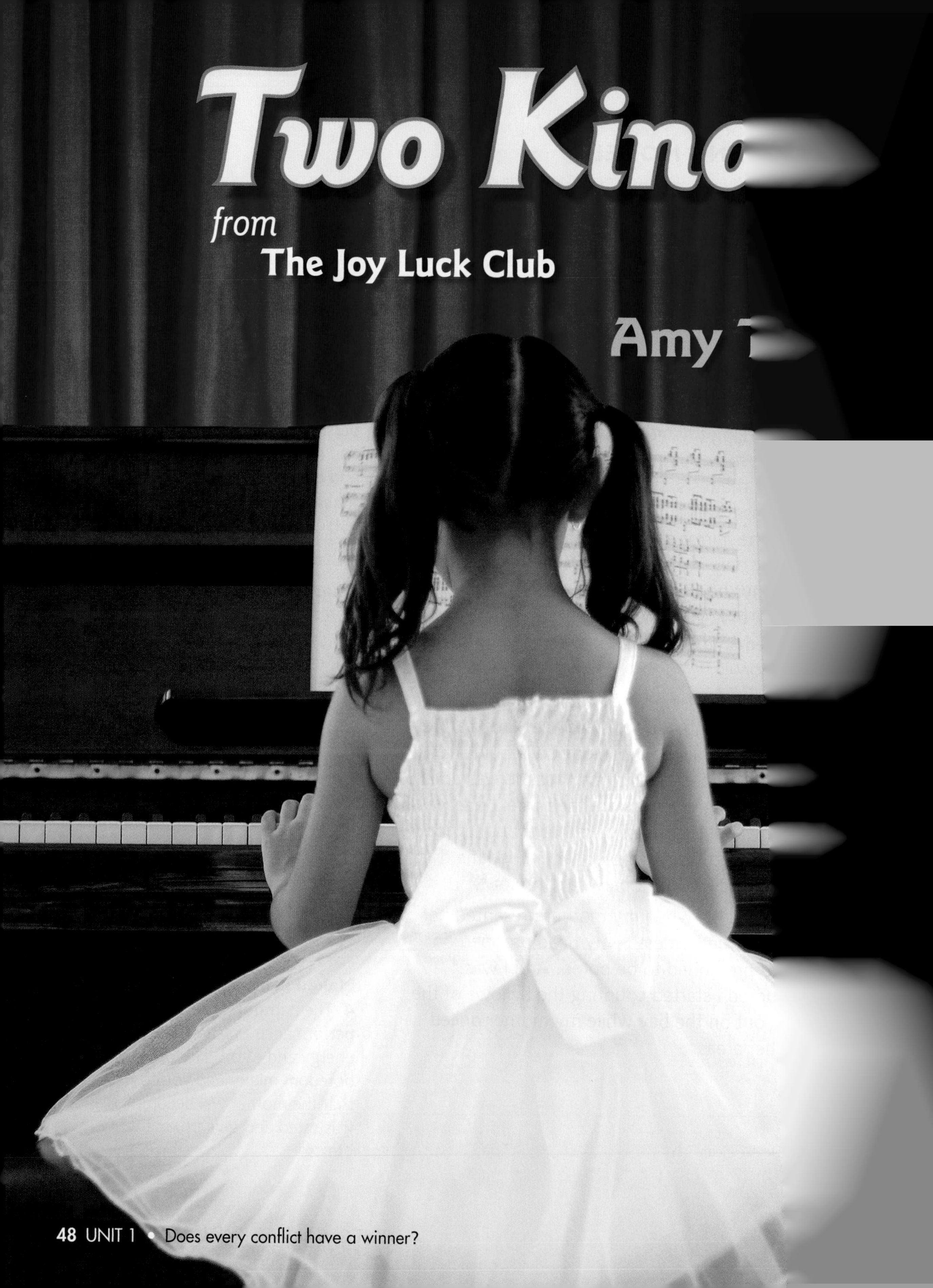

My mother believed you could be anything you wanted to be in America. You could open a restaurant. You could work for the government and get good retirement. You could buy a house with almost no money down. You could become rich. You could become instantly famous.

"Of course you can be prodigy,[1] too," my mother told me when I was nine. "You can be best anything. What does Auntie Lindo know? Her daughter, she is only best tricky."

America was where all my mother's hopes lay. She had come here in 1949 after losing everything in China: her mother and father, her family home, her first husband, and two daughters, twin baby girls. But she never looked back with regret. There were so many ways for things to get better.

**Character**
In what ways might the details in this paragraph contribute to the mother's motives?

老師

We didn't immediately pick the right kind of prodigy. At first my mother thought I could be a Chinese Shirley Temple.[2] We'd watch Shirley's old movies on TV as though they were training films. My mother would poke my arm and say, *"Ni kan"* [nē kän]—You watch. And I would see Shirley tapping her feet, or singing a sailor song, or pursing her lips into a very round O while saying, "Oh my goodness."

"*Ni kan,*" said my mother as Shirley's eyes flooded with tears. "You already know how. Don't need talent for crying!"

Soon after my mother got this idea about Shirley Temple, she took me to a beauty training school in the Mission district and put me in the hands of a student who could barely hold the scissors without shaking. Instead of getting big fat curls, I emerged with an uneven mass of crinkly black fuzz. My mother dragged me off to the bathroom and tried to wet down my hair.

"You look like Negro Chinese," she lamented, as if I had done this on purpose.

**Character**
What are the mother's motives for taking her daughter to beauty training school?

**Comprehension**
Whom does the narrator's mother want her to be like?

---

1. **prodigy** (präd′ ə jē) *n.* child of unusually high talent.
2. **Shirley Temple** American child star of the 1930s. She starred in her first movie at age three and won an Academy Award at age six.

The instructor of the beauty training school had to lop off these soggy clumps to make my hair even again. "Peter Pan is very popular these days," the instructor assured my mother. I now had hair the length of a boy's, with straight-across bangs that hung at a slant two inches above my eyebrows. I liked the haircut and it made me actually look forward to my future fame.

In fact, in the beginning, I was just as excited as my mother, maybe even more so. I pictured this prodigy part of me as many different images, trying each one on for size. I was a dainty ballerina girl standing by the curtains, waiting to hear the right music that would send me floating on my tiptoes. I was like the Christ child lifted out of the straw manger, crying with holy indignity. I was Cinderella stepping from her pumpkin carriage with sparkly cartoon music filling the air.

**Vocabulary ▶**
**reproach** (ri prōch′) *n.* disapproval; criticism

In all of my imaginings, I was filled with a sense that I would soon become *perfect.* My mother and father would adore me. I would be beyond **reproach**. I would never feel the need to sulk for anything.

But sometimes the prodigy in me became impatient. "If you don't hurry up and get me out of here, I'm disappearing for good," it warned. "And then you'll always be nothing."

老師

**Character**
Why is the mother interested in stories about remarkable children?

Every night after dinner, my mother and I would sit at the Formica kitchen table. She would present new tests, taking her examples from stories of amazing children she had read in *Ripley's Believe It or Not,* or *Good Housekeeping, Reader's Digest,* and a dozen other magazines she kept in a pile in our bathroom. My mother got these magazines from people whose houses she cleaned. And since she cleaned many houses each week, we had a great assortment. She would look through them all, searching for stories about remarkable children.

The first night she brought out a story about a three-year-old boy who knew the capitals of all the states and even most of the European countries. A teacher was quoted as saying the little boy could also pronounce the names of the foreign cities correctly.

"What's the capital of Finland?" my mother asked me, looking at the magazine story.

All I knew was the capital of California, because Sacramento was the name of the street we lived on in Chinatown. "Nairobi!"[3] I guessed, saying the most foreign word I could think of. She checked to see if that was possibly one way to pronounce "Helsinki" [hel siŋ′ kē] before showing me the answer.

The tests got harder—multiplying numbers in my head, finding the queen of hearts in a deck of cards, trying to stand on my head without using my hands, predicting the daily temperatures in Los Angeles, New York, and London.

One night I had to look at a page from the Bible for three minutes and then report everything I could remember. "Now Jehoshaphat had riches and honor in abundance and . . . that's all I remember, Ma," I said.

And after seeing my mother's disappointed face once again, something inside of me began to die. I hated the tests, the raised hopes and failed expectations. Before going to bed that night, I looked in the mirror above the bathroom sink and when I saw only my face staring back—and that it would always be this ordinary face—I began to cry. Such a sad, ugly girl! I made high-pitched noises like a crazed animal, trying to scratch out the face in the mirror.

And then I saw what seemed to be the prodigy side of me—because I had never seen that face before. I looked at my reflection, blinking so I could see more clearly. The girl staring back at me was angry, powerful. This girl and I were the same. I had new thoughts, willful thoughts, or rather thoughts filled with lots of won'ts. I won't let her change me, I promised myself. I won't be what I'm not.

So now on nights when my mother presented her tests, I performed listlessly, my head propped on one arm. I pretended to be bored. And I was. I got so bored I started counting the bellows of the foghorns out on the bay while my mother drilled me in other areas. The sound was comforting and reminded me of the cow jumping over the

**Predict**
How do you think the narrator will do on the harder tests? Read on to verify your prediction.

**Predict**
What is your prediction about the mother's reaction when the girl performs poorly on the tests? Why?

**Comprehension**
What would the narrator and her mother do every night after dinner?

---

3. **Nairobi** (nī rō′ bē) *n.* capital of Kenya, a country in east central Africa.

moon. And the next day, I played a game with myself, seeing if my mother would give up on me before eight bellows. After a while I usually counted only one, maybe two bellows at most. At last she was beginning to give up hope.

Two or three months had gone by without any mention of my being a prodigy again. And then one day my mother was watching *The Ed Sullivan Show*[4] on TV. The TV was old and the sound kept shorting out. Every time my mother got halfway up from the sofa to adjust the set, the sound would go back on and Ed would be talking. As soon as she sat down, Ed would go silent again. She got up, the TV broke into loud piano music. She sat down. Silence. Up and down, back and forth, quiet and loud. It was like a stiff embraceless dance between her and the TV set. Finally she stood by the set with her hand on the sound dial.

**▼ Critical Viewing**
How does the girl in this photograph compare with your image of the story's narrator?

She seemed entranced by the music, a little frenzied piano piece with this mesmerizing[5] quality, sort of quick passages and then teasing lilting ones before it returned to the quick playful parts.

"*Ni kan,*" my mother said, calling me over with hurried hand gestures. "Look here."

I could see why my mother was fascinated by the music. It was being pounded out by a little Chinese girl, about nine years old, with a Peter Pan haircut. The girl had the sauciness[6] of a Shirley Temple. She was proudly modest like a

4. ***The Ed Sullivan Show*** popular variety show, hosted by Ed Sullivan, that ran from 1948 to 1971.
5. **mesmerizing** (mez´ mər īz iŋ) *adj.* hypnotizing.
6. **sauciness** (sô´ sē nəs) *n.* liveliness; boldness; spirit.

proper Chinese child. And she also did this fancy sweep of a curtsy, so that the fluffy skirt of her white dress cascaded slowly to the floor like the petals of a large carnation.

In spite of these warning signs, I wasn't worried. Our family had no piano and we couldn't afford to buy one, let alone reams of sheet music and piano lessons. So I could be generous in my comments when my mother bad-mouthed the little girl on TV.

"Play note right, but doesn't sound good! No singing sound," complained my mother.

"What are you picking on her for?" I said carelessly. "She's pretty good. Maybe she's not the best, but she's trying hard." I knew almost immediately I would be sorry I said that.

"Just like you," she said. "Not the best. Because you not trying." She gave a little huff as she let go of the sound dial and sat down on the sofa.

The little Chinese girl sat down also to play an encore of "Anitra's Dance" by Grieg.[7] I remember the song, because later on I had to learn how to play it.

Three days after watching *The Ed Sullivan Show*, my mother told me what my schedule would be for piano lessons and piano practice. She had talked to Mr. Chong, who lived on the first floor of our apartment building. Mr. Chong was a retired piano teacher and my mother had traded housecleaning services for weekly lessons and a piano for me to practice on every day, two hours a day, from four until six.

When my mother told me this, I felt as though I had been sent to hell. I whined and then kicked my foot a little when I couldn't stand it anymore.

"Why don't you like me the way I am? I'm *not* a genius! I can't play the piano. And even if I could, I wouldn't go on TV if you paid me a million dollars!" I cried.

My mother slapped me. "Who ask you be genius?" she shouted. "Only ask you be your best. For you sake. You think I want you be genius? Hnnh! What for! Who ask you!"

"So ungrateful," I heard her mutter in Chinese. "If she

**Character**
What does this conversation indicate about the difference between the mother's and daughter's traits and motives?

**▲ Critical Viewing**
This television stood four feet tall. How have television and technology changed over the years?

**Comprehension**
Why does the mother decide that the narrator should play the piano?

7. **Grieg** (grēg) *n.* Edvard Grieg (1843–1907), Norwegian composer.

had as much talent as she has temper, she would be famous now."

Mr. Chong, whom I secretly nicknamed Old Chong, was very strange, always tapping his fingers to the silent music of an invisible orchestra. He looked ancient in my eyes. He had lost most of the hair on top of his head and he wore thick glasses and had eyes that always looked tired and sleepy. But he must have been younger than I thought, since he lived with his mother and was not yet married.

*He looked ancient...and had eyes that always looked tired and sleepy.*

I met Old Lady Chong once and that was enough. She had this peculiar smell like a baby that had done something in its pants. And her fingers felt like a dead person's, like an old peach I once found in the back of the refrigerator; the skin just slid off the meat when I picked it up.

I soon found out why Old Chong had retired from teaching piano. He was deaf. "Like Beethoven!"[8] he shouted to me. "We're both listening only in our head!" And he would start to conduct his frantic silent sonatas.

Our lessons went like this. He would open the book and point to different things, explaining their purpose: "Key! Treble! Bass! No sharps or flats! So this is C major! Listen now and play after me!"

**Predict**
How do you think the narrator will react to Old Chong's piano lessons? Read on to verify your prediction.

And then he would play the C scale a few times, a simple chord, and then, as if inspired by an old, unreachable itch, he gradually added more notes and running trills and a pounding bass until the music was really something quite grand.

I would play after him, the simple scale, the simple chord, and then I just played some nonsense that sounded like a cat running up and down on top of garbage cans. Old Chong smiled and applauded and then said, "Very good! But now you must learn to keep time!"

So that's how I discovered that Old Chong's eyes were too

8. **Beethoven** (bā´ tō´ vən) *n.* Ludwig van Beethoven (1770–1827), German composer who began to lose his hearing in 1801. Some of his greatest pieces were written when he was completely deaf.

slow to keep up with the wrong notes I was playing. He went through the motions in half-time. To help me keep rhythm, he stood behind me, pushing down on my right shoulder for every beat. He balanced pennies on top of my wrists so I would keep them still as I slowly played scales and arpeggios.[9] He had me curve my hand around an apple and keep that shape when playing chords. He marched stiffly to show me how to make each finger dance up and down, staccato[10] like an obedient little soldier.

He taught me all these things, and that was how I also learned I could be lazy and get away with mistakes, lots of mistakes. If I hit the wrong notes because I hadn't practiced enough, I never corrected myself. I just kept playing in rhythm. And Old Chong kept conducting his own private reverie.

So maybe I never really gave myself a fair chance. I did pick up the basics pretty quickly, and I might have become a good pianist at that young age. But I was so determined not to try, not to be anybody different that I learned to play only the most ear-splitting preludes, the most discordant hymns.

**Character**
What motivates the daughter to play piano badly?

Over the next year, I practiced like this, dutifully in my own way. And then one day I heard my mother and her friend Lindo Jong both talking in a loud bragging tone of voice so others could hear. It was after church, and I was leaning against the brick wall wearing a dress with stiff white petticoats. Auntie Lindo's daughter, Waverly, who was about my age, was standing farther down the wall about five feet away. We had grown up together and shared all the closeness of two sisters squabbling over crayons and dolls. In other words, for the most part, we hated each other. I thought she was snotty. Waverly Jong had gained a certain amount of fame as "Chinatown's Littlest Chinese Chess Champion."

**Comprehension**
What useful information does the narrator learn about her piano teacher?

9. **arpeggios** (är pej´ ē ōz) *n.* notes in a chord played separately in quick succession.
10. **staccato** (stə kät´ ō) *adv.* played crisply, with clear breaks between notes.

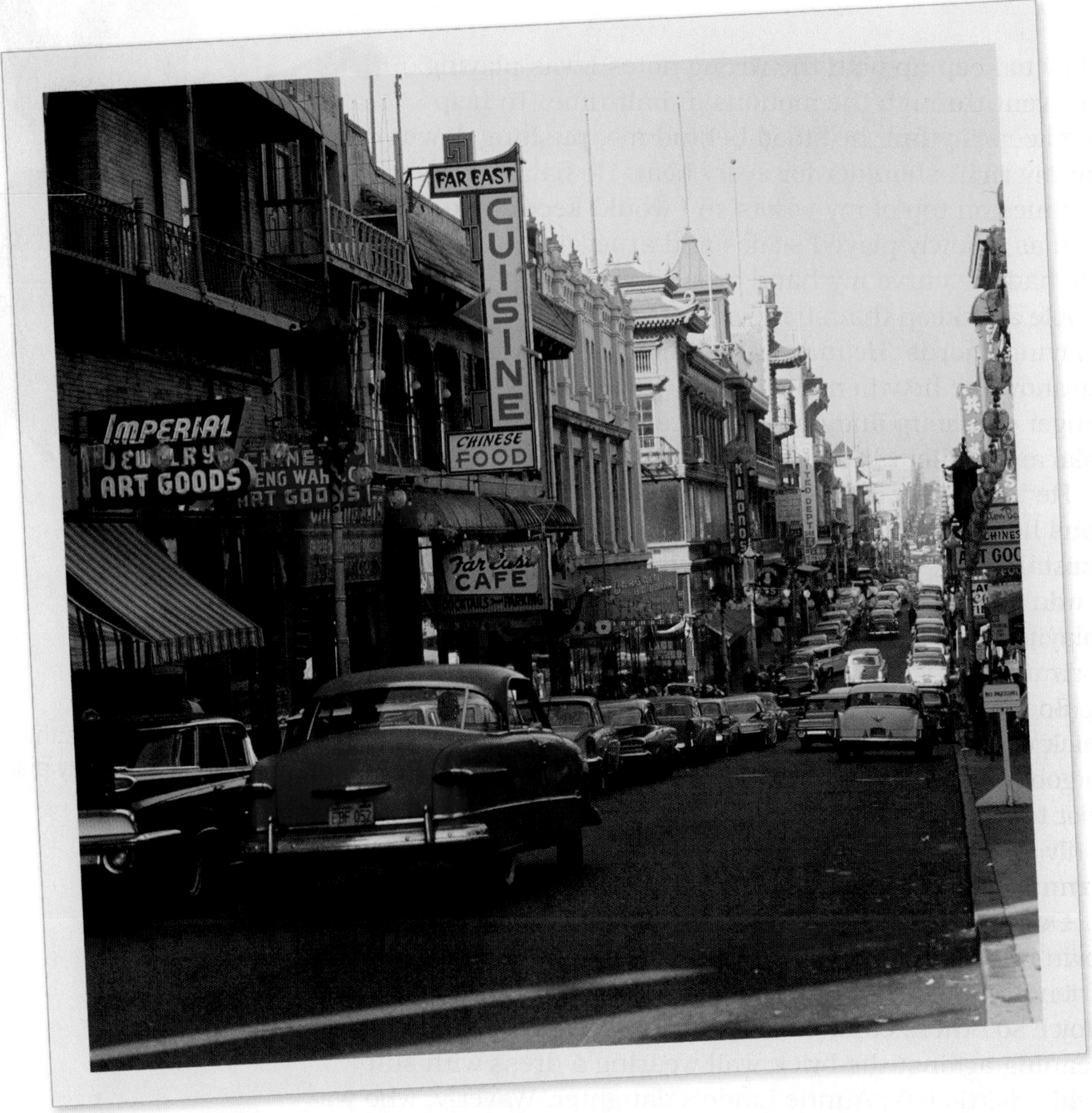


**▲ Critical Viewing** This photo shows the type of community and time period of the author's childhood. How may these surroundings have affected the story?

"She bring home too many trophy," lamented Auntie Lindo that Sunday. "All day she play chess. All day I have no time do nothing but dust off her winnings." She threw a scolding look at Waverly, who pretended not to see her.

"You lucky you don't have this problem," said Auntie Lindo with a sigh to my mother.

And my mother squared her shoulders and bragged: "Our problem worser than yours. If we ask Jing-mei wash dish, she hear nothing but music. It's like you can't stop this natural talent."

And right then, I was determined to put a stop to her foolish pride.

老師

A few weeks later, Old Chong and my mother **conspired** to have me play in a talent show which would be held in the church hall. By then, my parents had saved up enough to buy me a secondhand piano, a black Wurlitzer spinet with a scarred bench. It was the showpiece of our living room.

◀ **Vocabulary**
**conspired** (kən spīrd′) *v.* planned together secretly

For the talent show, I was to play a piece called "Pleading Child" from Schumann's[11] *Scenes from Childhood.* It was a simple, moody piece that sounded more difficult than it was. I was supposed to memorize the whole thing, playing the repeat parts twice to make the piece sound longer. But I dawdled over it, playing a few bars and then cheating, looking up to see what notes followed. I never really listened to what I was playing. I daydreamed about being somewhere else, about being someone else.

*And right then, I was determined to put a stop to her foolish pride.*

The part I liked to practice best was the fancy curtsy: right foot out, touch the rose on the carpet with a pointed foot, sweep to the side, left leg bends, look up and smile.

My parents invited all the couples from the Joy Luck Club[12] to witness my debut. Auntie Lindo and Uncle Tin were there. Waverly and her two older brothers had also come. The first two rows were filled with children both younger and older than I was. The littlest ones got to go first. They recited simple nursery rhymes, squawked out tunes on miniature violins, twirled Hula Hoops, pranced in pink ballet tutus, and when they bowed or curtsied, the audience would sigh in unison, "Awww," and then clap enthusiastically.

When my turn came, I was very confident. I remember

**Comprehension**
What do the narrator's mother and Auntie Lindo discuss?

---

**11. Schumann** (sho͞o′ män) Robert Alexander Schumann (1810–1856), German composer.
**12. Joy Luck Club** four Chinese women who have been meeting for years to socialize.

my childish excitement. It was as if I knew, without a doubt, that the prodigy side of me really did exist. I had no fear whatsoever, no nervousness. I remember thinking to myself, This is it! This is it! I looked out over the audience, at my mother's blank face, my father's yawn, Auntie Lindo's stiff-lipped smile, Waverly's sulky expression. I had on a white dress layered with sheets of lace, and a pink bow in my Peter Pan haircut. As I sat down I envisioned people jumping to their feet and Ed Sullivan rushing up to introduce me to everyone on TV.

And I started to play. It was so beautiful. I was so caught up in how lovely I looked that at first I didn't worry how I would sound. So it was a surprise to me when I hit the first wrong note and I realized something didn't sound quite right. And then I hit another and another followed that. A chill started at the top of my head and began to trickle down. Yet I couldn't stop playing, as though my hands were bewitched. I kept thinking my fingers would adjust themselves back, like a train switching to the right track. I played this strange jumble through two repeats, the sour notes staying with me all the way to the end.

**Predict**
How do you predict the mother will react to her daughter's poor piano playing?

When I stood up, I discovered my legs were shaking. Maybe I had just been nervous and the audience, like Old Chong, had seen me go through the right motions and had not heard anything wrong at all. I swept my right foot out, went down on my knee, looked up and smiled. The room was quiet, except for Old Chong, who was beaming and shouting, "Bravo! Bravo! Well done!" But then I saw my mother's face, her stricken face. The audience clapped weakly, and as I walked back to my chair, with my whole face quivering as I tried not to cry, I heard a little boy whisper loudly to his mother, "That was awful," and the mother whispered back, "Well, she certainly tried."

**Spiral Review**
**PLOT** Do you think the narrator's poor performance will inspire a change in her actions and attitude as the story progresses? Why or why not?

And now I realized how many people were in the audience, the whole world it seemed. I was aware of eyes burning into my back. I felt the shame of my mother and father as they sat stiffly throughout the rest of the show.

We could have escaped during intermission. Pride and some strange sense of honor must have anchored my parents to their chairs. And so we watched it all: the eighteen-year-old boy with a fake mustache who did a magic show and juggled flaming hoops while riding a unicycle. The breasted girl with white makeup who sang from *Madama Butterfly* and got honorable mention. And the eleven-year-old boy who won first prize playing a tricky violin song that sounded like a busy bee.

After the show, the Hsus, the Jongs, and the St. Clairs from the Joy Luck Club came up to my mother and father.

"Lots of talented kids," Auntie Lindo said vaguely, smiling broadly.

"That was somethin' else," said my father, and I wondered if he was referring to me in a humorous way, or whether he even remembered what I had done.

Waverly looked at me and shrugged her shoulders. "You aren't a genius like me," she said matter-of-factly. And if I hadn't felt so bad, I would have pulled her braids and punched her stomach.

*I felt the shame of my mother and father as they sat stiffly throughout the rest of the show.*

**Comprehension**
What happens at the talent show?

**◀ Critical Viewing**
How do you think the narrator felt watching the other children perform?

**Vocabulary ▸**
**devastated** (dev′ ə stāt′ əd) *v.* destroyed; completely upset
**nonchalantly** (nän′ shə länt′ lē) *adv.* seemingly uninterested

**Predict**
What do you predict the mother will say to her daughter now that the piano recital is over?

But my mother's expression was what **devastated** me: a quiet, blank look that said she had lost everything. I felt the same way, and it seemed as if everybody were now coming up, like gawkers at the scene of an accident, to see what parts were actually missing. When we got on the bus to go home, my father was humming the busy-bee tune and my mother was silent. I kept thinking she wanted to wait until we got home before shouting at me. But when my father unlocked the door to our apartment, my mother walked in and then went to the back, into the bedroom. No accusations. No blame. And in a way, I felt disappointed. I had been waiting for her to start shouting, so I could shout back and cry and blame her for all my misery.

老師

I assumed my talent-show fiasco meant I never had to play the piano again. But two days later, after school, my mother came out of the kitchen and saw me watching TV.

"Four clock," she reminded me as if it were any other day. I was stunned, as though she were asking me to go through the talent-show torture again. I wedged myself more tightly in front of the TV.

"Turn off TV," she called from the kitchen five minutes later.

I didn't budge. And then I decided. I didn't have to do what my mother said anymore. I wasn't her slave. This wasn't China. I had listened to her before and look what happened. She was the stupid one.

She came out from the kitchen and stood in the arched entryway of the living room. "Four clock," she said once again, louder.

"I'm not going to play anymore," I said **nonchalantly**. "Why should I? I'm not a genius."

She walked over and stood in front of the TV. I saw her chest was heaving up and down in an angry way.

"No!" I said, and I now felt stronger, as if my true self had finally emerged. So this was what had been inside me all along.

"No! I won't!" I screamed.

She yanked me by the arm, pulled me off the floor, snapped off the TV. She was frighteningly strong, half pulling, half carrying me toward the piano as I kicked the throw rugs under my feet. She lifted me up and onto the hard bench. I was sobbing by now, looking at her bitterly. Her chest was heaving even more and her mouth was open, smiling crazily as if she were pleased I was crying.

"You want me to be someone that I'm not!" I sobbed. "I'll never be the kind of daughter you want me to be!"

"Only two kinds of daughters," she shouted in Chinese. "Those who are obedient and those who follow their own mind! Only one kind of daughter can live in this house. Obedient daughter!"

"Then I wish I wasn't your daughter. I wish you weren't my mother," I shouted. As I said these things I got scared. It felt like worms and toads and slimy things crawling out of my chest, but it also felt good, as if this awful side of me had surfaced, at last.

"Too late change this," said my mother shrilly.

And I could sense her anger rising to its breaking point. I wanted to see it spill over. And that's when I remembered the babies she had lost in China, the ones we never talked about. "Then I wish I'd never been born!" I shouted. "I wish I were dead! Like them."

*" You want me to be someone that I'm not!" I sobbed. "I'll never be the kind of daughter you want me to be!"*

It was as if I had said the magic words. Alakazam!—and her face went blank, her mouth closed, her arms went slack, and she backed out of the room, stunned, as if she were blowing away like a small brown leaf, thin, brittle, lifeless.

It was not the only disappointment my mother felt in me. In the years that followed, I failed her so many times,

**Comprehension**
How does the narrator feel about her performance at the talent show?

**Vocabulary ▶**
**expectations** (ek´ spekt tā´ shənz) *n.* things looked forward to

each time asserting my own will, my right to fall short of **expectations**. I didn't get straight A's. I didn't become class president. I didn't get into Stanford. I dropped out of college.

For unlike my mother, I did not believe I could be anything I wanted to be. I could only be me.

And for all those years, we never talked about the disaster at the recital or my terrible accusations afterward at the piano bench. All that remained unchecked, like a betrayal that was now unspeakable. So I never found a way to ask her why she had hoped for something so large that failure was inevitable.

*For unlike my mother, I did not believe I could be anything I wanted to be. I could only be me.*

And even worse, I never asked her what frightened me the most: Why had she given up hope?

For after our struggle at the piano, she never mentioned my playing again. The lessons stopped. The lid to the piano was closed, shutting out the dust, my misery, and her dreams.

So she surprised me. A few years ago, she offered to give me the piano, for my thirtieth birthday. I had not played in all those years. I saw the offer as a sign of forgiveness, a tremendous burden removed.

**Predict**
How do you predict the narrator will respond to the gift of the piano?

"Are you sure?" I asked shyly. "I mean, won't you and Dad miss it?"

"No, this your piano," she said firmly. "Always your piano. You only one can play."

"Well, I probably can't play anymore," I said. "It's been years."

"You pick up fast," said my mother, as if she knew this was certain. "You have natural talent. You could been genius if you want to."

"No I couldn't."

"You just not trying," said my mother. And she was neither angry nor sad. She said it as if to announce a fact that could never be disproved. "Take it," she said.

But I didn't at first. It was enough that she had offered it to me. And after that, every time I saw it in my parents' living room, standing in front of the bay windows, it made me feel proud, as if it were a shiny trophy I had won back. ●

Last week I sent a tuner over to my parents' apartment and had the piano reconditioned, for purely **sentimental** reasons. My mother had died a few months before and I had been getting things in order for my father, a little bit at a time. I put the jewelry in special silk pouches. The sweaters she had knitted in yellow, pink, bright orange—all the colors I hated—I put those in moth-proof boxes. I found some old Chinese silk dresses, the kind with little slits up the sides. I rubbed the old silk against my skin, then wrapped them in tissue and decided to take them home with me.

After I had the piano tuned, I opened the lid and touched the keys. It sounded even richer than I remembered. Really, it was a very good piano. Inside the bench were the same exercise notes with handwritten scales, the same secondhand music books with their covers held together with yellow tape.

I opened up the Schumann book to the dark little piece I had played at the recital. It was on the left-hand side of

◀ **Vocabulary**
**sentimental** (sen tə ment′ əl) *adj.* emotional; showing tender feeling

**Predict**
What do you think the narrator will do now that the piano has been tuned after so many years?

**Comprehension**
What gift does the narrator receive for her 30th birthday? Why?

the page, "Pleading Child." It looked more difficult than I remembered. I played a few bars, surprised at how easily the notes came back to me.

And for the first time, or so it seemed, I noticed the piece on the right-hand side. It was called "Perfectly Contented." I tried to play this one as well. It had a lighter melody but the same flowing rhythm and turned out to be quite easy. "Pleading Child" was shorter but slower; "Perfectly Contented" was longer, but faster. And after I played them both a few times, I realized they were two halves of the same song.

老師

## Language Study

**Vocabulary** The words listed below appear in "Two Kinds." Make up an answer to each numbered question. Use a complete sentence that includes the italicized vocabulary word.

**reproach devastated nonchalantly expectations sentimental**

1. Why did the *reproach* bother him?
2. What kind of weather *devastated* the crops?
3. Why did he behave *nonchalantly* toward the girls?
4. Why don't the team's new uniforms meet your *expectations*?
5. Why are movies about pets often *sentimental*?

**WORD STUDY**

The **Latin root *-spir-*** means "breath."

If you say something "under your breath," you say it in secret. In this story, two characters **conspire**, or secretly plan, to have the narrator play piano in a talent show.

### Word Study

**Part A** Explain how the **Latin root *-spir-*** contributes to the meaning of the words *perspire* and *respiration*. Consult a dictionary if necessary.

**Part B** Use the context of the sentences and your knowledge of the Latin root *-spir-* to explain your answer to each question.

1. Is a *spirited* person lively or dull?
2. If something *inspires* you, does it make you feel excitement?

# Close Reading Activities

## Literary Analysis

### Key Ideas and Details

1. **(a)** In what ways does the mother pressure her daughter for change? **(b) Draw Conclusions:** How does the difference in their attitudes create problems? Support your answer with details from the text.
2. **Make Predictions (a)** What predictions did you make about how well the narrator would play at the recital? **(b)** On what details did you base each prediction? **(c)** Did reading ahead cause you to change your prediction?
3. **Make Predictions (a)** At what point in the story were you able to predict that the daughter would eventually refuse to play the piano? **(b)** What details in the text led you to make this prediction? **(c)** Did your prediction change as you read? Explain.

### Craft and Structure

4. **Character and Point of View** Using a diagram like the one shown, list the daughter's character traits, supporting your answers with story details.

5. **Character and Point of View (a)** What motives does the daughter have to rebel against her mother? Cite details from the text that reveal these motives. **(b)** What are the mother's character traits and motives that cause her to keep pushing her daughter? Cite textual evidence to support your answers.
6. **Character and Point of View** How might the story be different if it were told from the mother's point of view? Support your answer with details from the story.

### Integration of Knowledge and Ideas

7. **(a)** What are the titles of the two pieces in the Schumann book that the daughter plays at the end of the story? **(b) Connect:** In what ways do the titles and pieces reflect the daughter's feelings about herself?
8. **Make a Judgment:** Should the narrator's mother have pushed the daughter as she did? Explain, using examples from the text to support your opinion.

9. THE BIG ? **Does every conflict have a winner?** In this story, conflict results when a mother pushes her daughter to become a success. Is there a winner in this conflict? Explain.

**ACADEMIC VOCABULARY**

As you write and speak about "Two Kinds," use the words related to conflict that you explored on page 3 of this textbook.

## Conventions: **Personal and Possessive Pronouns**

A **personal pronoun** takes the place of a noun or another pronoun named elsewhere in the text. A **possessive pronoun** shows possession or ownership.

Pronouns are used every day in conversation. Writers use pronouns to avoid the awkwardness of repeating the same noun over and over.

| | |
|---|---|
| **Personal Pronouns** | I, me, we, us, you, he, him, she, her, it, they, them |
| **Possessive Pronouns** | my, mine, our, ours, your, yours, his, her, hers, its, their, theirs |

Personal and possessive pronouns must agree in number and in gender with the nouns or pronouns to which they refer.

**Singular:** Read this *book*. *It* is my favorite.
**Plural:** These are *the ranchers'* horses. The horses are *theirs*.
**Feminine:** Where is *Mary*? Here are *her* gloves.
**Masculine:** *Al's* dog was hungry. *His* dog ate the food.

### Practice A

Identify the personal pronoun in each item. Then, identify the noun it replaces.

1. When the daughter practices piano, she makes mistakes.
2. The mother has many magazines and enjoys reading them.
3. A three-year-old boy knows all the state capitals. He can also pronounce the names of foreign cities.

**Speaking Application** In "Two Kinds," find three sentences with personal pronouns. Recite these sentences to a partner and identify the personal pronouns.

### Practice B

Rewrite each sentence, using a possessive pronoun in place of each underlined word or words. Be sure the pronoun agrees with the noun it replaces in number and gender.

1. The mother's daily tests are boring.
2. The mother's and father's disappointment at the recital is clear.
3. Mr. Chong's piano lessons are useless.
4. The daughter does not take the piano, even though it is the daughter's.

**Writing Application** Write two sentences about the mother and daughter in "Two Kinds." Use possessive pronouns.

## Writing to Sources

**Narrative Text** Write a **journal entry** from the point of view of a character from "Two Kinds."

- Choose a character and a specific situation from the story.
- Write from the character's point of view, using the word *I*. Refer to details from the story to accurately represent the character's traits and motives.
- Describe the situation by presenting a clear sequence of events that unfolds naturally and logically.
- Use dialogue and descriptive details to convey the character's thoughts and feelings.

**Grammar Application** As you write, be sure to use personal and possessive pronouns correctly. Make sure your possessive pronouns agree in number and gender with the nouns or pronouns to which they refer.

## Research and Technology

**Build and Present Knowledge** Research traditional Chinese beliefs and customs about the relationship between parents and children. Then, write an **outline** that provides background information.

Follow these steps to complete the assignment:

- Generate a list of questions on your topic to guide your research.
- Consult a variety of library or Internet resources to answer your questions.
- Organize your thoughts by jotting down notes.
- In outline form, state briefly and in your own words the main points and key details of what you learned.
- Group your notes by category. Use Roman numerals (I, II, III) to number your most important points. Under each Roman numeral, use capital letters for each supporting detail.
- Share your findings with other students. Then, in small groups, discuss whether or not the traditional beliefs and customs are reflected in "Two Kinds."

Meet the Author

As a child, **Joan Aiken** (1924–2004) often walked in the fields near her home in England and created stories to amuse herself. She was inspired by her father, stepfather, and mother, who were all writers. She was also inspired by the classic novels her mother read to her when Aiken was young. By age five, Aiken was writing her own tales. Her stories, whether written for children or adults, often contain elements of horror, fantasy, and mystery.

## Does every conflict have a winner?

Think about the Big Question as you read "The Third Wish." Take notes on ways in which the story explores the nature of conflict.

## CLOSE READING FOCUS

### Key Ideas and Details: **Make Inferences**

Authors usually do not directly tell you everything about a story's characters, setting, and events. Instead, readers must **make inferences,** or develop logical ideas about unstated information.

- To form inferences, you must recognize details that the author states explicitly, or directly, in the story. Next, connect those details with what you know about life.
- Then, develop an informed idea, or inference, about the story's characters, setting, and events, based on that information.

### Craft and Structure: **Conflict and Resolution**

In most fictional stories, the plot centers on a **conflict**—a struggle between opposing forces. There are two kinds of conflict:

- When there is **external conflict,** a character struggles with an outside force, such as another character or nature.
- When there is **internal conflict,** a character struggles with himself or herself to overcome opposing feelings, beliefs, needs, or desires.

A story can have a series of small conflicts that contribute to the main conflict. The **resolution,** or outcome, often comes toward the end of the story, when the problem is settled in some way.

## Vocabulary

Copy the following words from "The Third Wish" into your notebook. Which two words share the same suffix? What part of speech is created when that suffix is used?

| **verge** | **dabbling** | **presumptuous** |
| --- | --- | --- |
| **rash** | **remote** | **malicious** |

## CLOSE READING MODEL

The passage below is from Joan Aiken's story "The Third Wish." The annotations to the right of the passage show ways in which you can use close reading skills to make inferences and analyze conflict and resolution.

### *from* "The Third Wish"

Leita made him a good wife. But as time went by Mr. Peters began to feel that she was not happy. She seemed restless,[1] wandered much in the garden, and sometimes when he came back from the fields he would find the house empty and she would return after half an hour or so with no explanation of where she had been. On these occasions she was always especially tender and would put out his slippers to warm and cook his favorite dish[2]—Welsh rarebit with wild strawberries—for supper.

One evening he was returning home along the river path when he saw Leita in front of him, down by the water. A swan had sailed up to the verge and she had her arms round its neck and the swan's head rested against her check.[3] She was weeping, and as he came nearer he saw that tears were rolling, too, from the swan's eyes.

"Leita, what is it?" he asked, very troubled.

"This is my sister," she answered. "I can't bear being separated from her."[4]

**Conflict and Resolution**

**1** Aiken describes Leita as "not happy" and "restless," feelings that suggest a possible internal conflict. You may expect that the story will explore the cause of Leita's conflict.

**Make Inferences**

**2** Leita's actions may lead you to infer that although she is sad, she cares deeply for her husband and wants him to be happy.

**Make Inferences**

**3** These physical gestures are tender and trusting. From them, you can infer that Leita and the swan have a close relationship. You might ask yourself how this relationship is related to Leita's sadness.

**Conflict and Resolution**

**4** Here readers learn the reason for Leita's unhappiness. You might wonder if Leita's internal conflict will begin to be resolved through a reunion with her sister.

# The Third Wish

Joan Aiken

ONCE THERE WAS A MAN WHO WAS DRIVING IN HIS CAR AT DUSK ON A SPRING EVENING THROUGH PART OF THE FOREST OF SAVERNAKE. HIS NAME WAS MR. PETERS. THE PRIMROSES WERE JUST BEGINNING BUT THE TREES WERE STILL BARE, AND IT WAS COLD; THE BIRDS HAD STOPPED SINGING AN HOUR AGO.

As Mr. Peters entered a straight, empty stretch of road he seemed to hear a faint crying, and a struggling and thrashing, as if somebody was in trouble far away in the trees. He left his car and climbed the mossy bank beside the road. Beyond the bank was an open slope of beech trees leading down to thorn bushes through which he saw the gleam of water. He stood a moment waiting to try and discover where the noise was coming from, and presently heard a rustling and some strange cries in a voice which was almost human—and yet there was something too hoarse about it at one time and too clear and sweet at another. Mr. Peters ran down the hill and as he neared the bushes he saw something white among them which was trying to extricate[1] itself; coming closer he found that it was a swan that had become entangled in the thorns growing on the bank of the canal.

The bird struggled all the more frantically as he approached, looking at him with hate in its yellow eyes, and when he took hold of it to free it, it hissed at him, pecked him, and thrashed dangerously with its wings which were powerful enough to break his arm. Nevertheless he managed to release it from the thorns, and carrying it tightly with one arm, holding the snaky head well away with

**◀ Critical Viewing**
What details of this picture could help you predict that this story has elements of fantasy?

**Conflict and Resolution**
What external conflict does Mr. Peters face after he finds the swan?

1. **extricate** (eks´ tri kāt´) *v.* set free.

the other hand (for he did not wish his eyes pecked out), he took it to the **verge** of the canal and dropped it in.

**Vocabulary ▶**
**verge** (vurj) *n.* edge; brink

**dabbling** (dab′ liŋ) *v.* wetting by dipping, splashing, or paddling in the water

**presumptuous** (prē zump′ cho͞o əs) *adj.* overconfident; lacking respect

The swan instantly assumed great dignity and sailed out to the middle of the water, where it put itself to rights with much **dabbling** and preening, smoothing its feathers with little showers of drops. Mr. Peters waited, to make sure that it was all right and had suffered no damage in its struggles. Presently the swan, when it was satisfied with its appearance, floated in to the bank once more, and in a moment, instead of the great white bird, there was a little man all in green with a golden crown and long beard, standing by the water. He had fierce glittering eyes and looked by no means friendly.

"Well, Sir," he said threateningly, "I see you are **presumptuous** enough to know some of the laws of magic. You think that because you have rescued—by pure good fortune—the King of the Forest from a difficulty, you should have some fabulous reward."

"I expect three wishes, no more and no less," answered Mr. Peters, looking at him steadily and with composure.[2]

**Spiral Review**
**PLOT** The King of the Forest grants Mr. Peters three wishes, but not without a warning. How does granting the wishes advance the plot? How does the warning hint at how the plot might develop?

"Three wishes, he wants, the clever man! Well, I have yet to hear of the human being who made any good use of his three wishes—they mostly end up worse off than they started. Take your three wishes then"—he flung three dead leaves in the air—"don't blame me if you spend the last wish in undoing the work of the other two."

Mr. Peters caught the leaves and put two of them carefully in his briefcase. When he looked up, the swan was sailing about in the middle of the water again, flicking the drops angrily down its long neck.

Mr. Peters stood for some minutes reflecting on how he should use his reward. He knew very well that the gift of three magic wishes was one which brought trouble more often than not, and he had no intention of being like the forester who first wished by mistake for a sausage, and then in a rage wished it on the end of his wife's nose, and then had to use his last wish in getting it off again. Mr. Peters had most of the things which he wanted and was very content with his life. The only thing that troubled him was that he was a little lonely, and had no companion for his old age. He decided to use his first wish and to keep the other two in case of an emergency. Taking a thorn he pricked his tongue with

2. **composure** (kəm pō′ zhər) *n.* calmness of mind.

it, to remind himself not to utter **rash** wishes aloud. Then holding the third leaf and gazing round him at the dusky undergrowth, the primroses, great beeches and the blue-green water of the canal, he said:

"I wish I had a wife as beautiful as the forest."

A tremendous quacking and splashing broke out on the surface of the water. He thought that it was the swan laughing at him. Taking no notice he made his way through the darkening woods to his car, wrapped himself up in the rug and went to sleep.

When he awoke it was morning and the birds were beginning to call. Coming along the track towards him was the most beautiful creature he had ever seen, with eyes as blue-green as the canal, hair as dusky as the bushes, and skin as white as the feathers of swans.

"Are you the wife that I wished for?" asked Mr. Peters.

"Yes, I am," she replied. "My name is Leita."

She stepped into the car beside him and they drove off to the church on the outskirts of the forest, where they were married. Then he took her to his house in a **remote** and lovely valley and showed her all his treasures—the bees in their white hives, the Jersey cows, the hyacinths, the silver candlesticks, the blue cups and the luster bowl for putting primroses in. She admired everything, but what pleased her most was the river which ran by the foot of his garden.

"Do swans come up there?" she asked.

"Yes, I have often seen swans there on the river," he told her, and she smiled.

Leita made him a good wife. But as time went by Mr. Peters began to feel that she was not happy. She seemed restless, wandered much in the garden, and sometimes when he came back from the fields he would find the house empty and she would return after half an hour or so with no explanation of where she had been. On these occasions she was always especially tender and would put out his slippers to warm and cook his favorite dish—Welsh rarebit[3] with wild strawberries—for supper.

One evening he was returning home along the river path when he saw Leita in front of him, down by the water. A swan had sailed up to the verge and she had her arms round its neck and the swan's head rested against her cheek. She was

3. **Welsh rarebit** a dish of melted cheese served on crackers or toast.

**◀ Vocabulary**

**rash** (rash) *adj.* too hasty

**remote** (ri mōt′) *adj.* far away from anything else

**Conflict and Resolution**
What inner conflict is resolved for Mr. Peters when he gets a wife?

**Make Inferences**
On what details does Mr. Peters base his inference that Leita is not happy?

**Comprehension**
What happens after Mr. Peters makes his first wish?

## LITERATURE IN CONTEXT

### Mythology Connection

**A Star Is Born**

The graceful, noble swan has been celebrated in the myths and literature of many cultures. It is also visible in the skies as a constellation, Cygnus the Swan.

In one version of how the constellation came to be, Phaethon, a human son of Apollo the sun god, borrowed his father's chariot. Phaethon drove dangerously, and to stop him, Zeus hurled a thunderbolt at him. It killed him instantly, and he fell from the sky.

Phaethon's friend Cygnus searched the river for him. As Apollo watched him dive in, he thought Cygnus resembled a swan. When Cygnus died of grief, Apollo took pity and changed him into a swan, placing him forever among the stars.

**Connect to the Literature**

What similarities can you find between the story of Cygnus and "The Third Wish"?

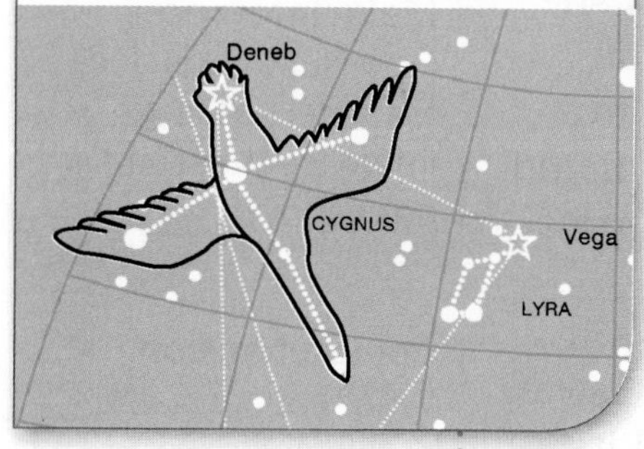


weeping, and as he came nearer he saw that tears were rolling, too, from the swan's eyes.

"Leita, what is it?" he asked, very troubled.

"This is my sister," she answered. "I can't bear being separated from her."

Now he understood that Leita was really a swan from the forest, and this made him very sad because when a human being marries a bird it always leads to sorrow.

"I could use my second wish to give your sister human shape, so that she could be a companion to you," he suggested.

"No, no," she cried, "I couldn't ask that of her."

"Is it so very hard to be a human being?" asked Mr. Peters sadly.

"Very, very hard," she answered.

"Don't you love me at all, Leita?"

"Yes, I do, I do love you," she said, and there were tears in her eyes again. "But I miss the old life in the forest, the cool grass and the mist rising off the river at sunrise and the feel of the water sliding over my feathers as my sister and I drifted along the stream."

"Then shall I use my second wish to turn you back into a swan again?" he asked, and his tongue pricked to remind him of the old King's words, and his heart swelled with grief inside him.

"Who will take care of you?"

"I'd do it myself as I did before I married you," he said, trying to sound cheerful.

She shook her head. "No, I could not be as unkind to you as that. I am partly a swan, but I am also partly a human being now. I will stay with you."

Poor Mr. Peters was very distressed on his wife's account and did his best to make her life happier, taking her for drives in the car, finding beautiful music for her to listen to on the radio, buying clothes for her and even suggesting a trip round the world. But she said no to that; she would prefer to stay in their own house near the river.

He noticed that she spent more and more time baking wonderful cakes—jam puffs, petits fours, éclairs and meringues. One day he saw her take a basketful down to the river and he guessed that she was giving them to her sister.

He built a seat for her by the river, and the two sisters spent hours together there, communicating in some wordless manner. For a time he thought that all would be well, but then he saw how thin and pale she was growing.

One night when he had been late doing the accounts he came up to bed and found her weeping in her sleep and calling:

"Rhea! Rhea! I can't understand what you say! Oh, wait for me, take me with you!"

Then he knew that it was hopeless and she would never be happy as a human. He stooped down and kissed her goodbye, then took another leaf from his notecase, blew it out of the window, and used up his second wish.

Next moment instead of Leita there was a sleeping swan lying across the bed with its head under its wing. He carried it out of the house and down to the brink of the river, and then he said, "Leita! Leita!" to waken her, and gently put her into the water. She gazed round her in astonishment for a moment, and then came up to him and rested her head lightly against his hand; next instant she was flying away over the trees towards the heart of the forest.

He heard a harsh laugh behind him, and turning round saw the old King looking at him with a **malicious** expression.

"Well, my friend! You don't seem to have managed so wonderfully with your first two wishes, do you? What will you do with the last? Turn yourself into a swan? Or turn Leita back into a girl?"

"I shall do neither," said Mr. Peters calmly. "Human beings and swans are better in their own shapes."

But for all that he looked sadly over towards the forest where Leita had flown, and walked slowly back to his house.

Next day he saw two swans swimming at the bottom of the garden, and one of them wore the gold chain he had given Leita after their marriage; she came up and rubbed her head against his hand.

Mr. Peters and his two swans came to be well known in that part of the country; people used to say that he talked to swans and they understood him as well as his neighbors. Many people were a little frightened of him. There was a story that once when thieves tried to break into his house they were set upon by two huge white birds which carried them off bodily and dropped them in the river.

**Conflict and Resolution**
Beyond what he has already done to resolve his wife's conflict, what else do you suggest Mr. Peters could do?

◀ **Vocabulary**
**malicious** (mə lish´ əs) *adj.* hateful; spiteful

**Comprehension**
Why does Leita want to be a swan again?

As Mr. Peters grew old everyone wondered at his contentment. Even when he was bent with rheumatism[4] he would not think of moving to a drier spot, but went slowly about his work, with the two swans always somewhere close at hand.

**Make Inferences**
What inferences can you make from knowing what Mr. Peters held in his hands when he died?

Sometimes people who knew his story would say to him: "Mr. Peters, why don't you wish for another wife?"

"Not likely," he would answer serenely. "Two wishes were enough for me, I reckon. I've learned that even if your wishes are granted they don't always better you. I'll stay faithful to Leita."

One autumn night, passers-by along the road heard the mournful sound of two swans singing. All night the song went on, sweet and harsh, sharp and clear. In the morning Mr. Peters was found peacefully dead in his bed with a smile of great happiness on his face. In his hands, which lay clasped on his breast, were a withered leaf and a white feather.

4. **rheumatism** (roo′ mə tiz′ əm) *n.* pain and stiffness of the joints and muscles.

## Language Study

**Vocabulary** The words listed below appear in "The Third Wish." Each word is used in a question. Answer each question, and then explain your response.

**verge** **presumptuous** **dabbling** **remote** **rash**

1. Does Australia seem *remote* to people who live in the U.S.?
2. Does it take a long time to make a *rash* decision?
3. Is it safe to stand on the *verge* of a steep cliff?
4. Is it *presumptuous* of a host to invite guests to a party?
5. If you see someone *dabbling* in a pool, is he in danger?

**WORD STUDY**
The **Latin prefix *mal-*** means "bad." In this story, the old King looks at Mr. Peters with a **malicious**, or hateful, look that shows a desire to cause him harm.

### Word Study

**Part A** Explain how the **Latin prefix *mal-*** contributes to the meanings of these words: *malfunction, maladjusted, malnutrition.* Consult a dictionary if necessary.

**Part B** Use the context of the sentences and your knowledge of the Latin prefix *mal-* to explain your answer to each question.

1. If something is *malodorous,* does it smell good?
2. What kind of physical *malady* might a player have after a football game?

# Close Reading Activities

## Literary Analysis

### Key Ideas and Details

1. **(a)** How does Mr. Peters get the opportunity to ask for three wishes? **(b) Connect:** Based on the King of the Forest's words, how did you think Mr. Peters's wishing would turn out? Was your prediction correct?
2. **(a)** How does Mr. Peters use his first wish? **(b) Speculate:** Why do you think he does not wish for riches? Cite textual support for your answer.
3. **Make Inferences** List details that support the inference that Mr. Peters loves Leita more than he loves himself.
4. **Make Inferences** List details that support the inference that Leita still loves Mr. Peters even after she changes back to a swan.
5. **Make Inferences (a)** Is Mr. Peters afraid to die? **(b)** What details from the text support your inference?

### Craft and Structure

6. **Conflict and Resolution (a)** What conflict does Mr. Peters's first wish introduce? **(b)** What resolution does Mr. Peters find for the conflict?
7. **Conflict and Resolution** In a chart like the one shown, identify two smaller conflicts that build toward Mr. Peters's main conflict, and tell how each is resolved.

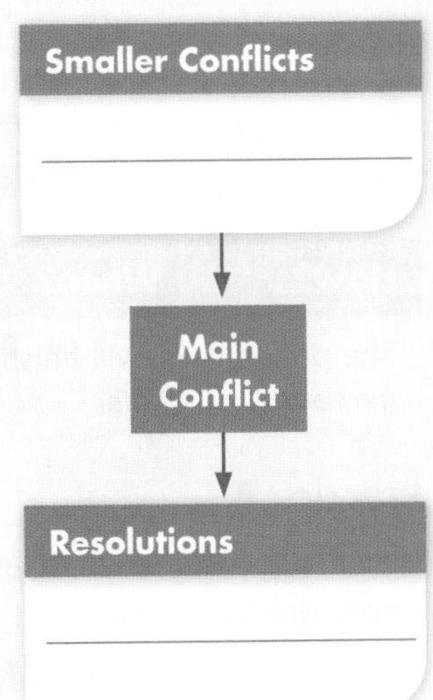


### Integration of Knowledge and Ideas

8. **(a) Make a Judgment:** Do you think Mr. Peters used his wishes wisely? **(b) Support:** What evidence from the story supports your opinion?
9. **Apply:** Many cultures have traditional tales about wishes that do not work out. Why might this kind of story be so common?

10. THE BIG ? **Does every conflict have a winner? (a)** Think about the decision Mr. Peters made to resolve his internal conflict. Was his decision wise? **(b)** What story details support your response? **(c)** Who were the "winners" in this story?

**ACADEMIC VOCABULARY**

As you write and speak about "The Third Wish," use the words related to conflict that you explored on page 3 of this textbook.

## Conventions: Adjectives and Adverbs

An **adjective** is a word that modifies or describes a noun or pronoun. An **adverb** is a word that modifies or describes a verb, an adjective, or another adverb.

**Adjectives** may answer the questions *What kind? How many? Which one?* or *Whose?* Possessive nouns and pronouns are used as adjectives to answer the question *Whose?*

**Coordinate adjectives** are two or more adjectives that modify the same noun and are separated by a comma. You can tell if adjectives are coordinate if the word *and* could be used in place of the comma.

| | | | |
|---|---|---|---|
| **What kind?** | Dan ate a hot, crusty roll. | **How many?** | We sold fifty tickets. |
| **Which one?** | Hand me that one. | **Whose?** | We saw Kathy's play. |

**Adverbs** provide information by answering the question *How? When? Where? How often?* or *To what extent?* Many adverbs end in the suffix *-ly.* This chart shows examples:

| How? | When? | Where? | How often? | To what extent? |
|---|---|---|---|---|
| She paced *nervously.* | I will finish it *later.* | The robins flew *away.* | Linda *always* laughs. | Luke moved *slightly.* Jo is *very* sad. |

### Practice A

Identify the adjective or adverb in each sentence. Then identify the word it modifies or describes.

1. Mr. Peters heard a faint cry.
2. The swan struggled frantically in the water.
3. Mr. Peters wished for a beautiful wife.
4. Mr. Peters used his second wish to please Leita.

**Reading Application** In "The Third Wish," find one sentence with two or more adjectives and one sentence with two or more adverbs. Then, identify the adjectives and adverbs.

### Practice B

Add adjectives or adverbs to each sentence based on the question in parentheses.

1. Mr. Peters was driving a car down a stretch of the road. (What kind of road?)
2. The swan was struggling in the canal. (How was it struggling?)
3. Leita was pleased by the river near the garden. (To what extent was she pleased?)

**Writing Application** Write two sentences in which you use coordinate adjectives to describe the relationship between Mr. Peters and Leita.

## Writing to Sources

**Narrative Text** Write an **anecdote**, or brief story, that tells what might have happened if Mr. Peters had not turned Leita back into a swan. Follow these steps:

- First, think of how the story would unfold with the new ending. Review "The Third Wish" to find details about Mr. Peters and Leita that indicate how each may have behaved if Leita had remained human.
- Then, jot down your ideas for a conflict that could have arisen. Is the conflict internal or external? Include descriptive details that vividly present the situation.
- Next, decide on a resolution to the conflict. As you draft your story, make sure that the resolution logically follows the event presented in the climax.
- Finally, conclude by describing how the characters grow or change as a result of their experiences.

**Grammar Application** Check your writing to be sure you have used adjectives and adverbs correctly. Include some coordinate adjectives in your anecdote.

## Speaking and Listening

**Presentation of Ideas** Write a **news story** based on "The Third Wish." In your story, announce the death of Mr. Peters and hail him as a local hero.
Follow these steps to complete the assignment:

- Reread the story, noting important details about Mr. Peters to include in your news story.
- Organize the story to present your details in the most effective order. For instance, you might present events in the order in which they occurred or in order of importance.
- Review your word choice to ensure that you have brought the news events to life and that you have maintained a formal tone.
- Practice reading your news story aloud, using proper grammar and a formal style, before presenting it to the class.

Meet the Author

**Laurence Yep** (b. 1948) was born in San Francisco. He grew up in an apartment above his family's grocery store in an African American neighborhood. As a child, Yep rode a bus to a bilingual school in Chinatown. He feels that these experiences with different cultures led him to write science fiction and fantasy stories in which characters face new worlds and learn new languages and customs. Yep was 18 when he sold his first story to a magazine for a penny a word.

## Does every conflict have a winner?

Think about the Big Question as you read "Ribbons." Take notes on how characters in the story work to resolve conflicts.

## CLOSE READING FOCUS

### Key Ideas and Details: **Make Inferences**

Stories present a wealth of details. Some details are stated explicitly; other details are unstated, or implied. An **inference** is a conclusion you draw about something that is not directly stated. Use details in the text to make inferences about a story. For example, if a story opens with a man running down a dark alley while looking over his shoulder, you might infer that the man is trying to get away from someone or something.

One way to make inferences is to read between the lines by asking questions, such as, "Who is the character running from?" and "Has the character done something wrong?"

### Craft and Structure: **Theme**

A story's **theme** is its central idea, message, or insight into life. Occasionally, the author states the theme directly. More often, however, the theme is implied.

As you read, look at what the characters say and do, where the story takes place, and what objects in the story seem important. These details will help you determine the theme—what the author wants to teach you about life.

## Vocabulary

You will encounter the following words in this story. Copy the words into your notebook. Circle the words that are adjectives. After you read, see how your knowledge of each word has increased.

| | | |
|---|---|---|
| **sensitive** | **meek** | **coax** |
| **laborious** | **exertion** | **furrowed** |

## CLOSE READING MODEL

The passage below is from Laurence Yep's story "Ribbons." The annotations to the right of the passage show ways in which you can use close reading skills to make inferences and determine theme.

### *from* "Ribbons"

Mom bowed formally as Grandmother reached the porch. "I'm so glad you're here," she said.

Grandmother gazed past us to the stairway leading up to our second-floor apartment. "Why do you have to have so many steps?" she said.

Mom sounded as meek as a child. "I'm sorry, Mother," she said.[1]

Dad tried to change the subject. "That's Stacy, and this little monster is Ian." *"Joe sun, Paw-paw,"* I said. "Good morning, Grandmother." It was afternoon, but that was the only Chinese I knew, and I had been practicing it.[2]

Mother had coached us on a proper Chinese greeting for the last two months, but I thought Grandmother also deserved an American-style bear hug. However, when I tried to put my arms around her and kiss her, she stiffened in surprise. "Nice children don't drool on people," she snapped at me.[3]

To Ian, anything worth doing was worth repeating, so he bowed again. *"Joe sun, Pawpaw."*

Grandmother brightened in an instant. "He has your eyes," she said to Mom.

Mom bent and hefted Ian into her arms. "Let me show you our apartment. You'll be in Stacy's room."

Grandmother didn't even thank me.[4]

**Make Inferences**

**1** The narrator describes Mom as "meek as a child." Since *meek* means "unwilling to argue," you might infer that Mom is respectful and obedient toward Grandmother.

**Make Inferences**

**2** From this greeting, you may infer that Grandmother is from China. Since the narrator has been practicing the greeting, you may also infer that she wants to impress Grandmother.

**Theme**

**3** Grandmother rejects a gesture of affection that is typical in western culture. Her reaction hints at a possible theme: the cultural differences between eastern and western traditions.

**Make Inferences**

**4** The first-person pronoun *me* tells you that the narrator is Stacy. Her words may lead you to infer that although she wants to impress Grandmother, she finds her grandmother to be a little rude.

# Ribbons

## *Laurence Yep*

The sunlight swept over the broad grassy square, across the street, and onto our living-room rug. In that bright, warm rectangle of light, I practiced my ballet.

Ian, my little brother, giggled and dodged around me while I did my exercises.

A car stopped outside, and Ian rushed to the window. "She's here! She's here!" he shouted excitedly. "Paw-paw's here!" *Paw-paw* is Chinese for grandmother—for "mother's mother."

I squeezed in beside Ian so I could look out the window, too. Dad's head was just disappearing as he leaned into the trunk of the car. A pile of luggage and cardboard boxes wrapped in rope sat by the curb. "Is that all Grandmother's?" I said. I didn't see how it would fit into my old bedroom.

Mom laughed behind me. "We're lucky she had to leave her furniture behind in Hong Kong." Mom had been trying to get her mother to come to San Francisco for years. Grandmother had finally agreed, but only because the British were going to return the city to the Chinese Communists in 1997. Because Grandmother's airfare and legal expenses had been so high,

**▲ Critical Viewing**
How do the pictures on these pages compare to the image you have of Grandmother? Explain.

there wasn't room in the family budget for Madame Oblomov's ballet school. I'd had to stop my daily lessons.

The rear car door opened, and a pair of carved black canes poked out like six-shooters. "Wait, Paw-paw," Dad said, and slammed the trunk shut. He looked sweaty and harassed.

Grandmother, however, was already using her canes to get to her feet. "I'm not helpless," she insisted to Dad.

Ian was relieved. "She speaks English," he said.

"She worked for a British family for years," Mom explained.

Turning, Ian ran toward the stairs. "I've got the door," he cried. Mom and I caught up with him at the front door and made him wait on the porch. "You don't want to knock her over," I said. For weeks, Mom had been rehearsing us for just this moment. Ian was supposed to wait, but in his excitement he began bowing to Grandmother as she struggled up the outside staircase.

Grandmother was a small woman in a padded silk jacket and black slacks. Her hair was pulled back into a bun behind her head. On her small feet she wore a pair of quilted cotton slippers

**Comprehension**
Why does the narrator have to stop her daily ballet lessons?

*"Paw-paw's here!" Paw-paw is Chinese for grandmother—for "mother's mother."*

**Make Inferences** Why might Grandmother have complained about "so many steps"?

**Vocabulary ▸**
**sensitive** (sen´ sə tiv) *adj.* easily hurt or affected
**meek** (mēk) *adj.* timid; not willing to argue
**coax** (kōks) *v.* use gentle persuasion
**laborious** (lə bôr´ ē əs) *adj.* taking much work or effort

shaped like boots, with furred tops that hid her ankles.

"What's wrong with her feet?" I whispered to Mom.

"They've always been that way. And don't mention it," she said. "She's **sensitive** about them."

I was instantly curious. "But what happened to them?"

"Wise grandchildren wouldn't ask," Mom warned. •

Mom bowed formally as Grandmother reached the porch. "I'm so glad you're here," she said.

Grandmother gazed past us to the stairway leading up to our second-floor apartment. "Why do you have to have so many steps?" she said.

Mom sounded as **meek** as a child. "I'm sorry, Mother," she said.

Dad tried to change the subject. "That's Stacy, and this little monster is Ian."

"*Joe sun, Paw-paw,*" I said. "Good morning, Grandmother." It was afternoon, but that was the only Chinese I knew, and I had been practicing it.

Mother had coached us on a proper Chinese greeting for the last two months, but I thought Grandmother also deserved an American-style bear hug. However, when I tried to put my arms around her and kiss her, she stiffened in surprise. "Nice children don't drool on people," she snapped at me.

To Ian, anything worth doing was worth repeating, so he bowed again. "*Joe sun, Paw-paw.*"

Grandmother brightened in an instant. "He has your eyes," she said to Mom.

Mom bent and hefted Ian into her arms. "Let me show you our apartment. You'll be in Stacy's room."

Grandmother didn't even thank me. Instead, she stumped up the stairs after Mom, trying to **coax** a smile from Ian, who was staring at her over Mom's shoulder.

Grandmother's climb was long, slow, **laborious.** *Thump, thump, thump.* Her canes struck the boards as she slowly mounted the steps. It sounded like the slow, steady beat of a mechanical heart.

Mom had told us her mother's story often enough. When Mom's

father died, Grandmother had strapped my mother to her back and walked across China to Hong Kong to escape the Communists who had taken over her country. I had always thought her trek was heroic, but it seemed even braver when I realized how wobbly she was on her feet.

I was going to follow Grandmother, but Dad waved me down to the sidewalk. "I need you to watch your grandmother's things until I finish bringing them up," he said. He took a suitcase in either hand and set off, catching up with Grandmother at the foot of the first staircase.

While I waited for him to come back, I inspected Grandmother's pile of belongings. The boxes, webbed with tight cords, were covered with words in Chinese and English. I could almost smell their exotic scent, and in my imagination I pictured sunlit waters lapping at picturesque docks. Hong Kong was probably as exotic to me as America was to Grandmother. Almost without thinking, I began to dance.

Dad came back out, his face red from **exertion**. "I wish I had half your energy," he said. Crouching, he used the cords to lift a box in each hand.

◀ **Vocabulary**
**exertion** (eg zʉr´ shən) *n.* physical work

I pirouetted,[1] and the world spun round and round. "Madame Oblomov said I should still practice every day." I had waited for this day not only for Grandmother's sake but for my own. "Now that Grandmother's here, can I begin my ballet lessons again?" I asked.

Dad turned toward the house. "We'll see, hon."

Disappointment made me protest. "But you said I had to give up the lessons so we could bring her from Hong Kong," I said. "Well, she's here."

Dad hesitated and then set the boxes down. "Try to understand, hon. We've got to set your grandmother up in her own apartment. That's going to take even more money. Don't you want your room back?"

Poor Dad. He looked tired and worried. I should have shut up, but I loved ballet almost as much as I loved him. "Madame put me in the fifth division even though I'm only eleven. If I'm absent much longer, she might make me start over again with the beginners."

"It'll be soon. I promise." He looked guilty as he picked up the boxes and struggled toward the stairs.

**Make Inferences**
What can you infer about Stacy from her dancing and her talk with Dad?

**Comprehension**
In whose room will Grandmother stay?

---

1. **pirouetted** (pir´ o͞o et´ əd) *v.* whirled around on one foot.

**▲ Critical Viewing** The shoes on the right are similar to the ones that Grandmother wore in China. How old do you think Grandmother was when she wore these shoes?

Dad had taken away the one hope that had kept me going during my exile[2] from Madame. Suddenly I felt lost, and the following weeks only made me more confused. Mom started laying down all sorts of new rules. First, we couldn't run around or make noise because Grandmother had to rest. Then we couldn't watch our favorite TV shows because Grandmother couldn't understand them. Instead, we had to watch Westerns on one of the cable stations because it was easier for her to figure out who was the good guy and who was the bad one.

Worst of all, Ian got all of her attention—and her candy and anything else she could bribe him with. It finally got to me on a warm Sunday afternoon a month after she had arrived. I'd just returned home from a long walk in the park with some friends. I was looking forward to something cool and sweet, when I found her giving Ian an ice cream bar I'd bought for

2. **exile** (eg´ zīl) *n.* a forced absence.

myself. "But that was *my* ice cream bar," I complained as he gulped it down.

"Big sisters need to share with little brothers," Grandmother said, and she patted him on the head to encourage him to go on eating.

When I complained to Mom about how Grandmother was spoiling Ian, she only sighed. "He's a boy, Stacy. Back in China, boys are everything."

**Theme**
What does Mom's comment tell you about the treatment of boys in China? What message about life do these details suggest?

It wasn't until I saw Grandmother and Ian together the next day that I thought I really understood why she treated him so much better. She was sitting on a kitchen chair with her head bent over next to his. She had taught Ian enough Chinese so that they could hold short, simple conversations. With their faces so close, I could see how much alike they were.

Ian and I both have the same brown eyes, but his hair is black, while mine is brown, like Dad's. In fact, everything about Ian looks more Chinese. Except for the shape of my eyes, I look as Caucasian as Dad. And yet people sometimes stare at me as if I were a freak. I've always told myself that it's because they're ignorant and never learned manners, but it was really hard to have my own grandmother make me feel that way.

Even so, I kept telling myself: Grandmother is a hero. She saved my mother. She'll like me just as much as she likes Ian once she gets to know me. And, I thought in a flash, the best way to know a person is to know what she loves. For me, that was the ballet.

Ever since Grandmother had arrived, I'd been practicing my ballet privately in the room I now shared with Ian. Now I got out the special box that held my satin toe shoes. I had been so proud when Madame said I was ready to use them. I was the youngest girl on pointe[3] at Madame's school. As I lifted them out, the satin ribbons fluttered down around my wrists as if in a welcoming caress. I slipped one of the shoes onto my foot, but when I tried to tie the ribbons around my ankles, the ribbons came off in my hands.

**Comprehension**
How do things change when Grandmother moves into the house?

3. **on pointe** (pwant) dancing on the tip of the toe (of the ballet shoe).

I could have asked Mom to help me reattach them, but then I remembered that at one time Grandmother had supported her family by being a seamstress.

Grandmother was sitting in the big recliner in the living room. She stared uneasily out the window as if she were gazing not upon the broad, green lawn of the square but upon a Martian desert.

"Paw-paw," I said, "can you help me?"

**Make Inferences**
What can you infer about Grandmother based on her reaction to the ribbons?

Grandmother gave a start when she turned around and saw the ribbons dangling from my hand. Then she looked down at my bare feet, which were callused from three years of daily lessons. When she looked back at the satin ribbons, it was with a hate and disgust that I had never seen before. "Give those to me." She held out her hand.

I clutched the ribbons tightly against my stomach. "Why?"

"They'll ruin your feet." She lunged toward me and tried to snatch them away.

Angry and bewildered, I retreated a few steps and showed her the shoe. "No, they're for dancing!"

All Grandmother could see, though, was the ribbons. She managed to totter to her feet without the canes and almost fell forward on her face. Somehow, she regained her balance. Arms reaching out, she stumbled clumsily after me.

"Lies!" she said.

"It's the truth!" I backed up so fast that I bumped into Mom as she came running from the kitchen.

Mom immediately assumed it was my fault. "Stop yelling at your grandmother!" she said.

By this point, I was in tears. "She's taken everything else. Now she wants my toe-shoe ribbons."

Grandmother panted as she leaned on Mom. "How could you do that to your own daughter?"

"It's not like you think," Mom tried to explain.

However, Grandmother was too upset to listen. "Take them away!"

*Grandmother gave a start when she turned around and saw the ribbons dangling from my hand.*

Mom helped Grandmother back to her easy chair. "You don't understand," Mom said.

All Grandmother did was stare at the ribbons as she sat back down in the chair. "Take them away. Burn them. Bury them."

Mom sighed. "Yes, Mother."

As Mom came over to me, I stared at her in amazement. "Aren't you going to stand up for me?"

But she acted as if she wanted to break any ties between us. "Can't you see how worked up Paw-paw is?" she whispered. "She won't listen to reason. Give her some time. Let her cool off." She worked the ribbons away from my stunned fingers. Then she also took the shoe.

For the rest of the day, Grandmother just turned away every time Mom and I tried to raise the subject. It was as if she didn't want to even think about satin ribbons.

That evening, after the dozenth attempt, I finally said to Mom, "She's so weird. What's so bad about satin ribbons?"

"She associates them with something awful that happened to her," Mom said.

That puzzled me even more. "What was that?"

She shook her head. "I'm sorry. She made me promise never to talk about it to anyone."

The next morning, I decided that if Grandmother was

**Spiral Review**
**CHARACTER** Based on the scene with the ribbons, list one detail you learn about each of these characters: Grandmother, Mom, and Stacy.

**Comprehension**
How does Grandmother react when she sees the ribbons from the ballet shoes?

going to be mean to me, then I would be mean to her. I began to ignore her. When she entered a room I was in, I would deliberately turn around and leave.

For the rest of the day, things got more and more tense. Then I happened to go into the bathroom early that evening. The door wasn't locked, so I thought it was unoccupied, but Grandmother was sitting fully clothed on the edge of the bathtub. Her slacks were rolled up to her knees and she had her feet soaking in a pan of water.

"Don't you know how to knock?" she snapped, and dropped a towel over her feet.

However, she wasn't quick enough, because I saw her bare feet for the first time. Her feet were like taffy that someone had stretched out and twisted. Each foot bent downward in a way that feet were not meant to, and her toes stuck out at odd angles, more like lumps than toes. I didn't think she had all ten of them, either.

"What happened to your feet?" I whispered in shock.

Looking ashamed, Grandmother flapped a hand in the air for me to go. "None of your business. Now get out."

*"Don't you know how to knock?" she snapped, and dropped a towel over her feet.*

## LITERATURE IN CONTEXT

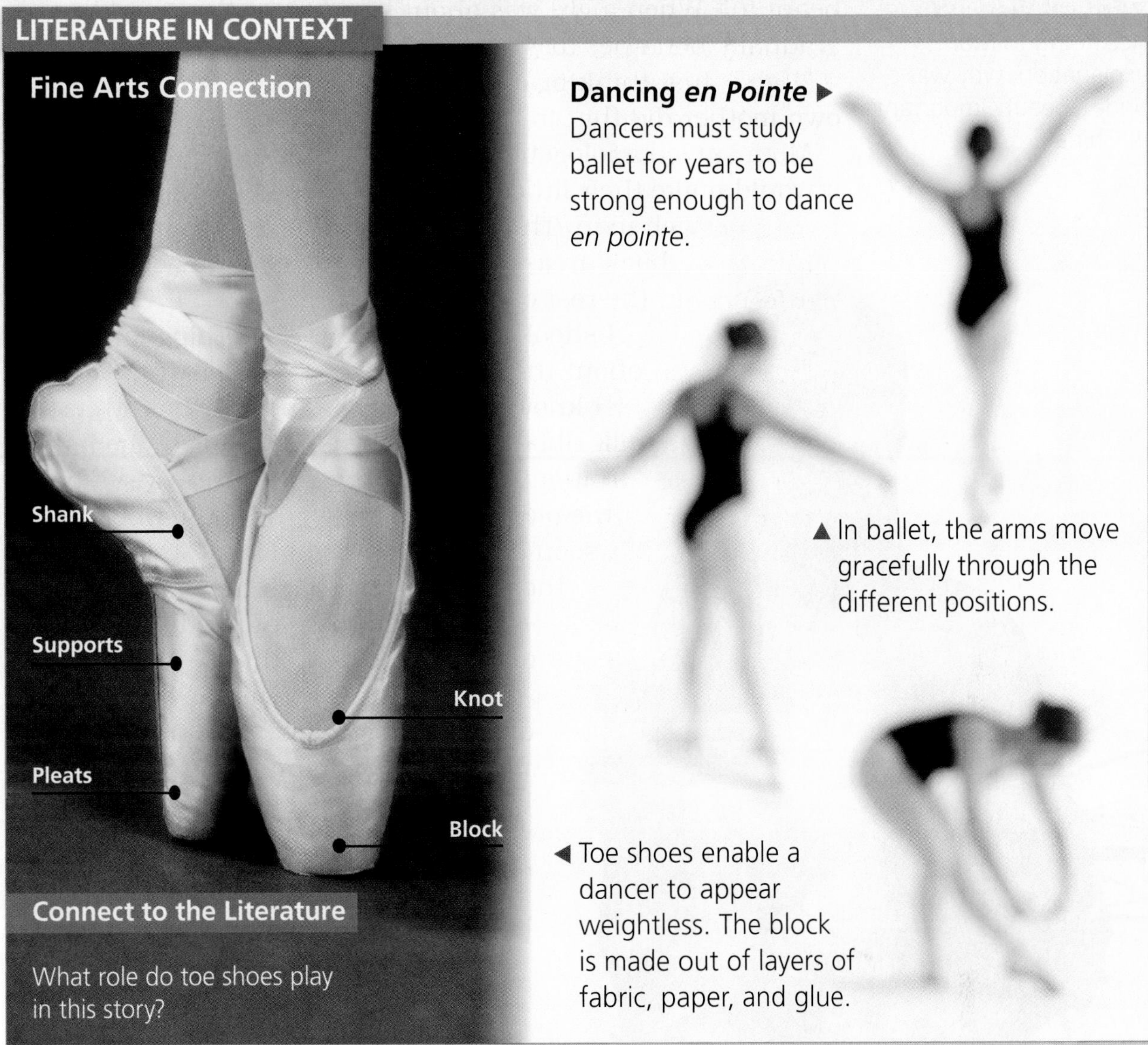


### Fine Arts Connection

**Dancing *en Pointe*** ▶ Dancers must study ballet for years to be strong enough to dance *en pointe*.

▲ In ballet, the arms move gracefully through the different positions.

◀ Toe shoes enable a dancer to appear weightless. The block is made out of layers of fabric, paper, and glue.

**Connect to the Literature**

What role do toe shoes play in this story?

She must have said something to Mom, though, because that night Mom came in and sat on my bed. Ian was outside playing with Grandmother. "Your grandmother's very upset, Stacy," Mom said.

"I didn't mean to look," I said. "It was horrible." Even when I closed my eyes, I could see her mangled feet.

I opened my eyes when I felt Mom's hand on my shoulder. "She was so ashamed of them that she didn't like even me to see them," she said.

"What happened to them?" I wondered.

Mom's forehead **furrowed** as if she wasn't sure how to explain things. "There was a time back in China when people thought women's feet had to be shaped a certain way to look

◀ **Vocabulary**
**furrowed** (fur′ōd) *v.* wrinkled

**Comprehension**
What did Stacy see that made Grandmother upset?

**▼Critical Viewing** According to Mom's explanation, why was a bride's beauty important in China?

beautiful. When a girl was about five, her mother would gradually bend her toes under the sole of her foot."

"Ugh." Just thinking about it made my own feet ache. "Her own mother did that to her?"

Mom smiled apologetically. "Her mother and father thought it would make their little girl attractive so she could marry a rich man. They were still doing it in some of the back areas of China long after it was outlawed in the rest of the country."

I shook my head. "There's nothing lovely about those feet."

"I know. But they were usually bound up in silk ribbons." Mom brushed some of the hair from my eyes. "Because they were a symbol of the old days, Paw-paw undid the ribbons as soon as we were free in Hong Kong—even though they kept back the pain."

I was even more puzzled now. "How did the ribbons do that?"

Mom began to brush my hair with quick, light strokes. "The ribbons kept the blood from circulating freely and bringing more feeling to her feet. Once the ribbons were gone, her feet ached. They probably still do."

I rubbed my own foot in sympathy. "But she doesn't complain."

"That's how tough she is," Mom said.

Finally the truth dawned on me. "And she mistook my toe-shoe ribbons for her old ones."

Mom lowered the brush and nodded solemnly. "And she didn't want you to go through the same pain she had."

I guess Grandmother loved me in her own way. When she came into the bedroom with Ian later that evening, I didn't leave. However, she tried to ignore me—as if I had become tainted by her secret.

When Ian demanded a story, I sighed. "All right. But only one."

Naturally, Ian chose the fattest story he could, which was my old collection of fairy tales by Hans Christian Andersen. Years of reading had cracked the spine so that the book fell open automatically in his hands to the story that had been my favorite when I was small. It was the original story of "The Little Mermaid"—not the cartoon. The picture illustrating the tale showed the mermaid posed like a ballerina in the middle of the throne room.

"This one," Ian said, and pointed to the picture of the Little Mermaid.

When Grandmother and Ian sat down on my bed, I began to read. However, when I got to the part where the Little Mermaid could walk on land, I stopped.

Ian was impatient. "Come on, read," he ordered, patting the page.

"After that," I went on, "each step hurt her as if she were walking on a knife." I couldn't help looking up at Grandmother.

This time she was the one to pat the page. "Go on. Tell me more about the mermaid."

So I went on reading to the very end, where the Little Mermaid changes into sea foam. "That's a dumb ending," Ian said. "Who wants to be pollution?"

"Sea foam isn't pollution. It's just bubbles," I explained. "The important thing was that she wanted to walk even though it hurt."

"I would rather have gone on swimming," Ian insisted.

"But maybe she wanted to see new places and people by going on the land," Grandmother said softly. "If she had kept her tail, the land people would have thought she was odd. They might even have made fun of her."

When she glanced at her own feet, I thought she might be talking about herself—so I seized my chance. "My satin ribbons aren't like your old silk ones. I use them to tie my toe shoes on when I dance." Setting the book down, I got out my other shoe. "Look."

Grandmother fingered the dangling ribbons and then pointed at my bare feet. "But you already have calluses there."

I began to dance before Grandmother could stop me. After a minute, I struck a pose on half-toe. "See? I can move fine."

She took my hand and patted it clumsily. I think it was the first time she had showed me any sign of affection. "When I

**Theme**
What details in this paragraph support a theme of understanding cultural differences?

**Comprehension**
What happened to Grandmother's feet when she was a child?

saw those ribbons, I didn't want you feeling pain like I do."

I covered her hands with mine. "I just wanted to show you what I love best—dancing."

"And I love my children," she said. I could hear the ache in her voice. "And my grandchildren. I don't want anything bad to happen to you."

Suddenly I felt as if there were an invisible ribbon binding us, tougher than silk and satin, stronger even than steel; and it joined her to Mom and Mom to me.

I wanted to hug her so badly that I just did. Though she was stiff at first, she gradually softened in my arms.

"'Let me have my ribbons and my shoes," I said in a low voice. "Let me dance."

"Yes, yes," she whispered fiercely.

I felt something on my cheek and realized she was crying, and then I began crying, too.

"So much to learn," she said, and began hugging me back. "So much to learn."

**Make Inferences**
Why do you think the narrator and her grandmother are crying?

## Language Study

**Vocabulary** The words below appear in "Ribbons." Use your knowledge of the words to answer each numbered question. Explain your responses.

**sensitive** **meek** **coax** **exertion** **furrowed**

1. If a girl is *meek,* how might she answer questions in class?
2. How would you *coax* someone to go somewhere with you?
3. What is your least favorite type of *exertion?*
4. If your forehead is *furrowed,* how might you feel?
5. If someone is *sensitive,* is it a good idea to tease him?

**WORD STUDY**
The **Latin suffix *-ious*** means "full of." In this story, the grandmother's walking is **laborious**, requiring much labor, or work, as she climbs the stairs.

### Word Study

**Part A** Explain how the **Latin suffix *-ious*** contributes to the meaning of the words *glorious, gracious,* and *harmonious*. Consult a dictionary if necessary.

**Part B** Use the context of the sentences and your knowledge of the Latin suffix *-ious* to explain your answer to each question.

1. If a meal is *nutritious,* what kinds of foods does it include?
2. Whom do you know with *ambitious* goals?

# Close Reading Activities

## Literary Analysis

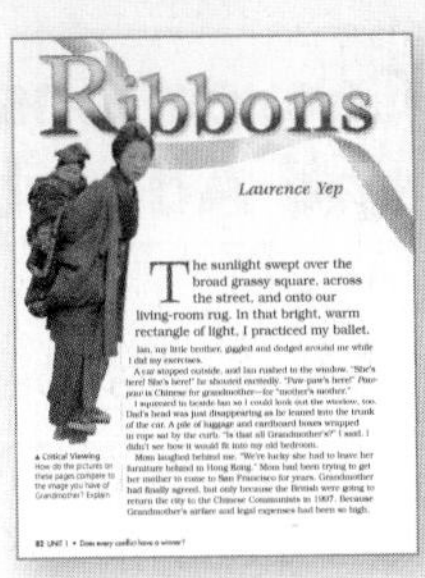

### Key Ideas and Details

1. **Make Inferences** The author describes Grandmother's arrival by saying, "The rear car door opened, and a pair of carved black canes poked out like six-shooters." **(a)** What first impression of Grandmother do these details create? **(b)** Why do you think the author includes these details instead of simply introducing the character by name?
2. **Make Inferences** Grandmother carried her daughter on her back to Hong Kong to escape her enemy. What questions might you ask to help you make an inference about Grandmother's life?
3. **(a)** Identify two examples from the story that show how Stacy's life changes when Grandmother arrives. **(b) Analyze Causes and Effects:** For each example, tell how you would expect Stacy to feel about these changes.
4. **(a)** How does Stacy learn the secret of Grandmother's feet? **(b) Connect:** How does Stacy's attitude change after her mother explains older Chinese customs? Support your response.

### Craft and Structure

5. **Theme** What theme does the story convey about understanding between grandparents and grandchildren? In a graphic organizer like the one shown, list details about the setting and characters that support the theme.
6. **(a) Deduce:** How does the author reveal differences between generations and cultures in this story? **(b) Support:** Support your answer with details from the story.

Setting → Theme ← Character

### Integration of Knowledge and Ideas

7. **Evaluate:** Discuss with a partner whether or not you sympathize with Stacy. Provide evidence from the text to support your view. Then, discuss how hearing your partner's responses and examples from the text did or did not change your view.

8. THE BIG ? **Does every conflict have a winner? (a)** How do Grandmother and Stacy finally overcome their conflict and begin to understand and appreciate one another? **(b)** What lessons does each character learn? What story details support your response?

### ACADEMIC VOCABULARY

As you write and speak about "Ribbons," use the words related to conflict that you explored on page 3 of this textbook.

## Conventions: Comparison of Adjectives and Adverbs

Most adjectives and adverbs have three degrees of comparison: the *positive*, the *comparative*, and the *superlative*.

The **positive** is used when no comparison is made: Hannah is a *fast* runner.

The **comparative** is used when two things are being compared: Eva is a *faster* runner than Hannah.

The **superlative** is used when three or more things are being compared: Emmy is the *fastest* runner on the team.

| Forming Comparative and Superlative Degrees | |
|---|---|
| **Use *-er* or *more* to form the comparative degree.** | faster, taller, more intelligent, more expressive |
| **Use *-est* or *most* to form the superlative degree.** | brightest, biggest, most nutritious, most sorrowful |
| **Use *more* and *most* with modifiers of three or more syllables.** | more popular, more intelligently, most popular, most intelligently |

### Practice A

Identify the adjective or adverb in each sentence. Then, identify the degree of comparison it indicates: *positive, comparative,* or *superlative.*

1. Ian was happy when Grandmother arrived.
2. The stairs were more dangerous for Grandmother than they were for Stacy.
3. Westerns were easier than comedies for Grandmother to understand.
4. The most difficult days in Grandmother's life were in the past.

**Reading Application** Find five adjectives and adverbs in "Ribbons," and indicate the degree of comparison each reflects: positive, comparative, or superlative.

### Practice B

Complete each sentence with the adjective or adverb described in parentheses.

1. For Stacy, the ________ activity is ballet dancing. (superlative form of *enjoyable*)
2. Grandmother and Ian have ________ conversations. (positive form of *simple*)
3. The more Grandmother favors Ian, the ________ Stacy gets. (comparative form of *angry*)

**Writing Application** Write at least three sentences about the relationship between Stacy and her grandmother. Use positive, comparative, and superlative adjectives and adverbs in your sentences.

## Writing to Sources

**Response to Literature** Write a **letter to the author** in which you tell whether or not you liked the story, making specific references to the text to support your opinion. As you draft, follow these steps:

- Begin with your overall reaction to "Ribbons."
- In several paragraphs, state and support your ideas about the story by referring to the text. You may wish to connect events in the story with your own experiences to demonstrate your understanding of the story.
- Draft your letter using correct business letter format. Refer to the Writing Handbook at the back of this textbook if you need help. Establish and maintain a formal writing style throughout your letter.
- End with a brief conclusion that summarizes the ideas you have presented in the body of your letter.

**Grammar Application** As you write, use positive, comparative, and superlative forms of adjectives and adverbs properly.

## Research and Technology

**Build and Present Knowledge** Create a **poster** based on "Ribbons." In your poster, give information about the basic arm and foot positions used in ballet and the benefits of learning to dance.

Follow these steps to complete the assignment:

- Identify the topic of your poster. Then, jot down questions to guide your research.
- Develop a research plan. Then, use the Internet and library resources to conduct your research.
- Use photos, drawings, and diagrams to illustrate your poster.
- Include information about the ballet terms that appear in the story, such as *pirouette* and *en pointe*.
- Present your poster and research to the class. You may want to add music or sound effects to emphasize key points.

## Does every conflict have a winner?

Explore the Big Question as you read these stories. Take notes to compare the ways that the main characters deal with the conflicts they face.

## READING TO COMPARE CHARACTERS

Authors James Thurber and Sherwood Anderson use many different techniques to portray the characters in their stories. After reading both stories, compare and contrast how the two authors bring their main characters to life.

### "The Night the Bed Fell"

**James Thurber** (1894–1961)
According to James Thurber, if you had lived in his Ohio home, you would have witnessed absurd events. While writing of such events, he always showed affection for his quirky relatives. Thurber's literary home was *The New Yorker* magazine, where he wrote essays that gently poked fun at the world. He often did line drawings to accompany his essays, even when his eyesight began to fail him.

### "Stolen Day"

**Sherwood Anderson** (1876–1941)
As a teenager, Sherwood Anderson worked as a newsboy, a housepainter, and a stable groom. Later, he fought in Cuba in the Spanish-American War. Even though Anderson did not begin to write professionally until he was forty years old, he is considered an important writer. His novel *Winesburg, Ohio* was published in 1919. In it, Anderson used simple, everyday language to capture the loneliness and hopelessness of characters living in a small town.

## Comparing Characters

A **character** is a person, animal, or being that takes part in the action of a literary work. In literature, you will find characters with a range of personalities and attitudes. For example, a character might be dependable and smart but also stubborn. The qualities that make each character unique are called **character traits.** Writers use the process of **characterization** to create and develop characters. There are two types of characterization:

- **Direct characterization:** The writer directly states or describes the character's traits.
- **Indirect characterization:** The writer reveals a character's personality through his or her words and actions and through the thoughts, words, and actions of others.

A character's responses may be internal or external. An **internal response** reveals a character's thoughts, while an **external response** consists of a character's actions or deeds. Writers use the internal and external responses of characters to develop the plot of a literary work. For example, the characters' responses can strongly influence the conflict—the problem or struggle that increases the tension in a story.

As you read the texts that follow, look for character traits that show each narrator's qualities, attitudes, and values. Use a chart like the one below to analyze how the writer of each text develops the narrator's character.

| | "The Night the Bed Fell" | "Stolen Day" |
|---|---|---|
| Main character | | |
| Direct description | | |
| Character's words and actions | | |
| What others say about character | | |

# THE NIGHT THE BED FELL

JAMES THURBER

I suppose that the high-water mark of my youth in Columbus, Ohio, was the night the bed fell on my father. It makes a better recitation (unless, as some friends of mine have said, one has heard it five or six times) than it does a piece of writing, for it is almost necessary to throw furniture around, shake doors, and bark like a dog, to lend the proper atmosphere and verisimilitude[1] to what is admittedly a somewhat incredible tale. Still, it did take place.

It happened, then, that my father had decided to sleep in the attic one night, to be away where he could think. My mother opposed the notion strongly because, she said, the old wooden bed up there was unsafe: it was wobbly and the heavy headboard would crash down on father's head in case the bed fell, and kill him. There was no dissuading him, however, and at a quarter past ten he closed the attic door behind him and went up the narrow twisting stairs. We later heard ominous creakings as he crawled into bed. Grandfather, who usually slept in the attic bed when he was with us, had disappeared some days before. On these occasions he was usually gone six or eight days and returned growling and out of temper, with the news that the

1. **verisimilitude** (ver′ ə si mil′ ə to͞od) *n.* appearance of truth or reality.

Federal Union[2] was run by a passel of blockheads and that the Army of the Potomac[3] didn't have a chance.

We had visiting us at this time a nervous first cousin of mine named Briggs Beall, who believed that he was likely to cease breathing when he was asleep. It was his feeling that if he were not awakened every hour during the night, he might die of suffocation. He had been accustomed to setting an alarm clock to ring at intervals until morning, but I persuaded him to abandon this. He slept in my room and I told him that I was such a light sleeper that if anybody quit breathing in the same room with me, I would wake instantly. He tested me the first night—which I had suspected he would—by holding his breath after my regular breathing had convinced him I was asleep. I was not asleep, however, and called to him. This seemed to allay his fears a little, but he took the precaution of putting a glass of spirits of camphor[4] on a little table at the head of his bed. In case I didn't arouse him until he was almost gone, he said, he would sniff the camphor, a powerful reviver. Briggs was not the only member of his family who had his crotchets.[5] Old Aunt Melissa Beall (who could whistle like a man, with two fingers in her mouth) suffered under the premonition that she was destined to die on South High Street, because she had been born on South High Street and married on South High Street. Then there was Aunt Sarah Shoaf, who never went to bed at night without the fear that a burglar was going to get in and blow chloroform[6] under her door through a tube. To avert this calamity—for she was in greater dread of anesthetics than of losing her household goods—she always piled her money, silverware, and other valuables in a neat stack just outside her bedroom, with a note reading: "This is all I have. Please take it and do not use your chloroform, as this is all I have." Aunt Gracie Shoaf also had a burglar phobia, but she met it with more fortitude. She was confident that burglars had been getting into her house every night for forty years. The fact that she never missed any thing was to her no proof to the contrary. She always claimed that she scared them off before they could take anything, by throwing shoes down the hallway. When she went to bed she piled, where she could get at them handily, all the shoes

◀ **Vocabulary**
**ominous** (äm′ ə nəs) *adj.* threatening

**Character**
What details about this character are probably exaggerated?

**Character**
What are the contrasts between the aunts' beliefs and reality?

**Comprehension**
What kind of a story does the narrator say he is going to tell?

---

2. **Federal Union** northern side during the Civil War of the 1860s. He is under the illusion that the Civil War has not yet ended.
3. **Army of the Potomac** one of the northern armies during the Civil War.
4. **spirits of camphor** liquid with a powerful odor.
5. **crotchets** (kräch′ its) *n.* peculiar ideas.
6. **chloroform** (klôr′ ə fôrm′) *n.* substance used at one time as an anesthetic.

**Some nights she threw them all.** by James Thurber

there were about her house. Five minutes after she had turned off the light, she would sit up in bed and say "Hark!" Her husband, who had learned to ignore the whole situation as long ago as 1903, would either be sound asleep or pretend to be sound asleep. In either case he would not respond to her tugging and pulling, so that presently she would arise, tiptoe to the door, open it slightly and heave a shoe down the hall in one direction, and its mate down the hall in the other direction. Some nights she threw them all, some nights only a couple of pair.

▲ **Critical Viewing** How would Gracie Shoaf defend the actions shown in this drawing?

But I am straying from the remarkable incidents that took place during the night that the bed fell on father. By midnight we were all in bed. The layout of the rooms and the disposition[7] of their occupants is important to an understanding of what later occurred. In the front room upstairs (just under father's attic bedroom) were my mother and my brother Herman, who sometimes sang in his sleep, usually "Marching Through Georgia" or "Onward, Christian Soldiers." Briggs Beall and myself were in a room adjoining this one. My brother Roy was in a room across the hall from ours. Our bull terrier, Rex, slept in the hall.

**Vocabulary ▶**
**perilous** (per′ ə ləs) *adj.* dangerous

My bed was an army cot, one of those affairs which are made wide enough to sleep on comfortably only by putting up, flat with the middle section, the two sides which ordinarily hang down like the sideboards of a drop-leaf table. When these sides are up, it is **perilous** to roll too far toward the edge, for then the cot is likely to tip completely over, bringing the whole bed down on top of one, with a tremendous banging crash. This, in fact, is precisely what happened about two o'clock in the morning. (It was my mother who, in recalling the scene later, first referred to it as "the night the bed fell on your father.")

7. **disposition** (dis′ pə zish′ ən) *n.* arrangement.

Always a deep sleeper, slow to arouse (I had lied to Briggs), I was at first unconscious of what had happened when the iron cot rolled me onto the floor and toppled over on me. It left me still warmly bundled up and unhurt, for the bed rested above me like a canopy. Hence I did not wake up, only reached the edge of consciousness and went back. The racket, however, instantly awakened my mother, in the next room, who came to the immediate conclusion that her worst dread was realized: the big wooden bed upstairs had fallen on father. She therefore screamed, "Let's go to your poor father!" It was this shout, rather than the noise of my cot falling, that awakened Herman, in the same room with her. He thought that mother had become, for no apparent reason, hysterical. "You're all right, Mamma!" he shouted, trying to calm her. They exchanged shout for shout for perhaps ten seconds: "Let's go to your poor father!" and "You're all right!" That woke up Briggs. By this time I was conscious of what was going on, in a vague way, but did not yet realize that I was under my bed instead of on it. Briggs, awakening in the midst of loud shouts of fear and apprehension, came to the

**▼ Critical Viewing**
What part of the story does this picture show?

**Character**
How does the mother's reaction make this situation humorous?

**Comprehension**
On what type of bed is the narrator sleeping?

**He came to the conclusion that he was suffocating.** by James Thurber

quick conclusion that he was suffocating and that we were all trying to "bring him out." With a low moan, he grasped the glass of camphor at the head of his bed and instead of sniffing it poured it over himself. The room reeked of camphor. "Ugf, ahfg," choked Briggs, like a drowning man, for he had almost succeeded in stopping his breath under the deluge of pungent spirits. He leaped out of bed and groped toward the open window, but he came up against one that was closed. With his hand, he beat out the glass, and I could hear it crash and tinkle on the alleyway below. It was at this juncture that I, in trying to get up, had the uncanny sensation of feeling my bed above me! Foggy with sleep, I now suspected, in my turn, that the whole uproar was being made in a frantic endeavor to extricate me from what must be an unheard-of and perilous situation. "Get me out of this!" I bawled. "Get me out!" I think I had the nightmarish belief that I was entombed in a mine. "Gugh," gasped Briggs, floundering in his camphor.

**Character**
What action does Briggs perform that helps to reveal his nervous personality?

By this time my mother, still shouting, pursued by Herman, still shouting, was trying to open the door to the attic, in order to go up and get my father's body out of the wreckage. The door was stuck, however, and wouldn't yield. Her frantic pulls on it only added to the general banging and confusion. Roy and the dog were now up, the one shouting questions, the other barking.

Father, farthest away and soundest sleeper of all, had by this time been awakened by the battering on the attic door. He decided that the house was on fire. "I'm coming, I'm coming!" he wailed in a slow, sleepy voice—it took him many minutes to regain full consciousness. My mother,

**▶ Critical Viewing**
How does the action in this drawing capture the mood of the story?

**Roy had to throw Rex.** by James Thurber

still believing he was caught under the bed, detected in his "I'm coming!" the mournful, resigned note of one who is preparing to meet his Maker. "He's dying!" she shouted.

"I'm all right!" Briggs yelled to reassure her. "I'm all right!" He still believed that it was his own closeness to death that was worrying mother. I found at last the light switch in my room, unlocked the door, and Briggs and I joined the others at the attic door. The dog, who never did like Briggs, jumped for him—assuming that he was the **culprit** in whatever was going on—and Roy had to throw Rex and hold him. We could hear father crawling out of bed upstairs. Roy pulled the attic door open, with a mighty jerk, and father came down the stairs, sleepy and irritable but safe and sound. My mother began to weep when she saw him. Rex began to howl. "What in the name of heaven is going on here?" asked father.

The situation was finally put together like a gigantic jigsaw puzzle. Father caught a cold from prowling around in his bare feet but there were no other bad results. "I'm glad," said mother, who always looked on the bright side of things, "that your grandfather wasn't here."

**Character**
What characteristics make the mother amusing?

◀ **Vocabulary**
**culprit** (kul′prit) *n.* guilty person

## Critical Thinking

1. **Key Ideas and Details (a)** Who is in the house on the night Thurber describes? **(b) Compare:** What quality or qualities do these characters share? **(c) Support:** What examples from the text illustrate the shared qualities?
2. **Key Ideas and Details (a)** Describe the layout of the rooms. **(b) Analyze:** Why is the placement of the rooms in the house important to the events?
3. **Key Ideas and Details (a)** What do Briggs, Aunt Sarah Shoaf, and Aunt Gracie Shoaf do before going to bed? **(b) Infer:** What do you suppose the author, looking back, thinks of this behavior? **(c) Make a Judgment:** Do you think the author treats his relatives fairly in the essay? Cite textual details in your response.
4. **Integration of Knowledge and Ideas (a)** Why do each of the people in the household have a different idea of what has happened? **(b)** How is the conflict among these ideas resolved? *[Connect to the Big Question: Does every conflict have a winner?]*

# Stolen Day

## Sherwood Anderson

It must be that all children are actors. The whole thing started with a boy on our street named Walter, who had inflammatory rheumatism.[1] That's what they called it. He didn't have to go to school.

Still he could walk about. He could go fishing in the creek or the waterworks pond. There was a place up at the pond where in the spring the water came tumbling over the dam and formed a deep pool. It was a good place. Sometimes you could get some big ones there.

I went down that way on my way to school one spring morning. It was out of my way but I wanted to see if Walter was there.

He was, inflammatory rheumatism and all. There he was, sitting with a fish pole in his hand. He had been able to walk down there all right.

It was then that my own legs began to hurt. My back too. I went on to school but, at the recess time, I began to cry. I did it when the teacher, Sarah Suggett, had come out into the schoolhouse yard.

She came right over to me.

"I ache all over," I said. I did, too.

**Character**
What can you tell about the narrator based on the pain he experiences?

---

1. **inflammatory rheumatism** (in flam′ ə tôr′ ē ro͞o′ mə tiz′ əm) *n.* a disease that causes the joints to swell painfully and gradually break down.

I kept on crying and it worked all right.

"You'd better go on home," she said.

So I went. I limped painfully away. I kept on limping until I got out of the schoolhouse street.

**Character**
Why does the narrator's pain suddenly disappear?

Then I felt better. I still had inflammatory rheumatism pretty bad but I could get along better.

I must have done some thinking on the way home.

"I'd better not say I have inflammatory rheumatism," I decided. "Maybe if you've got that you swell up."

I thought I'd better go around to where Walter was and ask him about that, so I did—but he wasn't there.

"They must not be biting today," I thought.

**Spiral Review**
**THEME** How might the narrator's so-called pain relate to a possible theme?

I had a feeling that, if I said I had inflammatory rheumatism, Mother or my brothers and my sister Stella might laugh. They did laugh at me pretty often and I didn't like it at all.

"Just the same," I said to myself, "I have got it." I began to hurt and ache again.

I went home and sat on the front steps of our house. I sat there a long time. There wasn't anyone at home but Mother and the two little ones. Ray would have been four or five then and Earl might have been three.

**Vocabulary**
**solemn** (säl′ əm) *adj.* serious; somber

It was Earl who saw me there. I had got tired sitting and was lying on the porch. Earl was always a quiet, **solemn** little fellow.

He must have said something to Mother for presently she came.

"What's the matter with you? Why aren't you in school?" she asked.

I came pretty near telling her right out that I had inflammatory rheumatism but I thought I'd better not. Mother and Father had been speaking of Walter's case at the table just the day before. "It affects the heart," Father had said. That frightened me when I thought of it. "I might die," I thought. "I might just suddenly die right here; my heart might stop beating."

I kept on crying and
it worked all right.

On the day before I had been running a race with my brother Irve. We were up at the fairgrounds after school and there was a half-mile track.

"I'll bet you can't run a half-mile," he said. "I bet you I could beat you running clear around the track."

And so we did it and I beat him, but afterwards my heart did seem to beat pretty hard. I remembered that lying there on the porch. "It's a wonder, with my inflammatory rheumatism and all, I didn't just drop down dead," I thought. The thought frightened me a lot. I ached worse than ever.

"I ache, Ma," I said. "I just ache."

She made me go in the house and upstairs and get into bed.

It wasn't so good. It was spring. I was up there for perhaps an hour, maybe two, and then I felt better.

I got up and went downstairs. "I feel better, Ma," I said.

Mother said she was glad. She was pretty busy that day and hadn't paid much attention to me. She had made me get into bed upstairs and then hadn't even come up to see how I was.

I didn't think much of that when I was up there but when I got downstairs where she was, and when, after I had said I felt better and she only said she was glad and went right on with her work, I began to ache again.

I thought, "I'll bet I die of it. I bet I do."

I went out to the front porch and sat down. I was pretty sore at Mother.

"If she really knew the truth, that I have the inflammatory rheumatism and I may just drop down dead any time, I'll bet

**▲ Critical Viewing**
Does this boy look genuinely upset, or do you think he is making himself cry, as the story's narrator does? Explain.

**Character**
What character trait do the narrator's thoughts suggest?

**Comprehension**
What does the narrator believe is wrong with him?

she wouldn't care about that either," I thought.

I was getting more and more angry the more thinking I did.

"I know what I'm going to do," I thought; "I'm going to go fishing."

I thought that, feeling the way I did, I might be sitting on the high bank just above the deep pool where the water went over the dam, and suddenly my heart would stop beating.

And then, of course, I'd pitch forward, over the bank into the pool and, if I wasn't dead when I hit the water, I'd drown sure.

They would all come home to supper and they'd miss me.

"But where is he?"

Then Mother would remember that I'd come home from school aching.

**Character**
Based on this imaginary scene, what words would you use to describe the narrator?

She'd go upstairs and I wouldn't be there. One day during the year before, there was a child got drowned in a spring. It was one of the Wyatt children.

Right down at the end of the street there was a spring under a birch tree and there had been a barrel sunk in the ground.

Everyone had always been saying the spring ought to be kept covered, but it wasn't.

So the Wyatt child went down there, played around alone, and fell in and got drowned.

Mother was the one who had found the drowned child. She had gone to get a pail of water and there the child was, drowned and dead.

This had been in the evening when we were all at home, and Mother had come running up the street with the dead, dripping child in her arms. She was making for the Wyatt house as hard as she could run, and she was pale.

She had a terrible look on her face, I remembered then.

"So," I thought, "they'll miss me and there'll be a search made. Very likely there'll be someone who has seen me sitting by the pond fishing, and there'll be a big alarm and all the town will turn out and they'll drag the pond."

I was having a grand time, having died. Maybe, after they found me and had got me out of the deep pool, Mother would grab me up in her arms and run home with me as she had run with the Wyatt child.

I got up from the porch and went around the house. I got my fishing pole and lit out for the pool below the dam. Mother was busy—she always was—and didn't see me go. When I got there I thought I'd better not sit too near the edge of the high bank.

By this time I didn't ache hardly at all, but I thought.

"With inflammatory rheumatism you can't tell," I thought.

"It probably comes and goes," I thought.

"Walter has it and he goes fishing," I thought.

I had got my line into the pool and suddenly I got a bite. It was a regular whopper. I knew that. I'd never had a bite like that.

I knew what it was. It was one of Mr. Fenn's big carp.

Mr. Fenn was a man who had a big pond of his own. He sold ice in the summer and the pond was to make the ice. He had bought some big carp and put them into his pond and then, earlier in the spring when there was a freshet,[2] his dam had gone out.

So the carp had got into our creek and one or two big ones had been caught—but none of them by a boy like me.

The carp was pulling and I was pulling and I was afraid he'd break my line, so I just tumbled down the high bank holding onto the line and got right into the pool. We had it out, there in the pool. We struggled. We wrestled. Then I got a hand under his gills and got him out.

He was a big one all right. He was nearly half as big as I was myself. I had him on the bank and I kept one hand under his gills and I ran.

I never ran so hard in my life. He was slippery, and now and then he wriggled out of my arms; once I stumbled and fell on him, but I got him home.

So there it was. I was a big hero that day. Mother got a washtub and filled it with water. She put the fish in it and all the neighbors came to look. I got into dry clothes and went down to supper—and then I made a break that spoiled my day.

**"I know what I'm going to do," I thought; "I'm going to go fishing."**

**Character**
What do the narrator's actions with the carp reveal about his physical condition?

**Comprehension**
What happened to the Wyatt child?

---

2. **freshet** (fresh′ it) a great rise or overflowing of a stream caused by heavy rains or melted snow.

# I was a BIG hero that day.

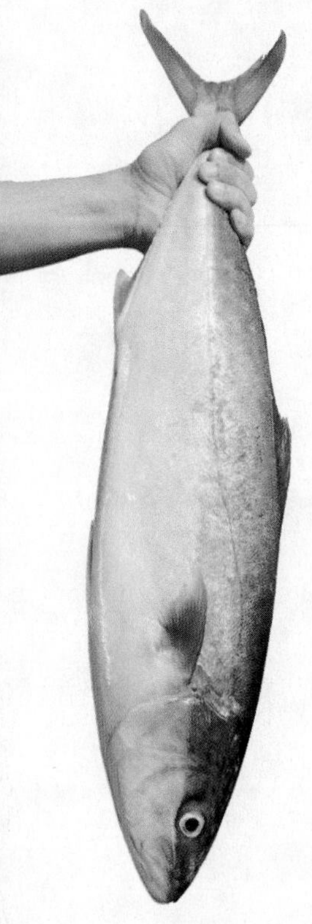

There we were, all of us, at the table, and suddenly Father asked what had been the matter with me at school. He had met the teacher, Sarah Suggett, on the street and she had told him how I had become ill.

"What was the matter with you?" Father asked, and before I thought what I was saying I let it out.

"I had the inflammatory rheumatism," I said—and a shout went up. It made me sick to hear them, the way they all laughed.

It brought back all the aching again, and like a fool I began to cry.

"Well, I *have* got it—I *have*, I *have*," I cried, and I got up from the table and ran upstairs.

I stayed there until Mother came up. I knew it would be a long time before I heard the last of the inflammatory rheumatism. I was sick all right, but the aching I now had wasn't in my legs or in my back.

## Critical Thinking

1. **Key Ideas and Details (a)** What inspires the narrator to think he has inflammatory rheumatism? **(b) Infer:** Why does the narrator think this would be an appealing disease to have? Support your response with textual evidence.
2. **Key Ideas and Details (a)** What does the narrator do after he gets home? **(b) Infer:** Why does his mother pay him little attention?
3. **Integration of Knowledge and Ideas (a)** How does his family respond when the narrator says he has inflammatory rheumatism? **(b) Defend:** Do you think the narrator's family should have been more understanding? Why or why not?
4. **Integration of Knowledge and Ideas** Does the story's ending resolve the conflict between what is true and what the narrator thinks is true? Explain, citing details from the story to support your response. ***[Connect to the Big Question: Does every conflict have a winner?]***

# Writing to Sources

## Comparing Characters

1. **Key Ideas and Details** Identify one example of direct characterization and one example of indirect characterization in each selection.
2. **Key Ideas and Details (a)** What happens to the narrator's army cot in "The Night the Bed Fell"? **(b)** What does his mother think happened?
3. **Key Ideas and Details (a)** What does the narrator of "Stolen Day" do that causes his teacher to send him home? **(b)** Why does he do this?
4. **Integration of Knowledge and Ideas** Use a chart like the one below to compare and contrast the narrators of both texts.

| | How similar? | How different? |
|---|---|---|
| Narrator: "Stolen Day" | A boy | Believes he is sick |
| Narrator: "The Night the Bed Fell" | | |

## Timed Writing

### Explanatory Text: Essay

In an essay, compare and contrast the narrators in these selections. Describe ways in which the narrators' internal and external responses to conflict affect the development of the plot. Cite evidence from the texts to support your analysis. **(30 minutes)**

### 5-Minute Planner

1. Read the prompt carefully and completely.
2. Answer these questions to help you gather your ideas.
   - How does each narrator respond to conflict? To what extent do the narrators' responses affect the plot of each selection?
   - Which narrator do you think will learn the most from his experiences? Why?
3. Create an outline in which you organize the details of your essay.
4. Reread the prompt, and then use your outline to draft your essay.

**USE ACADEMIC VOCABULARY**

As you write, use academic language, including the following words or their related forms:

**assumption**
**common**
**discover**
**perspective**

For more information about academic vocabulary, see pages xlvi-l.

# Language Study

## Using a Dictionary and Thesaurus

If you need to know the meaning, the pronunciation, or the part of speech of a word, you can find that information in a **dictionary.** In addition, a dictionary can show you a word's **etymology,** or origin. Etymologies explain how words come into the English language and how they change over time. Check the front or back of a dictionary for a guide to the symbols and abbreviations used in etymologies.

Here is an example of a dictionary entry. Notice what it tells you about the word *anthology.*

**Dictionary**

**anthology** (an thäl′ ə jē) *n., pl.* **-gies** [Gr. *anthologia,* a garland, collection of short poems < *anthologos,* gathering flowers < *anthos,* flower + *legein,* to gather] a collection of poems, stories, songs, excerpts, etc., chosen by the compiler

In a **thesaurus,** you will find a list of a word's synonyms, or words with similar meanings. You can use a thesaurus when you are looking for alternate word choices in your writing. Look at this example of a thesaurus entry.

**Thesaurus**

**clarify** *v.* interpret, define, elucidate, see EXPLAIN.

Note that a thesaurus does not provide definitions of words. Before you use a word you find in a thesaurus, check a dictionary to be sure you understand the word's meaning.

**Where To Find a Dictionary and Thesaurus** You can find these resources in book form at your school or library. You can also use *digital tools,* such as *online dictionaries* and *thesauruses,* to find the most precise words to express your ideas. Ask your teacher to recommend the best online word study resources.

**Practice A** Find each of the following words in a print or online dictionary. Write down the first pronunciation, part of speech, and definition of each word. Then, use each word in a sentence that shows its meaning.

**1.** voyage **2.** robust **3.** engulf **4.** intricate

**Practice B** Use a print or online thesaurus to find an alternate word for the italicized word in each sentence. Choose a more expressive word that means the same thing as the original. Verify the meaning of the word you choose in a dictionary.

**1.** I had to *run* down the street to catch the school bus on time.

**2.** After soccer practice, all we wanted to do was *sit* on the couch.

**3.** On our class trip to the nature trail, our assignment was to *find* as many bugs as possible.

**4.** After the storm, Damian had to *make* his storage shed again.

**5.** We had to *push* the trash down to make it fit in the can.

**Activity** Create a quick-reference thesaurus of some commonly used words. Make notecards like the one shown for the words *big*, *nice*, and *interesting*. Share your notecards with classmates and collect more synonyms. Then, with a partner, distinguish the shades of meaning that each word conveys. Use cards like these to help you find precise words when you write.

| |
|---|
| **Word:** |
| |
| **Part of speech:** |
| |
| **Definition:** |
| |
| **Synonym 1:** |
| |
| **Synonym 1 Definition:** |
| |
| **Shades of Meaning:** |
| |
| **Synonym 2:** |
| |
| **Synonym 2 Definition:** |
| |
| **Shades of Meaning:** |
| |

### Comprehension and Collaboration

With a partner, look up the meanings of the words *bolt* and *preserve*. Note that each word can be used as both a noun and a verb. For each word, write one sentence using the word as a noun and another sentence using the word as a verb.

## Delivering an Oral Summary

An **oral summary** shares many of the characteristics of a written summary. The guidelines below will help you plan what you want to say and help you say it with confidence.

### Learn the Skills

**Summarize.** Like its written counterpart, an oral summary should briefly state the main idea of a work, with only as many details as needed to give a complete, but concise, picture of the work.

**Organize your points in sequence.** To create a summary to use in an oral presentation, organize your ideas and record them on notecards.

Write the "main idea"—the overall statement of the work's content—on your first notecard. Include one or two key details that support the main idea. Make additional cards to present points from the beginning, middle, and end of the work. Write your conclusion on a separate card. Refer to your notecards as you deliver your presentation.

**Main Idea**
Giant pandas have become rare because hunters kill them.
**Facts:** There are only about 2,500 living in the wild. There are only about 150 in zoos.

**Show a comprehensive understanding.** As you prepare your presentation, do not just string together fact after fact. Ask yourself, "What does all this mean?" Try to convey a genuine understanding of what you have seen or read, not just the surface details.

**Consider your audience.** Include enough information so that your audience can follow the summary accurately.

**Conclusion**
If we can support the efforts to save pandas, maybe there will be more pandas in the world of our children and grandchildren.

**Plan your delivery.** Try to project confidence and a positive attitude. Plan and practice your delivery so that you stay focused when presenting.

- **Vary your sentence structure.** To add interest, vary your sentence structure just as you do when you write. Listen to your words and monitor yourself for errors in grammar.
- **Use your voice well.** Be energetic, but speak clearly and precisely. Enunciate every word. Vary the pitch and speed of your voice to keep your listeners engaged. Make sure that you are speaking loudly enough to be heard clearly.
- **Make eye contact.** Memorize as much of your summary as you can to enable you to make eye contact with listeners.

## Practice the Skills

**Presentation of Knowledge and Ideas** Use what you have learned in this workshop to complete the following activity.

ACTIVITY: **Prepare and Deliver an Oral Summary**

Choose an article, at least three pages long, from a magazine or Web site. Present an oral summary of the article to your class. Use the instruction on the previous page and the following steps to guide you:

- Begin with a strong opening statement. You might use a rhetorical question—a question asked for effect: *Does anyone wonder what happened to the plans for the new park?* You might use an impressive fact contained in the article: *It has been two years since the plans were first approved.*
- Use formal English, and vary the structure of your sentences.
- When presenting, project your voice so that everyone can hear you. Pronounce words clearly and make eye contact with your audience.
- End with a strong closing statement that relates to your opening statement. *So, that is what has happened to the park plans: repeated budget cuts.*

While your classmates give their presentations, use a checklist like the one below to rate their work.

### Presentation Evaluation Checklist

| Presentation Content | Presentation Delivery |
|---|---|
| Was the summary clear and easy to follow? Check all that apply.<br>❑ It has a strong beginning and ending.<br>❑ It includes all key points.<br>❑ I understood the main points of the work based on this summary. | Did the speaker deliver the summary effectively? Check all that apply.<br>❑ The speaker established good eye contact.<br>❑ The speaker enunciated clearly and maintained good volume.<br>❑ The speaker varied rate and pitch of voice.<br>❑ The speaker used formal English and varied sentence structure. |

**Comprehension and Collaboration** Ask your classmates to give you feedback by saying how they rated you on the Presentation Evaluation Checklist.

## Write a Narrative

### Autobiographical Narrative

**Defining the Form** Stories that tell of real events in a writer's life are called **autobiographical narratives.**

**Assignment** Write an autobiographical narrative about an event in your life that helped you grow or changed your outlook. Include

- ✓ a clear *sequence of events* involving you, the writer
- ✓ a problem or *conflict,* or a clear contrast between past and present viewpoints
- ✓ a *plot* line that includes a beginning, rising action, climax, and resolution, or *denouement*
- ✓ *pacing* that effectively builds the action
- ✓ *specific details and quotations*
- ✓ well-developed *major and minor characters*
- ✓ error-free writing, including *correct use of pronouns*

To preview the criteria on which your autobiographical narrative may be judged, see the rubric on page 125.

### FOCUS ON RESEARCH

When you write an autobiographical narrative, you might perform research to

- jog your memory about the event you are describing.
- discover other people's memories of the event.
- give your writing authenticity, or a true-to-life feel.

Research for an autobiographical work is more personal than other kinds of research. To gather information, interview people who were involved in the event; reread journal entries, letters, or emails from that time; and examine keepsakes and other objects that remind you of the event.

**READING-WRITING CONNECTION**

To get a feel for narrative nonfiction, read the excerpt from *Barrio Boy* by Ernesto Galarza on page 234.

## Prewriting/Planning Strategies

**Choose a topic.** To choose the right event from your life to narrate, use one of the following strategies:

- **Freewriting** Write for five minutes about whatever comes to mind on these general topics: *funny times, sad times,* and *lessons I have learned.* When you are finished, review what you have written and circle any ideas that could make a good topic for your purpose and audience.
- **Listing** Fill in a chart like the one below. In each column, list names or descriptions of memorable people and things that you know or have a particular viewpoint about from home, school, or travel. Review your chart to find connections between the items. For each connection you find, circle the two items and draw an arrow between them. Finally, review the connections you have found, and jot down ideas for engaging stories that they suggest.

| People | Places | Things | Events |
|---|---|---|---|
| | | | |
| | | | |

**Make a timeline.** Once you have decided on a topic, begin to gather the details that you will use in your narrative. Fill out a timeline like the one shown to organize your details in time order.

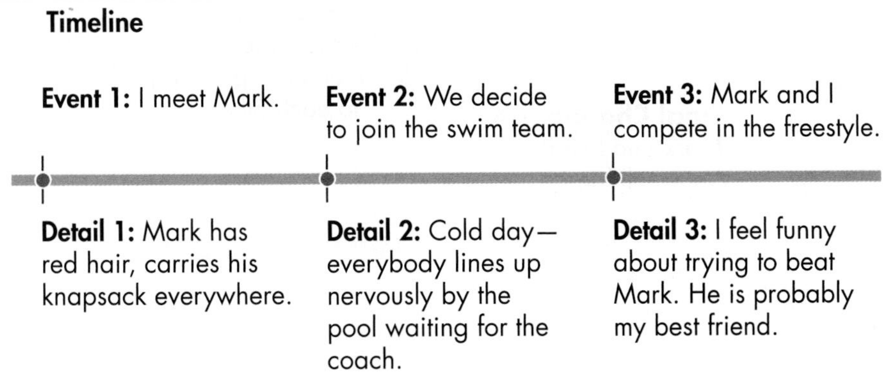
Timeline
Event 1: I meet Mark.
Event 2: We decide to join the swim team.
Event 3: Mark and I compete in the freestyle.
Detail 1: Mark has red hair, carries his knapsack everywhere.
Detail 2: Cold day—everybody lines up nervously by the pool waiting for the coach.
Detail 3: I feel funny about trying to beat Mark. He is probably my best friend.

## Drafting Strategies

**Map out your story.** Make a conflict chart like the one below. In the center, write a brief description of the conflict. Fill in linked circles with specific narrative action related to the conflict. Number the circles to help put the events of your story in order. As you draft, refer to your chart to help connect details to your central conflict.

**Develop the plot line.** Once you have mapped out the plot, make sure that you arrange the pace in the story so that the conflict intensifies during the **rising action.** The climax should be the highest point of interest in your story. **The resolution,** or **denouement,** should be the conclusion in which your conflict is resolved.

**Develop a setting.** A vivid setting can bring your story to life and help readers understand your characters. When describing a setting, try to appeal to several of your readers' senses. Draw a word picture of the place with precise and colorful nouns, adjectives, verbs, and adverbs.

> **Vague Description:** We lived in a small town.
>
> **Vivid Description:** Main Street smelled like pine trees because the woods were only steps away.

**Develop characters through dialogue.** Bring people to life by using dialogue—quoting what people said as they said it. Do not report everything a character says. Instead, create conversations that vividly show the character's feelings, gestures, and expressions as he or she reacts to events.

**Provide a conclusion.** Bring your narrative to a satisfying close by resolving conflicts and sharing insights or reflections with your readers.

**Background**
Mark and I were best friends.

**Event 1:**
Mark and I are matched in an important race.

**Central Conflict**
**My friendship with Mark vs. my desire to win.**

**Event 2:**
As the race approaches, Mark and I stop talking to each other.

**Final Change:**
Mark and I tied! We're still friends.

## Finding Your Voice

**Voice** describes a writer's distinctive style and can be influenced by word choice, sentence structure, and tone—the writer's attitude toward his or her subject. A professional writer usually has a distinct voice that makes his or her writing instantly recognizable. For example, think of how a jazz musician and a hip-hop artist might play "The Star-Spangled Banner" completely differently. Developing a unique voice can take time. These tips and activities will help get you started.

**Learning from the Professionals** Next time you read a passage that you enjoy in a literary work, think about the writer's voice. Filling in a chart like the one shown will help you analyze voice. The examples in this chart refer to Ernesto Galarza's *Barrio Boy,* which appears on pages 234–239, but you can use a similar chart for any text.

| | |
|---|---|
| **Word Choice** | *A new building, painted yellow; a straight sharp nose; her blond radiant face* |
| **Sentence Structure** | Long sentences that link together descriptive phrases |
| **Tone** | Observant, interested, and admiring, but not overly emotional |

**Refining Your Voice** As you write your autobiographical narrative, review your draft for word choice, sentence structure, and tone. Remember to consider your purpose and audience. Decide if your style of writing should be formal or informal. Are you happy with the voice you are using? If not, try revising some of these elements to adjust your voice. Ask yourself these questions:

- *Word Choice:* What kinds of words have I chosen? Have I used precise language to create a strong impression?
- *Sentence Structure:* How did I arrange the words in my sentences? What type of sentences do I typically create?
- *Tone:* How do I feel about my subject? Has my word choice helped convey my intended tone?

Ask a partner to read your draft and give feedback. By adjusting the elements above, you can adjust your voice. Many writers refer to this process as "finding their voice."

## Revising Strategies

**Review sequence of events.** Read through your narrative to make sure that the events you describe flow logically and are in chronological order. Add transition words, such as *first, next, later,* and *finally,* to clarify the sequence of events.

**Check your pacing.** A good story builds to a single most exciting moment, called the **climax.** The secret of building to a climax is **pacing**—the speed at which your story moves along. Pace your story to build suspense. To improve the pacing of your story, use the following strategies:

- Cut details and events that do not build suspense or heighten readers' interest.
- Revise or delete any paragraph that is not clearly connected to the central conflict.
- Make clear connections between other events to show readers how events relate to each other.

**Use specific, precise nouns.** Look for nouns that are vague or general and might leave the reader wondering *what kind.* Replace general and vague nouns with specific and precise ones. Review your draft, circling any nouns that do not answer the questions *What exactly?* and *What kind?* Replace these nouns with specific, precise nouns that convey a lively picture. Use a dictionary to confirm the precise meaning of the words you are using.

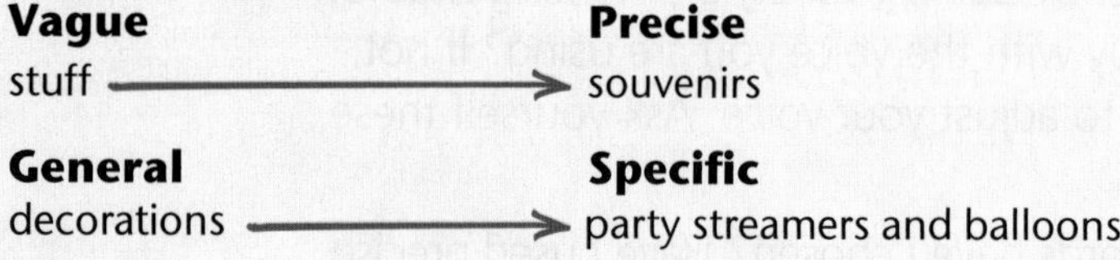


### Peer Review

Give your draft to one or two classmates to read. Ask them to highlight details that slow the story down or ideas that are unconnected to the central conflict. Use the feedback to eliminate any unnecessary details from your draft. As you review comments and revise your draft, adjust your writing to suit your purpose and audience as needed.

## Checking Pronoun-Antecedent Agreement

Incorrect pronoun-antecedent agreement occurs when a personal pronoun disagrees with its antecedent in person, number, or gender.

**Identifying Incorrect Pronoun-Antecedent Agreement** An **antecedent** is the word or words for which a pronoun stands. A pronoun's antecedent may be a noun, a group of words acting as a noun, or another pronoun.

**Antecedent** **Pronoun**

**Example:** I told Alexis to bring a bathing suit with her.

In this example, the pronoun *her* is third person and singular. It agrees with its feminine antecedent, *Alexis,* which is also third person (the person spoken about) and singular.

**Fixing Agreement Errors** To fix an incorrect pronoun-antecedent agreement, identify both the pronoun and the antecedent for which it stands. Then use one of the following methods.

1. **Identify the person of the antecedent** as first, second, or third. Choose a pronoun that matches the antecedent in person.
2. **Identify the number of the antecedent** as singular or plural. Choose a pronoun that matches the antecedent in number.
3. **Identify the gender of the antecedent** as masculine or feminine. Choose a pronoun that matches the antecedent in gender.

**Personal Pronouns**

| | Singular | Plural |
|---|---|---|
| **First Person** | I, me, my, mine | we, us, our, ours |
| **Second Person** | you, your, yours | you, your, yours |
| **Third Person** | **Feminine:** she, her, hers<br>**Masculine:** he, him, his<br>**Neutral:** it, its | they, them, their, theirs |

### Grammar in Your Writing

Read your draft. Draw an arrow from each personal pronoun to its antecedent. If the agreement is incorrect, fix it using one of the methods above.

## STUDENT MODEL: **Alexander Baker, Palos Verdes, CA**

### Bicycle Braking Blues

Crash! Once again, I found myself flying off my bike and toward the grass. At age eight, crashes were an everyday occurrence, and I reminded myself that it was better to practice braking here by the lawn than to risk another episode like "The Club Hill Clobbering."

With this hint, Alexander clearly connects his introduction to the central conflict of his story.

It all started when I arrived at my grandparents' house in Galesburg to spend the summer. I made many friends in their neighborhood, but they spent most of their time riding bikes, and I didn't have one. Then, my step-grandmother gave me the almost new, metallic green bike that her grandson had outgrown. I was overjoyed to have a bike. . . . I learned to ride it well enough—what I didn't learn was how to use the brakes. On the flat ground near my grandparents' house, I just let the bike slow down until I could put my feet down.

Adding this detail helps move the story along—it shows why a bike is so important to Alexander.

One day my babysitter took me for lunch at the club grill. She rode my grandfather's golf cart while I rode my bike. When we had to climb the big hill leading up to the club, I walked my bike alongside the cart. After lunch, I mounted my bike while Erika drove Grandpa's golf cart. As we headed toward home, neither of us gave a thought to . . . the HILL.

Alexander narrates events in clear sequence.

As we came around the corner of the bike path, I started picking up speed. By the time I realized what was happening, it was too late. "The hill!" I yelled to Erika. "Your brakes! Use your brakes!" she shouted. With the wind rushing in my ears, I could hardly hear her. Looking down the hill, I saw a golf cart was blocking the path. It seemed to be getting bigger and closer by the second. "Well," I thought to myself, "it's now or never." I steered my speeding bike toward the grass alongside the path and jumped off sideways. I leapt off and BAM! The world turned upside down and inside out. The next sound I heard was the grumbling of a golf cart engine. It sounded annoyed about the jumble of parts in its path. The next thing I saw was Erika's face. She was so scared that her face was stiff and pale. I stood up to show Erika that I was fine. The only damage I sustained was some dirt on my jeans, and the bike survived without too many scratches too. Also, my pride was hurt. How can you ride a bike if you can never go down hill? So every day, Erika took me to the hill and we'd go a little further up. That way, I learned to brake on a hill, little by little, rather than getting clobbered again!

Using this precise noun helps vividly convey the scene to readers.

Details such as *stiff* and *pale* help readers vividly imagine Erika's expression.

## Editing and Proofreading

Review your draft to correct errors in spelling, grammar, and punctuation.

**Focus on the Dialogue:** As you proofread your story, pay close attention to the correct punctuation of dialogue—the actual words spoken by a character. Use the examples as a guide. All dialogue should be enclosed in quotation marks. A split dialogue is when a quotation is split up with additional information in the middle, such as identifying the speaker.

*"She went home," I said.*

*"Wow!" I yelled. "I love it."*

**Spiral Review**
Earlier in the unit, you learned about **adjectives and adverbs** (p. 78). Check the use of these modifiers in your autobiographical narrative. Review your work to be sure you have used adjectives to describe nouns, and adverbs to describe verbs.

## Publishing and Presenting

Consider one of the following ways to share your writing:

**Present an oral narrative.** Practice telling your story, using notes rather than reading from your draft, until you can deliver it smoothly and naturally. Practice using gestures to emphasize key points. Tell your story to the class.

**Make a poster.** Arrange photos, artwork, or small souvenirs, along with a neat copy of your narrative, on posterboard to display in class.

## Reflecting on Your Writing

**Writer's Journal** Jot down your answer to this question:

*As you wrote, what new insights into your story did you have?*

### Rubric for Self-Assessment

Find evidence in your writing to address each category. Then, use the rating scale to grade your work.

| Criteria | Rating Scale |
|---|---|
| **Purpose/Focus** Clearly presents a narrative that develops real experiences and events | *not very* ............ *very*<br>1 2 3 4 |
| **Organization** Organizes events clearly and logically; presents a strong conclusion that follows from and reflects on events in the narrative | 1 2 3 4 |
| **Development of Ideas/Elaboration** Establishes a clear context and point of view; effectively uses narrative techniques, such as dialogue, pacing, and description | 1 2 3 4 |
| **Language** Uses precise words, descriptive details, and sensory language to convey experiences and events. | 1 2 3 4 |
| **Conventions** Uses proper grammar, including correct use of pronouns and antecedents | 1 2 3 4 |

## SELECTED RESPONSE

### I. Reading Literature

**Directions:** *Read this passage from "The Three Century Woman" by Richard Peck. Then, answer each question that follows.*

"I guess if you live long enough," my mom said to Aunt Gloria, "you get your fifteen minutes of fame."

Mom was on the car phone to Aunt Gloria. The minute Mom rolls out of the garage, she's on her car phone. It's state-of-the-art and better than her car.

We were heading for Whispering Oaks to see my great-grandmother Breckenridge, who's lived there since I was a little girl. They call it an Elder Care Facility. Needless to say, I hated going.

The reason for Great-grandmother's fame is that she was born in 1899. Now it's January 2001. If you're one of those people who claim the new century begins in 2001, not 2000, even you have to agree that Great-grandmother Breckenridge has lived in three centuries. This is her claim to fame.

We waited for a light to change along by Northbrook Mall, and I gazed <u>fondly</u> over at it. Except for the Multiplex, it was closed because of New Year's Day. I have a severe mall habit. But I'm fourteen, and the mall is a place without homework. Aunt Gloria's voice filled the car.

"If you take my advice," she told Mom, "you'll keep those Whispering Oaks people from letting the media in to interview Grandma. Interview her my foot! Honestly. She doesn't know where she is, let alone how many centuries she's lived in. The poor old soul. Leave her in peace. She's already got one foot in the—"

"Gloria, your trouble is you have no sense of history." Mom gunned across the intersection. "You got a C in history."

"I was sick a lot that year," Aunt Gloria said.

"Sick of history," Mom mumbled.

"I heard that," Aunt Gloria said.

They bickered on, but I tuned them out. Then when we turned in at Whispering Pines, a sound truck from IBC-TV was blocking the drive.

"Good grief," Mom murmured. "TV."

"I told you," Aunt Gloria said, but Mom switched her off. She parked in a frozen rut.

"I'll wait in the car," I said. "I have homework."

"Get out of the car," Mom said.

1. **Part A** Which of the following **character traits** best describes Aunt Gloria?

   A. bored
   B. silly
   C. shy
   D. concerned

   **Part B** Which detail from the passage best supports the answer to Part A?

   A. "Aunt Gloria's voice filled the car."
   B. "'I was sick a lot that year,' . . ."
   C. "'The poor old soul. Leave her in peace.'"
   D. "This is her claim to fame."

2. Which sentence from the passage shows the **first-person point of view?**

   A. "They call it an Elder Care Facility."
   B. "Now it's January 2001."
   C. "Needless to say, I hated going."
   D. "The minute mom rolls out of the garage, she's on her car phone."

3. What **conflict** does the narrator in the story face?

   A. She wants to go to the mall, but she has to do homework.
   B. She must visit her great-grandmother at the nursing home, but she hates going.
   C. She tries to tune out her mom and aunt bickering on the phone, but she can't.
   D. She has homework to do, but she forgot it at home.

4. Which of the following details from the passage is not part of the story's **plot?**

   A. "'She doesn't know where she is, let alone how many centuries she has lived in.'"
   B. "It's state-of-the-art and better than her car."
   C. "We were heading for Whispering Oaks to see my great-grandmother Breckenridge, who's lived there since I was a little girl."
   D. "'I guess if you live long enough,' my mom said to Aunt Gloria, 'you get your fifteen minutes of fame.'"

5. Which sentence best conveys a **theme** of the story?

   A. "Then when we turned in at Whispering Pines, a sound truck from IBC-TV was blocking the drive."
   B. "The reason for Great-grandmother's fame is that she was born in 1899."
   C. "Mom was on the car phone to Aunt Gloria."
   D. "'Gloria, your trouble is you have no sense of history.'"

6. Which of the following answer choices is an example of **direct characterization?**

   A. "Mom was on the car phone to Aunt Gloria."
   B. "They bickered on, but I tuned them out."
   C. "'I'll wait in the car.'"
   D. "I have a severe mall habit."

7. **Part A** Which answer choice is the best definition of the underlined word *fondly?*

   A. with affection
   B. tiredly
   C. with disgust
   D. uncaringly

   **Part B** Which context clue helps you determine the meaning of *fondly?*

   A. "along by Northbrook Mall"
   B. "I gazed"
   C. "it was closed because of New Year's Day"
   D. "I have a severe mall habit."

### Timed Writing

8. In a paragraph, explain how the writer uses **indirect characterization** to describe Mom. Support your ideas with at least three specific examples from the passage.

GO ON

## II. Reading Informational Text

**Directions:** *Read the passage. Then, answer each question that follows.*

### The American Alligator

**Appearance**

Alligators look like large lizards with thick bodies and tails. They have strong jaws and many sharp teeth. An alligator's eyes stick up above its skull, allowing it to see above the water while its body is beneath the surface. It swims by moving its powerful tail from side to side.

| Average Size | | | | |
|---|---|---|---|---|
| **Length when hatched** | **Length for adult male** | **Length for adult female** | **Weight for adult male** | **Weight for adult female** |
| 9 inches | 11–12 feet | 9 feet or less | 450–550 pounds | 160 pounds |

**Diet**

Alligators are meat-eating reptiles that eat birds, fish, snakes, turtles, frogs, and mammals. Alligators are good hunters, partly because they are not easily seen by their prey. That is because they swim with only their eyes and tough, scaly backs visible above the surface. To an unsuspecting creature, an alligator can look like a dead log floating in the water.

**1.** If you wanted to write a physical description of an American alligator, in which sections of this encyclopedia entry would you look for information?

**A.** Appearance *and* Length When Hatched
**B.** Appearance *and* Average Size
**C.** Appearance *and* Diet
**D.** Average Size *and* Diet

**2.** What are the subheads in this encyclopedia entry?

**A.** The American Alligator *and* Appearance
**B.** Appearance *and* Average Size
**C.** Appearance *and* Diet
**D.** Average Size *and* Diet

**3.** Which generalization is *not* supported by information in the encyclopedia entry?

**A.** Male alligators are bigger than females.
**B.** Alligators spend much of their time in the water.
**C.** Alligators do not live in the ocean.
**D.** Alligators use their sense of sight for hunting.

**4.** What can you infer from the information in the encyclopedia entry?

**A.** Alligators are dangerous.
**B.** Alligators are found in the South.
**C.** Alligators are easy to train.
**D.** Alligators live a long time.

## III. Writing and Language Conventions

**Directions:** *Read the passage. Then, answer each question that follows.*

(1) The Robert Johnson swimming Pool can be a flurry of activity in the summer. (2) Swimming pools have been around for centuries. (3) The squealing children jump repeatedly and excited into the turquoise water. (4) Across the pool is the sound of happy voices engaged in a "Marco Polo" game. (5) Childrens beach balls fly across the pool. (6) You can tell they are all having a great time swimming. (7) When the swimmers finally get out, the scorching pavement burns their feet. (8) Everyone is laughing and running for the towel. (9) Labor Day comes. (10) That unique feeling of summer ends when the lifeguard locks the gate, closing the pool until next year.

**1.** Which revision to sentence 8 shows correct **pronoun-antecedent agreement?**

**A.** Everyone is laughing and running for its towel.
**B.** Everyone is laughing and running for their towel.
**C.** Everyone is laughing and running for our towel.
**D.** Everyone is laughing and running for his or her towel.

**2.** Which sentence includes at least one **personal pronoun?**

**A.** sentence 9
**B.** sentence 5
**C.** sentence 6
**D.** sentence 4

**3.** Which revision shows the *best* way to correct the use of **adverbs** in sentence 3?

**A.** The squealing children jump repeatedly and excitedly into the turquoise water.
**B.** The squealing children jump repeated and excitedly into the turquoise water.
**C.** The squealing children repeated jump and excited into the turquoise water.
**D.** The squealing children jump repeatedly and excited into the turquoise water.

**4.** What is the correct way to capitalize the **proper nouns** in sentence 1?

**A.** The Robert Johnson swimming pool can be a flurry of activity in the Summer.
**B.** The Robert Johnson Swimming Pool can be a flurry of activity in the summer.
**C.** The Robert Johnson Swimming pool can be a flurry of activity in the summer.
**D.** The Robert johnson swimming pool can be a flurry of activity in the summer.

**5.** What is the correct way to punctuate the **possessive noun** in sentence 5?

**A.** Childrens beach ball's fly across the pool.
**B.** Childrens' beach ball fly across the pool.
**C.** Children's beach balls' fly across the pool.
**D.** Children's beach balls fly across the pool.

**6.** Which answer choice identifies the **adjectives** in sentence 10?

**A.** unique, summer
**B.** summer, next
**C.** unique, next
**D.** next, year

# CONSTRUCTED RESPONSE

**Directions:** *Follow the instructions to complete the tasks below as required by your teacher.*

*As you work on each task, incorporate both general academic vocabulary and literary terms you learned in Parts 1 and 2 of this unit.*

## Writing

**TASK 1** **Literature**

### Analyze Conflict and Character

*Write an essay in which you analyze how conflict shapes the main characters in two stories from Part 2.*

- Choose two stories and briefly summarize a conflict that the main character faces in each story.
- Analyze how the conflict and its resolution affects each main character's beliefs, thoughts, feelings, actions, and reactions. Tell whether or not each character changes or grows as a result of the conflict.
- Provide examples from both texts to support your analysis.
- Use appropriate transitions to clarify the relationships between ideas in your essay.

**TASK 2** **Literature**

### Analyze Characters' Points of View

*Write an essay in which you identify two characters' points of view from a story in Part 2. Analyze how the author develops and contrasts the points of view of these characters.*

- Identify two characters with distinct points of view in a story from Part 2. Describe what the characters believe and how they feel. Discuss their motives.
- Analyze how the author develops each character's point of view through narration, dialogue, and action. Include concrete details from the story to develop and support your analysis.
- Then, discuss how the author contrasts the points of view of your chosen characters through their dialogue, actions, and reactions.
- As you revise, check your writing for correct spelling and punctuation.

**TASK 3** **Literature**

### Evaluate Plot

*Write an essay in which you evaluate the plot in one of the stories in Part 2.*

**Part 1**

- Choose a story with a plot that you feel is developed in a particularly effective way.
- Reread the story, taking notes on the plot.
- Evaluate how effectively the parts of the plot work together to move the story forward. Focus on the exposition, rising action and conflict, climax, falling action, and resolution.

**Part 2**

- Write an essay in which you explain your evaluation of the plot. Cite specific examples of effective narrative techniques such as the use of foreshadowing, descriptive language, or specific details that build tension or suspense.
- Maintain a consistent style and tone in your writing.

## Speaking and Listening

**TASK 4** Literature

### Analyze and Develop Theme

*Write a brief narrative in which you develop the theme of a story from Part 2 in a different way. Read your story aloud to a group of classmates.*

- Choose a story from Part 2 with a theme that interests you. Note how the author develops the theme over the course of the story.
- Then, write a brief narrative in which you express the same theme in a new way. Consider using characters' words and actions, setting, symbols, or conflict to develop the theme.
- As you write, choose language that expresses your ideas clearly and effectively.
- Read your story aloud to a group of classmates.

**TASK 5** Literature

### Analyze Conflict Development

*Give a presentation in which you use multimedia or visual displays to clarify your analysis of how particular story elements interact to develop the conflict in a story from Part 2.*

- Prepare a presentation in which you identify the internal or external conflict faced by the main character in a story of your choice.
- Analyze how particular story elements, such as setting, plot, and other characters, interact to develop the conflict.
- Create a story map, a cause-and-effect chart, a slide show, or another graphic display to visually present the conflict's development.
- Accurately use appropriate vocabulary and content-area words as you present your display to the class.

## Research

**TASK 6** Literature

### Does every conflict have a winner?

In Part 2, you have read literature about different types of conflicts. Now you will conduct a short research project on a conflict that is happening in your community or in our country. Use both the literature you have read and your research to help reflect on this unit's Big Question. Review the following guidelines before you begin your research:

- Focus your research on one conflict.
- Gather relevant information from at least two reliable print or digital sources.
- Take careful notes as you conduct your research.
- Cite your sources accurately.

When you have completed your research, write a response to the Big Question. Discuss how your initial ideas about conflict have changed or been reinforced. Support your response with an example from the literature you read and an example from your research.

"Live daringly, boldly, fearlessly. Taste the relish to be found in **competition**—in having put forth the best within you."

**—Henry J. Kaiser**

PART 3

## TEXT SET DEVELOPING INSIGHT

# COMPETITION

The selections in this unit all relate to the Big Question: **Does every conflict have a winner?** Conflicts often arise from various competitive situations, ranging from sports to musical performances to academic achievements. The texts that follow offer different perspectives on competition. As you read, consider insights the authors present about the conflicts that can arise as a result of competition.

◀ CRITICAL VIEWING Do you think Henry J. Kaiser's quotation relates only to athletic competition, such as the competition between the two fencers in this photo? Explain.

### CLOSE READING TOOL

Use the **Close Reading Tool** to practice the strategies you learn in this unit.

### READINGS IN PART 3

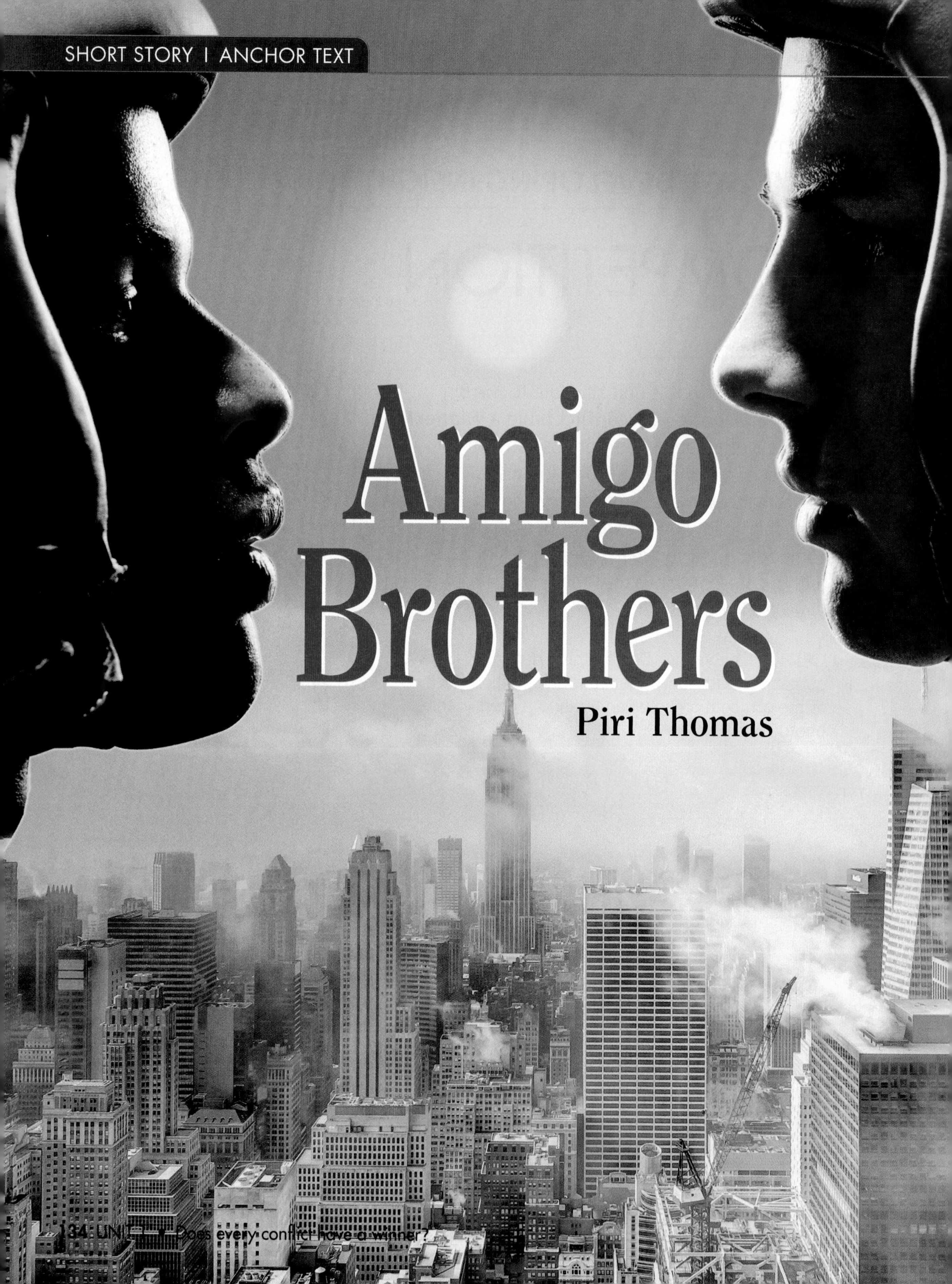

# Amigo Brothers

Piri Thomas

Antonio Cruz and Felix Vargas were both seventeen years old. They were so together in friendship that they felt themselves to be brothers. They had known each other since childhood, growing up on the lower east side of Manhattan in the same tenement building on Fifth Street between Avenue A and Avenue B.

Antonio was fair, lean, and lanky, while Felix was dark, short, and husky. Antonio's hair was always falling over his eyes, while Felix wore his black hair in a natural Afro style.

Each youngster had a dream of someday becoming lightweight champion of the world. Every chance they had the boys worked out, sometimes at the Boys Club on 10th Street and Avenue A and sometimes at the pro's gym on 14th Street. Early morning sunrises would find them running along the East River Drive, wrapped in sweat shirts, short towels around their necks, and handkerchiefs Apache style around their foreheads.

While some youngsters were into street negatives, Antonio and Felix slept, ate, rapped, and dreamt positive. Between them, they had a collection of *Fight* magazines second to none, plus a scrapbook filled with torn tickets to every boxing match they had ever attended, and some clippings of their own. If asked a question about any given fighter, they would immediately zip out from their memory banks divisions, weights, records of fights, knock-outs, technical knock-outs, and draws or losses.

Each had fought many bouts representing their community and had won two gold-plated medals plus a silver and bronze medallion. The difference was in their style. Antonio's lean form and long reach made him the better boxer, while Felix's short and muscular frame made him the better slugger. Whenever they had met in the ring for sparring sessions, it had always been hot and heavy.

Now, after a series of elimination bouts, they had been informed that they were to meet each other in the division finals that were scheduled for the seventh of August, two weeks away—the winner to represent the Boys Club in the Golden Gloves Championship Tournament.

The two boys continued to run together along the East River Drive. But even when joking with each other, they both sensed a wall rising between them.

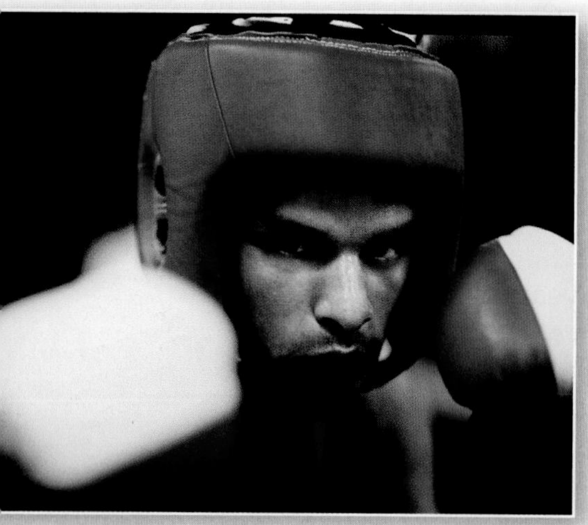

One morning less than a week before their bout, they met as usual for their daily work-out. They fooled around with a few jabs at the air, slapped skin, and then took off, running lightly along the dirty East River's edge.

Antonio glanced at Felix who kept his eyes purposely straight ahead, pausing from time to time to do some fancy leg work while throwing one-twos followed by upper cuts to an imaginary jaw. Antonio then beat the air with a barrage of body blows and short **devastating** lefts with an overhand jaw-breaking right. After a mile or so, Felix puffed and said, "Let's stop a while, bro. I think we both got something to say to each other."

**devastating ▶** (dev′ ə stāt′ iŋ) *adj.* destructive; overwhelming

Antonio nodded. It was not natural to be acting as though nothing unusual was happening when two ace-boon buddies were going to be blasting each other within a few short days.

They rested their elbows on the railing separating them from the river. Antonio wiped his face with his short towel. The sunrise was now creating day.

Felix leaned heavily on the river's railing and stared across to the shores of Brooklyn. Finally, he broke the silence.

"Man, I don't know how to come out with it."

Antonio helped. "It's about our fight, right?"

"Yeah, right." Felix's eyes squinted at the rising orange sun.

"I've been thinking about it too, *panín*. In fact, since we found out it was going to be me and you, I've been awake at night, pulling punches on you, trying not to hurt you."

"Same here. It ain't natural not to think about the fight. I mean, we both are *cheverote* fighters and we both want to win. But only one of us can win. There ain't no draws in the eliminations."

Felix tapped Antonio gently on the shoulder. "I don't mean to sound like I'm bragging, bro. But I wanna win, fair and square."

Antonio nodded quietly. "Yeah. We both know that in the ring the better man wins. Friend or no friend, brother or no . . ."

Felix finished it for him. "Brother. Tony, let's promise something right here. Okay?"

"If it's fair, *hermano*, I'm for it." Antonio admired the courage of a tugboat pulling a barge five times its welterweight size.

"It's fair, Tony. When we get into the ring, it's gotta be like we never met. We gotta be like two heavy strangers that want the same thing and only one can have it. You understand, don'tcha?"

"Sí, I know." Tony smiled. "No pulling punches. We go all the way."

"Yeah, that's right. Listen, Tony. Don't you think it's a good idea if we don't see each other until the day of the fight? I'm going to stay with my Aunt Lucy in the Bronx. I can use Gleason's Gym for working out. My manager says he got some sparring partners with more or less your style."

Tony scratched his nose pensively. "Yeah, it would be better for our heads." He held out his hand, palm upward. "Deal?"

"Deal." Felix lightly slapped open skin.

"Ready for some more running?" Tony asked lamely.

"Naw, bro. Let's cut it here. You go on. I kinda like to get things together in my head."

"You ain't worried, are you?" Tony asked.

"No way, man." Felix laughed out loud. "I got too much smarts for that. I just think it's cooler if we split right here. After the fight, we can get it together again like nothing ever happened."

The amigo brothers were not ashamed to hug each other tightly.

"Guess you're right. Watch yourself, Felix. I hear there's some pretty heavy dudes up in the Bronx. *Suavecito*, okay?"

"Okay. You watch yourself too, *sabe*?"

Tony jogged away. Felix watched his friend disappear from view, throwing rights and lefts. Both fighters had a lot of psyching up to do before the big fight.

The days in training passed much too slowly. Although they kept out of each other's way, they were aware of each other's progress via the ghetto grapevine.

The evening before the big fight, Tony made his way to the roof of his tenement. In the quiet early dark, he peered over the ledge. Six stories below the lights of the city blinked and the sounds of cars mingled with the curses and the laughter of children in the street. He tried not to think of Felix, feeling he had succeeded in psyching his mind. But only in the ring would he really know. To spare Felix hurt, he would have to knock him out, early and quick.

Up in the South Bronx, Felix decided to take in a movie in an effort to keep Antonio's face away from his fists. The flick was *The Champion* with Kirk Douglas, the third time Felix was seeing it.

The champion was getting hit hard. He was saved only by the sound of the bell.

Felix became the champ and Tony the challenger.

The movie audience was going out of its head. The challenger, confident that he had the championship in the bag, threw a left. The champ countered with a dynamite right.

Felix's right arm felt the shock. Antonio's face, superimposed[1] on the screen, was hit by the awesome blow. Felix saw himself in the ring, blasting Antonio against the ropes. The champ had to be forcibly restrained. The challenger was allowed to crumble slowly to the canvas.

When Felix finally left the theatre, he had figured out how to psyche himself for tomorrow's fight. It was Felix the Champion vs. Antonio the Challenger.

He walked up some dark streets, deserted except for small pockets of wary-looking kids wearing gang colors. Despite the fact that he was Puerto Rican like them, they eyed him as a stranger to their turf. Felix did a fast shuffle, bobbing and weaving, while letting loose a torrent of blows that would demolish whatever got in its way. It seemed to impress the brothers, who went about their own business.

Finding no takers, Felix decided to split to his aunt's. Walking the streets had not relaxed him, neither had the fight flick. All it had done was to stir him up. He let himself quietly into his Aunt Lucy's apartment and went straight to bed, falling into a fitful sleep with sounds of the gong for Round One.

Antonio was passing some heavy time on his rooftop. How would the fight tomorrow affect his relationship with Felix? After all, fighting was like any other profession. Friendship had nothing to do with it. A gnawing doubt crept in. He cut negative thinking real quick by doing some speedy fancy dance steps, bobbing and weaving like mercury.[2] The night air was blurred with **perpetual** motions of left hooks and right crosses. Felix, his *amigo* brother, was not going to be Felix at all in the ring. Just an opponent with another face. Antonio went to sleep, hearing the opening bell for the first round. Like his friend in the South Bronx, he prayed for victory, via a quick clean knock-out in the first round.

**perpetual ▶** (pər pech′ o͞o əl) *adj.* constant; unending

Large posters plastered all over the walls of local shops announced the fight between Antonio Cruz and Felix Vargas as the main bout.

The fight had created great interest in the neighborhood. Antonio and Felix were well liked and respected. Each had his own loyal following. Antonio's fans counted on his boxing skills. On the other side, Felix's admirers trusted in his dynamite-packed fists.

Felix had returned to his apartment early in the morning of August 7th and stayed there, hoping to avoid seeing Antonio. He turned the radio on to salsa music sounds and then tried to read while waiting for word from his manager.

---

1. **superimposed** (so͞o′ pər im pōzd′) *adj.* put or stacked on top of something else.
2. **mercury** (mʉr′ kyo͞or ē) *n.* the element mercury, also known as quicksilver because it is so quick and fluid.

The fight was scheduled to take place in Tompkins Square Park. It had been decided that the gymnasium of the Boys Club was not large enough to hold all the people who were sure to attend. In Tompkins Square Park, everyone who wanted could view the fight, whether from ringside or window fire escapes or tenement rooftops.

The morning of the fight Tompkins Square was a beehive of activity with numerous workers setting up the ring, the seats, and the guest speakers' stand. The scheduled bouts began shortly after noon and the park had begun filling up even earlier.

The local junior high school across from Tompkins Square Park served as the dressing room for all the fighters. Each was given a separate classroom with desk tops, covered with mats, serving as resting tables. Antonio thought he caught a glimpse of Felix waving to him from a room at the far end of the corridor. He waved back just in case it had been him.

The fighters changed from their street clothes into fighting gear. Antonio wore white trunks, black socks, and black shoes. Felix wore sky blue trunks, red socks, and white boxing shoes. Each had dressing gowns to match their fighting trunks with their names neatly stitched on the back.

The loudspeakers blared into the open windows of the school. There were speeches by dignitaries, community leaders, and great boxers of yesteryear. Some were well prepared, some improvised on the spot. They all carried the same message of great pleasure and honor at being part of such a historic event. This great day was in the tradition of champions emerging from the streets of the lower east side.

Interwoven with the speeches were the sounds of the other boxing events. After the sixth bout, Felix was much relieved when his trainer Charlie said, "Time change. Quick knock-out. This is it. We're on."

Waiting time was over. Felix was escorted from the classroom by a dozen fans in white T-shirts with the word FELIX across their fronts.

Antonio was escorted down a different stairwell and guided through a roped-off path.

As the two climbed into the ring, the crowd exploded with a roar. Antonio and Felix both bowed gracefully and then raised their arms in acknowledgment.

Antonio tried to be cool, but even as the roar was in its first birth, he turned slowly to meet Felix's eyes looking directly into his. Felix nodded his head and Antonio responded. And both as one, just as quickly, turned away to face his own corner.

Bong—bong—bong. The roar turned to stillness.

"Ladies and Gentlemen. *Señores y Señoras.*"

The announcer spoke slowly, pleased at his bilingual efforts.

"Now the moment we have all been waiting for—the main event between two fine young Puerto Rican fighters, products of our lower east side. In this corner, weighing 134 pounds, Felix Vargas. And in this corner, weighing 133 pounds, Antonio Cruz. The winner will represent the Boys Club in the tournament of champions, the Golden Gloves. There will be no draw. May the best man win."

The cheering of the crowd shook the window panes of the old buildings surrounding Tompkins Square Park. At the center of the ring, the referee was giving instructions to the youngsters.

"Keep your punches up. No low blows. No punching on the back of the head. Keep your heads up. Understand. Let's have a clean fight. Now shake hands and come out fighting."

Both youngsters touched gloves and nodded. They turned and danced quickly to their corners. Their head towels and dressing gowns were lifted neatly from their shoulders by their trainers' nimble fingers. Antonio crossed himself. Felix did the same.

BONG! BONG! ROUND ONE. Felix and Antonio turned and faced each other squarely in a fighting pose. Felix wasted no time. He came in fast, head low, half hunched toward his right shoulder, and lashed out with a straight left. He missed a right cross as Antonio slipped the punch and countered with one-two-three lefts that snapped Felix's head back, sending a mild shock coursing through him. If Felix had any small doubt about their friendship affecting their fight, it was being neatly dispelled.

Antonio danced, a joy to behold. His left hand was like a piston pumping jabs one right after another with seeming ease. Felix bobbed and weaved and never stopped boring in. He knew that at long range he was at a disadvantage. Antonio had too much reach on him. Only by coming in close could Felix hope to achieve the dreamed-of knockout.

Antonio knew the dynamite that was stored in his *amigo* brother's fist. He ducked a short right and missed a left hook. Felix trapped him against the ropes just long enough to pour some punishing rights and lefts to Antonio's hard midsection. Antonio slipped away from Felix, crashing two lefts to his head, which set Felix's right ear to ringing.

Bong! Both *amigos* froze a punch well on its way, sending up a roar of approval for good sportsmanship.

Felix walked briskly back to his corner. His right ear had not stopped ringing. Antonio gracefully danced his way toward his stool none the worse, except for glowing glove burns, showing angry red against the whiteness of his midribs.

"Watch that right, Tony." His trainer talked into his ear. "Remember Felix always goes to the body. He'll want you to drop your hands for his overhand left or right. Got it?"

Antonio nodded, spraying water out between his teeth. He felt better as his sore midsection was being firmly rubbed.

Felix's corner was also busy.

"You gotta get in there, fella." Felix's trainer poured water over his curly Afro locks. "Get in there or he's gonna chop you up from way back."

*Bong! Bong!* Round two. Felix was off his stool and rushed Antonio like a bull, sending a hard right to his head. Beads of water exploded from Antonio's long hair.

Antonio, hurt, sent back a blurring barrage of lefts and rights that only meant pain to Felix, who returned with a short left to the head followed by a looping right to the body. Antonio countered with his own flurry, forcing Felix to give ground. But not for long.

Felix bobbed and weaved, bobbed and weaved, occasionally punching his two gloves together.

Antonio waited for the rush that was sure to come. Felix closed in and feinted[3] with his left shoulder and threw his right instead. Lights suddenly exploded inside Felix's head as Antonio slipped the blow and hit him with a pistonlike left catching him flush on the point of his chin.

Bedlam[4] broke loose as Felix's legs momentarily buckled. He fought off a series of rights and lefts and came back with a strong right that taught Antonio respect.

Antonio danced in carefully. He knew Felix had the habit of playing possum when hurt, to sucker an opponent within reach of the powerful bombs he carried in each fist.

A right to the head slowed Antonio's pretty dancing. He answered with his own left at Felix's right eye that began puffing up within three seconds.

Antonio, a bit too eager, moved in too close and Felix had him entangled into a rip-roaring, punching toe-to-toe slugfest that brought the whole Tompkins Square Park screaming to its feet.

---

3. **feinted** (fānt′ əd) *v.* pretended to make a blow.
4. **Bedlam** (bed′ ləm) *n.* condition of noise and confusion.

**evading ▶**
(ē vād′ iŋ) *v.* avoiding

Rights to the body. Lefts to the head. Neither fighter was giving an inch. Suddenly a short right caught Antonio squarely on the chin. His long legs turned to jelly and his arms flailed out desperately. Felix, grunting like a bull, threw wild punches from every direction. Antonio, groggy, bobbed and weaved, **evading** most of the blows. Suddenly his head cleared. His left flashed out hard and straight catching Felix on the bridge of his nose.

Felix lashed back with a haymaker,[5] right off the ghetto streets. At the same instant, his eye caught another left hook from Antonio. Felix swung out trying to clear the pain. Only the frenzied screaming of those along ringside let him know that he had dropped Antonio. Fighting off the growing haze, Antonio struggled to his feet, got up, ducked, and threw a smashing right that dropped Felix flat on his back.

Felix got up as fast as he could in his own corner, groggy but still game. He didn't even hear the count. In a fog, he heard the roaring of the crowd, who seemed to have gone insane. His head cleared to hear the bell sound at the end of the round. He was very glad. His trainer sat him down on the stool.

In his corner, Antonio was doing what all fighters do when they are hurt. They sit and smile at everyone.

The referee signaled the ring doctor to check the fighters out. He did so and then gave his okay. The cold water sponges brought clarity to both *amigo* brothers. They were rubbed until their circulation ran free.

*Bong*! Round three—the final round. Up to now it had been tic-tac-toe, pretty much even. But everyone knew there could be no draw and this round would decide the winner.

This time, to Felix's surprise, it was Antonio who came out fast, charging across the ring. Felix braced himself but couldn't ward off the barrage of punches. Antonio drove Felix hard against the ropes.

The crowd ate it up. Thus far the two had fought with *mucho corazón*. Felix tapped his gloves and commenced his attack anew. Antonio, throwing boxer's caution to the winds, jumped in to meet him.

Both pounded away. Neither gave an inch and neither fell to the canvas. Felix's left eye was tightly closed. Claret red blood poured from Antonio's nose. They fought toe-to-toe.

The sounds of their blows were loud in contrast to the silence of a crowd gone completely mute. The referee was stunned by their savagery.

---

**5. haymaker** punch thrown with full force.

*Bong! Bong! Bong!* The bell sounded over and over again. Felix and Antonio were past hearing. Their blows continued to pound on each other like hailstones.

Finally the referee and the two trainers pried Felix and Antonio apart. Cold water was poured over them to bring them back to their senses.

They looked around and then rushed toward each other. A cry of alarm surged through Tompkins Square Park. Was this a fight to the death instead of a boxing match?

The fear soon gave way to wave upon wave of cheering as the two *amigos* embraced.

No matter what the decision, they knew they would always be champions to each other.

BONG! BONG! BONG! "Ladies and Gentlemen. *Señores* and *Señoras*. The winner and representative to the Golden Gloves Tournament of Champions is . . ."

The announcer turned to point to the winner and found himself alone. Arm in arm the champions had already left the ring.

## ABOUT THE AUTHOR

### Piri Thomas (1928–2011)

Growing up on the streets of New York City's Spanish Harlem, Piri Thomas faced tough challenges like poverty, gangs, and racism. He later related those struggles in his best-selling autobiographical novel, *Down These Mean Streets*. The book introduced many non-Hispanics to the world of *el barrio*—"the neighborhood."

When he was young, Thomas tried to avoid the difficult world around him by surrounding himself with books. "My one island of refuge in *el barrio* was the public library," Thomas has recalled. "I gorged myself on books. . . . Reading helped me to realize that there was a world out there far vaster than the narrow confines of *el barrio*."

# Close Reading Activities

## READ

### Comprehension

Reread all or part of the text to help you answer the following questions.

1. What dream do Antonio and Felix share?
2. What deal do Antonio and Felix make?
3. What do Antonio and Felix do during their time apart?
4. Why are so many people in the neighborhood interested in the fight?
5. Who wins the fight? Explain.

**Research: Clarify Details** Choose at least one detail in this story that is unfamiliar to you and briefly research it. Explain how your research sheds light on an aspect of the story.

**Summarize** Write an objective summary of the story. Remember that an objective summary is free from opinion and evaluation.

### Language Study

**Selection Vocabulary** The following passages are from the story. Identify synonyms for each boldfaced word. Then, use each word in a sentence.

- Antonio then beat the air with … short **devastating** lefts. . . .
- The night air was blurred with **perpetual** motions of left hooks and right crosses.
- Antonio, groggy, bobbed and weaved, **evading** most of the blows.

**Diction and Style** Study this sentence from the story and answer the questions that follow.

> If asked a question about any given fighter, they would immediately zip out from their memory banks divisions, weights, records of fights, knock-outs, technical knock-outs, and draws or losses.

1. **(a)** Use context to define *zip*. **(b)** Why does the author use *zip* instead of a synonym?
2. **(a)** To what does the term *memory banks* refer? **(b)** What is the connotation, or connected image or emotion, of the phrase in context?

**Conventions** Read this passage from the story. Identify the proper nouns in the passage. Explain what effect their use adds to the story.

> Up in the South Bronx, Felix decided to take in a movie in an effort to keep Antonio's face away from his fists. The flick was *The Champion* with Kirk Douglas, the third time Felix was seeing it.

### Academic Vocabulary

The following academic vocabulary words appear in blue in the questions on the facing page.

**effective** **literally** **communication**

Categorize the words. Decide whether you know each one well, a little, or not at all. Look up definitions of the words you are unsure of or do not know.

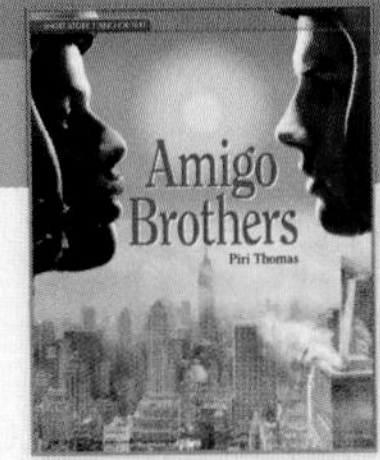


## Literary Analysis

Reread the passages and answer the questions:

**Focus Passage 1** *(p. 136)*

Antonio helped. "It's about our fight, right?" ... We go all the way."

### Key Ideas and Details

1. **(a)** What does Felix want to discuss with Antonio? **(b)** How does Antonio respond? **(c)** What understanding do the boys reach?

### Craft and Structure

2. **(a) Interpret:** Why does the author choose to use Spanish words in passages of dialogue? **(b) Evaluate:** Would the story be as **effective** without the use of Spanish? Explain.

3. **(a)** What does Antonio mean, **literally** and figuratively, by "not pulling punches"? **(b) Interpret:** In what way is this whole passage about "not pulling punches"?

### Integration of Knowledge and Ideas

4. **(a) Compare:** How are the boys alike in their worries, their **communication,** and their hopes? **(b) Synthesize:** In what way might the boys' similarities lead to fierce competition?

**Focus Passage 2** *(p. 141)*

Antonio waited for the rush ... screaming to its feet.

### Key Ideas and Details

1. **(a)** What is happening in this passage? **(b)** What details bring these events to life?

### Craft and Structure

2. **(a)** From what point of view is this sequence narrated? **(b) Evaluate:** How does this point of view affect reader sympathies?

3. **Analyze:** The fight is described as a "rip-roaring, punching, toe-to-toe slugfest." In what way does the author's word choice enhance the pacing and suspense of the passage? Cite details to support your response.

### Integration of Knowledge and Ideas

4. **(a) Analyze:** How does this characterization, or description, of the friends differ from the beginning of the story? **(b) Evaluate:** What does this change indicate about the nature of competition?

## Conflict

A conflict is a struggle between opposing forces. An **internal conflict** takes place within a character's mind. In an **external conflict,** a character struggles against some outside force, such as another person. Reread the story, taking notes on conflict.

1. **(a)** What external conflict do the boys face? **(b)** What internal conflict do they face? **(c)** In what ways are the two conflicts similar and different?

2. **Competition** How does the author develop the idea of competition and cooperation? Cite details from the story in your answer.

# DISCUSS

## From Text to Topic **Group Discussion**

Discuss the following passage with a group of classmates. Take notes. Contribute your own ideas, and support them with examples from the text.

> "Ladies and Gentlemen. *Señores* and *Señoras*. The winner and representative to the Golden Glove Tournament of Champions is..." The announcer turned to point to the winner and found himself alone. Arm in arm, the champions had already left the ring.

**QUESTIONS FOR DISCUSSION**

1. Why does the story not name the winner?
2. What makes both boys "champions"?
3. What insight about competition does this story reveal?

# WRITE

## Writing to Sources **Explanatory Text**

**Assignment**

Write an **analytical essay** in which you identify a theme of "Amigo Brothers" and explore its development.

**Prewriting and Planning** Reread the story, noting details that describe the two friends and the conflicts they face. Analyze the story's title for clues to theme, and look for ways in which the characters' words and actions reveal growth. Then, formulate a statement about the theme, or insight about life revealed in the story.

**Drafting** Begin your draft by introducing your overall analysis of theme. Then, support your analysis by describing ways in which the story's title, plot, and characters' actions reveal theme. Support your ideas by citing specific textual evidence. Conclude your essay by summarizing your findings.

**Revising** Review your draft and rearrange details, where necessary, to strengthen your argument. Use transitions to help readers make connections between your ideas. Add supporting details where needed, and delete details that detract from your main points.

**Editing and Proofreading** Review your word choice, and replace informal or imprecise words with more formal, specific words. Take note of your use of pronouns to be sure that each is used correctly and has a clear antecedent. Proofread carefully to ensure your writing is free from errors in spelling and grammar.

**CONVENTIONS**

Check the pronouns in your essay to ensure they agree in number with their subjects.

## RESEARCH

### Research **Investigate the Topic**

**Healthy and Unhealthy Competition** Although Felix and Antonio fight hard, many readers may view their competition as a healthy one. However, not all competitions are viewed this way.

> **Assignment**
> Conduct research to find a variety of opinions on competition. Use the Internet, library databases, and the library catalog. Take notes by paraphrasing and summarizing ideas, and be sure your notes include your sources. Share your findings in a **visual presentation** for the class.

**PREPARATION FOR ESSAY**

You may use the knowledge you gain during this research assignment to support your claims in an essay you will write at the end of this section.

**Formulate a Plan** Before you begin, create a research plan. Jot down specific questions that will guide your exploration.

**Gather Sources** Once you have completed a research plan, consult a variety of credible sources. For example, you may use library databases to locate journal or magazine articles. Use the Internet to find up-to-date information from a variety of experts on competition.

**Take Notes** Take notes on each source. Jot down what each source says about competition—healthy or unhealthy, positive or negative. Use an organized note-taking strategy:

- Make a source card or spreadsheet column for each source. Number each source 1, 2, 3, and so on.
- As you create each notecard, put the number of the source in the corner of the card or enter the note into the appropriate spreadsheet column.
- Remember to take notes using your own words, and clearly identify direct quotations.

**Synthesize Multiple Sources** Pull together your findings by creating a poster. Draw a line horizontally across a large sheet of poster board. Label the ends *Negative* and *Positive*. Draw points on the line to show the relative attitudes of your different sources toward competition. Briefly label the source's stance, or attitude, above each point and identify the source below.

**Present Ideas** When your poster is complete, display it and present the ideas from negative to positive, expanding on what the labels show. Then, sum up for the class what your diagram reveals about attitudes toward competition.

# Get More From Competition

Christopher Funk

Whether you are in sports or business, whether you compete for fun or profit, there are hidden strategies both to boost your performance and find more enjoyment in the process. Here are five such strategies.

**maximize ▶** (mak´sə mīz´) *v.* make the most of

**First, to maximize your likelihood of winning (whether a game or a contract), forget about winning!**

The more that you think about the outcome, the more mental focus is drained away from the process of getting there. To do your best, all your mental energy needs to be concentrated in the present. If you stay focused on the immediate demands that are right in front of you, winning will take care of itself. A bit cliché, but true.

**Second, think of the contest as an opportunity to stretch yourself. Focus on how you can gain.**

This is particularly valuable when you can think of how you can benefit, even if you end up losing. Perhaps you can gain new insights that will help you compete better the next time around. The attitude that "nothing is gained in a losing effort" not only robs you of potential gains, but makes losing more likely.

**optimal ▶** (äp´tə məl) *adj.* best or most favorable; optimum

**deteriorates ▶** (dē tir´ē ə rāts) *v.* gets worse

**Third, find the middle ground between stress and relaxation. You cannot "force" optimal performance by putting yourself under increased pressure.**

Performance **deteriorates** under high stress. On the other hand, you need a certain amount of stress to shift your mind and body into full gear. So if you tend to be rather lax, fire yourself up. Kick yourself in the pants. Tell yourself that it really does matter and that you must do well. But if you tend to get too serious or worried, take the opposite approach. Bring a dimension of play to your competing. Even when the consequences are important (in fact, especially when they are very important), relax and have some fun. People handle serious situations best when they lighten up. Take this strategy and you'll enjoy yourself more, and you'll perform better.

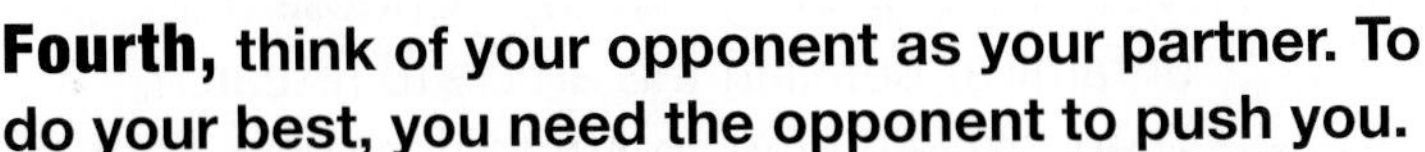

**Fourth, think of your opponent as your partner. To do your best, you need the opponent to push you.** You gain the most when you have tough competitors. Good competition comes about when all competitors are doing well. So appreciate your opponents; without them, you would not be able to reach the same heights of performance. While you want to defeat your opponents, opponents are not enemies.

**Fifth, compete with a sense of deep purpose. If you are simply competing to gain personal benefit (whether material benefit or ego), you are going to perform less well than if you are dedicated to values, goals, and ideals that are beyond yourself.** So know what is important to you and find your center of gravity beyond yourself. . . . Find your mission and you'll perform at your peak. Just as important, you'll have an enduring sense of satisfaction.

# Close Reading Activities

## READ

### Comprehension

Reread all or part of the text to help you answer these questions.

1. What is the purpose of this article?
2. On what does the author advise readers to focus?
3. According to the author, what is better than competing for personal gain?

**Research: Clarify Details** Choose one unfamiliar detail in this article to research. Then, explain how your research sheds light on the article.

**Summarize** Write an objective summary of the article. Remember to leave out opinions and judgements.

### Language Study

**Selection Vocabulary** The following sentences appear in the selection. Define each boldfaced word, and then use the word in a sentence of your own.

- First, to **maximize** your likelihood of winning (whether a game or a contract), forget about winning!
- You cannot "force" **optimal** performance by putting yourself under increased pressure.
- Performance **deteriorates** under high stress.

### Literary Analysis

Reread to answer the questions.

**Focus Passage** *(p. 148)*
Performance deteriorates … and you'll perform better.

#### Key Ideas and Details

1. **(a)** According to the author, what should you do if you are too relaxed? What should you do if you are too worried? **(b)** What is the benefit of having the right **attitude**?

#### Craft and Structure

2. The author uses repetition and parallel structures: "Kick yourself...," and "Tell yourself..." **Analyze:** Explain the effect of these language choices on readers.
3. **(a)** Is the author's tone in this passage formal or informal? **(b) Analyze:** What is the overall effect of the author's tone?

#### Integration of Knowledge and Ideas

4. **(a)** What is the author's overall advice on the challenge of competing? **(b) Evaluate:** Does the author provide **sufficient** support for his main points? Cite details from the text in your response.

### Structure

***Structure*** refers to the organization of a text. Elements that contribute to a text's structure include formatting and the order in which ideas are presented.

1. What is the relationship between the boldfaced headings and the text that follows?
2. How does the structure of this article contribute to its effectiveness?

# DISCUSS • RESEARCH • WRITE

## From Text to Topic **Partner Discussion**

Discuss the following passage with a partner. Contribute your own ideas, and support them with examples from the text.

> So know what is important to you and find your center of gravity beyond yourself.... Find your mission and you'll perform at your peak. Just as important, you'll have an enduring sense of satisfaction.

### QUESTIONS FOR DISCUSSION

1. What does Funk mean by "center of gravity beyond yourself"?
2. For Funk, what is more important in competition, the mind or the body? Explain.

## Research **Investigate the Topic**

**Mind and Body** The mind-body connection is a big topic in sports. It may be that some sports are best played by "mind first" athletes, while others are best played by "body first" athletes.

**Assignment**

Conduct research to define the mind-body connection. Then define and cite examples of athletes who might be considered "mind first" or "body first." Consult Web sites or magazine articles. Take clear notes and identify your sources so that you can easily access the information later. Share your findings in an **informal speech** to the class. Draw a conclusion about which athletes tend to be stronger competitors—those who are "mind first" or those who are "body first."

### PREPARATION FOR ESSAY

You may use the results of your research to support your claims in an essay you will write at the end of this section.

### ACADEMIC VOCABULARY

Academic terms appear in blue on these pages. If these words are not familiar to you, use a dictionary to find their definitions. Then, use the words as you speak and write about the text.

## Writing to Sources **Narrative**

Funk's article gives some specific recommendations for success.

**Assignment**

Write a **fictional narrative** in which a character follows some or all of Funk's advice. Make sure your story has a **resolution,** which may or may not include winning a contest. Follow these steps:

- Introduce characters, setting, and conflict in the exposition.
- Create a smooth progression of plot events that build on one another and lead to a climax.
- Use dialogue and description to develop the character and events.
- Bring events to a satisfying conclusion in the story's resolution.

WEB ARTICLE

# Forget Fun, Embrace Enjoyment

*Adam Naylor, EdD*

After years of sitting and listening to competitive coaches, I am struck by their relationship with fun. They will talk at length about offense, defense, discipline, and effort … and a bit after the fact say, "and yeah, it needs to be fun." Sometimes a shrug of the shoulder accompanies this afterthought. Ultimately, a rather unconvincing **advocacy** for fun. Coaches get regularly called to task by more politically correct sects[1] for being out of touch and borderline abusive … and sometimes rightfully so. Yet, not in this case, the shrug and "well sure I guess it's important," approach to fun is onto something.

**advocacy** ▶ (ad′və kə sē) *n.* support for a particular idea or mission

There is a problem with fun. It is the wrong word that creates the wrong idea … especially at more adult levels of competition (teenage years on). Words matter. They create cognitive schemas[2] and shape behaviors. Fun is the right idea, but the wrong mental message.

Fun sends a message of **trivialness** and purposeless living. Fun, in the pleasurable sense, is hedonistic.[3] This is why

**trivialness** ▶ (triv′ē əl nes) *n.* state of having little importance

1. **more politically correct sects** groups that focus more on ways in which certain ideas or practice might be unjust or give offense to certain groups.
2. **cognitive schemas** (skē′məz) *n.* mental networks of ideas, beliefs, knowledge, and associations.
3. **hedonistic** (hē də nis′ tik) *adj.* pleasure loving.

it does not seem to sit right with many people who are engaged in competitive sport. Fun is a lazy tropical vacation, not an early morning row on the river. Fun is dinner with friends and a movie, not racing around a soccer pitch on a rainy afternoon. The word "fun" occupies space in many minds that does not fit the emotion of striving on the playing field.

So abandon the idea altogether? Certainly not. Refine thinking and reword things a bit.

At the foundation of play is "enjoyment." An activity that engages interest and challenges the individual appropriately. Mihaly Csikszentmihalyi, father of Flow,[4] articulates this concept so well: "[competitive sport] that stretches one's ability is enjoyable"; "after an enjoyable event, we know that we have changed"; "enjoyment happens only as a result of unusual investments of attention" (Csikszentmihalyi and Csikszentmihalyi, 1998). Enjoyment involves effort, both mental and physical. It does not occur during trivial **endeavors,** but rather as part of a purpose driven life. Effortful and purpose driven … sounds like sports.

◀ **endeavors** (en dev´ərz) *n.* attempts; efforts

Sports at all levels ought to be enjoyable. This comes from embracing the many challenges of competition. It also comes from abandoning the juvenile concept of fun. The youngest athletes get enjoyment—they experiment with new techniques, they dare opponents to strike them out, they relish the brisk fall afternoons of play, and they strive with healthy grimaces on their faces. To a casual observer, it would look like they are having fun … sure maybe, but truly they have mastered the enjoyment necessary for success at all stages and ages of sport.

---

4. **Flow** (flō) *n.* a mental state defined by psychologist Mihaly Csikszentmihalyi of being completely absorbed in what you are doing.

## ABOUT THE AUTHOR

### Adam Naylor (b. 1974)

A professor at Boston University, Adam Naylor does not just teach college students. He has also educated Olympic medalists, US Open players, and Stanley Cup champions by using sports psychology as a means to inner and outer success. On the subject of competition, Naylor says that the "hard stuff"—things like diving for the goal and running at full tilt through the finish line—is most meaningful. He adds that "the black and white stuff on the scoreboard or stat sheet" just does not compare.

# Close Reading Activities

## READ

### Comprehension

Reread the text as needed to answer these questions.

1. What is the topic of this article?
2. What main point does the author make about the topic?

**Research: Clarify Details** Research at least one unfamiliar detail in this article. Explain how your research clarified your understanding.

**Summarize** Write an objective summary of the text to confirm your comprehension.

### Language Study

**Selection Vocabulary** Create a word map for each boldfaced word from the selection. Then, use each word in a sentence of your own.

- . . . a rather unconvincing **advocacy** for fun.
- Fun sends a message of **trivialness** and purposeless living.
- It does not occur during trivial **endeavors**....

### Literary Analysis

Reread the passage and answer the following questions.

**Focus Passage** *(pp. 152–153)*
Funs sends a message … striving on the playing field.

#### Key Ideas and Details

1. **(a)** According to Naylor, what message does the word *fun* send? **(b)** How do some athletes **perceive** the word *fun*?

#### Craft and Structure

2. **(a)** How does the author use repetition in this paragraph? **(b) Evaluate:** What is the effect of this repetition?
3. **(a)** What descriptive examples does Naylor use in this paragraph? **(b) Draw Conclusions:** What message about fun does Naylor convey through these examples?

#### Integration of Knowledge and Ideas

4. **(a) Generalize:** What is the author's claim, or main argument? **(b) Evaluate: Explain** how elements of word choice and style help support the claim.

### Persuasive Techniques

A **persuasive technique** is a strategy an author uses to persuade readers. Two common persuasive techniques are the use of **loaded language**—or highly-charged emotional words—and the use of **expert opinions**.

1. **(a)** What do *hedonistic* and *striving* mean? **(b)** How does this loaded language create a contrast?
2. Why does the author **cite** the testimony of Csikszentmihalyi?
3. **Competition** For the author, is competition "fun" or "enjoyment"? Explain how persuasive techniques contrast the two ideas.

# DISCUSS • RESEARCH • WRITE

## From Text to Topic **Debate**

With a partner, informally debate the ideas in the following passage. Support your ideas with details from the text as well as examples drawn from real life.

> Words matter. They create cognitive schemas and shape behaviors. Fun is the right idea, but the wrong mental message.

### QUESTIONS FOR DISCUSSION

1. In contrast to *fun,* what ideas does the word *enjoyment* inspire?
2. Can words really shape behavior by making a difference in how and why we compete? Cite evidence from the text in your discussion.

## Research **Investigate the Topic**

**Coaching and Competition** Adam Naylor begins his argument by mentioning athletic coaches' attitude toward fun.

**Assignment**

Conduct research to find out how professional coaches regard the notion of fun in competitive sports. Use a library database to find journal articles about the topic, or use a variety of online sources to find web articles and media clips. Take clear notes and carefully identify your sources so that you can easily access the information later. Record your findings in an **annotated listing**.

### PREPARATION FOR ESSAY

You may use the results of your research to support your ideas in the essay you will write at the end of this section.

## Writing to Sources **Argument**

In the article, Naylor makes the claim that even young athletes know how to get enjoyment from competition.

**Assignment**

Write an **argument** in which you agree or disagree with Naylor about young athletes and competition. Follow these steps as you write your argument:

- State your claim telling whether you agree or disagree with Naylor.
- In the body of your essay, state your reasons, supporting them with examples from the text and from your own research.
- Organize your details logically, using transitions to connect your ideas.
- Use a formal style.
- Sum up your argument in a concluding paragraph or section.

### ACADEMIC VOCABULARY

Academic terms appear in blue on these pages. Use the words as you speak and write about the text.

# Video Game Competitiveness, Not Violence, Spurs Aggression, Study Suggests

*Jennifer LaRue Huget*

**aggressive** ▶ (ə gres′iv) *adj.* forceful, especially in a destructive or mean way

**spur** ▶ (spʉr) *v.* cause

For years, researchers having been trying to tease out the relationship between video game violence and **aggressive** behavior on the part of people who play such games. So far, it's seemed that violence in video games may **spur** aggression in players, at least in the first few minutes after the game is played.

A study published Aug. 17 in the American Psychological Association journal "Psychology of Violence" adds the useful insight that it might not be the games' violent content itself that sparks aggression but instead their level of competitiveness.

In a series of small experiments involving college undergraduates, researchers had participants play one of two games that were equally matched for competitiveness, difficulty and pace of action. One of the games had been determined to be substantially more violent than the other. When the games ended, participants took part in a second task they thought to be unrelated to the game-playing experiment (which they had been told was about eye movement, not aggressive behavior): They were asked to prepare a hot-sauce mixture for a taster who they knew had reported a dislike for hot and spicy food. Those who played the violent video game were no more likely to create a large quantity of spicy food—an act that has been established in the realm of psychological research as an aggressive act—than those who played the nonviolent game.

But in a second experiment, games were selected on the basis of how competitive they were. After the game playing, participants again took part in the "hot sauce paradigm"[1] portion of the research. Those whose games had been determined to be more competitive were far more likely to create large quantities of very spicy sauce for their poor tasters. They also had significantly higher heart rates.

The authors point out that many violent video games also tend to be extremely competitive. So separating out the effect of the level of competitiveness could open new channels for both understanding the link between video games and aggressive behavior and also, perhaps, figuring out how to **blunt** that effect.

**blunt** ▶ (blunt) *v.* lessen; make less forceful

1. **paradigm** (par′ə dīm′) *n.* approach based on a theory.

## READ • WRITE

### Comprehension

Reread the text as needed to answer these questions.

1. What does the article say about video games?
2. **(a)** What happened in the first **experiment**? **(b)** How did the second experiment vary from the first one?

### Language Study

**Selection Vocabulary** Define each boldfaced word from the selection, and use the word in a sentence of your own.

- **aggressive**
- **spur**
- **blunt**

### Literary Analysis

Reread the selection to answer the following questions.

**Key Ideas and Details**

1. **(a)** In the past, what did researchers believe caused aggressive behavior in people who play violent video games? **(b)** What new information on this topic appeared in the study published in "Psychology of Violence"?

**Craft and Structure**

2. **(a)** What word or phrase most clearly shows the relationship between the two experiments in the study? **(b) Draw Conclusions:** What type of relationship does this word convey?
3. **Deduce:** Why does the author use the words *could* and *perhaps* in the last sentence?

**Integration of Knowledge and Ideas**

4. **(a)** What is the main **insight** in this article? **(b) Speculate:** How might video game developers respond to this article? Explain.

### Writing to Sources **Informative Text**

This article reports on the relationship between aggression and competition.

**Assignment**

Write an **essay** in which you evaluate the author's conclusion. Introduce your main idea, and then support it using details from the text and outside research. Choose precise details to make your ideas clear, and strive to achieve a formal tone.

**ACADEMIC VOCABULARY**

Academic terms appear in blue on these pages. If these words are not familiar to you, use a dictionary to find their definitions. Then, use the words as you speak and write about the text.

MAGAZINE ARTICLE

# Win Some, Lose Some

Charles Osgood

**aversion** ▶ (ə vʉr′zhən) *n.* intense dislike

The victor may get the spoils,[1] but the true rewards go to those who are good sports. We all have little victories and defeats in our lives, and some big ones too. Rare is the day that we don't add to both our "Win" and "Loss" columns. Obviously we would like the Ws to outweigh the Ls, but our appetite for victory and our **aversion** to defeat seem to have sharpened in recent years. We don't handle either one very well anymore.

1. **the victor may get the spoils** person who wins not only has the pleasure of winning but gets additional benefits.

The role models we get from the worlds of entertainment, sports and politics have not been terribly helpful. You'd think that these public individuals, who must deal with winning and losing on a regular basis, would set a sportsmanlike example for the rest of us.

Whatever happened to the old gladiator mantra[2] "We who are about to die salute you"? It gets me to thinking about that Joe Raposo song "(Here's to the) Winners." Is it any surprise that he never bothered to write a song called "Here's to the Losers"? (Truth be told, someone else did.)

It feels wonderful to win, but how should winners express their satisfaction in the moment of victory? How should they comport themselves in the presence of those they've vanquished? As if they had just conquered Nazi Germany or found a cure for cancer? Conversely, how should the losers express their frustration and disappointment in moments of defeat? A sense of perspective is difficult to come by in hard-fought contests.

For their part, today's sports fans haven't come that far from the days of the gladiator. They know that their teams can't win 'em all, but they do want to see the thrill of victory and the agony of defeat acted out. And so the players, who are also players in the theatrical sense, celebrate not only game victories but completely routine plays as well. You'll see some NFL players doing a little dance to taunt the opposition every time they catch a pass or make a tackle. It's a far cry from the days when Tom Landry of the Dallas Cowboys would tell Hollywood Henderson to try to look as if he'd done it before. Landry himself used to stand stoically on the sidelines like a man waiting for a bus. You could not tell from his facial expression or bearing whether his team was ahead or behind.

In the poem "If," his famous litany[3] of what it takes to "be a man, my son," Rudyard Kipling observes, "If you can meet with triumph and disaster,/And treat those two **impostors** just the same...." They are impostors, you know. A musician friend of mine has a sign on his studio wall that reads "Show Me a Good Loser and I'll Show You a Loser!" Do musicians think in terms of winners and losers too? Are they that competitive?

◀ **impostors** (im päs′tərz) *n.* people or things pretending to be someone or something else

2. **mantra** (man′trə) *n.* statement repeated often, much like or as a chant or song refrain.
3. **litany** (lit′ ′n ē) *n.* list.

Many of them are. For in the arts, as in virtually every kind of human endeavor, there is an element of competition.

There's a story, apocryphal[4] perhaps, about Fritz Kreisler, the virtuoso violinist, sitting in the audience at a Berlin Philharmonic concert next to pianist Josef Hofmann. The twelve-year-old prodigy Jascha Heifetz was performing a solo in Tchaikovsky's Violin Concerto in D Major.

Nobel Peace Prize Medal

"It's very hot in here, isn't it?" Kreisler is supposed to have whispered to Hofmann between movements.

Without a moment's hesitation, Hofmann is said to have whispered back, "Not for pianists."

Artists may not like to admit it, but in the arts, as in virtually every endeavor, there is an element of competition. It's human nature to want to do better than somebody else. Victory is better than defeat, just as surely as health, wealth and wisdom are better than sickness, poverty and ignorance. With winning comes not only the thrill of victory but also the gold medal, the job, the Oscar, the Nobel, the presidency or the Lombardi Trophy—the prize that goes to the winner of the Super Bowl.

That coveted award is named for Vince Lombardi, the legendary football coach often credited (if "credit" is the appropriate word here) with saying "Winning isn't everything. It's the only thing!" In fact, he never said it. It may have been another coach, UCLA's Red Sanders, who uttered those words.

While he was in college, Lombardi was one of Fordham University's "Seven Blocks of Granite." (Fordham is my alma mater.[5]) After graduation, he taught Latin and chemistry and coached at St. Cecilia High School (also my alma mater) in Englewood, New Jersey. What he said, according to people there who knew him well, was "Winning isn't everything, but wanting to win is."

Later, as a coach for the Green Bay Packers, he pushed his players to work hard. And you bet he wanted to imbue[6] them with a strong desire to win—but not at all costs. That would have been inconsistent with character. And to Lombardi, character was what counted most—on the field and in life.

In the end, we do seem to save our respect for the individuals who show the most character when faced with situations of triumph or loss. We admire

4. **apocryphal** (ə päk′rə fəl) *adj.* most likely not true but repeated as if true nevertheless.
5. **alma mater** (al′mə mät′ər) school, university, or college that someone attended.
6. **imbue** (im byo͞o′) *v.* to convey in a way that causes someone or something to become filled with or saturated by what is conveyed.

people like Joe DiMaggio, Jacqueline Kennedy, Billie Jean King, Michael Jordan and Christopher Reeve[7]—a partial list, but you get the idea.

For all of its melodrama and legal wrangling, even our drawn-out presidential election last fall may have taught us some valuable lessons. When he ultimately conceded the contest, Vice-President Gore[8] made a statement that was sportsmanlike and unequivocal. He called on those who had voted for him to join him in supporting President Bush and wishing him well.

At his inauguration a month later, Bush publicly thanked President Clinton for his years of service and acknowledged Gore as a worthy opponent. It was an election campaign "conducted with spirit and ended with grace," Bush said. That was graceful on his part.

I recently took my seventeen-year-old son, Jamie, a high school senior, to the campus of a college to which he was applying on an early decision basis. I waited with other parents as our children went in for their interviews. In most cases, as each one **emerged**, you could tell right away whether the outcome was a W or an L. Some of the kids came running out grinning and with thumbs up. Others came out looking crushed or in tears. A few parents of the latter seemed angry and berated their offspring for not having done well enough. When Jamie came through the door, I caught his eye across the room, and he smiled. I swear there was no way to tell from his face or manner how things had gone. I could not have been more proud.

◀ **emerged** (ē murjd′) *v.* came out

7. **Christopher Reeve** actor who became paralyzed but went on to become a spokesperson for those with spinal cord injuries.
8. **Vice-President Gore** candidate who lost to George W. Bush in the presidential election of 2000.

## ABOUT THE AUTHOR

### Charles Osgood (b. 1933)

Known for his witty comments and signature bow tie, Charles Osgood has entertained radio listeners and television watchers for decades. Osgood, who writes his own stories, gets up each morning at 2:30 so that he can arrive in the office by 3:30 and get started on the morning news cycle. An economist by training, Osgood says he just fell into radio. He developed his own unique style by adding "little rhymes" to his reports. This habit earned him the title of "poet in residence" and eventually helped lead to jobs in television. In addition to broadcasting, Osgood has appeared on screen as the narrator of Dr. Seuss's *Horton Hears a Who*. He is also the author of six books and the winner of many prizes and awards for journalism.

# Close Reading Activities

## READ

### Comprehension

Reread to answer these questions.

1. How has sportsmanship decreased, according to Osgood?
2. What qualities should both winners and losers have?
3. What did Osgood's son do that made the author proud?

**Research: Clarify Details** Choose at least one unfamiliar detail in this article, and research it. Then, explain how your research clarifies your understanding of the article.

**Summarize** Write an objective summary of the article. Do not include your opinions or evaluations.

### Language Study

**Selection Vocabulary** Define each boldfaced word from the text, and then write a synonym for each.

- …our **aversion** to defeat…
- …treat those two **impostors** just the same. …
- As each one **emerged,** you could tell…

### Literary Analysis

Reread the focus passage and answer the following questions.

**Focus Passage** *(p. 160)*
Artists may not like to admit it... the winner of the Super Bowl.

#### Key Ideas and Details

1. According to Osgood, what desire is "just human nature"?

#### Craft and Structure

2. **(a)** What sound devices are present in the phrase "health, wealth, and wisdom"? What effect is created? **(b) Contrast:** What effect is created by the phrase "sickness, poverty, and ignorance"? **(c) Analyze:** Why do you think Osgood chose these phrases to present his ideas?
3. **(a)** Find examples of hyperbole, or exaggeration, in this passage. **(b) Connect:** In what way does the use of hyperbole help Osgood make his point?

#### Integration of Knowledge and Ideas

4. **(a) Generalize:** What is the main idea of this passage? **(b) Interpret:** What is the author's **attitude** toward winning?

### Rhetorical Devices

A **rhetorical device** is the use of language to persuade or **convince** a reader. Take notes on the author's use of rhetorical devices.

1. **(a)** Cite two examples of *rhetorical questions,* or questions the author uses to make a point. **(b)** What ideas do the implied answers convey?
2. **Competition (a)** Why are the words *winners* and *losers* repeated so often in this article? **(b) Infer:** What larger insight about competition does Osgood convey? Explain.

# DISCUSS • RESEARCH • WRITE

## From Text to Topic **Panel Discussion**

Discuss the following passage with a group of classmates. Take notes as you listen. When you speak, contribute your own ideas and support them with examples from the text.

> "For their part, today's sports fans haven't come far from the days of the gladiator. They know that their teams can't win 'em all, but they do want to see the thrill of victory and the agony of defeat acted out. And so the players, who are also players in the theatrical sense, celebrate not only game victories but completely routine plays as well."

### QUESTIONS FOR DISCUSSION

1. What comparisons does Osgood make in the passage?
2. What insights about competitive sports does the passage reveal?

## Research **Investigate the Topic**

**A Model of Character** Osgood cites examples from Vince Lombardi's life in his arguments.

**Assignment**

Conduct research to learn more about Lombardi's views on triumph and loss in competition. Find a biography in your library's online database or a good online encyclopedia. Take clear notes and carefully identify your sources so that you can easily access the information later. Share your findings in an **informal presentation** for the class.

### PREPARATION FOR ESSAY

You may use the results of your research to support your ideas in the essay you will write at the end of this section.

### ACADEMIC VOCABULARY

Academic terms appear in blue on these pages. If these words are unfamiliar, look up their definitions in a dictionary. Then, use the words as you to speak and write about the text.

## Writing to Sources **Argument**

Osgood argues that "true rewards go to those who are good sports."

**Assignment**

Write an **argument** in which you either agree or disagree with Osgood's claim. Follow these steps:

- State your own claim clearly and introduce opposing claims.
- Support your claims with relevant evidence from the text and from additional research. Refute opposing claims.
- Logically organize your argument, and use transitional words, phrases, and clauses to create cohesion.
- Establish and maintain a formal style through word choice and tone.

# Orlando Magic

## Leroy Neiman

# Close Reading Activities

## READ • DISCUSS • WRITE

### Comprehension

Study the painting to answer the following questions.

**1.** Where does the action in this painting take place?

**2.** Describe what is happening in the painting.

### Critical Analysis

#### Key Ideas and Details

**1. (a)** Which player is identified by name? **(b) Speculate:** Why might the artist have chosen to identify only one player?

#### Craft and Structure

**2. (a) Distinguish:** Describe the qualities of the colors the artist uses in this painting. **(b) Analyze:** Which colors draw the eye? **(c) Evaluate:** Why do they do so?

**3. (a) Analyze:** Which images in the painting are in focus? Which images are out of focus? **(b) Evaluate:** What effect does the contrast between clear and blurry images have upon the viewer?

#### Integration of Knowledge and Ideas

**4. Synthesize:** What ideas about competition does this painting **illustrate**? Explain, using details from the painting to support your response.

**ACADEMIC VOCABULARY**

Academic terms appear in blue on these pages. If these words are not familiar to you, use a dictionary to find their definitions. Then, use them as you speak and write about the text.

### From Text to Topic **Debate**

Form teams to **debate** this question: Is this painting mainly about competition, or is it mainly about a specific player? Discuss the painting with your team to prepare.

### Writing to Sources **Argument**

Write a brief **argument** in which you compare and contrast the depiction of competition in this painting with the depiction of competition in another nonfiction selection in this section. Explain and support reasons why one of the two selections is a more accurate, meaningful, or exciting way to show competition. As you incorporate specific details from the painting and from the other selection, be sure to use words, phrases, and clauses to clarify the relationships between your ideas.

# Assessment: Synthesis

## Speaking and Listening: **Group Discussion**

**Competition and Conflict** The texts in this section vary in genre, length, style, and perspective. However, all of the texts explore ideas about competition and conflict. The ways in which we view competition, and the things we gain and lose as we compete, are related to the Big Question addressed in this unit: **Does every conflict have a winner?**

▲ Refer to the selections you read in Part 3 as you complete the activities on this assessment.

### Assignment

**Conduct discussions.** With a small group of classmates, conduct a discussion about the issues of competition and conflict. Refer to the texts in this section, other texts you have read, and your personal experience and knowledge to support your ideas. Begin your discussion by addressing the following questions:

- How does competition create conflict?
- How can our attitudes toward competing change our experiences?
- How do competition and conflict bring out the best and the worst in us?
- How can we compete in positive ways?

**Summarize and present your ideas.** After you have fully explored the topic, summarize your discussion and present your findings to the class as a whole.

## Criteria for Success

✓ **Organizes the group effectively**
Appoint a group leader and a timekeeper. The group leader should present the discussion questions. The timekeeper should make sure the discussion takes no longer than 20 minutes.

✓ **Maintains focus of discussion**
As a group, stay on topic and avoid straying into other subject areas.

✓ **Involves all participants equally and fully**
No one person should monopolize the conversation. Rather, everyone should take turns speaking and contributing ideas.

✓ **Follows the rules for collegial discussion**
As each group member speaks, others should listen carefully. Build on one another's ideas, and support viewpoints and opinions with sound reasoning and evidence. Express disagreement respectfully.

**USE NEW VOCABULARY**

As you speak and share ideas, work to use the vocabulary words you have learned in this section. The more you use new words, the more you will "own" them.

## Writing: **Narrative**

**Competition and Conflict** We all face conflicts. Some of these conflicts relate to competition in sports, in school, and even in friendships. Often, such conflicts change how we think or behave, in big or little ways.

> **Assignment**
> Write a **personal narrative,** or a true story of events from your life. Begin by introducing a conflict you have experienced that is related to competition. Tell what happened to increase the conflict and describe if and how you resolved it. In your conclusion, reflect on what you learned or how you changed as a result of your experience.

### Criteria for Success

**Purpose/Focus**

✓ **Connects specific incidents with larger ideas**
Make meaningful connections between your experiences and the texts you have read in this section.

✓ **Clearly conveys the significance of the story**
Provide a conclusion in which you reflect on what you experienced.

**Organization**

✓ **Sequences events logically**
Structure your narrative so that individual events build on one another to create a coherent whole.

**Development of Ideas/Elaboration**

✓ **Supports insights**
Include both personal examples and details from the texts you have read in this section.

✓ **Uses narrative techniques effectively**
Although a personal narrative is a work of nonfiction, it may include storytelling elements like those found in fiction. Consider using dialogue to help readers "hear" how characters sound.

**Language**

✓ **Uses description effectively**
Use vivid descriptive details to help readers picture settings and characters.

**Conventions**

✓ **Does not have errors**
Check your narrative to eliminate errors in grammar, spelling, and punctuation.

**WRITE TO EXPLORE**

Writing is a way to explore what you feel and think: You may change your mind or get new ideas as you work. As you write your personal narrative, explore your ideas on the topic of competition and conflict.

## Writing to Sources: Argument

**Competition and Conflict** The readings in this section present many ideas about competition and conflict. They raise questions, such as the following, about various aspects of competition and conflict.

- How can competition help us become better people?
- How can communication change our experience of conflict and competition?
- What is the relationship between competition and aggression?
- Can we learn to win and lose with grace and dignity?

Focus on the question that intrigues you the most, and then complete the following assignment.

### Assignment

Write an **argumentative essay** in which you state and defend a claim about values, problems, or advice related to competition and conflict. Build evidence for your claim by analyzing the presentation of competition and conflict in two or more texts from this section. Clearly present, develop, and support your ideas with examples and details from the texts.

## Prewriting and Planning

**Choose texts.** Review the texts in the section to determine which ones you will cite in your essay. Select at least two texts that will provide strong material to support your argument.

**Gather details and craft a working thesis, or claim.** Use a chart like the one shown to develop your claim.

**Focus Question: How can communication change our experience of conflict and competition?**

| Text | Passage | Notes |
|---|---|---|
| "Amigo Brothers" | "No pulling punches. We go all the way." | Tony and Felix talk about their competition and how they will deal with it. |
| "Forget Fun, Embrace Enjoyment" | "Words matter. They create cognitive schemas and shape behaviors." | Author argues that good competition is enjoyable and brings out our best. |
| **Example Claim:** Communicating our ideas can help us understand and benefit from competition and conflict. | | |

**Prepare counterarguments.** Note possible objections to your claim and evidence. Plan to include and address the strongest of these counterclaims in your essay.

**INCORPORATE RESEARCH**

As you write your argument, refer to the research you conducted as you read the texts in this section. Choose appropriate details from your research to support your claims and build your argument.

## Drafting

**Structure your ideas and evidence.** Create an informal outline or list of ideas you want to present. Decide where you will include evidence and which evidence you will use to support each of your main points.

**Address counterclaims.** Strong argumentation takes differing ideas into account and addresses them directly. As you organize your ideas, build in sections in which you explain opposing opinions or differing interpretations. Then, write a reasoned, well-supported response to those counterclaims.

**Frame and connect ideas.** Write an introduction that will grab readers' attention. Consider beginning with a compelling quotation or a surprising detail. Use words, phrases, and clauses to link the major sections of your essay and to clarify the relationships between your claims and the evidence that supports them. Finally, sum up your ideas in a strong concluding paragraph.

## Revising and Editing

**Review content.** Make sure that your claim is clearly stated and that you have supported it with convincing evidence from the texts in this section. Underline main ideas in your paper and confirm that each one is supported. Add more proof as needed.

**Review style.** Revise to cut wordy passages. Check to be sure you have found the clearest, simplest way to communicate your ideas. Review your word choice to ensure your tone is objective and your style is formal.

### CITE RESEARCH CORRECTLY

Take note of the evidence from outside sources you have included in your argument. Follow accepted conventions to cite your sources. See the Citing Sources pages in the Introductory Unit of this textbook for additional guidance.

### Self-Evaluation Rubric

Use the following criteria to evaluate the effectiveness of your essay.

| Criteria | Rating Scale |
|---|---|
| **Purpose/Focus** Introduces a precise claim and distinguishes the claim from alternative or opposing claims; provides a concluding section that follows from and supports the argument presented | *not very ... very*<br>1 2 3 4 |
| **Organization** Establishes a logical organization; uses words, phrases and clauses to link the major sections of the text, create cohesion, and clarify relationships among claims, reasons, and evidence, and between claims and counterclaims | 1 2 3 4 |
| **Development of Ideas/Elaboration** Develops the claim and counterclaims fairly, supplying evidence for each while pointing out the strengths and limitations of both | 1 2 3 4 |
| **Language** Establishes and maintains a formal style and objective tone | 1 2 3 4 |
| **Conventions** Attends to the norms and conventions of the discipline | 1 2 3 4 |

# Independent Reading

## Titles for Extended Reading

In this unit, you have read texts in a variety of genres. Continue to read on your own. Select works that you enjoy, but challenge yourself to explore new authors and works of increasing depth and complexity. The titles suggested below will help you get started.

### INFORMATIONAL TEXT

**Geeks: How Two Lost Boys Rode the Internet out of Idaho**
by Jon Katz
Villard Books, 2000
EXEMPLAR TEXT

In this **nonfiction** book, Jesse and Eric, two computer "geeks" with few social skills or future prospects, meet the reporter Jon Katz, who convinces them that they can use their computer savvy to create a better life.

**Discoveries: Working It Out**

What role does conflict play in social studies, science, music, and mathematics? The **essays** and **stories** in this book explore different types of conflicts and how they are worked out.

**The Emperor's Silent Army**
by Jane O'Connor

In 1974, farmers digging in China uncovered an army of life-sized clay soldiers buried for over 2,000 years. This work of **historical nonfiction** tells that story.

### LITERATURE

**The Devil's Arithmetic**
by Jane Yolen

In this **historical novel,** a girl finds herself whisked back in time to a Polish village to experience firsthand the horrors her relatives experienced during the Holocaust.

**The Collected Poems of Langston Hughes**
by Langston Hughes
Vintage, 1994
EXEMPLAR TEXT

Langston Hughes was just nineteen when his first poem, "The Negro Speaks of Rivers," was published. This collection of **poetry** spans Hughes's long and brilliant career.

**White Fang and The Call of the Wild**
by Jack London

*White Fang* tells the story of a wild wolf who suffers hardships and cruelty until a man adopts him. In *The Call of the Wild,* a pampered dog is stolen from his home and forced to become a sled dog in the Yukon. In both novels, animals rely on instinct to survive in brutal environments.

**Heat**
by Mike Lupica
Philomel, 2006

Michael Arroyo is such a skilled pitcher that coaches of rival baseball teams demand proof of his age. In this **novel,** Michael must struggle to find a way to play the game that he loves and to cope with his difficult home life.

**ONLINE TEXT SET**

ARTICLE
**The Fall of the Hindenburg** Michael Morrison

NOVEL EXCERPT
***from* Letters from Rifka** Karen Hesse

EDITORIAL
**Veteran Returns, Becomes Symbol** Minneapolis Star and Tribune

## Preparing to Read Complex Texts

**Attentive Reading** As you read on your own, ask yourself questions like these to enrich your reading experience.

**When reading narratives, ask yourself...**

### Comprehension: **Key Ideas and Details**

- Can I clearly picture the setting of the story? Which details help me do so?
- Can I picture the characters clearly in my mind? Why or why not?
- Do the characters speak and act like real people? Why or why not?
- Which characters do I like? Why? Which characters do I dislike? Why?
- Do I understand why the characters act as they do? Why or why not?
- What does the story mean to me? Does it express a meaning or an insight I find important and true?

### Text Analysis: **Craft and Structure**

- Does the story grab my attention right from the beginning? Why or why not?
- Do I want to keep reading? Why or why not?
- Can I follow the sequence of events in the story? Am I confused at any point? If so, what information would make the sequence clearer?
- Do the characters change as the story progresses? If so, do their changes seem believable?
- Are there any passages that I find especially moving, interesting, or well written? If so, why?

### Connections: **Integration of Knowledge and Ideas**

- How is this story similar to and different from other stories I have read?
- Do I care what happens to the characters? Do I sympathize with them? Why or why not?
- How do my feelings toward the characters affect my experience of reading the story?
- Did the story teach me something new or cause me to look at something in a new way? If so, what did I learn?
- Would I recommend this story to others? Why or why not?
- Would I like to read other works by this author? Why or why not?

# UNIT 2

THE BIG ?

# What should we learn?

## UNIT PATHWAY

PART 1
**SETTING EXPECTATIONS**

- INTRODUCING THE BIG QUESTION
- CLOSE READING WORKSHOP

PART 2
**TEXT ANALYSIS**
GUIDED EXPLORATION

EXPLORING IDEAS

PART 3
**TEXT SET**
DEVELOPING INSIGHT

MOTIVATION

PART 4
**DEMONSTRATING INDEPENDENCE**

- INDEPENDENT READING
- ONLINE TEXT SET

### CLOSE READING TOOL

Use this tool to practice the close reading strategies you learn.

### STUDENT eTEXT

Bring learning to life with audio, video, and interactive tools.

### ONLINE WRITER'S NOTEBOOK

Easily capture notes and complete assignments online.

Find all Digital Resources at **pearsonrealize.com.**

# Introducing the Big Question

## What should we learn?

Everyone has their own ideas about what is important to learn. Some people believe we should learn information that helps us develop practical skills. Others believe we should explore topics driven by our curiosity and talents.

When you think about what we should learn, remember that knowledge includes skills you learn in school and lessons you learn from others. It also includes information that helps you understand other cultures, and ideas that inspire you to investigate the world around you. No matter what is most important to you, the drive to discover new things is something we all have in common.

## Exploring the Big Question

**Collaboration: Group Discussion** Start thinking about the Big Question by making a list of things you believe are important to learn. Describe an example for each of the following:

- A skill that could save someone's life
- A subject you would like to study in school
- A job that requires specific knowledge
- An idea that might make the world a better place
- A personal interest of yours

With a small group, discuss why you think some of these items are more important to learn than others. During your discussion, speak when it is your turn and listen to others without interrupting. Assign a discussion leader to keep ideas moving forward and a group recorder to list the items in the order of importance the group agrees to support. Ask a timekeeper to monitor your discussion and limit it to fifteen minutes. Finally, choose a speaker to present your group's ideas to the class.

**Connecting to the Literature** The texts in this unit explore the different ways we learn—from experience, from others, and from ourselves. Each reading will give you additional insight into the Big Question.

## Vocabulary

**Acquire and Use Academic Vocabulary** The term "academic vocabulary" refers to words you typically encounter in scholarly and literary texts and in technical and business writing. Review the definitions of these academic vocabulary words. Then, practice using these words in your writing and academic discussions.

**analyze** (an′ə līz′) *v.* break into parts in order to study closely

**discover** (di skuv′ər) *v.* find something hidden or previously unknown; find out

**evaluate** (ē val′yo͞o āt′) *v.* judge or rate

**examine** (eg zam′ ən) *v.* study in depth in order to find or check something

**explore** (ek splôr′) *v.* travel through an unfamiliar area to find out what it is like; thoroughly discuss a topic

**facts** (fakts) *n.* true information about a topic

**inquire** (in kwīr′) *v.* ask someone for information

**investigate** (in ves′tə gāt′) *v.* examine thoroughly

**Gather Vocabulary Knowledge** Additional words related to learning are listed below. Categorize the words by deciding whether you know each one well, know it a little bit, or do not know it at all.

| | | |
|---|---|---|
| **curiosity** | **interview** | **question** |
| **experiment** | **knowledge** | **understand** |
| **information** | | |

Then, do the following:

1. Write the definitions of the words you know.
2. Verify the definitions by looking up each word in a print or online dictionary. Revise your definitions as needed.
3. Continue to use the dictionary to look up the meanings and pronunciations of the unknown words.
4. Then, write a paragraph, using all the vocabulary words, about the types of things you think are important to learn.

# Close Reading Workshop

In this workshop, you will learn an approach to reading that will deepen your understanding of literature and will help you better appreciate the author's craft. The workshop includes models for close reading, discussion, research, and writing. After you have reviewed the strategies and models, practice your skills with the Independent Practice selection.

## CLOSE READING: **NONFICTION**

In Part 2 of this unit you will focus on reading various types of nonfiction. Use these strategies as you read the texts.

### Comprehension: **Key Ideas and Details**

- Read first to unlock basic meaning.
- Use context clues to help you determine the meanings of unfamiliar words.
- Identify unfamiliar details that you might need to clarify through research.
- Distinguish between what is stated directly and what must be inferred.

**Ask yourself questions such as these:**

- What is the author's central idea or thesis?
- What evidence does the author present to explain or support the central idea?

### Text Analysis: **Craft and Structure**

- Think about the genre of the work and how the author presents ideas.
- Analyze the overall structure and organization of the work.
- Consider how the author's word choice expresses his or her attitude toward the subject or audience.

**Ask yourself questions such as these:**

- What is the author's point of view or opinion? How does the author's point of view affect my understanding of the topic?
- What is the author's purpose in writing this piece?

### Connections: **Integration of Knowledge and Ideas**

- Look for relationships among key ideas. Identify causes and effects, and comparisons and contrasts.
- Analyze the author's arguments and evaluate the supporting evidence.
- Compare and contrast this work with other nonfiction texts you have read.

**Ask yourself questions such as these:**

- How has this work increased my knowledge of a subject, issue, or event?
- Have I changed my attitude or beliefs based on the information in the selection? Why or why not?

## Read

As you read this excerpt, take note of the annotations that model ways to closely read the text.

### Reading Model

#### from *Freedom Walkers: The Story of the Montgomery Bus Boycott* by Russell Freedman

Not so long ago in Montgomery, Alabama, the color of your skin determined where you could sit on a public bus.[1] If you happened to be an African American, you had to sit in the back of the bus, even if there were empty seats up front.

Back then, racial segregation was the rule throughout the American South. Strict laws—called "Jim Crow" laws—enforced a system of white supremacy that discriminated against blacks and kept them in their place as second-class citizens.[2]

People were separated by race from the moment they were born in segregated hospitals until the day they were buried in segregated cemeteries. Blacks and whites did not attend the same schools, worship in the same churches, eat in the same restaurants, sleep in the same hotels, drink from the same water fountains, or sit together in the same movie theaters.

In Montgomery, it was against the law for a white person and a Negro to play checkers on public property or ride together in a taxi.[3]

Most southern blacks were denied their right to vote. The biggest obstacle was the poll tax, a special tax that was required of all voters but was too costly for many blacks and for poor whites as well. Voters also had to pass a literacy test to prove that they could read, write, and understand the U.S. Constitution. These tests were often rigged to disqualify even highly educated blacks. Those who overcame the obstacles and insisted on registering as voters faced threats, harassment, and even physical violence. As a result, African Americans in the South could not express their grievances in the voting booth, which, for the most part, was closed to them. But there were other ways to protest, and one day a half century ago, the black citizens in Montgomery rose up in protest and united to demand their rights—by walking peacefully.[4]

It all started on a bus.[5]

**Key Ideas and Details**

**1** Quick research reveals that Freedman's book was published in 2006; by using the phrase "Not so long ago," the author emphasizes that segregation is part of our recent history.

**Craft and Structure**

**2** The author uses highly charged language such as "white supremacy" and "kept them in their place" to reveal his negative attitude toward segregation.

**Key Ideas and Details**

**3** These examples vividly show how "Jim Crow" laws affected people's lives.

**Integration of Knowledge and Ideas**

**4** This paragraph builds to its main idea—African Americans finally "rose up in protest."

**Craft and Structure**

**5** The author uses *foreshadowing* by hinting at events to come. This sentence engages readers and makes them curious about what "started on a bus."

## Jo Ann Robinson

Looking back, she remembered it as the most humiliating experience of her life, "a deep hurt that would not heal."[6] It had happened just before Christmas in 1949. She was about to visit relatives in Cleveland, Ohio, where she would spend the holidays.

Earlier that day she had driven out to Dannelly Field, the Montgomery, Alabama, airport, and checked her luggage for the flight to Cleveland. Then she drove back to the campus of Alabama State, an all-black college where she had been hired that fall as a professor of English. After parking her car in the campus garage, she took her armful of Christmas gifts, walked to the nearest bus stop, and waited for a ride back to the airport.[7]

Soon a Montgomery City Lines bus rolled into view and pulled up at the stop. Balancing her packages, Jo Ann Robinson stepped aboard and dropped her dime into the fare box. She saw that the bus was nearly empty. Only two other passengers were aboard—a black man in a seat near the back and a white woman in the third seat from the front. Without thinking, Robinson took a seat two rows behind the white woman.

"I took the fifth-row seat from the front and sat down," she recalled, "immediately closing my eyes and envisioning, in my mind's eye, the wonderful two-week vacation I would have with my family and friends in Ohio."[8]

Jolted out of her reverie by an angry voice, she opened her eyes and sat upright. The bus driver had come to a full stop and turned in his seat. He was speaking to her. "If you can sit in the fifth row from the front seat of the other buses in Montgomery," he said, "suppose you get off and ride in one of them."

The driver's message didn't register at first. Robinson was still thinking about her holiday trip. Suddenly the driver rose from his seat, went over to her, and stood with his arm drawn back, as if to strike her. "Get up from there!" he yelled. "Get up from there!"[8]

Shaken and alarmed, Robinson bolted to her feet and stumbled off the bus in tears, packages falling from her arms. She had made the mistake of sitting in one of the front ten seats, which were reserved for white riders only.

"I felt like a dog," she wrote later. "And I got mad, after this was over, and I realized I was a human being, and just as intelligent and far more [educationally] trained than that bus driver was.[9] But I think he wanted to hurt me, and he did. I cried all the way to Cleveland."

**Key Ideas and Details**
**6** Detailed recollections and quotations emphasize a key idea: Jo Ann Robinson suffered a "humiliating experience."

**Key Ideas and Details**
**7** The author establishes Robinson's status as a valued member of her community and describes the innocent nature of her trip.

**Craft and Structure**
**8** The harsh threats from the bus driver sharply contrast with the earlier image of Robinson envisioning her Christmas vacation.

**Integration of Knowledge and Ideas**
**9** The title of the book and textual details suggest that the author's purpose is to inform readers about the Montgomery bus boycott while also giving the human side of the story.

## Discuss

Sharing your own ideas and listening to the ideas of others can deepen your understanding of a text and help you look at a topic in a whole new way. As you participate in collaborative discussions, work to have a genuine exchange in which classmates build upon one another's ideas. Support your points with evidence and ask meaningful questions.

### Discussion Model

**Student 1:** This author gives so many examples of how people were segregated "from the moment they were born . . . until the day they were buried." This was everyday life in the United States!

**Student 2:** What struck me was the image of the woman with an armful of packages being treated "like a dog" by the bus driver. I could really picture that scene in my mind.

**Student 3:** The author chose words that really show you segregation's cruelty. The idea that people were thought of as "second-class citizens" and kept "in their place" is terrible.

**Student 2:** The story ended before describing the Montgomery bus boycott. I wonder if Robinson was involved in the protest.

## Research

Targeted research can clarify unfamiliar details and shed light on various aspects of a text. Consider questions that arise in your mind as you read, and use those questions as the basis for research.

### Research Model

**Questions:** *What was the Montgomery bus boycott? Was Jo Ann Robinson involved?*

**Key Words for Internet Search:** "Montgomery bus boycott" AND "Jo Ann Robinson"

**Result:** Encyclopedia of Alabama: Montgomery Bus Boycott; Encyclopedia of Alabama: Jo Ann Robinson

**What I Learned:** The Montgomery bus boycott was an important protest in the civil rights movement. It led to the United States Supreme Court barring segregation on public transportation. Robinson helped start the boycott after Rosa Parks, an African American, was arrested for refusing to give up her bus seat to a white man. Martin Luther King, Jr., was heavily involved in the protest.

## Write

Writing about a text will deepen your understanding of it and will also allow you to share your ideas more formally with others. The following model essay evaluates Russell Freedman's use of powerful language and descriptive details, and cites evidence to support the main ideas.

### Writing Model: Informative Text

#### Language and Description in *Freedom Walkers: The Story of the Montgomery Bus Boycott*

The early 1950s was a difficult time for African Americans in Montgomery, Alabama. They were commonly denied their rights, and segregation on public buses was the law. In this passage from his book, Russell Freedman uses expressive language and descriptive details to make the terrible effects of segregation in Montgomery real for readers.

The writer establishes the essay's thesis in the opening paragraph.

In the first section, Freedman's choice of highly charged words and phrases paints a grim picture of everyday life in Alabama. African Americans were "kept ... in their place as second-class citizens" by a "system of white supremacy" and were separated "from the moment they were born ... until the day they were buried." These details create an image of a society that was so unfair that it had to change. The section ends by foreshadowing an event on a bus that would lead to a protest against this injustice.

The writer supports claims with specific examples of "highly charged" words and phrases.

The second section describes what happened on a Montgomery bus in 1949. The author portrays Jo Ann Robinson as a busy professional woman cheerfully boarding a bus at the beginning of a holiday trip to visit relatives. Her statement that she was "envisioning, in my mind's eye, the wonderful two-week vacation I would have with my family and friends in Ohio" strengthens the image of Robinson as an innocent victim. That peaceful moment is shattered, however, when the bus driver "with his arm drawn back, as if to strike her" yells at her to "Get up from there!" She had taken a seat reserved for whites. The contrast between the two images effectively expresses the cruelty of the incident. The additional description that "shaken and alarmed, Robinson bolted to her feet and stumbled off the bus in tears, packages falling from her arms" further emphasizes this contrast. The selection ends with Robinson's comment that "I cried all the way to Cleveland."

The writer uses direct quotations to support the analysis.

Although the excerpt ends before discussion of the Montgomery bus boycott itself, the author's detailed description of Robinson's fear, anger, and outrage at the injustice of segregation makes it clear why, years later, she became one of the leaders of the Montgomery bus boycott.

Details from outside research can be used to fill in gaps in information.

As you read the following text, apply the close reading strategies you have learned. You may need to read the article multiple times.

# from *What Makes a Rembrandt a Rembrandt?*

by Richard Mühlberger

## *Meet the Author*

**Richard Mühlberger** (b. 1938) has been an author, an art critic, and an educator at art museums. Many of his books—including *What Makes a Van Gogh a Van Gogh?* and *What Makes a Leonardo a Leonardo?*—bring to life the works of the world's greatest artists.

### *Citizen Soldiers*

A Dutch poet of Rembrandt's day wrote, "When the country is in danger, every citizen is a soldier." That was the idea behind the militia, or civic guard companies, which trained citizens how to fight and shoot in case their city was attacked. Each company drilled in archery, the crossbow, or the musket. By Rembrandt's time, militia companies were as much social clubs as military organizations.

Captain Frans Banning Cocq, out to impress everyone, chose Rembrandt to paint his militia company, with members of the company paying the artist to have their portraits included in the painting. The huge canvas was to be hung in the new hall of the militia headquarters, where it would be seen at receptions and celebrations along with other militia paintings.

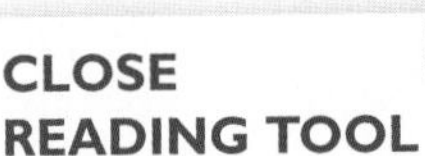

**CLOSE READING TOOL**

Read and respond to this selection online using the **Close Reading Tool.**

By the mid-seventeenth century, there were more than one hundred big militia paintings hanging in public halls in the important cities of the Netherlands. In all of these group portraits, the men were evenly lined up so that each face got equal attention, just as they had been in traditional anatomy lesson paintings. Rembrandt did not like this way of presenting the scene. He had seen militia companies in action, and there were always people milling about who were not militiamen but who took part in their exercises and parades. To add realism to the piece, he decided to include some of these people, as well as a dog. There was room on the wall for a canvas about sixteen feet wide, large enough for Rembrandt to do what no other painter had ever done before. His idea was to show the exciting commotion before a parade began.

### *Two Handsome Officers*

Everywhere in the painting, Rembrandt used sharp contrasts of dark and light. Everything that honors the citizen soldiers and their work is illuminated; everything else is in shadow. Captain Frans Banning Cocq is the man dressed in black with a red sash under his arm, striding forward in the center. Standing next to him is the most brightly lighted man in the painting, Lieutenant Willem van Ruytenburgh, attired in a glorious gold and yellow uniform, silk sash, soft leather cavalry boots, and a high hat with white ostrich plumes. His lancelike weapon, called a partisan, and the steel gorget[1] around his neck—a leftover from the days when soldiers wore full suits of armor—are the only hints that he is a military man. Rembrandt links him to Banning Cocq by contrasting the colors of their clothing and by painting the shadow of Banning Cocq's hand on the front of van Ruytenburgh's coat. The captain is giving orders to his lieutenant for the militia company to march off.

Banning Cocq is dressed in a black suit against a dark background, yet he does not disappear. Rembrandt made him the most important person in the composition. Van Ruytenburgh turns to listen to him, which shows his respect for his commander. Banning Cocq's face stands out above his bright red sash and white collar. How well Rembrandt knew that darkness makes faces shine! The captain's self-assured pace, the movement of the tassels at his knees, and the angle of his walking staff are proof of the energy and dignity of his stride.

---

1. **gorget** (gôr′ jit) *n.* a piece of armor for the throat.

### *Muskets and Mascots*

On either side of these two handsome officers, broad paths lead back into the painting

Rembrandt knew that when the huge group scene was placed above eye level on the wall of the militia headquarters, these empty areas would be the first to be seen. He wanted them to lead the eyes of viewers to figures in the painting who did not have the advantage of being placed in the foreground. In the middle of one of these paths is a man in red pouring gunpowder into the barrel of his musket. Behind the captain, only partially seen, another man shoots his gun into the air, and a third militiaman, to the right of van Ruytenburgh, blows on his weapon to clean it. Loading, shooting, and cleaning were part of the standard drill for musketeers, and so they were included in the painting to demonstrate the men's mastery of their weapons.

Walking in a stream of bright light down the path on the left is a blond girl dressed in yellow with a dead chicken tied to her waist. She has a friend in blue behind her. In their public shows, the militia would choose two young girls to carry the emblems[2] of their company, here the claws of a bird. The yellow and blue of the girls' costumes are the militia's colors. In the parade that is being organized, these mascots will take a prominent place, the fair-haired girl holding aloft the chicken's claws.

Many of the background figures stand on stairs so that their faces can be seen. The man above the girl in yellow is Jan Corneliszoon Visscher, after Banning Cocq and van Ruytenburgh the highest-ranking person in the militia company. He waves a flag that combines the colors of the militia company with the three black crosses of Amsterdam. While Rembrandt did not pose him in bright light, he made him important by placing him high up on the stairs, by showing the sheen in his costume, and by giving him the large flag to unfurl.

---

2. **emblems** *n.* objects that stand for something else; symbols.

### *A Red Ribbon and Fine Old Clothes*

In spite of his partial appearance, the drummer on the right seems ready to come forward to lead a march with his staccato beat. The sound seems to bother the dusty dog below. Behind the drummer, two men appear to be figuring out their places in the formation. The one in the white collar and black hat outranks many of the others in the scene. His prestige is signaled in an unusual way: A red ribbon dangles over his head, tied to the lance of the man in armor behind van Ruytenburgh. Additional lances can be counted in the darkness, some leaning against the wall, others carried by militiamen. Their crisscross patterns add to the feeling of commotion that Rembrandt has captured everywhere on the huge canvas.

The costumes worn in this group portrait are much more ornate and colorful than what Dutchmen ordinarily wore every day. Some, like the breeches and helmet of the man shooting his musket behind Banning Cocq, go back a hundred years to the beginnings of the militia company. In the eyes of many Dutchmen, clothing associated with a glorious past brought special dignity to the company. What an opportunity for Rembrandt, perhaps the greatest lover of old clothes in Amsterdam!

### *Not a Night Watch*

*Night Watch* is a mistaken title that was given to the painting over a hundred years after Rembrandt died, but it has stuck, and is what the painting is almost universally called. Although the exaggerated chiaroscuro[3] does give an impression of nighttime, there is daylight in the scene. It comes from the left, as the shadows under Banning Cocq's feet prove. And it is clear that no one in the painting is on watch, alert to the approach of an enemy. The official title of the painting is *Officers and Men of the Company of Captain Frans Banning Cocq and Lieutenant Willem van Ruytenburgh.*

Rembrandt completed the painting in 1642, when he was thirty-six years old. He probably had no idea that it would be the most famous Dutch painting of all time. In 1678, one of his former students wrote that it would "outlive all its rivals," and within another century the painting was considered one of the wonders of the world.

3. **chiaroscuro** (kē är´ ə skoor´ ō) *n.* a dramatic style of light and shade in a painting or drawing.

# Close Reading Activities

## Read

### Comprehension: **Key Ideas and Details**

1. **(a)** Why was Rembrandt hired to paint the militia company? **(b) Analyze:** How did Rembrandt change the way military group portraits were painted?
2. **(a) Interpret:** According to the article, what techniques does Rembrandt use to emphasize higher-ranking figures? **(b) Support:** How does the painter make the background figures visible?
3. **(a) Classify:** Which two people in the painting are not actual militia members? **(b) Hypothesize:** Would these people have been included in a more traditional militia portrait? Explain.
4. **Summarize:** What details in the painting suggest that a parade is being organized?

### Text Analysis: **Craft and Structure**

5. **(a) Analyze:** What are two possible purposes the author had for writing this article? **(b) Support:** Cite details from the text that support each purpose.
6. **(a) Distinguish:** What organizational pattern does the author use to describe "Two Handsome Officers"? **(b) Assess:** Is this organization appropriate for the section? Explain.

### Connections: **Integration of Knowledge and Ideas**

#### Discuss

In this article, the author mixes historical details with details about the painting he describes. In a **small-group discussion,** share your ideas about whether or not this technique is effective. Use evidence from the text to support your main points.

#### Research

*Night Watch* is one of Rembrandt's most famous works. Find a larger reproduction of the painting. Then, conduct research to find an article about it. Compare this new article to Mühlberger's, considering the ways the authors describe and evaluate Rembrandt's painting techniques, including his use of color, light, and shadow.

Take notes as you perform your research. Then, write a brief **explanation** comparing and contrasting the articles' discussions of Rembrandt's painting techniques.

#### Write

Good literary nonfiction typically presents key ideas in a logical order. Write an **essay** in which you evaluate the organization of key ideas in this selection. Cite details from the article to support your analysis.

#### THE BIG ? What should we learn?

Consider how reading about art helps you learn more about it. What might Rembrandt be trying to teach through his artwork? Explain.

"The **mind**, once **expanded**
to the dimensions of larger ideas,
**never returns** to its original size."

**—Oliver Wendell Holmes**

PART 2

# TEXT ANALYSIS GUIDED EXPLORATION

# EXPLORING IDEAS

The authors in this section introduce and explore ideas through different forms of nonfiction. As you read, think about whether the information in each text is new to you, or whether it helps you explore a familiar topic in a new way. The quotation on the opposite page will help you start thinking about the ways in which learning new information and reexamining familiar ideas can alter our perception and broaden our understanding.

◀ CRITICAL VIEWING Explain your interpretation of the picture on the opposite page. How does the image relate to the concept of exploring ideas?

## READINGS IN PART 2

**CLOSE READING TOOL**

Use the **Close Reading Tool** to practice the strategies you learn in this unit.

# Focus on Craft and Structure

## Elements of Nonfiction

Nonfiction is writing about actual people, ideas, and events.

**Nonfiction** writing presents information that is true or thought to be true. Two broad categories of nonfiction are **functional texts,** which are practical documents that help readers perform everyday tasks, and **literary nonfiction,** which features some of the same literary elements and techniques as fiction.

Authors of nonfiction write with one or more **purposes,** or goals, in mind. Usually, these are to inform, describe, or persuade. To fulfill his or her purpose, the writer organizes information in a logical **structure,** or arrangement of parts, using patterns of organization such as these:

- **Chronological,** which presents events in the order in which they happened
- **Spatial,** which describes items as they appear in space—for example, left to right
- **Comparison-and-contrast,** which groups ideas based on their similarities and differences
- **Cause-and-effect,** which explains how one event causes another
- **Problem-and-solution,** which examines a problem and proposes ways to solve it

**Literary Nonfiction** In addition to informing, describing, or persuading, literary nonfiction may have an additional purpose: to entertain. When a work of literary nonfiction tells a story, it is called **narrative nonfiction.** It may include the elements listed in the right-hand column of the chart below.

**Storytelling Elements in Narrative Nonfiction**

| In Fiction | In Narrative Nonfiction |
| --- | --- |
| **Characters** are developed through<br>• **direct characterization,** or statements about what the characters are like;<br>• **indirect characterization,** or descriptions of what the characters do, say, and think. | **Direct** and **indirect characterization** reveal the personalities of **real people.** |
| **Setting** is revealed through<br>• **vivid descriptions** of **time, place,** and **customs;**<br>• **figurative language,** or unusual comparisons, such as similes. | **Vivid descriptions** and **figurative language** describe **real places, real historical eras,** and **real customs.** |
| **Plot,** or the sequence of fictional events in a story, is **artfully paced and organized** to sustain readers' interest. | **Artful pacing and organization** describe **actual events.** |

## Forms of Literary Nonfiction

In addition to narrative nonfiction, three common forms of literary nonfiction are articles, essays, and speeches.

**Articles** are short prose works that present facts about a subject. They may appear in print sources, such as newspapers, or in online sources, such as Web sites.

**Essays** are also short prose works that focus on a particular subject. They may be more personal than articles, however. The author of an essay often has a deep emotional connection to the subject.

**Speeches** are written texts that are delivered orally to an audience. Like an essay, a speech expresses the speaker's point of view, or perspective, on a topic.

## Types of Nonfiction

Just as there are different *forms* of nonfiction, there are also different *types*—each with its own general purpose. The chart below shows the most common types of nonfiction and gives examples of ways that a work of each type might address the same general subject: pets.

**Types and Purposes of Nonfiction**

| Type | Purpose | Examples |
|---|---|---|
| **Expository** | to present facts and ideas or to explain a process | an online article that explores ways to keep your dog healthy |
| **Persuasive** | to convince readers to take an action or to adopt a point of view | a speech urging the audience to adopt a pet |
| **Narrative** | to tell the story of a real-life experience | an essay about a dog who saved a person's life |
| **Descriptive** | to provide a vivid picture of something | an essay about the writer's favorite pet |
| **Reflective** | to explain the writer's insights about an event or experience | an essay describing lessons about life the writer learned from owning a pet |
| **Humorous** | to entertain and amuse | an article about the challenges of training a very frisky puppy |
| **Analytical** | to break a large idea into parts to show how the parts work as a whole | an article that discusses the criteria used for judging champion show dogs |

## Analyzing Structure and Relationships in Literary Nonfiction

The **structure** of a nonfiction work provides clues to the **author's purpose.**

Writers of nonfiction deliberately arrange their words, sentences, paragraphs, and sections in ways that clearly develop their key ideas.

**Text Features** You can often tell how a nonfiction work is organized by looking at its arrangement on the page. **Text features,** such as subheads and charts, can provide clues about the author's purpose.

| If a text has . . . | It is probably organized . . . | Its purpose may be . . . |
|---|---|---|
| steps or dates | in time order | • to tell a story<br>• to explain a process |
| section headings | by topic | • to inform<br>• to describe |

**Key Ideas** All nonfiction works communicate one or more key ideas. The opening sentences of a work usually state or suggest the key idea and hint at the author's purpose:

> I was only three when I first smelled the fresh, damp soil of Grandma's garden. Somewhere inside me, a seed of love sprouted and began to grow.

These sentences convey the key idea that the writer began gardening at a very young age. The author's purpose might be to reflect on a personal experience.

**Point of View** The author's **point of view** is his or her basic beliefs about a subject. The opening sentences in the previous example tell you that the author has a passion for gardening. Her point of view is that gardening is a worthwhile pursuit.

**Major Sections** Nonfiction may be organized into **sections** arranged under headings. Each section supports a key idea and helps fulfill the author's purpose. Consider the section headings in an article about New York City:

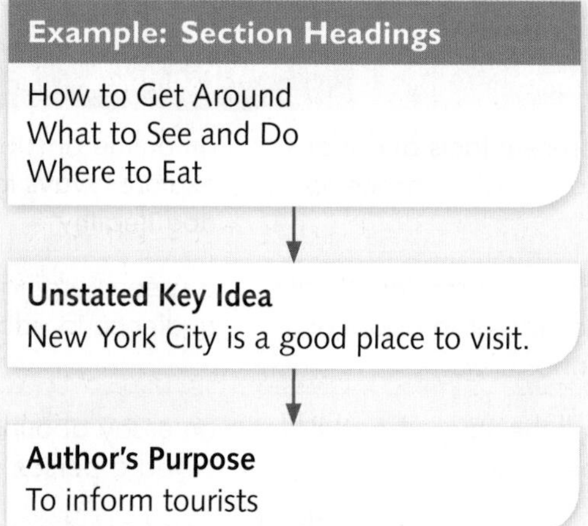

Example: Section Headings
How to Get Around
What to See and Do
Where to Eat
Unstated Key Idea
New York City is a good place to visit.
Author's Purpose
To inform tourists


The structure, key idea, and purpose of a text are interrelated. The headings suggest that there are a lot of things to do in New York City. The information presented indicates that the article is meant for visitors. These elements combine to express the author's purpose to offer guidance to tourists.

**Logical Relationships** Nonfiction works show their subjects in relationship to the larger world. For instance, they may show cause-and-effect relationships, such as ways in which people are affected by events and ideas—and vice versa. Here are some specific examples.

| If a text is about . . . | It might show . . . |
|---|---|
| the Civil War | • what events and ideas caused the war<br>• who suffered during the war |
| the author's life as a spy | • what caused her career choice<br>• how her actions affected others |
| social networks | • how they have impacted users' lives<br>• why they have become so popular |

People do not always agree about the causes or effects of an event. Two writers, given the same facts, may express different opinions. Each writer's point of view affects his or her interpretation of information. In some nonfiction works, the writer may be *biased,* expressing a one-sided opinion. However, a writer is not necessarily biased just because he or she has a particular point of view.

**Word Choice** Looking closely at an author's choice of words can help you detect his or her point of view. Word choice can also help reveal an author's **tone,** or attitude toward his or her subject and audience. In particular, notice words with positive or negative **connotations,** or emotional associations. For example, the words *curious* and *nosy* have the same basic meaning. However, calling someone "curious" conveys positive connotations, while calling that same person "nosy" conveys negative connotations.

**Figurative Language** In literary nonfiction, writers often use figurative language, or unusual comparisons, to bring an idea to life and to create a certain tone. Look at the example below, in which a girl is described in three very different ways.

| Example | Lily is compared to . . . | Tone |
|---|---|---|
| *"Cyclone Lily" strikes again.* | a cyclone | sarcastic |
| *Lily sheds her things like a tree sheds leaves.* | a tree | matter-of-fact |
| *Lily is bursting with life. She can't help but drop petals along the way.* | a flower | adoring |

## What should we learn?

Think about the Big Question as you read "Life Without Gravity." Take note of how a lack of gravity can affect the human body.

### Meet the Author

As a boy, **Robert Zimmerman** (b. 1953) loved science-fiction books. They appealed to him because "the time was the early 1960s, when the first humans were going into space, and these books had an optimistic and hopeful view of that endeavor, as well as the future." As a child, Zimmerman viewed the blastoff of NASA's first manned spacecraft. He recalls thinking, "This is the United States. We can do anything if we put our minds to it!"

## CLOSE READING FOCUS

### Key Ideas and Details: Main Idea

The **main idea** is the central point of a nonfiction text. While most texts focus on one main idea, some may address two or more closely related central ideas. The main idea of a paragraph is often stated in a topic sentence. The rest of the paragraph presents **supporting details** that give examples, explanations, or reasons.

When you read nonfiction, adjust your reading rate to recognize main ideas.

- **Skim,** or look over the text quickly, to get a sense of the main ideas before you begin reading.
- **Read closely** to learn what the central ideas are.
- **Scan,** or run your eyes over the text, to find answers to questions, to clarify, or to find supporting details.

### Craft and Structure: Expository Essay

An **expository essay** is a short piece of nonfiction in which an author explains, defines, or interprets ideas, events, or processes. The organization, or structure, of the information depends on the topic and on the author's purpose, or reason for writing. Ideas may be developed in sections or in related paragraphs. Transitional words, such as *finally* and *since*, may clarify the development of ideas. As you read, analyze the structure the author uses to present ideas.

## Vocabulary

You will encounter the following words in "Life Without Gravity." Copy the words into your notebook. If there are words you do not know, circle the part of each word that seems familiar and might be a clue to its meaning.

| | | |
|---|---|---|
| **manned** | **spines** | **feeble** |
| **blander** | **globules** | **readapted** |

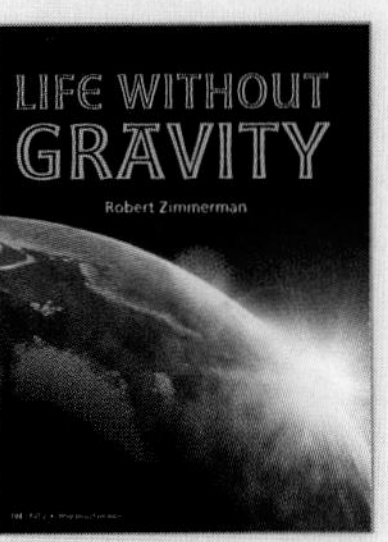


## CLOSE READING MODEL

The passage below is from Robert Zimmerman's expository essay "Life Without Gravity." The annotations to the right of the passage show ways in which you can use close reading skills to identify main ideas and supporting details and to understand an expository essay.

### *from* "Life Without Gravity"

Being weightless in space seems so exciting.[1] Astronauts bounce about from wall to wall, flying! They float, they weave, they do somersaults and acrobatics without effort. Heavy objects can be lifted like feathers, and no one ever gets tired because nothing weighs anything.[2] In fact, everything is fun, nothing is hard.

NOT! Since the first manned space missions in the 1960s, scientists have discovered that being weightless in space isn't just flying around like Superman.[3] Zero gravity is alien stuff. As space tourist Dennis Tito said when he visited the international space station, "Living in space is like having a different life, living in a different world."

Worse, weightlessness can sometimes be downright unpleasant. Your body gets upset and confused. Your face puffs up, your nose gets stuffy, your back hurts, your stomach gets upset, and you throw up.[4] If astronauts are to survive a one-year journey to Mars—the shortest possible trip to the Red Planet—they will have to learn how to deal with this weird environment.

**Main Idea**
**1** In the topic sentence, the author clearly states the main idea of this paragraph: Weightlessness in space seems exciting.

**Main Idea**
**2** In the body of the paragraph, the author supports the main idea. He provides specific examples that show why weightlessness is exciting.

**Expository Essay**
**3** The author emphasizes the word *NOT!* to grab your attention and introduce a contrasting view—the view he actually holds. Now you may guess that the purpose of this essay is to explain why weightlessness is not actually fun.

**Main Idea**
**4** In this paragraph, the author uses vivid and surprising examples to support the idea that weightlessness can be "downright unpleasant."

# LIFE WITHOUT GRAVITY

Robert Zimmerman

Being weightless in space seems so exciting. Astronauts bounce about from wall to wall, flying! They float, they weave, they do somersaults and acrobatics without effort. Heavy objects can be lifted like feathers, and no one ever gets tired because nothing weighs anything. In fact, everything is fun, nothing is hard.

NOT! Since the first **manned** space missions in the 1960s, scientists have discovered that being weightless in space isn't just flying around like Superman. Zero gravity is alien stuff. As space tourist Dennis Tito said when he visited the international space station, "Living in space is like having a different life, living in a different world."

Worse, weightlessness can sometimes be downright unpleasant. Your body gets upset and confused. Your face puffs up, your nose gets stuffy, your back hurts, your stomach gets upset, and you throw up. If astronauts are to survive a one-year journey to Mars—the shortest possible trip to the Red Planet—they will have to learn how to deal with this weird environment. •

Our bodies are adapted to Earth's gravity. Our muscles are strong in order to overcome gravity as we walk and run. Our inner ears[1] use gravity to keep us upright. And because gravity wants to pull all our blood down into our legs, our hearts are designed to pump hard to get blood up to our brains.

In space, the much weaker gravity makes the human body change in many unexpected ways. In microgravity,[2] your blood is rerouted, flowing from the legs, which become thin and sticklike, to the head, which swells up. The extra liquid in your head also makes you feel like you're hanging upside down or have a stuffed-up nose.

The lack of gravity causes astronauts to routinely "grow" between one and three inches taller. Their **spines** straighten

◀ **Vocabulary**

**manned** (mand) *adj.* having human operators on board

**spines** (spīnz) *n.* backbones

**Expository Essay**
What information do you learn about the human body in these paragraphs?

**Spiral Review**
**AUTHOR'S POINT OF VIEW** How does the author regard space travel? Explain your answer.

**Comprehension**
What are some disadvantages of weightlessness?

1. **inner ears** (in′ ər irz) *n.* internal parts of the ears that give people a sense of balance.
2. **microgravity** (mī′ krō grav′ i tē) *n.* state of near-weightlessness that astronauts experience as their spacecraft orbits Earth.

Vocabulary ▶

**feeble** (fē′ bəl)
*adj.* weak

**blander** (bland′ ər)
*adj.* more tasteless

**globules** (gläb′ yo͞olz)
*n.* drops of liquid

out. The bones in the spine and the disks between them spread apart and relax.

But their bones also get thin and spongy. The body decides that if the muscles aren't going to push and pull on the bones, it doesn't need to lay down as much bone as it normally does. Astronauts who have been in space for several months can lose 10 percent or more of their bone tissue. If their bones got much weaker, they would snap once the astronauts returned to Earth.

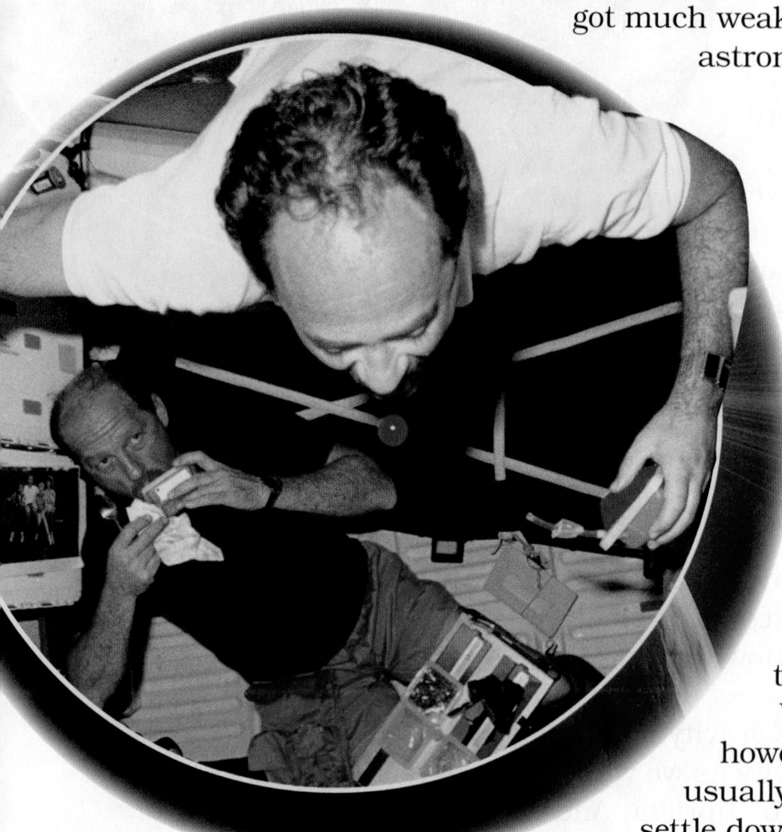

And their muscles get weak and flabby. Floating about in space is too easy. If astronauts don't force themselves to exercise, their muscles become so **feeble** that when they return to Earth they can't even walk.

Worst of all is how their stomachs feel. During the first few days in space, the inner ear—which gives people their sense of balance—gets confused. Many astronauts become nauseous. They lose their appetites. Many throw up. Many throw up a lot! •

Weightlessness isn't all bad, however. After about a week people usually get used to it. Their stomachs settle down. Appetites return (though astronauts always say that food tastes **blander** in space). The heart and spine adjust.

▲ **Critical Viewing**
Why do you think the red liquid in this picture is floating around? Explain.

**Main Idea**
What is the main idea in this paragraph?

Then, flying around like a bird becomes fun! Rooms suddenly seem much bigger. Look around you: The space above your head is pretty useless on Earth. You can't get up there to work, and anything you attach to the ceiling is simply something you'll bump your head on.

In space, however, that area is useful. In fact, equipment can be installed on every inch of every wall. In weightlessness you choose to move up or down and left or right simply by pointing your head. If you turn yourself upside down, the ceiling becomes the floor.

And you can't drop anything! As you work you can let your tools float around you. But you'd better be organized and neat. If you don't put things back where they belong when you are finished, tying them down securely, they will float away. Air currents will then blow them into nooks and crannies, and it might take you days to find them again.

In microgravity, you have to learn new ways to eat. Don't try pouring a bowl of cornflakes. Not only will the flakes float all over the place, the milk won't pour. Instead, big balls of milk will form. You can drink these by taking big bites out of them, but you'd better finish them before they slam into a wall, splattering apart and covering everything with little tiny milk **globules**.

Some meals on the space station are eaten with forks and knives, but scooping food with a spoon doesn't work. If the food isn't gooey enough to stick to the spoon, it will float away.

Everyone in space drinks through a straw, since liquid simply refuses to stay in a glass. The straw has to have a clamp at one end, or else when you stop drinking, the liquid will continue to flow out, spilling everywhere.

To prevent their muscles and bones from becoming too weak for life on Earth, astronauts have to follow a boring two-hour exercise routine every single day. Imagine having to run on a treadmill for one hour in the morning and then ride an exercise bicycle another hour before dinner. As Russian astronaut Valeri Ryumin once said, "Ye-ech!"

Even after all this exercise, astronauts who spend more than two months in space are usually weak and uncomfortable when they get back to Earth. Jerry Linenger, who spent more than four months on the Russian space station, *Mir,* struggled to walk after he returned. "My

## LITERATURE IN CONTEXT

### Science Connection

**Weighted Down** Your weight in pounds is actually the measure of the downward force of gravity upon your body. How much force gravity puts on you depends on the size and mass of the planet on which you are standing.

Imagine that on Earth you weigh 100 pounds. Because the surface gravity of Jupiter is 2.64 times that of Earth, you would weigh 264 pounds on Jupiter without eating a forkful more. On the other hand, surface gravity on the moon is one-sixth of Earth's gravity. That means your moon weight would be just under 17 pounds, though you would look exactly the same.

Of course, when you are not on a planet or moon, you are out of gravity's pull, so you weigh nothing at all.

### Connect to the Literature

Is weightlessness as described in "Life Without Gravity" something you would like to experience? Why or why not?

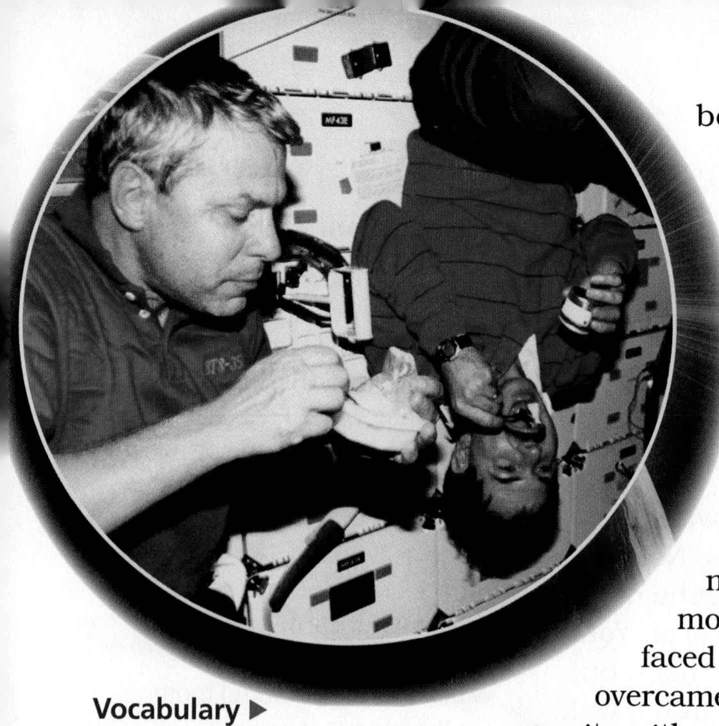

body felt like a 500 pound barbell," he said. He even had trouble lifting and holding his fifteen-month-old son, John.

When Linenger went to bed that first night, his body felt like it was being smashed into the mattress. He was constantly afraid that if he moved too much, he would float away and out of control.

And yet, Linenger recovered quickly. In fact, almost two dozen astronauts have lived in space for more than six months, and four have stayed in orbit for more than a year. These men and women faced the discomforts of weightlessness and overcame them. And they all readapted to Earth gravity without problems, proving that voyages to Mars are possible . . . even if it feels like you are hanging upside down the whole time!

**Vocabulary ▶**
**readapted** (rē ə dapt′ əd) *v.* gradually adjusted again

## Language Study

**Vocabulary** The words in blue appear in "Life Without Gravity." Rewrite each sentence so that it includes a word from the list that conveys the same basic meaning as the italicized word or phrase.

**manned** **spines** **blander** **globules** **readapted**

**1.** My cold makes this food seem *less tasty*.
**2.** Space flights *with humans aboard* took place in the 1960s.
**3.** When the thermometer broke, *tiny drops* of mercury spilled out.
**4.** With no *bones in our backs,* we would not be able to stand.
**5.** After being away on vacation, we have *gotten used to* being home.

**WORD STUDY**

The **Old English suffix *-ness*** means "the condition or quality of being." It usually indicates that the word is a noun. In this essay, the author explains that **feebleness**, a weakened condition, can be brought on by a lack of gravity.

### Word Study

**Part A** Explain how the **Old English suffix *-ness*** contributes to the meanings of the words *dreariness, togetherness,* and *greatness.* Consult a dictionary if necessary.

**Part B** Use what you know about the Old English suffix *-ness* to explain your answer to each question.

**1.** If Sara is known for her *nastiness,* does she treat people well?
**2.** Could *laziness* prevent someone from being productive?

# Close Reading Activities

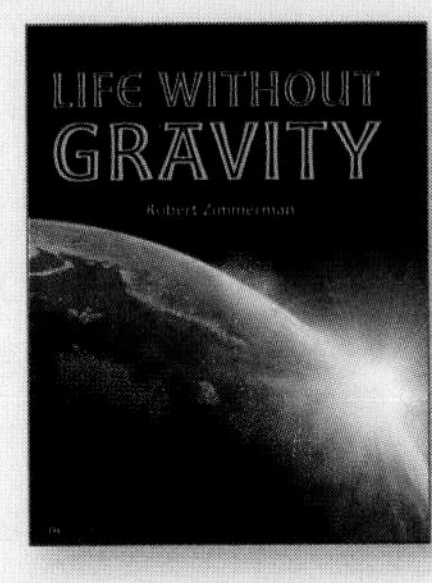


## Literary Analysis

### Key Ideas and Details

1. **Main Idea** What ideas did you identify from skimming the essay before you read it?
2. **Main Idea (a)** What are three main ideas in the essay? **(b)** What supporting details does the author provide for each idea?
3. **(a)** List three unpleasant effects of weightlessness that are explained in the essay. **(b) Cause and Effect:** Describe the cause of each unpleasant effect.

### Craft and Structure

4. **Expository Essay (a)** Fill out a chart like the one on the right to organize the information provided in the essay. **(b)** Does the organization of the essay enable the author to achieve his purpose? Why or why not?
5. **Expository Essay (a)** Explain why "Life Without Gravity" is an expository essay. **(b) Support:** Give examples from the text to support your answer.

| What Is Weightlessness? |
|---|
| |
| **What Are Its Advantages?** |
| |
| **What Are Its Disadvantages?** |
| |
| **Author's Conclusion** |
| |

### Integration of Knowledge and Ideas

6. **Relate:** What do you think you would like most about being weightless? What effect of weightlessness would be most difficult for you? Use details from the essay to support your answers.
7. **(a) Synthesize** If the astronauts quoted in the article were offered another trip in space, what advice would you give them about the wisdom of taking the trip again? Use evidence from the essay to support your advice. **(b) Discuss:** Talk about your advice in a small group. As a group, choose three important pieces of advice to share with the class.

8. THE BIG ? **What should we learn? (a)** How do the experiences of other people—such as those of the astronauts in this essay—help us to learn about the world? **(b)** What can we learn from people who experiment with something new? Explain.

**ACADEMIC VOCABULARY**

As you write and speak about "Life Without Gravity," use the words related to learning that you explored on page 175 of this textbook.

## Conventions: Action Verbs and Linking Verbs

A **verb** is a word that expresses an action or a state of being. Every complete sentence must have at least one verb.

- An **action verb** tells what action someone or something is doing.
- A **linking verb** joins the subject of a sentence with a word or phrase that describes or renames the subject. The most common linking verbs are forms of *be*, such as *am, is, are, was, were, has been,* and *will be*. Other linking verbs include *seem, become, stay, feel, taste,* and *look*. Several of these verbs can also be used as action verbs.

| Action Verbs | Linking Verbs |
|---|---|
| I *smelled* the roses. | The roses *smelled* fresh. |
| He *tastes* the apples. | The apple *tastes* sour. |
| The farmers *grow* corn. | The corn *grows* tall. |
| She *felt* the turtle's shell. | The shell *felt* hard. |

### Practice A

Identify the verb or verbs in each sentence, and indicate whether they are action verbs or linking verbs.

**1.** Weightlessness is sometimes unpleasant.
**2.** A weightless person experiences back pain.
**3.** Our muscles are strong because of gravity.
**4.** Astronauts learn new ways to eat.

**Reading Application** In "Life Without Gravity," find one sentence with a linking verb and one with an action verb.

### Practice B

Write a sentence for each item, using the subject indicated and a form of the linking verb in parentheses.

**1.** astronaut (seem)
**2.** space camp (be)
**3.** equipment (stay)
**4.** gravity (become)

**Writing Application** Choose a photo from the essay and write two sentences about it, one using a linking verb, and one using an action verb.

## Writing to Sources

**Explanatory Text** An **analogy** makes a comparison between two or more things that are alike in some ways but otherwise different. For example: *A follower without a leader is like a planet without a sun.*

- Use this sentence starter to write a basic analogy based on what you learned from the essay: "Life without gravity is like ___________."
- Then, write several sentences to develop your analogy. Support your statements with details from the essay. You may also use anecdotes (personal stories), examples from real life, and facts or statistics to explain your ideas.

**Grammar Application** Reread your analogy to make sure you have used action verbs and linking verbs correctly.

## Speaking and Listening

**Presentation of Ideas** Listen to the audio version of "Life Without Gravity," which is available in the eText version of your textbook. As you listen, take notes on the main ideas and supporting details in the essay. Then, in a small group, compare and contrast the audio and text versions. Discuss the elements that make each version compelling. Finally, use your notes to help you prepare and deliver an **oral summary** of your findings.

- Be objective. In your own words, outline the main ideas and supporting details of the essay. Compare ways in which the text and audio version present key ideas. Then, provide points of contrast between the two versions.
- Gather your notes and organize them logically.
- Assign presentation roles. Rehearse your presentation, adjusting the volume of your voice and perfecting your pronunciation of words.
- Present your summary to the class. Strive to maintain eye contact as you speak.
- After your presentation, invite comments and feedback from the class.

# Building Knowledge

Meet the Author

**Chief Dan George** (1899–1981), the son of a tribal chief, was named Geswanouth Slahoot but was also known as Dan Slaholt. At age five, he was sent to a mission boarding school, where his last name was changed to George. Years later, George won the role of an aging Indian in a TV series. He won acting awards and earned parts in major motion pictures. With fame, George became a spokesperson for Native Americans.

## What should we learn?

Explore the Big Question as you read "I Am a Native of North America." Take notes on what can be learned from the values and lifestyle of Native Americans.

## CLOSE READING FOCUS

### Key Ideas and Details: **Main Idea**

The **main** or **central idea** is the most important idea in a literary work or a passage of text. A single main idea may grow out of two or more important ideas that the author develops throughout the text. Sometimes the author directly states the main idea and then provides the key points that support it. These key points are supported in turn by details such as examples and descriptions.

Other times, the main idea is unstated. Readers must make inferences from the text in order to determine the main idea. To do this, notice how the writer groups details, and then look for sentences that pull details together.

### Craft and Structure: **Reflective Essay**

A **reflective essay** is a brief prose work that presents a writer's thoughts and feelings—or reflections—about an experience or idea. The purpose is to communicate these thoughts and feelings so that readers will respond with thoughts and feelings of their own. As you read a reflective essay, think about the ideas the writer is sharing and analyze the interactions between individuals, events, and ideas in the text.

## Vocabulary

You will encounter the following words in this reflective essay. Copy the words into your notebook, noting which ones you know, which ones you know a little bit, and which ones you do not know at all. After reading the essay, see how your knowledge of each word has increased.

| | | |
|---|---|---|
| **distinct** | **communal** | **justifies** |
| **promote** | **hoarding** | **integration** |

## CLOSE READING MODEL

The passage below is from "I Am a Native of North America." The annotations to the right of the passage show ways in which you can use close reading skills to identify and make inferences about main ideas and to understand a reflective essay.

### *from* "I Am a Native of North America"

Love is something you and I must have.[1] We must have it because our spirit feeds upon it. We must have it because without it we become weak and faint. Without love our self-esteem weakens. Without it our courage fails. Without love we can no longer look out confidently at the world. Instead we turn inwardly and begin to feed upon our own personalities and little by little we destroy ourselves.[2]

You and I need the strength and joy that comes from knowing that we are loved. With it we are creative. With it we march tirelessly. With it, and with it alone, we are able to sacrifice for others.[3]

There have been times when we all wanted so desperately to feel a reassuring hand upon us . . . there have been lonely times when we so wanted a strong arm around us . . . I cannot tell you how deeply I miss my wife's presence when I return from a trip. Her love was my greatest joy, my strength, my greatest blessing.[4]

**Main Idea**

**1** This paragraph begins with a topic sentence that directly states a main idea. You can expect to find support for this idea in the sentences to come.

**Main Idea**

**2** The author provides supporting details that focus on the universal human need for love. These details explain why love is so important.

**Reflective Essay**

**3** The author uses emotionally-charged language to express his thoughts and feelings about love. As you explore these ideas, you may respond with your own thoughts and feelings on the subject.

**Reflective Essay**

**4** Here, the author offers an example from his own experience. The power and emotion of this personal detail may prompt you to consider who is important in your own life.

# I Am a Native of North America

Chief Dan George

Vocabulary ▶
**distinct** (di stiŋkt′) *adj.* separate and different

**communal** (kə myo͞on′ əl) *adj.* shared by all

In the course of my lifetime I have lived in two distinct cultures. I was born into a culture that lived in communal houses. My grandfather's house was eighty feet long. It was called a smoke house, and it stood down by the beach along the inlet.[1] All my grandfather's sons and their families lived in this large dwelling. Their sleeping apartments were separated by blankets made of bull rush reeds, but one open fire in the middle served the cooking needs of all. In houses like these, throughout the tribe, people learned to live with one another; learned to serve one another; learned to respect the rights of one another. And children shared the thoughts of the adult world and found themselves surrounded by aunts and uncles and cousins who loved them and did not threaten them. My father was born in such a house and learned from infancy how to love people and be at home with them.

And beyond this acceptance of one another there was a deep respect for everything in nature that surrounded them. My father loved the earth and all its creatures. The earth was his second mother. The earth and everything it contained was a gift from See-see-am[2] . . . and the way to thank this great spirit was to use his gifts with respect.

**Reflective Essay**
What experience or idea is the author reflecting on here?

1. **inlet** (in′ let′) *n.* narrow strip of water jutting into a body of land from a river, a lake, or an ocean.
2. **See-see-am** the name of the Great Spirit, or "The Chief Above," in the Salishan language of Chief George's people.

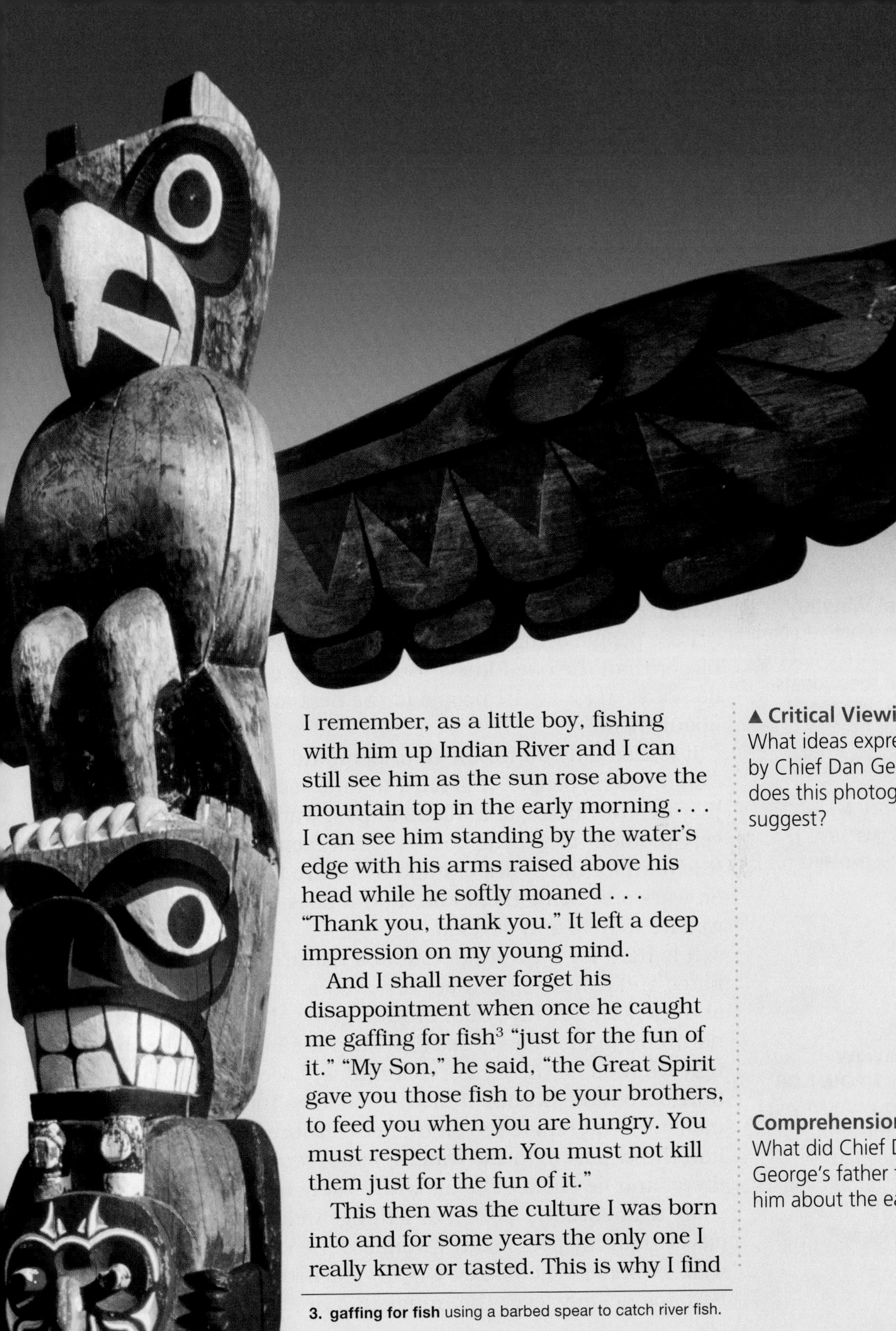

I remember, as a little boy, fishing with him up Indian River and I can still see him as the sun rose above the mountain top in the early morning . . . I can see him standing by the water's edge with his arms raised above his head while he softly moaned . . . "Thank you, thank you." It left a deep impression on my young mind.

And I shall never forget his disappointment when once he caught me gaffing for fish[3] "just for the fun of it." "My Son," he said, "the Great Spirit gave you those fish to be your brothers, to feed you when you are hungry. You must respect them. You must not kill them just for the fun of it."

This then was the culture I was born into and for some years the only one I really knew or tasted. This is why I find

**▲ Critical Viewing**
What ideas expressed by Chief Dan George does this photograph suggest?

**Comprehension**
What did Chief Dan George's father teach him about the earth?

3. **gaffing for fish** using a barbed spear to catch river fish.

▲ **Critical Viewing** Based on what you have read, describe what the people in these boats might be doing.

**Vocabulary ▶**
**justifies** (jus´ tə fīz´) *v.* excuses; explains

**Spiral Review**
**AUTHOR'S POINT OF VIEW** How would you describe the author's attitude toward his subject? Support your answer with details from the essay.

it hard to accept many of the things I see around me.

I see people living in smoke houses hundreds of times bigger than the one I knew. But the people in one apartment do not even know the people in the next and care less about them.

It is also difficult for me to understand the deep hate that exists among people. It is hard to understand a culture that **justifies** the killing of millions in past wars, and is at this very moment preparing bombs to kill even greater numbers. It is hard for me to understand a culture that spends more on wars and weapons to kill, than it does on education and welfare to help and develop.

It is hard for me to understand a culture that not only hates and fights its brothers but even attacks nature and abuses her. I see my white brother going about blotting out nature from his cities. I see him strip the hills bare, leaving ugly wounds on the face of mountains. I see him tearing things from the bosom of mother earth as though she were a monster, who refused to share her treasures with him. I see him throw poison in the waters, indifferent to the life he kills there; and he chokes the air with deadly fumes.

My white brother does many things well for he is more clever than my people but I wonder if he knows how to love well. I wonder if he has ever really learned to love at all. Perhaps he only loves the things that are his own but never learned to love the things that are outside and beyond him. And this is, of course, not love at all, for man must love all creation or he will love none of it. Man must love fully or he will become the lowest of the animals. It is the power to love that makes him the greatest of them all . . . for he alone of all animals is capable of love.

Love is something you and I must have. We must have it because our spirit feeds upon it. We must have it because without it we become weak and faint. Without love our self-esteem weakens. Without it our courage fails. Without love we can no longer look out confidently at the world. Instead we turn inwardly and begin to feed upon our own personalities and little by little we destroy ourselves.

You and I need the strength and joy that comes from knowing that we are loved. With it we are creative. With it we march tirelessly. With it, and with it alone, we are able to sacrifice for others.

There have been times when we all wanted so desperately to feel a reassuring hand upon us . . . there have been lonely times when we so wanted a strong arm around us . . . I cannot tell you how deeply I miss my wife's presence when I return from a trip. Her love was my greatest joy, my strength, my greatest blessing.

I am afraid my culture has little to offer yours. But my culture did prize friendship and companionship. It did not look on privacy as a thing to be clung to, for privacy builds up walls and walls **promote** distrust. My culture lived in big family communities, and from infancy people learned to live with others.

My culture did not prize the **hoarding** of private possessions; in fact, to hoard was a shameful thing to do among my people. The Indian looked on all things in nature as belonging to him and he expected to share them with others and to take only what he needed.

Everyone likes to give as well as receive. No one wishes only to receive all the time. We have taken much from your culture . . . I wish you had taken something from our culture . . . for there were some beautiful and good things in it.

**Main Idea**
What key words or sentences so far have helped you determine the essay's main idea?

**Reflective Essay**
What experiences does the author reflect on here?

**◀ Vocabulary**

**promote** (prə mōt′) *v.* encourage; contribute to the growth of

**hoarding** (hôr′ diŋ) *n.* accumulation and storage of items or supplies

**Vocabulary ▶**
**integration** (inˊ tə grāˊ shən) *n.* the end of separation of cultural or racial groups

Soon it will be too late to know my culture, for **integration** is upon us and soon we will have no values but yours. Already many of our young people have forgotten the old ways. And many have been shamed of their Indian ways by scorn and ridicule. My culture is like a wounded deer that has crawled away into the forest to bleed and die alone.

The only thing that can truly help us is genuine love. You must truly love us, be patient with us and share with us. And we must love you—with a genuine love that forgives and forgets . . . a love that forgives the terrible sufferings your culture brought ours when it swept over us like a wave crashing along a beach . . . with a love that forgets and lifts up its head and sees in your eyes an answering love of trust and acceptance.

This is brotherhood . . . anything less is not worthy of the name.

I have spoken.

## Language Study

**Vocabulary** The words boldfaced below appear in "I Am a Native of North America." For each, choose its **antonym,** or word that is opposite in meaning, from among the three choices given. Explain your answers.

**1. distinct: (a)** similar **(b)** different **(c)** decided

**2. communal: (a)** busy **(b)** private **(c)** organized

**3. promote: (a)** encourage **(b)** advance **(c)** prevent

**4. hoarding: (a)** storing **(b)** distributing **(c)** saving

**5. integration: (a)** segregation **(b)** assimilation **(c)** mixing

**WORD STUDY**

The **Latin root *-just-*** means "law" or "fair and right." In this essay, Chief Dan George cannot understand a culture that **justifies**, or defends as right, the killing of others in a war.

### Word Study

**Part A** Explain how the **Latin root *-just-*** contributes to the meanings of the words *justice, adjust,* and *injustice.* Consult a dictionary if necessary.

**Part B** Use the context of the sentences and your knowledge of the Latin root *-just-* to explain your answer to each question.

**1.** If a decision is *unjust,* is it fair?

**2.** If there is no *justification* for your error, are you to blame?

# Close Reading Activities

## Literary Analysis

### Key Ideas and Details

1. **(a)** What details does Chief Dan George provide about his father's relationship with nature? **(b)** Find a sentence from the essay that pulls these details together.
2. **(a)** Name three things that people learn from growing up in communal homes. Use examples from the essay to support your answer. **(b) Compare and Contrast:** Identify several differences between the "two distinct cultures" in which Chief Dan George lived.
3. **Main Idea** **(a)** What is the main idea of the essay? **(b)** Is the main idea stated directly, or do you have to determine it by making inferences? **(c)** What key points and supporting details contribute most to the development of the main idea?

### Craft and Structure

4. **Reflective Essay** Analyze the reflective essay in a chart like the one on the right. In the top box, write George's reflections on three points. In the middle box, write your response to each point. Trade charts with a partner and discuss your responses. Then, in the last box, explain whether your responses changed based on your discussion.
5. **Reflective Essay** **(a)** What three things puzzle Chief Dan George about his "white brother"? **(b) Interpret:** When Chief Dan George says, "My white brother . . . is more clever than my people," what does he mean by *clever*? **(c) Support:** What details in the text support your interpretation?

| George's Reflections |
| --- |
| |
| **My Responses** |
| |
| **After Discussion** |
| |

### Integration of Knowledge and Ideas

6. **(a) Analyze:** What is the "brotherhood" that Chief Dan George talks about in the essay? **(b) Evaluate:** Is this brotherhood important? Why or why not?
7. **Make a Judgment:** Can people maintain a sense of cultural identity while interacting with members of another group that does not have the same culture? Explain your answer, using evidence from the text to support your ideas.

8. THE BIG ? **What should we learn? (a)** Why is it important to know the beliefs and traditions of those who came before us? **(b)** What could happen if we ignore the past?

**ACADEMIC VOCABULARY**

As you write and speak about "I Am a Native of North America," use words related to learning that you explored on page 175 of this textbook.

# Close Reading Activities Continued

## Conventions: The Principal Parts of Verbs

A verb has four **principal parts:** *present, present participle, past,* and *past participle.*

The chart below shows the four principal parts of *talk,* a regular verb, as well as the principal parts of several commonly misused irregular verbs. Notice that when you use the present participle or the past participle, you include a helping verb. Common helping verbs include *has, have, had, am, is, are, was,* and *were.* A verb combined with its helping verb is called a *verb phrase.*

| | Present | Present Participle | Past | Past Participle |
|---|---|---|---|---|
| **Regular** | talk | (is) talking | talked | (has) talked |
| **Irregular** | sit | (is) sitting | sat | (has) sat |
| **Irregular** | am, is, are | (is) being | was | (has) been |
| **Irregular** | has, have | (is) having | had | (has) had |
| **Irregular** | begin | (is) beginning | began | (has) begun |

### Practice A

Identify the verb or verb phrase in each sentence. Then identify its principal part.

1. Chief Dan George's family lived in a large communal house.
2. He had learned much from his grandfather.
3. He is yearning for greater tolerance in America.
4. Chief Dan George believes in love.

**Reading Application** In "I Am a Native of North America," locate at least three of the principal parts of verbs.

### Practice B

Complete each sentence, using a principal part of the verb in parentheses. Identify the principal part you have used.

1. People once (know) Chief Dan George as Dan Slaholt.
2. By the age of 17, he (work) at different jobs.
3. Before appearing in movies, he (act) in TV shows.
4. Chief Dan George (call) on his readers to love one another.

**Writing Application** Choose an idea or image mentioned in the essay and write four sentences about it, using each of the four principal parts of verbs.

## Writing to Sources

**Informative Text** Make an **outline** to show the main idea and supporting details in "I Am a Native of North America." Build your outline using this format:

At the top of your outline, write a sentence that states the main ideas of the essay in your own words. Then, list subtopics for each main idea, and finally, list details. Refer back to the text to find and confirm specific details.

- Use Roman numerals to identify each key point.
- Use capital letters to identify supporting details.

Once you have completed your outline, write a brief summary of the essay.

**Grammar Application** Check your writing to be sure you have used the principal parts of verbs correctly.

## Speaking and Listening

**Presentation of Ideas** In a small group, present a **response** to an audio version of "I Am a Native of North America." Access the audio recording, which is available in the eText version of your textbook. Follow these steps to complete your response.

- Listen to the audio version as a group, taking notes on the impact of the selection as it is read aloud. For example, note whether the audio version brings certain words and phrases to life, or if it conveys a certain tone that is not evident in the print version.
- Next, discuss with the group ways in which the audio version enhanced or detracted from the meaning and tone of the printed version. Replay the audio and reread the print version to find specific examples that support your group's ideas.
- After your discussion, plan a presentation to the class in which you share your response.
- Assign presenter roles, and rehearse your presentation.
- At the conclusion of your presentation, invite questions and comments from your audience.

# Building Knowledge

*Meet the Author*

**Barbara Jordan** (1936–1996) inherited her skill at public speaking from her father, a Baptist minister. As a high school student in Houston, Texas, Jordan won public speaking competitions. In 1966, Jordan was elected to the Texas Senate, and she became a member of Congress in 1972. During the 1976 Democratic National Convention, she became the first African American to deliver the keynote speech at a major party's political convention. In 1990, the National Women's Hall of Fame voted Jordan one of the most influential women of the twentieth century.

## What should we learn?

Think about the Big Question as you read "All Together Now." Note ways in which the persuasive essay can help you learn about tolerance.

## CLOSE READING FOCUS

### Key Ideas and Details: **Classifying Fact and Opinion**

When you read nonfiction, it is important to classify types of information. Distinguishing between fact and opinion is a key skill.

- A **fact** is something that can be proved.
- An **opinion** is a person's judgment or belief. It may be supported by factual evidence, but it cannot be proved.

As you read, recognize clues that indicate an opinion, such as the phrases *I believe* or *in my opinion*. Also look for words such as *always, never, must, cannot, best, worst,* and *all,* which may be part of broad statements that reveal personal judgments.

### Craft and Structure: **Persuasive Essay**

A **persuasive essay** is a work of nonfiction that presents a series of arguments to convince readers to believe or act in a certain way. When you read persuasive essays, be alert for the use of persuasive techniques. Then, decide whether a particular technique represents reasonable and relevant support that convinces you to accept or act on the author's ideas. As you read, identify and analyze the persuasive techniques defined below.

- **Appeals to authority** use the statements of experts and well-known people.
- **Appeals to emotion** use words that convey strong feelings.
- **Appeals to reason** use logical arguments backed by facts.

## Vocabulary

You will encounter the following words in this persuasive essay. Copy the words into your notebook. Write antonyms—words with opposite meanings—for as many words as you can.

| | | |
|---|---|---|
| **legislation** | **tolerant** | **culminated** |
| **fundamental** | **equality** | **optimist** |

## CLOSE READING MODEL

The passage below is from Barbara Jordan's persuasive essay "All Together Now." The annotations to the right of the passage show ways in which you can use close reading skills to classify fact and opinion and to understand a persuasive essay.

### *from* "All Together Now"

When I look at race relations today I can see that some positive changes have come about. But much remains to be done, and the answer does not lie in more legislation. We *have* the legislation we need; we have the laws. Frankly, I don't believe that the task of bringing us all together can be accomplished by government.[1] What we need now is soul force—the efforts of people working on a small scale to build a truly tolerant, harmonious society. And parents can do a great deal to create that tolerant society.[2]

We all know that race relations in America have had a very rocky history. Think about the 1960s when Dr. Martin Luther King, Jr., was in his heyday and there were marches and protests against segregation and discrimination. The movement culminated in 1963 with the March on Washington.[3]

Following that event, race relations reached an all-time peak. . . . At last, black people and white people seemed ready to live together in peace.

But that is not what happened. By the 1990's the good feelings had diminished. Today the nation seems to be suffering from compassion fatigue, and issues such as race relations and civil rights have never regained momentum.[4]

**Fact and Opinion**

**1** The phrase, "I don't believe" indicates that the author is expressing an opinion.

**Persuasive Essay**

**2** In this sentence, Jordan introduces the cornerstone of her argument by appealing to readers' sense of community. She uses the term "soul force" to stir and empower readers to take action on the issue.

**Fact and Opinion**

**3** The author strengthens her argument with facts. She mentions actual dates, people, and events—the 1960s, Martin Luther King, Jr., and the March on Washington.

**Persuasive Essay**

**4** Here Jordan changes her tone. She uses the words "diminished," "suffering," and "compassion fatigue" to develop an emotional appeal. Jordan's message is that past gains in race relations are in danger of slipping away due to inaction.

# All Together Now

Barbara Jordan

**Vocabulary ▶**
**legislation** (lej′ is lā′ shən) *n.* law-making

**tolerant** (täl′ ər ənt) *adj.* accepting; free from bigotry or prejudice

**culminated** (kul′ mə nāt′ əd) *v.* reached its highest point, or climax

**fundamental** (fun′ də ment′ 'l) *adj.* basic; forming a foundation

**▼ Critical Viewing**
Based on this photo and the title, what do you think this essay will be about?

When I look at race relations today I can see that some positive changes have come about. But much remains to be done, and the answer does not lie in more **legislation**. We *have* the legislation we need; we have the laws. Frankly, I don't believe that the task of bringing us all together can be accomplished by government. What we need now is soul force—the efforts of people working on a small scale to build a truly **tolerant**, harmonious society. And parents can do a great deal to create that tolerant society.

We all know that race relations in America have had a very rocky history. Think about the 1960s when Dr. Martin Luther King, Jr., was in his heyday and there were marches and protests against segregation[1] and discrimination. The movement **culminated** in 1963 with the March on Washington.

Following that event, race relations reached an all-time peak. President Lyndon B. Johnson pushed through the Civil Rights Act of 1964, which remains the **fundamental** piece of civil rights legislation in this century. The Voting Rights Act of 1965 ensured that everyone in our country could vote. At last, black people and white people seemed ready to live together in peace.

---

1. **segregation** (seg′ rə gā′ shən) *n.* the practice of forcing racial groups to live apart from each other.

But that is not what happened. By the 1990's the good feelings had diminished. Today the nation seems to be suffering from compassion fatigue, and issues such as race relations and civil rights have never regained momentum.

Those issues, however, remain crucial. As our society becomes more diverse, people of all races and backgrounds will have to learn to live together. If we don't think this is important, all we have to do is look at the situation in Bosnia[2] today.

How do we create a harmonious society out of so many kinds of people? The key is tolerance—the one value that is indispensable in creating community.

If we are concerned about community, if it is important to us that people not feel excluded, then we have to do something. Each of us can decide to have one friend of a different race or background in our mix of friends. If we do this, we'll be working together to push things forward.

One thing is clear to me: We, as human beings, must be willing to accept people who are different from ourselves. I must be willing to accept people who don't look as I do and don't talk as I do. It is crucial that I am open to their feelings, their inner reality.

What can parents do? We can put our faith in young people as a positive force. I have yet to find a racist baby. Babies come into the world as blank slates and, with their beautiful innocence, see others not as different but as enjoyable companions. Children learn ideas and attitudes from the adults who nurture them. I absolutely believe that children do not adopt prejudices unless they absorb them from their parents or teachers.

The best way to get this country faithful to the American dream of tolerance and **equality** is to start small. Parents can actively encourage their children to be in the company of people who are of other racial and ethnic backgrounds. If a child thinks, "Well, that person's color is not the same as mine, but she must be okay because she likes to play with the same things I like to play with," that child will grow up with a broader view of humanity.

I'm an incurable **optimist**. For the rest of the time that I have left on this planet I want to bring people together. You

**Persuasive Essay**
Which persuasive technique does Jordan use with this reference to Bosnia?

**Spiral Review**
**STRUCTURE** The author organizes her ideas by asking and then answering a question. Do you think this structure is effective? Explain.

**◄ Vocabulary**
**equality** (ē kwôl′ə tē) *n.* social state in which all people are treated the same

**optimist** (äp′ tə mist) *n.* someone who takes the most hopeful view of matters

**Fact and Opinion**
What clue words in this paragraph show that the author is expressing an opinion?

**Comprehension**
What did the Voting Rights Act of 1965 do?

---

2. **Bosnia** (bäz′ nē ə) *n.* country, located on the Balkan Peninsula in Europe, that was the site of a bloody civil war between different ethnic and religious groups during the 1990s.

▲ **Critical Viewing** Does this photograph reflect the attitude Jordan conveys in the essay? Explain.

might think of this as a labor of love. Now, I know that love means different things to different people. But what *I* mean is this: I care about you because you are a fellow human being and I find it okay in my mind, in my heart, to simply say to you, I love you. And maybe that would encourage you to love me in return.

It is possible for all of us to work on this—at home, in our schools, at our jobs. It is possible to work on human relationships in every area of our lives.

## Language Study

**Vocabulary** The words listed below appear in "All Together Now." Answer each numbered question by writing a complete sentence that includes the italicized vocabulary word. Explain your answers.

**tolerant** **culminated** **fundamental** **equality** **optimist**

1. Is reading a *fundamental* part of education?
2. If Joan is an *optimist,* does she believe things will end well?
3. If people are *tolerant,* are they likely to accept others?
4. If a soccer team's season *culminated* in victory, what happened?
5. If a country is founded on *equality,* are some people treated differently than others?

**WORD STUDY**

The **Latin root *-leg-*** means "law." In this essay, Barbara Jordan argues that we need more than just **legislation**, or the act of making laws, to improve race relations.

### Word Study

**Part A** Explain how the **Latin root *-leg-*** contributes to the meanings of the words *allegation, legacy,* and *privilege*. Consult a dictionary if necessary.

**Part B** Use your knowledge of the Latin root *-leg-* to explain your answer to each question.

1. Is a thief likely to give a *legitimate* account of his actions?
2. Would you expect an honest person to do something *illegal*?

# Close Reading Activities

## Literary Analysis

### Key Ideas and Details

1. **Classifying Fact and Opinion** List two facts Jordan uses to support her ideas.
2. **Classifying Fact and Opinion** In a chart like the one on the right, record three opinions Jordan expresses, and list the clues from the text that helped you identify each opinion.
3. **(a)** How does Jordan summarize the history of race relations from the 1960s to the 1990s? Use examples from the essay to support your answer. **(b) Interpret:** In your own words, describe what Jordan means by "compassion fatigue."

| Opinion |
|---|
| |
| |
| **Clues** |
| |
| |

### Craft and Structure

4. **Persuasive Essay** Identify one appeal to authority, one appeal to emotion, and one appeal to reason that Jordan uses in this persuasive essay.
5. **(a)** According to Jordan, how do children learn ideas and attitudes? Support your answer with a quotation from the essay. **(b) Interpret:** What does Jordan mean when she says "I have yet to find a racist baby"?
6. **Persuasive Essay (a)** What is the most convincing argument Jordan makes? **(b)** Why is it convincing?

### Integration of Knowledge and Ideas

7. **(a)** What "one value" is necessary to create "a harmonious society"? **(b) Analyze:** Why does Jordan suggest Americans "start small" to promote this value? **(c) Apply:** What types of behavior might help reduce the problems Jordan describes?
8. **(a)** What does Jordan suggest parents do to foster a sense of community? **(b) Evaluate:** Do you think that Jordan's ideas could work to promote tolerance? Explain your answer using textual details.

9. THE BIG ? **What should we learn?** Discuss the following questions in a small group. **(a)** How can learning about the history of race relations help us in the future? **(b)** What can this knowledge teach us?

**ACADEMIC VOCABULARY**

As you write and speak about "All Together Now," use the words related to learning that you explored on page 175 of this textbook.

# Close Reading Activities Continued

## Conventions: **Conjunctions and Interjections**

**Conjunctions** connect words or groups of words. **Coordinating conjunctions,** such as *but* and *so,* connect words or groups of words of the same kind, such as two or more nouns or verbs.

In the following examples, the coordinating conjunctions are boldfaced. The words or groups of words they connect are italicized.

**Nouns:** The *pen* **and** *paper* contained fingerprints.

**Verbs:** Shall we *walk* **or** *ride* our bicycles?

**Groups of words:** *He ran out the door,* **but** *the bus had already left.*

| Coordinating Conjunctions | | |
|---|---|---|
| and | nor | so |
| but | or | yet |
| for | | |

An **interjection** is a part of speech that expresses a feeling, such as pain or excitement. An interjection may be set off with a comma or an exclamation point. Interjections can add emphasis and are especially useful for writing realistic dialogue.

In these examples, notice how the interjections are punctuated and how they make the writing sound more realistic.

**Pain:** Ouch! I hit my toe.

**Excitement:** Wow, Melissa can run really fast!

| Common Interjections | |
|---|---|
| Wow | Hey |
| Whew | Boy |
| Well | Yikes |
| Oh | Oops |

### Practice A

In each sentence, identify the coordinating conjunction and the words or groups of words connected by the conjunction.

1. My great-grandmother and great-grandfather grew up during segregation.
2. As young kids they attended all-black schools, but their high school was integrated.
3. Great-grandma had to work to help the family, so she waited tables after school.
4. Great-grandpa wrote and edited articles for the African-American newspaper.

**Reading Application** In "All Together Now," find two coordinating conjunctions, and identify the words they connect.

### Practice B

Rewrite each sentence, adding an interjection and the appropriate punctuation.

1. Many brave people put their lives on the line in the 1960s.
2. Did you know that some people actually died while fighting for civil rights?
3. Dr. Martin Luther King, Jr., inspired many people.
4. Do you know of any books I should read about the Civil Rights Movement?

**Writing Application** Write a paragraph about the ways that people can work together to bring about positive change. Use at least two coordinating conjunctions and two interjections.

## Writing to Sources

**Argument** Write a brief **persuasive letter** to community leaders advising them how people in the community can promote tolerance. Use examples from Jordan's essay to support your ideas and arguments. Demonstrate understanding of your topic as you draft.

- Clearly state your claim, or position. For example, "Promoting tolerance in our community would . . . ."
- Identify your goals. Then, use details from the text and other reliable sources to explain how to meet those goals.
- Defend your claims with logical reasoning and relevant evidence. Be sure to address alternate or opposing claims.
- Review your letter to ensure you have used correct formatting and that your tone is respectful and formal.

**Grammar Application** Check your writing to make sure you have used and punctuated conjunctions properly. To maintain a formal tone, you may decide not to use interjections in your letter.

## Speaking and Listening

**Comprehension and Collaboration** In a small group, write a **public service announcement** (PSA) on promoting the fair treatment of all people. Follow these steps to complete the assignment.

- Begin by brainstorming for ideas. Give all group members a chance to speak. Record everyone's ideas, and then as a group decide which ideas you will use in your PSA.
- Identify your audience, then draft your PSA. Support your claims with examples from "All Together Now." You may wish to include other relevant information that supports your main idea and appeals to your audience.
- Make your PSA memorable by using persuasive techniques such as those Jordan used in her essay.
- Present your PSA to the class. After your presentation, ask for feedback from your classmates.

# Building Knowledge

## Meet the Author

After starting out as a journalist, **Marjorie Kinnan Rawlings** (1896–1953) quit and moved to a farm she bought in northern Florida. There, her experiences and close exposure to nature inspired her to write several novels, including the 1939 Pulitzer Prize–winning book, *The Yearling.* While working on *The Yearling,* Rawlings prepared for key scenes by participating in bear hunts. Her writing reflects an intimate understanding and appreciation of the outdoors.

## What should we learn?

Explore the Big Question as you read "Rattlesnake Hunt." Take notes on the ways that learning about rattlesnakes helps the author learn about herself.

## CLOSE READING FOCUS

### Key Ideas and Details: **Classifying Fact and Opinion**

As you read nonfiction, note details a writer uses to support an idea. You can classify these details into two basic categories. A **fact** is information you can prove. An **opinion** is a judgment.

- **Fact:** The room measures ten feet by twelve feet.
- **Opinion:** Green is the best color for the room.

Be aware that some writers present opinions or beliefs as facts. To get to the truth, use resources to check facts.

### Craft and Structure: **Word Choice, or Diction**

A writer's **word choice,** or **diction,** can make writing seem difficult or easy, formal or informal. Diction includes not only individual words but also the phrases and expressions the writer uses. The answers to these questions shape a writer's diction:

- ***What does the audience already know about the topic?*** The writer may have to define terms or use simpler language.
- ***What feeling will this work convey?*** The use of casual or formal language can make a work serious or funny, academic or personal. The type of language and the length and style of the sentences can make a work seem simple or complex.

As you read, notice how the author's word choice affects the way you respond to a text.

## Vocabulary

You will encounter the following words in this essay. Write the words in your notebook, circling the one that has an opposite meaning from *life.* Explain how you arrived at your answer.

| | | |
|---|---|---|
| **adequate** | **desolate** | **forage** |
| **translucent** | **arid** | **mortality** |

## CLOSE READING MODEL

The passage below is from Marjorie Kinnan Rawlings's essay "Rattlesnake Hunt." The annotations to the right of the passage show ways in which you can use close reading skills to classify fact and opinion and to analyze the author's word choice, or diction.

### *from* "Rattlesnake Hunt"

I hope never in my life to be so frightened as I was in those first few hours. I kept on Ross' footsteps, I moved when he moved, sometimes jolting into him when I thought he might leave me behind. He does not use the forked stick of conventional snake hunting, but a steel prong, shaped like an L, at the end of a long stout stick.[1] He hunted casually, calling my attention to the varying vegetation, to hawks overhead, to a pair of the rare whooping cranes that flapped over us. In mid-morning he stopped short, dropped his stick, and brought up a five-foot rattlesnake draped limply over the steel L. It seemed to me that I should drop in my tracks.[2]

"They're not active at this season," he said quietly. "A snake takes on the temperature of its surroundings.[3] They can't stand too much heat for that reason, and when the weather is cool, as now, they're sluggish."[4]

The sun was bright overhead, the sky a translucent blue, and it seemed to me that it was warm enough for any snake to do as it willed.

**Word Choice, or Diction**

**1** Rawlings knows that many of her readers may be unfamiliar with snake-hunting tools. She defines her terms clearly and uses simple comparisons to help you visualize the prong that Ross uses.

**Word Choice, or Diction**

**2** Rawlings creates a conversational tone with the use of informal language and a detail about her intense personal reaction to the sight of the snake.

**Fact and Opinion**

**3** Here Rawlings provides facts that explain the snake's behavior. These facts help her—and her readers—feel less intimidated by the snake.

**Word Choice, or Diction**

**4** *Sluggish* means "slow to respond or react." This informal but vivid word is effective in helping you understand the snake's current state.

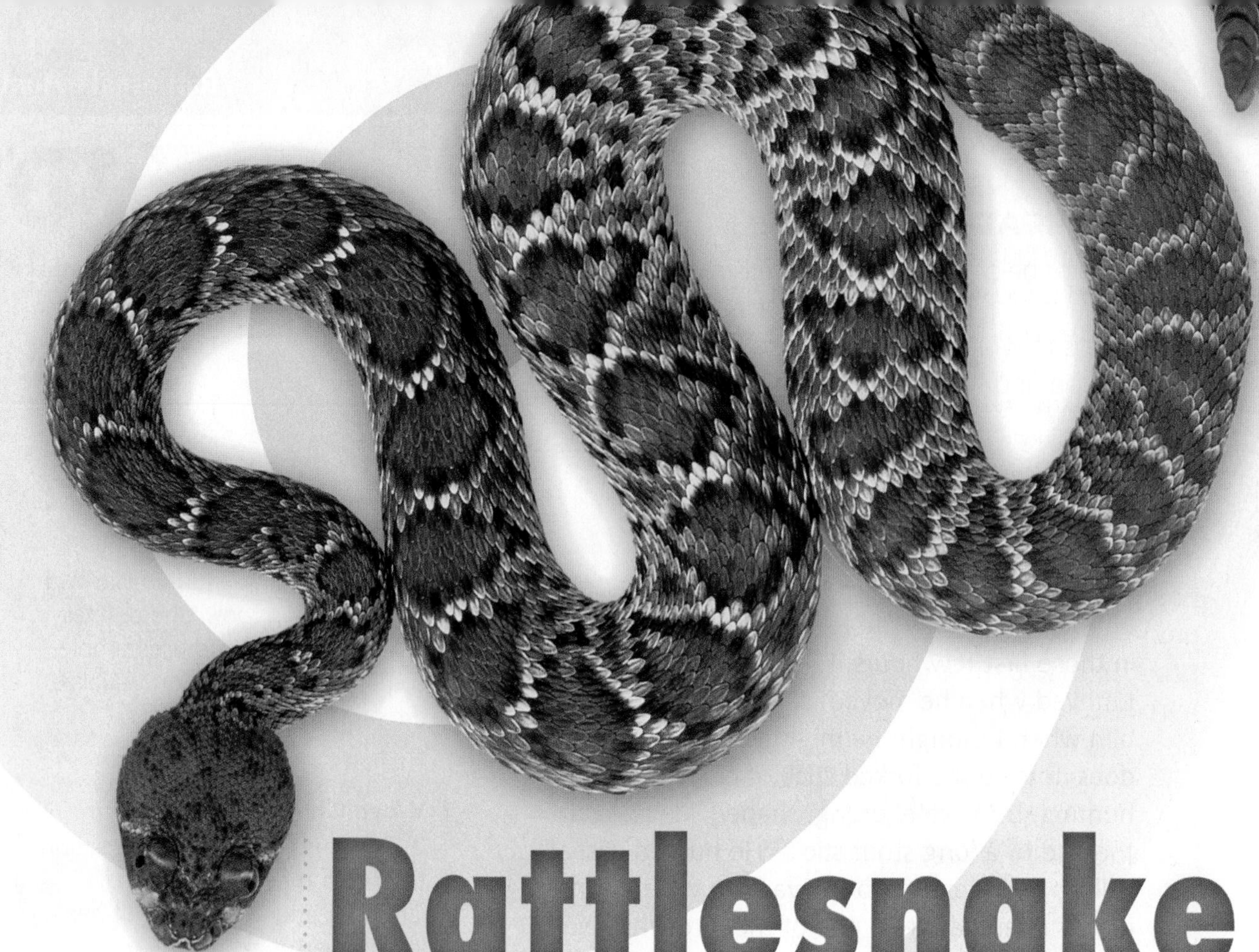

# Rattlesnake Hunt

Marjorie Kinnan Rawlings

▲ **Critical Viewing**
Would seeing a snake like this one frighten you? Why or why not?

**Vocabulary ▶**
**adequate** (ad′ i kwət) *adj.* sufficient; enough

Ross Allen, a young Florida herpetologist,[1] invited me to join him on a hunt in the upper Everglades[2]—for rattlesnakes. Ross and I drove to Arcadia in his coupé[3] on a warm January day.

I said, "How will you bring back the rattlesnakes?"

"In the back of my car."

My courage was not adequate to inquire whether they were thrown in loose and might be expected to appear between our feet. Actually, a large portable box of heavy close-meshed wire made a safe cage. Ross wanted me to

1. **herpetologist** (hʉr′ pə täl′ ə jist) *n.* someone who studies reptiles and amphibians.
2. **Everglades** large region of marshes in southern Florida, about one hundred miles long and averaging fifty miles in width.
3. **coupé** (ko͞o pā′) *n.* small two-door automobile.

write an article about his work and on our way to the unhappy hunting grounds I took notes on a mass of data that he had accumulated in years of herpetological research. The scientific and dispassionate detachment of the material and the man made a desirable approach to rattlesnake territory. As I had discovered with the insects and varmints,[4] it is difficult to be afraid of anything about which enough is known, and Ross' facts were fresh from the laboratory.

**Spiral Review**
**AUTHOR'S POINT OF VIEW** What is the author's attitude toward snakes? Which words in this paragraph show her perspective on the topic?

The hunting ground was Big Prairie, south of Arcadia and west of the northern tip of Lake Okeechobee. Big Prairie is a **desolate** cattle country, half marsh, half pasture, with islands of palm trees and cypress and oaks. At that time of year the cattlemen and Indians were burning the country, on the theory that the young fresh wire grass that springs up from the roots after a fire is the best cattle **forage**. Ross planned to hunt his rattlers in the forefront of the fires. They lived in winter, he said, in gopher holes, coming out in the midday warmth to forage, and would move ahead of the flames and be easily taken. We joined forces with a big man named Will, his snake-hunting companion of the territory, and set out in early morning, after a long rough drive over deep-rutted roads into the open wilds.

◀ **Vocabulary**
**desolate** (des´ ə lit) *adj.* lonely; solitary

**forage** (fôr´ ij) *n.* food for domestic animals

I hope never in my life to be so frightened as I was in those first few hours. I kept on Ross' footsteps, I moved when he moved, sometimes jolting into him when I thought he might leave me behind. He does not use the forked stick of conventional snake hunting, but a steel prong, shaped like an L, at the end of a long stout stick. He hunted casually, calling my attention to the varying vegetation, to hawks overhead, to a pair of the rare whooping cranes that flapped over us. In mid-morning he stopped short, dropped his stick, and brought up a five-foot rattlesnake draped limply over the steel L. It seemed to me that I should drop in my tracks.

**Fact and Opinion**
What reference source could confirm the fact in the last paragraph about a snake's temperature?

"They're not active at this season," he said quietly. "A snake takes on the temperature of its surroundings. They can't stand too much heat for that reason, and when the weather is cool, as now, they're sluggish."

**Comprehension**
Why is the narrator going on a rattlesnake hunt?

4. **varmints** (vär´ mənts) *n.* animals regarded as troublesome.

**Vocabulary ▶**
**translucent** (trans lo͞o´ sənt) *adj.* allowing some light through

**arid** (ar´id) *adj.* getting little rain, and therefore very dry

The sun was bright overhead, the sky a **translucent** blue, and it seemed to me that it was warm enough for any snake to do as it willed. The sweat poured down my back. Ross dropped the rattler in a crocus sack and Will carried it. By noon, he had caught four. I felt faint and ill. We stopped by a pond and went swimming. The region was flat, the horizon limitless, and as I came out of the cool blue water I expected to find myself surrounded by a ring of rattlers. There were only Ross and Will, opening the lunch basket. I could not eat. Will went back and drove his truck closer, for Ross expected the hunting to be better in the afternoon. The hunting was much better. When we went back to the truck to deposit two more rattlers in the wire cage, there was a rattlesnake lying under the truck.

Ross said, "Whenever I leave my car or truck with snakes already in it, other rattlers always appear. I don't know whether this is because they scent or sense the presence of other snakes, or whether in this **arid** area they come to the car for shade in the heat of the day."

**▼ Critical Viewing**
What makes the snake in this photograph appear dangerous?

The problem was scientific, but I had no interest. •

That night Ross and Will and I camped out in the vast spaces of the Everglades prairies.

We got water from an abandoned well and cooked supper under buttonwood bushes by a flowing stream. The camp fire blazed cheerfully under the stars and a new moon lifted in the sky. Will told tall tales of the cattlemen and the Indians and we were at peace.

Ross said, "We couldn't have a better night for catching water snakes."

After the rattlers, water snakes seemed innocuous[6] enough. We worked along the edge of the stream and here Ross did not use his L-shaped steel. He reached under rocks and along the edge of the water and brought out harmless reptiles with his hands. I had said nothing to him of my fears, but he understood them. He brought a small dark snake from under a willow root.

"Wouldn't you like to hold it?" he asked. "People think snakes are cold and clammy, but they aren't. Take it in your hands. You'll see that it is warm."

Again, because I was ashamed, I took the snake in my hands. It was not cold, it was not clammy, and it lay trustingly in my hands, a thing that lived and breathed and had **mortality** like the rest of us. I felt an upsurgence of spirit.

The next day was magnificent. The air was crystal, the sky was aquamarine, and the far horizon of palms and oaks lay against the sky. I felt a new boldness and followed Ross bravely. He was making the rounds of the gopher holes. The rattlers came out in the mid-morning warmth and were never far away. He could tell by their trails whether one had come out or was still in the hole. Sometimes the two men dug the snake out. At times it was down so long and winding a tunnel that the digging was hopeless. Then they blocked the entrance and went on to other holes. In an hour or so they made the original rounds, unblocking the holes. The rattler in every case came out hurriedly, as though anything were preferable to being shut in. All the time Ross talked to me, telling me the scientific facts he had discovered about the habits of the rattlers. •

"They pay no attention to a man standing perfectly still," he said, and proved it by letting Will unblock a hole while he stood at the entrance as the snake came out. It was exciting to

**▲ Critical Viewing**
Snakes are often pictured in art and on artifacts such as this Native American basket. Why do you think that is so?

**◀ Vocabulary**
**mortality** (môr tal′ ə tē) *n.* the condition of being mortal, or having to die eventually

**Comprehension**
How are the narrator's feelings changing?

6. **innocuous** (in näk′ yo͞o əs) *adj.* harmless.

watch the snake crawl slowly beside and past the man's legs. When it was at a safe distance he walked within its range of vision, which he had proved to be no higher than a man's knee, and the snake whirled and drew back in an attitude[7] of fighting defense. The rattler strikes only for paralyzing and killing its food, and for defense.

**Fact and Opinion**
Is Ross stating fact or opinion in this paragraph? How do you know?

"It is a slow and heavy snake," Ross said. "It lies in wait on a small game trail and strikes the rat or rabbit passing by. It waits a few minutes, then follows along the trail, coming to the small animal, now dead or dying. It noses it from all sides, making sure that it is its own kill, and that it is dead and ready for swallowing."

**Word Choice, or Diction**
How would you rephrase "as the sun mounted in the sky and warmed the moist Everglades" in less formal language?

A rattler will lie quietly without revealing itself if a man passes by and it thinks it is not seen. It slips away without fighting if given the chance. Only Ross' sharp eyes sometimes picked out the gray and yellow diamond pattern, camouflaged among the grasses. In the cool of the morning, chilled by the January air, the snakes showed no fight. They could be looped up limply over the steel L and dropped in a sack or up into the wire cage on the back of Will's truck. As the sun mounted in the sky and warmed the moist Everglades earth, the snakes were warmed too, and Ross warned that it was time to go more cautiously. Yet having learned that it was we who were the aggressors; that immobility meant complete safety; that the snakes, for all their lightning flash

7. **attitude** (at′ ə to͞od′) *n.* a position or posture of the body.

in striking, were inaccurate in their aim, with limited vision; having watched again and again the liquid grace of movement, the beauty of pattern, suddenly I understood that I was drinking in freely the magnificent sweep of the horizon, with no fear of what might be at the moment under my feet. I went off hunting by myself, and though I found no snakes, I should have known what to do.

The sun was dropping low in the west. Masses of white cloud hung above the flat marshy plain and seemed to be tangled in the tops of distant palms and cypresses. The sky turned orange, then saffron. I walked leisurely back toward the truck. In the distance I could see Ross and Will making their way in too. The season was more advanced than at the Creek, two hundred miles to the north, and I noticed that spring flowers were blooming among the lumpy hummocks. I leaned over to pick a white violet. There was a rattlesnake under the violet.

If this had happened the week before, if it had happened the day before, I think I should have lain down and died on top of the rattlesnake, with no need of being struck and poisoned. The snake did not coil, but lifted its head and whirred its rattles lightly. I stepped back slowly and put the violet in a buttonhole. I reached forward and laid the steel L across the snake's neck, just back of the blunt head. I called to Ross:

"I've got one."

He strolled toward me.

"Well, pick it up," he said.

I released it and slipped the L under the middle of the thick body.

"Go put it in the box."

He went ahead of me and lifted the top of the wire cage. I made the truck with the rattler, but when I reached up the six feet to drop it in the cage, it slipped off the stick and dropped on Ross' feet. It made no effort to strike.

"Pick it up again," he said. "If you'll pin it down lightly and reach just back of its head with your hand, as you've seen me do, you can drop it in more easily."

I pinned it and leaned over.

**LITERATURE IN CONTEXT**

## Language Connection

### Scientific Words From Greek Origins

Ross Allen studies herpetology. The word *herpetology* comes from the Greek words *herpein*, meaning "to creep," and *logo*, meaning "word." Other scientific words derived from Greek and ending with the suffix *-ology* (meaning "science or theory of") include *biology*, the study of animals and plants; *anthropology*, the study of humans; *ichthyology*, the study of fish; and *paleontology*, the study of life forms from the past, especially fossils.

**Connect to the Literature**

How does the origin of the word *herpetology* explain why herpetologists study snakes?

**Comprehension**
What will a rattler do if it thinks it is not seen?

**Word Choice, or Diction**
On this page, find an example of an informal expression that is used by the author.

"I'm awfully sorry," I said, "but you're pushing me a little too fast."

He grinned. I lifted it on the stick and again as I had it at head height, it slipped off, down Ross' boots and on top of his feet. He stood as still as a stump. I dropped the snake on his feet for the third time. It seemed to me that the most patient of rattlers might in time resent being hauled up and down, and for all the man's quiet certainty that in standing motionless there was no danger, would strike at whatever was nearest, and that would be Ross.

I said, "I'm just not man enough to keep this up any longer," and he laughed and reached down with his smooth quickness and lifted the snake back of the head and dropped it in the cage. It slid in among its mates and settled in a corner. The hunt was over and we drove back over the uneven trail to Will's village and left him and went on to Arcadia and home. Our catch for the two days was thirty-two rattlers.

I said to Ross, "I believe that tomorrow I could have picked up that snake."

Back at the Creek, I felt a new lightness. I had done battle with a great fear, and the victory was mine.

## Language Study

**Vocabulary** The words listed below appear in "Rattlesnake Hunt." For each item, write a single sentence correctly using the words indicated.

**adequate** **forage** **translucent** **arid** **mortality**

**1.** arid, farmer

**2.** mortality, medicine

**3.** adequate, light

**4.** forage, horse

**5.** translucent, marbles

**WORD STUDY**

The **Latin root *-sol-*** means "alone." Rawlings's hunting trip takes her into **desolate**, or lonely, territory.

### Word Study

**Part A** Explain how the **Latin root *-sol-*** contributes to the meaning of the words *soliloquy, consolidate,* and *soloist*. Consult a dictionary if necessary.

**Part B** Use the sentence context and your knowledge of the Latin root *-sol-* to explain your answer to each question.

**1.** How many people can play a game of *solitaire*?

**2.** If you seek *solitude*, do you want others around?

## Literary Analysis

### Key Ideas and Details

1. **Classifying Fact and Opinion** Identify one fact and one opinion in the essay.
2. **(a)** Why does Rawlings go on the hunt? **(b) Infer:** Why do Rawlings's feelings about snakes change when she holds one? Support your inference using details from the text.
3. **Classifying Fact and Opinion** What resource would you use to check the facts about a rattlesnake's vision?
4. **Classifying Fact and Opinion** How do both facts and opinions help Rawlings explain her experience with snakes? Cite details from the text in your response.

### Craft and Structure

5. **Word Choice, or Diction** Review the author's word choice, or diction, by completing a chart like the one on the right. Then, summarize the effect of the writer's word choice, or diction.
6. **Word Choice, or Diction** Reread the top of page 227. How do phrases like "the liquid grace of movement, the beauty of pattern" reflect the author's new attitude toward snakes?
7. **(a)** Note two ways in which Rawlings shows that she has partly overcome her fears. **(b) Infer:** Why does the author announce at the end of the hunt that she has won a "victory"?

| Technical Vocabulary |
| --- |
| |
| **Formal Language** |
| |
| **Informal Language** |
| |

### Integration of Knowledge and Ideas

8. **Analyze:** How is the information presented about snakes the same as or different from information found in works of fiction, popular media, or textbooks? Support your answer with specific examples from the essay.
9. **Evaluate:** How successful was the author in sharing her experiences with readers? Explain.

10. THE BIG ? **What should we learn? (a)** In what ways does the hunt change how Rawlings thinks about nature and herself? **(b)** How does conquering our fears allow us greater freedom to learn about the world? Support your response with examples.

**ACADEMIC VOCABULARY**

As you write and speak about "Rattlesnake Hunt," use the words related to learning that you explored on page 175 of this textbook.

## Conventions: Simple and Compound Subjects and Predicates

Every sentence has a **subject** and a **predicate,** which together express a complete thought. The subject describes whom or what the sentence is about. The predicate is a verb that tells what the subject does, what is done to the subject, or what the condition of the subject is.

- A **simple subject** is the main noun or pronoun. A **complete subject** is a simple subject and all the words that modify it.
- A **simple predicate** is the main verb or verb phrase. A **complete predicate** is a simple predicate and all the words that modify or complete it.
- A **compound subject** contains two or more subjects that share the same verb. The subjects are joined by a conjunction such as *and* or *or.*
- A **compound predicate** contains two or more verbs that share the same subject. The predicates are joined by a conjunction.

| Simple Subject/ Simple Predicate | Complete Subject/ Complete Predicate | Compound Subject | Compound Predicate |
|---|---|---|---|
| The well-known author wrote many stories. | The talented writer described her life in Florida. | Rawlings and the hunter walked carefully. | Snakes sleep or wake on their own schedules. |

### Practice A

Rewrite these sentences. Underline the simple subjects, double underline the simple predicates, and circle any compound subjects and compound predicates.

1. The author follows a snake hunter.
2. He and the author hunt snakes in the upper Everglades.
3. The man knows the area well.
4. The snake hunter finds and captures rattlesnakes.

**Reading Application** In "Rattlesnake Hunt," identify the subjects and predicates in three different sentences.

### Practice B

Write sentences using the subjects and predicates listed.

1. snake; slithers
2. herons, whooping cranes; fly
3. gopher; hid
4. Ross, Will; hiked, hunted
5. hawk; waits, watches

**Writing Application** Write three sentences about snakes. Then, circle the simple subjects and the predicates. Finally, draw a line between the complete subjects and complete predicates.

## Writing to Sources

**Informative Text** Write an **adaptation** of an incident described in "Rattlesnake Hunt." Retell the incident for a new audience, such as a group of kindergarteners or a class of students learning English. Follow these steps:

- Review the essay, and choose an incident to retell. Then, decide on an audience.
- Draft to reflect the needs and interests of your audience.
- Use precise words and sensory language to add life and immediacy to your description. Include quotations from the selection to highlight important parts of the incident.
- Finally, revise to organize ideas logically, making sure you have met both your purpose and the needs of your audience.

**Grammar Application** Make sure to use subjects and predicates correctly in your essay. Compound subjects joined with *and* share the same verb and take the plural form. Compound subjects joined with *or* take the form of the verb that agrees with the subject closest to the verb.

## Research and Technology

**Build and Present Knowledge** Write a **help-wanted ad** for a person to work with Ross Allen, the herpetologist. Before you write, use online search terms, such as *herpetologist, experience required,* and *scientist* to find related help-wanted ads to use as models. To determine the necessary qualifications to describe in your ad, refer to details in the essay.

- Notice the concise writing style of ads, and review what the ads cover, including job responsibilities, education, experience, skills, and personal traits the employer seeks.
- Use language that is appropriate for a business ad, including correct grammar and tone.
- Type your ad on a computer and use the spell-check feature.
- Add clip art or other visual displays to enhance key ideas, clarify a point, or add interest.
- Experiment with typefaces to emphasize main ideas.

## What should we learn?

Explore the Big Question as you read these selections. Take notes on what the main characters learn and how that knowledge helps them face their situations.

## READING TO COMPARE FICTION AND NONFICTION

As you read a short story by Ernest Hemingway and an autobiographical narrative by Ernesto Galarza, compare and contrast the ways that these authors use elements of fiction and nonfiction.

AUTOBIOGRAPHY

SHORT STORY

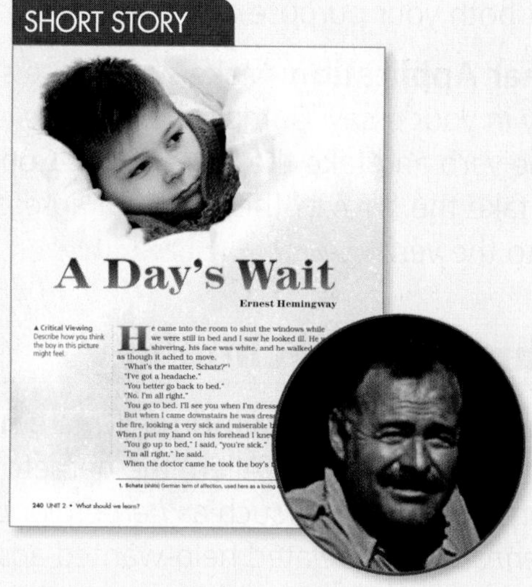


### from *Barrio Boy*

**Ernesto Galarza** (1905–1984) When he was a young child, Ernesto Galarza moved with his family from Mexico to California. There, his family harvested crops and struggled to make ends meet. Galarza learned English quickly and won a scholarship for college. From 1936 to 1947, Galarza worked to improve education and workers' lives in Latin America. When he returned to California, he worked to gain rights for farm workers.

### "A Day's Wait"

**Ernest Hemingway** (1899–1961) A true adventurer, Ernest Hemingway based much of his writing on his own experiences. He served as an ambulance driver in World War I, worked as a journalist, traveled the world, and enjoyed outdoor sports. Hemingway's fiction celebrates his spirit of adventure. Among his most famous works are *A Farewell to Arms, For Whom the Bell Tolls,* and *The Old Man and the Sea.*

## Comparing Fiction and Nonfiction

**Fiction** is prose writing that tells about imaginary characters and events. Novels, novellas, and short stories are types of fiction. **Literary nonfiction** is prose writing that tells about real people, places, objects, or events. Biographies, memoirs, and historical accounts are types of nonfiction.

While one is fiction and the other nonfiction, the selections that follow are both examples of **narrative writing** that include the following elements:

- a *narrator* who tells the story
- *characters*, or people living the story
- *dialogue*, or the conversations that the characters have
- story *events* that make up the action
- a *theme* or *central idea*

These elements work together to develop the narratives. For example, both writers use dialogue to convey the impact that a specific event or situation has upon the characters.

The use of a narrator is another important element of fiction and literary nonfiction. The narrator in the excerpt from *Barrio Boy* tells about an important real event in the writer's life. In contrast, the narrator in "A Day's Wait" tells the story of an imagined boy on a single day. As you read, use a chart like the one shown to note ways in which the elements and features of the works are similar and different.

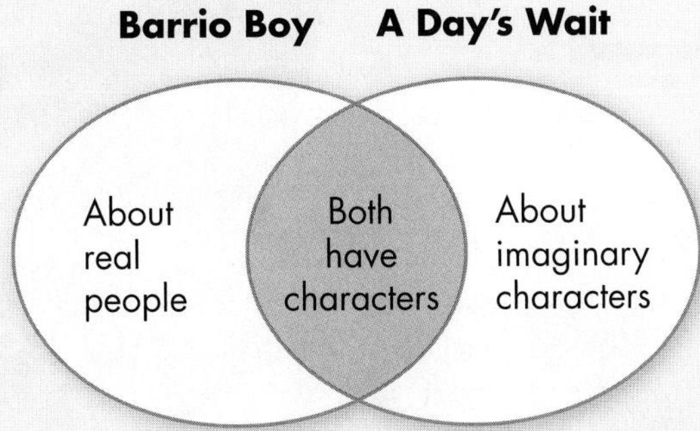

from

# Barrio Boy

Ernesto Galarza

My mother and I walked south on Fifth Street one morning to the corner of Q Street and turned right. Half of the block was occupied by the Lincoln School. It was a three-story wooden building, with two wings that gave it the shape of a double-T connected by a central hall. It was a new building, painted yellow, with a shingled roof that was not like the red tile of the school in Mazatlán. I noticed other differences, none of them very **reassuring**.

We walked up the wide staircase hand in hand and through the door, which closed by itself. A mechanical **contraption** screwed to the top shut it behind us quietly.

Up to this point the adventure of enrolling me in the school had been carefully rehearsed. Mrs. Dodson had told us how to find it and we had circled it several times on our walks. Friends in the *barrio*[1] explained that the director was called a principal, and that it was a lady and not a man. They assured us that there was always a person at the school who could speak Spanish.

Exactly as we had been told, there was a sign on the door in both Spanish and English: "Principal." We crossed the hall and entered the office of Miss Nettie Hopley.

Miss Hopley was at a roll-top desk to one side, sitting in a swivel chair that moved on wheels. There was a sofa against the opposite wall, flanked by two windows and a door that opened on a small balcony. Chairs were set around a table and framed pictures hung on the walls of a man with long white hair and another with a sad face and a black beard.

The principal half turned in the swivel chair to look at us

**◀ Critical Viewing**
Does this picture convey the emotions that a child might feel as he enrolls in a new school? Explain.

**◀ Vocabulary**
**reassuring**
(rē ə shoo͞r′ iŋ)
*adj.* having the effect of restoring confidence

**contraption**
(kən trap′ shən)
*n.* strange device or machine

**Nonfiction**
Who is the narrator of this work? How can you tell?

1. **barrio** (bär′ ē ō) *n.* part of a town or city where most of the people are Hispanic.

▲ **Critical Viewing**
Do you think the narrator would feel comfortable in a classroom like this one? Why or why not?

over the pinch glasses crossed on the ridge of her nose. To do this she had to duck her head slightly as if she were about to step through a low doorway.

What Miss Hopley said to us we did not know but we saw in her eyes a warm welcome and when she took off her glasses and straightened up she smiled wholeheartedly, like Mrs. Dodson. We were, of course, saying nothing, only catching the friendliness of her voice and the sparkle in her eyes while she said words we did not understand. She signaled us to the table. Almost tiptoeing across the office, I maneuvered myself to keep my mother between me and the gringo lady. In a matter of seconds I had to decide whether she was a possible friend or a menace.[2] We sat down.

**Vocabulary ▶**
**formidable**
(fôr′ mə də bəl) *adj.* impressive

Then Miss Hopley did a **formidable** thing. She stood up. Had she been standing when we entered she would have seemed tall. But rising from her chair she soared. And what she carried up and up with her was a buxom superstructure,[3] firm shoulders, a straight sharp nose, full cheeks slightly molded by a curved line along the nostrils, thin lips that moved like steel springs, and a high forehead topped by hair gathered in a bun. Miss Hopley was not a giant in body but when she mobilized[4] it to a standing position she seemed

2. **menace** (men′ əs) *n.* danger; threat.
3. **buxom superstructure** full figure.
4. **mobilized** (mō′ bə līzd′) *v.* put into motion.

a match for giants. I decided I liked her.

She strode to a door in the far corner of the office, opened it and called a name. A boy of about ten years appeared in the doorway. He sat down at one end of the table. He was brown like us, a plump kid with shiny black hair combed straight back, neat, cool, and faintly obnoxious.

Miss Hopley joined us with a large book and some papers in her hand. She, too, sat down and the questions and answers began by way of our interpreter. My name was Ernesto. My mother's name was Henriqueta. My birth certificate was in San Blas. Here was my last report card from the Escuela Municipal Numero 3 para Varones of Mazatlán,[5] and so forth. Miss Hopley put things down in the book and my mother signed a card.

My name was Ernesto. My mother's name was Henriqueta. My birth certificate was in San Blas.

As long as the questions continued, Doña[6] Henriqueta could stay and I was secure. Now that they were over, Miss Hopley saw her to the door, dismissed our interpreter and without further ado took me by the hand and strode down the hall to Miss Ryan's first grade.

Miss Ryan took me to a seat at the front of the room, into which I shrank—the better to survey her. She was, to skinny, somewhat runty me, of a withering height when she patrolled the class. And when I least expected it, there she was, crouching by my desk, her blond radiant face level with mine, her voice patiently maneuvering me over the awful idiocies of the English language.

During the next few weeks Miss Ryan overcame my fears of tall, energetic teachers as she bent over my desk to help me with a word in the pre-primer. Step by step, she loosened me and my classmates from the safe anchorage of the desks for recitations at the blackboard and consultations at her desk. Frequently she burst into happy announcements to the whole class. "Ito can read a sentence," and small Japanese Ito, squint-eyed and shy, slowly read aloud while the class listened in wonder: "Come, Skipper, come. Come and run." The Korean, Portuguese, Italian, and

**Comprehension**
How did the principal welcome the narrator and his mother?

---

5. **Escuela Municipal Numero 3 para Varones of Mazatlán** (es kwā lä mo͞o nē sē päl′ no͞o′ me rō trās pä′ rä bä rō′ nesuv mä sät län′) Municipal School Number 3 for Boys of Mazatlán.
6. **Doña** (dō′ nyä) Spanish title of respect meaning "lady" or "madam."

Polish first graders had similar moments of glory, no less shining than mine the day I conquered "butterfly," which I had been persistently pronouncing in standard Spanish as boo-ter-flee. "Children," Miss Ryan called for attention. "Ernesto has learned how to pronounce *butterfly*!" And I proved it with a perfect imitation of Miss Ryan. From that celebrated success, I was soon able to match Ito's progress as a sentence reader with "Come, butterfly, come fly with me."

Like Ito and several other first graders who did not know English, I received private lessons from Miss Ryan in the closet, a narrow hall off the classroom with a door at each end. Next to one of these doors Miss Ryan placed a large chair for herself and a small one for me. Keeping an eye on the class through the open door she read with me about sheep in the meadow and a frightened chicken going to see the king, coaching me out of my phonetic ruts in words like *pasture, bow-wow-wow, hay,* and *pretty,* which to my Mexican ear and eye had so many unnecessary sounds and letters. She made me watch her lips and then close my eyes as she repeated words I found hard to read. When we came to know each other better, I tried interrupting to tell Miss Ryan how we said it in Spanish. It didn't work. She only said "oh" and went on with *pasture, bow-wow-wow,* and *pretty.* It was as if in that closet we were both discovering together the secrets of the English language and grieving together over the tragedies of Bo-Peep. The main reason I was graduated with honors from the first grade was that I had fallen in love with Miss Ryan. Her radiant, no-nonsense character made us either afraid not to love her or love her so we would not be afraid, I am not sure which. It was not only that we sensed she was with it, but also that she was with us. Like the first grade, the rest of the Lincoln School was a sampling of the lower part of town where many races made their home. My pals in the second grade were Kazushi, whose parents spoke only Japanese; Matti, a skinny Italian boy; and Manuel, a fat Portuguese who would never get into a fight but wrestled you to the ground and just sat on you. Our assortment of nationalities included Koreans, Yugoslavs, Poles, Irish, and home-grown Americans.

At Lincoln, making us into Americans did not mean scrubbing away what made us originally foreign. The teachers called us as our parents did, or as close as they could pronounce our names in Spanish or Japanese. No one was ever scolded or punished for speaking in his native tongue on

**Nonfiction**
What details in this section help you appreciate the importance of the author's actual experience?

**Nonfiction**
What details in this passage tell about each character in the narrative?

**Spiral Review**
**CENTRAL IDEA** How do Galarza's memories of Lincoln School relate to a central idea?

the playground. Matti told the class about his mother's down quilt, which she had made in Italy with the fine feathers of a thousand geese. Encarnación acted out how boys learned to fish in the Philippines. I astounded the third grade with the story of my travels on a stagecoach, which nobody else in the class had seen except in the museum at Sutter's Fort. After a visit to the Crocker Art Gallery and its collection of heroic paintings of the golden age of California, someone showed a silk scroll with a Chinese painting. Miss Hopley herself had a way of expressing wonder over these matters before a class, her eyes wide open until they popped slightly. It was easy for me to feel that becoming a proud American, as she said we should, did not mean feeling ashamed of being a Mexican.

▲ **Critical Viewing** What do you think it would be like to travel in a stagecoach like the one in this picture?

## Critical Thinking

1. **Key Ideas and Details** Describe Galarza's experiences as a newcomer in school. Provide specific textual details in your summary.
2. **Key Ideas and Details (a)** Why is Galarza afraid of Miss Ryan at first? **(b) Interpret:** What does Galarza mean when he says Miss Ryan "was with it" and "with us"?
3. **Integration of Knowledge and Ideas** What experiences in Lincoln School help Galarza realize his dream of "becoming a proud American"? Cite details to support your analysis.
4. **Integration of Knowledge and Ideas (a)** What is the unknown that frightens Galarza in this story? **(b)** What does Galarza learn about himself and those around him from his experiences at school? **(c)** Why is this learning process important? ***[Connect to the Big Question: What should we learn?]***

# A Day's Wait

**Ernest Hemingway**

▲ **Critical Viewing**
Describe how you think the boy in this picture might feel.

He came into the room to shut the windows while we were still in bed and I saw he looked ill. He was shivering, his face was white, and he walked slowly as though it ached to move.

"What's the matter, Schatz?"[1]

"I've got a headache."

"You better go back to bed."

"No. I'm all right."

"You go to bed. I'll see you when I'm dressed."

But when I came downstairs he was dressed, sitting by the fire, looking a very sick and miserable boy of nine years. When I put my hand on his forehead I knew he had a fever.

"You go up to bed," I said, "you're sick."

"I'm all right," he said.

When the doctor came he took the boy's temperature.

1. **Schatz** (shäts) German term of affection, used here as a loving nickname.

"What is it?" I asked him.

"One hundred and two."

Downstairs, the doctor left three different medicines in different colored capsules with instructions for giving them. One was to bring down the fever, another a purgative, the third to overcome an acid condition. The germs of influenza can only exist in an acid condition, he explained. He seemed to know all about influenza and said there was nothing to worry about if the fever did not go above one hundred and four degrees. This was a light **epidemic** of flu and there was no danger if you avoided pneumonia.

◀ **Vocabulary**
**epidemic** (epʹ ə demʹ ik) *n.* outbreak of a contagious disease

Back in the room I wrote the boy's temperature down and made a note of the time to give the various capsules.

"Do you want me to read to you?"

"All right. If you want to," said the boy. His face was very white and there were dark areas under his eyes. He lay still in the bed and seemed very detached from what was going on.

I read aloud from Howard Pyle's *Book of Pirates*; but I could see he was not following what I was reading.

"How do you feel, Schatz?" I asked him.

"Just the same, so far," he said.

I sat at the foot of the bed and read to myself while I waited for it to be time to give another capsule. It would have been natural for him to go to sleep, but when I looked up he was looking at the foot of the bed, looking very strangely.

"Why don't you try to go to sleep? I'll wake you up for the medicine."

"I'd rather stay awake."

After a while he said to me, "You don't have to stay in here with me, Papa, if it bothers you."

"It doesn't bother me."

"No. I mean you don't have to stay if it's going to bother you."

I thought perhaps he was a little lightheaded and after giving him the prescribed capsules at eleven o'clock I went out for a while.

It was a bright, cold day, the ground covered with a sleet that had frozen so that it seemed as if all the bare trees, the bushes, the cut brush and all the grass and the bare ground had been varnished with ice. I took the young Irish setter for a little walk up the road and along a frozen creek, but it was difficult to stand or walk on the glassy surface and the red dog slipped and slithered and I fell twice, hard, once dropping my gun and having it slide away over the ice.

We **flushed** a covey of quail under a high clay bank with overhanging brush and I killed two as they went out of sight

**Vocabulary ▶**
**flushed** (flusht) *v.* drove from hiding

**Fiction**
Who is the narrator of this work? How do you know?

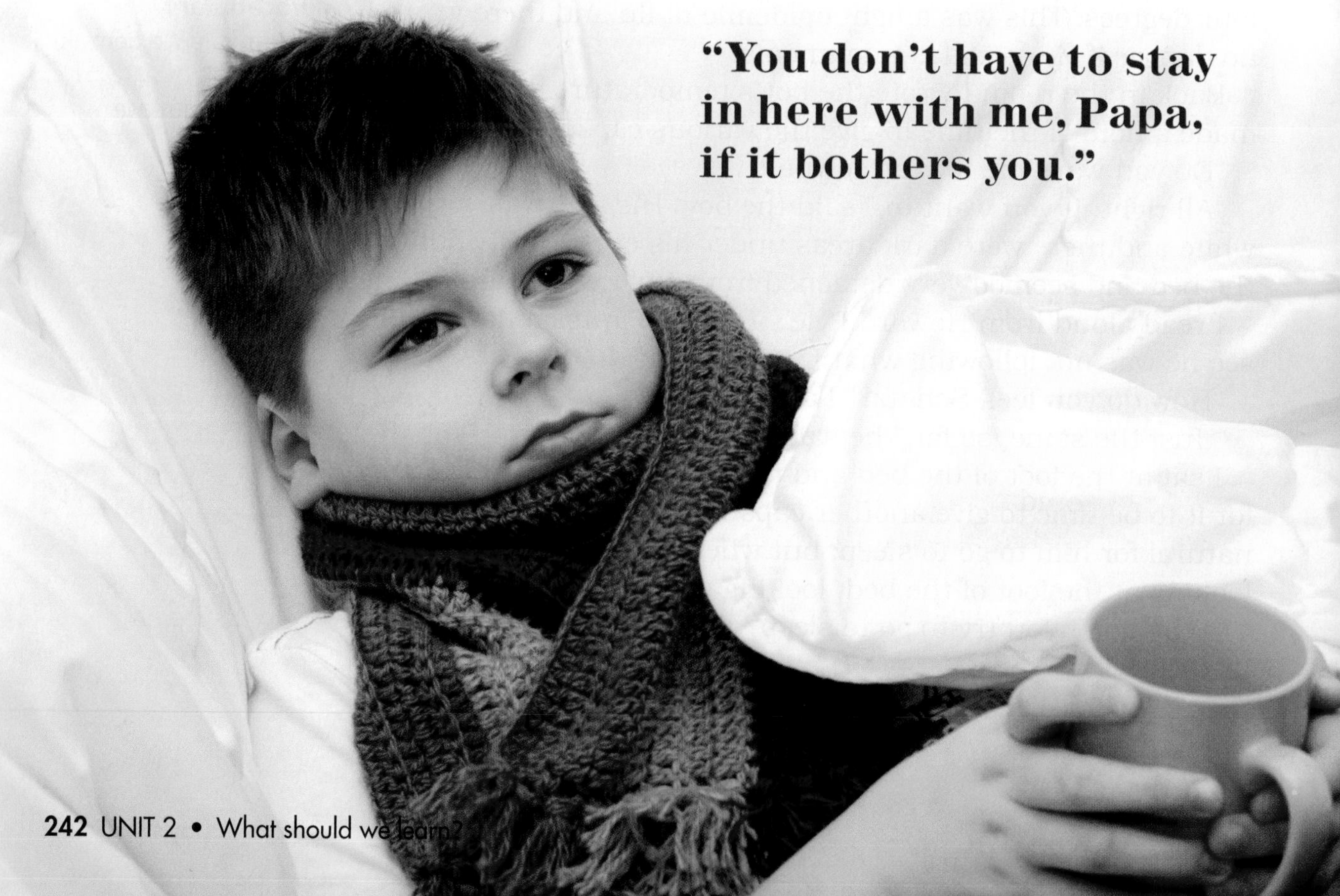

**"You don't have to stay in here with me, Papa, if it bothers you."**

over the top of the bank. Some of the covey lit in trees but most of them scattered into brush piles and it was necessary to jump on the ice-coated mounds of brush several times before they would flush. Coming out while you were poised unsteadily on the icy, springy brush they made difficult shooting, and I killed two, missed five, and started back pleased to have found a covey close to the house and happy there were so many left to find on another day.

At the house they said the boy had refused to let anyone come into the room.

"You can't come in," he said. "You mustn't get what I have."

I went up to him and found him in exactly the position I had left him, white-faced, but with the tops of his cheeks flushed by the fever, staring still, as he had stared at the foot of the bed.

I took his temperature.

"What is it?"

"Something like a hundred," I said. It was one hundred and two and four tenths.

"It was a hundred and two," he said.

"Who said so?"

"The doctor."

"Your temperature is all right," I said. "It's nothing to worry about."

"I don't worry," he said, "but I can't keep from thinking."

"Don't think," I said. "Just take it easy."

"I'm taking it easy," he said and looked straight ahead. He was **evidently** holding tight on to himself about something.

"Take this with water."

"Do you think it will do any good?"

"Of course it will."

I sat down and opened the *Pirate* book and commenced to read, but I could see he was not following, so I stopped.

"About what time do you think I'm going to die?" he asked.

"What?"

"About how long will it be before I die?"

"You aren't going to die. What's the matter with you?"

"Oh, yes, I am. I heard him say a hundred and two."

## LITERATURE IN CONTEXT

### Science Connection

**Temperature Scales**
You might have been taught that ice and snow melt when the temperature is 32°F, or Fahrenheit. Another commonly known temperature is 98.6°F—normal body temperature. Using the Celsius scale is another matter. Water freezes at 0° Celsius, or C, and boils at 100°C.

When temperature is expressed one way and must be converted to the other, there are formulas or conversion charts to help. Today, only the United States and Jamaica still use Fahrenheit as the standard for most measurements.

**Connect to the Literature**

Why is the boy's temperature important to him and his father?

◀ **Vocabulary**
**evidently** (ev´ ə dent´ lē) *adv.* clearly; obviously

**Comprehension**
How does the boy know his temperature?

"People don't die with a fever of one hundred and two. That's a silly way to talk."

"I know they do. At school in France the boys told me you can't live with forty-four degrees. I've got a hundred and two."

He had been waiting to die all day, ever since nine o'clock in the morning.

"You poor Schatz," I said. "Poor old Schatz. It's like miles and kilometers. You aren't going to die. That's a different thermometer. On that thermometer thirty-seven is normal. On this kind it's ninety-eight."

"Are you sure?"

"Absolutely," I said. "It's like miles and kilometers. You know, like how many kilometers we make when we do seventy miles in the car?"

"Oh," he said.

But his gaze at the foot of the bed relaxed slowly. The hold over himself relaxed too, finally, and the next day it was very slack and he cried very easily at little things that were of no importance.

**Spiral Review**
**THEME** What critical information has the boy learned from this conversation with his father? How does his reaction relate to a possible theme?

## Critical Thinking

1. **Key Ideas and Details (a)** Why does the boy tell his father to leave the sickroom? **(b) Infer:** What does this action reveal about the boy?
2. **Key Ideas and Details (a)** Why does the boy think he will die? Use details from the story to support your response. **(b) Interpret:** What is the meaning of the story's title?
3. **Key Ideas and Details (a) Analyze:** Which of the boy's words and actions give clues that he believes something terrible is wrong? **(b) Evaluate:** Do you think the story is about the boy's bravery or about the boy's fear? Explain. **(c) Speculate:** What might have happened if the boy had shared his fears?
4. **Integration of Knowledge and Ideas** When the truth of the boy's illness is explained to him, what has he learned about his own character? ***[Connect to the Big Question: What should we learn?]***

# Writing to Sources

## Comparing Fiction and Nonfiction

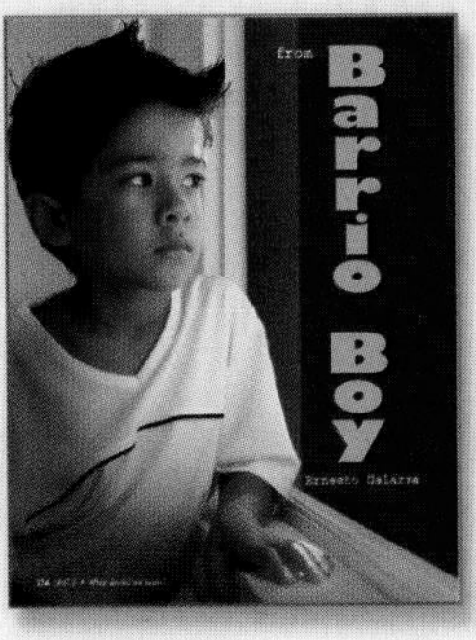

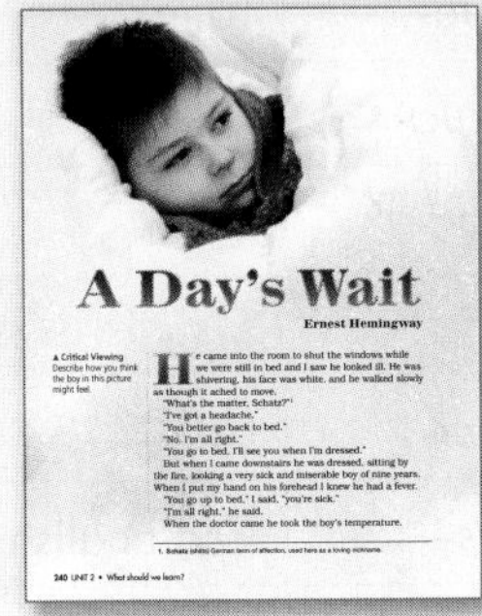

1. **Craft and Structure (a)** For each selection, tell whether the narrator and events are real or imagined. **(b)** Based on your answer, what rules about truth and accuracy did each writer follow for writing these selections?
2. **Key Ideas and Details** Complete a chart like the one shown to help you analyze one character in each story.

| Character | Detail | Fiction or Nonfiction? |
|---|---|---|
| The boy in "A Day's Wait" | | |
| Miss Ryan in *Barrio Boy* | | |

3. **Integration of Knowledge and Ideas (a)** How might "A Day's Wait" be different if it were nonfiction? **(b)** How might *Barrio Boy* change if it were fiction?

## Timed Writing

### Explanatory Text: Essay

In a brief essay, compare and contrast the narrators of *Barrio Boy* and "A Day's Wait." State your topic in the introduction and discuss how the narrator presents the events in each work. Consider adding a chart to show what is the same and different. **(40 minutes)**

### 5-Minute Planner

1. Gather your ideas by jotting down answers to these questions:
   - Which work includes more personal details about the narrator?
   - Do the narrator's thoughts and actions build toward a specific theme or insight? Why or why not?
   - Which narrator is central to the narrative's action?
2. Choose an organizational strategy. If you use the block method, present all the details about one narrator, then all the details about the other narrator. If you use the point-by-point method, discuss one aspect of both narrators, then another aspect of both narrators, and so on.
3. Reread the prompt and then draft your essay.

**USE ACADEMIC VOCABULARY**

As you write, use academic language, including the following words or their related forms:

**adaptation**
**culture**
**diversity**
**tradition**

For more information about academic vocabulary, see pp. xlvi-l.

# Language Study

## Word Origins

A word's **origin,** or **etymology,** tells the history of the word. Knowing the history of a word or word part can help you understand its meaning. This chart gives the meanings of several Latin, Greek, Old English, and Middle English word parts.

| Latin and Greek Word Parts | | | |
|---|---|---|---|
| **Roots** | **Origin** | **Meaning** | **Examples** |
| *-aud-* | Latin | to hear | audio, audience |
| *-struct-* | Latin | to build | structure, instruct |
| *-port-* | Latin | to carry | portable, transport |
| **Prefixes** | **Origin** | **Meaning** | **Examples** |
| *inter-* | Latin | among, between | Internet, international |
| *mis-* | Old English | wrong, not | misbehave, misfortune |
| *tele-* | Greek | distant | telephone, telescope |
| **Suffixes** | **Origin** | **Meaning** | **Examples** |
| *-ful* | Middle English | full of | joyful, fearful |
| *-less* | Middle English | without | careless, thoughtless |

### Practice A

For each word in italics, underline the root, prefix, or suffix. Then, explain how the meaning of the word part contributes to the meaning of the word. If necessary, consult a print or online dictionary.

1. The *construction* of the new bank building is on schedule.
2. When Samuel *interrupts* me, I can't remember what I have been saying.
3. When the roads are slick, electronic signs alert drivers to be *careful.*
4. The *auditorium* was full of people eager to hear the new symphony.
5. The losing candidate suspected that the votes had been *miscounted.*

Many words and phrases in English come from **Latin, Greek, and Anglo-Saxon mythology.** Study the chart below to learn the origins of some of these words and phrases.

| Words and Phrases From Mythology | | |
|---|---|---|
| **Word or Phrase** | **Origin** | **Meaning** |
| January | Janus, a Roman god, had two faces— one looking forward and one looking backward. | The first month of our calendar year |
| Achilles heel | Achilles, a great Greek warrior, was known to be weak only in his foot. | A weakness or weak point |
| herculean effort | The Greek hero Hercules was known for his strength and for completing twelve difficult tasks. | A difficult task requiring great strength |
| high horse | In medieval England, nobles were given tall horses to show their importance. The phrase "get off your high horse" developed from this practice. | A superior attitude |

### Comprehension and Collaboration

Trade your odyssey story (see Activity below) with a partner. Rewrite your partner's story to include three new words based on word parts from the chart on the previous page. You may use words that appear in this Language Study, other words you know, or new words you find in a dictionary.

### Practice B

Identify the word or phrase from the chart that is associated with each sentence.

1. When Byron bragged about his new car we told him not to be too proud of himself.
2. It is always good to have a fresh start in the new year.
3. I can usually stick to a healthy diet, but my weakness is brownies.
4. Beating the other team will require us to be stronger than ever.

**Activity** An **allusion** is a reference to a well-known person, event, literary work, or work of art. Many works of literature contain allusions. For example, a writer might describe a long or difficult journey as an "odyssey." This is an allusion to *the Odyssey*, a long epic poem that was written sometime between 600 and 800 B.C. In the poem, the ancient Greek hero Odysseus takes a long, difficult voyage to reach his home. Another ancient Greek hero is Hercules, who was famous for completing amazingly difficult tasks. Write a short tale about an odyssey in which the hero must make a herculean effort. Your story can be set in either the past or the present.

## Evaluating a Persuasive Presentation

A **persuasive presentation** is similar to a persuasive composition. Its purpose is to persuade the listener to do, buy, or believe something. Use these strategies to assess persuasive presentations.

### Learn the Skills

**Evaluate content.** Like its written counterpart, an effective persuasive presentation includes a clear statement of the speaker's position and relevant supporting evidence. Listen to every word of a persuasive presentation in order to explain the speaker's purpose. Evaluate the speaker's claims, and identify whether the speaker is appealing to your emotions or using facts, statistics, and other information that can be proved.

**Determine the speaker's attitude.** Ask yourself these questions to determine how the speaker feels about his or her subject:

- Does the speaker appeal to emotion or to reason?
- Does he or she use words that convey strong images or associations?
- What do the speaker's body language and facial expressions suggest?
- What is the speaker's tone of voice?

**Listen for a logical organization.** Follow the argument from point to point. Listen for the connections between ideas. Also, listen for a convincing introduction and conclusion.

**Listen for strong evidence.** Think about the anecdotes, descriptions, facts, statistics, and specific examples that support the speaker's position. Is the reasoning sound? Does the speaker provide sufficient and convincing evidence? Why or why not?

**Ask questions.** Never be afraid to ask questions. You will discover how well the speaker has researched the topic by seeing how he or she responds to questions about the evidence.

**Challenge bias or faulty logic.** If you disagree with something the presenter has said, express your opinion. Respect the speaker's viewpoints if you identify bias or faulty logic. If you suspect a piece of evidence is wrong, ask the speaker to cite its source.

**Clarify and contribute.** Paraphrase a speaker's key points to clarify what you have heard. You might also share a personal anecdote or observation that affirms the speaker's position.

## Practice the Skills

**Presentation of Knowledge and Ideas** Use what you have learned in this workshop to complete the following activity.

### ACTIVITY: **Evaluating a Persuasive Presentation**

Watch a persuasive sales pitch, either live or on videotape or television.

- Identify the speaker's message.
- Determine if the speaker's purpose is to inform or to influence the audience.
- Explain how you felt listening to the message.
- List questions that the speaker's claims raise for you.
- Jot down notes about the presentation, such as the speaker's tone of voice, body language, and facial expressions.
- Draw conclusions about the speaker's message by considering verbal and nonverbal cues.

Use the Assessment Guide below to interpret the content and delivery of the persuasive presentation you watched.

| Assessment Guide |
| --- |
| What is the speaker's message? |
| Is the speaker's purpose to inform or to influence the audience? |
| Is the speaker's reasoning sound? |
| Does the speaker provide sufficient and relevant evidence to support his or her claims? |
| How could you research the speaker's claims? |
| What does the speaker hope you will do after hearing the message? |
| On what points would you challenge the speaker? |
| How effective was the delivery of the presentation? |
| What can you conclude about the speaker's verbal and nonverbal communication, including tone of voice, gestures, and facial expressions? |

**Comprehension and Collaboration** Compare your findings with those of your classmates. As a group, discuss how you can use the strategies above to evaluate other messages, such as advertisements, commercials, and other persuasive presentations.

## Write an Argumentative Text

### Argumentative Essay

**Defining the Form** In an **argumentative essay,** the writer states and supports a claim based on factual evidence. You might use elements of this form in writing editorials or reviews.

**Assignment** Write an argumentative essay in which you use logic and reasoning to convince readers to agree with your claim. Your essay should feature the following elements:

- ✓ a *clear statement of your position* on an issue that has more than one side
- ✓ the *context* surrounding the issue
- ✓ *persuasive evidence* and *logical reasoning* that support your claims
- ✓ statements that *acknowledge opposing views and offer counterarguments*
- ✓ an *appropriate organizational structure* for an argument
- ✓ formal language that appeals *mainly to reason*
- ✓ error-free writing, including *effectively combined sentences*

To preview the criteria on which your argumentative essay may be judged, see the rubric on page 257.

#### FOCUS ON RESEARCH

When you write an argumentative essay, be sure to use strong evidence to support your claim.

- Evidence should be credible, or come from a trustworthy source. Generally, the most reliable Web sites are those from government organizations, major museums, and academic institutions.
- As you gather information, make sure that sources agree on basic facts. If you find one source with facts that are contradicted by other sources, that source is probably inaccurate.
- Cite your sources properly in your essay. The Research Workshop in the Introductory Unit provides useful information on citations.

#### READING-WRITING CONNECTION

To get the feel for argumentative writing, read "All Together Now" by Barbara Jordan, on page 214.

## Prewriting/Planning Strategies

**Hold a roundtable.** With a group, hold a roundtable discussion of problems in your school. Raise as many different issues as possible. Jot down topics that spark strong feelings in you. Choose from these subjects for your essay topic.

**Make a quick list.** Fold a piece of paper in thirds lengthwise. In the first column, write issues and ideas that interest you. In the second column, write a descriptive word for each idea. In the third column, give an example that supports your description. Make sure each issue has an opposing side. Choose the issue or idea that interests you most.

Issues and Ideas
Cafeteria food
Water pollution
New playground
Descriptive Word
tasteless
scary
needed
Examples
macaroni and cheese
streams polluted by
fertilizer runoff
child hurt on slide


**Narrow your focus.** Evaluate your topic to be sure you can fully and effectively discuss it. For example, the topic "violence in the media" would cover violence on news reports, in movies, in video games, and on television. To write an effective argumentative essay, you should consider focusing on violence in one medium, not all four.

**Gather evidence to support your position.** Conduct research either in the library, on the Internet, or by interviewing experts on your topic. Gather the following types of support from accurate, credible sources:

**Facts:** statements that can be proved true

**Statistics:** facts presented in the form of numbers

**Anecdotes:** brief stories that illustrate a point

**Quotations from Authorities:** statements from leading experts

**Examples:** facts, ideas, or events that support a general idea

**Anticipate counterarguments.** Make a list of the arguments people might have against your position. For each, identify a response that you can use to address the issues in your essay.

## Drafting Strategies

**Develop and support your claim.** To make your position clear to your readers, review your notes and develop a *thesis statement*—one strong sentence that states your claim. Include this statement in your introduction.

**Organize to emphasize your arguments and address counterarguments.** As you draft, present the supporting evidence you have gathered, starting with your least important points and building toward your most important ones. Use transitional words and phrases to unify your writing and show the relationships among your ideas. Address opposing concerns and counterarguments directly—do not avoid them. Delete information that does not support or add anything to your argument. Write a powerful conclusion that follows the logic of the evidence and supports your argument. Consider the method shown in the pyramid.

Introduction and claim

- First set of arguments
- Supporting details

- Concerns and counterarguments
- Statements proving opposition is weak or incorrect

- Strongest argument
- Supporting details

Conclusions

**Choose precise words.** Forceful language helps convey your point and builds support for your position. Create a speaker's voice by using precise, lively words that will appeal to readers' sense of reason and stir their emotions.

**Vague:** a *good* candidate

**Precise:** a *trustworthy* candidate
an *intelligent* candidate

**Appeal to your audience.** Use words that your audience will understand. If you are writing for teenagers, use informal language, but avoid slang and maintain standard English. If you are writing to a government official, use a formal style and serious language. Also, choose words that add interest and encourage readers to continue reading.

## Revising for Correct Verb Tense

A verb expresses an action or a state of being. Verbs have tenses, or different forms, that tell when something happens or exists.

**Identifying Verb Tense** In standard English, verbs have six tenses: present, past, future, present perfect, past perfect, and future perfect.

**Present** indicates an action that happens regularly or states a general truth: *I walk my dog Squeegee every morning. He is happy.*

**Past** indicates an action that has already happened: *We walked earlier than usual yesterday. It was sunny.*

**Future** indicates an action that will happen: *We will walk on the beach this summer. The sand will feel hot.*

**Present perfect** indicates an action that happened some time in the past or an action that happened in the past and is still happening now: *We have walked here every day for two years.*

**Past perfect** indicates an action that was completed before another action in the past: *We had walked around the corner before Squeegee barked.*

**Future perfect** indicates an action that will have been completed before another: *We will have walked two hundred miles before I need new shoes.*

**Fixing Incorrect Verb Tense** To fix an incorrect form of a verb, first identify any questionable verbs in your essay. Then, verify the correct form using one of the following methods.

1. **Review the basic forms of the six tenses.** First, identify the time—present, past, or future—in which the action occurs. Then, review the examples above to determine which form corresponds with that time. Avoid shifting tenses needlessly.
2. **Rewrite the sentence.** Consider which verb tense will make your ideas as precise as possible. Revise using that tense.

### Grammar in Your Writing

Choose a paragraph in your draft. Underline the verbs in each sentence of the paragraph. If the tense for any verb is faulty or shifts needlessly, fix it using one of the methods described above.

## Revising Strategies

**Highlight your main points.** To check your organization, highlight each main point. Then, use one or more of these strategies:

- If a reader needs to know one main point in order to understand a second one, make sure the first main point comes *before* the second.
- If one main point means the same as another, combine them, or combine the paragraphs in which they appear.
- If one main point is stronger than the others, move it to the end of your essay.

**Model: Revising to Highlight Main Points**

The best way a person can make his or her voice heard is by voting on Election Day! In the United States, the government is elected by each and every voting citizen. In some other countries, people do not have the right to vote. Their leaders are in power, and the people sometimes do not have a way to make their opinion heard. Their voices are silent, and they must listen to what their leaders tell them to do. Our system is not always perfect, but it does give us the chance to keep trying to make things better.

**Combine sentences to show connections.** To improve your writing, combine short, choppy sentences to stress the connections between ideas.

**Similar Ideas:** The town permits skating on the lake. We don't have the money to open a rink.

**Combined:** The town permits skating on the lake ***because*** we don't have the money to open a rink.

**Opposing Ideas:** The food is better heated. Most classrooms do not have microwave ovens.

**Combined:** The food is better heated, ***but*** most classrooms do not have microwave ovens.

**Peer Review**

Read your draft to a group of peers. Ask if the order of your main points is logical. Consider their responses as you revise.

## Revising to Combine Sentences Using Conjunctions

Too many short sentences in a row can make your writing choppy—that is, your writing will seem to have a repetitive stop-start quality. Using conjunctions to combine sentences will help you create a smoother, more varied writing style. It will also create cohesion and clarify the relationships among claims, reasons, and evidence.

**Identifying Sentences to Combine** Combine sentences that express similar ideas by using words that clarify the relationship between the ideas. Here are two common ways to combine sentences:

**Use a coordinating conjunction, such as *and* or *but*.**

**CHOPPY:** I really wanted to sleep. I had to walk my dogs.

**COMBINED:** I really wanted to sleep, **but** I had to walk my dogs.

**Add a subordinating conjunction, such as *after* or *until*.**

**CHOPPY:** You cannot read the book. I want a chance.

**COMBINED:** You cannot read the book **until** I get a chance.

**Fixing Choppy Sentences** To fix choppy sentences, rewrite them using the following method.

1. **Identify relationships between sentences.** Look for a series of related short sentences. Identify whether the ideas in the sentences are of equal importance or unequal importance.
2. **Combine sentences.** Combine sentences showing equal importance by using coordinating conjunctions. Use subordinating conjunctions to combine sentences of unequal importance.

| Coordinating Conjunctions | Common Subordinating Conjunctions |
|---|---|
| and, or, so, for, but, nor, yet | after, although, as, as if, as long as, because, before, even though, if, in order that, since, so that, than, though, unless, until, when, whenever, where, wherever, while |

### Grammar in Your Writing

Read your draft aloud, highlighting any passages that sound choppy. Then, revise by combining sentences using the method described.

## STUDENT MODEL: **Amanda Wintenburg, Daytona Beach, FL**

### Decide the Future

To you, voting may seem like just a waste of time, just a mere piece of paper with boxes on it, that you have to go through to mark which person you want for that particular job. But to me, it's something more, much more. . . it's your chance to decide the future. Everyone who is eligible should take advantage of the right to vote.

In the opening paragraph, Amanda points out the two "sides" to the voting issue. She follows with her thesis statement.

I'm not the only one who thinks voting should be a top priority for people. For years, companies and organizations have supplied numerous reminders and reasons to explain when and why you vote. You've seen the commercials; they've all told us about it. Voting is important for a number of reasons. Politicians decide how much government support we will get for college tuition, how many jobs will be available, and who will pay more taxes.

This evidence supports the statement that others think voting is a top priority.

This evidence supports the idea that voting matters.

Eenie, meenie, miney mo, . . . maybe you don't want to vote because you feel as if you don't know enough about the candidates to make an informed decision. However, newspapers, television broadcasts, performance records—all these fact-based sources of information are available to the interested voter who wants to make a responsible choice. Find out what the candidates have been doing and what they plan to do. Make your decision based on information.

Here, Amanda identifies and addresses readers' concerns and counterarguments.

In many countries, voting is not an option. In countries with kings and queens, leaders are born into their positions. In other countries, the leaders take control rather than being voted into a leadership role. Often leaders who are not elected can be corrupt or tyrannical, because the people can't remove them from power. We are citizens of a free country in which we have the right to vote. Whether or not the system works perfectly, it is better than a system with no voting. Vote because you can. Remind yourself that not everyone is as lucky.

Here, Amanda gives two examples of types of countries where voting is not an option. She also discusses the negative results of this fact.

Amanda reminds readers that not everyone has the right to vote. She uses language that appeals to both reason and emotion.

If you don't vote, you have less control over your own life. Voting is your chance to make your voice heard. It's your chance to decide the future.

## Editing and Proofreading

Review your draft to correct errors in spelling, grammar, and punctuation errors.

**Focus on Spelling Irregular Plurals**

- Change the *y* to *i* and add *-es* to nouns that end in a consonant and *y* (*memory/memories*).
- Do not change the *y* but add *-s* to nouns that end in a vowel and *y* (*play/plays, key/keys*).
- For most nouns ending in *fe,* change the *fe* to *ve* and and *-s* (*elf/elves, wife/wives*).

**Spiral Review**

Earlier in the unit, you learned about **principal parts of verbs** (p. 210) and **conjunctions** (p. 218). Review your essay to be sure that you have used verbs and coordinating conjunctions correctly.

## Publishing and Presenting

Consider one of the following ways to share your writing:

**Deliver a speech.** Use your argumentative essay as the basis for a speech that you give to your classmates.

**Post your essay.** Many local newspapers will publish well-written argumentative essays if they appeal to the newspaper's audience. Submit your composition and see what happens.

## Reflecting on Your Writing

**Writer's Journal** Jot down your answer to this question:

*What part of the writing process was most challenging? Explain.*

### Rubric for Self-Assessment

Find evidence in your writing to address each category. Then, use the rating scale to grade your work.

| Criteria | Rating Scale |
|---|---|
| **Purpose/Focus** Clearly presents a position on an issue that has at least two sides | *not very* ............ *very*<br>1 2 3 4 |
| **Organization** Introduces the topic and make a clear claim; organizes reasons and evidence logically; provides a concluding section that follows from the argument presented | 1 2 3 4 |
| **Development of Ideas/Elaboration** Supports the claim with clear reasons and relevant evidence, using credible sources; addresses counterarguments; establishes and maintains a formal style | 1 2 3 4 |
| **Language** Uses precise language to strengthen the argument; uses words, phrases, and clauses to clarify the relationships among claims and reasons | 1 2 3 4 |
| **Conventions** Uses proper grammar, including correct use of conjunctions | 1 2 3 4 |

## SELECTED RESPONSE

### I. Reading Literature/Informational Text

**Directions:** *Read the excerpt from "The Eternal Frontier" by Louis L'Amour. Then, answer each question that follows.*

The question I am most often asked is, "Where is the frontier now?"

The answer should be obvious. Our frontier lies in outer space. The moon, the asteroids, the planets, these are mere stepping stones, where we will test ourselves, learn needful lessons, and grow in knowledge before we attempt those frontiers beyond our solar system. Outer space is a frontier without end, the eternal frontier, an everlasting challenge to explorers not [only] of other planets and other solar systems but also of the mind of man.

All that has gone before was preliminary. We have been preparing ourselves mentally for what lies ahead. Many problems remain, but if we can avoid a devastating war we shall move with a rapidity scarcely to be believed. In the past seventy years we have developed the automobile, radio, television, transcontinental and transoceanic flight, and the electrification of the country, among a multitude of other such developments. In 1900 there were 144 miles of surfaced road in the United States. Now there are over 3,000,000. Paved roads and the development of the automobile have gone hand in hand, the automobile being civilized man's antidote to overpopulation.

What is needed now is leaders with perspective; we need leadership on a thousand fronts, but they must be men and women who can take the long view and help to shape the outlines of our future. There will always be the nay-sayers, those who cling to our lovely green planet as a baby clings to its mother, but there will be others like those who have taken us this far along the path to a limitless future. We are a people born to the frontier. It has been a part of our thinking, waking, and sleeping since men first landed on this continent. The frontier is the line that separates the known from the unknown wherever it may be, and we have a driving need to see what lies beyond . . .

1. Which answer choice most clearly identifies the passage as an example of a **persuasive essay?**
   **A.** the author clearly defines an unfamiliar topic
   **B.** the author attempts to convince readers by presenting well-supported claims
   **C.** the author shares personal reflections and insights
   **D.** the author uses vivid language to describe a person, place, or thing

2. What is the author's main **argument** in this passage?
   **A.** We should be concerned about the problem of overpopulation.
   **B.** We should explore outer space beyond what has already been discovered.
   **C.** We should prepare ourselves mentally for the future.
   **D.** We should cling to our planet.

3. Which answer choice states the most likely reason for L'Amour's **word choice** in referring to outer space as "the eternal frontier"?
   **A.** A frontier is an unknown or unexplored area.
   **B.** The frontier is a popular setting for movies.
   **C.** Books about frontiers are often bestsellers.
   **D.** Many readers will think the frontier is an interesting topic.

4. Which claim from the passage appeals most strongly to readers' emotions?
   **A.** "Outer space is a frontier without end, the eternal frontier"
   **B.** "We have developed the automobile, radio, television, transcontinental and transoceanic flight"
   **C.** "We are a people born to the frontier. It has been part of our thinking, waking, and sleeping"
   **D.** "The frontier is the line that separates the known from the unknown wherever it may be"

5. Which phrase from the passage is an example of a **fact?**
   **A.** "if we can avoid a devastating war"
   **B.** "we shall move with a rapidity scarcely to be believed"
   **C.** "In 1900 there were 144 miles of surfaced road in the United States"
   **D.** "The automobile being civilized man's antidote to overpopulation"

6. Which phrase from the passage is an example of an **opinion?**
   **A.** "'Where is the frontier now?'"
   **B.** "The answer should be obvious."
   **C.** "We have developed the automobile, radio, television, transcontinental and transoceanic flight"
   **D.** "Paved roads and the development of the automobile have gone hand in hand."

7. **Part A** Which answer choice states the best definition of the underlined word *preliminary?*
   **A.** logical
   **B.** leading up to
   **C.** historic
   **D.** concluding

   **Part B** Which context clue in the passage helps you define *preliminary?*
   **A.** "beyond our solar system"
   **B.** "also of the mind of man"
   **C.** "All that has gone before"
   **D.** "preparing ourselves mentally"

## Timed Writing

8. Make a list of the **author's main arguments.** In an essay, evaluate whether the author supports each **argument** with **facts** or only offers **opinions** to persuade readers to accept his ideas. Cite evidence from the text to support your analysis.

GO ON

## II. Reading Informational Text

**Directions:** *Read the passage. Then, answer each question that follows.*

### Salamander Population at Risk in Oasis Springs

The Agency for Natural Habitats recently discovered a rare species of salamander living in Oasis Springs, a popular spring-fed pool. We have found that the process used for cleaning the pool is endangering these creatures. To keep the water safe for swimmers, the pool staff currently uses a combination of bleach and brushing to treat algae. This treatment kills the salamanders. Today, we are announcing to the public the steps we will take to preserve the salamander population in Oasis Springs.

Our most important solution involves a new cleaning process. The pool will be cleaned without brushes or bleach. Divers will wipe the rocky bottom with special cloths. No soap products will be used.

We will also participate in a special breeding program to foster the growth of the salamander population. Ten salamanders will be taken from the pool each month to reproduce. They will then be reintroduced into the pool. This program has been successful in other locations with endangered salamander populations.

Finally, specialists will visit the pool each week to monitor the salamander population. An expert committee will then review the results and report on the program's success.

These crucial steps will allow both salamanders and people to enjoy Oasis Springs for many years to come.

**1. Part A** What is the main purpose of the passage?

- **A.** to persuade the public to help save the salamanders
- **B.** to explain how to clean the spring-fed pool without harming people
- **C.** to inform the public about the proposed steps to save the salamander population
- **D.** to explore the life of a salamander

**Part B** Which of the following answer choices *best* shows the author's purpose?

- **A.** "Today, we are announcing to the public the steps we will take to preserve the salamander population in Oasis Springs."
- **B.** "An expert committee will then review the results"
- **C.** "The Agency for Natural Habitats recently discovered a rare species of salamander"
- **D.** "This program has been successful in other locations"

**2.** Which answer choice is a proposed solution to the problem?

- **A.** Ban swimming in the pool.
- **B.** Clean the pool without bleach or brushes.
- **C.** Close the pool to the public.
- **D.** Bring divers in to clean the salamanders.

# III. Writing and Language Conventions

**Directions:** *Read the passage below. Then, answer each question that follows.*

(1) "Seventh Grade" is a funny and believable story. (2) In it, a boy named Victor likes a girl named Teresa. (3) To impress her, Victor pretends to speak French in class. (4) Although he seems smart, he did not really know French. (5) Victor's teacher knows Victor is faking. (6) However, the teacher is very cool. (7) He does not tell the class that Victor has answered incorrectly. (8) That is because he will remember his own life as a teenager.

**1.** Which of the following sentences contains a **linking verb?**

**A.** sentence 2
**B.** sentence 3
**C.** sentence 4
**D.** sentence 7

**2.** Identify the **complete subject** and **complete predicate** of sentence 1.

**A.** "Seventh Grade" is / a funny and believable story.
**B.** "Seventh Grade" / is
**C.** "Seventh Grade" is a / funny and believable story.
**D.** "Seventh Grade" / is a funny and believable story.

**3.** Which revision of sentence 6 uses an **action verb?**

**A.** However, the teacher seems very cool.
**B.** However, the teacher was very cool.
**C.** However, the teacher has a very cool attitude.
**D.** However, the teacher will be very cool.

**4.** What is the best way to revise the **tenses** of the verbs in sentence 8?

**A.** Change *will remember* to the present tense.
**B.** Change *is* to the past tense.
**C.** Change *is* to the present perfect tense.
**D.** Change *is* to the past perfect tense.

**5.** What **principal part** of the verb *tell* appears in sentence 7?

**A.** present
**B.** present participle
**C.** past
**D.** past participle

**6.** Which revision to sentence 4 creates agreement by presenting all verbs in the **present tense?**

**A.** Although he was smart, he did not really know French.
**B.** Although he seemed smart, he does not really know French.
**C.** Although he seems smart, he does not really know French.
**D.** All the verbs are already in the present tense.

# CONSTRUCTED RESPONSE

**Directions:** *Follow the instructions to complete the tasks below as assigned by your teacher.*

*As you work on each task, incorporate both general academic vocabulary and literary terms you learned in Part 2.*

## Writing

**TASK 1 Informational Text**

### Analyze Structure and Purpose

*Write an essay in which you compare the characteristics of two different types of nonfiction selections from Part 2.*

- Choose two selections that represent different types of nonfiction.
- Describe how information is organized in each selection.
- Analyze the author's purpose for writing each selection, and evaluate the connection between that purpose and the selection's organization.
- Discuss the similarities and differences in purpose and structure.
- Each paragraph should have a central idea supported by details from the selections.
- Revise your essay to eliminate unnecessary information and to correct any errors.

**TASK 2 Informational Text**

### Analyze Text Structure

*Write an essay in which you analyze the structure an author uses to organize a work of literary nonfiction in Part 2.*

- Identify and describe the structure the author uses to organize the text you chose.
- Explain how the major sections contribute to the text as a whole and to the development of the author's ideas.
- Cite evidence from the text to support your analysis while presenting your ideas in an organized manner.
- Review your essay to ensure that each sentence has a subject and a predicate. Revise your essay using transitions, such as conjunctions, to combine choppy sentences.

**TASK 3 Informational Text**

### Determine an Author's Point of View

*Write an essay in which you identify and analyze the author's point of view in a selection from Part 2.*

**Part 1**

- Choose a selection in which the author establishes a clear point of view on a topic. Begin by stating the topic and describing the author's perspective on it.
- Analyze how the author presents his or her perspective: Is some evidence emphasized more than other evidence? Does the author include facts or just an interpretation of facts?
- Make notes on the author's perspective and use of supporting facts. Answer the following question: Do you think the author conveys his or her point of view effectively?

**Part 2**

- Write an essay in which you explain the author's point of view and describe how the author uses facts and evidence to support his or her perspective.
- In your conclusion, state whether you think the author conveys his or her point of view effectively. Support your opinion with examples from the text.
- Revise your essay, adding transitions to create cohesion and clarify the relationships among ideas.

## Speaking and Listening

**TASK 4** Informational Text

### Evaluate Arguments

*With a small group of classmates, decide on a text from Part 2 that will be the basis for individual oral presentations. Work independently to evaluate the author's argument. Then, present your ideas to the group and evaluate the presentations of other members.*

- As the basis for your presentation, write an essay in which you trace and evaluate the author's argument and specific claims. Include your assessment of the author's reasoning and evidence.
- Use precise language to express your ideas and appeal to your audience.
- Take turns presenting your evaluations.
- Evaluate your classmates' presentations by assessing their use of clear reasoning and relevant and sufficient evidence.

**TASK 5** Informational Text

### Analyze the Impact of Word Choice

*Give an oral presentation in which you analyze how word choice and diction impact the meaning and tone of a text from Part 2.*

- Select a work from Part 2 and explain why you chose it. Then, choose a specific passage to use as the focus of your analysis.
- Describe the tone of the selection (for example, formal or informal, serious or funny)
- Analyze how the author's word choice affects your response to the text. Consider specific words, sentence length and style, and the overall feeling conveyed. Include supporting examples and quotations from the text.
- Consider whether the author could have achieved a completely different effect by using different words or by changing the structure.
- During your presentation, establish eye contact, speak with appropriate volume, and pronounce words clearly.

## Research

**TASK 6** Informational Text

### What should we learn?

In Part 2, you have read literary nonfiction about ideas and subjects that are important to learn. Now, conduct a short research project about something you believe is important to learn. Perhaps it is a specific skill, a subject you would like to study, or an interesting career. Use the literary nonfiction you have read in Part 2 and your research to reflect on this unit's Big Question. Review the following guidelines before you begin:

- Focus your research on one specific topic.
- Gather relevant information from at least two reliable print or digital sources.
- Take notes as you research your topic.
- Cite your sources according to accepted conventions.

When you have completed your research, write a response to the Big Question. Discuss whether your initial ideas have changed or been reinforced. Support your response with examples from the Part 2 selections as well as examples from your research.

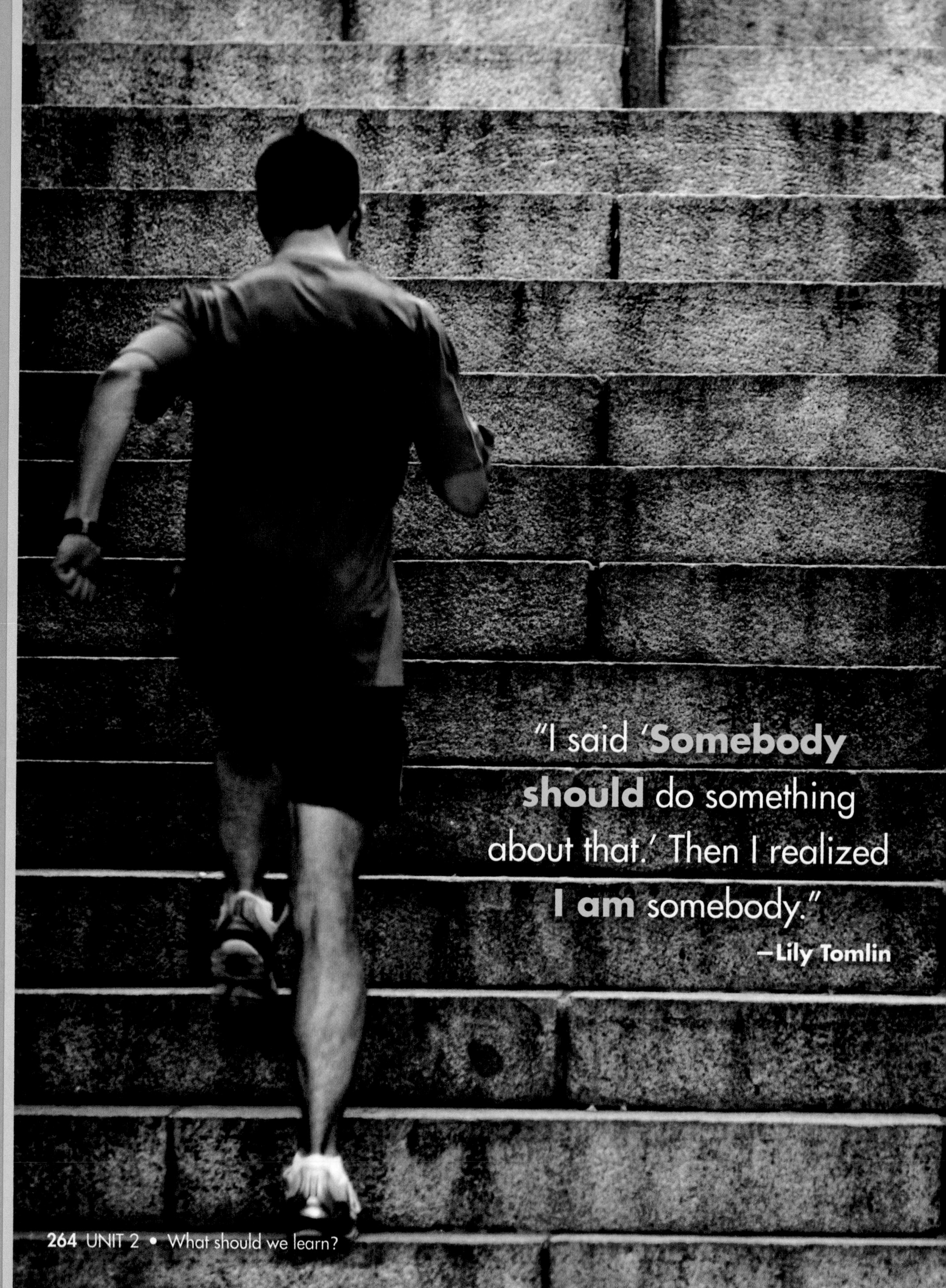
"I said 'Somebody should do something about that.' Then I realized I am somebody."
—Lily Tomlin

PART 3

# TEXT SET DEVELOPING INSIGHT

# MOTIVATION

The selections in this unit all deal with the Big Question: **What should we learn?** In this section, texts in various genres explore ideas about human behavior and motivation. As you read, consider whether motivation comes from within or is learned from others, and think about the ways that a person's goals and behavior may change as a result of learning.

◀ CRITICAL VIEWING Does this photograph make you feel motivated? Why or why not?

**CLOSE READING TOOL**

Use the **Close Reading Tool** to practice the strategies you learn in this unit.

## READINGS IN PART 3

AUTOBIOGRAPHY | ANCHOR TEXT

# NO GUMPTION

RUSSELL BAKER

I began working in journalism when I was eight years old. It was my mother's idea. She wanted me to "make something" of myself and, after a level-headed appraisal[1] of my strengths, decided I had better start young if I was to have any chance of keeping up with the competition.

The flaw in my character which she had already spotted was lack of "**gumption**." My idea of a perfect afternoon was lying in front of the radio rereading my favorite Big Little Book,[2] *Dick Tracy Meets Stooge Viller.* My mother despised inactivity. Seeing me having a good time in repose, she was powerless to hide her disgust. "You've got no more gumption than a bump on a log," she said. "Get out in the kitchen and help Doris do those dirty dishes."

My sister Doris, though two years younger than I, had enough gumption for a dozen people. She positively enjoyed washing dishes, making beds, and cleaning the house. When she was only seven she could carry a piece of short-weighted cheese back to the A&P, threaten the manager with legal action, and come back triumphantly with the full quarter-pound we'd paid for and a few ounces extra thrown in for forgiveness. Doris could have made something of herself if she hadn't been a girl. Because of this defect, however, the best she could hope for was a career as a

**gumption** ▶
(gump′ shən) *n.*
determination; initiative

1. **appraisal** (ə prāz′ əl) *n.* judgment; evaluation.
2. **Big Little Book** a small, inexpensive picture book that often portrayed the adventures of comic-strip heroes like Dick Tracy.

nurse or schoolteacher, the only work that capable females were considered up to in those days.

This must have saddened my mother, this twist of fate that had allocated all the gumption to the daughter and left her with a son who was content with Dick Tracy and Stooge Viller. If disappointed, though, she wasted no energy on self-pity. She would make me make something of myself whether I wanted to or not. "The Lord helps those who help themselves," she said. That was the way her mind worked.

She was realistic about the difficulty. Having sized up the material the Lord had given her to mold, she didn't overestimate what she could do with it. She didn't insist that I grow up to be President of the United States.

Fifty years ago parents still asked boys if they wanted to grow up to be President, and asked it not jokingly but seriously. Many parents who were hardly more than paupers still believed their sons could do it. Abraham Lincoln had done it. We were only sixty-five years from Lincoln. Many a grandfather who walked among us could remember Lincoln's time. Men of grandfatherly age were the worst for asking if you wanted to grow up to be President. A surprising number of little boys said yes and meant it.

I was asked many times myself. No, I would say, I didn't want to grow up to be President. My mother was present during one of these interrogations.[3] An elderly uncle, having posed the usual question and exposed my lack of interest in the Presidency, asked, "Well, what do you want to be when you grow up?"

I loved to pick through trash piles and collect empty bottles, tin cans with pretty labels, and discarded magazines. The most desirable job on earth sprang instantly to mind. "I want to be a garbage man," I said.

My uncle smiled, but my mother had seen the first distressing evidence of a bump budding on a log. "Have a little gumption, Russell," she said. Her calling me Russell was a signal of unhappiness. When she approved of me I was always "Buddy."

When I turned eight years old she decided that the job of starting me on the road toward making something of myself

3. **interrogations** (in ter ə´ gā´ shənz) *n.* situations in which a person is formally questioned.

could no longer be safely delayed. "Buddy," she said one day, "I want you to come home right after school this afternoon. Somebody's coming and I want you to meet him."

When I burst in that afternoon she was in conference in the parlor with an executive of the Curtis Publishing Company. She introduced me. He bent low from the waist and shook my hand. Was it true as my mother had told him, he asked, that I longed for the opportunity to conquer the world of business?

My mother replied that I was blessed with a rare determination to make something of myself.

"That's right," I whispered.

"But have you got the grit, the character, the never-say-quit spirit it takes to succeed in business?"

My mother said I certainly did.

"That's right," I said.

He eyed me silently for a long pause, as though weighing whether I could be trusted to keep his confidence, then spoke man-to-man. Before taking a **crucial** step, he said, he wanted to advise me that working for the Curtis Publishing Company placed enormous responsibility on a young man. It was one of the great companies of America. Perhaps the greatest publishing house in the world. I had heard, no doubt, of the *Saturday Evening Post*?

**crucial ▶** (kroo͞´ shəl) *adj.* important; critical

Heard of it? My mother said that everyone in our house had heard of the *Saturday Post* and that I, in fact, read it with religious devotion.

Then doubtless, he said, we were also familiar with those two monthly pillars of the magazine world, the *Ladies Home Journal* and the *Country Gentleman.*

Indeed we were familiar with them, said my mother.

Representing the *Saturday Evening Post* was one of the weightiest honors that could be bestowed in the world of business, he said. He was personally proud of being a part of that great corporation.

My mother said he had every right to be.

Again he studied me as though debating whether I was worthy of a knighthood. Finally: "Are you trustworthy?"

My mother said I was the soul of honesty.

"That's right," I said.

The caller smiled for the first time. He told me I was a lucky young man. He admired my spunk. Too many young men thought life was all play. Those young men would not go far in this world. Only a young man willing to work and save and keep his face washed and his hair neatly combed could hope to come out on top in a world such as ours. Did I truly and sincerely believe that I was such a young man?

"He certainly does," said my mother.

"That's right," I said.

He said he had been so impressed by what he had seen of me that he was going to make me a representative of the Curtis Publishing Company. On the following Tuesday, he said, thirty freshly printed copies of the *Saturday Evening Post* would be delivered at our door. I would place these magazines, still damp with the ink of the presses, in a handsome canvas bag, sling it over my shoulder, and set forth through the streets to bring the best in journalism, fiction, and cartoons to the American public.

He had brought the canvas bag with him. He presented it with reverence fit for a chasuble.[4] He showed me how to drape the sling over my left shoulder and across the chest so that the pouch lay easily accessible[5] to my right hand, allowing the best in journalism, fiction, and cartoons to be swiftly extracted and sold to a citizenry whose happiness and security depended upon us soldiers of the free press.

The following Tuesday I raced home from school, put the canvas bag over my shoulder, dumped the magazines in, and, tilting to the left to balance their weight on my right hip, embarked on the highway of journalism.

We lived in Belleville, New Jersey, a commuter town at the northern fringe of Newark. It was 1932, the bleakest year of the Depression. My father had died two years before, leaving us with a few pieces of Sears, Roebuck furniture and not much else, and my mother had taken Doris and me to live with one of her younger brothers. This was my Uncle Allen. Uncle Allen had made something of himself by 1932. As salesman for a soft-drink bottler in Newark, he had an income of $30 a week; wore pearl-gray spats,[6] detachable collars, and a three-piece suit; was happily married; and took in threadbare relatives.

With my load of magazines I headed toward Belleville Avenue. That's where the people were. There were two filling stations at the intersection with Union Avenue, as well as an A&P, a fruit stand, a bakery, a barber shop, Zuccarelli's

---

4. **chasuble** (chaz´ ə bəl) *n.* sleeveless outer garment worn by priests.
5. **accessible** (ak ses´ ə bəl) *adj.* available.
6. **spats** (spats) *n.* cloth or leather material that covers the upper part of shoes or ankles.

drugstore, and a diner shaped like a railroad car. For several hours I made myself highly visible, shifting position now and then from corner to corner, from shop window to shop window, to make sure everyone could see the heavy black lettering on the canvas bag that said *The Saturday Evening Post.* When the angle of the light indicated it was suppertime, I walked back to the house.

"How many did you sell, Buddy?" my mother asked.

"None."

"Where did you go?"

"The corner of Belleville and Union Avenues."

"What did you do?"

"Stood on the corner waiting for somebody to buy a *Saturday Evening Post.*"

"You just stood there?"

"Didn't sell a single one."

"For God's sake, Russell!"

Uncle Allen intervened. "I've been thinking about it for some time," he said, "and I've about decided to take the *Post* regularly. Put me down as a regular customer." I handed him a magazine and he paid me a nickel. It was the first nickel I earned.

Afterwards my mother instructed me in salesmanship. I would have to ring doorbells, address adults with charming self-confidence, and break down resistance with a sales talk pointing out that no one, no matter how poor, could afford to be without the *Saturday Evening Post* in the home.

I told my mother I'd changed my mind about wanting to succeed in the magazine business.

"If you think I'm going to raise a good-for-nothing," she replied, "you've got another think coming." She told me to hit the streets with the canvas bag and start ringing doorbells the instant school was out next day. When I objected that I didn't feel any **aptitude** for salesmanship, she asked how I'd like to lend her my leather belt so she could whack some sense into me. I bowed to superior will and entered journalism with a heavy heart.

**aptitude ▶** (ap´ tə to͞od) *n.* talent; ability

My mother and I had fought this battle almost as long as I could remember. It probably started even before memory began, when I was a country child in northern Virginia and my mother, dissatisfied with my father's plain workman's life, determined that I would not grow up like him and his people, with calluses on their hands, overalls on their backs, and fourth-grade educations in their heads. She had fancier ideas of life's possibilities. Introducing me to the *Saturday Evening Post*, she was trying to wean me as early as possible from my father's world where men left with lunch pails at sunup, worked with their hands until the grime ate into the pores, and died with a few sticks of mail-order furniture as their legacy. In my mother's vision of the better life there were desks and white collars, well-pressed suits, evenings of reading and lively talk, and perhaps—if a man were very, very lucky and hit the jackpot, really made something important of himself—perhaps there might be a fantastic salary of $5,000 a year to support a big house and a Buick with a rumble seat[7] and a vacation in Atlantic City.

And so I set forth with my sack of magazines. I was afraid of the dogs that snarled behind the doors of potential buyers. I was timid about ringing the doorbells of strangers, relieved when no one came to the door, and scared when someone did. Despite my mother's instructions, I could not deliver an engaging sales pitch. When a door opened I simply asked, "Want to buy a *Saturday Evening Post*?" In Belleville few persons did. It was a town of 30,000 people, and most weeks I rang a fair majority of its doorbells. But I rarely sold my thirty copies. Some weeks I canvassed the entire town for six days and still had four or five unsold magazines on Monday evening; then I dreaded the coming of Tuesday morning, when a batch of thirty fresh *Saturday Evening Posts* was due at the front door.

"Better get out there and sell the rest of those magazines tonight," my mother would say.

I usually posted myself then at a busy intersection where a traffic light controlled commuter flow from Newark. When the light turned red I stood on the curb and shouted my sales pitch at the motorists.

"Want to buy a *Saturday Evening Post*?"

One rainy night when car windows were sealed against me I came back soaked and with not a single sale to report. My mother beckoned to Doris.

"Go back down there with Buddy and show him how to sell these magazines," she said.

---

7. **rumble seat** in the rear of early automobiles, a seat that could be folded shut.

Brimming with zest, Doris, who was then seven years old, returned with me to the corner. She took a magazine from the bag, and when the light turned red she strode to the nearest car and banged her small fist against the closed window. The driver, probably startled at what he took to be a midget assaulting his car, lowered the window to stare, and Doris thrust a *Saturday Evening Post* at him.

"You need this magazine," she piped, "and it only costs a nickel."

Her salesmanship was irresistible. Before the light changed half a dozen times she disposed of the entire batch. I didn't feel humiliated. To the contrary. I was so happy I decided to give her a treat. Leading her to the vegetable store on Belleville Avenue, I bought three apples, which cost a nickel, and gave her one.

"You shouldn't waste money," she said.

"Eat your apple." I bit into mine.

"You shouldn't eat before supper," she said. "It'll spoil your appetite."

Back at the house that evening, she dutifully reported me for wasting a nickel. Instead of a scolding, I was rewarded with a pat on the back for having the good sense to buy fruit instead of candy. My mother reached into her bottomless supply of maxims[8] and told Doris, "An apple a day keeps the doctor away."

By the time I was ten I had learned all my mother's maxims by heart. Asking to stay up past normal bedtime, I knew that a refusal would be explained with, "Early to bed and early to rise, makes a man healthy, wealthy, and wise." If I whimpered about having to get up early in the morning, I could depend on her to say, "The early bird gets the worm."

The one I most despised was, "If at first you don't succeed, try, try again." This was the battle cry with which she constantly sent me back into the hopeless struggle whenever I moaned that I had rung every doorbell in town and knew there wasn't a single potential buyer left in Belleville that week. After listening to my explanation, she handed me the canvas bag and said, "If at first you don't succeed . . ."

Three years in that job, which I would gladly have quit after the first day except for her insistence, produced at least one valuable result. My mother finally concluded that I would never

---

**8. maxims** (mak′ simz) *n.* wise sayings.

make something of myself by pursuing a life in business and started considering careers that demanded less competitive zeal.

One evening when I was eleven I brought home a short "composition" on my summer vacation which the teacher had graded with an A. Reading it with her own schoolteacher's eye, my mother agreed that it was top-drawer seventh grade prose and complimented me. Nothing more was said about it immediately, but a new idea had taken life in her mind. Halfway through supper she suddenly interrupted the conversation.

"Buddy," she said, "maybe you could be a writer."

I clasped the idea to my heart. I had never met a writer, had shown no previous urge to write, and hadn't a notion how to become a writer, but I loved stories and thought that making up stories must surely be almost as much fun as reading them. Best of all, though, and what really gladdened my heart, was the ease of the writer's life. Writers did not have to trudge through the town peddling from canvas bags, defending themselves against angry dogs, being rejected by surly strangers. Writers did not have to ring doorbells. So far as I could make out, what writers did couldn't even be classified as work.

I was enchanted. Writers didn't have to have any gumption at all. I did not dare tell anybody for fear of being laughed at in the schoolyard, but secretly I decided that what I'd like to be when I grew up was a writer.

ABOUT THE AUTHOR

**Russell Baker** (b. 1925)

Newspaper columnist, author, and humorist Russell Baker grew up during the Great Depression, a period in the 1930s of poor business conditions and major unemployment. Baker began his career as a journalist for *The Baltimore Sun* and *The New York Times*. He later won a Pulitzer Prize for his "Observer" column that was published for more than thirty years in the *Times*. He won a second Pulitzer Prize for his autobiography *Growing Up*, from which "No Gumption" comes.

# Close Reading Activities

## READ

### Comprehension

Reread all or part of the text to help you answer the following questions.

1. What is young Russell Baker's problem?
2. What job does Baker get?
3. What skill does Doris have that Baker does not have?

**Research: Clarify Details** Choose at least one unfamiliar detail from the text and briefly research it. Then, explain how the information sheds light on an aspect of the autobiography.

**Summarize** Write an objective summary of the autobiography. Remember that an objective summary does not contain opinions.

### Language Study

**Selection Vocabulary** The following passages are from the autobiography. Define each boldfaced word, and then use the word in a sentence.

- The flaw in my character which she had already spotted was lack of **"gumption."**
- Before taking a **crucial** step, he said, he wanted to advise me that working for the Curtis Publishing Company . . .
- When I objected that I didn't feel any **aptitude** for salesmanship, she asked how I'd like to lend her my leather belt . . .

**Diction and Style** Study the following sentence from the autobiography. Then, answer the questions that follow.

> She wanted me to "make something" of myself and, after a level-headed appraisal of my strengths, decided I had better start young if I was to have any chance of keeping up with the competition.

1. **(a)** What is a synonym for *strengths* in this sentence? **(b)** What other meaning does *strength* have?
2. **(a)** Who is "the competition"? **(b)** In what other context is the word *competition* often used? **(c)** Why do you think the author chose to use "the competition" rather than another term?

**Conventions** Read this passage from the autobiography. Identify the verbs in the compound predicate in the passage. Then, explain what idea is emphasized in the compound predicate.

> The following Tuesday I raced home from school, put the canvas bag over my shoulder, dumped the magazines in, and, tilting to the left to balance their weight on my right hip, embarked on the highway of journalism.

### Academic Vocabulary

The following words appear in blue in the instructions and questions on the facing page.

**identify** **insight** **purpose**

Categorize the words by deciding whether you know each one well, know it a little bit, or do not know it at all. Then, use a print or online dictionary to look up the definitions of the words you are unsure of or do not know at all.

## Literary Analysis

Reread the identified passages. Then, respond to the questions.

**Focus Passage 1** *(pp. 266–267)*

The flaw in my character which she had already spotted...were considered up to in those days.

### Key Ideas and Details

1. **Interpret:** What does Baker's mother mean when she says he has no "gumption"?
2. **Define:** Citing details from the passage, explain why Doris has gumption.

### Craft and Structure

3. **(a)** In this passage, point out one example of direct characterization and one example of indirect characterization. **(b) Evaluate:** Which type of characterization is more effective? Explain.
4. **(a) Identify** details that show this autobiography is set in the past. **(b) Analyze Cause and Effect:** How will the time period in which she grows up affect Doris's work choices in the future?

### Integration of Knowledge and Ideas

5. **Draw Conclusions:** Infer what makes Baker happy and what makes Doris happy. Then, draw a conclusion about happiness.

**Focus Passage 2** *(p. 272)*

Brimming with zest, Doris, who was then seven...which cost a nickel, and gave her one.

### Key Ideas and Details

1. **(a)** What is the driver's response to Doris's actions? **(b) Contrast:** How does Doris's approach to selling differ from Baker's approach?
2. **Interpret:** What is Baker's reaction to his sister's salesmanship?

### Craft and Structure

3. **(a)** What words does the author use to describe Doris? **(b) Analyze:** How do these words show why she is successful?
4. **Evaluate:** How does the author use exaggeration to create humor in this passage? Cite details from the text in your answer.

### Integration of Knowledge and Ideas

5. **Connect:** The author's mother has said he has "no gumption." What **insight** does this passage provide into the meaning of *gumption*?

## Autobiography

In an **autobiography,** the writer communicates details about his or her own life. Autobiographical writing may tell about a person's whole life or only a part of it.

1. What does Baker's humorous tone suggest about his **purpose** for writing?
2. **Motivation** What might Baker want to communicate about himself, his mother, and Doris?
3. Cite textual examples that show how Baker uses conflict, suspense, and resolution to develop the plot.

# DISCUSS

## From Text to Topic **Group Discussion**

Discuss the following passage with a group of classmates. Take notes during the discussion. Contribute your own ideas, and support them with examples from the text.

> "Buddy," she said, "maybe you could be a writer."...
> So far as I could make out, what writers did couldn't even be classified as work. (p. 273)

**QUESTIONS FOR DISCUSSION:**

1. How does this passage show Baker's sense of humor?
2. What idea about a writing career does Baker find motivating? What makes this observation humorous?

# WRITE

## Writing to Sources **Argument**

**Assignment**

Write a **persuasive essay** in which you agree or disagree with the following statement: *Money provides the best motivation for success.* Consider both Baker's goals for himself and his mother's goals for him.

**Prewriting and Planning** Choose your position. Then, reread the autobiography, looking for details that support your claim. Record your notes in a web diagram. Put your claim and counterclaim(s) in the center and supporting details in the outer circles.

**Drafting** Draft a strong introduction, body, and conclusion.

- **Introduction** State your claim, or your position on the issue.
- **Body** Acknowledge opposing opinions, or counterclaims. Present facts, reasons and examples to support your position and refute counterclaims. Cite specific details from the text and other relevant evidence.
- **Conclusion** Sum up your argument in a strong concluding statement.

**Revising** Reread your essay, making sure you have strongly supported your claim and addressed counterclaims. Make clear connections between your claim and the evidence that supports it by using transitional words and phrases, such as those below.

| | | |
|---|---|---|
| *for example* | *specifically* | *in particular* |
| *because* | *such as* | *for this reason* |

**Editing and Proofreading** Double-check your essay for commonly confused words, such as *accept/except, than/then,* and *are/our.* Make any necessary corrections.

**CONVENTIONS**

Check your use of pronouns to ensure each pronoun has a clear antecedent, and that all antecedents agree with their pronouns in gender and number.

# RESEARCH

## Research **Investigate the Topic**

**Goals and Motivation** In this autobiography, Baker's own aims in life differ from his mother's goals for him. Many people believe there is a clear link between motivation and goals. For example, some people believe success depends on setting achievable goals.

**Assignment**

Conduct research to learn what experts say about the relationship between goals and motivation. Consult a dictionary for definitions and search print and online sources using key words such as *goals* and *motivation*. Take clear notes and carefully identify your sources so that you can easily access the information later. Share your findings in an **oral presentation** for the class.

**PREPARATION FOR ESSAY**

You may use the knowledge you gain during this research assignment to support your claims in an essay you will write at the end of this section.

**Gather Sources** Locate a variety of print and electronic sources. For example, you might consult a published study by experts that explains the findings of a study or research project. You may also look for information in news articles and reference books. Choose sources that feature expert authors and up-to-date information.

**Take Notes** Take notes on each source, either electronically or on notecards. Use an organized note-taking strategy.

- Use key words like *incentives* and abbreviations such as *e.g.* (for example).
- Use separate notecards to organize subtopics.
- If you plan to include a direct quotation, use the exact words of the source and place the words inside quotation marks. Otherwise, paraphrase by putting the information in your own words.

**Synthesize Multiple Sources** Assemble data from your sources and organize it into a cohesive presentation. Draw conclusions about the relationship between goals and motivation. Use your notes to construct an outline for your presentation. Create a Works Cited list as described in the Research Workshop in the Introductory Unit of your textbook.

**Organize and Present Ideas** Review your outline and practice delivering your presentation. Be prepared to answer questions from your audience.

# Intrinsic Motivation Doesn't Exist, Researcher Says

Jeff Grabmeier

COLUMBUS, Ohio—While some **psychologists** still argue that people perform better when they do something because they want to—rather than for some kind of reward, such as money—Steven Reiss suggests we shouldn't even make that distinction.

Reiss, a professor of psychology at Ohio State University, argues that a diverse range of human motivations can't be forced into these categories of intrinsic and extrinsic motivations. Psychologists say intrinsic motivations are those that arise from within—doing something because you want to—while extrinsic motivations mean people are seeking a reward, such as money, a good grade in class, or a trophy at a sporting event.

"They are taking many diverse human needs and motivations, putting them into just two categories, and then saying one type of motivation is better than another," said Reiss, who outlines his argument in the current issue of the journal *Behavior Analyst*.

"But there is no real evidence that intrinsic motivation even exists."

The issue is more than academic, Reiss said. Many sports psychology books, and books advising how to motivate students and business people, **tout** the value of intrinsic motivation and warn that extrinsic rewards can undermine people's performance.

The argument is that people should do something because they enjoy it, and that rewards only sabotage natural desire.

Reiss disagrees.

"There is no reason that money can't be an effective motivator, or that grades can't motivate students in school," he said. "It's all a matter of individual differences. Different people are motivated in different ways."

Reiss has developed and tested a theory of motivation that states there are 16 basic desires that guide nearly all meaningful behavior, including power, independence, curiosity, and acceptance. Whether you agree there are 16 desires or not, he said there is not any way to reduce all of these desires to just two types.

In addition to trying to fit all motivations into two types, Reiss said proponents of intrinsic motivation are also making value judgments by saying some types of motivation are better than others.

"For example, some people have said that wealth and materialism lead to inferior quality happiness, but there is no real proof of that," he said.

"Individuals differ enormously in what makes them happy—for some competition, winning and wealth are the greatest sources of happiness, but for others, feeling competent or socializing may be more satisfying. The point is that you can't say some motivations, like money, are inherently inferior."

In the article, Reiss points to some of the problems he sees with the theories and studies connected to intrinsic motivation. One problem is that people who tout the value of intrinsic motivation have several different definitions for what that means, and these definitions change depending on circumstances.

One common definition, for example, is that intrinsic motivation is that which is inherently pleasurable, while extrinsic motivation is not. For example, the argument is that children are naturally curious and enjoy learning for the joy it brings them. Grades, they argue, are an extrinsic reward that **fosters** competition and makes learning less pleasurable.

◀ **psychologists** (sī käl′ ə jists) *n.* experts who study the human mind and behavior

◀ **tout** (tout) *v.* promote

◀ **fosters** (fôs′tərz) *v.* promotes the growth or development of

However, Reiss said his research has found people show a wide range of curiosity—some people are very curious and enjoy spending a great deal of time learning on their own. However, many people are not very curious and don't enjoy learning for its own sake.

"There are many children for whom the important reward to them is the grades they get, the competition among classmates," Reiss said. "This goes against what some psychologists say, who think competition is bad and a non-competitive attitude is good, and that learning and curiosity are intrinsic values that everyone shares. They are pushing their own value system on to everybody."

**"There are many children for whom the important reward to them is the grades they get, the competition among classmates. . ."**

Another way of defining intrinsic motivation is the means-end definition, which says intrinsic motivation is doing what we want, whereas extrinsic motivation is doing something to get something else. For example, some might argue that children playing baseball are intrinsically motivated by the joy of playing, while a professional baseball player is extrinsically motivated, by money and championships.

But Reiss said this definition confuses means and ends. A child playing baseball may be satisfying his need for physical exercise, while the professional player is satisfying his parental instinct by providing a good income for his family.

For children and professionals, baseball is a means to two different ends.

Reiss also criticized many of the studies, which proponents say prove the existence of intrinsic motivation, and how it can be undermined by extrinsic rewards.

For example, many studies have purportedly shown how people who enjoy doing a specific activity—such as children who enjoy drawing—do that activity less after they are offered rewards. But when the results show the subjects continue the activity even after the rewards are offered, the researchers have argued that this just shows the subjects expect to get a reward and no longer are intrinsically motivated.

"The results are always turned around to prove their hypothesis."

Also, researchers have assumed that rewards simply make people

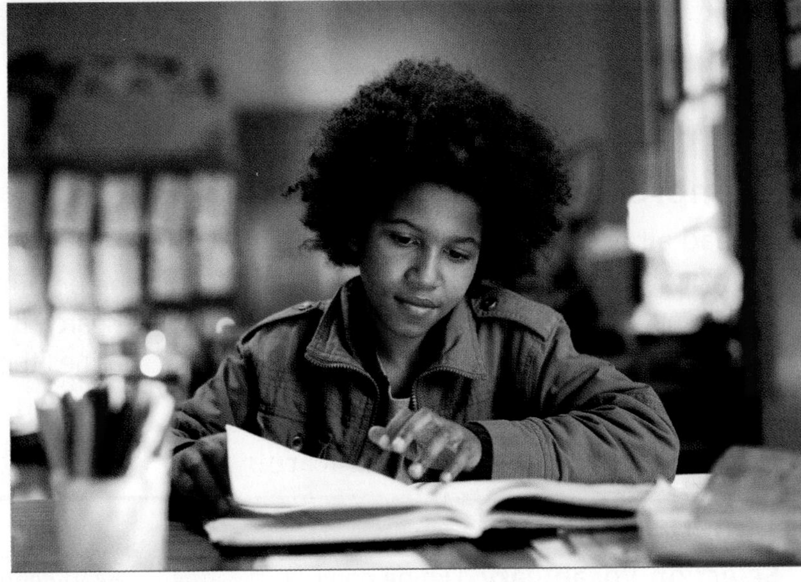

less interested in the intrinsic joys of an activity. But Reiss said many of these studies haven't considered the possibility that the negative effect of rewards has nothing to do with intrinsic or extrinsic motivations. Instead, rewards may cause some people to pursue an activity less because of the negative feelings they cause, such as performance anxiety.[1] Avoiding an activity because of performance anxiety related to a reward is not the same as avoiding it simply because the reward undermines intrinsic motivation.

"Too many studies that supposedly prove intrinsic motivation have serious flaws in logic, or too many important uncontrolled variables,"[2] he said. "There needs to be more scientific rigor."

1. **performance anxiety** fear of performing for an audience.
2. **uncontrolled variables** things in an experiment that could give false results.

## ABOUT THE AUTHOR

### Jeff Grabmeier

Jeff Grabmeier serves as Senior Director of Research and Innovation Communications at Ohio State University, where he writes about research in social sciences, business, and humanities. He is also co-chair of the Education Committee of the National Association of Science Writers. This organization supports teachers of science writing and people who want to become science writers by sponsoring workshops and fellowships.

# Close Reading Activities

## READ

### Comprehension

Reread all or part of the text to help you answer the following questions.

1. How do psychologists define *intrinsic* and *extrinsic* motivation?
2. What does Reiss say is wrong about many studies on intrinsic motivation?

**Research: Clarify Details** Choose at least one unfamiliar detail from the text and briefly research it. Then, explain how your research clarifies the article.

**Summarize** Write an objective summary of the article that is free from opinions.

### Language Study

**Selection Vocabulary** Define each boldfaced word from the article, then use it in a sentence of your own.

- …some **psychologists** still argue that people perform better when they do something because they want to…
- Many sports psychology books, and books advising how to motivate students and business people, **tout** the value of intrinsic motivation…
- Grades, they argue, are an extrinsic reward that **fosters** competition…

### Literary Analysis

Reread the identified passage. Then, respond to the following questions.

**Focus Passage** *(pp. 279–280)*
One common definition…don't enjoy learning for its own sake.

#### Key Ideas and Details

1. **(a)** What is an example of each type of motivation? **(b)** Which is more pleasurable according to common definitions?
   **(c) Connect:** What evidence contradicts these **perceptions**?

#### Craft and Structure

2. **(a)** What transition words does the author use to connect ideas in the passage?
   **(b) Connect:** What relationship do the words show? **(c) Analyze:** Why are transitions especially important in informational texts such as this one?

#### Integration of Knowledge and Ideas

3. **Speculate:** Based on this passage, what might people find if they **investigate** the connection between grades and motivation?

### Expository Writing

**Expository writing** explains or informs. In an expository article, the author provides information that supports the main idea and his or her purpose for writing.

1. **(a)** What is the main idea of the article?
   **(b)** What types of details does the author provide to support the main idea?
2. **(a)** What is the author's most likely purpose for writing this article? **(b)** What is a possible secondary purpose?

# DISCUSS • RESEARCH • WRITE

## From Text to Topic Group Discussion

Discuss the following passage with a group of classmates. Take notes during the discussion. Contribute your own ideas and support them with examples from the text.

> "There is no reason that money can't be an effective motivator, or that grades can't motivate students in school," he said. "It's all a matter of individual differences. Different people are motivated in different ways."

### QUESTIONS FOR DISCUSSION

1. How does Reiss feel about money as a motivator?
2. What does Reiss believe about the ways in which people are motivated?

## Research Investigate the Topic

**Money and Grades** According Steven Reiss, money can be an effective motivator. Some people think it is a good idea to give students financial rewards for getting good grades. Others disagree.

**Assignment**

Conduct research to find out what experts say about the idea of motivating students to get good grades by offering them money. Consult print and digital sources for information about studies on the pros and cons of this practice. Take clear notes and carefully identify your sources so that you can easily access the information later. Share your findings in an **informal speech** for the class.

### PREPARATION FOR ESSAY

You may use the results of your research to support your ideas in the essay you will write at the end of this section.

## Writing to Sources Argument

This article introduces the idea that people are motivated by a variety of factors and that extrinsic rewards, such as money, may be good motivators. Do you agree or disagree?

**Assignment**

Write an **argument** in which you take a position for or against the practice of rewarding good grades with money. Follow these steps:

- Introduce your claim and **acknowledge** an opposing claim.
- Support your claim with evidence from your research.
- Use words and phrases that clearly show the relationships between your claims and the evidence that supports them.
- Establish and maintain a formal style.

### ACADEMIC VOCABULARY

Academic terms appear in blue on these pages. If these words are not familiar to you, use a dictionary to find their definitions. Then, use the words as you speak and write about the text.

# The Cremation of Sam McGee

Robert Service

*There are strange things done in the midnight sun*
*By the men who moil[1] for gold;*
*The Arctic trails have their secret tales*
*That would make your blood run cold;*
*The Northern Lights have seen queer sights,*
*But the queerest they ever did see*
*Was that night on the marge[2] of Lake Lebarge*
*I **cremated** Sam McGee.*

**cremated** ▶ (krē´māt´ id) *v.* burned a dead body to ashes

Now Sam McGee was from Tennessee,
where the cotton blooms and blows.
Why he left his home in the South to roam
'round the Pole, God only knows.
He was always cold, but the land of gold
seemed to hold him like a spell;
Though he'd often say in his homely way
that "he'd sooner live in hell."

On a Christmas Day we were mushing our way
over the Dawson trail.
Talk of your cold! through the parka's fold
it stabbed like a driven nail.
If our eyes we'd close, then the lashes froze
til sometimes we couldn't see;
It wasn't much fun, but the only one
to **whimper** was Sam McGee.

**whimper** ▶ (hwim´ pər) *v.* make low, crying sounds

1. **moil** (moil) *v.* toil and slave.
2. **marge** (märj) *n.* poetic word for the shore of the lake.

And that very night, as we lay packed tight
in our robes beneath the snow,
And the dogs were fed, and the stars o'erhead
were dancing heel and toe,
He turned to me, and "Cap," says he,
"I'll cash in this trip, I guess;
And if I do, I'm asking that you
won't refuse my last request."
Well, he seemed so low that I couldn't say no;
then he says with a sort of moan:
"It's the cursed cold, and it's got right hold
till I'm chilled clean through to the bone.
Yet 'tain't being dead—it's my awful dread
of the icy grave that pains;
So I want you to swear that, foul or fair,
you'll cremate my last remains."

A pal's last need is a thing to heed,
so I swore I would not fail;
And we started on at the streak of dawn;
but God! he looked ghastly pale.
He crouched on the sleigh, and he raved all day
of his home in Tennessee;
And before nightfall a corpse was all
that was left of Sam McGee.

There wasn't a breath in that land of death,
and I hurried, horror-driven,
With a corpse half hid that I couldn't get rid,
because of a promise given;
It was lashed to the sleigh, and it seemed to say:
"You may tax your brawn[3] and brains,
But you promised true, and it's up to you
to cremate those last remains."

3. **brawn** (brôn) *n.* physical strength.

**loathed** ▶
(lōthd) *v.* hated

Now a promise made is a debt unpaid,
and the trail has its own stern code.
In the days to come, though my lips were dumb,
in my heart how I cursed that load.
In the long, long night, by the lone firelight,
while the huskies, round in a ring,
Howled out their woes to the homeless snows—
O God! how I **loathed** the thing.
And every day that quiet clay
seemed to heavy and heavier grow;
And on I went, though the dogs were spent
and the grub was getting low;
The trail was bad, and I felt half mad,
but I swore I would not give in;
And I'd often sing to the hateful thing,
and it hearkened with a grin.

Till I came to the marge of Lake Lebarge,
and a derelict[4] there lay;
It was jammed in the ice, but I saw in a trice
it was called the "Alice May."
And I looked at it, and I thought a bit,
and I looked at my frozen chum;
Then "Here," said I, with a sudden cry,
"is my cre-ma-tor-eum."

Some planks I tore from the cabin floor,
and I lit the boiler fire;
Some coal I found that was lying around,
and I heaped the fuel higher;
The flames just soared, and the furnace roared—
such a blaze you seldom see;
And I burrowed a hole in the glowing coal,
and I stuffed in Sam McGee.

Then I made a hike, for I didn't like
to hear him sizzle so;
And the heavens scowled, and the huskies howled,
and the wind began to blow.
It was icy cold, but the hot sweat rolled
down my cheeks, and I don't know why;

4. **derelict** (der′ ə likt′) *n.* abandoned ship.

And the greasy smoke in an inky cloak
went streaking down the sky.

I do not know how long in the snow
I wrestled with grisly fear;
But the stars came out and they danced about
ere again I ventured near;
I was sick with dread, but I bravely said:
"I'll just take a peep inside.
I guess he's cooked, and it's time I looked"; . . .
then the door I opened wide.

And there sat Sam, looking cool and calm,
in the heart of the furnace roar;
And he wore a smile you could see a mile,
and he said: "Please close that door.
It's fine in here, but I greatly fear
you'll let in the cold and storm—
Since I left Plumtree, down in Tennessee,
it's the first time I've been warm."

*There are strange things done in the midnight sun*
*By the men who moil for gold;*
*The Arctic trails have their secret tales*
*That would make your blood run cold;*
*The Northern Lights have seen queer sights,*
*But the queerest they ever did see*
*Was that night on the marge of Lake Lebarge*
*I cremated Sam McGee.*

## ABOUT THE AUTHOR

### **Robert Service** (1874–1958)

A writer of novels, poetry, and ballads, Robert Service was born in England and raised in Scotland. At age twenty he went to work for a bank in Vancouver, British Columbia, in Canada. After two years, he was assigned to a Yukon branch of the bank. While in the Yukon Territory, he met fur trappers and gold prospectors. After leaving the bank, Service traveled in the Arctic, where he observed the people living there and recorded his adventures.

# Close Reading Activities

## READ

### Comprehension

Reread all or part of the text to help you answer the following questions.

1. Why is Sam McGee in the Arctic?
2. What promise does the speaker make to Sam?
3. What is surprising about the poem's conclusion?

**Research: Clarify Details** Choose at least one unfamiliar detail in the poem and briefly research it. Then, explain how your research sheds light on the poem.

**Summarize** Write an objective summary of the poem. Remember that an objective summary is free from opinion and evaluation.

### Language Study

**Selection Vocabulary** Define each boldfaced word. Then, identify the part of speech that the three words share. Finally, use the words in sentences of your own.

- … I **cremated** Sam McGee.
- … the only one to **whimper** was Sam McGee.
- … O God! How I **loathed** the thing.

### Literary Analysis

Reread the identified passage. Then, respond to the following questions.

**Focus Passage** *(p. 286)*

Now a promise made…and it hearkened with a grin.

**Key Ideas and Details**

1. **(a)** What is the speaker's struggle in this passage? **(b) Analyze:** Why does he refuse to give in?
2. **Deduce:** Why is the speaker's task so difficult?

**Craft and Structure**

3. **Interpret:** How do the rhyming words in the middle and ends of lines affect the sound of the poem?
4. **(a)** What are two vivid **images** in this stanza? **(b) Evaluate:** What specific words make these images vivid? Why?

**Integration of Knowledge and Ideas**

5. **Connect:** How does the setting **contribute** to the action?

### Characters

A **character** is a person or an animal that takes part in the action in a literary work. Reread the poem, and take notes on ways in which the author develops characters to show their motivations.

1. **Motivation** What motivates Sam McGee to stay in the Arctic?
2. **(a)** Why does McGee want to be cremated? **(b)** Why does the speaker agree to McGee's request?
3. **Motivation** How does the **outcome** relate to McGee's character and motivation?

# DISCUSS • RESEARCH • WRITE

## From Text to Topic **Partner Discussion**

Discuss the following passage with a partner. Contribute your own ideas, support them with examples from the text, and respond to your partner's ideas.

> I do not know how long in the snow
> I wrestled with grisly fear;
> But the stars came out and they danced about
> ere again I ventured near;
> I was sick with dread, but I bravely said:
> "I'll just take a peep inside.
> I guess he's cooked, and it's time I looked"; ...
> then the door I opened wide.

### QUESTIONS FOR DISCUSSION

1. What words in this passage create a tense mood?
2. How do the words *cooked* and *looked* break the tense mood and create humor?

## Research **Investigate the Topic**

**Klondike Gold Rush** In "The Cremation of Sam McGee," poet Robert Service captures the excitement and danger that prospectors faced during the Klondike Gold Rush of the 1890s.

**Assignment**

Conduct research to learn what motivated prospectors to join the Klondike Gold Rush. Consult print and electronic sources. Take clear notes and carefully identify your sources. Share your findings in a **brief research paper.**

### PREPARATION FOR ESSAY

You may use the results of your research assignment to support your ideas in the essay you will write at the end of this section.

### ACADEMIC VOCABULARY

Academic terms appear in blue on these pages. If these words are not familiar to you, use a dictionary to find their definitions. Then, use the words as you speak and write about the text.

## Writing to Sources **Narrative**

"The Cremation of Sam McGee" describes the adventures of two gold prospectors during the Klondike Gold Rush.

**Assignment**

Write a **fictional narrative** in which you imagine you are searching for gold during the Klondike Gold Rush. Describe your adventures.

- Write from the first-person point of view.
- Use time-order words, such as *first, next,* and *last,* to show a clear sequence of events.
- Use precise words and sensory language to capture the action.
- Provide a satisfying conclusion that follows from the narrated experience.

# A Special Gift—The Legacy of "Snowflake" Bentley

Barbara Eaglesham

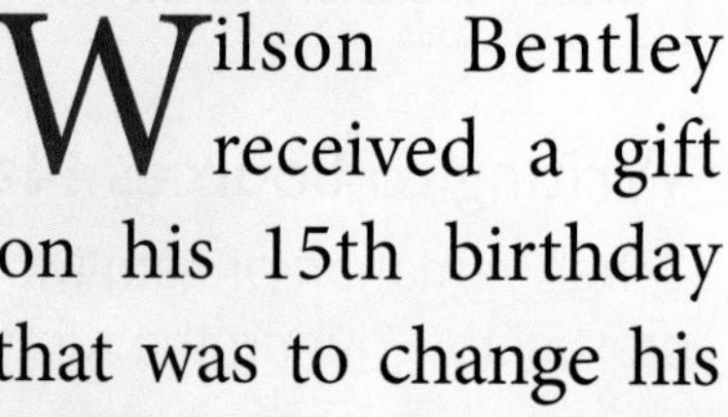

Wilson Bentley received a gift on his 15th birthday that was to change his life—an old microscope his mother had once used in teaching. As birthday gifts go, it might not have seemed like much, but to this 1880s Vermont farm boy it was special indeed.

"When the other boys of my age were playing with popguns and sling-shots, I was absorbed in studying things under this microscope," he later wrote.

And nothing fascinated him more than snowflakes. It would become a passion that would last a lifetime, earn him the nickname "Snowflake Bentley," and make him known around the world.

## Focused on Beauty

If you have ever seen a snowflake design on a mug, or on jewelry, or maybe on a tote bag, chances are it was based on one of Bentley's more than 5,000 photomicrographs[1] of snow crystals (snow crystals are the building blocks of snowflakes).

At first, though, Bentley did not own a camera. He had only his eyes and his microscope, and no way to share his enjoyment of the delicate **hexagons** other than to draw them. As soon as the snow started to fly (and if his chores were done), he would collect some snow crystals on a board painted black. He'd spend hours inside his woodshed, where he had his microscope, picking up the most perfect ones on the end of a piece of straw from a broom and transferring them to a microscope slide. There, he would flatten them with a bird feather. Then, holding his breath, he would observe the crystal and hurry to draw what he saw before it **evaporated** into thin air. It was a frustrating business to try to capture all the details in a drawing while simultaneously being in a race against time.

Eventually, a few years later, Bentley noticed an advertisement for a microscope and camera that he knew was the answer to his dreams. The problem was, the equipment cost $100—equal to a whopping $2,000 today. His father, being a serious, hard-working farmer, felt that looking through a microscope was a waste of time. "Somehow my mother got him to spend the money," Bentley wrote, "but he

◀ **evaporated** (ē vap´ ə rāt əd) *v.* changed from a liquid to a gas

◀ **hexagons** (hek´ sə gänz´) *n.* six-sided figures

1. **photomicrographs** photographs made through a microscope.

never came to believe it had been worthwhile." That was probably a feeling shared by the locals of Jericho, who nicknamed him "Snowflake" Bentley.

Undeterred, he began his quest to photograph a snow crystal. Once he attached the microscope to the camera and rigged up a way to focus it without running back and forth (he couldn't reach the focus knob from behind the camera), he began experimenting with photography. In the 1880s, few people owned a camera, so Bentley had no one to ask for help. Time after frustrating time, his **negatives** appeared blank. Not until the following winter did he figure out that too much light was reaching the camera lens. His solution was to place a metal plate with a pinhole in the center beneath the stage of the microscope, to cut down the stray light and allow only the light waves carrying the image to reach the camera.

**negatives ▶** (neg´ ə tivz) *n.* photograhic images in which the light and dark areas are reversed

This was the key, and on January 15, 1885, at the age of 19, Bentley finally photographed a snowflake! Many hours over the next 45 years were spent in his tiny darkroom beneath the stairs developing negatives that he then carried, often by lantern-light, to the brook for washing. In all that time, he never saw two snow crystals that were exactly alike, although he realized that if he were able to collect two crystals side-by-side from the same cloud, there was a good chance that they might look the same. (Scientist Nancy Knight did just that in 1988, and indeed found two identical snow crystals!)

An artist as well as a scientist, Bentley wanted to find a way to make the shape of the crystal stand out more from the white background of the photo paper. He couldn't bring himself to alter his original glass plate negatives, so he began making copies of them and scraping the photographic emulsion away from the edges of the images with a knife, a time-consuming trick that allowed sunlight through, turning the background black when printed by sunlight.

Bentley's book, *Snow Crystals,* containing 2,453 of his photographs, was finally published and delivered to his house just weeks before his death in 1931.

Bentley was pleased. He never made more than a few thousand dollars from his work, but it had been a labor of love and he was satisfied to know that he would finally be able to share the beauty of his snow crystals with the world.

He is remembered primarily for this accomplishment, but to his friends and family, he was kind, gentle, and funny "Willie." He was the man who would sometimes tie an insect to a blade of grass to photograph it covered with dew the next morning, and who always chewed every bite 36 times. He was a gifted pianist who also played the violin and clarinet. He was the bachelor farmer who lived in the same farmhouse all his life. To scientists, he was the untrained researcher who not only photographed snow crystals, but also kept a detailed daily log of local weather conditions throughout his life and developed a method to measure the size of raindrops. To the people of Jericho, he is remembered as the not-so-flaky-after-all "Snowflake" Bentley.

ABOUT THE AUTHOR

**Barbara Eaglesham** (b. 1957)

A lab instructor in microbiology at Cornell University, Barbara Eaglesham loves looking through a microscope. "I get very jazzed about science," Eaglesham confesses. "I love to attempt to communicate complicated subjects to young people." Eaglesham has written an article about diamonds, titled "Fire and Ice." Her piece about "Snowflake" Bentley was originally published in *ODYSSEY: Adventures in Science.*

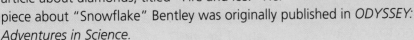

# Close Reading Activities

## READ

### Comprehension

Reread all or part of the text to help you answer the following questions.

1. What gift changed Wilson Bentley's life?
2. Before he had a camera, how did Bentley capture the shapes of snowflakes?
3. Why did Bentley's first photographs appear blank?

**Research: Clarify Details** Choose at least one unfamiliar detail from this article and briefly research it. Then, explain how your research sheds light on an aspect of the article.

**Summarize** Write an objective summary of the article. Remember that an objective summary is free from opinion and evaluation.

### Language Study

**Selection Vocabulary** Define each boldfaced word from the article, and then use the word in a sentence of your own.

- … and no way to share his enjoyment of the delicate **hexagons** other than to draw them.
- … he would observe the crystal and hurry to draw what he saw before it **evaporated** into thin air.
- Time after frustrating time his **negatives** appeared blank.

### Literary Analysis

Reread the identified passage. Then, respond to the following questions.

**Focus Passage** *(p. 292)*
This was the key, and on January 15… when printed by sunlight.

**Key Ideas and Details**

1. **Interpret:** What did Bentley **observe** that makes each snow crystal special?
2. **Analyze:** How did Bentley make the shape of the crystals more visible in his photographs?

**Craft and Structure**

3. **(a)** List two details that show the writer conducted research in order to write this article. **(b) Speculate:** What sources might she have consulted in her research?
4. **(a) Interpret:** What is the tone of this passage? **(b) Support:** What details convey the tone?

**Integration of Knowledge and Ideas**

5. **Relate:** In what ways was Bentley's work beneficial to science?

### Biography

A **biography** is a form of nonfiction in which a writer tells the life story of another person. Reread this biographical article, and note how the author uses characterization to portray Bentley and show his motivation.

1. **Motivation** How did Bentley's curiosity give his life **focus**?
2. What details in the selection lead to insights about Bentley?

# DISCUSS • RESEARCH • WRITE

## From Text to Topic **Partner Discussion**

Discuss the following passage with a partner. Take notes during the discussion. Share your own ideas, and support them with examples from the text.

> Bentley's book, *Snow Crystals*, containing 2,453 of his photographs, was finally published and delivered to his house just weeks before his death in 1931. Bentley was pleased. He never made more than a few thousand dollars from his work, but it had been a labor of love and he was satisfied to know that he would finally be able to share the beauty of his snow crystals with the world.

### QUESTIONS FOR DISCUSSION

1. What idea is emphasized by the words *finally* and *just weeks* in the first sentence?
2. What is Bentley's "labor of love"? What does this phrase reveal about Bentley's motivation for his work?

## Research **Investigate the Topic**

**Snow Crystals** Snow crystals fascinated Wilson Bentley, and they continue to fascinate people today.

**Assignment**

Conduct research to learn more about snow crystals. Consult print and Internet sources. Take clear notes and carefully identify your sources. Share your findings in an **annotated poster.** Include a paragraph in which you explain what motivated Wilson Bentley to devote his life's work to the study of snow crystals.

### PREPARATION FOR ESSAY

You may use the results of your research to support your ideas in the essay you will write at the end of this section.

## Writing to Sources **Informative Text**

"The Legacy of 'Snowflake' Bentley" focuses on one man's study of snow crystals. Consider what you learned about scientific **inquiry** from his method of study.

**Assignment**

Write an **informative essay** in which you explain how curiosity motivated Wilson Bentley to make a lasting contribution to science.

- Introduce the topic clearly, and briefly preview what your essay will cover.
- Develop the topic with facts and details, using science terms such as *evidence* and *hypothesis* when appropriate.
- Organize your ideas in a logical sequence.
- Maintain a formal style and tone.

### ACADEMIC VOCABULARY

Academic terms appear in blue on these pages. If these words are not familiar to you, use a dictionary to find their definitions. Then, use the words as you speak and write about the text.

# All Stories Are Anansi's

African Folk Tale ◆ Harold Courlander

In the beginning, all tales and stories belonged to Nyame (nē ä′ mē), the Sky God. But Kwaku Anansi (kwä′ ko͞o ə nän′ sē), the spider, yearned to be the owner of all the stories known in the world, and he went to Nyame and offered to buy them.

The Sky God said: "I am willing to sell the stories, but the price is high. Many people have come to me offering to buy, but the price was too high for them. Rich and powerful families have not been able to pay. Do you think you can do it?"

Anansi replied to the Sky God: "I can do it. What is the price?"

"My price is three things," the Sky God said. "I must first have Mmoboro (mō bô′ rō), the hornets. I must then have Onini (ō nē′ nē), the great python. I must then have Osebo (ō sā′ bō), the leopard. For these things I will sell you the right to tell all stories."

Anansi said: "I will bring them."

He went home and made his plans. He first cut a gourd from a vine and made a small hole in it. He took a large calabash[1] and filled it with water. He went to the tree where the hornets lived. He poured some of the water over himself, so that he was dripping. He threw some water over the hornets, so that they too were dripping. Then he put the calabash on his head, as though to protect himself from a storm, and called out to the hornets: "Are you foolish people? Why do you stay in the rain that is falling?"

The hornets answered: "Where shall we go?"

"Go here, in this dry gourd," Anansi told them.

The hornets thanked him and flew into the gourd through the small hole. When the last of them had entered, Anansi plugged the hole with a ball of grass, saying: "Oh, yes, but you are really foolish people!"

He took his gourd full of hornets to Nyame, the Sky God. The Sky God accepted them. He said: "There are two more things."

Anansi returned to the forest and cut a long bamboo pole and some strong vines. Then he walked toward the house of

---

1. **calabash** (kal′ ə bash′) *n.* large fruit that is dried and made into a bowl or cup.

Onini, the python, talking to himself. He said: "My wife is stupid. I say he is longer and stronger. My wife says he is shorter and weaker. I give him more respect. She gives him less respect. Is she right or am I right? I am right, he is longer. I am right, he is stronger."

When Onini, the python, heard Anansi talking to himself, he said: "Why are you arguing this way with yourself?"

**dispute ▶** (di spyoot′) *n.* disagreement

The spider replied: "Ah, I have had a **dispute** with my wife. She says you are shorter and weaker than this bamboo pole. I say you are longer and stronger."

Onini said: "It's useless and silly to argue when you can find out the truth. Bring the pole and we will measure."

So Anansi laid the pole on the ground, and the python came and stretched himself out beside it.

"You seem a little short," Anansi said.

The python stretched further.

"A little more," Anansi said.

"I can stretch no more," Onini said.

"When you stretch at one end, you get shorter at the other end," Anansi said. "Let me tie you at the front so you don't slip."

He tied Onini's head to the pole. Then he went to the other end and tied the tail to the pole. He wrapped the vine all around Onini, until the python couldn't move.

**opinion ▶** (ə pin′ yən) *n.* belief based on what seems true or probable to one's own mind

"Onini," Anansi said, "it turns out that my wife was right and I was wrong. You are shorter than the pole and weaker. My **opinion** wasn't as good as my wife's. But you were even more foolish than I, and you are now my prisoner."

Anansi carried the python to Nyame, the Sky God, who said: "There is one thing more."

Osebo, the leopard, was next. Anansi went into the forest and dug a deep pit where the leopard was accustomed to walk. He covered it with small branches and leaves and put dust on it, so that it was impossible to tell where the pit was. Anansi went away and hid. When Osebo came prowling in the black of night, he stepped into the trap Anansi had prepared and fell to the bottom. Anansi heard the sound of the leopard falling, and he said: "Ah, Osebo, you are half-foolish!"

When morning came, Anansi went to the pit and saw the leopard there.

"Osebo," he asked, "what are you doing in this hole?"

"I have fallen into a trap," Osebo said. "Help me out."

"I would gladly help you," Anansi said. "But I'm sure that if I bring you out, I will have no thanks for it. You will get hungry, and later on you will be wanting to eat me and my children."

"I swear it won't happen!" Osebo said.

"Very well. Since you swear it, I will take you out," Anansi said.

He bent a tall green tree toward the ground, so that its top was over the pit, and he tied it that way. Then he tied a rope to the top of the tree and dropped the other end of it into the pit.

"Tie this to your tail," he said.

Osebo tied the rope to his tail.

"Is it well tied?" Anansi asked.

"Yes, it is well tied," the leopard said.

"In that case," Anansi said, "you are not merely half-foolish, you are all-foolish."

And he took his knife and cut the other rope, the one that held the tree bowed to the ground. The tree straightened up with a snap, pulling Osebo out of the hole. He hung in the air head downward, twisting and turning. And while he hung this way, Anansi killed him with his weapons.

Then he took the body of the leopard and carried it to Nyame, the Sky God, saying: "Here is the third thing. Now I have paid the price."

Nyame said to him: "Kwaku Anansi, great warriors and chiefs have tried, but they have been unable to do it. You have done it. Therefore, I will give you the stories. From this day onward, all stories belong to you. Whenever a man tells a story, he must **acknowledge** that it is Anansi's tale."

In this way Anansi, the spider, became the owner of all stories that are told. To Anansi all these tales belong.

◂ **acknowledge** (ak näl′ ij) *v.* recognize and admit

ABOUT THE AUTHOR

## Harold Courlander (1908–1996)

Harold Courlander is best known for his collections of folk tales from around the world. He once told an interviewer that his interest in folk tales arose from the rich multicultural environment in his hometown of Detroit, Michigan. During Courlander's career, he published more than thirty-five books. As he traveled around the world, he made sound recordings of the music and stories of African, African American, and Native American cultures. When asked about his work, Courlander has said, "I think of myself primarily as a narrator. I have always had a special interest in using fiction and nonfiction narration to bridge communication between other cultures and our own."

# Close Reading Activities

## READ

### Comprehension

Reread all or part of the text to help you answer the following questions.

1. What price does the Sky God ask for his stories?
2. What is Anansi's attitude toward the other animals?
3. Why does Anansi succeed when warriors and chiefs have failed?

**Research: Clarify Details** Choose at least one unfamiliar detail from the story and briefly research it. Then, explain how the information sheds light on an aspect of the folk tale.

**Summarize** Write an objective summary of the folk tale. Remember that an objective summary is free from opinion and evaluation.

### Language Study

**Selection Vocabulary** Identify at least one synonym for each boldfaced word from the selection. Then, use each word in a sentence of your own.

- "Ah, I have had a **dispute** with my wife."
- My **opinion** wasn't as good as my wife's.
- Whenever a man tells a story, he must **acknowledge** that it is Anansi's tale.

### Literary Analysis

Reread the identified passage. Then, respond to the following questions.

**Focus Passage** *(p. 298)*

The spider replied: "Ah, I have had a dispute … and you are now my prisoner."

**Key Ideas and Details**

1. **(a)** How does Anansi gain Onini's trust? **(b) Analyze:** How does Anansi convince the python to let himself be tied to the bamboo pole?
2. **Infer:** What is Anansi's opinion of Onini? Cite evidence from the text to support your answer.

**Craft and Structure**

3. **Infer:** Based on this passage, what is one possible theme, or lesson, of the folk tale?

**Integration of Knowledge and Ideas**

4. **(a) Interpret:** What characteristics of Anansi are revealed in his encounter with Onini? **(b) Apply:** How does Onini's behavior resemble that of a human?

### Folk Tales

A **folk tale** is a story composed orally and then passed from person to person by word of mouth. Reread the folk tale, and take notes on ways in which the author uses animal characters to **communicate** a lesson about human motivation.

1. In what ways are the animal characters like humans?
2. **Motivation (a)** What motivates the hornets, the python, and the leopard to listen to Anansi? **(b)** What motivates Anansi to succeed?

## DISCUSS • RESEARCH • WRITE

### From Text to Topic **Small Group Discussion**

Discuss the following passage with three or four classmates. Take notes during the discussion. **Contribute** your own ideas, and support them with examples from the text.

> The Sky God said: "I am willing to sell the stories, but the price is high. Many people have come to me offering to buy, but the price was too high for them. Rich and powerful families have not been able to pay. Do you think you can do it?"
> Anansi replied to the Sky God: "I can do it. What is the price?"

#### QUESTIONS FOR DISCUSSION

1. What idea is emphasized by the Sky God's statements about payment? Why do you think he does not simply name a price?
2. What do you learn about Anansi when he says "I can do it" before he knows the Sky God's price?

### Research **Investigate the Topic**

**Tricksters in Folk Tales** Trickster characters are common in the **tradition** of folk literature. These characters use their cleverness to try to trick others. The coyote, the fox, and the rabbit are common trickster animals in folk literature.

**Assignment**

Conduct research to find out about common trickster characters and to learn what types of feelings and desires typically motivate their actions. Consult print and digital sources. Take clear notes and carefully identify your sources. Share your findings in an **informal presentation** for the class.

#### PREPARATION FOR ESSAY

You may use the results of your research assignment to support your ideas in the essay you will write at the end of this section.

### Writing to Sources **Narrative**

This folk tale tells about a trickster spider that outsmarts other characters and succeeds in owning all the stories in the world.

**Assignment**

Write your own **folk tale** about the trickster character of your choice.

- Introduce your trickster character and explain his or her motivation.
- Describe the main events in the story using vivid verbs and descriptive language.
- Conclude by telling whether or not the trickster got what he or she wanted, and why.

#### ACADEMIC VOCABULARY

Academic terms appear in blue on these pages. If necessary, use a dictionary to find their definitions. Then, use the words as you speak and write about the text.

# Maslow's Theory of Motivation and Human Needs

5 Self-Actualization
4 Self-Esteem
3 Love & Relationships
2 Your Family & Work
1 Your Body

| LEVELS OF NEEDS | MOTIVATION & BEHAVIOR |
|---|---|
| **LEVEL 5 = Self-Actualization** | |
| **FULFILLMENT OF GOALS & DREAMS** Need for self-fulfillment. Desire to realize your full potential and become the best you are capable of becoming. | **CREATIVITY** Be a self-starter, have enthusiasm, be creative, be dedicated, enjoy challenges, love to accomplish results! |
| **LEVEL 4 = Self-Esteem** | |
| **SELF RESPECT & ACCEPTANCE** Need for reputation, prestige, and recognition from others. Contains the desire to feel important, strong and significant. | **BRAINPOWER** Display your talents and skills, have self-confidence, appreciate attention and recognition from others. |
| **LEVEL 3 = Love & Relationships** | |
| **COMMUNICATION & RESPONSE** Need to be loved and to love. Includes the desire for affection and belonging. | **VALIDATION** Join and be active in clubs and groups, be able to talk to others, contribute to society, marry and have a family. |
| **LEVEL 2 = Your Family & Work** | |
| **SOCIAL SAFETY & SECURITY** Need to be safe from physical and psychological harm in the present and future, and trust in a predictable future. | **SURVIVAL SKILLS** Work, save for future, improve skills and talents, be responsible, and want an organized predictable world. |
| **LEVEL 1 = Your Body** | |
| **PHYSICAL SAFETY & SECURITY** Need to stay alive! Biological and cultural imperatives to live. Includes having enough healthy food, air, and water to survive. | **SURVIVAL SKILLS** Eat, sleep, and take care of your bodily needs, provide for clothing, shelter, comfort, be free from pain. |

## READ • RESEARCH

### Comprehension

Review the infographic to answer the following questions.

1. **(a)** What is the subject of the chart? **(b)** What is the relationship between the two columns in the chart?
2. **(a)** What information about the chart does the pyramid **diagram** show? **(b)** Which level of needs and motivations is the highest?

### Critical Analysis

#### Key Ideas and Details

1. **(a) Compare and Contrast:** How are the two columns in the chart for Level 1 alike and different? **(b) Draw Conclusions:** Who do you think experiences Level 1 needs, motivation, and behavior? **Explain** your reasoning.
2. **Analyze:** Explain the focus of Level 4.

#### Craft and Structure

3. **(a) Interpret:** What are the fundamental differences between the levels at the top of the pyramid and the levels at the bottom? **(b) Hypothesize:** Maslow's **theory** is always shown in a pyramid diagram. Why do you think he chose this shape in which to visually represent his theory?

#### Integration of Knowledge and Ideas

4. **Draw Conclusions:** Based on the pyramid diagram, does Maslow think most adults achieve self-actualization, or is this group a small percentage of the population? Explain your reasoning.

**ACADEMIC VOCABULARY**

Academic terms appear in blue on these pages. If these words are not familiar to you, use a dictionary to find their definitions. Then, use the words as you speak and write about the chart.

### Research **Investigate the Topic**

**Abraham Maslow** Abraham Maslow pioneered a branch of psychology called humanistic psychology. Maslow's ideas are illustrated in this chart.

**Assignment**

Conduct research to find out more about Abraham Maslow, Maslow's Theory of Morivation, and the focus of humanistic psychology. Take careful notes and identify your sources. Share your findings in a **brief research report.**

## Speaking and Listening: **Group Discussion**

**Motivation and Learning** The texts in this section vary in genre, length, style, and perspective. However, all of the texts present ideas related to human behavior and the factors that motivate us. The issue of motivation, and whether it comes from within or is learned from others, is fundamentally related to the Big Question addressed in this unit: **What should we learn?**

### Assignment

**Conduct discussions.** With a small group of classmates, conduct a discussion about the issues of motivation and learning. Refer to the texts in this section, other texts you have read, and your personal experience and knowledge to support your ideas. Begin your discussion by addressing the following questions:

- What are some factors that motivate people? Does every action have a motivation?
- To what extent can goals and behavior change as a result of learning?
- Why are some people more motivated than others? Can we learn to be more motivated?
- What effects can time and place have on motivation and learning?

**Summarize and present your ideas.** After you have fully explored the topic, summarize your discussion and present your findings to the class as a whole.

▲ Refer to the selections you read in Part 3 as you complete the activities on this assessment.

## Criteria for Success

✓ **Organizes the group effectively**
Appoint a group leader and a timekeeper. The group leader should present the discussion questions. The timekeeper should make sure the discussion takes no longer than 20 minutes.

✓ **Maintains focus of discussion**
As a group, stay on topic and avoid straying into other subject areas.

✓ **Involves all participants equally and fully**
No one person should monopolize the conversation. Rather, everyone should take turns speaking and contributing ideas.

✓ **Follows the rules for collegial discussion**
As each group member speaks, others should listen carefully. Build on one another's ideas and support viewpoints and opinions with sound reasoning and evidence. Express disagreement respectfully.

**USE NEW VOCABULARY**

As you speak and share ideas, work to use the vocabulary words you have learned in this unit. The more you use new words, the more you will "own" them.

## Writing: **Narrative**

**Motivation and Learning** The texts in this section portray different individuals who learned important lessons when they came to understand the factors that motivated themselves or others.

> **Assignment**
>
> Write an **autobiographical narrative,** or a true story about your own life, in which you discuss a time when you were motivated by a goal that was at odds with the expectations of your family, a friend, or your community. Describe what you wanted and what the other person or group wanted. Tell about the conflict that resulted and how the conflict was resolved. In your conclusion, explain what you learned from the experience.

### Criteria for Success

**Purpose/Focus**

✓ **Connects specific incidents with larger ideas**
Make meaningful connections between your experiences and the texts you have read in this section.

✓ **Clearly conveys the significance of the story**
Provide a conclusion in which you reflect upon what you experienced.

**Organization**

✓ **Sequences events logically**
Structure your narrative so that individual events build on one another to create a coherent whole.

**Development of Ideas/Elaboration**

✓ **Supports insights**
Include both personal examples and details from the texts you have read in this section.

✓ **Uses narrative techniques effectively**
Even though an autobiographical narrative is nonfiction, it may include storytelling elements like those found in fiction. Consider using dialogue to help readers "hear" how characters sound.

**Language**

✓ **Uses description effectively**
Use descriptive details to bring settings and characters to life.

**Conventions**

✓ **Does not have errors**
Check your narrative to eliminate errors in grammar, spelling, and punctuation.

**WRITE TO EXPLORE**

Writing is a way to explore what you feel and think: You may change your mind or get new ideas as you work. As you write your autobiographical narrative, explore your ideas on motivation and learning.

## Writing to Sources: **Informative Text**

**Motivation and Learning** The related readings in this section present a range of ideas about what motivates people to take action. The selections raise questions, such as the following, about whether motivation comes from within or is a result of an outside factor or experience:

- What can we learn when a goal conflicts with a promise or commitment?
- When is it important to reconsider our motivations?
- Can a goal that comes from an inner motivation be beneficial to society?

Focus on the question that intrigues you the most, and then complete the following assignment.

### Assignment

Write an **informative essay** in which you explore the connection between learning and motivation. Develop your essay by analyzing relevant ideas and information in two or more texts from this section. Choose a strategy for organizing your essay. For example, you might compare and contrast the motivations of characters in the selections. Clearly present, develop, and support your ideas with examples, details, and quotations from the texts.

**INCORPORATE RESEARCH**

As you write your informative essay, refer to the research you conducted as you read the texts in this section. Choose appropriate ideas and details from your research to support your thesis statement.

### Prewriting and Planning

**Choose texts.** Review the texts in this section to determine which ones you will cite in your essay. Select at least two texts that will provide strong material to support your examination of motivation and learning.

**Gather details and craft a working topic.** Use a chart like the one shown to develop your topic. Though you may refine or change your ideas as you write, details in your chart can help you establish a clear direction.

**Focus Question: What effect does motivation have on learning?**

| Text | Passage | Notes |
|---|---|---|
| "The Legacy of 'Snowflake' Bentley" | "When the other boys of my age were playing…I was absorbed in studying things under this micro-scope," he later wrote. | At a young age, Bentley was curious and motivated by learning |
| "Intrinsic Motivation Doesn't Exist, Researcher Says" | "Individuals differ enormously in what makes them happy—for some competition, winning and wealth are the greatest sources of happiness…" | Researcher says competi-tion, winning, and wealth motivate some people |
| **Example Topic:** Some people are motivated by an inner desire to learn, but others are motivated to learn by a desire for recognition or a reward. | | |

## Drafting

**Develop a thesis statement.** Review your notes to help you develop a thesis statement—one strong sentence that sums up your main idea about motivation. Include this statement in your introduction.

**Organize to connect supporting ideas and details.** Create an informal outline or list of ideas you want to present. Decide which facts, definitions, details, quotations, or examples best support each idea. Then, as you draft, make sure the relationships among your ideas are clear. For example, you might explore comparisons and contrasts by noting similarities and differences in the motivations of two characters. You might analyze cause and effect by showing the relationship between the setting and achievement of a goal.

**Use topic-related terms.** Give your essay a scholarly tone by using terms you have learned from your reading and research. Review the definitions of terms such as *intrinsic motivation,* and *Maslow's Theory,* and use them where appropriate in your essay.

## Revising and Editing

**Review content.** Make sure your thesis is clearly stated and that you have supported it with facts, details, and examples from the texts you read. Underline main ideas in your essay and confirm that each one is supported.

**Review style.** Revise rambling sentences that are hard to follow, and omit unnecessary words. Check that you have found the clearest, simplest way to communicate your ideas.

**CITE RESEARCH CORRECTLY**

Take note of the evidence from outside sources that you have included in your informative essay. Be sure to cite those sources in your final draft. Refer to the Citing Sources pages in the Introductory Unit of this textbook for additional guidance.

### Self-Evaluation Rubric

Use the following criteria to evaluate the effectiveness of your essay.

| Criteria | Rating Scale | | | |
|---|---|---|---|---|
| **Purpose/Focus** Introduces a specific topic; provides a concluding section that follows from and supports the information or explanation presented | *not very* ............*very*<br>1 | 2 | 3 | 4 |
| **Organization** Organizes complex ideas, concepts, and information to make important connections and distinctions; uses appropriate and varied transitions to link the major sections, create cohesion, and clarify relationships among ideas | 1 | 2 | 3 | 4 |
| **Development of Ideas/Elaboration** Develops the topic with well-chosen, relevant and sufficient facts, extended definitions, concrete details, quotations or other information and examples appropriate to the audience's knowledge of the topic | 1 | 2 | 3 | 4 |
| **Language** Uses precise language and domain-specific vocabulary to clearly convey ideas | 1 | 2 | 3 | 4 |
| **Conventions** Uses correct conventions of grammar, spelling, and punctuation | 1 | 2 | 3 | 4 |

# Independent Reading

## Titles for Extended Reading

In this unit, you have read texts in a variety of genres, including literary nonfiction. Continue to read on your own. Select books that you enjoy, but challenge yourself to explore new topics, new authors, and works of increasing depth and complexity. The titles suggested below will help you get started.

### INFORMATIONAL TEXT

**Barrio Boy**
by Ernesto Galarza

As a young boy in the early twentieth century, Galarza moved from a tiny Mexican village to a bustling Latino neighborhood in Sacramento, California. Follow him on his journey in this **memoir** of his early life.

**Astronomy & Space** EXEMPLAR TEXT
Edited by Phillis Engelbert

Explore outer space in this three-volume **encyclopedia,** which includes a timeline, photographs, biographies, and a glossary of important words to know.

**Discoveries: Finding Our Place in the World**

This collection of **essays** explores four subject areas. In it, you will find "Stonehenge: Groundbreaking Discoveries," "Where on Earth Are You?" "From Bricks to Mortar to Cyberspace: Art Museums Online," and "Testing the Market."

**Nonfiction Readings Across the Curriculum**

This collection of **essays** and **stories** features writers such as Beverly Cleary, Gary Paulsen, Joe Namath, and more. Delve into its pages to find interesting observations about sports, literature, science, and social studies.

**Green Lantern's Book of Inventions**
by Clare Hibbert

With a comic book superhero as your guide, learn about great inventions through the ages—from the wheel to the Internet—in this **nonfiction** book.

### LITERATURE

**Child of the Owl**
by Laurence Yep

When her father is hospitalized, twelve-year-old Casey is sent to live with her grandmother in the strange and unfamiliar world of Chinatown. This **novel** follows Casey as she learns to accept her new situation, drawing strength from family history and Chinese legend.

**Slow Dance Heart Break Blues**
by Arnold Adoff

In this collection of **poetry,** Adoff uses a hip-hop style and modern imagery to explore issues important to teenagers, such as love, loss, and identity.

### ONLINE TEXT SET

SHORT STORY
**Suzy and Leah** Jane Yolen

EXPOSITORY ESSAY
**Conversational Ballgames**
Nancy Masterson Sakamoto

DRAMATIC MONOLOGUE
**My Head Is Full of Starshine**
Peg Kehret

## Preparing to Read Complex Texts

**Attentive Reading** As you read on your own, ask yourself questions like these to enrich your reading experience.

**When reading literary nonfiction, ask yourself...**

### Comprehension: **Key Ideas and Details**

- Is the author writing about a personal experience or a topic he or she has studied? In either case, what are my expectations about the work?
- Are the ideas the author expresses important? Why or why not?
- Did the author live at a different time and place than the present? If so, how does that affect his or her choice of topic and attitude?
- Does the author express beliefs that are very different from mine? If so, how does that affect what I understand and feel about the text?
- Does any one idea seem more important than the others? Why?
- What can I learn from this work?

### Text Analysis: **Craft and Structure**

- Does the author organize ideas so that I can understand them? If not, what is unclear?
- Is the work interesting right from the start? If so, what has the author done to capture my interest? If not, why?
- Does the author give me a new way of looking at a topic? If so, how? If not, why?
- Is the author an expert on the topic? How do I know?
- Does the author use a variety of evidence that makes sense? If not, what is weak?
- Does the author use words in ways that are both interesting and clear? If so, are there any sections that I enjoy more than others?

### Connections: **Integration of Knowledge and Ideas**

- Does the work seem believable? Why or why not?
- Do I agree or disagree with the author's arguments or ideas? Why?
- Does this work remind me of others I have read? If so, in what ways?
- Does this work make me want to read more about this topic? Does it make me want to explore a related topic? Why or why not?

# What is the best way to communicate?

## UNIT PATHWAY

**PART 1**
**SETTING EXPECTATIONS**

- INTRODUCING THE BIG QUESTION
- CLOSE READING WORKSHOP

**PART 2**
**TEXT ANALYSIS**
GUIDED EXPLORATION

SOUNDS AND IMAGES

**PART 3**
**TEXT SET**
DEVELOPING INSIGHT

HEROES AND OUTLAWS

**PART 4**
**DEMONSTRATING INDEPENDENCE**

- INDEPENDENT READING
- ONLINE TEXT SET

**CLOSE READING TOOL**

Use this tool to practice the close reading strategies you learn.

**STUDENT eTEXT**

Bring learning to life with audio, video, and interactive tools.

**ONLINE WRITER'S NOTEBOOK**

Easily capture notes and complete assignments online.

Find all Digital Resources at **pearsonrealize.com.**

## What is the best way to communicate?

We communicate for different reasons and in different ways. Through communication, we can send a message to another person. The message may entertain or inform, and it may be made in person or transmitted through technology. We use telephones, television, and the Internet to send messages, videos, and music to many people or to those far away. We can also express ourselves through art, music, and photography. Sometimes, we read, or watch, or listen to communication created by someone else. With so many reasons and ways to communicate, we often have to choose the *best* way to express ourselves.

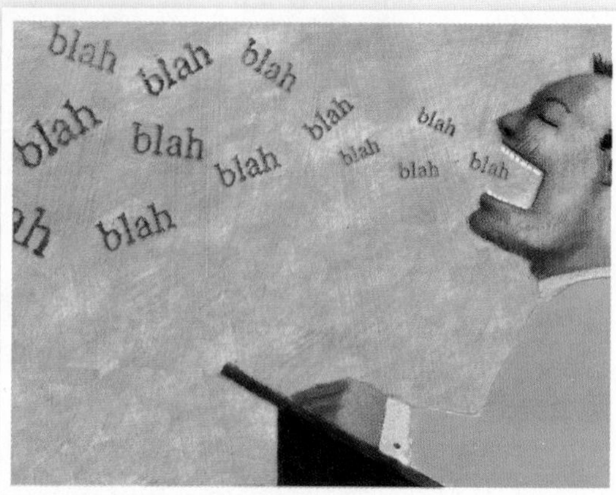


## Exploring the Big Question

**Collaboration: One-on-One Discussion** Start thinking about the Big Question by making a list of ways that people communicate. Describe one specific example of each of these types of communication:

- telling stories
- transmitting messages through technology
- talking to friends or family members
- filming an event
- speaking in public
- creating music or art

Share your examples with a partner. With your partner, discuss which items on your lists are the best ways to communicate and why. Build on your partner's ideas, responding to each with related ideas of your own. Ask questions to make sure you have understood each other's points, and clarify your meaning as needed. As you exchange ideas, build upon each other's comments. You may want to use the vocabulary words on the next page in your discussion.

**Connecting to the Literature** The texts in this unit explore the different ways we communicate our thoughts and ideas. Each reading will give you additional insight into the Big Question.

## Vocabulary

**Acquire and Use Academic Vocabulary** The term "academic vocabulary" refers to words you typically encounter in scholarly and literary texts and in technical and business writing. Review the definitions of these academic vocabulary words. Then, practice using these words in your writing and academic discussions.

**communicate** (kə myo͞o′ ni kāt′) *v.* share ideas, thoughts, or feelings; make known to others

**contribute** (kən trib′ yo͞ot) *v.* add to; enrich

**inform** (in fôrm′) *v.* tell; give information about

**media** (mē′ dē ə) *n. pl.* sources of information, such as newspapers, television, and the Internet

**produce** (prə do͞os′) *v.* make; create

**react** (rē akt′) *v.* respond to

**speak** (spēk′) *v.* use oral language

**technology** (tek näl′ ə jē) *n.* machines, equipment, and ways of doing things that are based on modern knowledge about science

**transmit** (trans mit′) *v.* send or give out

**Gather Vocabulary Knowledge** Additional words related to communication are listed below. Categorize the words by deciding whether you know each one well, know it a little bit, or do not know it at all.

| | | |
|---|---|---|
| **enrich** | **express** | **listen** |
| **entertain** | **learn** | **teach** |

Then, do the following:

1. Work with a partner to write each word on one side of an index card and its definition on the other side.
2. Verify the definitions by looking them up in a print or online dictionary and revising your cards as needed.
3. Place the cards with the words facing up in a pile.
4. Take turns drawing a word card, pronouncing the word and then using it in an original sentence.

# Close Reading Workshop

In this workshop, you will learn an approach to reading that will deepen your understanding of literature and will help you better appreciate the author's craft. The workshop includes models for close reading, discussion, research, and writing. After you have reviewed the models, practice your skills with the Independent Practice selection.

## CLOSE READING: **POETRY**

In Part 2 of this unit you will focus on reading various poems. Use these strategies as you read the texts.

### Comprehension: **Key Ideas and Details**

- Read first to unlock basic meaning.
- Use context clues to help you determine the meanings of unfamiliar words.
- Identify unfamiliar details that you might need to clarify through research.
- Distinguish between what is stated directly and what must be inferred.

**Ask yourself questions such as these:**

- What is this poem about?
- Who is the speaker of the poem?
- To which senses do the poem's images appeal?
- How does the speaker feel about the topic?

### Text Analysis: **Craft and Structure**

- Notice the poet's creative and unusual use of language.
- Consider how rhythm, repetition, and other sound devices develop the poem's meaning.
- Consider how the poem's structure relates to its meaning.

**Ask yourself questions such as these:**

- How does the poet's word choice create vivid images?
- What ideas do those images convey?
- How do the poem's sounds and structure affect meaning?

### Connections: **Integration of Knowledge and Ideas**

- Look for relationships among key ideas. Identify causes and effects, and comparisons and contrasts.
- Look for imagery and analyze its deeper meaning.
- Synthesize to determine the poem's theme.

**Ask yourself questions such as these:**

- How has this work increased my knowledge of a subject, author, or genre?
- What theme, or insight about life, does this poem express?

## Read

As you read this poem, take note of the annotations that model ways to closely read the text.

### Reading Model

### "The Railway Train" by Emily Dickinson

I like to see it lap the miles,
And lick[1] the valleys up,
And stop to feed itself at tanks;
And then, prodigious, step

Around a pile of mountains,[2]
And supercilious, peer
In shanties by the sides of roads;
And then a quarry pare

To fit its sides, and crawl between,
Complaining all the while
In horrid, hooting stanza;
Then chase itself down hill

And neigh[3] like Boanerges;[4]
Then, punctual as a star,
Stop—docile and omnipotent[5]—
At its own stable door.

**Craft and Structure**

**1** The repeated *l* sounds at the beginnings of the words *lap* and *lick* help build a playful image of a speeding train.

**Key Ideas and Details**

**2** The context clue "step/ Around a pile of mountains" can help you infer that *prodigious* means "very big." This image supports the idea that the train is powerful.

**Craft and Structure**

**3** Throughout the poem, the speaker compares the train to an animal. The word *neigh*, which imitates a horse's whinny, reinforces this comparison.

**Key Ideas and Details**

**4** Research can help you determine that *Boanerges* is a Biblical reference to a loud, fiery speaker. This line repeats the idea of the train's power.

**Integration of Knowledge and Ideas**

**5** *Docile* means "easily managed," and *omnipotent* means "all-powerful." The contrast between these words implies that the speaker has conflicting ideas about the train.

## Discuss

Sharing your own ideas and listening to the ideas of others can deepen your understanding of a text and help you look at a topic in a whole new way. As you participate in collaborative discussions, work to have a genuine exchange in which classmates build upon one another's ideas. Support your points with evidence and ask meaningful questions.

### Discussion Model

**Student 1:** It's interesting that Emily Dickinson talks about the train as if it were alive. The words *lap, lick, feed,* and *stable* make me think of a giant workhorse.

**Student 2:** That's what I picture, too. I notice that every stanza has words that make the train seem like a living thing. She builds on that idea throughout the poem by including more lifelike features, such as the train "peering," "crawling," "complaining," and "hooting."

**Student 3:** The thing I find most interesting is that the speaker says she enjoys watching the train in line 1, but a lot of the descriptions are not very positive. She claims that the train is proud and she says it complains. I wonder what Dickinson thought of trains, which were just becoming popular in her time.

## Research

Targeted research can clarify unfamiliar details and shed light on various aspects of a text. Consider questions that arise in your mind as you read, and use those questions as the basis for research.

### Research Model

**Question:** *How did the growth of the railroad affect Americans in the late 1800s?*

**Key Words for Internet Search:** expansion AND railroad AND 1800s

**Result:** U.S. History.org, Early American Railroads; How Stuff Works, Railroad Expansion

**What I Learned:** The railroad's introduction and expansion in the United States during the 1800s had an enormous impact. On one hand, trains made shipping and travel easier than ever before. However, railroads threatened small businesses, railroad owners took advantage of workers, and some protestors were so strongly opposed to the railway that they turned to violence to stop its expansion.

## Write

Writing about a text will deepen your understanding of it and will also allow you to share your ideas more formally with others. The following model essay analyzes the use of poetic elements to express the speaker's point of view, and cites evidence to support its main ideas.

### Writing Model: Informative Text

#### "The Railway Train"—Good, Bad, or Both?

Emily Dickinson compares a train to a horse in her poem "The Railway Train." Her word choice and use of poetic elements create vivid images of the powerful train while expressing the speaker's conflicting feelings.

The writer clearly states the essay's thesis in the first paragraph, preparing readers for the ideas to follow.

The poem begins by setting up the comparison between the train and a horse, using descriptions, such as "lap the miles," as if the train was going to race around a track and then "stop to feed itself at tanks." Dickinson builds the comparison and imagery by continuing sentences across stanzas. The poem ends with a sense of completion as the train/horse returns to "its own stable door."

Direct quotations and examples support the writer's claims.

Within this image of the horse running its course and returning home, Dickinson uses sound devices that allow readers to "hear" the train and its "horrid, hooting." Word choice, sound devices, and extended comparisons end in an image of power with the stopped train "docile and omnipotent / At its own stable door." Given this description, the speaker obviously respects the "beast's" power but seems to hold some negative sentiment toward it as well.

The writer makes a direct connection between the quotation and the thesis.

In line 1, the speaker declares, "I like to see it." However, it becomes apparent that the speaker's feelings about the train are complicated: She likes and dislikes it at the same time. By the second stanza, the train is described as snobbish and looking down on the shanties. In the third stanza, there are more negative descriptions—*complaining* and *horrid.* By the end, though, positive feelings return with words like *punctual* and *docile*. The speaker is uncertain, showing both her appreciation of and her hesitation regarding the train. She likes to watch it, but thinks it is loud and out of place.

The speaker of the poem shares the mixed feelings people of the time had about the railroad and its expansion. Through comparisons, descriptions, sound devices, and word choice, Dickinson paints a vivid picture of the train and expresses the speaker's doubt about the new invention that would soon take over transportation in the United States.

By including information gathered during research, the writer connects the poem to a real historical event: the birth and expansion of the railroad.

As you read the following poems, apply the close reading strategies you have learned. You may need to read the poems multiple times.

*Meet the Author*

Born in El Paso, Texas, in 1942, **Pat Mora** enjoys writing about the Mexican-American heritage of the Southwest. Bilingual and bicultural, she writes poetry in English and Spanish and often includes Spanish words and phrases in her English-language poems.

**Vocabulary ▶**
**maestro** (mīs′ trō) *n.* great musician

**snare** (sner) *v.* catch; capture

**CLOSE READING TOOL**

Read and respond to this selection online using the **Close Reading Tool.**

# Maestro

by Pat Mora

He hears her
when he bows.
Rows of hands clap
again and again he bows
to stage lights and upturned faces
but he hears only his mother's voice

years ago in their small home
singing Mexican songs
one phrase at a time
while his father strummed the guitar
or picked the melody with quick fingertips.
Both cast their music in the air
for him to **snare** with his strings,
songs of *lunas*[1] and *amor*[2]
learned bit by bit.
She'd nod, smile, as his bow slid
note to note, then the trio
    *voz,*[3] *guitarra,*[4] *violín*[5]
would blend again and again
to the last pure note
sweet on the tongue.

---

1. **lunas** (lo͞o′ näs) *n.* Spanish for "moons."
2. **amor** (ä′ môr′) *n.* Spanish for "love."
3. **voz** (vōs) *n.* Spanish for "voice."
4. **guitarra** (gē tär′ rä) *n.* Spanish for "guitar."
5. **violín** (vē ō lēn′) *n.* Spanish for "violin."

# The Desert Is My Mother

by Pat Mora

I say feed me.
She serves red prickly pear[1] on a spiked cactus.

I say tease me.
She sprinkles raindrops in my face on a sunny day.

I say frighten me.
She shouts thunder, flashes lightning.

I say hold me.
She whispers, "Lie in my arms."

I say heal me.
She gives me chamomile, oregano, peppermint.

I say caress me.
She strokes my skin with her warm breath.

I say make me beautiful.
She offers turquoise for my fingers,
a pink blossom for my hair.

I say sing to me.
She chants her windy songs.

I say teach me.
She blooms in the sun's glare,
the snow's silence,
the driest sand.

The desert is my mother.
*El desierto es mi madre.*
The desert is my strong mother.

1. **prickly pear** *n.* a species of cactus with sharp spines and an edible fruit.

# Bailando[1]

by Pat Mora

I will remember you dancing,
spinning round and round
a young girl in Mexico,
your long, black hair free in the wind,
spinning round and round
a young woman at village dances
your long, blue dress swaying
to the beat of *La Varsoviana,*[2]
smiling into the eyes of your partners,
years later smiling into my eyes
when I'd reach up to dance with you,
my dear aunt, who years later
danced with my children,
you, white-haired but still young
waltzing on your ninetieth birthday,
more beautiful than the orchid
pinned on your shoulder,
tottering now when you walk
but saying to me, *"Estoy*[3] *bailando,"*
and laughing.

1. **Bailando** (bī län´ dō) *v.* Spanish for "dancing."
2. **La Varsoviana** (lä bär´ sō byä´ nä) *n.* a lively folk dance.
3. **Estoy** (es toi´) *v.* Spanish for "I am."

# Close Reading Activities

## Read

### Comprehension: **Key Ideas and Details**

1. **(a)** What scene is described in lines 1–5 of "Maestro"? **(b) Interpret:** What does the speaker mean by "he hears only his mother's voice" (line 6)? **(c) Infer:** Which means more to the maestro—his present audience or his childhood memories? Explain.
2. **Interpret:** What does the speaker mean by saying "The Desert Is My Mother"?
3. **(a)** Describe three of the times the aunt dances in "Bailando." **(b) Connect:** What key idea do these images convey?
4. **Summarize:** Write a brief, objective summary of each poem. Cite details from the poems in your writing, but do not include your opinions or evaluations.

### Text Analysis: **Craft and Structure**

5. **(a)** Find one image that appeals to the sense of touch, one that appeals to sight, and one that appeals to hearing in "The Desert Is My Mother." **(b) Analyze:** Do these images help paint an effective picture of the desert? Explain.
6. **Analyze:** How does the one-sentence, one-stanza structure of "Bailando" reinforce the poem's key ideas?
7. **(a)** Identify one example of repetition in each poem. **(b) Analyze:** Explain how each example conveys an idea or helps structure the poem.

### Connections: **Integration of Knowledge and Ideas**

#### Discuss

Conduct a **small-group discussion** in which you analyze how the poet uses imagery and figurative language to express the theme of each poem.

#### Research

Briefly research the effect Mora's culture has had on her work. Consider the following:

**a.** Mora's use of Spanish words in her poetry

**b.** the melding of American and Mexican cultures

**c.** the geography of Mora's childhood

Take notes as you research. Then, write a brief **analysis** of how Mora's cultural background influences one of the poems you read.

#### Write

Choose one of the poems and identify a lesson it suggests about life. In an **essay,** explain how well this lesson applies to life in general. Give examples to support your evaluation.

#### What is the best way to communicate?

Consider how people communicate without using words. Why do you think Mora uses poetry to describe these wordless ways of communicating? Explain.

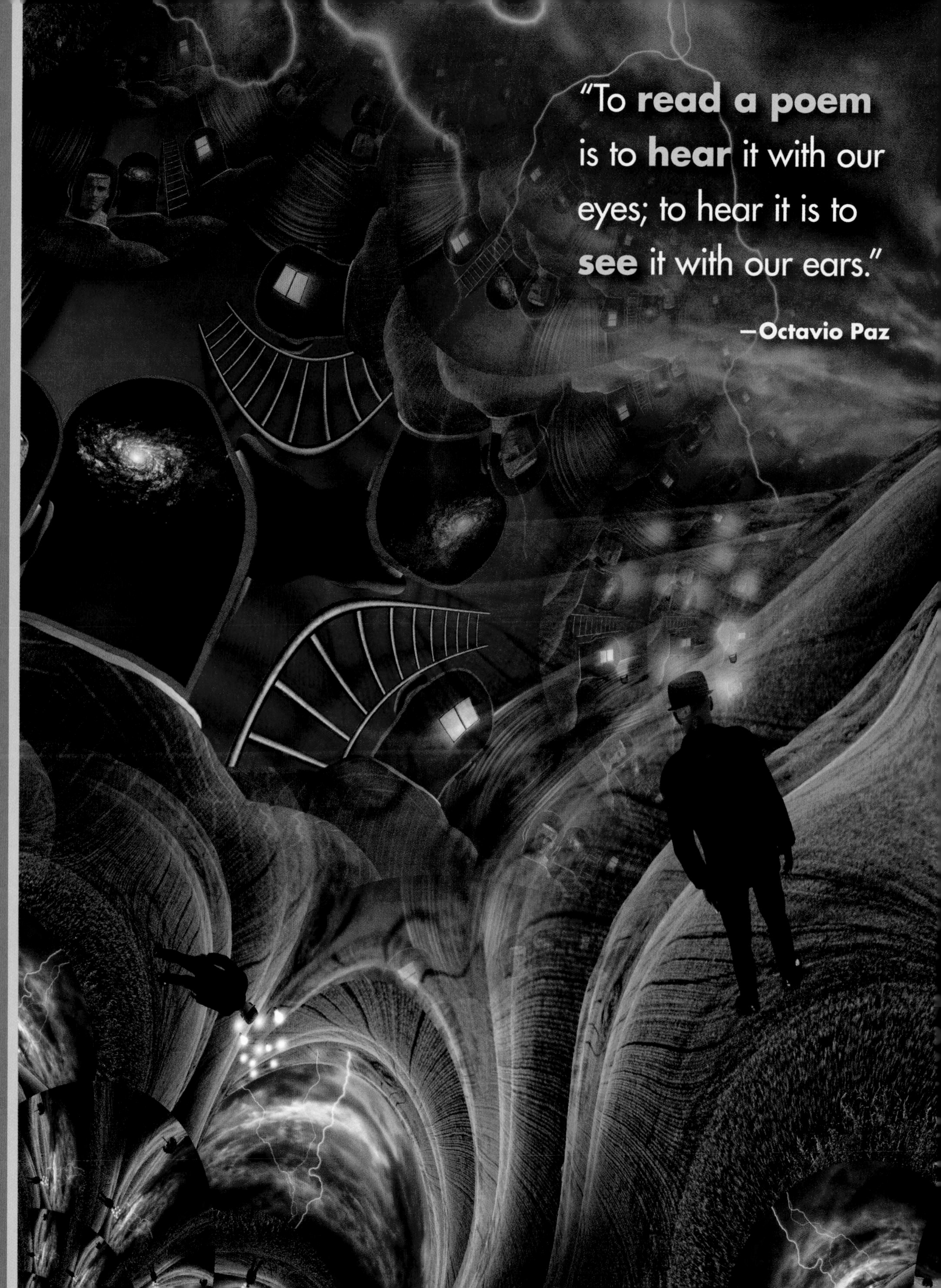
"To **read a poem** is to **hear** it with our eyes; to hear it is to **see** it with our ears."
—Octavio Paz

PART 2

## TEXT ANALYSIS GUIDED EXPLORATION

# SOUNDS AND IMAGES

As you read the poetry in this section, analyze how the poets use the written word to create distinct images and sounds. The quotation on the opposite page will help you start thinking about the ways in which poetic sounds and images can communicate unique ideas and important themes.

◀ CRITICAL VIEWING What ideas about sounds and images does this picture communicate to you?

### READINGS IN PART 2



**CLOSE READING TOOL**

Use the **Close Reading Tool** to practice the strategies you learn in this unit.

# Focus on Craft and Structure

## Elements of Poetry

**Poetry** uses the rhythms and sounds of words as well as their meanings to set the imagination in motion.

**Poetry** is a type of literature that uses the sounds, rhythms, and meanings of words to describe the world in striking and imaginative ways. Poetry comes in many forms, from structured traditional verse to contemporary poems that follow few rules. However varied their forms may be, many poems are made up of the same elements.

**Lines and Stanzas** Poetry is divided into **lines,** or groups of words. In some poems, the first word of each line is capitalized, even if it is not the beginning of a sentence. A sentence in a poem may stretch over several lines. The first one or two lines may *break,* or end, before the sentence is finished. However, good readers of poetry know that they should read the sentence as a whole, without pausing at the end of every line.

In many poems, lines are organized in units of meaning called **stanzas.** The lines in a stanza work together to express one key idea. A blank line, called a **stanza break,** signals that one stanza has ended and a new stanza is beginning.

As you read the poem below, think about the key idea in each stanza, and identify the relationship between ideas.

**Refrains and Repetition** Like a catchy song, a poem may repeat lines, either identically or with variations. A line or group of lines that is repeated at regular intervals in a poem is called a **refrain.** In a refrain, a poet reminds readers and listeners of a key idea, image, or event. Often, a refrain is repeated at the end of each stanza. A poet may also repeat lines with **variations**—changing one or more words with each repetition.

As you read the poem at the bottom of the page, notice how the poet uses repetition, including a refrain, to emphasize his key ideas.

**"Life"**
by Paul Laurence Dunbar

A crust of bread and a corner to sleep in,
A minute to smile and an hour to weep in,
A pint of joy to a peck of trouble,
And never a laugh but the moans come double;
        And that is life!

This five-line **stanza** compares life's joys to its sorrows. Together, the lines **focus on one key idea:** Life has more sorrow than joy.

A crust and a corner that love makes precious,
With a smile to warm and the tears to refresh us;
And joy seems sweeter when cares come after,
And a moan is the finest of foils for laughter;
        And that is life!

The **focus changes,** and a **new stanza** starts. Here, the speaker describes life's joys. **The key idea** is that sorrow intensifies joy.

## Sound Devices

**Rhythm and Meter** Most poems have **rhythm,** or a beat, created by the stressed and unstressed syllables in words. To sustain a pattern of rhythm, or **meter,** a poet may arrange words and break lines at certain points.

Meter is measured in **feet,** or units of stressed and unstressed syllables. As you read the following lines, look for the pattern in the arrangement of stressed syllables (´) and unstressed syllables (˘). Feet are divided by slashes (/).

> Whĕn Í / sĕe bírch / ĕs bénd /
> tŏ léft / ănd ríght
> Ăcróss / thĕ línes / ŏf stráight / ĕr
> dárk / ĕr trées,
> Ĭ líke / tŏ thínk / sŏme bóy's /
> bĕen swíng / ĭng thém.
> (from "Birches," Robert Frost)

In this example, each foot consists of one unstressed syllable followed by one stressed syllable. This down-up, down-up rhythmic pattern fits the subject of an imagined boy swinging on the branches of trees.

Poets may break a metrical pattern for effect. For example, Frost shifts the accent to the first syllable in this line from "Birches": "Kicking his way down through the air to the ground." The shift emphasizes the boy's movement.

**Rhyme** Some poems also contain **rhyme,** or the repetition of vowel and consonant sounds at the ends of words, as in <u>tin</u> and <u>pin</u>. In many poems, the **rhymes** follow a particular pattern, or rhyme **scheme.** In the following example, the first line rhymes with the third line, and the second line rhymes with the fourth line. This rhyme scheme is indicated by using a different letter for each rhyme sound: *abab*.

**Rhyme Scheme**

| | |
|---|---|
| How doth the little crocodile | a |
| Improve his shining tail, | b |
| And pour the waters of the Nile | a |
| On every golden scale! | b |

(from "How Doth the Little Crocodile," Lewis Carroll)

## Additional Sound Devices

Poets may also use other sound devices to enhance mood and meaning in their poems.

- **Alliteration** is the repetition of consonant sounds in the beginnings of words, as in *slippery slope*.
- **Repetition** is the use of any element of language—a sound, word, or phrase—more than once.
- **Onomatopoeia** is the use of words that imitate sounds. *Splat, hiss,* and *gurgle* are all examples of onomatopoeia.

## Analyzing Language, Form, and Structure in Poetry

**Poetic language** is specific, imaginative, and rich with emotion. Every **form** of poetry has its own **structure**.

Poetic language begins when a writer weaves together the images and associations called up by words and says something unique that could not be said in different words.

**Shade of Meaning** The **denotation** of a word is its literal, dictionary definition. The **connotation** consists of the ideas and feelings that the word brings to mind. The chart below lists several words that refer to dogs. Consider the differences in the words' connotations (printed in darker type).

| Denotative and Connotative Meanings | |
|---|---|
| canine ⟶ | dog |
| pooch ⟶ | **friendly, lovable** dog |
| mongrel ⟶ | **mean, ugly** mixed-breed dog |

The technical term *canine* has a neutral connotation, neither positive nor negative. By contrast, the word *pooch* conveys positive feelings, while *mongrel* conveys negative feelings.

**Imagery** To create vivid word pictures, poets use **imagery,** or descriptions that appeal to the five senses. Imagery helps poets convey what they see, hear, smell, taste, or touch.

The example below appeals to the senses of taste, hearing, and smell.

**Example: Imagery**

Taste the green in the lettuce,
Hear the crunch of its freshness,
Smell its earth perfume.

**Figurative Language** To help readers share their perceptions and insights, poets may also use **figurative language,** or language that is not meant to be taken literally. Many types of figurative language are comparisons that show how things are alike in surprising ways. Three common types of figurative language are similes, metaphors, and personification.

A **simile** uses the word *like* or *as* to compare two seemingly unlike things.

- *His hands were as cold as steel.*

A **metaphor** describes one thing as if it were something else.

- *My chores were a mountain waiting to be climbed.*

In **personification,** the writer gives human qualities to a nonhuman subject.

- *The fingertips of the rain tapped a steady beat on the windowpane.*

There are many different forms of poetry. A poet chooses the form that best suits his or her intended meaning.

**Narrative** poetry tells a story in verse. Narrative poems have elements similar to those in short stories, such as plot and characters.

**Haiku** is a three-line Japanese form that describes something in nature. The first and third lines each have five syllables, and the second line has seven.

**Free Verse** poetry is defined by its lack of structure. It has no regular meter, rhyme, fixed line length, or specific stanza pattern.

**Lyric** poetry expresses the thoughts and feelings of a single speaker, often in highly musical verse.

**Ballads** are songlike poems that tell stories. They often deal with adventure or romance.

**Concrete** poems are shaped to look like their subjects. The poet arranges the lines to create a picture on the page.

**Limericks** are humorous, rhyming five-line poems with a specific rhythm pattern and rhyme scheme.

Look at the lyric poem below to see how the structural elements of rhythm, rhyme, and imagery help reinforce the poet's meaning.

| Analysis of Lines from "Tiare Tahiti," Rupert Brooke | | |
|---|---|---|
| *Taü here,* Mamua! | **a** | • The poem's meter emphasizes the commands "crown" and "come." |
| Crown the hair, and come away! | **b** | |
| Hear the calling of the moon, | **c** | • The *b* rhyme sound ties lines 3–5 together, reflecting their focus on the night's beauty. This focus is developed with **imagery**. |
| And the whispering scents that stray | **b** | |
| About the idle warm lagoon. | **c** | |
| Hasten, hand in human hand, | **d** | • The new *c* rhyme sound in lines 6–7 introduces a new idea: the speaker urges Mamua to come to the lagoon. The **alliteration** of the *h, w,* and *d* sounds reinforces this idea. |
| Down the dark, the flowered way, | **b** | |
| Along the whiteness of the sand, | **d** | |
| And in the water's soft caress, | **e** | • Lines 9–10 rhyme, interrupting the pattern of alternating rhymes. The interruption shows that these lines express a key idea: Nature can ease the mind. |
| Wash the mind of foolishness, | **e** | |
| Mamua, until the day. | **b** | |

# Building Knowledge

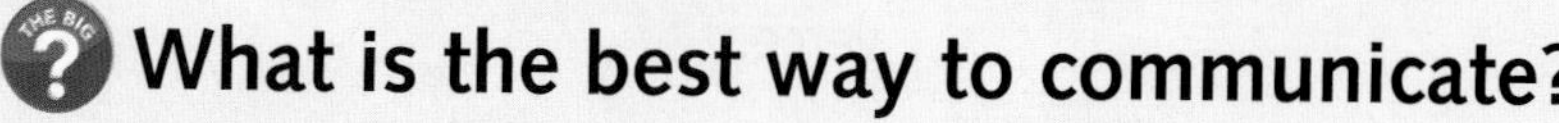

## What is the best way to communicate?

Explore the Big Question as you read Poetry Collection 1. Take notes on how each poet arranges words to communicate meaning.

## CLOSE READING FOCUS

### Key Ideas and Details: **Draw Conclusions**

The techniques a poet uses may require readers to think critically to determine a poem's meaning. When you **draw conclusions**, you arrive at an overall meaning or understanding by pulling together various details. Drawing conclusions helps you recognize ideas that are not directly stated.

Asking questions like the ones that follow can help you identify details and make connections that enable you to draw conclusions.

- What details does the writer include and emphasize?
- How are the details related? Is there a pattern?
- What do the details mean all together?

### Craft and Structure: **Forms of Poetry**

There are many different **forms of poetry**. Each form has specific rules that guide the structure and content.

- A **lyric poem** expresses the poet's thoughts and feelings about a single image or idea in vivid, musical language.
- In a **concrete poem,** the poet arranges the letters and lines to create a visual image that suggests the poem's subject.
- **Haiku** is a traditional form of Japanese poetry that is often about nature. The first and third lines always have five syllables, and the second line always has seven syllables.

## Vocabulary

You will encounter the following words in Poetry Collection 1. In your notebook, make three columns: *verbs, nouns,* and *adjectives*. Write each word in the appropriate column.

| | | |
|---|---|---|
| **translates** | **luminous** | **minnow** |
| **swerve** | **utter** | **fragrant** |

## CLOSE READING MODEL

The passages below are from William Jay Smith's "Seal" and Bashō's "Haiku." The annotations to the right of the passages show ways in which you can use close reading skills to draw conclusions and recognize forms of poetry.

### *from* "Seal"

See how he dives
From the rocks with a zoom!
See how he darts[1]
Through his watery room

**Draw Conclusions**

**1** The words *dives, zoom,* and *darts* suggest grace and speed. These details may help you conclude that seals are able to move through the water quickly and easily.

### *from* "Haiku"

On sweet plum blossoms[2]
The sun rises suddenly.
Look, a mountain path![3]

**Draw Conclusions**

**2** From this detail, you might draw the conclusion that this scene takes place in the springtime, when flowers "blossom," or bloom.

**Forms of Poetry**

**3** The five-syllable, seven-syllable, five-syllable structure tells you immediately that this poem is haiku.

## Meet the Poets

### "Winter"

**Nikki Giovanni** (b. 1943) is not only a poet but also a college professor who teaches both English literature and African American studies. She has won numerous awards for her poetry, including three NAACP Image Awards for Literature.

### "The Rider"

When **Naomi Shihab Nye** (b. 1952) was fourteen, her family moved from Missouri to the Middle East. Though she now values learning about her Arab heritage, the move was not easy for her. Nye has published volumes of poetry as well as books for children.

### "Seal"

**William Jay Smith** (b. 1918) was born in Winnfield, Louisiana. He has taught college students, written poetry and essays, translated Russian and French poetry, and even served in the Vermont State Legislature.

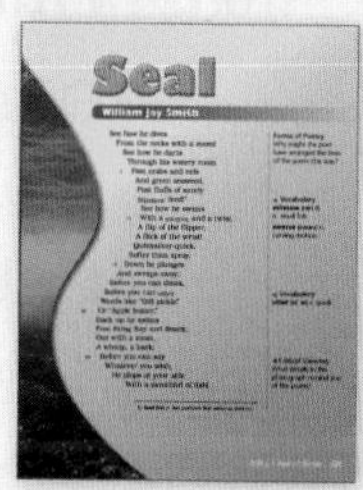

### "Haiku"

**Matsuo Bashō** (1644–1694) was born in Japan and began studying poetry at an early age. He wrote poetry, taught poetry, served as a noble in the court, and lived in a monastery. He remains one of Japan's most famous poets.

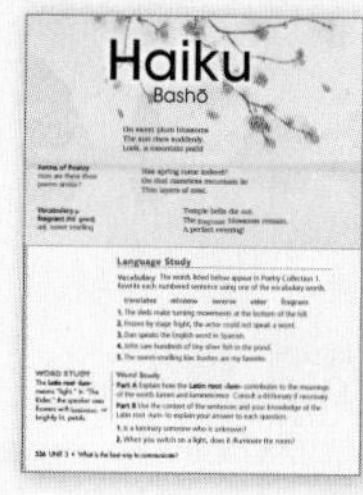

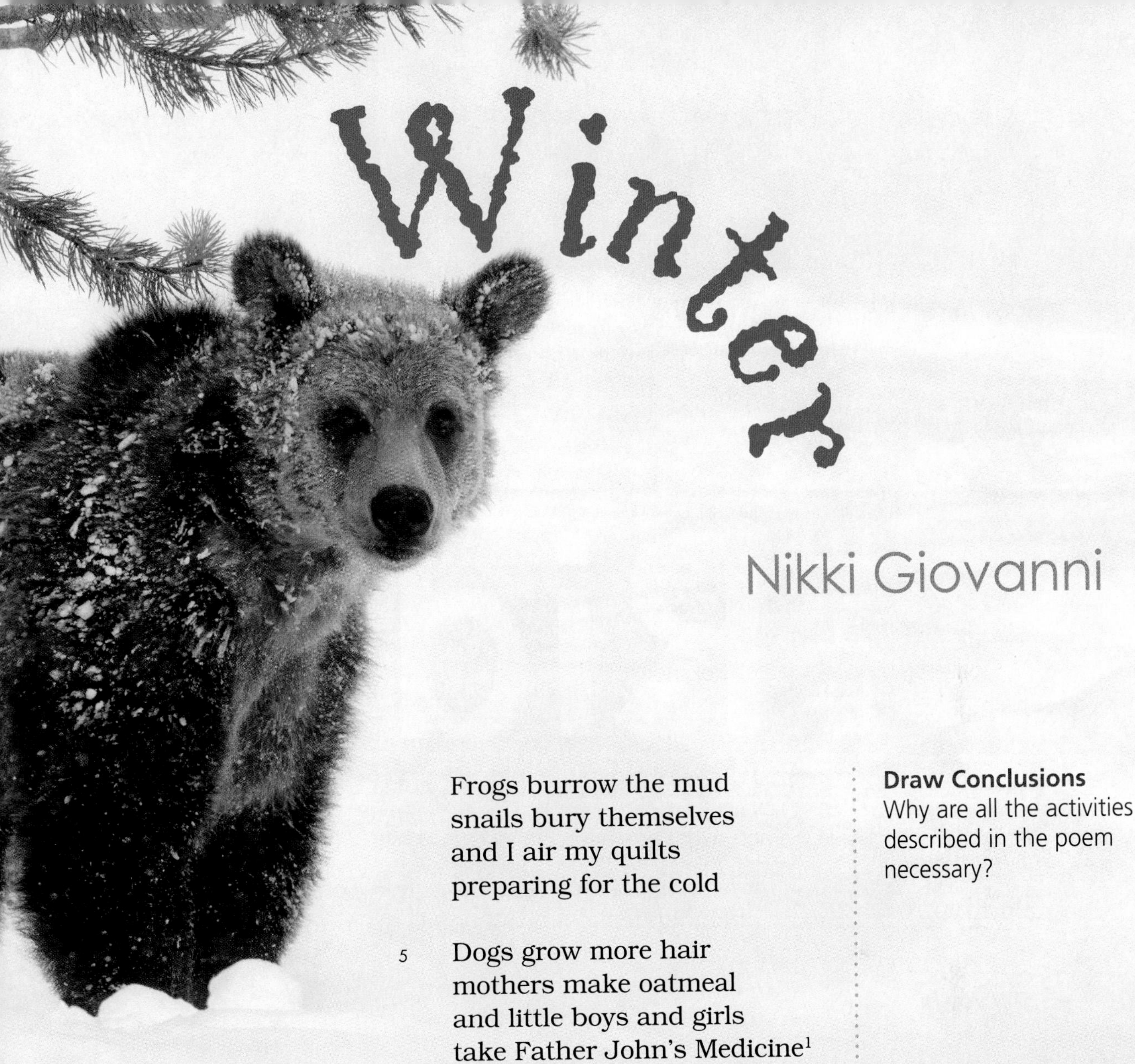

# Winter

Nikki Giovanni

Frogs burrow the mud
snails bury themselves
and I air my quilts
preparing for the cold

Dogs grow more hair
mothers make oatmeal
and little boys and girls
take Father John's Medicine[1]

Bears store fat
chipmunks gather nuts
and I collect books
For the coming winter

**Draw Conclusions**
Why are all the activities described in the poem necessary?

1. **Father John's Medicine** old-fashioned cough syrup.

# THE Rider

## Naomi Shihab Nye

A boy told me
if he rollerskated fast enough
his loneliness couldn't catch up to him,

the best reason I ever heard
for trying to be a champion.

What I wonder tonight
pedaling hard down King William Street
is if it translates to bicycles.

A victory! To leave your loneliness
panting behind you on some street corner
while you float free into a cloud of sudden azaleas,
luminous pink petals that have
never felt loneliness,
no matter how slowly they fell.

**Vocabulary ▶**
**translates** (trans´ lāts) *v.* expresses the same thing in another form

**luminous** (lo͞o´ mə nəs) *adj.* giving off light

**Forms of Poetry**
Whose feelings does the poem express—"a boy's" or the speaker's? Explain.

**◀ Critical Viewing**
What details in this photograph convey the feelings the poem describes?

# Seal

## William Jay Smith

See how he dives
From the rocks with a zoom!
See how he darts
Through his watery room
Past crabs and eels
And green seaweed,
Past fluffs of sandy
Minnow feed![1]
See how he swims
With a swerve and a twist,
A flip of the flipper,
A flick of the wrist!
Quicksilver-quick,
Softer than spray,
Down he plunges
And sweeps away;
Before you can think,
Before you can utter
Words like "Dill pickle"
Or "Apple butter,"
Back up he swims
Past Sting Ray and Shark,
Out with a zoom,
A whoop, a bark;
Before you can say
Whatever you wish,
He plops at your side
With a mouthful of fish!

**Forms of Poetry**
Why might the poet have arranged the lines of the poem this way?

**◄ Vocabulary**
**minnow** (min ō) *n.* small fish

**swerve** (swurv) *n.* curving motion

**◄ Vocabulary**
**utter** (ut′ ər) *v.* speak

**◄ Critical Viewing**
What details in this photograph remind you of the poem?

1. **feed** (fēd) *n.* tiny particles that minnows feed on.

# Haiku

## Bashō

On sweet plum blossoms
The sun rises suddenly.
Look, a mountain path!

**Forms of Poetry**
How are these three poems similar?

Has spring come indeed?
On that nameless mountain lie
Thin layers of mist.

**Vocabulary ▶**
**fragrant** (frā´ grənt) *adj.* sweet smelling

Temple bells die out.
The **fragrant** blossoms remain.
A perfect evening!

## Language Study

**Vocabulary** The words listed below appear in Poetry Collection 1. Rewrite each numbered sentence using one of the vocabulary words.

**translates** **minnow** **swerve** **utter** **fragrant**

1. The sleds make turning movements at the bottom of the hill.
2. Frozen by stage fright, the actor could not speak a word.
3. Dan speaks the English word in Spanish.
4. John saw hundreds of tiny silver fish in the pond.
5. The sweet-smelling lilac bushes are my favorite.

**WORD STUDY**

The **Latin root *-lum-*** means "light." In "The Rider," the speaker sees flowers with **luminous**, or brightly lit, petals.

### Word Study

**Part A** Explain how the **Latin root *-lum-*** contributes to the meanings of the words *lumen* and *luminescence*. Consult a dictionary if necessary.

**Part B** Use the context of the sentences and your knowledge of the Latin root *-lum-* to explain your answer to each question.

1. Is a *luminary* someone who is unknown?
2. When you switch on a light, does it *illuminate* the room?

# Close Reading Activities

## Literary Analysis

### Key Ideas and Details

1. **Draw Conclusions** For each poem, ask a question that helps you draw the conclusion given. **(a)** The speaker in "Winter" accepts the changing seasons as part of the natural cycle of life. **(b)** The speaker in "The Rider" values speed. **(c)** The seal in "Seal" zooms around quickly. **(d)** The speakers in the three haiku value nature.
2. **(a)** What two sports are discussed in "The Rider"? **(b) Compare:** What do the two sports have in common? Include details from the poem to support your answer.

### Craft and Structure

3. **Forms of Poetry** In a chart like the one on the right, write the name of the poems from this collection that have the characteristics described in the left column.
4. **Forms of Poetry** How is the form of each poem suited to the ideas it conveys? Cite specific textual evidence to support your claims.
5. **Forms of Poetry** Based on the three haiku, how would you describe Bashō's attitude toward nature? Use specific details from the poems to support your answer.
6. **(a)** Identify six words that describe the movement of the seal in "Seal." **(b) Infer:** How would you describe the mood or feeling that these words create?

| Characteristics of Poem | Poem |
|---|---|
| Three lines; 17 syllables | |
| Lines shaped like subject | |
| Thoughts of one speaker | |
| Single image or idea | |
| Musical language | |

### Integration of Knowledge and Ideas

7. **(a)** What actions do the animals and people take in "Winter"? **(b) Connect:** How do these actions reflect winter in your experience? Explain.
8. **(a) Relate:** Which poem in this collection did you enjoy the most? Why? **(b) Speculate:** Do you think these poems are meaningful for people your age? Explain.

9. THE BIG ? **What is the best way to communicate? (a)** Which techniques or words convey ideas, pictures, or feelings most effectively in these poems? **(b)** How does form or structure help communicate a poem's meaning? Explain your answer, citing evidence from the poems.

**ACADEMIC VOCABULARY**

As you write and speak about Poetry Collection 1, use the words related to communication that you explored on page 313 of this textbook.

# Close Reading Activities Continued

## Conventions: Sentence Functions and End Marks

Sentences are classified into four categories based on their **functions**. Each type of sentence calls for its own specific punctuation mark(s).

| Category | Function | End Marks | Example |
|---|---|---|---|
| **Declarative** | to make statements | .<br>period | Our cat chased a squirrel up a tree. |
| **Interrogative** | to ask questions | ?<br>question mark | Where did I put my jacket? |
| **Imperative** | to give commands | . *or* !<br>period or exclamation point | Put your books away. *or* Don't touch that stove! |
| **Exclamatory** | to call out or exclaim | !<br>exclamation point | That's a great idea! |

### Practice A

Identify the function of each sentence.

1. How fast can that boy rollerskate?
2. The bike rider noticed some pink azaleas.
3. That seal is so sleek and graceful!
4. What do seals like to eat?
5. Smell the fragrant flowers.
6. Has spring come at last?
7. Prepare your house for winter.
8. It is so cozy here by the fire!

**Reading Application** In Poetry Collection 1, find one declarative sentence, one interrogative sentence, one imperative sentence, and one exclamatory sentence.

### Practice B

Follow the directions to write a sentence that performs the indicated function.

1. Make a statement about bike riding.
2. Ask a question about winter.
3. Issue a command that one of the haiku speakers might give.
4. Make an exclamation about a seal.

**Writing Application** Write four sentences about the poems in this collection. Use one declarative sentence, one interrogative sentence, one imperative sentence, and one exclamatory sentence.

## Writing to Sources

**Poetry** Write a **lyric poem, concrete poem,** or **haiku** to share your thoughts in new, creative ways.

- Choose a subject that interests you. Write the subject in the center of a piece of paper, and create a cluster diagram around it.
- Brainstorm by listing vivid descriptions, action words, thoughts, and feelings in the cluster diagram.
- Review the characteristics of each poetic form and decide which form is best suited to your topic. Next, review the poem or poems in Poetry Collection 1 that have the form you have chosen. Note techniques the poet uses that you could replicate in your own work. Then, use your notes to draft your poem. Add a creative title to capture your readers' interest.
- Use one or more computer programs, such as a word-processing or drawing program, to write and format your poem. Use punctuation, line length, and word arrangement to create the desired effect. Publish your poem by posting it on an approved Web site or in your classroom.

**Grammar Application** Check to be sure you have correctly punctuated your writing.

## Speaking and Listening

**Presentation of Ideas** In the library or online, find a recording of a poet reading his or her own lyric poetry. Listen to one or more of the poems with a small group of classmates as you read the written version of each poem. Then, in a brief **presentation** to your group, compare the experience of reading a poem to the experience of hearing it read aloud. Follow these steps:

- Analyze the effects of hearing the words in comparison with reading them. Support your opinion with specific reasons and examples from the recording and the text.
- Listen carefully to each person's opinions and weigh them against your own.
- With your group, acknowledge new information expressed by others and discuss whether or not your opinion changed after listening to other responses.

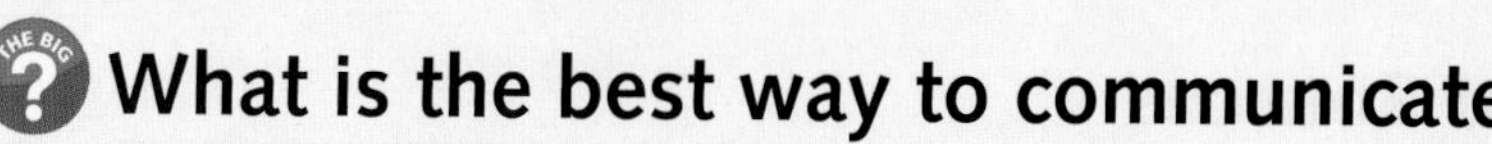

## What is the best way to communicate?

Explore the Big Question as you read Poetry Collection 2. Take notes on the ways in which the poems explore ways of communicating.

## CLOSE READING FOCUS

### Key Ideas and Details: **Draw Conclusions**

To interpret meaning in poetry, **draw conclusions** by connecting important details. For example, if the speaker in a poem describes beautiful flowers, bright sunshine, and happy children, you might conclude that he or she has a positive outlook. As you read, identify important details. Then, look at the details together to draw a conclusion about the poem's meaning.

### Craft and Structure: **Figurative Language**

**Figurative language** is language that is not meant to be taken literally. Writers use figures of speech, or figurative language, to express ideas in vivid and imaginative ways. Common figures of speech include the following:

- A **simile** compares two unlike things by using the word *like* or *as*: *My love is like a red, red rose.*
- A **metaphor** compares two unlike things by saying that one thing *is* another: *Life is a bowl of cherries.*
- In **personification,** a nonhuman subject is given human characteristics: *The stars were dancing.*
- A **symbol** is a thing that represents something other than itself. For example, a dove may symbolize peace.

## Vocabulary

You will encounter the following words in Poetry Collection 2. Decide whether you know each word well, know it a little bit, or do not know it at all. After you read, use each word in a sentence that shows the word's meaning.

| | |
|---|---|
| **fascinated** | **granite** |
| **crystal** | **haunches** |

## CLOSE READING MODEL

The passages below are from Naomi Long Madgett's "Life" and Langston Hughes's "Mother to Son." The annotations to the right of the passages show ways in which you can use close reading skills to draw conclusions and analyze figurative language.

### *from* "Life"

Life is but a toy that swings on a bright gold chain[1]
Ticking for a little while[2]
To amuse a fascinated infant,

**Figurative Language**

**1** The speaker says life *is* a toy. This metaphor creates a strong opening image for the poem.

**Draw Conclusions**

**2** When you connect the phrase *ticking for a little while* with the image of a gold chain, you may visualize a pocket watch. From this image, you may conclude that the speaker believes life passes swiftly.

### *from* "Mother to Son"

Well, son, I'll tell you:
Life for me ain't been no crystal stair.[3]
It's had tacks in it,
And splinters,

**Draw Conclusions**

**3** The speaker uses informal language to describe life's struggles. You may conclude that she has little formal education, but her life experience has given her great wisdom.

## Meet the Poets

### "Life"

**Naomi Long Madgett** (b. 1923) first discovered poetry at the age of seven or eight, while reading in her father's study. She was most inspired by the poets Alfred, Lord Tennyson and Langston Hughes, though their styles are quite different. Madgett once said, "I would rather be a good poet than anything else." Her ambition to create good poetry has led her to write more than seven collections of poems.

### "The Courage That My Mother Had"

**Edna St. Vincent Millay** (1892–1950) was the daughter of a hard-working nurse who encouraged her daughters to be independent and to love reading. Millay's mother had a powerful influence on young Edna, who grew up to be a widely published writer and political activist. Born in Rockland, Maine, Millay published her first poem at the age of fourteen. In 1923, she became the first woman to win the Pulitzer Prize for poetry.

### "Mother to Son"

**Langston Hughes** (1902–1967) published his first work just a year after his high school graduation. Though he wrote in many genres, Hughes is best known for his poetry. He was one of the main figures in the Harlem Renaissance, a creative movement among African Americans that took place in the 1920s in New York City.

### "Fog"

**Carl Sandburg** (1878–1967) was born in Illinois to Swedish immigrant parents. Although he won the Pulitzer Prize in both poetry and history, he was not a typical scholar. By the time his first book appeared, he had tried many different occupations, including farm worker, stagehand, railroad worker, soldier, and cook.

# Life

Naomi Long Madgett

Life is but a toy that swings on a bright gold chain
Ticking for a little while
To amuse a fascinated infant,
Until the keeper, a very old man,
Becomes tired of the game
And lets the watch run down.

◀ **Vocabulary**
**fascinated** (fas´ ə nāt´ əd) *adj.* very interested

# The Courage That My Mother Had

## Edna St. Vincent Millay

The courage that my mother had
Went with her, and is with her still:
Rock from New England quarried;[1]
Now **granite** in a granite hill.

The golden brooch[2] my mother wore
She left behind for me to wear;
I have no thing I treasure more:
Yet, it is something I could spare.

Oh, if instead she'd left to me
The thing she took into the grave!—
That courage like a rock, which she
Has no more need of, and I have.

**Vocabulary ▶**
**granite** (gran´ it) *n.* hard, gray rock

**Draw Conclusions**
What detail in the third stanza shows how the speaker feels about her mother?

1. **quarried** (kwôr´ ēd) *adj.* carved out of the ground.
2. **brooch** (brōch) *n.* large ornamental pin.

# Mother to Son

## Langston Hughes

Well, son, I'll tell you:
Life for me ain't been no crystal stair.
It's had tacks in it,
And splinters,
And boards torn up,
And places with no carpet on the floor—
Bare.
But all the time
I'se been a-climbin' on,
And reachin' landin's,
And turnin' corners,
And sometimes goin' in the dark
Where there ain't been no light.
So boy, don't you turn back.
Don't you set down on the steps
'Cause you finds it's kinder hard.
Don't you fall now—
For I'se still goin', honey,
I'se still climbin',
And life for me ain't been no crystal stair.

◀ **Vocabulary**
**crystal** (kris´ təl) *adj.* made of clear, brilliant glass

**Figurative Language**
What does the staircase symbolize?

**Draw Conclusions**
What details in the poem support the conclusion that life has not been easy for the mother?

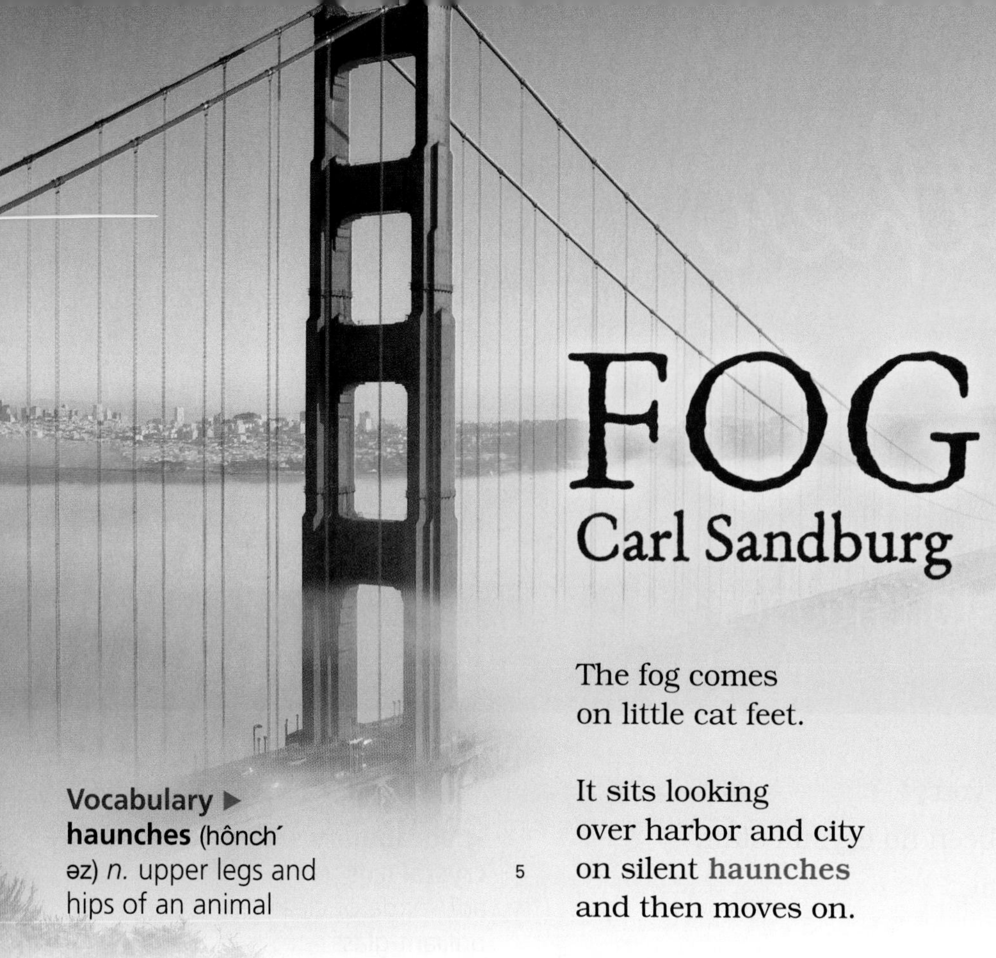

# FOG

## Carl Sandburg

The fog comes
on little cat feet.

It sits looking
over harbor and city
on silent **haunches**
and then moves on.

**Vocabulary ▶**
**haunches** (hônch´ əz) *n.* upper legs and hips of an animal

## Language Study

**Vocabulary** The words listed below appear in Poetry Collection 2. Explain your answer to each numbered question.

**fascinated** **granite** **crystal** **haunches**

**1.** If Michael is *fascinated* by the show, is he bored?

**2.** If something is made of *granite*, will it break easily?

**3.** If a glass is made of *crystal*, is it fragile?

**4.** Is it possible for a dog to sit on its *haunches*?

**WORD STUDY**

The **suffix *-er***, means "one who." The watch in "Life" has a **keeper**, someone who winds the watch to keep it going.

### Word Study

**Part A** Explain how the **suffix *-er*** contributes to the meanings of the words *writer, climber,* and *thinker*. Consult a dictionary if necessary.

**Part B** Use the context of the sentences and your knowledge of the suffix *-er* to explain your answer to each question.

**1.** Is a champion *swimmer* likely to win a prize in running?

**2.** What does a *photographer* enjoy doing?

# Close Reading Activities

## Literary Analysis

### Key Ideas and Details

1. **(a)** In "Life," what image does Naomi Long Madgett use to describe life? **(b) Evaluate:** Is it an effective image? Why or why not?
2. **Draw Conclusions** Use a graphic organizer like the one on the right to connect details from the poem "Life" to reach the conclusion given.
3. **Draw Conclusions** Which details from "The Courage That My Mother Had" support the conclusion that the speaker admires her mother?
4. **Draw Conclusions (a)** What qualities does the mother in "Mother to Son" demonstrate through her words and actions? Cite specific examples from the poem. **(b)** Why does the mother need these qualities?

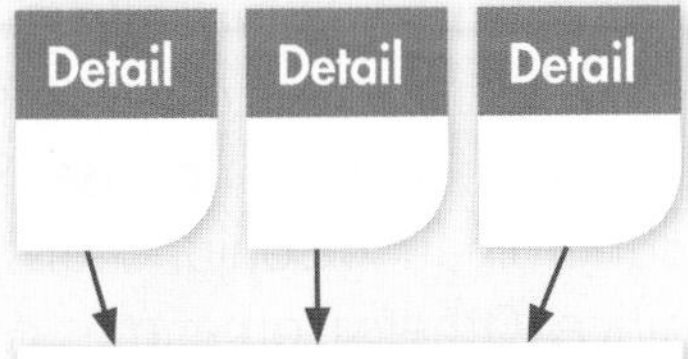


**Conclusion:** The speaker believes that people lose interest in life as they grow older.

### Craft and Structure

5. **Figurative Language (a)** In "Fog," to what is fog compared? **(b)** How are these two things alike? **(c)** What type of figurative language does the author use? How can you tell?
6. **Figurative Language (a)** What is a symbol of hardship in "Mother to Son"? What is a symbol of ease and luxury? **(b)** How are these things alike and different?
7. **Figurative Language (a)** What is a symbol for strength in "The Courage That My Mother Had"? **(b)** How do you know?

### Integration of Knowledge and Ideas

8. **Interpret:** In "The Courage That My Mother Had," why would the speaker rather have her mother's character than the physical item her mother left her?
9. **(a)** What three things does the fog do in "Fog"? **(b) Connect:** What qualities of fog make it a good subject for a poem?

10. THE BIG ? **What is the best way to communicate?** How can a poet use figures of speech to communicate ideas in new and different ways?

**ACADEMIC VOCABULARY**

As you write and speak about Poetry Collection 2, use the words related to communication that you explored on page 313 of this textbook.

## Conventions: Independent and Dependent Clauses

A **clause** is a group of words with its own subject and verb. The two major types of clauses are independent clauses and dependent clauses.

An **independent clause** can stand by itself as a complete sentence. A **dependent clause** (also called a **subordinate clause**) cannot stand alone as a complete sentence but instead adds information to an independent clause. Some dependent clauses begin with subordinating conjunctions, such as *if, when, because, where,* and *since.* Others (sometimes called **relative clauses**) begin with relative pronouns, such as *who, whom, whose, which,* and *that.*

| Comparing Two Kinds of Clauses | |
|---|---|
| **Independent** | **Dependent** |
| The mosque (S) has (V) a golden dome. | *since* the mosque (S) has (V) a dome |
| I (S) planted (V) the heirloom tomatoes in May. | *that* I (S) planted (V) in May |

### Practice A

Identify the independent and dependent clauses in each sentence.

1. The infant was amused when the watch was swinging back and forth.
2. She had courage that was like granite.
3. When the fog came in, we could not see ten feet ahead.
4. The mother climbed stairs where there was no light.

**Reading Application** In Poetry Collection 2, find a sentence with an independent and a dependent clause. Explain the role of each clause.

### Practice B

Identify the dependent clause in each sentence. Then, use the dependent clause to write a new sentence.

1. When we were driving, the fog made it difficult to see.
2. If these stairs were repaired, they would be safer.
3. This watch, which is made of gold, is quite valuable.

**Writing Application** Write two sentences about poetry that both include dependent clauses. Label each independent and dependent clause.

## Writing to Sources

**Explanatory Text** Create a **metaphor** using one of the following topics from the poems in this collection as inspiration:

- life
- a quality, such as courage
- an idea, such as nature

Before you write, review the poems in Poetry Collection 2, and note techniques the authors use to create effective metaphors. Use precise language to compare your topic to something else, such as an object, an idea, or an animal. Then, extend the metaphor by making several connected comparisons. Use vivid images and descriptive language to develop your metaphor.

**Grammar Application** Check your writing to make sure it is free from grammatical errors.

## Research and Technology

**Build and Present Knowledge** Working with a partner, write a **scientific explanation** of fog. Present your findings to the class in an oral report.

- Use library resources to research the natural phenomenon of fog. If you are using a reference book, scan the table of contents to see if your topic is addressed. Then, review the index for key words.
- Look up unfamiliar or scientific terms in a glossary or dictionary.
- Find out how, why, and when fog forms, and why it disappears. As you write your explanation, support it with factual details.
- Use diagrams, illustrations, photographs, maps, or other visuals to clarify your findings and emphasize key points.
- Conclude your report by briefly analyzing Carl Sandburg's poem and evaluating the effectiveness of his comparison between fog and a cat. Support your claims with details from your research and from the poem. Be sure to communicate information in your own words.

## What is the best way to communicate?

Think about the Big Question as you read Poetry Collection 3. Note ways in which the poets use sound devices to communicate ideas.

## CLOSE READING FOCUS

### Key Ideas and Details: **Paraphrase**

When you **paraphrase**, you restate something in your own words. To paraphrase a poem, you must first understand its meaning. Begin by looking for the poem's main idea and the details that support it. Reading aloud according to punctuation can help you identify complete thoughts in a poem. Observe these rules:

- Keep reading when a line has no end punctuation.
- Pause at commas; pause slightly longer at dashes and semicolons.
- Stop at periods, question marks, or exclamation points.

### Craft and Structure: **Sound Devices**

**Sound devices** use the sounds of words to create musical effects that appeal to the ear. These sound devices are used in poetry:

- **Onomatopoeia** is the use of words with sounds that suggest their meanings: the *shooshing* of skis
- **Alliteration** is the repetition of sounds at the beginnings of words: *maggie* and *millie* and *mollie* and *may*
- **Repetition** is the repeated use of words, phrases, or rhythms: To the swinging and the ringing / *of the bells, bells, bells*
  *Of the bells, bells, bells, bells*

## Vocabulary

You will encounter the following words in Poetry Collection 3. Write the words in your notebook and circle the word that you associate with a sound. Then, use the word in a sentence.

| | | |
|---|---|---|
| **groves** | **fathom** | **withered** |
| **curdled** | **sputters** | **smattering** |

## CLOSE READING MODEL

The passages below are from Shel Silverstein's "Sarah Cynthia Sylvia Stout Would Not Take the Garbage Out" and William Shakespeare's "Full Fathom Five." The annotations to the right of the passages show ways in which you can use close reading skills to paraphrase as you read and analyze sound devices.

### *from* "Sarah Cynthia Sylvia Stout Would Not Take the Garbage Out"

It filled the can, it covered the floor,
It cracked the window and blocked the door[1]
With bacon rinds and chicken bones,
Drippy ends of ice cream cones,
Prune pits, peach pits, orange peel,
Gloppy glumps of cold oatmeal,...[2]

**Sound Devices**
**1** By repeating the phrase, "It ___ the ___," the poet creates a strong rhythm and a sense of the unstoppable force of the garbage.

**Sound Devices**
**2** The nonsense phrase *gloppy glumps* calls to mind the real words *sloppy lumps,* which can help you understand its meaning. Alliteration makes the phrase sound silly, which adds to the poem's bouncy rhythm and humorous tone.

### *from* "Full Fathom Five"

Full fathom five thy father lies;
Of his bones are coral made;
Those are pearls that were his eyes;[3]
Nothing of him that doth fade....

**Paraphrase**
**3** When you encounter unfamiliar or difficult language, slow down, reread, and then try to paraphrase the lines. You might paraphrase these lines like this: "Your father lies under five fathoms of water. His bones are now made of coral, and his eyes are made of pearls."

## Meet the Poets

### "Train Tune"

**Louise Bogan** (1897–1970) grew up in Maine and attended the Girls' Latin School in Boston, where she developed an interest in poetry. During her writing career, she became known for her compact use of language and for the traditional form of her poems. A very private person, Bogan struggled with her fame as a highly respected poet, critic, and lecturer.

Train Tune
Louise Bogan

### "Full Fathom Five"

**William Shakespeare** (1564–1616) is widely regarded as the greatest writer in the English language. He wrote thirty-seven plays, many of which are still performed frequently today. They include *Romeo and Juliet, Hamlet,* and *A Midsummer Night's Dream.*

FULL FATHOM FIVE
WILLIAM SHAKESPEARE

### "Sarah Cynthia Sylvia Stout Would Not Take the Garbage Out"

**Shel Silverstein** (1932–1999) was a cartoonist, composer, folk singer, and writer. He began writing poetry at an early age, before he had a chance to study any of the great poets. "I was so lucky that I didn't have anyone to copy," he once said.

Sarah Cynthia Sylvia Stout Would Not Take the Garbage Out
Shel Silverstein

### "Onomatopoeia"

**Eve Merriam** (1916–1992) became fascinated with words when she was quite young. "I remember being enthralled by the sound of words," she said. This fascination led her to write poetry, fiction, nonfiction, and drama.

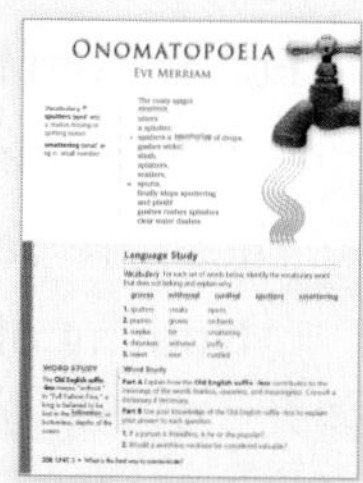
ONOMATOPOEIA
EVE MERRIAM

# Train Tune

Louise Bogan

Back through clouds
Back through clearing
Back through distance
Back through silence

Back through **groves**
Back through garlands
Back by rivers
Back below mountains

Back through lightning
Back through cities
Back through stars
Back through hours

Back through plains
Back through flowers
Back through birds
Back through rain

Back through smoke
Back through noon
Back along love
Back through midnight

◀ **Vocabulary**
**groves** (grōvz) *n.* small groups of trees

# FULL FATHOM FIVE

**WILLIAM SHAKESPEARE**

**Vocabulary ▶**
**fathom** (fa*th*´ əm)
*n.* unit of length used to measure the depth of water

**Paraphrase**
After which lines do you come to a complete stop when reading?

Full **fathom** five thy father lies;
Of his bones are coral made;
Those are pearls that were his eyes;
Nothing of him that doth fade
But doth suffer a sea change
Into something rich and strange.
Sea nymphs hourly ring his knell;[1]
Ding-dong.
Hark! Now I hear them—Ding-dong bell.

1. **knell** (nel) *n.* funeral bell.

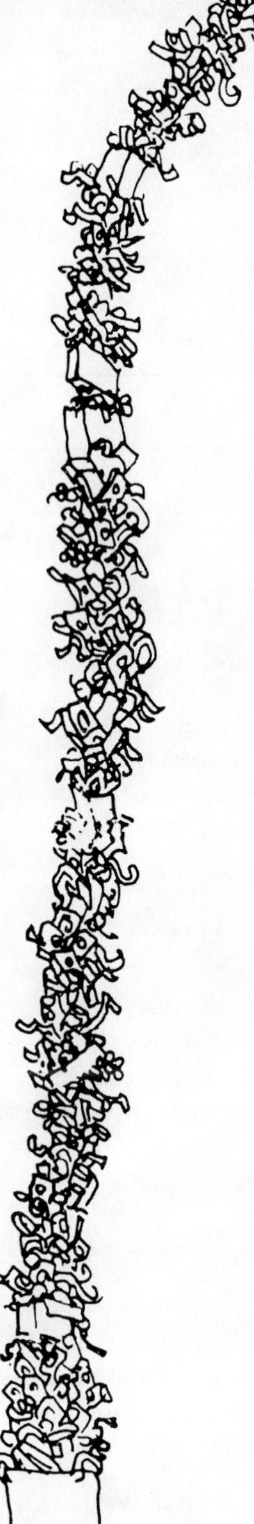

# Sarah Cynthia Sylvia Stout Would Not Take the Garbage Out

## *Shel Silverstein*

Sarah Cynthia Sylvia Stout
Would not take the garbage out!
She'd scour[1] the pots and scrape the pans,
Candy[2] the yams and spice the hams,
And though her daddy would scream and shout,
She simply would not take the garbage out.
And so it piled up to the ceilings:
Coffee grounds, potato peelings,
Brown bananas, rotten peas,
Chunks of sour cottage cheese.
It filled the can, it covered the floor,
It cracked the window and blocked the door
With bacon rinds[3] and chicken bones,
Drippy ends of ice cream cones,
Prune pits, peach pits, orange peel,
Gloppy glumps of cold oatmeal,
Pizza crusts and **withered** greens,
Soggy beans and tangerines,
Crusts of black burned buttered toast,

1. **scour** (skour) *v.* clean by rubbing vigorously.
2. **candy** (kan′ dē) *v.* coat with sugar.
3. **rinds** (rīndz) *n.* tough outer layers or skins.

Gristly bits of beefy roasts . . .
The garbage rolled on down the hall,
It raised the roof, it broke the wall . . .
Greasy napkins, cookie crumbs,
Globs of gooey bubble gum,
Cellophane from green baloney,
Rubbery blubbery macaroni,
Peanut butter, caked and dry,
**Curdled** milk and crusts of pie,
Moldy melons, dried-up mustard,
Eggshells mixed with lemon custard,
Cold french fries and rancid meat,
Yellow lumps of Cream of Wheat.
At last the garbage reached so high
That finally it touched the sky.
And all the neighbors moved away,
And none of her friends would come to play.
And finally Sarah Cynthia Stout said,
"OK, I'll take the garbage out!"
But then, of course, it was too late . . .
The garbage reached across the state,
From New York to the Golden Gate.
And there, in the garbage she did hate,
Poor Sarah met an awful fate,
That I cannot right now relate[4]
Because the hour is much too late.
But children, remember Sarah Stout
And always take the garbage out!

4. **relate** (ri lāt′) *v.* tell.

◀ **Vocabulary**
**withered** (with′ ərd) *adj.* dried up

**Sound Devices**
Which sound device does the poet use in line 24? Explain.

◀ **Vocabulary**
**curdled** (kurd′ 'ld) *adj.* rotten

**Spiral Review**
**TONE** Which words and phrases on this page contribute to a humorous, lighthearted tone? Explain.

◀ **Critical Viewing**
The author drew the cartoons that accompany the poem. How does the art add to the poem's humor?

# ONOMATOPOEIA

## EVE MERRIAM

**Vocabulary ▶**
**sputters** (sput´ ərz) *v.* makes hissing or spitting noises

**smattering** (smat´ ər iŋ) *n.* small number

The rusty spigot
**sputters,**
utters
a splutter,
spatters a **smattering** of drops,
gashes wider;
slash,
splatters,
scatters,
spurts,
finally stops sputtering
and plash!
gushes rushes splashes
clear water dashes.

## Language Study

**Vocabulary** For each set of words below, identify the vocabulary word that does not belong and explain why.

**groves withered curdled sputters smattering**

1. sputters creaks opens
2. prairies groves orchards
3. surplus bit smattering
4. shrunken withered puffy
5. sweet sour curdled

**WORD STUDY**
The **Old English suffix *-less*** means "without." In "Full Fathom Five," a king is believed to be lost in the **fathomless,** or bottomless, depths of the ocean.

### Word Study

**Part A** Explain how the **Old English suffix *-less*** contributes to the meanings of the words *fearless, ceaseless,* and *meaningless.* Consult a dictionary if necessary.

**Part B** Use your knowledge of the Old English suffix *-less* to explain your answer to each question.

1. If a person is *friendless,* is he or she popular?
2. Would a *worthless* necklace be considered valuable?

# Close Reading Activities

## Literary Analysis

### Key Ideas and Details

1. **Paraphrase** In a chart like the one on the right, write an example from each poem in which you read according to punctuation rather than stopping at the end of a line. Then, paraphrase each example.
2. **(a)** What emotion does the speaker mention in "Train Tune"? **(b) Speculate:** Why do you think the poet includes this detail? Support your answer.
3. **(a)** Name two changes that the speaker describes happening to the father in "Full Fathom Five." **(b) Interpret:** Why does the poet call these changes "rich and strange"?

| Poem Title and Example | Paraphrase |
|---|---|
| | |
| | |
| | |
| | |

### Craft and Structure

4. **Sound Devices (a)** Find two examples of alliteration in "Sarah Cynthia..." **(b)** How does alliteration add to the humor of the poem?
5. **Sound Devices (a)** Identify the repetition in "Train Tune." **(b)** What effect does this sound device have when you read the poem out loud?
6. **Sound Devices (a)** Identify three words from "Onomatopoeia" that sound like falling water. **(b) Analyze:** How do the sounds of the words help convey the author's meaning?
7. **Sound Devices (a)** What sound device is used in the title "Full Fathom Five"? **(b)** Find an example of another sound device in the poem.

### Integration of Knowledge and Ideas

8. **Evaluate:** Which of these poems has the most musical quality? Give examples from the poem to support your answer.
9. **(a) Infer:** What lesson might readers learn from "Sarah Cynthia . . ."? **(b) Analyze:** Do you think the poet intended to teach a lesson? Why or why not?

10. **What is the best way to communicate? (a)** Which poem evokes the strongest response in you? Explain. **(b)** How do the sounds of the poem contribute to your response? Cite specific examples from the poem.

**ACADEMIC VOCABULARY**

As you write and speak about Poetry Collection 3, use the words related to communication that you explored on page 313 of this textbook.

## Conventions: Sentence Structures

A **simple sentence** consists of one independent clause—a group of words that has a subject and a verb and can stand by itself as a complete thought. A **compound sentence** consists of two or more independent clauses linked by a word such as *and, but,* or *or*. A **complex sentence** contains one independent clause and one or more dependent clauses—a group of words that has a subject and verb but is not a complete thought. A **compound-complex sentence** consists of two or more independent clauses and one or more dependent clauses.

**Simple sentence:** We planned a picnic.

**Compound sentence:** We planned a picnic (ind. clause), but it rained (ind. clause).

**Complex sentence:** Because there is rain (dep. clause), which has lasted all day (dep. clause), we are indoors (ind. clause).

**Compound-complex sentence:** Because it rained (dep. clause), we are indoors (ind. clause), but it is still a fun time (ind. clause).

### Practice A

Identify each sentence as simple, compound, complex, or compound-complex.

1. The garbage piled up to the ceiling.
2. The man, who lies beneath the sea, has pearls for eyes.
3. The train that chugs along the tracks passes by a river, but it does not go through a tunnel.
4. The spigot is rusty, and its handle does not turn easily.

**Reading Application** In Poetry Collection 3, find a simple sentence, a compound sentence, a complex sentence, and a compound-complex sentence.

### Practice B

For each item, write a sentence and then identify its structure. Use at least three different sentence structures.

1. Tell why a poet would use humor.
2. Describe why a poet would use onomatopoeia.
3. Explain why a poet would choose to express himself or herself through poetry.
4. Describe a scene from one of the poems you have read.

**Writing Application** Write a paragraph from the perspective of Sarah Cynthia Sylvia Stout. Use all four sentence structures.

## Writing to Sources

**Informative Text** Write a **paraphrase** of one of the poems you read in Poetry Collection 3.

- Carefully reread each stanza of the poem to identify the poet's main idea.
- Use a dictionary to define words you do not know. Replace these words with familiar synonyms, or words that have the same meaning.
- Restate the entire poem in your own words.
- Reread your paraphrase to make sure it has the same meaning as the original. Make revisions as necessary.

**Grammar Application** Check your writing to be sure your sentence structures are effective.

## Speaking and Listening

**Presentation of Ideas** Present a **poetry reading** of one of the poems from Poetry Collection 3.

Follow these guidelines as you prepare:

- Rehearse your reading with a small group.
- Be sure you are pronouncing each word correctly, and reading according to punctuation.
- To help you read with the appropriate expression, consider the poet's intentions in writing the poem. Did the poet mean to convey a serious tone or a silly tone? What type of rhythm did the poet want the poem to have?
- Practice reading slowly and expressively. You may decide to emphasize certain words or ideas by raising or lowering the volume of your voice. Do not read with a singsong tone. Be sure that your reading sounds natural.
- Speak clearly, and make eye contact periodically with your audience.
- Ask a partner for feedback on your reading, and make changes based on his or her suggestions.

After you have finished rehearsing, hold a reading for the class.

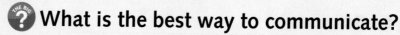

## What is the best way to communicate?

Think about the Big Question as you read Poetry Collection 4. Take notes on how each poet uses sound devices to explore the nature of communication.

## CLOSE READING FOCUS

### Key Ideas and Details: **Paraphrase**

When you **paraphrase**, you restate something in your own words to make the meaning clear to yourself. If you are unsure of a poem's meaning, reread the poem to clarify ideas.

- First, look up the definitions of unfamiliar words in the original passage and replace them with words you know.
- Identify the poet's main ideas. Restate the passage, using your own everyday words.
- Reread the passage to make sure your version makes sense.

### Craft and Structure: **Sound Devices**

**Rhythm and rhyme** are two techniques poets use to give poems a musical quality. Rhythm is a poem's pattern of stressed (ʹ) and unstressed (˘) syllables. Rhyme is the repetition of sounds at the ends of words. A poem's rhythmical pattern is called **meter.** Meter is measured in *feet,* or units of stressed and unstressed syllables. A **rhyme scheme** is a pattern of rhymes. In this example, the words *sire* and *fire* create a rhyme. Each metrical foot is set off by slashes.

Hálf / ĭn dreáms / hĕ sáw / hĭs síre /
Wíth / hĭs gréat / hănds fúll / ŏf fíre.

## Vocabulary

You will encounter the following words in Poetry Collection 4. In your notebook, write two words that have both prefixes and suffixes. How do these affixes affect the meaning of each word?

| | | |
|---|---|---|
| **incessantly** | **uncommonly** | **supple** |
| **downy** | **coveted** | **envying** |

## CLOSE READING MODEL

The passage below is from Edgar Allan Poe's poem "Annabel Lee." The annotations to the right of the passage show ways in which you can use close reading skills to paraphrase and to analyze sound devices.

### *from* "Annabel Lee"

It was many and many a year ago,
    In a kingdom by the sea,[1]
That a maiden there lived whom you may know
    By the name of Annabel Lee;
And this maiden she lived with no other thought
    Than to love and be loved by me.[2]

*I* was a child and *she* was a child,
    In this kingdom by the sea.
But we loved with a love that was more than love—
    I and my Annabel Lee—
With a love that the wingèd seraphs of Heaven
    Coveted her and me.[3]

**Sound Devices**
**1** Poe establishes a strong pattern of stressed and unstressed syllables. Notice how this rhythm suggests the ebb and flow of ocean waves.

**Paraphrase**
**2** You may need to clarify the meaning of these lines to fully understand Poe's language. First, reread the lines, then restate them in your own words. For example, "Annabel Lee was a young woman who was deeply in love with the speaker, who was also deeply in love with her."

**Sound Devices**
**3** The repetition of the long *e* sound at the ends of the words *sea, Lee,* and *me* creates a rhyme scheme that reinforces the poem's musical quality.

## Meet the Poets

### "Stopping by Woods on a Snowy Evening"

**Robert Frost** (1874–1963) was born in San Francisco but moved to New England when he was eleven. That region of the country proved to be inspirational for him as a writer. His most popular poems describe New England country life and landscapes. Frost won the Pulitzer Prize four times—more than any other poet.

### "Annabel Lee"

**Edgar Allan Poe** (1809–1849) won great literary success but suffered much personal loss in his life. His mother died when he was just two years old. Later in life, he also suffered the loss of his beloved wife, Virginia. After her death, Poe became depressed and antisocial. Much of his writing reflects this loss of an ideal love.

### "Father William"

**Lewis Carroll** (1832–1898) is the pen name of Charles Dodgson, a mathematics professor who was born in England. Under his pen name, Dodgson wrote *Alice's Adventures in Wonderland* and *Through the Looking Glass.* Like these classic novels, his poems are noted for their clever wordplay, nonsensical meanings, and delightfully zany words.

### "Jim"

**Gwendolyn Brooks** (1917–2000) began writing at the age of seven and published her first poem, "Eventide," at age thirteen. As an adult, Brooks wrote hundreds of poems, many of which focus on the African American experience. In 1950, she became the first African American to win a Pulitzer Prize.

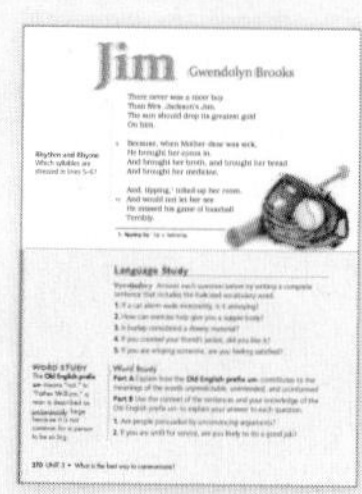

# Stopping by Woods on a Snowy Evening

Robert Frost

Whose woods these are I think I know.
His house is in the village, though;
He will not see me stopping here
To watch his woods fill up with snow.

My little horse must think it queer
To stop without a farmhouse near
Between the woods and frozen lake
The darkest evening of the year.

He gives his harness bells a shake
To ask if there is some mistake.
The only other sound's the sweep
Of easy wind and **downy** flake.

The woods are lovely, dark, and deep,
But I have promises to keep,
And miles to go before I sleep,
And miles to go before I sleep.

**Rhythm and Rhyme**
In lines 1–8, which lines end with rhyming words?

◀ **Vocabulary**
**downy** (dou´ nē) *adj.* soft and fluffy

# Annabel Lee

Edgar Allan Poe

**Rhythm and Rhyme**
Which syllables are stressed in the first two lines?

**Vocabulary ▶**
**coveted** (kuv′ it əd)
*v.* wanted; desired

It was many and many a year ago,
  In a kingdom by the sea,
That a maiden there lived whom you may know
  By the name of Annabel Lee;
And this maiden she lived with no other thought
  Than to love and be loved by me.

*I* was a child and *she* was a child,
  In this kingdom by the sea.
But we loved with a love that was more than love—
  I and my Annabel Lee—
With a love that the wingèd seraphs[1] of Heaven
  **Coveted** her and me.

And this was the reason that, long ago,
  In this kingdom by the sea,
A wind blew out of a cloud, chilling
  My beautiful Annabel Lee;
So that her highborn kinsmen came
  And bore her away from me,
To shut her up in a sepulcher[2]
  In this kingdom by the sea.

1. **wingèd seraphs** (ser′ efs) *n.* angels.
2. **sepulcher** (sep′ əl kər) *n.* vault or chamber for burial; tomb.

The angels, not half so happy in Heaven,
    Went **envying** her and me:—
Yes! that was the reason (as all men know,
    In this kingdom by the sea)
That the wind came out of a cloud by night,
    Chilling and killing my Annabel Lee.

But our love it was stronger by far than the love
    Of those who were older than we—
    Of many far wiser than we—
And neither the angels in Heaven above
    Nor the demons down under the sea
Can ever dissever[3] my soul from the soul
    Of the beautiful Annabel Lee;

For the moon never beams, without bringing
    me dreams
Of the beautiful Annabel Lee;
And the stars never rise, but I feel the bright eyes
    Of the beautiful Annabel Lee;
And so, all the night-tide, I lie down by the side
Of my darling—my darling—my life and my bride,
    In her sepulcher there by the sea—
    In her tomb by the sounding sea.

◀ **Vocabulary**
**envying** (en´ vē iŋ) *v.* wanting something that someone else has

**Paraphrase**
How would you paraphrase lines 15–18?

3. **dissever** (di sev´ ər) *v.* separate; divide.

**▲ Critical Viewing** Read the poem to identify which group of lines this drawing illustrates.

# Father William

Lewis Carroll

"You are old, Father William," the young man said,
"And your hair has become very white;
And yet you **incessantly** stand on your head—
Do you think, at your age, it is right?"

"In my youth," Father William replied to his son,
"I feared it might injure the brain;
But, now that I'm perfectly sure I have none,
Why, I do it again and again."

"You are old," said the youth, "as I mentioned before.
And have grown most **uncommonly** fat;
Yet you turned a back-somersault in at the door—
Pray, what is the reason of that?"

"In my youth," said the sage, as he shook his gray locks,
"I kept all my limbs very **supple**
By the use of this ointment—one shilling[1] the box—
Allow me to sell you a couple?"

"You are old," said the youth, "and your jaws are too weak
For anything tougher than suet;[2]
Yet you finished the goose, with the bones and the beak—
Pray, how did you manage to do it?"

"In my youth," said his father, "I took to the law,
And argued each case with my wife;
And the muscular strength, which it gave to my jaw,
Has lasted the rest of my life."

"You are old," said the youth, "one would hardly suppose
That your eye was as steady as ever;
Yet you balanced an eel on the end of your nose—
What made you so awfully clever?"

"I have answered three questions, and that is enough,"
Said his father; "don't give yourself airs!
Do you think I can listen all day to such stuff?
Be off, or I'll kick you downstairs!"

---

1. **shilling** (shil′iŋ) *n.* British coin.
2. **suet** (so͞o′it) *n.* fat used in cooking.

◀ **Vocabulary**

**incessantly** (in ses′ ənt lē) *adv.* without stopping

**uncommonly** (un käm′ ən lē) *adv.* remarkably

**supple** (sup′ əl) *adj.* able to bend easily; flexible

**Paraphrase**
How would you paraphrase "Don't give yourself airs!"?

# Jim
## Gwendolyn Brooks

There never was a nicer boy
Than Mrs. Jackson's Jim.
The sun should drop its greatest gold
On him.

Because, when Mother-dear was sick,
He brought her cocoa in.
And brought her broth, and brought her bread.
And brought her medicine.

And, tipping,[1] tidied up her room.
And would not let her see
He missed his game of baseball
Terribly.

**Rhythm and Rhyme** Which syllables are stressed in lines 5–6?

1. **tipping** (tip′ iŋ) *v.* tiptoeing.

## Language Study

**Vocabulary** Answer each question below by writing a complete sentence that includes the italicized vocabulary word.

**1.** If a car alarm wails *incessantly,* is it annoying?

**2.** How can exercise help give you a *supple* body?

**3.** Is burlap considered a *downy* material?

**4.** If you *coveted* your friend's jacket, did you like it?

**5.** If you are *envying* someone, are you feeling satisfied?

**WORD STUDY**

The **Old English prefix *un-*** means "not." In "Father William," a man is described as **uncommonly** large because it is not common for a person to be so big.

### Word Study

**Part A** Explain how the **Old English prefix *un-*** contributes to the meanings of the words *unpredictable, unintended,* and *uninformed*.

**Part B** Use the context of the sentences and your knowledge of the Old English prefix *un-* to explain your answer to each question.

**1.** Are people persuaded by *unconvincing* arguments?

**2.** If you are *unfit* for service, are you likely to do a good job?

## Literary Analysis

### Key Ideas and Details

1. **Paraphrase** Paraphrase the following lines:
   **(a)** lines 11–12 of "Stopping by Woods on a Snowy Evening"
   **(b)** lines 9–10 of "Annabel Lee"
   **(c)** lines 13–16 of "Father William"
   **(d)** lines 3–4 of "Jim"
2. **Paraphrase** Identify two words in these poems that you might look up in a dictionary to help you paraphrase meaning.
3. **(a)** In "Jim," what tasks does the boy perform for his mother? **(b) Infer:** What detail tells you that Jim is not selfish?
4. **(a)** In "Annabel Lee," how does the speaker react to Annabel Lee's death? Provide a quotation from the poem to support your answer. **(b) Infer:** What will prevent the separation of the speaker's soul from Annabel Lee's soul? Support your answer.

### Craft and Structure

5. **Sound Devices (a)** Do all the poems have rhythmic patterns? Explain. **(b)** Which poem has the most interesting rhythm? Support your opinion with examples from the text.
6. **Sound Devices** Use a chart like the one on the right to analyze rhyme in each poem.
7. **Sound Devices (a)** What words in Frost's poem describe sights and sounds? **(b)** What is the mood, or feeling, of the poem?

| Poem | Rhyming Words |
|---|---|
| Father William | |
| Stopping by Woods . . . | |
| Jim | |
| Annabel Lee | |

### Integration of Knowledge and Ideas

8. **(a)** In "Stopping by Woods on a Snowy Evening," why has the speaker stopped? **(b) Infer:** What about the place captures his attention? **(c) Speculate:** Why do you think Frost uses the image of a snowy night to communicate the idea of the journey through life?
9. **(a)** Identify two misconceptions about older people that Carroll pokes fun at in "Father William." **(b) Synthesize:** What misconceptions do you think people have today about older people? Explain why they are misconceptions.

10. THE BIG ? **What is the best way to communicate? (a)** Which of these poems do you think expresses the most emotion toward its subject? **(b)** How is emotion most clearly communicated in the poem? Explain, citing textual details.

**ACADEMIC VOCABULARY**

As you write and speak about Poetry Collection 4, use the words related to communication that you explored on page 313 of this textbook.

## Conventions: Subject-Verb Agreement

To maintain correct **subject-verb agreement,** subjects and verbs must agree in number.

To check subject-verb agreement, determine whether the subject is singular or plural and then make sure the verb matches.

**Singular subject and verb:** Sarah enjoys swimming.
**Plural subject and verb:** They enjoy bowling.

A compound subject consists of two subjects joined by a conjunction such as *and, or,* or *nor.* When the subjects joined are plural, they take a plural verb. When the subjects joined are singular, refer to the rules in the chart below.

| Rule | Example |
|---|---|
| Two or more singular subjects joined by *and* take a plural verb. | *Running* **and** *tennis* **are** both fun sports. |
| Singular subjects joined by *or* or *nor* take a singular verb. | *Running* **or** *walking* **is** good exercise.<br>Neither *running* **nor** *walking* **is** a waste of time. |
| When singular and plural subjects are joined by *or* or *nor,* the verb must agree with the closer subject. | Neither the *roast* **nor** the *potatoes* **are** cooking.<br>Concert *tickets* **or** a fancy *dinner* **is** a great gift. |

### Practice A

Complete each sentence with one of the verbs in parentheses.

1. Mrs. Jackson's son Jim (were/was) a very nice boy.
2. The man and his horse (stop/stops) by the woods.
3. Neither Father William nor his son (play/plays) baseball.
4. Annabel Lee and her kinsmen (go/goes) away from the speaker.

**Reading Application** In Poetry Collection 4, find three subjects and verbs that illustrate subject-verb agreement.

### Practice B

Complete each sentence with a subject that agrees with the verb.

1. Neither _______ nor his _______ feels well.
2. Either the _______ or the _______ has filled up with snow.
3. _______ and _______ have a conversation about getting old.

**Writing Application** Write three sentences about poetry. Include one sentence with a singular subject, one with a plural subject, and one with a compound subject. Make sure subjects and verbs agree.

## Writing to Sources

**Poetry** Write a **poem** about a person you know.

- Review the poems in this collection and note techniques and words the poets use to effectively portray a person.
- Then, choose someone to whom you would like to pay tribute or who evokes a strong emotion in you.
- Collect your thoughts by taking notes that describe the person and convey your feelings about him or her.
- Draft your lines. After you have expressed your ideas and feelings, revise your poem using rhythm to add a musical quality.
- Type your poem on a computer using a word-processing or publishing program. Use text-editing features such as the thesaurus and spell-check as you revise and edit your poem. Post your poem on the classroom Web site.

**Grammar Application** Check your writing to make sure your subjects and verbs agree.

## Research and Technology

**Build and Present Knowledge** Conduct a **survey** in which you ask classmates to rate the poems from Poetry Collection 4 according to specific categories. These categories may include best character description, best use of language, or best rhythm, rhyme, and meter.

- Formulate the survey questions. Evaluate your questions to be sure they are clear and answerable.
- Count the number of votes that each poem receives in each category. Then, note which poems received the most votes in each category.
- With a small group, discuss the survey results. Generate questions to evaluate whether the survey was or was not effective and why. Refer to specific examples and details from the poems to support your evaluations.

## What is the best way to communicate?

Explore the Big Question as you read these poems. Take notes on the ways in which each poem communicates a particular view of the world.

## READING TO COMPARE IMAGERY

Poets Walt Whitman and E. E. Cummings use imagery to paint vivid pictures in the minds of readers. As you read the poems, consider how descriptive language can make the reader "see" exactly what the writer sees. Compare the role imagery plays in each poem.

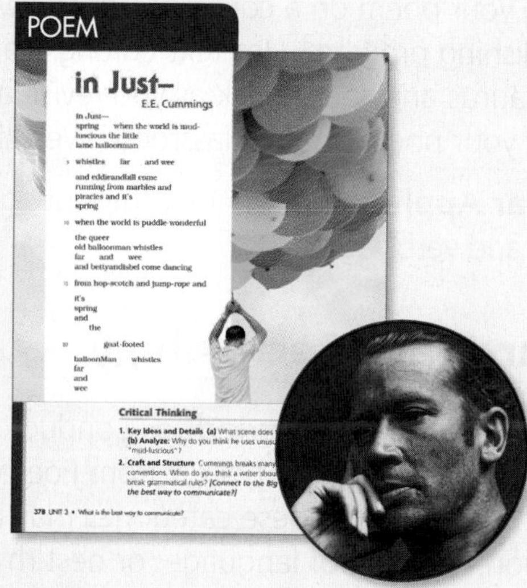
POEM

in Just–

E.E. Cummings

in Just–
spring     when the world is mud-
luscious the little
lame balloonman

whistles     far     and wee

and eddieandbill come
running from marbles and
piracies and it's
spring

when the world is puddle-wonderful

the queer
old balloonman whistles
far     and     wee
and bettyandisbel come dancing

from hop-scotch and jump-rope and

it's
spring
and
    the

        goat-footed

balloonMan     whistles
far
and
wee

**Critical Thinking**

1. **Key Ideas and Details (a)** What scene does
**(b) Analyze:** Why do you think he uses unus
"mud-luscious"?

2. **Craft and Structure** Cummings breaks many
conventions. When do you think a writer shou
break grammatical rules? ***[Connect to the Big***
***the best way to communicate?]***

378 UNIT 3 • What is the best way to communicate?

### "Miracles"

**Walt Whitman** (1819–1892)
Walt Whitman worked at many occupations during his life. He was a printer, a teacher, and a newspaper reporter. In 1855, Whitman first published *Leaves of Grass.* In this book, he abandoned regular rhyme and rhythm in favor of free verse, which followed no set pattern. Now considered a masterpiece, the book led critics to regard Whitman as the father of American poetry.

### "in Just—"

**E. E. Cummings** (1894–1962)
Edward Estlin Cummings published his first collection of poetry in the early 1920s. The work stood out for many reasons, including Cummings's original use of language and unusual punctuation, capitalization, and spacing. Cummings often wrote poems that were playful and humorous. These poems reflected his attitude that "the most wasted of all days is one without laughter."

## Comparing Imagery

In poetry, an **image** is a word or phrase that appeals to one or more of the five senses. Poets use **imagery** to bring their poems to life with descriptions of how their subjects look, sound, feel, taste, and smell. Here are two examples:

- The phrase "the sweet, slippery mango slices" appeals to the senses of taste and touch.
- The phrase "glaring lights and wailing sirens" appeals to the senses of sight and hearing.

Writers also create **mood** through their use of images, words, and descriptive details. Mood is the feeling created in the reader by a literary work or passage. The mood of a work may be described with adjectives such as *joyous, gloomy, cozy,* or *frightening*.

To fully appreciate images and experience the mood in a poem, determine the meanings of any unfamiliar words the poet uses—including words the poet has made up. Also, pay close attention to the *connotations*—or emotional associations—of words, as well as to their figurative, or nonliteral, meanings.

Both "Miracles" and "in Just—" contain images that appeal to the senses. In a chart like the one below, keep track of the images in the two poems. Note the sense that an image appeals to and write the image in the appropriate box. Keep in mind that some images may appeal to more than one sense, so you may put an image into more than one box. After you read, use your chart to help you compare and contrast the authors' use of imagery.

| Sense | Images | |
|---|---|---|
| | "Miracles" | "in Just—" |
| Sight | | |
| Hearing | | |
| Touch/Movement | | |
| Taste | | |
| Smell | | |

# Miracles

Walt Whitman

Why, who makes much of a miracle?
As to me I know of nothing else but miracles,
Whether I walk the streets of Manhattan,
Or dart my sight over the roofs of houses toward the sky,
Or wade with naked feet along the beach just in the edge
of the water,
Or stand under trees in the woods,
Or talk by day with any one I love . . .
Or sit at table at dinner with the rest,
Or look at strangers opposite me riding in the car,
Or watch honey-bees busy around the hive of a summer
forenoon,
Or animals feeding in the fields,
Or birds, or the wonderfulness of insects in the air,
Or the wonderfulness of the sundown, or of stars shining
so quiet and bright,
Or the exquisite delicate thin curve of the new moon in
spring;
These with the rest, one and all, are to me miracles,
The whole referring, yet each distinct and in its place.

To me every hour of the light and dark is a miracle,
Every cubic inch of space is a miracle,
Every square yard of the surface of the earth is spread
with the same,
Every foot of the interior swarms with the same.

To me the sea is a continual miracle,
The fishes that swim—the rocks—the motion of the
waves—the ships with men in them,
What stranger miracles are there?

◀ **Critical Viewing**
Does this photograph convey the feelings expressed by the speaker in the poem? Explain.

**Imagery**
Which image in the first seven lines appeals to the sense of touch?

◀ **Vocabulary**
**exquisite** (eks´ kwiz it) *adj.* beautiful in a delicate way

**distinct** (di stiŋkt´) *adj.* separate and different

## Critical Thinking

1. **Key Ideas and Details (a) Classify:** List events that the speaker calls miracles. **(b) Infer:** Why is the sea a "continual miracle"?
2. **Integration of Knowledge and Ideas** Why do you think Whitman decided to use poetry to describe the beauty around him? *[Connect to the Big Question: What is the best way to communicate?]*

# in Just–

E.E. Cummings

in Just—
spring          when the world is mud-
luscious the little
lame balloonman

whistles          far          and wee

and eddieandbill come
running from marbles and
piracies and it's
spring

when the world is puddle-wonderful

the queer
old balloonman whistles
far          and          wee
and bettyandisbel come dancing

from hop-scotch and jump-rope and

it's
spring
and
          the

                    goat-footed

balloonMan          whistles
far
and
wee

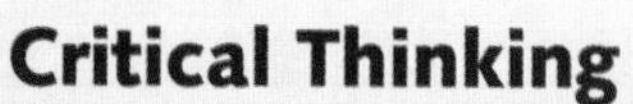

## Critical Thinking

1. **Key Ideas and Details (a)** What scene does the speaker describe? **(b) Analyze:** Why do you think he uses unusual words such as "mud-luscious"?
2. **Craft and Structure** Cummings breaks many language conventions. When do you think a writer should be allowed to break grammatical rules? *[Connect to the Big Question: What is the best way to communicate?]*

## Comparing Imagery

1. **Craft and Structure** Give an example from each poem of an image that appeals to the senses listed below. Then, explain the meaning, including the connotations, of key words in each image. **(a)** hearing **(b)** touch
2. **Craft and Structure** **(a)** Using a chart like the one shown, identify and explain sight images in each poem. Explain the meaning, including the connotations, of key words in each image. **(b)** Which poem has more vivid sight images? Why?

| Miracles | in Just— |
|---|---|
| Image: | Image: |
| Effect: | Effect: |

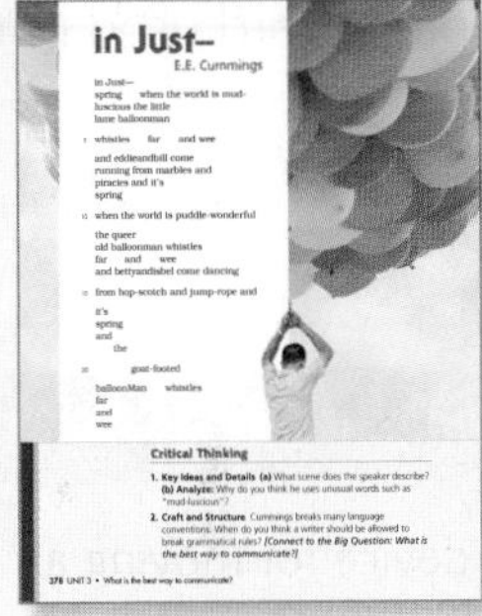


## Timed Writing

### Argument: Recommendation

Write an essay in which you recommend one of the two poems to someone your age. Choose the poem that you believe provides more effective examples of imagery. Include details from the text to support your claim. **(40 minutes)**

### 5-Minute Planner

1. Read the prompt carefully and completely.
2. Gather your ideas by jotting down answers to these questions:
   - What do you find fascinating or distinctive about the imagery in the poem you recommend?
   - Which images are most meaningful to you?
   - In what ways is the imagery in your chosen poem more effective than the imagery in the other poem?
3. To help you address the questions above, review the graphic organizer you completed as you read the poems.
4. Reread the prompt, and then draft your essay. Remember to support your argument with clear reasons and relevant textual evidence.

### USE ACADEMIC VOCABULARY

As you write, use academic language, including the following words or their related forms:

**appreciate**
**insight**
**perceive**
**unique**

For more information about academic vocabulary, see pages xlvi–l.

## Words With Multiple Meanings

A **multiple-meaning word** is a word that has more than one definition. Many words in English have multiple meanings; for example, *peach* can be defined as a color or a fruit. To determine the meaning intended in a sentence, you must consider the context, or the overall meaning of the sentence or paragraph in which the word appears. You also need to look at the function of the word in the sentence. Some words with multiple meanings can be used as different parts of speech. The following chart shows a multiple-meaning word used in two different sentences.

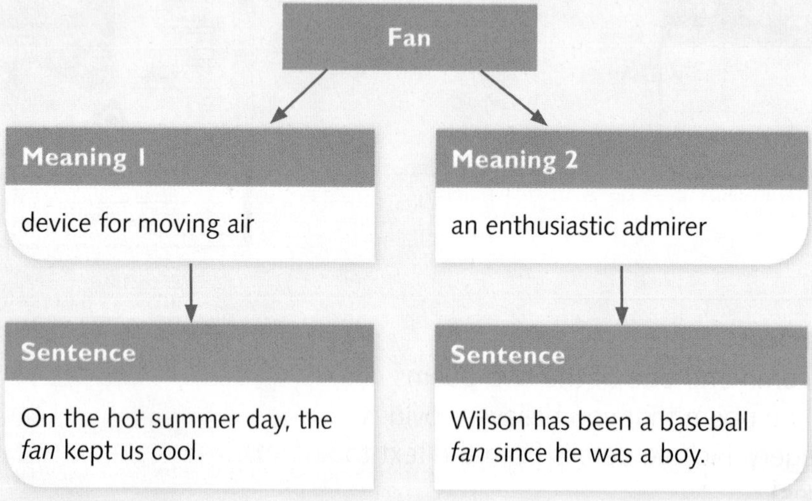

Fan
Meaning 1
device for moving air
Meaning 2
an enthusiastic admirer
Sentence
On the hot summer day, the *fan* kept us cool.
Sentence
Wilson has been a baseball *fan* since he was a boy.

## Practice A

Write the meaning of each italicized word. Verify the meaning in a dictionary.

1. a. When the *bats* swooped down on my head, I let out a scream.
   b. I wish we could get new *bats* for our softball team this year.
2. a. Julian was not *present* to collect the prize he won.
   b. I decided to make my sister's birthday *present* this year.
3. a. The *second* hand on the clock ticked loudly.
   b. Liliana won *second* prize at the science fair.
4. a. We saved the *rest* of the cake for the next class.
   b. After running a mile in track, we all needed a *rest*.

## Practice B

For each word listed, write two sentences that use different meanings of the word. If necessary, look up the meanings in a dictionary.

1. kind
2. object
3. express
4. ring
5. dash
6. season
7. desert
8. seal

**Activity** Use a print or digital dictionary to learn about the following multiple-meaning words: *power, degree, dynamite, file,* and *patient.* Write each word on a separate notecard like the one shown. Fill in the left column of the notecard with one of the word's meanings. Fill in the right column with another of the word's meanings. Then, trade notecards with a partner, and discuss the different meanings and uses of the words that each of you found.

| Word: ________________ | |
|---|---|
| **Part of Speech:** | **Part of Speech:** |
| **Definition:** | **Definition:** |
| **Example Sentence:** | **Example Sentence:** |

### Comprehension and Collaboration

Work with two or three classmates to write a sentence that uses two different meanings of each of the following words. For example: *While we sat in a traffic* jam, *I was able to eat my breakfast of* toast *and* jam.

- **fair**
- **long**
- **last**

## Evaluating Media Messages and Advertisements

Media messages and advertisements appear on television, the radio, and the Internet. To ensure you understand and respond appropriately to these messages, critically evaluate them using the strategies in this lesson.

### Learn the Skills

**Determine the purpose.** Identify the purpose, or goal, of the message. Some messages are meant to inform, to persuade, or to entertain. Some messages are attempts to sell you something or to convince you to do something.

**Analyze images and sounds.** Think critically about what you see and hear. Notice how the mood created by music and sounds influences your response to the message. Analyze the differences between images and sounds used in messages designed to sell and those used in messages designed to inform.

**Challenge the claims and evidence.** Analyze the accuracy of the claims. Consider whether the reasoning is logical and whether sufficient and relevant evidence supports the claims.

**Identify propaganda techniques.** To effectively analyze the logic of the messages, be alert to techniques involving faulty reasoning.

- **Slant and Bias:** Beware of any message that presents only one side of a many-sided issue.
- **Bandwagon Appeal:** Beware of messages that suggest you will feel left out if you do not do or buy something.
- **Spokespersons:** Ask yourself whether the spokesperson for the message has the knowledge to back up his or her claims.

**Analyze the use of language.** Advertisers use language to appeal to certain groups of people. For example, formal language can make messages seem more accurate. While informal language and popular slang are often used to appeal to a younger audience.

**Interpret visual techniques.** Lighting can draw attention to specific parts of an image or create a certain mood. Camera angles can influence the way you view an image. For instance, a close-up shot can focus your attention on a single subject, whereas a panoramic shot will show you the larger context but with few details. Special visual effects can change or enhance an existing image to increase audience appeal or interest.

## Practice the Skills

**Presentation of Knowledge and Ideas** Use what you have learned in this workshop to complete the following activity.

ACTIVITY: **Evaluate Media Advertisements**

Watch three television commercials. Then, follow these steps:

- Identify the message and interpret the purpose of each commercial.
- Ask questions that help you evaluate the evidence that supports the claims in each commercial.
- Explain how each commercial makes you feel.
- List memorable details from each commercial, such as special effects, camera angles, lighting, and music. Explain how these elements support the purpose of the commercial.
- Use the Interpretation Guide to interpret the advertisements.

Use the Interpretation Guide to analyze the content of each commercial.

**Interpretation Guide**

**Visual Techniques**
Which visual techniques are evident in the advertisement? Briefly explain each.

- ❑ camera angles
- ❑ special effects
- ❑ special lighting
- ❑ other visual

**Sound Techniques**
Which sound techniques are evident in the advertisement? Briefly explain each.

- ❑ music
- ❑ special effects
- ❑ other visual techniques

**Messages**
What is the ad's message? How can you tell?

**Claims and Evidence**
Does the advertisement conatin claims about a product? If so, what are they? What evidence is provided to support the claims? Is the evidence relevant? Is there enough reasonable evidence to support the claims? Explain.

**Purpose**
What is the purpose of the advertisement?

**Comprehension and Collaboration** Compare your findings with those of your classmates. As a group, interpret how visual and sound techniques influence the message in an advertisement.

## Write an Explanatory Text

### Comparison-and-Contrast Essay

**Defining the Form** In a **comparison-and-contrast essay,** the writer analyzes the similarities and differences between two or more related subjects. You might use elements of this form in persuasive essays, journals, and reviews.

**Assignment** Write a comparison-and-contrast essay that helps readers make a decision or see old things in a fresh way. Your essay should feature these elements:

- ✓ A *topic involving two or more things* that are neither nearly identical nor extremely different
- ✓ *Relevant facts, descriptions and examples* that illustrate *both similarities and differences*
- ✓ *A clear organization* that highlights the points of comparison
- ✓ An *introduction* that grabs readers' interest, and a strong, memorable *conclusion*
- ✓ error-free writing, including the correct use of *sentence structures that clarify relationships*

To preview the criteria on which your comparison-and-contrast essay may be judged, see the rubric on page 391.

### FOCUS ON RESEARCH

When you write a comparison-and-contrast essay, you might conduct research to

- learn background information about each subject.
- locate facts, statistics, or other details that describe each subject.
- find quotations that highlight key details about each subject.

When presenting your research, be sure to cite your sources properly. The Research Workshop in the Introductory Unit contains information on how to cite sources.

## Prewriting/Planning Strategies

**Choose a topic.** To choose a topic for your essay, use one of these strategies:

- **Quicklist** Fold a piece of paper in thirds lengthwise. In the first column, list recent choices you have made—for instance, products you have bought or activities you have completed. In the second column, next to each choice, write a precise descriptive phrase. In the third column, give an alternative to your choice.
  **Example:** polka-dot sweatshirt / playful, silly / team jacket
  Review your list, and choose the most interesting pairing to compare and contrast.
- **BUT Chart** Write the word BUT down the center of a piece of paper. On the left, list items with something in common. List differences among them on the right. Then, choose your topic from this list.

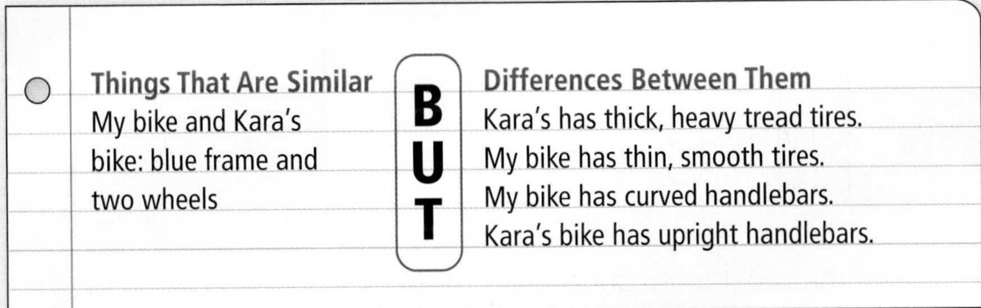


**Get specific.** You may find that your topic is too broad to cover in a brief essay. Use the following strategies to narrow your topic.

- **Describe it** to someone who is not familiar with it.
- **Apply it,** explaining what you can do with it, on it, or to it.
- **Analyze it** by breaking it into parts.
- **Argue for or against it,** explaining good and bad points, while maintaining a formal style.

Examine the specific details from your notes and circle those that can be connected to create a focused topic.

**Show similarities and differences.** Focus on gathering details that show similarities and differences between your subjects. Use a Venn diagram to organize your details. Fill in details about one subject on the left side of the diagram and details about the other on the right side. Use the middle section to list common features.

## Drafting Strategies

**Organize the body of your draft.** Your essay should be easy for readers to follow and understand. There are two main ways to organize a comparison-and-contrast essay. Choose the organization that is most appropriate to your topic and purpose.

- **Block Method** Present all the details about one of your subjects, and then present all the details about your next subject. This method works well if you are writing about more than two subjects or if your topic is complex.
- **Point-by-Point Method** Discuss one aspect of both subjects, then another aspect of both subjects, and so on.

**Methods of Organization**

| Block Method |
|---|
| A. Theater |
| 1. Amount of variety |
| 2. Intensity |
| 3. Realism |
| B. Television |
| 1. Amount of variety |
| 2. Intensity |
| 3. Realism |

| Point-by-Point Comparison |
|---|
| A. Amount of Variety |
| 1. Theater |
| 2. Television |
| B. Intensity |
| 1. Theater |
| 2. Television |
| C. Realism |
| 1. Theater |
| 2. Television |

**Layer ideas using SEE.** Often, the most interesting parts of an essay are the details you offer to support your main ideas. Use the SEE method to ensure that your main ideas are supported with strong elaboration.

- ***S****tate* your main idea in every paragraph to stay on topic.
- ***E****xtend* the idea with an example that proves the main idea.
- ***E****laborate* by offering further details to describe your example.

**Include formatting, graphics, and multimedia.** Use headings to highlight the main sections in your paper. Graphics, such as charts and tables, or multimedia, such as a tape recording or slide show, can strengthen your ideas and further audience comprehension.

**Clarify relationships.** Use words and phrases to show relationships between ideas. Transitions that show comparisons include *also, just as, like,* and *similarly.* Transitions that show contrasts include *although, but, however, on the other hand, whereas,* and *while.*

## Developing Your Ideas

**Ideas** make up the content of any piece of writing. In your comparison-and-contrast essay, you may have several thoughts about your subjects that are based on your own experience. Other ideas may come from your research. Follow these tips to develop your ideas.

**Focus on important features.** Begin by listing all the features you can think of for each subject. Then, review your list to identify features that are very important and those that are less important. Write "key" next to the important features. These are the ideas you should focus on as you write your essay.

**Choose relevant details.** Make sure that the details you include are relevant. For example, in an essay comparing Walt Whitman's free verse to rhyming poetry, the lives of Whitman or another poet are probably not relevant. Instead, you should focus on the characteristics of each kind of poetry.

**Make comparisons complete.** To make your comparisons effective, provide similar information on each subject. For example, suppose you are writing to compare the cities of New York and London. If you write about the size, diversity, and industries of New York, you should write about the same features of London in order to present a balanced comparison. Of course, you may describe a feature found in one subject but not in the other to show an important difference between your subjects. For example, if you are comparing two kinds of birds, the fact that penguins can swim but eagles cannot may be a significant detail. Use a chart similar to the one below to organize your points of comparison.

| Feature | Subject 1 | Subject 2 |
|---|---|---|
| Feature 1 | | |
| Feature 2 | | |
| Feature 3 | | |
| Feature 4 | | |

## Revising Strategies

**Heighten interest.** Check your essay to make sure it grabs and holds your readers' attention. Use the following strategies:

- Sharpen your introduction to intrigue readers, and encourage them to read further. Consider including a strong image, a surprising comparison, or a thought-provoking question or quotation.
- Add details that are surprising, colorful, and important.
- Add headings, relevant graphics, or multimedia.
- Add language, such as transitions, to emphasize similarities or differences.
- Rework your conclusion to add impact or leave readers with a lingering question. Be sure your conclusion makes the value of the comparison and contrast clear.

**Model: Revising to Heighten Interest**

When actors are filming a movie, they can do a retake if they forget a line or

*The audience never gets to see or hear the hilarious verbal or physical mistakes of film actors.*

if they "flub" it. In live theater, however, there are no second chances!

**Avoid repetition.** Check your writing for unnecessary repetition. Sometimes writers will repeat a point but add something slightly different the second time. You can avoid repetition by combining the two sentences to include the additional information while increasing interest with sentence variety.

**Repetitive:** Lastly, the best thing about theater is it's real. What I mean is you see when people make mistakes. You see people being human by making mistakes every so often.

**Combined:** Lastly, the best thing about theater is it's human and real. You can see when people make mistakes.

**Peer Review**

Read your revised draft to a teacher or classmate. Ask whether you repeated information. Together, look for ways to make your writing clearer and less repetitive.

## Revising Sentence Structures to Clarify Relationships

**Coordination** relates two clauses of equal importance. **Subordination** relates a less important clause to a more important clause. Choosing the correct word to link these clauses will clarify the relationships.

**Revising Sentences to Clarify Coordination** If two clauses are related and of equal weight, use **coordinating conjunctions.** *And* can be used to join related clauses. Often, though, the conjunctions *or, but,* or *so* can make the relationship between the clauses clearer, as in this example:

**Original sentence:** It was raining, *and we* took the car.

**Revised sentence:** It was raining, *so we* took the car.

**Revising Sentences to Clarify Subordination** If the clauses are not equal, you must use a **subordinating conjunction** or a **relative pronoun.** Conjunctions such as *after, before,* and *when* indicate time. *Because* or *since* show cause and effect, as in this example:

*When* the curtain fell, the audience burst into applause.

**Avoiding Dangling and Misplaced Modifiers** Be careful to avoid dangling and misplaced modifiers. A **dangling modifier** does not modify any word in the sentence; a **misplaced modifier** modifies the wrong word. Revise your writing to fix these problems.

**Fixing a Dangling Modifier**

**Incorrect:** After beginning to boil, we turned the heat off.

**Correct:** After the water began to boil, we turned the heat off.

**Fixing a Misplaced Modifier**

**Incorrect:** I viewed a video on my computer that I had never seen before.

**Correct:** On my computer, I viewed a video that I had never seen before.

### Grammar in Your Writing

Review your draft, looking for relationships between ideas that you can clarify by using coordination or subordination. In addition, look for dangling or misplaced modifiers. Revise your comparison-and-contrast essay to fix these issues.

## STUDENT MODEL: **Mackenzie Ames, Daytona Beach, FL**

### Stage vs. Set

Theater or television? If you are under eighteen, you more than likely said "television." Have you ever stopped to consider what the magical world of theater has to offer?

In the first paragraph, Mackenzie introduces the comparison in a way that grabs the reader's attention. She compares things that are alike, yet different.

Anyone who has been to the theater can tell you that there is nothing like the feeling of sitting and watching people perform. Actors get something special out of theater, too. Knowing that hundreds of people are watching your every move creates a special kind of excitement.

There's also variety. In live theater, every show is different. When you watch a rerun on television, it's the exact same thing every time. With theater, you get a different experience every night. You can go to see the same show with a different cast or director and the performance will be totally different. Even if you go to a show with the same cast and director, it will be different. An actor might forget a line and improvise or suddenly decide to change the way he or she is playing a character in a scene. The audience never knows exactly what will happen.

Mackenzie develops her argument by including examples and explanations, using the point-by-point method of organization.

Theater is also larger than the drama you see on television. I don't care how big a screen your television has, theater will always be BIGGER—the emotion more passionate, the voices louder, and the effect more profound. In theater, you have to project your voice and movements so that they carry to the back rows of the audience. In television, actors just need to be seen and heard by the cameras and microphones.

Mackenzie uses elaboration to support her main points.

Lastly, the best thing about theater is it's human and real. You see when people make mistakes. On television, everything has to be perfect or they do a retake. You never see television actors miss a line or trip over their feet. Since there is no second chance in theater, everything is more spontaneous. When a performance takes an unexpected turn, the audience gets to see the professionalism of the actors as they respond to something new.

Next time you're channel surfing and there's nothing good on, why not take some time to check out what's playing in your community playhouse? Who knows? Maybe you'll discover a rising talent. Even better, maybe you'll decide you want to become an actor or actress after you see how thrilling a live production really is.

In the final paragraph, Mackenzie offers a strong conclusion that challenges the reader to accept her point of view.

## Editing and Proofreading

Review your draft to correct errors in grammar, spelling, and punctuation.

**Focus on empty language.** Review your work to delete words that do not add value or meaning. Consider cutting words such as *very* and *really* and clauses such as *I think, as I said,* and *you know.*

**Spiral Review**
Earlier in the unit, you learned about **independent and dependent clauses** (p. 348) and about **sentence structures** (p. 360). Review your essay to be sure that subjects and verbs agree in number and that you have a variety of sentence structures to add interest to your essay.

## Publishing and Presenting

Consider one of the following ways to share your writing.

**Be a consumer watchdog.** If your essay contains information that is useful to consumers, form a Consumer Information Panel. Post your essays to a class blog or school Web site. Include links to reliable, related sites, such as government Web sites that focus on health and safety or consumer issues.

**Submit it to a magazine.** Submit your essay to a magazine that specializes in the subject you have chosen. You can find publishing information and an address in a recent edition of the magazine.

## Reflecting on Your Writing

**Writer's Journal** Jot down your answer to this question:
*What was the most important improvement you made when revising?*

### Rubric for Self-Assessment

Find evidence in your writing to address each category. Then, use the rating scale to grade your work.

| Criteria | Rating Scale | | | |
|---|---|---|---|---|
| | *not very* | ............ | | *very* |
| **Purpose/Focus** Clearly analyzes the similarities and differences between two or more related subjects | 1 | 2 | 3 | 4 |
| **Organization** Introduces the topic in a way that grabs the reader's interest; provides clear organization that highlights the major points of comparison; uses appropriate transitions to create cohesion and clarify relationships among ideas; provides a strong, memorable conclusion | 1 | 2 | 3 | 4 |
| **Development of Ideas/Elaboration** Creates an informative and explanatory text that examines a topic using a comparison/contrast organization; develops the topic with concrete details that illustrate both similarities and differences between the subjects; provides relevant facts, definitions, quotations, and examples; establishes and maintains a formal style | 1 | 2 | 3 | 4 |
| **Language** Uses variety of sentence structures; uses precise language and domain-specific vocabulary to compare and contrast a topic | 1 | 2 | 3 | 4 |
| **Conventions** Uses proper grammar, including correct use of coordination and subordination to clarify relationships | 1 | 2 | 3 | 4 |

# Assessment: Skills

## SELECTED RESPONSE

### I. Reading Literature

**Directions:** *Read "The Village Blacksmith" by Henry Wadsworth Longfellow. Then, answer each question that follows.*

Under a spreading chestnut tree
The village smithy stands;
The smith, a mighty man is he,
With large and sinewy hands;
And the muscles of his brawny arms
Are strong as iron bands.

His hair is crisp, and black, and long,
His face is like the tan;
His brow is wet with honest sweat,
He earns whate'er he can,
And looks the whole world in the face,
For he owes not any man.

Week in, week out, from morn till night,
You can hear his bellows blow;
You can hear him swing his heavy sledge
With measured beat and slow,
Like a sexton ringing the village bell,
When the evening sun is low.

And children coming home from school
Look in at the open door;
They love to see the flaming forge,
And hear the bellows roar,
And catch the burning sparks that fly
Like chaff from a threshing-floor.

He goes on Sunday to the church,
And sits among his boys;
He hears the parson pray and preach,
He hears his daughter's voice,
Singing in the village choir,
And it makes his heart rejoice.
It sounds to him like her mother's voice,
Singing in Paradise!
He needs must think of her once more,
How in the grave she lies;
And with his hard, rough hand he wipes
A tear out of his eyes.

Toiling—rejoicing—sorrowing,
Onward through life he goes;
Each morning sees some task begin,
Each evening sees it close;
Something attempted, something done,
Has earned a night's repose.

Thanks, thanks to thee, my worthy friend,
For the lesson thou hast taught!
Thus at the flaming forge of life
Our fortunes must be wrought;
Thus on its sounding anvil shaped
Each burning deed and thought.

1. **Part A** "The Village Blacksmith" is an example of which **form of poetry?**

   **A.** haiku
   **B.** free verse
   **C.** narrative poem
   **D.** limerick

   **Part B** Which answer choice best supports your answer to Part A?

   **A.** The lines of the poem have a particular number of syllables.
   **B.** The poem is humorous.
   **C.** The poem has a rhyme scheme.
   **D.** The poem tells a story.

2. **Part A** Which line from the poem contains an example of **imagery?**

   **A.** "His brow is wet with honest sweat"
   **B.** "The village smithy stands"
   **C.** "And children coming home from school"
   **D.** "Has earned a night's repose"

   **Part B** The imagery from Part A appeals to which of the following senses?

   **A.** sight and hearing
   **B.** touch and hearing
   **C.** sight and touch
   **D.** taste and smell

3. Which lines from the poem contain the best example of the sound device **rhyme**?

   **A.** "And children coming home from school / Look in at the open door"
   **B.** "It sounds like his mother's voice / Singing in Paradise!"
   **C.** "With measured beat and slow / Like a sexton ringing the village bell / When the evening sun is low"
   **D.** "Thus on its sounding anvil shaped / Each burning deed and thought"

4. Which lines contain an example of a **simile?**

   **A.** lines 47–48
   **B.** lines 3–5
   **C.** lines 15–17
   **D.** lines 29–30

5. Which line contains the **sound device** of allieration?

   **A.** "He hears the parson pray and preach"
   **B.** "A tear out of his eyes"
   **C.** "With measured beat and slow"
   **D.** "It sounds to him like her mother's voice"

6. Identify the type of **figurative langauge** contained in the following lines:

   "They love to see the flaming forge, / And hear the bellows roar"

   **A.** simile
   **B.** metaphor
   **C.** symbol
   **D.** personification

7. Which answer choice states the best definition of the underlined word *repose?*

   **A.** work
   **B.** rest
   **C.** worry
   **D.** entertainment

## Timed Writing

8. Identify one **simile,** one **metaphor,** and one example of **personification** in the poem. In an essay, explain how this **figurative language** contributes to the poem's overall meaning.

GO ON

## II. Reading Informational Text

**Directions:** *Read the passage below. Then, answer each question that follows.*

### How to Set up an E-mail Filter

An e-mail filter sorts your e-mail, deletes unwanted junk mail, and helps you avoid e-mail scams. Follow these steps to make your e-mail inbox easier to navigate and to avoid annoying junk e-mails.

**Step 1** Open your e-mail account and locate the "Tools," "Filters," or "Options" menu items. Usually, these are listed at the top of the screen.

**Step 2** Once you have found the Filters option, click on "New" to create a new folder. **TIP:** Name the folder "Junk Mail" so it is easy to find.

**Step 3** Set up the rules, or conditions, for the filter. The rules enable you to control what happens to e-mail that is delivered to your account. **TIP:** One rule you can set is to send e-mails from unknown senders to your new folder. This means that any message from a sender who is not listed in your address book will be sent to the Junk Mail folder.

**Step 4** Specify the action you want the filter to execute. Filters can sort e-mails into a folder, delete e-mails, or take other actions your e-mail provider offers. **TIP:** If your filter sends unwanted e-mails to a folder, be sure to check the folder periodically to see if a *wanted* e-mail has been sent there by mistake.

**Step 5** Click "OK" or "Save" to save your new folder. **TIP:** You can add new filters for different uses, such as organizing e-mail correspondence related to school, work, or family.

**1. Part A** Which of the following is a key step in setting up an e-mail filter?

**A.** open your junk mail first
**B.** avoid e-mail scams
**C.** check your junk mail folder for wanted e-mails
**D.** set up the conditions of the filter

**Part B** Which action is part of the key step you identified in Part A?

**A.** Add new filters for different uses.
**B.** Click "OK" or "save" to save to your new folder.
**C.** Make a rule to send e-mails from unknown senders to a folder.
**D.** Name the folder "Junk Mail" so it is easy to find.

**2.** What is the purpose of the tips that follow each step?

**A.** They provide additional information and advice.
**B.** They summarize the main points of the steps.
**C.** They provide definitions for technical terms.
**D.** They clarify difficult concepts.

## III. Writing and Language Conventions

**Directions:** *Read the script for the multimedia report. Then, answer each question that follows.*

**Slide 1** (1) Visual: Title Slide: Stick Insects (2) *Script:* There is 2,000 species of stick insects, including 41 that exist in North America. (3) They are the coolest bugs in your backyard!
**Slide 2** (4) *Visual:* Walking Stick (5) *Script:* Adults look like sticks, and their eggs resemble seeds. (6) This is called camouflage. (7) Birds cannot eat bugs that they cannot see.
**Slide 3** (8) *Visual:* Huge walking stick on man's face (9) *Script:* India is home to some of the world's biggest stick insects
(10) Some are over twelve inches long. (11) There are not any this large in the United States.

**1.** Which of the following revisions changes sentence 9 to a **interrogative sentence?**

**A.** India is home to some of the world's biggest stick insects!
**B.** India is home to some of the world's biggest stick insects.
**C.** Did you know that India is home to some of the world's biggest stick insects?
**D.** You might not know that India is home to some of the world's biggest stick insects.

**2.** Which of these sentences contains a **dependent clause?**

**A.** sentence 3
**B.** sentence 5
**C.** sentence 6
**D.** sentence 7

**3.** What is the **function** of sentence 10?

**A.** to ask a question
**B.** to call out or exclaim
**C.** to make a statement
**D.** to give a command

**4.** Which is the *best* way to combine sentences 10 and 11 to make a **compound sentence?**

**A.** Some are over twelve inches long, but there are not any this large in the United States.
**B.** Some are over twelve inches long there are not any this large in the United States.
**C.** Some are over twelve inches long, there are not any that large in the United States.
**D.** Some are over twelve inches long, so there are not any that large in the United States.

**5.** How should sentence 2 be revised to fix incorrect **subject-verb agreement?**

**A.** There are 2,000 species of stick insects, including 41 that exists in North America.
**B.** There are 2,000 species of stick insects, including 41 that exist in North America.
**C.** There is 2,000 species of stick insects, including 41 that exists in North America.
**D.** The sentence contains no error in subject-verb agreement.

# CONSTRUCTED RESPONSE

**Directions:** *Follow the instructions to complete the tasks below as required by your teacher.*

*As you work on each task, incorporate both general academic vocabulary and literary terms you learned in Parts 1 and 2.*

## Writing

**TASK 1** **Informational Text**

### Compare and Contrast Forms of Poetry

*Write an essay in which you compare and contrast two poetic forms.*

- Review the specific rules that guide the structure of each of these poetic forms: lyric poetry, concrete poetry, and haiku. Choose two forms to compare and contrast in your essay.
- Select one or more poems of each form from Part 2 of this unit.
- In your essay, compare and contrast the characteristics of each poetic form. Support your analysis with specific examples from the poems you have chosen.
- Explain how each characteristic you discuss contributes to the meaning of the poem.
- Include your topic sentence in the introductory paragraph. Organize the body of your comparison-and-contrast essay to clearly show comparisons and contrasts.

**TASK 2** **Literature**

### Analyze Word Choice

*Write an essay in which you use the literal and implied meanings of words to help you interpret a poem in Part 2.*

- Choose a poem that features powerful words and images.
- Note examples of figurative language—such as similes, metaphors, and personification—and imagery that appeals to the five senses. Analyze the impact of each example.
- Cite evidence from the poem to support your analysis.
- As you edit, make sure you have used correct punctuation, including commas to separate items in a series.

**TASK 3** **Literature**

### Analyze a Poem's Form and Structure

*Write an essay in which you analyze the form and structure of a poem in Part 2.*

**Part 1**

- Choose a poem from Part 2 to use as the basis of your analysis.
- Read the poem several times, taking notes on these elements of form and structure: rhyme, rhythm and meter, line length, stanza divisions, punctuation, capitalization, and spacing. Explain how these elements, both individually and together, contribute to the poem's meaning and effect.

**Part 2**

- Write an essay in which you analyze the form and structure of your chosen poem. Include the elements listed above in Part 1.
- Revise your work to correct any run-on sentences or sentence fragments. Place phrases and clauses within sentences to clarify the relationships among ideas.
- Publish your finished essay in the classroom library. Include a copy of the original text of the poem.

## Speaking and Listening

**TASK 4** **Literature**

### Analyze the Impact of Sound Devices

*Give an oral presentation of an essay in which you analyze the impact of sound devices in a poem in Part 2.*

- Analyze the impact of rhyme and other sound devices, such as repetition or alliteration, in a poem from Part 2. Consider how the sound devices affect the poem's mood, meaning, and tone.
- Organize your key points and support them with examples from the poem.
- Before your presentation, consult a print or online dictionary to find the pronunciations of unknown words.
- Deliver your presentation to the class. Use appropriate eye contact, adequate volume, and clear pronunciation.

**TASK 5** **Literature**

### Lead a Discussion About Word Choice

*Lead a small-group discussion about the effects of word choice in a poem from Part 2.*

- Choose a poem with powerful language to use as the basis for your discussion. Prepare by jotting down words from the poem that you find particularly effective. Note the figurative or connotative meanings of these words.
- Ask someone in your group to read the poem aloud. Then, allow group members to share their opinions and ideas about word choice in the poem. Follow general rules for discussion, taking turns speaking.
- Pose questions and respond to others' questions. Acknowledge new information and adjust your own ideas in response if necessary.
- Use formal English and academic vocabulary as you discuss the poem.

## Research

**TASK 6** **Literature**

### What is the best way to communicate?

In Part 2 of this unit, you have read literature about ways people communicate. Now you will conduct a short research project on one type of communication. Use both the literature you have read and your research to reflect on this unit's Big Question. Review the following guidelines before you begin:

- Focus your research on one type of communication.
- Gather relevant information from at least two reliable print or digital sources.
- Take notes as you research your topic.
- Cite your sources accurately.

When you have completed your research, write a response to the Big Question. Discuss how your initial ideas have been either changed or reinforced. Support your response with an example from literature and an example from your research.

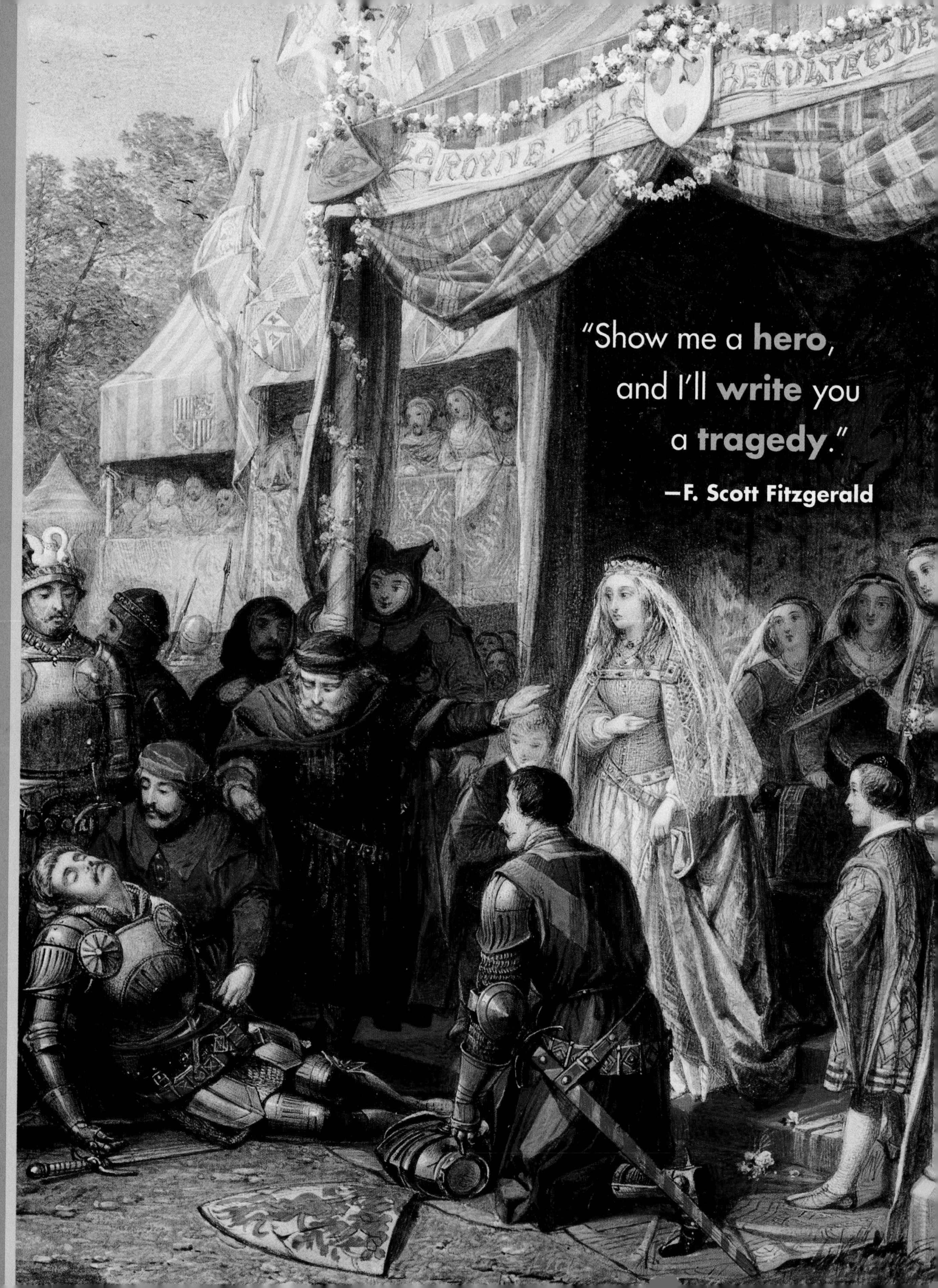
"Show me a **hero**,
and I'll **write** you
a **tragedy**."
—F. Scott Fitzgerald

PART 3

# TEXT SET DEVELOPING INSIGHT

# HEROES AND OUTLAWS

The selections in this unit all deal with the Big Question: **What is the best way to communicate?** Often, the information that is communicated about a person shapes our ideas about whether that person is a hero or an outlaw. As you read the texts in this section, analyze how the authors depict heroes and outlaws, and notice how the difference between the two can sometimes blur.

◀ CRITICAL VIEWING How does the scene depicted in this painting connect to the idea of heroes and outlaws?

**CLOSE READING TOOL**

Use the **Close Reading Tool** to practice the strategies you learn in this unit.

## READINGS IN PART 3

# The Highwayman

Alfred Noyes

## PART ONE

The wind was a **torrent** of darkness among the gusty trees.
The moon was a ghostly galleon[1] tossed upon cloudy seas.
The road was a ribbon of moonlight over the purple moor,[2]
And the highwayman came riding—
Riding—riding—
The highwayman came riding, up to the old inn door.

He'd a French cocked-hat on his forehead, a bunch of lace at his chin,
A coat of the claret velvet, and breeches of brown doeskin.
They fitted with never a wrinkle. His boots were up to the thigh.
And he rode with a jeweled twinkle,
His pistol butts a-twinkle,
His rapier hilt[3] a-twinkle, under the jeweled sky.

◀ **torrent** (tôr´ ənt) *n.* flood

Over the cobbles he clattered and clashed in the dark innyard.
He tapped with his whip on the shutters, but all was locked and barred.
He whistled a tune to the window, and who should be waiting there
But the landlord's black-eyed daughter,
Bess, the landlord's daughter,
Plaiting a dark red love knot into her long black hair.

And dark in the dark old innyard a stable wicket creaked
Where Tim the ostler[4] listened. His face was white and peaked.

1. **galleon** (gal´ ē ən) *n.* large Spanish sailing ship.
2. **moor** (moor) *n.* open, rolling land with swamps.
3. **rapier** (rā´ pē ər) **hilt** large cup-shaped handle of a rapier, which is a type of sword.
4. **ostler** (äs´ lər) *n.* stable worker.

His eyes were hollows of madness, his hair like moldy hay,
But he loved the landlord's daughter,
The landlord's red-lipped daughter.
Dumb as a dog he listened, and he heard the robber say—
"One kiss, my bonny[5] sweetheart, I'm after a prize tonight,
But I shall be back with the yellow gold before the morning light;
Yet, if they press me sharply, and harry me through the day,
Then look for me by moonlight,
Watch for me by moonlight,
I'll come to thee by moonlight, though hell should bar the way."

He rose upright in the stirrups. He scarce could reach her hand,
But she loosened her hair in the casement.[6] His face burnt like a brand[7]
As the black cascade of perfume came tumbling over his breast;
And he kissed its waves in the moonlight,
(O, sweet black waves in the moonlight!)
Then he tugged at his rein in the moonlight, and galloped away to the west.

## PART TWO

He did not come in the dawning. He did not come at noon;
And out of the tawny sunset, before the rise of the moon,
When the road was a gypsy's ribbon, looping the purple moor,
A redcoat troop came marching—
Marching—marching—
King George's men[8] came marching, up to the old inn door.

---

5. **bonny** (bän´ ē) *adj.* Scottish for "pretty."
6. **casement** (kās´ mənt) *n.* window frame that opens on hinges.
7. **brand** (brand) *n.* piece of burning wood.
8. **King George's men** soldiers serving King George of Great Britain.

They said no word to the landlord. They drank his ale
  instead
But they gagged his daughter, and **bound** her, to the foot
  of her narrow bed.
Two of them knelt at her casement, with muskets at their
  side!
There was death at every window;
    And hell at one dark window;
For Bess could see, through her casement, the road that
  *he* would ride.

They had tied her up to attention, with many a sniggering
  jest.[9]
They had bound a musket beside her, with the muzzle
  beneath her breast!
"Now, keep good watch!" and they kissed her. She heard
  the doomed man say—
*Look for me by moonlight;*
    *Watch for me by moonlight;*
*I'll come to thee by moonlight, though hell should bar*
  *the way!*

She twisted her hands behind her; but all the knots held
  good!
She writhed her hands till her fingers were wet with
  sweat or blood!
They stretched and strained in the darkness, and the
  hours crawled by like years,
Till, now, on the stroke of midnight,
    Cold, on the stroke of midnight,
The tip of one finger touched it! The trigger at least was
  hers!

The tip of one finger touched it. She **strove** no more for
  the rest.
Up, she stood up to attention, with the muzzle beneath
  her breast.
She would not risk their hearing; she would not strive
  again;

◄ **bound** (bound) *v.* tied

◄ **strove** (strōv) *v.* struggled; made great efforts

---

9. **sniggering** (snig´ ər iŋ) **jest** sly joke.

For the road lay bare in the moonlight;
Blank and bare in the moonlight;
And the blood of her veins, in the moonlight, throbbed to her love's refrain.

*Tlot-tlot; tlot-tlot!* Had they heard it? The horsehoofs ringing clear;
*Tlot-tlot, tlot-tlot,* in the distance? Were they deaf that they did not hear?
Down the ribbon of moonlight, over the brow of the hill,
The highwayman came riding—
Riding—riding—
The redcoats looked to their priming![10] She stood up, straight and still.

*Tlot-tlot,* in the frosty silence! *Tlot-tlot,* in the echoing night!
Nearer he came and nearer. Her face was like a light.
Her eyes grew wide for a moment; she drew one last deep breath,
Then her finger moved in the moonlight,
Her musket shattered the moonlight,
Shattered her breast in the moonlight and warned him—with her death.

He turned. He spurred to the west; he did not know who stood
Bowed, with her head o'er the musket, drenched with her own blood!
Not till the dawn he heard it, and his face grew gray to hear
How Bess, the landlord's daughter,
The landlord's black-eyed daughter,
Had watched for her love in the moonlight, and died in the darkness there.

Back, he spurred like a madman, shouting a curse to the sky,
With the white road smoking behind him and his rapier brandished[11] high.

---

**10. priming** (prī′ miŋ) *n.* explosive used to set off the charge in a gun.
**11. brandished** (bran′ dishd) *adj.* waved in a threatening way.

Blood-red were his spurs in the golden noon; wine-red was his velvet coat;
When they shot him down on the highway,
Down like a dog on the highway,
And he lay in his blood on the highway, with a bunch of lace at his throat.

*And still of a winter's night, they say, when the wind is in the trees,*
*When the moon is a ghostly galleon tossed upon cloudy seas,*
*When the road is a ribbon of moonlight over the purple moor,*
*A highwayman comes riding—*
*Riding—riding—*
*A highwayman comes riding, up to the old inn door.*

*Over the cobbles he clatters and clangs in the dark innyard.*
*He taps with his whip on the shutters, but all is locked and barred.*
*He whistles a tune to the window, and who should be waiting there*
*But the landlord's black-eyed daughter,*
*Bess, the landlord's daughter,*
*Plaiting a dark red love knot into her long black hair.*

## ABOUT THE AUTHOR

### Alfred Noyes (1880–1958)

Englishman Alfred Noyes's love for learning led him to a career as a poet, an author, a professor, and a critic. Noyes published his first volume of poetry at the age of 21, and became quite popular with the reading public. Despite his great love for England's history and landscape, he moved to the United States, where he taught at Harvard University and Princeton University and lectured around the country. In 1913, Noyes received an honorary Ph.D. from Yale University.

# Close Reading Activities

## READ

### Comprehension

Reread all or part of the text to help you answer the following questions.

1. Where and when does the action of the poem take place?
2. Who overheard what the highwayman told Bess?
3. When does the highwayman plan to return?
4. What does the highwayman do when he hears Bess's warning?

**Research: Clarify Details** Choose a detail or reference in the poem that is unfamiliar to you and briefly research it. Then, explain how your research helped you understand an aspect of the poem.

**Summarize** Write an objective summary of the poem. Remember to omit your opinions and evaluations.

### Language Study

**Selection Vocabulary** Identify synonyms for the boldfaced words from the poem, and then use the words in sentences of your own.

- The wind was a **torrent** of darkness among the gusty trees.
- But they gagged his daughter, and **bound** her, to the foot of her narrow bed.
- She **strove** no more for the rest.

**Diction and Style** Study the passage below. Then, answer the questions that follow.

> Yet, if they press me sharply, and harry me through the day, … I'll come to thee by moonlight, though hell should bar the way.

1. **(a)** What does "press me sharply" mean here? **(b)** What connotations, or feelings, associated with the word *sharply* affect the tone of the sentence?
2. **(a)** Use context to determine the meaning of *harry*. Use a dictionary to confirm your answer. **(b)** Why is *harry* a more effective word in this context than a synonym would be?

**Conventions** Reread the lines below and identify the dependent clause in the stanza. Tell which subordinating conjunction introduces the clause, and then explain what information the dependent clause provides.

> He rose upright in the stirrups. He scarce could reach her hand,/ But she loosened her hair in the casement. His face burnt like a brand/ As the black cascade of perfume came tumbling over his breast;/ And he kissed its waves in the moonlight, / (O, sweet black waves in the moonlight!)/ Then he tugged at his reign in the moonlight, and galloped away to the west.

### Academic Vocabulary

The following words appear in blue in the instructions and questions on the facing page.

**contrast** **identify** **opposing**

Decide whether you know each word well, know it a little bit, or do not know it at all. Then, look up the definitions of the words you do not know well.

## Literary Analysis

Reread the identified passages. Then, respond to the following questions.

**Focus Passage 1** *(p. 401)*

The wind was a torrent of darkness… His rapier hilt a-twinkle under the jeweled sky.

### Key Ideas and Details

1. **Summarize:** In your own words, describe the character, setting, and action presented in these stanzas.

### Craft and Structure

2. **(a) Analyze:** What examples of figurative language does the poet use to describe the night? **(b) Interpret:** What mood does this description establish?
3. **Analyze:** What do the poem's descriptive details suggest about the highwayman? Support your answer.

### Integration of Knowledge and Ideas

4. **Compare and Contrast:** How does the description of the setting compare and **contrast** with the description of the highwayman?

**Focus Passage 2** *(p. 404)*

*Tlot-tlot; tlot-tlot!* Had they heard it?… and warned him—with her death.

### Key Ideas and Details

1. **(a)** What does Bess do in this passage? **(b) Interpret:** Why does she do it?

### Craft and Structure

2. **(a) Distinguish: Identify** the sound device that Noyes uses in lines 67, 68, and 73. **(b) Analyze:** How does the use of this sound device create a feeling of tension in the poem?
3. **Analyze:** What effect does Noyes achieve by repeating "riding" in lines 70–71?

### Integration of Knowledge and Ideas

4. **(a) Interpret:** In the second stanza from this passage, what two words with **opposing** connotations are linked together with rhyme? **(b) Analyze:** What is the effect of this contrast?

## Repetition

Poets use the **repetition** of words or phrases to link and emphasize ideas. A repeated phrase in a poem can make an image more powerful. Reread "The Highwayman," noting how the poet uses repetition.

1. **(a)** Identify the repetition in lines 28–30. **(b)** What effect does this repetition achieve?
2. **Heroes and Outlaws (a)** In lines 40–42, how does Noyes use repetition and rhythm to complement the visual image he creates? **(b)** Explain how the repetition in these lines creates a connection between the soldiers and the highwayman.

## DISCUSS

### From Text to Topic **Group Discussion**

Discuss lines 19–27 with a group of classmates. Contribute your own ideas, and support them with examples from the poem.

> And dark in the dark old innyard a stable wicket creaked ... before the morning light; (pp. 401–402)

**QUESTIONS FOR DISCUSSION:**

1. Do you think Bess is aware of Tim's feelings for her? Why or why not?
2. What details in the poet's description of Tim characterize Tim as a villain or a hero?

## WRITE

### Writing to Sources **Informative Text**

**Assignment**

Write a **character analysis** of the highwayman. Review the poet's descriptions of the highwayman's character and actions to determine whether he is a hero, an outlaw, or a little bit of both.

**Prewriting and Planning** As you review the poem, record details about the highwayman, including his characteristics, motivations, and actions. Review your notes to develop your analysis of the highwayman's character.

**Drafting** Begin with a thesis statement—one sentence in which you present your main idea about the highwayman's character. In the body of your essay, support your thesis by presenting the reasons for your interpretation of the highwayman's character. Support each reason with details from the poem and, when appropriate, from real life. In your conclusion, explain why the poet characterized the highwayman as he did.

**Revising** Reread your essay to ensure that you have clearly supported your main points. If your main points require additional support, consider adding direct quotations from the poem. If you add quotations, be sure to use quotation marks to clearly distinguish them from your own writing.

**Editing and Proofreading** Make sure that the pronouns in your essay match their antecedents. Then, edit your essay to clarify relationships between facts, characters, and events. One way to clarify relationships in your writing is by adding transitions, such as *as a result, because of,* and *in other words.*

**CONVENTIONS**

Pronouns must agree with their antecedents in number and gender. Use singular pronouns with singular antecedents and plural pronouns with plural antecedents.

THE HIGHWAYMAN
Alfred Noyes

# RESEARCH

## Research **Investigate the Topic**

**Heroes and Outlaws in Literature** Heroes and outlaws have been subjects in literature for thousands of years. Sometimes, outlaws are portrayed as heroes. Robin Hood, a folk hero of British literature, is one such heroic outlaw.

> **Assignment**
> Conduct research to learn about an outlaw hero of folk literature. Investigate where and when the person or character lived, and why he or she was considered both an outlaw and a hero. Consult print and electronic resources. Take clear notes that carefully identify your sources. Compare and contrast the subject of your research with the highwayman in the poem. Share your findings in an **informal presentation** to the class.

**PREPARATION FOR ESSAY**
You may use the knowledge you gain during this research assignment to support your claims in an essay you will write at the end of this section.

**Gather Sources** Locate authoritative print and digital sources. Use library catalogs and databases to find books, stories, and articles about outlaw heroes. To find online sources, use Internet databases and search engines. Remember not all online sources are reliable, so you must verify the validity of the information you find.

**Take Notes** Take notes on each source using an organized note-taking strategy. You may write your notes on notecards or record them in one or more electronic files.

- For sources that provide historical information, such as articles and encyclopedias, make a separate note for each source. Label the top of each note with the type of information it contains.
- For sources that provide stories about outlaw heroes, identify the source, and write a brief summary of the story in your own words.
- For Internet sources, record the Web site and the date you accessed the information.

**Synthesize Multiple Sources** Assemble the information from your research into a cohesive presentation. Select and organize important historical facts and other information you want to share. Draw conclusions about why your subject is both an outlaw and a hero, and compare his or her story with that of the highwayman. Then, outline your presentation.

**Organize and Present Ideas** Review your outline and practice delivering your presentation. Be ready to answer questions from your audience.

# CARNEGIE HERO *Fund Commission*

### *History*

*"I do not expect to stimulate or create heroism by this fund, knowing well that heroic action is impulsive; but I do believe that, if the hero is injured in his bold attempt to serve or save his fellows, he and those dependent upon him should not suffer pecuniarily."*[1]

—Andrew Carnegie

### Heroes of Civilization

A massive coal mine disaster in 1904 prompted Andrew Carnegie to establish a commission to recognize acts of civilian[2] heroism.

Pittsburgh steelmaker Andrew Carnegie had long held the idea that ordinary citizens who perform extraordinary acts of heroism should be recognized for their deeds. A massive explosion on January 25, 1904, in a coal mine at Harwick, Pa., near Pittsburgh, claiming 181 lives, inspired him to act … two of the victims had entered the mine after the explosion in ill-fated rescue attempts.

Within three months of the disaster, Carnegie had set aside $5 million under the care of a commission to recognize "civilization's heroes" … and to provide financial assistance for those disabled and the dependents of those killed helping others.

The **Carnegie Hero Fund Commission** carries out the founder's wishes by awarding the **Carnegie Medal** throughout the United States and Canada.

Over the 108 years of its existence, the Fund has awarded more

---

1. **pecuniarily** (pi kyo͞o´nē er´ i lē) *adv.* monetarily; relating to money.
2. **civilian** (sə vil´yən) *n.* any person not an active member of the armed forces and not employed as a police officer or firefighter.

*"We live in a heroic age."*

The Carnegie Medal

than 9,500 medals and $34 million in accompanying grants, including scholarship aid and continuing assistance. Ten hero funds established in Europe carry out a similar mission. The Carnegie Hero Fund Trust for Great Britain was set up in 1908 and was followed a year later by the Foundation Carnegie in France. In quick succession came hero funds in Germany, Norway, Switzerland, the Netherlands, Sweden, Denmark, Belgium, and Italy.

**commemorated** ▶ (kə mem′ə rāt′ id) *v.* honored the memory of

The Hero Fund's heritage was **commemorated** in 1996 by the Pennsylvania Historical and Museum Commission through the issuance of a roadside marker, which was installed along Pittsburgh Street in Springdale, Pa., near the sites of both the mine and the cemetery in which many of the disaster's victims are buried. More than 2,000 such markers have been issued by the state since the program's inception in 1946. The blue and gold signs dotting the state's highways commemorate subjects having meaningful impact and statewide or national significance.

**prompted** ▶ (prämpt′id) *v.* urged into action

The Harwick explosion, remaining one of the worst U.S. mining disasters of the century, claimed 179 lives. It was the deaths of the two rescuers which **prompted** Carnegie to act on his thoughts about civilian heroism. Within three months of the explosion, Carnegie established a $5 million trust and appointed a 21-member commission to carry out his wish that "heroes and those dependent upon them should be freed from pecuniary cares resulting from their heroism." Further, the heroic acts were to be recognized by the granting of a medal.

More than a century later, the Carnegie Hero Fund Commission continues to carry out those goals.

### What Is a Hero?

The Commission's definition of a hero has been largely unchanged since 1904: A civilian who knowingly risks his or her own life to an extraordinary degree while saving or attempting to save the life of another person. The cases submitted for consideration—in excess of 85,000 to date—are scrutinized by a full-time staff before formal review by the Commission itself. Persons selected for recognition receive a bronze medal and a financial grant, and each becomes **eligible** for scholarship aid. Those disabled in their heroic acts or the dependents of those killed are eligible for additional benefits, including ongoing aid to meet living expenses.

◀ **eligible** (elʹi jə bəl) *adj.* fit to be chosen; qualified

Approximately 20 percent of the awards are made posthumously,[3] reflecting a verse from the New Testament embossed on each medal: "Greater love hath no man than this, that a man lay down his life for his friends" (John 15:13).

## A Heroic Age

*The marker in Dunfermline reads, "The false heroes of barbarous man are those who can only boast of the destruction of their fellows. The true heroes of civilisation are those alone who save or greatly serve them. Young Hunter was one of those and deserves an enduring monument."*—Carnegie

"We live in a heroic age," Carnegie wrote in 1904 in the opening lines of the fund's deed of trust. "Not seldom are we thrilled by deeds of heroism where men or women are injured or lose their lives in attempting to preserve or rescue their fellows; such the heroes of civilization. The heroes of barbarism maimed or killed theirs."

Similar thinking first surfaced in 1886, when Carnegie donated toward the cost of a marker honoring a 17-year-old boy who drowned in a rescue attempt in Carnegie's native Scotland. The philanthropist's[4] thoughts on heroism are chiseled into the youth's stone marker in a cemetery in Dunfermline, Carnegie's boyhood home.

The deaths of the Harwick rescuers 18 years later provided impetus for Carnegie to act on his peace-loving convictions, and he took great satisfaction in the establishment of the Hero Fund. Carnegie biographer Joseph Frazier Wall (Andrew Carnegie, Oxford University Press, New York), writes, "Every other philanthropic fund that Carnegie had ever established had been proposed to him—often forced upon him—by others. The Hero Fund came out of his own head and heart, and it delighted him."

---

3. **posthumously** (päsʹchoo məsʹ lē) *adv.* after one's death.
4. **philanthropist** (fə lanʹthrə pist) *n.* wealthy person who helps others, especially through gifts or charity.

# Close Reading Activities

## READ

### Comprehension

Reread the text as needed to answer the following questions.

1. Who was Andrew Carnegie?
2. What event inspired Carnegie to create the Hero Fund?
3. What is the purpose of the fund?

**Research: Clarify Details** Choose an unfamiliar detail from the article and conduct research to learn more. Then, explain how your research helped you understand the article.

**Summarize** Write an objective summary of the article. Remember to leave out your opinions and evaluations.

### Language Study

**Selection Vocabulary** Write two related words for each boldfaced word from the selection (example: *assist, assistance, assisted*).

- The Hero Fund's heritage was **commemorated** in 1996 ...
- It was the deaths of the two rescuers which **prompted** Carnegie to act...
- ... the dependents of those killed are **eligible** for additional benefits ...

### Literary Analysis

Reread the identified passage. Then, respond to the following questions.

**Focus Passage** *(p. 413)*

**A Heroic Age** The marker in Dunfermline reads ... Carnegie's boyhood home.

**Key Ideas and Details**

1. **(a)** Who is "young Hunter"? **(b) Interpret:** How does he fit the **definition** of a hero that appears on the marker in Dunfermline?

**Craft and Structure**

2. **(a) Interpret: Explain** in your own words what "Not seldom are we thrilled by deeds of heroism" means. **(b) Evaluate:** Explain the effect of the negative construction "Not seldom."

**Integration of Knowledge and Ideas**

3. **(a)** What groups that are commonly considered heroes might Carnegie call "heroes of barbarous man"? **(b)** According to Carnegie, what is the key **characteristic** of a "true hero of civilization"?

### Structure

The **structure** of a text helps determine the organization of key ideas. Features such as headings, type size and style, and placement on a page reveal a text's structure. Take notes on this Web article's structure.

1. What text features identify the key ideas of the article? Cite examples.
2. **Heroes and Outlaws (a)** Why is the first section set off from the rest of the text? **(b)** What key idea about heroes does this section present?

CARNEGIE HERO
*Fund Commission*

# DISCUSS • RESEARCH • WRITE

## From Text to Topic **Group Discussion**

Discuss the following passage with a group of classmates. Take notes during the discussion. Contribute your own ideas, and support them with examples from the text.

> The Commission's definition of a hero has been largely unchanged since 1904: A civilian who knowingly risks his or her own life to an extraordinary degree while saving or attempting to save the life of another person.

### QUESTIONS FOR DISCUSSION

1. What words in this passage define who is eligible for an award? Who might not be eligible?
2. Why do you think these restrictions are in place? Do you agree with them? Explain.

## Research **Investigate the Topic**

**Civilization's Heroes** Carnegie's fund has been in place since 1904, and thousands of cases of heroism are still submitted every year for review.

**Assignment**

Conduct research to learn the story of a past winner of the Carnegie Hero Fund Commission award. Consult the Internet to find a winner and learn the basic details of his or her story. Then, consult news sources to learn additional details. Take clear notes and carefully identify your sources so that you can easily access the information later. Share your findings in a brief **hero profile**.

### PREPARATION FOR ESSAY

You may use the results of your research to support your ideas in the essay you will write at the end of this section.

## Writing to Sources **Argument**

The Carnegie Hero Fund Commission selects winners from nominations that are submitted by members of the public.

**Assignment**

Write a **persuasive letter** in which you nominate someone you have read or heard about for a Carnegie Medal. Follow these steps:

- State your intention of nominating the person for the medal.
- Describe in detail the nature of the person's heroic act and its outcome.
- Present strong evidence that your nominee knowingly risked his or her life to save someone.
- Conclude by reflecting on why you consider the person a hero.

### ACADEMIC VOCABULARY

Academic terms appear in blue on these pages. If these words are not familiar to you, use a dictionary to find their definitions. Then, use the words as you speak and write about the text.

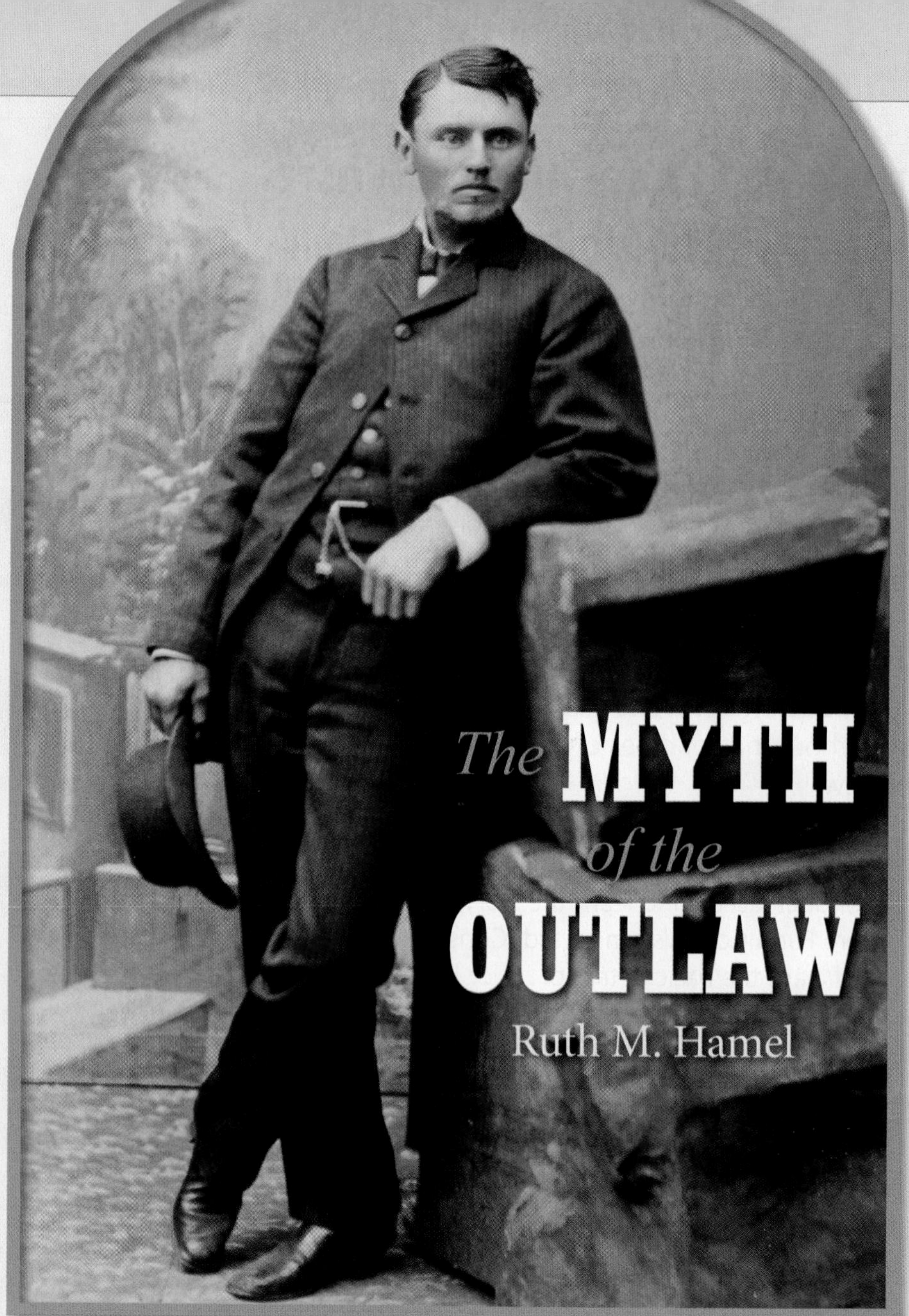

# *The* MYTH *of the* OUTLAW

Ruth M. Hamel

Jesse James, 1875

Life in the United States was hard after the Civil War. In many places, farmland had been ruined, factories burned, and homes destroyed. Not much work was available for the returning soldiers. But not only was life hard, it also was dull. People needed heroes to liven things up.

Outlaws such as Billy the Kid, Jesse James, William Quantrill, Belle Starr, and Sam Bass led lives that sounded exciting to many Americans. Their crimes were written up in newspapers and told around campfires, and the stories changed each time they were told.

Eventually, it seemed, every outlaw was on the side of the poor.

Outlaws also were featured in the new "dime novels." These small paperbacks sold for ten cents—affordable for the common man—and were filled with exciting stories of heroes such as Deadeye Dick and Fearnot Fred. Often the stories were purely fictional.

In 1882, the year after Pat Garrett killed Billy the Kid, Garrett's book *Billy the Kid* was published. He said that so many lies had been told about Billy that someone had to tell the truth. Billy himself had invented some of the lies. For instance, he had bragged about killing twenty-one men by the time he was twenty-one years old, but records show that he had killed only four and helped in the killing of five others.

In stories and songs, Billy is handsome and generous, having been forced into a life of crime when someone insulted his mother. But instead of having a face "fine and fair," Billy was, according to one source, "**nondescript**, narrow-chested, stoop-shouldered and **repulsive** looking." He was a cattle thief and a killer, but after his death someone said, "The Kid had principle … outside of some loose notions about rustling cattle.[1] This was stealing, but I don't believe it struck him that way."

Similarly, Jesse James was portrayed in a sympathetic light both while he was alive and after he was dead. Indeed, seventeen men claimed to be the "real" Jesse James after his death, and at last count four hundred fifty articles and movies tell of his life and crimes. *Jesse James at Bay* portrays James as a kind of Robin Hood who helped widows and orphans.

When artist Thomas Hart Benton was **commissioned** to paint a mural celebrating the state of Missouri at the state capitol in 1935 … , he included a handsome picture of James. In addition, one of Benton's best-known lithographs[2] is of James killing two men during a train robbery.

Just in case the outlaws might be forgotten, a set of trading cards was issued in the 1930s. The cards were called "The Roundup Series," and all of the outlaws pictured look handsome, likable, kind, and generous. Just the way they were in real life—at least in people's minds.

◄ **commissioned** (kə mish′ənd) *v.* appointed or hired to carry out a duty or task

◄ **nondescript** (nän′di skript′) *adj.* hard to describe; not interesting

◄ **repulsive** (ri pul′siv) *adj.* causing intense dislike; disgusting

1. **rustling cattle** stealing cattle.
2. **lithographs** (lith′ə grafs′) *n.* prints made from a flat stone or metal plate.

# Close Reading Activities

## READ

### Comprehension

Reread all or part of the text to help you answer the following questions.

1. What was life like after the Civil War? Why?
2. In the years following the Civil War, how were outlaws portrayed?
3. What is the author's attitude toward these stories?

**Research: Clarify Details** Choose an unfamiliar detail from the article and briefly research it. Then, explain how your research helps you understand the article.

**Summarize** Write an objective summary of the article. Remember to omit any opinions or evaluations.

### Language Study

**Selection Vocabulary** List a synonym for each boldfaced word from the article. Then, use the boldfaced word in a sentence of your own.

- Billy was, according to one source, "**nondescript,** narrow-chested, stoop-shouldered and **repulsive** looking."
- When artist Thomas Hart Benton was **commissioned** to paint a mural…

### Literary Analysis

Reread the passage indicated below.

**Focus Passage** *(p. 417)*

In stories and songs … helped widows and orphans.

**Key Ideas and Details**

1. **Compare and Contrast:** What are two contrasting ideas about Billy the Kid?

**Craft and Structure**

2. **(a) Infer:** What does the comment about Billy the Kid's "loose notions" suggest about the **attitude** of the person who made this remark? **(b) Speculate:** Why does the author include this quotation?
3. **(a) Analyze:** Why does the author begin the paragraph about Jesse James with the word *similarly*? **(b) Draw Conclusions:** What does this suggest about James?

**Integration of Knowledge and Ideas**

4. **Connect:** How does the information in this passage **reflect** the title of the article? Cite details from the article to support your answer.

### Diction

Through **diction**, or word choice, an author can create vivid images and reveal his or her **viewpoint** on a subject. Take notes on the author's diction in this article.

1. **(a)** In the opening paragraph, what vivid words does the author use to describe life after the Civil War? **(b)** What image do these words create?
2. **Heroes and Outlaws (a)** What image of Billy the Kid does the word "repulsive" create? **(b)** Why does the author include a quotation with this word in the article?

# DISCUSS • RESEARCH • WRITE

## From Text to Topic **Partner Discussion**

Discuss the following passage with a partner. Take notes, contribute your own ideas, and support them with examples from the text.

> When artist Thomas Hart Benton was commissioned to paint a mural celebrating the state of Missouri at the state capitol in 1935 ..., he included a handsome picture of James. In addition, one of Benton's best-known lithographs is of James killing two men during a train robbery.

### QUESTIONS FOR DISCUSSION

1. What does James's portrayal in the mural suggest about the state's attitude toward him?
2. Can art affect the ways in which people perceive a hero or an outlaw? Explain.

## Research **Investigate the Topic**

**Outlaws After the Civil War** Many outlaws besides Billy the Kid and Jesse James became famous after the Civil War.

**Assignment**

Conduct research to learn about a famous outlaw of the post-Civil War era. Use Web sites to find the popular version of his or her story. Consult biography databases and authoritative print sources to find more objective accounts. Take clear notes and identify sources for different accounts of the same information. Share your findings in a brief **oral report** to the class.

### PREPARATION FOR ESSAY

You may use the results of your research to support your ideas in the essay you will write at the end of this section.

### ACADEMIC VOCABULARY

Academic terms appear in blue on these pages. If these words are not familiar to you, use a dictionary to find their definitions. Then, use the words as you speak and write about the text.

## Writing to Sources **Argument**

There was considerable controversy about several scenes, including the image of Jesse James, in Thomas Hart Benton's mural *A Social History of the State of Missouri.*

**Assignment**

Write an **argument** in which you recommend preserving the mural as it is, or removing the scene with Jesse James because it glorifies criminal activity. Follow these steps:

- Go online to view a reproduction of Benton's mural.
- State your position in your opening paragraph.
- Present your reasons and evidence in body paragraphs.
- Acknowledge opposing arguments and respond to them.
- Use a formal tone that is free from slang.
- Provide a concluding paragraph.

# The Real Story of a Cowboy's Life

Geoffrey C. Ward

discipline ▶ (dis′ ə plin′) *n.* strict control

gauge ▶ (gāj) *v.* estimate or judge

A drive's success depended on **discipline** and planning. According to Teddy Blue,[1] most Texas herds numbered about 2,000 head with a trail boss and about a dozen men in charge—though herds as large as 15,000 were also driven north with far larger escorts. The most experienced men rode "point" and "swing," at the head and sides of the long herd; the least experienced brought up the rear, riding "drag" and eating dust. At the end of the day, Teddy Blue remembered, they "would go to the water barrel . . . and rinse their mouths and cough and spit up . . . black stuff. But you couldn't get it up out of your lungs."

They had to learn to work as a team, keeping the herd moving during the day, resting peacefully at night. Twelve to fifteen miles a day was a good pace. But such steady progress could be interrupted at any time. A cowboy had to know how to **gauge** the temperament of his cattle, how to chase down

1. **Teddy Blue** Edward C. Abbot, a cowboy who rode in a successful trail drive in the 1880s.

a stray without alarming the rest of the herd, how to lasso a steer using the horn of his saddle as a tying post. His saddle was his most prized possession; it served as his chair, his workbench, his pillow at night. Being dragged to death was the most common death for a cowboy, and so the most feared occurrence on the trail was the nighttime stampede.

As Teddy Blue recalled, a sound, a smell, or simply the sudden movement of a jittery cow could set off a whole herd.

> If . . . the cattle started running—you'd hear that low rumbling noise along the ground and the men on herd wouldn't need to come in and tell you, you'd know—then you'd jump for your horse and get out there in the lead, trying to head them and get them into a mill[2] before they scattered. It was riding at a dead run in the dark, with cut banks and prairie dog holes all around you, not knowing if the next jump would land you in a shallow grave.

Most cowboys had guns, but rarely used them on the trail. Some outfits made them keep their weapons in the chuck wagon to eliminate any chance of gunplay. Charles Goodnight[3] was still more **emphatic**: "Before starting on a trail drive, I made it a rule to draw up an article of agreement, setting forth what each man was to do. The main clause stipulated[4] that if one shot another he was to be tried by the outfit and hanged on the spot, if found guilty. I never had a man shot on the trail."

◀ **emphatic** (em fat′ ik) *adj.* expressing strong feeling

Regardless of its ultimate destination, every herd had to ford[5] a series of rivers—the Nueces, the Guadalupe, the Brazos, the Wichita, the Red.

A big herd of longhorns swimming across a river, Goodnight remembered, "looked like a million floating rocking chairs," and crossing those rivers one after another, a cowboy recalled, was like climbing the rungs of a long ladder reaching north.

"After you crossed the Red River and got out on the open plains," Teddy Blue remembered, "it was sure a pretty sight to see them strung out for almost a mile, the sun shining on their horns." Initially, the

2. **mill** (mil) *n.* slow movement in a circle.
3. **Charles Goodnight** cowboy who rode successful trail drives beginning in the 1860s.
4. **stipulated** (stip′ yə lāt′ əd) *v.* stated as a rule.
5. **ford** (fôrd) *v.* cross a river at a shallow point.

land immediately north of the Red River was Indian territory, and some tribes charged tolls for herds crossing their land—payable in money or beef. But Teddy Blue remembered that the homesteaders, now pouring onto the Plains by railroad, were far more nettlesome:

> There was no love lost between settlers and cowboys on the trail. Those jay-hawkers would take up a claim right where the herds watered and charge us for water. They would plant a crop alongside the trail and plow a furrow around it for a fence, and then when the cattle got into their wheat or their garden patch, they would come cussing and waving a shotgun and yelling for damages. And the cattle had been coming through there when they were still raising punkins in Illinois.

The settlers' hostility was entirely understandable. The big herds ruined their crops, and they carried with them a disease, spread by ticks and called "Texas fever," that devastated domestic livestock. Kansas and other territories along the route soon established quarantine lines,[6] called "deadlines," at the western fringe of settlement, and insisted that trail drives not cross them. Each year, as settlers continued to move in, those deadlines moved farther west.

Sometimes, farmers tried to enforce their own, as John Rumans, one of Charles Goodnight's hands, recalled:

> Some men met us at the trail near Canyon City, and said we couldn't come in. There were fifteen or twenty of them, and they were not going to let us cross the Arkansas River. We didn't even stop. . . . Old man [Goodnight] had a shotgun loaded with buckshot and led the way, saying: "John, get over on that point with your Winchester and point these cattle in behind me." He slid his shotgun across the saddle in front of him and we did the same with our Winchesters. He rode right across, and as he rode up to them, he said: "I've monkeyed as long as I want to with you," and they fell back to the sides, and went home after we had passed.

There were few diversions on the trail. Most trail bosses banned liquor. Goodnight prohibited gambling, too. Even the songs for which cowboys became famous grew directly out of doing a job, remembered Teddy Blue:

> The singing was supposed to soothe [the cattle] and it did; I don't know why, unless it was that a sound they was used to

6. **quarantine** (kwôr´ ən tēn) **lines** *n.* boundaries created to prevent the spread of disease.

would keep them from spooking at other noises. I know that if you wasn't singing, any little sound in the night—it might be just a horse shaking himself—could make them leave the country; but if you were singing, they wouldn't notice it.

The two men on guard would circle around with their horses on a walk, if it was a clear night and the cattle was bedded down and quiet, and one man would sing a verse of song, and his partner on the other side of the herd would sing another verse; and you'd go through a whole song that way. . . . "Bury Me Not on the Lone Prairie" was a great song for awhile, but . . . they sung it to death. It was a saying on the range that even the horses nickered it and the coyotes howled it; it got so they'd throw you in the creek if you sang it.

The number of cattle on the move was sometimes staggering: once, Teddy Blue rode to the top of a rise from which he could see seven herds strung out behind him; eight more up ahead; and the dust from an additional thirteen moving parallel to his. "All the cattle in the world," he remembered, "seemed to be coming up from Texas."

At last, the herds neared their destinations. After months in the saddle—often wearing the same clothes every day, eating nothing but biscuits and beef stew at the chuck wagon, drinking only water and coffee, his sole companions his fellow cowboys, his herd, and his horse—the cowboy was about to be paid for his work, and turned loose in town.

## ABOUT THE AUTHOR

### Geoffrey C. Ward (b. 1940)

Historian Geoffrey C. Ward strives to present an accurate portrayal of the past. He has written more than a dozen books about the United States and the people who played key roles in its growth. Ward's book *A First-Class Temperament,* about Franklin D. Roosevelt, won the 1989 National Book Critics Circle Award for biography. Ward has also written biographies of Mark Twain, Susan B. Anthony, Harry Truman, and Billy the Kid. In addition to his books, Ward has written or co-written more than twenty screenplays for films, many of which have appeared on public television. Ward teamed up with filmmaker Ken Burns to create the Emmy Award-winning PBS documentaries *The Civil War* and *Baseball.*

# Close Reading Activities

## READ

### Comprehension

Reread to answer these questions.

1. How did trail bosses reduce the likelihood of violence between cowboys?
2. Why did cowboy songs become commonplace?
3. What was the relationship between cowboys and settlers?

**Research: Clarify Details** Choose an unfamiliar reference from the essay and briefly research it. Then, explain how your research helps you understand the essay.

**Summarize** Write an objective summary of the essay. Remember that an objective summary is free from opinion and evaluation.

### Language Study

**Selection Vocabulary** Define each boldfaced word from the essay, and then use each word in a sentence.

- **discipline**
- **gauge**
- **emphatic**

### Literary Analysis

**Reread the identified passage. Then, respond to the following questions.**

**Focus Passage** *(pp. 421–422)*
"After you crossed the Red River and got out on the open plains," … when they were still raising punkins in Illinois."

#### Key Ideas and Details

1. **(a)** What **challenge** did some Indian tribes present for the cowboys? **(b)** How did the cowboys deal with this challenge?

#### Craft and Structure

2. **Interpret:** A nettle is a plant with painful, stinging fibers. How does the word *nettlesome* characterize the settlers?
3. **Analyze:** *Jay hawker* is a slang term for "thief." How does Teddy Blue's use of the term contribute to the meaning and mood of the passage?

#### Integration of Knowledge and Ideas

4. **Connect:** How does Blue's comment about "raising punkins in Illinois" sum up his **attitude** toward the settlers?

### Primary Sources

Quotations from **primary sources**—original, first-hand accounts of an event—lend strong credibility and vivid details to an author's writing. **Evaluate** how Geoffrey Ward uses primary sources in this essay.

1. Why is Teddy Blue's description of a nighttime stampede more effective than a description by the author would be?
2. **Heroes and Outlaws** How do the primary sources strengthen or weaken the popular opinion that cowboys are ideal folk heroes?

# DISCUSS • RESEARCH • WRITE

## From Text to Topic **Debate**

Debate the following passage in small groups, with half the group taking the cowboys' side and half the group taking the settlers' side. Respond to the previous speaker's ideas, and contribute your own ideas, supporting them with examples from the text.

> The settlers' hostility was entirely understandable… and they fell back to the sides, and went home after we had passed. (p. 422)

### QUESTIONS FOR DISCUSSION

1. Should decades of cattle drives have established the cowboys' rights to the land? Explain.
2. Does Goodnight's behavior in this passage characterize him as a hero or an outlaw? Explain.

## Research **Investigate the Topic**

**Cowboys and Settlers** Cowboys were not the only ones who had a difficult time in the Great Plains of the 1880s. The settlers who moved west faced harsh conditions, disease, and separation from their families, as well as opposition from the cowboys.

**Assignment**

Conduct research about Great Plains settlers during the 1880s to learn about the challenges they faced. Take notes on the books, magazines, and Internet resources you consult, and record your sources. Share your findings in a brief **research report**. Explain whether you consider the settlers heroes, outlaws, or a combination of the two.

### PREPARATION FOR ESSAY

You may use the results of your research to support your ideas in the essay you will write at the end of this section.

## Writing to Sources **Argument**

The cowboys in the essay blamed the settlers for disputes between the groups. The settlers blamed the cowboys.

**Assignment**

Write an **argument** in which you agree or disagree that the cowboys had the right to drive their cattle along the same trails and lands they had always used, even after famers settled that land. Follow these steps:

- Begin by introducing the issue and stating your position.
- Present your arguments in the body of your essay. Cite facts and details from the essay to support your claims.
- Anticipate and address opposing arguments.
- Write a strong conclusion that reflects on the importance of your position.

### ACADEMIC VOCABULARY

Academic terms appear in blue on these pages. If these words are not familiar to you, use a dictionary to find their definitions. Then, use the words as you speak and write about the text.

# After Twenty Years

## O. Henry

**spectators** ▶ (spek´ tāt´ erz) *n.* people who watch

**intricate** ▶ (in´ tri kit) *adj.* complex; detailed

The policeman on the beat moved up the avenue impressively. The impressiveness was habitual and not for show, for spectators were few. The time was barely 10 o'clock at night, but chilly gusts of wind with a taste of rain in them had well nigh[1] de-peopled the streets.

Trying doors as he went, twirling his club with many intricate and artful movements, turning now and then to cast his watchful eye down the pacific thoroughfare,[2] the officer, with his stalwart form and slight swagger, made a fine picture of a guardian of the peace. The vicinity was one that kept early hours. Now and then you might see the lights of a cigar store or of an all-night lunch counter; but the majority of the doors belonged to business places that had long since been closed.

When about midway of a certain block the policeman suddenly slowed his walk. In the doorway of a darkened hardware store a man leaned, with an unlighted cigar in his mouth. As the policeman walked up to him the man spoke up quickly.

"It's all right, officer," he said, reassuringly. "I'm just waiting for a friend. It's an appointment made twenty years ago.

1. **well nigh** *adv.* very nearly.
2. **pacific thoroughfare** calm street.

Sounds a little funny to you, doesn't it? Well, I'll explain if you'd like to make certain it's all straight. About that long ago there used to be a restaurant where this store stands—'Big Joe' Brady's restaurant."

"Until five years ago," said the policeman. "It was torn down then."

The man in the doorway struck a match and lit his cigar. The light showed a pale, square-jawed face with keen eyes, and a little white scar near his right eyebrow. His scarfpin was a large diamond, oddly set.

"Twenty years ago tonight," said the man, "I dined here at 'Big Joe' Brady's with Jimmy Wells, my best chum, and the finest chap in the world. He and I were raised here in New York, just like two brothers, together. I was eighteen and Jimmy was twenty. The next morning I was to start for the West to make my fortune. You couldn't have dragged Jimmy out of New York; he thought it was the only place on earth. Well, we agreed that night that we would meet here again exactly twenty years from that date and time, no matter what our conditions might be or from what distance we might have to come. We figured that in twenty years each of us ought to have our destiny worked out and our fortunes made, whatever they were going to be."

"It sounds pretty interesting," said the policeman. "Rather a long time between meets, though, it seems to me. Haven't you heard from your friend since you left?"

"Well, yes, for a time we corresponded," said the other. "But after a year or two we lost track of each other. You see, the West is a pretty big proposition, and I kept hustling around over it pretty lively. But I know Jimmy will meet me here if he's alive, for he always was the truest, stanchest old chap in the world. He'll never forget. I came a thousand miles to stand in this door tonight, and it's worth it if my old partner turns up."

The waiting man pulled out a handsome watch, the lids of it set with small diamonds.

"Three minutes to ten," he announced. "It was exactly ten o'clock when we parted here at the restaurant door."

**simultaneously** (sĭ́ məl tā́ nē əs lē) *adv.* at the same time

"Did pretty well out West, didn't you?" asked the policeman.

"You bet! I hope Jimmy has done half as well. He was a kind of plodder, though, good fellow as he was. I've had to compete with some of the sharpest wits going to get my pile. A man gets in a groove in New York. It takes the West to put a razor-edge on him."

The policeman twirled his club and took a step or two.

"I'll be on my way. Hope your friend comes around all right. Going to call time on him sharp?"

"I should say not!" said the other. "I'll give him half an hour at least. If Jimmy is alive on earth he'll be here by that time. So long, officer."

"Good-night, sir," said the policeman, passing on along his beat, trying doors as he went.

There was now a fine, cold drizzle falling, and the wind had risen from its uncertain puffs into a steady blow. The few foot passengers astir in that quarter hurried dismally and silently along with coat collars turned high and pocketed hands. And in the door of the hardware store the man who had come a thousand miles to fill an appointment, uncertain almost to absurdity,[3] with the friend of his youth, smoked his cigar and waited.

About twenty minutes he waited, and then a tall man in a long overcoat, with collar turned up to his ears, hurried across from the opposite side of the street. He went directly to the waiting man.

"Is that you, Bob?" he asked, doubtfully.

"Is that you, Jimmy Wells?" cried the man in the door.

"Bless my heart!" exclaimed the new arrival, grasping both the other's hands with his own. "It's Bob, sure as fate. I was certain I'd find you here if you were still in existence. Well, well, well!—twenty years is a long time. The old restaurant's gone, Bob; I wish it had lasted, so we could have had another dinner there. How has the West treated you, old man?"

"Bully;[4] it has given me everything I asked it for. You've changed lots, Jimmy. I never thought you were so tall by two or three inches."

"Oh, I grew a bit after I was twenty."

"Doing well in New York, Jimmy?"

"Moderately. I have a position in one of the city departments. Come on, Bob; we'll go around to a place I know of, and have a good long talk about old times."

The two men started up the street, arm in arm. The man from

3. **absurdity** (ab sʉr′ də tē) *n.* nonsense.

4. **bully** *interj.* very good.

the West, his egotism enlarged by success, was beginning to outline the history of his career. The other, submerged in his overcoat, listened with interest.

At the corner stood a drug store, brilliant with electric lights. When they came into this glare each of them turned **simultaneously** to gaze upon the other's face.

The man from the West stopped suddenly and released his arm.

"You're not Jimmy Wells," he snapped. "Twenty years is a long time, but not long enough to change a man's nose from a Roman to a pug."[5]

"It sometimes changes a good man into a bad one," said the tall man. "You've been under arrest for ten minutes, 'Silky' Bob. Chicago thinks you may have dropped over our way and wires us she wants to have a chat with you. Going quietly, are you? That's sensible. Now, before we go to the station here's a note I was asked to hand to you. You may read it here at the window. It's from Patrolman Wells."

The man from the West unfolded the little piece of paper handed him. His hand was steady when he began to read, but it trembled a little by the time he had finished. The note was rather short.

*Bob,*
*I was at the appointed place on time.*
*When you struck the match to light your*
*cigar I saw it was the face of the man*
*wanted in Chicago. Somehow I couldn't*
*do it myself, so I went around and got a*
*plain clothes man to do the job.*
*Jimmy.*

5. **change a man's nose from a Roman to a pug** A Roman nose has a high, prominent bridge, but a pug nose is short, thick, and turned up at the end.

## ABOUT THE AUTHOR

### O. Henry (1862–1910)

O. Henry is the pen name of William Sydney Porter. He is known for his warm, witty short stories featuring ordinary people. Born and raised in Greensboro, North Carolina, Porter moved to Texas at the age of 20. While he was working at a bank, a discrepancy was found with the accounts and Porter was accused of stealing bank funds. He was tried, found guilty, and sentenced to prison. While in prison, Porter began to write short stories. Upon his release, he moved to New York City and started a career as a writer. He used the name O. Henry to hide the fact that he had been in prison. Many of his 300 stories are inspired by his time in prison, where he gained an understanding of people on both sides of the law.

# Close Reading Activities

## READ

### Comprehension

Reread all or part of the text to help you answer the following questions.

1. For whom is the man in the doorway waiting?
2. Why has it been so long since the two men have seen each other?
3. Who finally comes to meet Bob?

**Research: Clarify Details** Choose an unfamiliar detail from the story and briefly research it. Explain how your research helps you understand the story.

**Summarize** Write an objective summary of the story. Remember to omit your opinions and evaluations.

### Language Study

**Selection Vocabulary** Define each boldfaced word from the story, and then write a paragraph that includes all three words.

- … for **spectators** were few.
- … twirling his club with many **intricate** and artful movements…
- … each of them turned **simultaneously** …

### Literary Analysis

Reread the identified passage. Then, respond to the following questions.

**Focus Passage** *(p. 426)*

The policeman on the beat … that had long since been closed.

#### Key Ideas and Details

1. Why is the street deserted?
2. **(a) Infer:** Does this story more likely take place in the country or the city? **(b) Support:** What details support your answer?

#### Craft and Structure

3. **(a) Evaluate:** Cite details that convey a clear picture of the policeman. **(b) Interpret:** Based on the text, describe the policeman in your own words.

#### Integration of Knowledge and Ideas

4. **(a) Analyze:** How does the author use details about the setting to **communicate** a mood? **(b) Draw Conclusions:** What impact does this mood have on the reader's expectations for the rest of the story?

### Irony

**Irony** is a literary element that involves a **contradiction** or contrast. In *situational irony,* something takes place that is the opposite of what you expect to happen. Take notes on O. Henry's use of irony in this story.

1. **(a)** Is Bob's description of Jimmy as "the truest, stanchest old chap in the world" accurate? **(b)** What makes the description ironic?
2. **(a)** In what way is the story's ending ironic? **(b)** If Jimmy had let Bob go free, would the story's ending still create irony? Explain.

# DISCUSS • RESEARCH • WRITE

## From Text to Topic **Group Discussion**

Discuss Jimmy's note with a group of classmates. **Contribute** your own ideas, and support them with examples from the text.

> Bob,
> I was at the appointed place on time. When you struck the match to light your cigar I saw it was the face of the man wanted in Chicago. Somehow I couldn't do it myself, so I went around and got a plain clothes man to do the job.
> Jimmy

### QUESTIONS FOR DISCUSSION

1. Was it right for Jimmy to send someone else to arrest Bob? Explain.
2. Should Jimmy have turned Bob in? Why or why not?

## Research **Investigate the Topic**

**Police Heroes** Although Jimmy did not face obvious danger in this story, police officers often do encounter situations that require courage and, sometimes, heroism.

**Assignment**

Conduct research to learn about one or more police officers who have been heroes. Consult electronic news sources as well as books and magazines. Take clear notes and carefully identify your sources so that you can easily access the information later. Share your findings about one of the heroes in a **group discussion** with the class.

### PREPARATION FOR ESSAY

You may use the results of your research to support your ideas in the essay you will write at the end of this section.

## Writing to Sources: **Narrative**

O. Henry's story ends with a surprising and ironic twist. But until the very end, the story could have gone in another direction.

**Assignment**

Develop a **fictional narrative** by writing a different ending to "After Twenty Years." Keep the first part of O. Henry's story, but then cut away to your own narrative before Bob meets the plainclothes policeman. Follow these instructions:

- Refer to the text to make sure that your characters' new actions are consistent with what has already happened.
- Address the concept of "heroes and outlaws" in your narrative.
- Make sure your story has a conflict and a climax in the plot.
- Use realistic dialogue and detailed descriptions.

### ACADEMIC VOCABULARY

Academic terms appear in blue on these pages. If these words are not familiar to you, use a dictionary to find their definitions. Then, use the words as you speak and write about the text.

# Harriet Tubman

*Africans in America: America's Journey Through Slavery* PBS

Harriet Tubman is perhaps the most well-known of all the Underground Railroad's "conductors." During a ten-year span she made 19 trips into the South and escorted over 300 slaves to freedom. And, as she once proudly pointed out to Frederick Douglass, in all of her journeys she "never lost a single passenger."

Tubman was born a slave in Maryland's Dorchester County around 1820. At age five or six, she began to work as a house servant. Seven years later she was sent to work in the fields. While she was still in her early teens, she suffered an injury that would follow her for the rest of her life. Always ready to stand up for someone else, Tubman blocked a doorway to protect another field hand from an angry overseer.[1] The overseer picked up and threw a two-pound weight at the field hand. It fell short, striking Tubman on the head. She never fully recovered from the blow, which **subjected** her to spells in which she would fall into a deep sleep.

Around 1844 she married a free black named John Tubman and took his last name. (She was born Araminta Ross; she later changed her first name to Harriet, after her mother.) In 1849, in fear that she, along with other slaves on the plantation, was to be sold, Tubman resolved to run away. She set out one night on foot. With some assistance from a friendly white woman, Tubman was on her way. She followed the North Star by night, making her way to Pennsylvania and soon after to Philadelphia, where she found work and saved her money. The following year she returned to Maryland and escorted her sister and her sister's

1. **overseer** (ō´vər sē´ər) *n.* person hired by a landowner to run a plantation and supervise slaves.

two children to freedom. She made the dangerous trip back to the South soon after to rescue her brother and two other men. On her third return, she went after her husband, only to find he had taken another wife. Undeterred, she found other slaves seeking freedom and escorted them to the North.

Tubman returned to the South again and again. She devised clever techniques that helped make her "forays" successful, including using the master's horse and buggy for the first leg of the journey; leaving on a Saturday night, since runaway notices couldn't be placed in newspapers until Monday morning; turning about and heading south if she encountered possible slave hunters; and carrying a drug to use on a baby if its crying might put the fugitives in danger. Tubman even carried a gun which she used to threaten the fugitives if they became too tired or decided to turn back, telling them, "You'll be free or die."

By 1856, Tubman's capture would have brought a $40,000 reward from the South. On one occasion, she overheard some men reading her wanted poster, which stated that she was illiterate. She promptly pulled out a book and **feigned** reading it. The ploy was enough to fool the men.

Tubman had made the perilous trip to slave country 19 times by 1860, including one especially challenging journey in which she rescued her 70-year-old parents. Of the famed heroine, who became known as "Moses," Frederick Douglass said, "Excepting John Brown—of sacred memory—I know of no one who has willingly encountered more perils and hardships to serve our enslaved people than [Harriet Tubman]."

And John Brown, who **conferred** with "General Tubman" about his plans to raid Harpers Ferry, once said that she was "one of the bravest persons on this continent."

Becoming friends with the leading abolitionists of the day, Tubman took part in antislavery meetings. On the way to such a meeting in Boston in 1860, in an incident in Troy, New York, she helped a fugitive slave who had been captured.

During the Civil War Harriet Tubman worked for the Union as a cook, a nurse, and even a spy. After the war she settled in Auburn, New York, where she would spend the rest of her long life. She died in 1913.

◀ **feigned** (fānd) *v.* pretended or imitated

◀ **subjected** (səb jekt′ id) *v.* caused one to experience

◀ **conferred** (kən fʉrd′) *v.* met to discuss

# Close Reading Activities

## READ

### Comprehension

Reread all or part of the text to help you answer the following questions.

1. For what is Harriet Tubman famous?
2. How was Tubman injured as a teen?
3. What "techniques" did Tubman use to make successful journeys?

**Research: Clarify Details** Choose an unfamiliar detail from the article and research it. Explain how your research helps you understand the article.

**Summarize** Write an objective summary of the article. Do not include opinions.

### Language Study

**Selection Vocabulary** Define each boldfaced word from the article, and use it in a sentence of your own. What part of speech do all the words share?

- She never fully recovered from the blow, which **subjected** her to spells …
- She promptly pulled out a book and **feigned** reading it.
- And John Brown, who **conferred** with "General Tubman" about his plans to raid Harper's Ferry …

### Literary Analysis

Reread the identified passage. Then, answer the following questions.

**Focus Passage** *(pp. 432–433)*
Around 1844 … escorted them to the North.

**Key Ideas and Details**

1. Why did Tubman first decide to run away?
2. What did Tubman do before she attempted to help her sister escape to freedom?

**Craft and Structure**

3. **(a)** What organizational pattern does the author use in this paragraph? **(b)** What words and phrases establish this pattern? **(c) Evaluate:** Why is this organizational pattern appropriate for the subject?

**Integration of Knowledge and Ideas**

4. **(a) Interpret:** What point does the author make in describing Tubman as "undeterred"? **(b) Support:** What details in the passage support the idea that Tubman was often "undeterred"?

### Author's Viewpoint

An **author's viewpoint** includes the author's attitudes, opinions, and feelings toward a subject. Viewpoint is revealed through word choice and tone. Take notes on how the author's viewpoint is expressed in this article.

1. **Heroes and Outlaws (a)** Does the author portray Harriet Tubman as an outlaw or a hero? **(b)** What details in the text support this viewpoint?
2. Why does the author include quotations from Frederick Douglass and John Brown?

# DISCUSS • RESEARCH • WRITE

## From Text to Topic **Group Discussion**

Discuss the following passage with a group of classmates. Take notes during the discussion. Contribute your own ideas, and support them with examples from the text.

> Tubman even carried a gun which she used to threaten the fugitives if they became too tired or decided to turn back, telling them, "You'll be free or die."

### QUESTIONS FOR DISCUSSION

1. What does Tubman's threat tell you about the way she viewed her mission?
2. Was Tubman an outlaw, a hero, or both? Explain.

## Research **Investigate the Topic**

**The Underground Railroad** Harriet Tubman was a "conductor" on the Underground Railroad, a network of safe houses and routes that slaves used to escape to free northern states and Canada.

**Assignment**

Conduct research to find out more about the heroes and outlaws who helped slaves escape to freedom on the Underground Railroad. Consult books and articles on the topic, and search the Internet to find information. Take clear notes and identify your sources. Create or find illustrative charts and graphics, and use them in an **informal media presentation** for the class.

### PREPARATION FOR ESSAY

You may use the results of your research to support your ideas in the essay you will write at the end of this section.

## Writing to Sources **Narrative**

This article describes some of the steps Tubman and her "passengers" had to take in order to escape to freedom.

**Assignment**

As one of Tubman's "passengers," write a **fictional narrative** in the form of several diary entries. Writing from the perspective of a runaway slave, describe the problems you encounter and explain how you **solve** them by using some of Tubman's techniques that are described in the article. Follow these steps:

- Use diary format and style. Write from the first-person perspective, using the pronouns *I, me,* and *mine*.
- Include two or three entries in your diary.
- In each entry, use vivid details to describe the events of the day, what Tubman said and did, and your **reactions** to your experiences.

### ACADEMIC VOCABULARY

Academic terms appear in blue on these pages. If these words are not familiar to you, use a dictionary to find their definitions. Then, use the words as you speak and write about the text.

# WANTED

**Harriet Tubman, Abolitionist**

She is a "Conductor" of the underground RailRoad that leads slave up north and away from our plantations causing a shortage in laborers. She threatens to shoot her passangers who want to make the right discion and turn back. She had never allowed on of our slaves to escape her grasp. This illiterate woman attends the insolent antislave meetings. The sooner she is turned in, the better it is for all us Southerners.

Tubman was born a slave in Maryland's Dorchester County and worked as a house servent around age five. About seven years later, she was sent to work in the fields. In her early teen years, she quite problematic for the overseers, constantly getting in the was of their slaves disapline. Later, she ran away from the plantation, then procceeded to set other slaves free too.

# $40,000

# REWARD

## READ • RESEARCH • WRITE

### Comprehension

Review the poster to help you answer the following questions.

1. Who might have produced and displayed this poster? Cite details to support your answer.
2. According to the poster, what damage was Tubman causing?

### Critical Analysis

#### Key Ideas and Details

1. **Analyze:** What was the author's purpose for creating this poster?

#### Craft and Structure

2. **Generalize:** Based on the grammar and language of the poster, is it surprising that Tubman is referred to as "illiterate"? Explain.
3. **Analyze:** How does the poster appeal to the viewer's desire to belong to a group? Cite an example from the poster.

#### Integration of Knowledge and Ideas

4. **(a) Evaluate:** How important was Tubman's capture to the people who would have displayed this poster? **(b) Support:** What details support your answer?

**ACADEMIC VOCABULARY**

Academic terms appear in blue on these pages. If these words are not familiar to you, use a dictionary to find their definitions. Then, use the words as you speak and write about the text.

### Research **Investigate the Topic**

**Abolitionist Leader** Conduct research to find out about another hero of the American abolitionist movement during the 1800s. Note the qualities that made the person both a hero and an outlaw. Share your findings in an **informal presentation** for the class.

### Writing to Sources **Explanatory Text**

Review the Web article about Harriet Tubman on pages 432–433. Then, write a **comparison-and-contrast essay** in which you examine the similarities and differences in the ways in which Tubman is portrayed in the article and in the wanted poster. Analyze the use of visual images and word choice as well as the impact of the information each author chose to include. Follow these steps:

- Organize your essay to show comparisons and contrasts.
- Use details from the selections, such as examples of logical reasoning, **facts**, and moral claims, to support your ideas.
- **Conclude** by evaluating which medium's portrayal is more **convincing**.

# Assessment: Synthesis

## Speaking and Listening: Group Discussion

**Heroes and Outlaws** The texts in this section vary in genre, length, style, and perspective. However, all of the texts address, in some way, our fascination with heroes and outlaws. The ways in which we define both heroes and outlaws are related to the Big Question addressed in this unit: **What is the best way to communicate?**

▲ Refer to the selections you read in Part 3 as you complete the activities on this assessment.

### Assignment

**Conduct discussions.** With a small group of classmates, conduct a discussion on how we communicate our ideas about heroes and outlaws. Refer to the texts in this section, other texts you have read, and your personal experience and knowledge to support your ideas. Begin your discussion by addressing the following questions:

- What defines a "hero"? Is everyone's definition the same? Why or why not?
- Why are certain individuals seen as heroes to some people and outlaws to others?
- Do heroes and outlaws create themselves, or do we create them through the ideas we communicate about them?

**Summarize and present your ideas.** After you have fully explored the topic, summarize your discussion and present your findings to the class as a whole.

## Criteria for Success

✓ **Organizes the group effectively**
Appoint a group leader and a timekeeper. The group leader should present the discussion questions. The timekeeper should make sure the discussion takes no longer than 20 minutes.

✓ **Maintains focus of discussion**
As a group, stay on topic and avoid straying into other subject areas.

✓ **Involves all participants equally and fully**
No one person should monopolize the conversation. Rather, everyone should take turns speaking and contributing ideas.

✓ **Follows the rules for collegial discussion**
As each group member speaks, others should listen carefully. Build on one another's ideas and support viewpoints and opinions with sound reasoning and evidence. Express disagreement respectfully.

**USE NEW VOCABULARY**

As you speak and share ideas, work to use the vocabulary words you have learned in this unit. The more you use new words, the more you will "own" them.

## Writing: **Narrative**

**Heroes and Outlaws** Heroes and outlaws have been the subjects of popular stories for thousands of years. Sometimes, the same person may be a hero in some stories and an outlaw (or villain) in others. The difference may be simply a matter of communication: how the character is described and how the events are presented.

> **Assignment**
> Write a **fictional narrative** about a hero, an outlaw, or a combination of the two in which communication plays a role in introducing or resolving a conflict. The "outlaw" in your story can be someone who actually breaks the law, or someone who simply breaks rules. Use the knowledge and insights you gained in this section to help you compose your story.

### Criteria for Success

#### Purpose/Focus

✓ **Connects specific incidents with larger ideas**
Make clear connections between your characters and plot and the texts you have read in this section.

✓ **Clearly conveys the significance of the story**
Provide a conclusion in which the conflict is resolved, either positively or negatively, in a satisfying and logical manner.

#### Organization

✓ **Sequences events logically**
Structure your narrative so that individual events build on one another to create a coherent whole.

#### Development of Ideas/Elaboration

✓ **Supports insights**
Include examples and details that draw from the texts you have read in this section.

✓ **Uses narrative techniques effectively**
Use narrative techniques, such as flashback and foreshadowing, to build interest and suspense.

#### Language

✓ **Uses description effectively**
Use descriptive details to paint word pictures that help readers see settings and characters.

#### Conventions

✓ **Does not have errors**
Check your narrative to eliminate errors in grammar, spelling, and punctuation.

**WRITE TO EXPLORE**

Writing is a way to explore what you feel and think: This means that you may change your mind or get new ideas as you work. As you write your fictional narrative, explore your ideas on the role communication plays in depicting heroes and outlaws.

## Writing to Sources: **Explanatory Text**

**Heroes and Outlaws** The authors in this section communicate their ideas about what makes a hero and what makes an outlaw in many different ways. They raise questions, such as the following:

- Are people who follow a law always right? Are people who break a law always wrong?
- How does the way we communicate through literature and other media affect our own and others' perceptions of heroes and outlaws?
- Can a person be both a hero and an outlaw?

Focus on the question that intrigues you the most, and then complete the following assignment.

**Assignment**

Write an **explanatory essay** in which you compare and contrast the ways in which two or more of the selections portray heroes and outlaws. As you analyze each selection, pay particular attention to the ways in which the author's attitude toward the subject influences his or her portrayal of a hero or an outlaw. Clearly present, develop, and support your ideas with examples and details from the texts.

**INCORPORATE RESEARCH**

In your essay, use the information you gathered as you completed the brief research assignments related to the selections in this section.

### Prewriting and Planning

**Choose texts.** Review the texts in this section to determine the ones you will cite in your essay. Select at least two that will provide strong material to support your main idea.

**Gather details and identify key ideas.** Use a chart like the one shown to develop your key ideas.

**Focus Question: How does the way we communicate in literature and other media affect our perception of heroes and outlaws?**

| Text | Passage | Notes |
|---|---|---|
| The Highwayman | They had tied her up to attention, with many a sniggering jest. They had bound a musket beside her, with the muzzle beneath her breast! | The author portrays the legal authorities (King George's soldiers) as cruel and evil—moral outlaws. |
| Harriet Tubman | She devised clever techniques that helped make her "forays" successful, including using the master's horse and buggy for the first leg of the journey; | The author implies that, though Tubman broke laws, she was a hero because she protected a basic human right. |
| **Example Key Idea:** An author may apply moral standards rather than legal standards in defining and portraying heroes and outlaws. | | |

**Organize your details.** Gather the descriptions, examples, and quotations you will use to make comparisons and contrasts. Organize your details in a Venn diagram or two-column chart. Make sure you have details that support all of your main points.

## Drafting

**Follow an appropriate organizational pattern.** To show comparisons and contrasts among two or more selections, you may decide to use the block method of organization. In this organization, present all the details about one selection first, then all the details about the second selection, and so on.

**Plan your introduction.** Begin your essay with a strong introductory paragraph that does the following:

- presents the selections you are comparing and contrasting
- identifies the features of heroes and outlaws that you will discuss
- states a main idea about your subjects

## Revising and Editing

**Review supporting details.** Underline the key ideas in your essay. Confirm that each one is supported with details from the texts in this section or from your research. Add additional support if necessary.

**Check subject-verb agreement.** Circle the verbs in your essay. Make sure that sentences with singular subjects have singular verbs, and sentences with plural subjects have plural verbs.

### CITE RESEARCH CORRECTLY

Avoid plagiarism by properly crediting the ideas of others. Refer to the Citing Sources pages in the Introductory Unit for information on citing sources.

### Self-Evaluation Rubric

Use the following criteria to evaluate the effectiveness of your essay.

| Criteria | Rating Scale |
|---|---|
| **Purpose/Focus** Clearly analyzes the similarities and differences between two or more related subjects | *not very ... very*<br>1 2 3 4 |
| **Organization** Provides a clear organization that highlights the major points of comparison; uses appropriate transitions to create cohesion and clarify relationships among ideas; provides a strong introduction | 1 2 3 4 |
| **Development of Ideas/Elaboration** Develops the topic with concrete details that illustrate both similarities and differences between the subjects; provides relevant facts, definitions, quotations, and examples | 1 2 3 4 |
| **Language** Uses precise language and domain-specific vocabulary to compare and contrast a topic or topics | 1 2 3 4 |
| **Conventions** Uses proper grammar, including correct subject-verb agreement | 1 2 3 4 |

# Independent Reading

## Titles for Extended Reading

In this unit, you have read texts in a wide variety of genres. Continue to read on your own. Select works that you enjoy, but challenge yourself to explore new authors and works of increasing depth and complexity. The titles suggested below will help you get started.

### INFORMATIONAL TEXT

**Discoveries: Pushing the Boundaries**

In this book, you can read about many different ways to communicate. The **nonfiction articles** in this collection include "The Samurai of Feudal Japan" and "Challenging Assumptions."

**This Land Was Made for You and Me: The Life and Songs of Woody Guthrie**
by Elizabeth Partridge

EXEMPLAR TEXT

During the Great Depression of the 1930s, folk singer Woody Guthrie wandered the nation, meeting everyday people and writing songs. This **biography** of Guthrie includes photographs, posters, letters, and drawings.

**Vincent van Gogh: Portrait of an Artist**
by Jan Greenberg and Sandra Jordan

EXEMPLAR TEXT

The painter Vincent van Gogh surprised the art world of the late nineteenth century with his broad brushstrokes, vivid colors, and dreamlike landscapes. Meet Van Gogh in this exciting **biography**.

### LITERATURE

**It Doesn't Always Have to Rhyme**
by Eve Merriam

This **poetry** collection is full of playful poems about poetry, including "How to Eat a Poem," "Metaphor," and "Onomatopoeia."

**The Poetry of Robert Frost: The Collected Poems**
by Robert Frost

EXEMPLAR TEXT

In his poetry, Robert Frost can capture a single thought or moment in a way that is personal but also universal. This **poetry** collection includes many of Frost's most popular poems.

**When I Dance**
by James Berry

James Berry was born in Jamaica but moved to England as a young man. Many of the poems in this **poetry** collection pulse with the rhythms of life in the Caribbean.

**The Music of Dolphins**
by Karen Hesse

After a plane crash, the main character in this exciting **novel** is raised by dolphins until the Coast Guard finds her. Mila "the Dolphin Girl" learns to speak, but she longs to return to the sea.

**ONLINE TEXT SET**

AUTOBIOGRAPHY
***from* Angela's Ashes** Frank McCourt

SHORT STORY
**Seventh Grade** Gary Soto

WEB SITE
**Safe Routes to School**

## Preparing to Read Complex Texts

**Attentive Reading** As you read on your own, ask yourself questions like these to enrich your reading experience.

**When reading poetry, ask yourself…**

### Comprehension: **Key Ideas and Details**

- Who is the speaker of the poem? What kind of person does the speaker seem to be? How do I know?
- What is the poem about?
- If the poem is telling a story, who are the characters and what happens to them?
- Does any one line or section state the poem's theme, or meaning, directly? If so, what is that line or section?
- If there is no direct statement of a theme, what details help me to see the poem's deeper meaning?

### Text Analysis: **Craft and Structure**

- How does the poem look on the page? Is it long and rambling or short and concise? Does it have long or short lines?
- Does the poem have a formal structure or is it free verse?
- Do I notice repetition, rhyme, or meter? Do I notice other sound devices? How do these techniques affect how I read the poem?
- Even if I do not understand every word, do I like the way the poem sounds? Why or why not?
- Do any of the poet's word choices seem especially interesting or unusual? Why?
- What images do I notice? Do they create clear word-pictures in my mind? Why or why not?

### Connections: **Integration of Knowledge and Ideas**

- Has the poem helped me understand its subject in a new way? If so, how?
- Does the poem remind me of others I have read? If so, how?
- In what ways is the poem different from others I have read?
- What information, ideas, or insights have I gained from reading this poem?
- Would I like to read more poems by this poet? Why or why not?

# UNIT 4

# Do others see us more clearly than we see ourselves?

## UNIT PATHWAY

**PART 1**
**SETTING EXPECTATIONS**

- INTRODUCING THE BIG QUESTION
- CLOSE READING WORKSHOP

**PART 2**
**TEXT ANALYSIS**
GUIDED EXPLORATION

DRAMATIC TRANSFORMATIONS

**PART 3**
**TEXT SET**
DEVELOPING INSIGHT

LEADERS AND FOLLOWERS

**PART 4**
**DEMONSTRATING INDEPENDENCE**

- INDEPENDENT READING
- ONLINE TEXT SET

## CLOSE READING TOOL

Use this tool to practice the close reading strategies you learn.

## STUDENT eTEXT

Bring learning to life with audio, video, and interactive tools.

## ONLINE WRITER'S NOTEBOOK

Easily capture notes and complete assignments online.

Find all Digital Resources at **pearsonrealize.com.**

# Introducing the Big Question

## Do others see us more clearly than we see ourselves?

We are constantly learning about ourselves through our experiences and our interactions with others. Sometimes we feel that another person truly knows and understands us. Other times, however, we might suspect that someone is making an assumption about us based on appearance or other factors. To see ourselves and others clearly, it helps to reflect on the unique characteristics of each person. Our individual qualities and beliefs about ourselves influence how others see us and how we react to the people around us.

## Exploring the Big Question

**Collaboration: Group Discussion** Start thinking about the Big Question by making a list of the ways you form impressions about other people and the ways that other people form impressions about you. Describe one specific example of each of the following:

- An impression based on appearance
- An impression influenced by prejudice, or bias
- An insight about the way another person treats you or others
- A time another person seemed to understand your thoughts
- A perception based on another person's reaction to a difficult situation

Share your examples with a small group. Discuss whether or not each situation helped someone see another person more clearly. As you conduct your discussion, use the words related to self-perception listed on the next page.

**Connecting to the Literature** Each reading in this unit will give you additional insight into the Big Question.

## Vocabulary

**Acquire and Use Academic Vocabulary** The term "academic vocabulary" refers to words you typically encounter in scholarly and literary texts and in technical and business writing. Review the definitions of these academic vocabulary words.

**appreciate** (ə prē´ shē āt´) *v.* be thankful for

**assumption** (ə sump´ shən) *n.* act of accepting something as true without proof

**bias** (bī´ əs) *n.* slanted or prejudiced viewpoint

**characteristic** (kar´ ək tər is´ tik) *n.* trait; feature

**define** (dē fīn´) *v.* describe; explain

**focus** (fō´ kəs) *n.* direction; point of concentration

**identify** (ī den´ tə fī´) *v.* recognize; point out

**ignore** (ig nôr´) *v.* pay no attention to

**Gather Vocabulary Knowledge** Additional words related to self-perception are listed below. Categorize the words by deciding whether you know each one well, know it a little bit, or do not know it at all.

**appearance**
**image**
**perception**
**perspective**
**reaction**
**reflect**
**reveal**

Then, do the following:

1. Work with a partner to determine and write each word's definition.
2. Verify definitions by looking them up in a print or online dictionary and revising as needed.
3. Then, for each word, write an original sentence about how we see ourselves and others. Provide enough information so the meaning of each word is clear.
4. Exchange sentences with your partner to see if he or she agrees with your main points and your use of the vocabulary words.

# Close Reading Workshop

In this workshop, you will learn an approach to reading that will deepen your understanding of literature and will help you better appreciate the author's craft. The workshop includes models for close reading, discussion, research, and writing. After you have reviewed the strategies and models, practice your skills with the Independent Practice selection.

## CLOSE READING: **DRAMA**

In Part 2 of this unit you will focus on reading excerpts from various dramas. Use these strategies as you read the texts.

### Comprehension: **Key Ideas and Details**

- Read first to unlock basic meaning.
- Use context clues to help you determine the meanings of unfamiliar words.
- Identify unfamiliar details that you might need to clarify through research.

**Ask yourself questions such as these:**

- Who are the main characters?
- When and where does the action take place?
- What conflicts do the characters face?

### Text Analysis: **Craft and Structure**

- Think about the genre of the work and how the author presents ideas.
- Consider how stage directions can convey information about characters, sound effects, lighting, and props.
- Analyze how dialogue is used to reveal characters' personalities and emotions.

**Ask yourself questions such as these:**

- How does the author reveal information about characters and their conflicts?
- How do characters' actions advance the plot?
- How do stage directions help bring the drama to life?

### Connections: **Integration of Knowledge and Ideas**

- Look for relationships among key ideas.
- Analyze how the author develops characters. Then, synthesize details about the characters to determine theme.
- Compare and contrast this work with similar works you have read.

**Ask yourself questions such as these:**

- How has this work broadened my knowledge of drama?
- How do elements work together to help the reader "see" the drama?
- Would I recommend this work to others? Why or why not?

## Read

As you read this excerpt from a drama, take note of the annotations that model ways to closely read the text.

### Reading Model

#### from *Sorry, Wrong Number* by Lucille Fletcher

[SCENE: *As curtain rises, we see a divided stage, only the center part of which is lighted and furnished as* Mrs. Stevenson's *bedroom. Expensive, rather fussy furnishings.*[1] *A large bed, on which* Mrs. Stevenson, *clad in bed-jacket, is lying. A night-table close by, with phone, lighted lamp, and pill bottles. A mantle, with clock, R. A closed door, R. A window, with curtains closed, rear. The set is lit by one lamp on night-table. It is enclosed by three flats. Beyond this central set, the stage, on either side, is in darkness.*[1]

Mrs. Stevenson *is dialing a number on the phone, as curtain rises. She listens to phone, slams down receiver in irritation.*[2]

*As she does so, we hear sound of a train roaring by in the distance. She reaches for her pill bottle, pours herself a glass of water, shakes out pill, swallows it, then reaches for the phone again, dials number nervously.*][2]

**Sound**: *Number being dialed on phone: Busy signal.*

**Mrs. Stevenson** *(A querulous, self-centered neurotic.)*[2] : Oh—dear! *(Slams down receiver, dials* **Operator**.*)*

[SCENE: *A spotlight, L. of side flat, picks up out of peripheral darkness, figure of* **1st Operator**, *sitting with headphones at a small table. If spotlight not available, use flashlight, clicked on by* **1st Operator**, *illuminating her face.*][3]

**Operator:** Your call, please?

**Mrs. Stevenson:** Operator? I've been dialing Murray Hill 4-0098 now for the last three-quarters of an hour, and the line is always busy. But I don't see how it could be that busy that long. Will you try it for me, please?

**Operator:** Murray Hill 4-0098? One moment, please. [SCENE: *She makes gesture of plugging in call through a switchboard.*]

**Mrs. Stevenson:** I don't see how it could be busy all this time. It's my husband's office. He's working late tonight, and I'm all alone here in the house. My health is very poor—and I've been feeling so nervous all day. . . .[4]

**Operator:** Ringing Murray Hill 4-0098. ... (SOUND: *Phone buzz. It rings three times. Receiver is picked up at other end.)*

**Craft and Structure**

**1** Stage directions give details that help create the mood. The description of a "fussy" bedroom surrounded by darkness conveys an unsettling feeling.

**Key Ideas and Details**

**2** You might consult a dictionary to learn that *querulous* means "complaining" and a *neurotic* is an anxious person. If you combine these details with the other character traits described, you may conclude that Mrs. Stevenson is easily upset.

**Craft and Structure**

**3** In this stage direction, the playwright gives specific instructions for lighting the scene in order to create the desired atmosphere.

**Integration of Knowledge and Ideas**

**4** Mrs. Stevenson's dialogue reveals an internal conflict. She is uneasy because she is sick, alone, and cannot reach her husband.

[SCENE: *Spotlight picks up figure of a heavyset man, seated at desk with phone on right side of dark periphery of stage. He is wearing a hat. Picks up phone, which rings three times.*][5]

**MAN:** Hello.

**MRS. STEVENSON:** Hello ...? *(A little puzzled)* Hello. Is Mr. Stevenson there?

**MAN**: *(into phone, as though he had not heard.)* Hello. ... *(Louder)* Hello.

[SCENE: *Spotlight on left now moves from* **OPERATOR** *to another man,* **GEORGE**. *A killer type,*[6] *also wearing a hat, but standing as in a phone booth. A three-sided screen may be used to suggest this.*]

**2ND MAN:** *(slow, heavy quality, faintly foreign accent).* Hello.

**1ST MAN:** Hello, George?

**GEORGE:** Yes, sir.

MRS. STEVENSON: *(louder and more imperious, to phone).* Hello. Who's this? What number am I calling, please?[7]

**1ST MAN:** We have heard from our client. He says the coast is clear for tonight.

**GEORGE:** Yes, sir.

**1ST MAN:** Where are you now?

**GEORGE:** In a phone booth.

**1ST MAN:** OK. You should know the address. At eleven o'clock the private patrolman goes around to the bar on Second Avenue for a beer. Be sure that all the lights downstairs are out. There should be only one light visible from the street. At eleven-fifteen a subway train crosses the bridge. It makes a noise in case her window is open and she should scream.

**MRS. STEVENSON:** *(shocked).* Oh—HELLO! What number is this, please?

**GEORGE:** OK. I understand.

**1ST MAN:** Make it quick. As little blood as possible. Our client does not wish to make her suffer long.

**GEORGE:** A knife OK, sir?

**1ST MAN:** Yes. A knife will be OK. And remember—remove the rings and bracelets and the jewelry in the bureau drawer. Our client wishes it to look like simple robbery.[8]

**GEORGE:** OK—I get—[SCENE: *Spotlight suddenly goes out on* **GEORGE**.]

*(SOUND: A bland buzzing signal)*

**Craft and Structure**

**5** These stage directions indicate a scene change. They describe the new setting and introduce a new character.

**Key Ideas and Details**

**6** The playwright includes this detail to communicate that George is a threatening character. Stage directions like this can help a director choose the right actor for the role.

**Integration of Knowledge and Ideas**

**7** Mrs. Stevenson can hear the two men, but they cannot hear her. This situation emphasizes her isolation and develops the theme.

**Craft and Structure**

**8** This dialogue builds tension and suspense, and moves the action forward.

## Discuss

Sharing your own ideas and listening to the ideas of others can deepen your understanding of a text and help you look at a topic in a whole new way. As you participate in collaborative discussions, work to have a genuine exchange in which classmates build upon one another's ideas. Support your points with evidence and ask meaningful questions.

### Discussion Model

**Student 1:** The playwright includes a lot of information about Mrs. Stevenson in stage directions. Stage directions describe her "expensive, rather fussy" bedroom. They also describe Mrs. Stevenson's slamming down the receiver and picking it up again, which shows she feels frustrated.

**Student 2:** We also learn about Mrs. Stevenson through dialogue. She tells the operator that she's been trying to reach her husband, and that she's alone, sick, and nervous. When she overhears the dialogue between the men, we see her confusion and anxiety build—she keeps asking what number she is calling.

**Student 3:** What I noticed is that the dialogue clearly shows that this scene takes place decades ago. Mrs. Stevenson is calling "Murray Hill 4-0098." What does *Murray Hill* mean in a phone number?

## Research

Targeted research can clarify unfamiliar details and shed light on various aspects of a text. Consider questions that arise in your mind as you read, and use those questions as the basis for research.

### Research Model

**Questions:** *What does* Murray Hill *mean in a phone number? Where would someone with this phone number be located?*

**Key Words for Internet Search:** "Murray Hill" + name + telephone

**Result:** New York City telephone exchanges after December 1930.

**What I Learned:** Numbers that include names such as *Murray Hill* came into usage during the 1930s and '40s. Each name was a separate telephone exchange, and Murray Hill covered part of Manhattan in New York City.

## Write

The following model essay evaluates Lucille Fletcher's use of stage directions and dialogue to reveal important details.

### Writing Model: Argument

### Stage Directions and Dialogue in *Sorry, Wrong Number*

If a play does not have a narrator to provide important details about characters and story events, the playwright must rely on stage directions and dialogue to convey information to readers. In this scene from *Sorry, Wrong Number,* Lucille Fletcher skillfully uses detailed stage directions and dialogue to reveal the main character's personality and move the action forward.

In the first paragraph, the writer introduces the main argument by providing a strong thesis statement.

Fletcher's stage directions are a major source of crucial details. As the scene opens, a long stage direction describes the setting: Mrs. Stevenson's "expensive, rather fussy" bedroom. This description does three important things. First, it suggests that Mrs. Stevenson herself is wealthy and fussy. Second, it helps readers picture the room clearly. Finally, by mentioning the darkness surrounding the room, it conveys a feeling of isolation and unease.

The writer makes a claim and supports it with specific details.

As the scene unfolds, stage directions provide further details about Mrs. Stevenson's personality and her growing internal conflict. The first time Mrs. Stevenson fails to reach her husband by phone, she slams down the receiver. She then takes a pill and dials a second time, nervously. She is described as a "querulous, self-centered neurotic." These details portray a character who is impatient, selfish, and anxious.

The writer draws a conclusion based on specific details provided in the stage directions.

Dialogue is another source of important details in this scene. Mrs. Stevenson tells the operator that she has been trying to reach her husband for almost an hour, and that she is alone, in poor health, and nervous. The dialogue also reveals specific information about the setting. The Murray Hill telephone exchange Mrs. Stevenson asks the operator for once covered a part of Manhattan. This detail reveals that her husband works somewhere in New York City.

By incorporating evidence from research, the writer provides an interesting fact about the setting.

When Mrs. Stevenson overhears two men plotting a murder, she keeps asking what number she is calling. The confusion further develops her mounting anxiety. The men cannot hear her and continue discussing their murder plans. As the tension and suspense build, the action of the play moves forward.

Through her skillful use of stage directions and dialogue, Lucille Fletcher reveals important details enabling readers to picture the scene and experience the building tension and suspense.

The conclusion restates the main idea and provides a strong closing.

As you read the following text, apply the close reading strategies you have learned. You may need to read the drama excerpt multiple times.

# from the novel *Dragonwings*

by Laurence Yep

I do not know when I fell asleep, but it was already way past sunrise when I woke up. The light crept through the cracks in the walls and under the shutters and seemed to delight especially in dancing on my eyes. Father lay huddled, rolled up in his blanket. He did not move when the knock came at our door. I was still in my clothes because it was cold. I crawled out of the blankets and opened the side door.

The fog lay low on the hill. Tendrils drifted in through the open doorway. At first I could not see anything but shadows, and then a sudden breeze whipped the fog away from the front of our barn. Hand Clap stood there as if he had appeared by magic. He bowed.

"There you are." He turned and called over his shoulder. "Hey, everybody, they're here."

I heard the clink of harness and the rattle of an old wagon trying to follow the ruts in the road. Toiling up the hill out of the fog was Red Rabbit, and behind him I saw Uncle on the wagon seat. The rest of the wagon was empty—I suppose to give Red Rabbit less of a load to pull. Behind the wagon came the Company, with coils of ropes over their shoulders and baskets of food. I ran down the hill, my feet pounding against the hard, damp earth. I got up on the seat and almost bowled Uncle over. For once Uncle did not worry about his dignity but caught me up and returned my hug.

## Meet the Author

"Sometimes I think of myself as a professional daydreamer," **Laurence Yep** (b. 1948) once said. His vivid imagination—along with the influences of his Chinese-American background and his interest in mythology and fantasy—have led him to write more than sixty novels, stories, and plays.

**CLOSE READING TOOL**

Read and respond to this selection online using the **Close Reading Tool.**

"Ouch," he said, and pushed me away. He patted himself lightly on his chest. "I'm not as young as I used to be."

Then Hand Clap, Lefty, and White Deer crowded around.

"Am I ever glad you're here," I said. "Poor Father—"

Uncle held up his hands. "We know. That's why we came."

"But how? Why?" I was bursting with a dozen questions all at once.

"Why, to help you get that thing up to the top of the hill," Uncle said. "Why else would we close up our shop and take a boat and climb this abominable hill, all on the coldest, wettest day ever known since creation?"

"But you don't believe in flying machines."

"I still don't," Uncle said sternly. "But I still feel as if I owe you something for what was done to you by that man who once was my son.[1] I'll be there to haul your machine up the hill, and I'll be there to haul it back down when it doesn't fly."

"We were all getting fat anyway," White Deer said, "especially Uncle."

---

1. **man who once was my son** Black Dog, who robbed the narrator and his father.

# from the dramatization of *Dragonwings*

by Laurence Yep

| | |
|---|---|
| **Red Rabbit** a horse that pulls the company's laundry wagon | **Moon Shadow** the narrator of the story |
| **Uncle Bright Star** another laundry owner | **Miss Whitlaw** owner of a stable in San Francisco where the narrator and his father live |
| **White Deer** the third laundry owner | **Windrider** Moon Shadow's father |

**Scene 9** *Piedmont, later that day outside the stable.*

**Moon Shadow:** September twenty-second, Nineteen-ought-nine. Dear Mother. I have bad news. We are going to lose Dragonwings before father can fly it. Black Dog stole all we have, and the landlord will not give us an extension on our rent. So we'll have to move and leave Dragonwings behind. We have asked Miss Whitlaw for help, but her new house has taken up all of her money. And even if Uncle would speak to us, he has probably spent all he has on rebuilding his laundry.

[**Uncle Bright Star** and **Miss Whitlaw** *enter from L.*]

**Miss Whitlaw:** I could have gotten down from the wagon by myself.

**Uncle Bright Star:** Watch gopher hole.

**Miss Whitlaw:** I'm younger than you.

**Moon Shadow:** Uncle, Miss Whitlaw!

**Miss Whitlaw:** How are you?

*[Shaking* **Moon Shadow's** *hand.* **Windrider** *enters from U. He now wears a cap.]*

**Windrider:** Come to laugh, Uncle?

**Uncle Bright Star:** I came to help you fly your contraption.

**Moon Shadow:** But you don't believe in flying machines.

**Uncle Bright Star:** And I'll haul that thing back down when it doesn't fly. Red Rabbit and me were getting fat anyway. But look at how tall you've grown. And how thin. And ragged. *[Pause.]* But you haven't broken your neck which was more than I ever expected.

**Miss Whitlaw:** As soon as I told your uncle, we hatched the plot together. You ought to get a chance to fly your aeroplane.

**Uncle Bright Star:** Flat purse, strong backs.

**Windrider:** We need to pull Dragonwings to the very top.

**Uncle Bright Star:** That hill is a very steep hill.

**Windrider:** It has to be that one. The winds are right.

**Uncle Bright Star:** Ah, well, it's the winds.

**Windrider:** Take the ropes. *[Pantomimes taking a rope over his shoulder as he faces the audience.]* Got a good grip?

**Others:** *[Pantomiming taking the ropes.]* Yes, right, etc.

**Windrider:** Then pull.

*[They strain. **Moon Shadow** stumbles but gets right up. Stamping his feet to get better footing, he keeps tugging.]*

**Moon Shadow:** *[Giving up.]* It's no good.

**Uncle Bright Star:** Pull in rhythm. As we did on the railroad.[1]
*[In demonstration, **Uncle Bright Star** stamps his feet in a slow rhythm to set the beat and the others repeat. The rhythm picks up as they move.]*
Ngúng, ngúng.
Dew gùng

**Others:** Ngúng, ngúng.
Dew gùng

**Uncle Bright Star:** *[Imitating the intonation of the Cantonese.]*
Púsh, púsh.
Wòrk, wòrk.

**Others:** Púsh, púsh.
Wòrk, wòrk.

**Uncle Bright Star:** Seen gà,
Gee gá.

*[High rising tone on the last syllable.]*

**Others:** Seen gà,
Gee gá.

*[High rising tone on the last syllable.]*

---

1. **railroad** Uncle Bright Star had helped dig tunnels through the mountains for the railroad.

**Uncle Bright Star:** Get rìch,
Go hóme.

**Others:** Get rìch,
Go hóme.

*[**Moon Shadow, Windrider, Uncle Bright Star** and **Miss Whitlaw** arrive D.]*

**Moon Shadow:** *[Panting.]* We made it. Tramp the grass down in front.

*[**Windrider** stands C as the others stamp the grass. They can't help smiling and laughing a little.]*

**Windrider:** That's enough.

**Moon Shadow:** [To ***Miss Whitlaw.***] Take that propeller.

*[**Miss Whitlaw** takes her place before the right propeller with her hands resting on the blade. **Moon Shadow** takes his place beside the left propeller. **Windrider** faces U., his back to the audience.]*

**Miss Whitlaw:** Listen to the wind on the wings.

**Uncle Bright Star:** It's alive.

**Windrider:** All right.

[***Moon Shadow*** and ***Miss Whitlaw*** pull down at the propellers and back away quickly. We hear a motor cough into life. Propellers begin to turn with a roar.]

**Uncle Bright Star:** *[Slowly turning.]* What's wrong? Is it just going to roll down the hill?

*[**Miss Whitlaw** crosses her fingers as they all turn to watch the aeroplane.]*

**Miss Whitlaw:** He's up!

*[**Windrider** starts to do his flight ballet.]*

**Moon Shadow:** *[Pointing.]* He's turning.

**Uncle Bright Star:** He's really flying.

**Miss Whitlaw:** I never thought I'd see the day. A human up in the sky. Off the ground.

*[They turn and tilt their heads back.]*

**Miss Whitlaw:** *[Cont'd.]* Free as an eagle.

**Uncle Bright Star:** *[Correcting her.]* Like dragon.

**Moon Shadow:** Father, you did it. *[Wonderingly.]* You did it.

*[The aeroplane roars loudly overhead.* **Moon Shadow** *as adult steps forward and addresses the audience.]*

**Moon Shadow:** I thought he'd fly forever and ever. Up, up to heaven and never come down. But then some of the guy wires[2] broke, and the right wings separated. Dragonwings came crashing to earth. Father had a few broken bones, but it was nothing serious. Only the aeroplane was wrecked. Uncle took him back to the laundry to recover. Father didn't say much, just thought a lot—I figured he was busy designing the next aeroplane. But when Father was nearly well, he made me sit down next to him.

**Windrider:** Uncle says he'll make me a partner if I stay. So the western officials would have to change my immigration class. I'd be a merchant, and merchants can bring their wives here. Would you like to send for Mother?

**Moon Shadow:** *[Going to* **Windrider.***]* But Dragonwings?

**Windrider:** When I was up in the air, I tried to find you. You were so small. And getting smaller. Just disappearing from sight. *[Handing his cap to* **Moon Shadow.***]* Like you were disappearing from my life. *[He begins his ballet again.]* I knew it wasn't the time. The Dragon King[3] said there would be all sorts of lessons.

*[***Moon Shadow** *turns to audience as an adult.]*

**Moon Shadow:** We always talked about flying again. Only we never did. *[Putting on cap.]* But dreams stay with you, and we never forgot.

*[***Windrider** *takes his final pose. A gong sounds.]*

---

2. **guy wires** wires that help to steady the plane's two sets of wings.
3. **Dragon King** In Chinese legends, most dragons are not evil creatures. Earlier in the story, Windrider relates a dream sequence in which he was given his name by the Dragon King and learned he had once been a flying dragon.

# Close Reading Activities

## Read

### Comprehension: **Key Ideas and Details**

1. In the novel excerpt, what reason does Uncle Bright Star give for helping Windrider?
2. **(a)** In the novel excerpt, how does Uncle plan to get the flying machine up the hill? **(b) Compare:** In the scene from the drama, what helps the audience grasp how Dragonwings will be moved?
3. **(a)** What happens to Dragonwings? **(b) Infer:** How is Windrider changed by his flight? **(c) Interpret:** What does Moon Shadow mean when he says, "dreams stay with you, and we never forgot"?
4. **Summarize:** Write a brief, objective summary of Scene 9 from *Dragonwings.* Include important textual details.

### Text Analysis: **Craft and Structure**

5. **(a) Interpret:** Why does the playwright have the characters chant? **(b) Draw Conclusions:** Why do they chant in both Chinese and English?
6. **Analyze:** If *Dragonwings* were a three-act play, in which act do you think you would find the excerpt you read? Explain.
7. **(a) Compare and Contrast:** How is the dialogue in the drama similar to and different from the dialogue in the novel excerpt? **(b) Analyze:** Which version—the novel or the drama—is more effective in helping you picture the action? Why?

### Connections: **Integration of Knowledge and Ideas**

#### Discuss

Conduct a **small-group discussion** about the stage directions in this scene. Find and discuss examples of directions that show action, reveal thoughts and feelings, or describe the setting. Then, answer this question: Are stage directions as useful to readers as they are to actors? Explain your answer.

#### Research

In his final speech, Windrider mentions the Dragon King, a character from Chinese mythology. Briefly research the Dragon King to find out what he looks like and what powers he has. Take notes as you perform your research. Then, write a brief **explanation** of why the Dragon King is important to Windrider.

#### Write

Conflicts can lead people to change their goals. In an **essay,** identify Windrider's original goal and explain how conflict changed it. Support your analysis with details from the scene.

#### Do others see us more clearly than we see ourselves?

Based on his letter and his words and actions in the scene, what qualities do you see in Moon Shadow that he may not see in himself?

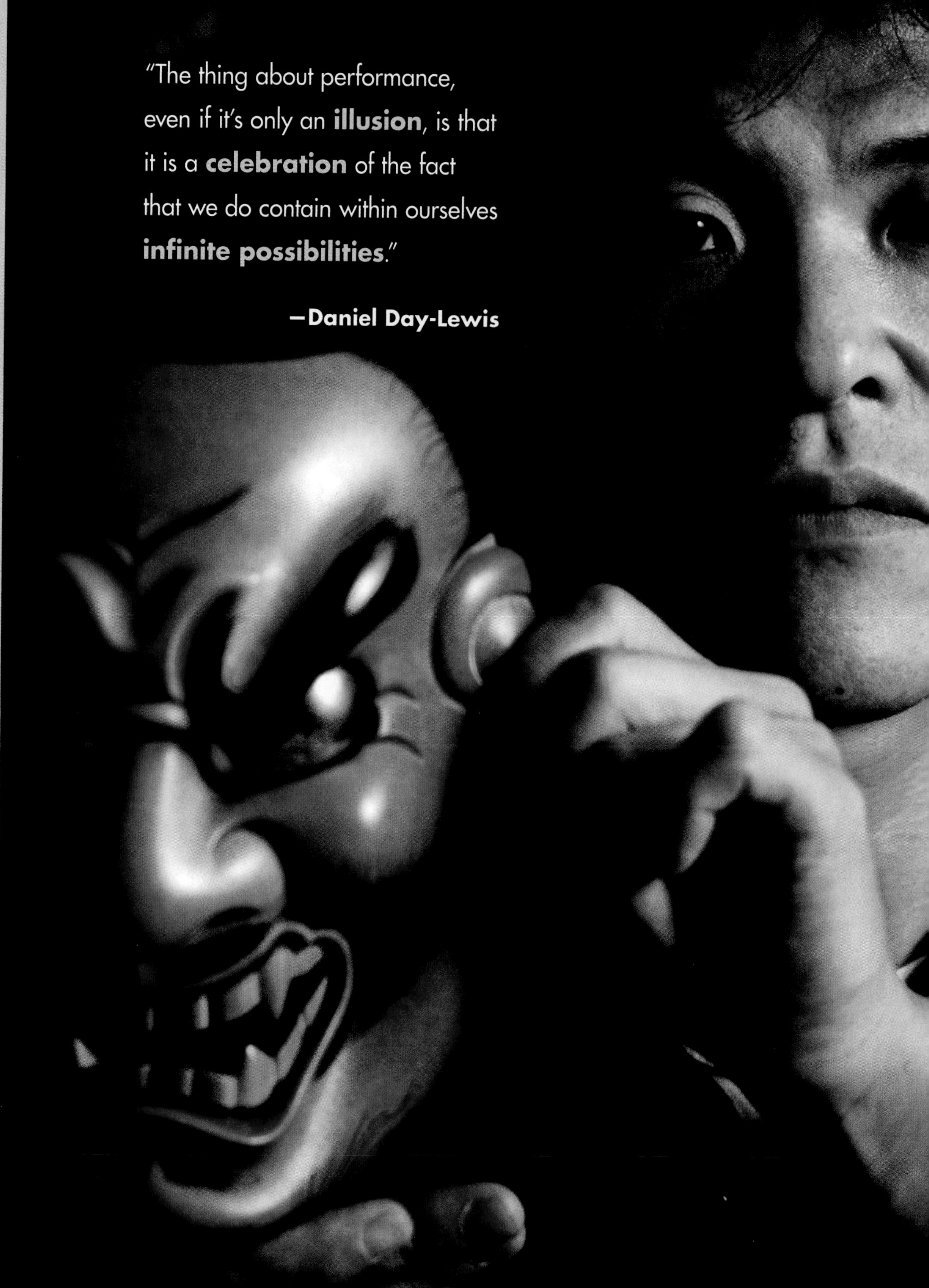
"The thing about performance, even if it's only an **illusion**, is that it is a **celebration** of the fact that we do contain within ourselves **infinite possibilities**."
**—Daniel Day-Lewis**

PART 2

# TEXT ANALYSIS GUIDED EXPLORATION

# DRAMATIC TRANSFORMATIONS

As you read the drama in this section, pay careful attention to the ways in which characters change and grow in reaction to both internal and external conflicts. The quotation on the opposite page will help you explore the idea that everyone possesses the potential for change.

◀ CRITICAL VIEWING What dramatic transformation is about to take place in the photo on the opposite page?

## READINGS IN PART 2

**CLOSE READING TOOL**

Use the **Close Reading Tool** to practice the strategies you learn in this unit.

# Focus on Craft and Structure

## Elements of Drama

A **drama** is a story that is meant to be performed.

A **drama,** or **play,** is a story that is performed for an audience. Some dramas are presented live on a stage, while others are recorded on film. No matter what the form, a drama brings to life the words of its author, the **playwright.**

Drama is similar to fiction in many ways. Like fiction, drama focuses on **characters,** made-up people who interact in a particular **setting,** or environment. The characters are caught up in a struggle, or **conflict.** This drives the **plot**—a series of actions that build to a **climax.** The climax is the highest point of tension. The action then winds down in a **resolution.**

Unlike fiction, drama is meant to be performed. Instead of *reading* a playwright's words, audiences see and hear actors speak the words.

The written text of a drama is called a **script.** A script consists of **dialogue,** the words spoken by the actors, and **stage directions,** the playwright's instructions about how the drama should be performed. **Acts** are the units of action in a drama. Acts are often divided into parts called **scenes.**

| Elements of Drama | |
|---|---|
| **Stage Directions** | Stage directions are the playwright's instructions about how to perform the drama. They tell how actors should speak and move, and give details about lighting, sound effects, and costumes. These abbreviations are often used in stage directions:<br>**C:** center stage<br>**D:** downstage (nearest to audience)<br>**U:** upstage (farthest from audience)<br>**L:** stage left (audience's right)<br>**R:** stage right (audience's left) |
| **Dialogue** | Dialogue is conversation between or among characters. |
| **Set/Scenery** | *Set* and *scenery* are terms used to describe the construction onstage that suggests the time and place of the action. |
| **Props** | Props are small movable items, such as a doctor's clipboard or a student's notebook, that actors use to make their actions look realistic. |
| **Acts and Scenes** | Acts and scenes are the basic units of action in a drama. A full-length drama may consist of several acts. |

## Changing Forms of Drama

**Early Drama** The earliest known written dramas came to us from the ancient Greeks. The Greeks divided drama into two basic categories that we still use today: **comedy** and **tragedy.**

| | |
|---|---|
| Comedy | • features ordinary people in funny or ridiculous situations<br>• usually has a happy ending<br>• is meant to entertain, but also may point out human weaknesses and the faults of a society |
| Tragedy | • shows the downfall of the main character, known as the **tragic hero**<br>• the tragic hero may be an admirable person with a fault that brings about his or her destruction<br>• the hero might also be an ordinary person destroyed by an evil force in society |

The biggest difference between a comedy and a tragedy is the way that the story ends. Comedies end in happy events, such as reunions or weddings. Tragedies end in sad events, such as deaths or partings. After the great plays of the ancient Greeks, drama went into a decline that lasted more than one thousand years. It bloomed again during the time of English playwright William Shakespeare (1564–1616). Shakespeare and his fellow dramatists wrote both comedies and tragedies.

**Drama Today** The modern period has seen a tremendous growth in dramatic writing, and this growth has brought change—even in the meaning of the term *drama.* Contemporary plays and films that treat serious subjects tend to be called *dramas* now, rather than *tragedies*. These serious works are different from contemporary comedies, which, as expected, are lighter and more entertaining.

An even more important change is the way different media have altered people's experience with drama. For several thousand years, people saw dramas in only one way: live. Today, the world of drama is not limited to the stage. Here are some other common types of dramas:

- **Screenplays** are the scripts for films. They include camera angles and can allow for more scene changes than a stage play.
- **Teleplays** are scripts written for television. They contains elements similar to those in a screenplay.
- **Radio plays** are written to be performed as radio broadcasts. They include sound effects and do not require a set.

## Analyzing Drama

Drama has its own unique way of telling stories about **characters**.

**Structure in Drama** The **structure,** or framework, of a drama affects the way the audience or reader finds meaning in the performance or script. The following is a typical structure for a three-act drama.

| | |
|---|---|
| Act I | The characters, setting, and **conflict**, or problem, are introduced in the **exposition**. |
| Act II | In the **rising action**, the main character, or **protagonist**, tries to solve the conflict, but faces obstacles that prevent an easy solution. |
| Act III | The **climax**, or highest point of interest, represents a turning point in the drama. During the **falling action**, the plot moves toward the **resolution** of the conflict. |

Of course, not all dramas follow a three-act structure. Many classic dramas, including most works by the Ancient Greeks and by Shakespeare, consist of five acts. One-act plays, on the other hand, contain a single act. Some one-act plays are divided into multiple scenes.

**Conflict in Drama** Dramatic action is driven by **conflict,** or struggle. There are two types of conflict in drama. **External conflict** occurs between a character and an outside force, such as another character. **Internal conflict** occurs within the mind of a character, as when a character is torn between opposing feelings or goals.

**Example: External Conflict**

- Two young people want to marry, but their parents will not allow it.
- A family must flee their war-torn country.

**Example: Internal Conflict**

- A girl must decide if she should turn in her friend, who has committed a crime.
- A man struggles to overcome a violent past.

### Action: Showing, Not Telling

Drama is moved forward entirely by spoken dialogue and physical action. Audiences who watch a play or film are not *told* what is happening. Rather, they are *shown* what happens. For example, the audience may recognize conflict by hearing anger in an actor's voice or seeing tension in his body. As a drama unfolds, various elements work together to bring the story to life. A dimly lit stage may create an emotional effect; one character's tone of voice may make another character respond in a certain way.

Obviously, the experience of reading a drama differs from that of seeing it performed. Readers experience a script more fully if they imagine the setting described in the stage directions and the way the actors' voices and movements bring the dialogue to life.

**Character Development** In drama, two elements are key to the development of character: stage directions and dialogue. Playwrights use **stage directions** to tell how characters speak, move, and interact with other characters. Playwrights create **dialogue** to reveal character in several ways.

- A character may directly express private thoughts, feelings, and conflicts in a speech.
- Personality traits may be revealed as a character interacts with other characters.
- A character may comment on another character.

In addition, playwrights may have characters deliver different types of speeches.

- A **monologue** is a long, uninterrupted speech spoken by one character to another.
- A **soliloquy** is a speech in which a character is alone and reveals private thoughts. Sometimes a soliloquy is spoken to the audience. Other times, the character is speaking only to himself or herself.
- An **aside** is a comment made by a character to the audience. It is not meant to be heard by the other characters.

To engage the audience and reader, playwrights create **complex characters** who resemble real people. Complex characters are involved in complicated relationships. These characters change as a play progresses.

**Theme in Drama** As in most other literary genres, drama conveys **themes,** or insights about life and human nature.

**Examples of Theme in Drama**

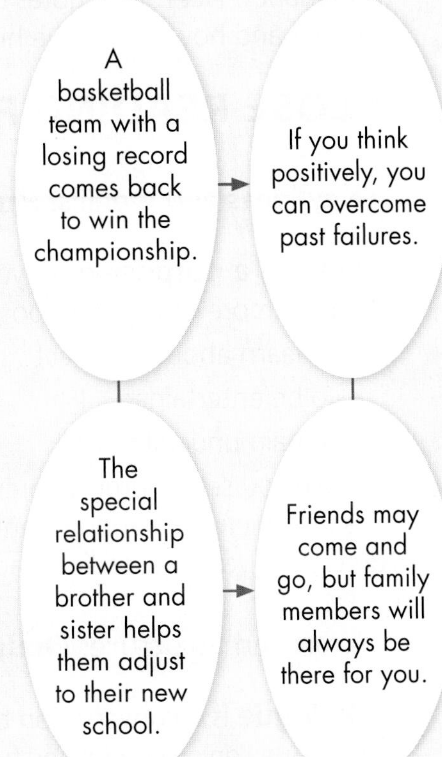

Dramatic Subject
Theme
A basketball team with a losing record comes back to win the championship.
If you think positively, you can overcome past failures.
The special relationship between a brother and sister helps them adjust to their new school.
Friends may come and go, but family members will always be there for you.


The various elements of a drama work together to convey its theme. To determine and analyze the theme of a drama, notice how the characters respond to conflicts and decide whether they change or grow as a result of their experiences. Consider how the setting impacts characters or events. Finally, look for central ideas that are emphasized throughout the drama through the words and actions of the characters. Considering all of these elements will lead you to the central insight in a dramatic work.

# Building Knowledge

## Meet the Author

As a teenager, **Israel Horovitz** (b. 1939) did not like books by Charles Dickens. As he got older, however, he came to appreciate Dickens's style and stories. Today, Horovitz refers to Dickens as "a masterful storyteller." He imagines that if Dickens were alive today, he would be "our greatest television writer, or perhaps screenwriter." As Horovitz adapted Dickens's novel into a play, he thought about which character was his favorite. Surprisingly, it is Scrooge, who reminds Horovitz of his own father.

## Do others see us more clearly than we see ourselves?

Explore the Big Question as you read *A Christmas Carol: Scrooge and Marley,* Act I. Take notes on how the main character sees himself and how others see him.

## CLOSE READING FOCUS

### Key Ideas and Details: Purpose for Reading

**Setting a purpose** gives you a focus as you read. You may set one or more of these purposes:

- To learn about a subject
- To be entertained
- To gain understanding
- To take action or make a decision
- To be inspired
- To complete a task

To help you set a purpose, preview a text before reading. Look at the title, pictures, captions, and beginnings of passages to help you determine your reason for reading the text.

### Craft and Structure: Dialogue

**Dialogue** is a conversation between characters. In a play, dialogue serves several key functions. When the play is viewed as a performance, the characters are developed entirely through dialogue. Characters' words and speech patterns give clues to their personalities. Dialogue also advances the plot and develops the conflict. In a dramatic script, a character's name appears before the lines he or she speaks, as in the following example.

**Mrs. Perez.** Come on, kids! We're leaving.
**Jen.** Wait for me! *Please* wait for me!

## Vocabulary

You will encounter the following words in *A Christmas Carol: Scrooge and Marley,* Act I. Copy the words into your notebook, and record their definitions.

| | | |
|---|---|---|
| **implored** | **morose** | **destitute** |
| **void** | **conveyed** | **gratitude** |

## CLOSE READING MODEL

The passage below is from Israel Horovitz's play *A Christmas Carol: Scrooge and Marley,* Act I. The annotations to the right of the passage show ways in which you can use close reading skills to set a purpose for reading and to analyze dialogue.

### from *A Christmas Carol: Scrooge and Marley,* Act I

**MARLEY.** How is it that I appear before you in a shape that you can see, I may not tell. I have sat invisible beside you many and many a day. That is no light part of my penance. I am here tonight to warn you that you have yet a chance and hope of escaping my fate.[1] A chance and hope of my procuring, Ebenezer.

**SCROOGE.** You were always a good friend to me. Thank'ee!

**MARLEY.** You will be haunted by Three Spirits.[2]

**SCROOGE.** Would that be the chance and hope you mentioned, Jacob?

**MARLEY.** It is.

**SCROOGE.** I think I'd rather not.

**MARLEY.** Without their visits, you cannot hope to shun the path I tread. Expect the first one tomorrow, when the bell tolls one.

**SCROOGE.** Couldn't I take 'em all at once, and get it over, Jacob?[3]

**MARLEY.** Expect the second on the next night at the same hour. The third upon the next night when the last stroke of twelve has ceased to vibrate.[4] Look to see me no more. Others may, but you may not. And look that, for your own sake, you remember what has passed between us!

**Purpose for Reading**

**1** At this point, your purpose for reading may be to learn more about Scrooge and to discover what hope there is for him to escape his fate.

**Dialogue**

**2** You may sense from this dialogue that Marley's remarks will have a strong impact on the plot.

**Dialogue**

**3** Based on his words, Scrooge seems nervous about what is to come. By revealing Scrooge's unease, this dialogue helps you gain new insight into Scrooge's personality.

**Purpose for Reading**

**4** Marley has revealed that Scrooge's "chance and hope" lies in the visits from three spirits. At this point, your purpose for reading may broaden. You may read on to find out what role the Three Spirits play in Scrooge's fate.

# A Christmas Carol: Scrooge and Marley

Israel Horovitz
*from* A Christmas Carol
*by* Charles Dickens

**Jacob Marley,** a specter
**Ebenezer Scrooge,** not yet dead, which is to say still alive
**Bob Cratchit,** Scrooge's clerk
**Fred,** Scrooge's nephew
**Thin Do-Gooder**
**Portly Do-Gooder**
**Specters (Various),** carrying money-boxes
**The Ghost of Christmas Past**
**Four Jocund Travelers**
**A Band of Singers**
**A Band of Dancers**
**Little Boy Scrooge**
**Young Man Scrooge**
**Fan,** Scrooge's little sister
**The Schoolmaster**
**Schoolmates**
**Fezziwig,** a fine and fair employer
**Dick,** young Scrooge's co-worker
**Young Scrooge**
**A Fiddler**
**More Dancers**
**Scrooge's Lost Love**
**Scrooge's Lost Love's Daughter**
**Scrooge's Lost Love's Husband**
**The Ghost of Christmas Present**
**Some Bakers**
**Mrs. Cratchit,** Bob Cratchit's wife
**Belinda Cratchit,** a daughter
**Martha Cratchit,** another daughter
**Peter Cratchit,** a son
**Tiny Tim Cratchit,** another son
**Scrooge's Niece,** Fred's wife
**The Ghost of Christmas Future,** a mute Phantom
**Three Men of Business**
**Drunks, Scoundrels, Women of the Streets**
**A Charwoman**
**Mrs. Dilber**
**Joe,** an old second-hand goods dealer
**A Corpse,** very like Scrooge
**An Indebted Family**
**Adam,** a young boy
**A Poulterer**
**A Gentlewoman**
**Some More Men of Business**

# ACT I

*THE PLACE OF THE PLAY* Various locations in and around the City of London, including Scrooge's Chambers and Offices; the Cratchit Home; Fred's Home; Scrooge's School; Fezziwig's Offices; Old Joe's Hide-a-Way.

*THE TIME OF THE PLAY* The entire action of the play takes place on Christmas Eve, Christmas Day, and the morning after Christmas, 1843.

## SCENE 1

[*Ghostly music in auditorium. A single spotlight on* JACOB MARLEY, D.C. *He is ancient; awful, dead-eyed. He speaks straight out to auditorium.*]

**MARLEY.** [*Cackle-voiced*] My name is Jacob Marley and I am dead. [*He laughs.*] Oh, no, there's no doubt that I am dead. The register of my burial was signed by the clergyman, the clerk, the undertaker . . . and by my chief mourner . . . Ebenezer Scrooge . . . [*Pause; remembers*] I am dead as a doornail.

[*A spotlight fades up, Stage Right, on* SCROOGE, *in his counting-house,*[1] *counting. Lettering on the window behind* SCROOGE *reads: "*SCROOGE AND MARLEY, LTD.*" The spotlight is tight on* SCROOGE*'s head and shoulders. We shall not yet see into the offices and setting. Ghostly music continues, under.* MARLEY *looks across at* SCROOGE; *pitifully. After a moment's pause*]

I present him to you: Ebenezer Scrooge . . . England's most tightfisted hand at the grindstone, Scrooge! a squeezing, wrenching, grasping, scraping, clutching, covetous, old sinner! secret, and self-contained, and solitary as an oyster. The cold within him freezes his old features, nips his pointed nose, shrivels his cheek, stiffens his gait; makes his eyes red, his thin lips blue; and speaks out shrewdly in his grating voice. Look at him. Look at him . . .

[SCROOGE *counts and mumbles.*]

**SCROOGE.** They owe me money and I will collect. I will have

**Purpose for Reading**
Based on the images, title, and other information you can quickly preview, what is your purpose for reading this play?

**Comprehension**
Where and when does this drama take place?

1. **counting-house** office for keeping financial records and writing business letters.

them jailed, if I have to. They owe me money and I will collect what is due me.

[MARLEY *moves towards* SCROOGE*; two steps. The spotlight stays with him.*]

**Dialogue**
What do these lines reveal about Marley's character?

**MARLEY.** [*Disgusted*] He and I were partners for I don't know how many years. Scrooge was my sole executor, my sole administrator, my sole assign, my sole residuary legatee,[2] my sole friend and my sole mourner. But Scrooge was not so cut up by the sad event of my death, but that he was an excellent man of business on the very day of my funeral, and solemnized[3] it with an undoubted bargain. [*Pauses again in disgust*] He never painted out my name from the window. There it stands, on the window and above the warehouse door: Scrooge and Marley. Sometimes people new to our business call him Scrooge and sometimes they call him Marley. He answers to both names. It's all the same to him. And it's cheaper than painting in a new sign, isn't it? [*Pauses; moves closer to* SCROOGE] Nobody has ever stopped him in the street to say, with gladsome looks, "My dear Scrooge, how are you? When will you come to see me?" No beggars **implored** him to bestow a trifle, no children ever ask him what it is o'clock, no man or woman now, or ever in his life, not once, inquire the way to such and such a place. [MARLEY *stands next to* SCROOGE *now. They share, so it seems, a spotlight.*] But what does Scrooge care of any of this? It is the very thing he likes! To edge his way along the crowded paths of life, warning all human sympathy to keep its distance.

**Vocabulary ▶**
**implored** (im plôrd′) *v.* begged

[*A ghostly bell rings in the distance.* MARLEY *moves away from* SCROOGE, *now, heading* D. *again. As he does, he "takes" the light:* SCROOGE *has disappeared into the black void beyond.* MARLEY *walks* D.C., *talking directly to the audience. Pauses*]

The bell tolls and I must take my leave. You must stay a while with Scrooge and watch him play out his scroogey

2. **my sole executor** (eg zek′ yo͞o tər), **my sole administrator, my sole assign** (ə sīn′), **my sole residuary legatee** (ri zij′ o͞o er′ ē leg′ ə tē′) legal terms giving one person responsibility to carry out the wishes of another who has died.
3. **solemnized** (säl′ əm nīzd′) *v.* honored or remembered. Marley is being sarcastic.

life. It is now the story: the once-upon-a-time. Scrooge is busy in his counting-house. Where else? Christmas eve and Scrooge is busy in his counting-house. It is cold, bleak, biting weather outside: foggy withal: and, if you listen closely, you can hear the people in the court go wheezing up and down, beating their hands upon their breasts, and stamping their feet upon the pavement stones to warm them . . .

[*The clocks outside strike three.*]

Only three! and quite dark outside already: it has not been light all day this day.

[*This ghostly bell rings in the distance again.* MARLEY *looks about him. Music in.* MARLEY *flies away.*]

[*N.B.* MARLEY'S *comings and goings should, from time to time, induce the explosion of the odd flash-pot. I.H.*]

**▼ Critical Viewing**
How does this portrayal of Scrooge compare with the image you picture as you read?

## SCENE 2

[*Christmas music in, sung by a live chorus, full. At conclusion of song, sound fades under and into the distance. Lights up in set: offices of Scrooge and Marley, Ltd.* SCROOGE *sits at his desk, at work. Near him is a tiny fire. His door is open and in his line of vision, we see* SCROOGE'S *clerk,* BOB CRATCHIT, *who sits in a dismal tank of a cubicle, copying letters. Near* CRATCHIT *is a fire so tiny as to barely cast a light: perhaps it is one pitifully glowing coal?* CRATCHIT *rubs his hands together, puts on a white comforter*[4] *and tries to heat his hands around his candle.* SCROOGE'S NEPHEW *enters, unseen.*]

**SCROOGE.** What are you doing, Cratchit? Acting cold, are you? Next, you'll be asking to replenish your coal from my coal-box, won't you? Well, save your breath, Cratchit! Unless you're prepared to find employ elsewhere!

**NEPHEW.** [*Cheerfully; surprising* SCROOGE] A merry Christmas to you, Uncle! God save you!

**SCROOGE.** Bah! Humbug![5]

**Comprehension**
What was Marley's relationship to Scrooge?

4. **comforter** (kum´ fər tər) *n.* long, woolen scarf.
5. **Humbug** (hum´ bug´) *interj.* nonsense.

**Nephew.** Christmas a "humbug," Uncle? I'm sure you don't mean that.

**Scrooge.** I do! Merry Christmas? What right do you have to be merry? What reason have you to be merry? You're poor enough!

**Nephew.** Come, then. What right have you to be dismal? What reason have you to be **morose**? You're rich enough.

**Vocabulary ▶**
**morose** (mə rōs´) *adj.* gloomy; ill-tempered

**Scrooge.** Bah! Humbug!

**Nephew.** Don't be cross, Uncle.

**Scrooge.** What else can I be? Eh? When I live in a world of fools such as this? Merry Christmas? What's Christmastime to you but a time of paying bills without any money; a time for finding yourself a year older, but not an hour richer. If I could work my will, every idiot who goes about with "Merry Christmas" on his lips, should be boiled with his own pudding, and buried with a stake of holly through his heart. He should!

**Nephew.** Uncle!

**Scrooge.** Nephew! You keep Christmas in your own way and let me keep it in mine.

**Nephew.** Keep it! But you don't keep it, Uncle.

**Scrooge.** Let me leave it alone, then. Much good it has ever done you!

**Nephew.** There are many things from which I have derived good, by which I have not profited, I daresay. Christmas among the rest. But I am sure that I always thought of Christmas time, when it has come round—as a good time: the only time I know of, when men and women seem to open their shut-up hearts freely, and to think of people below them as if they really were fellow-passengers to the grave, and not another race of creatures bound on other journeys. And therefore, Uncle, though it has never put a scrap of gold or silver in my pocket, I believe that it *has* done me good, and that it *will* do me good; and I say, God bless it!

[*The* Clerk *in the tank applauds, looks at the furious* Scrooge *and pokes out his tiny fire, as if in exchange for the moment of impropriety.* Scrooge *yells at him.*]

**Scrooge.** [*To the clerk*] Let me hear another sound from *you* and you'll keep your Christmas by losing your situation. [*To the nephew*] You're quite a powerful speaker, sir. I wonder you don't go into Parliament.[6]

**Nephew.** Don't be angry, Uncle. Come! Dine with us tomorrow.

**Scrooge.** I'd rather see myself dead than see myself with your family!

**Nephew.** But, why? Why?

**Scrooge.** Why did you get married?

**Nephew.** Because I fell in love.

**Scrooge.** That, sir, is the only thing that you have said to me in your entire lifetime which is even more ridiculous than "Merry Christmas"! [*Turns from* Nephew] Good afternoon.

**Nephew.** Nay, Uncle, you never came to see me before I married either. Why give it as a reason for not coming now?

**Scrooge.** Good afternoon, Nephew!

**Dialogue**
How does this exchange between Scrooge and his nephew show the contrast between the two characters?

**Comprehension**
What invitation does Scrooge's nephew offer?

6. **Parliament** (pär´ lə mənt) national legislative body of Great Britain, in some ways like the United States Congress.

**Nephew.** I want nothing from you; I ask nothing of you; why cannot we be friends?

**Scrooge.** Good afternoon!

**Nephew.** I am sorry with all my heart, to find you so resolute. But I have made the trial in homage to Christmas, and I'll keep my Christmas humor to the last. So A Merry Christmas, Uncle!

**Scrooge.** Good afternoon!

**Nephew.** And A Happy New Year!

**Scrooge.** Good afternoon!

**Dialogue**
What can you infer about the nephew's character from his words to Cratchit?

**Nephew.** [*He stands facing* Scrooge.] Uncle, you are the most . . . [*Pauses*] No, I shan't. My Christmas humor is intact . . . [*Pause*] God bless you, Uncle . . . [Nephew *turns and starts for the door; he stops at* Cratchit's *cage.*] Merry Christmas, Bob Cratchit . . .

**Cratchit.** Merry Christmas to you sir, and a very, very happy New Year . . .

**Scrooge.** [*Calling across to them*] Oh, fine, a perfection, just fine . . . to see the perfect pair of you: husbands, with wives and children to support . . . my clerk there earning fifteen shillings a week . . . and the perfect pair of you, talking about a Merry Christmas! [*Pauses*] I'll retire to Bedlam![7]

**Nephew.** [*To* Cratchit] He's impossible!

**Cratchit.** Oh, mind him not, sir. He's getting on in years, and he's alone. He's noticed your visit. I'll wager your visit has warmed him.

**Nephew.** Him? Uncle Ebenezer Scrooge? *Warmed?* You are a better Christian than I am, sir.

**Cratchit.** [*Opening the door for* Nephew*; two* Do-Gooders *will enter, as* Nephew *exits*] Good day to you, sir, and God bless.

**Nephew.** God bless . . . [*One man who enters is portly, the other is thin. Both are pleasant.*]

**Cratchit.** Can I help you, gentlemen?

---

**7. Bedlam** (bed′ ləm) hospital in London for the mentally ill.

**Thin Man.** [*Carrying papers and books; looks around* Cratchit *to* Scrooge] Scrooge and Marley's, I believe. Have I the pleasure of addressing Mr. Scrooge, or Mr. Marley?

**Scrooge.** Mr. Marley has been dead these seven years. He died seven years ago this very night.

**Portly Man.** We have no doubt his liberality[8] is well represented by his surviving partner . . . [*Offers his calling card*]

**Scrooge.** [*Handing back the card; unlooked at*] . . . Good afternoon.

**Thin Man.** This will take but a moment, sir . . .

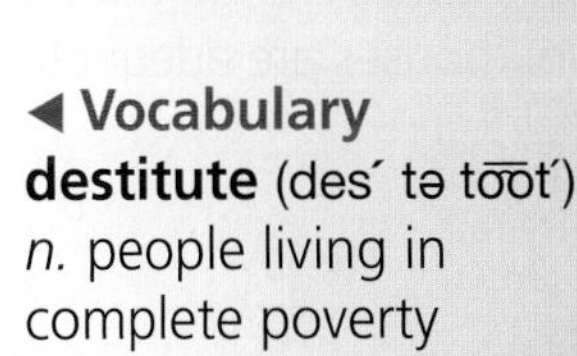

**Portly Man.** At this festive season of the year, Mr. Scrooge, it is more than usually desirable that we should make some slight provision for the poor and **destitute**, who suffer greatly at the present time. Many thousands are in want of common necessities; hundreds of thousands are in want of common comforts, sir.

◂ **Vocabulary**
**destitute** (des′ tə to̅o̅t′) *n.* people living in complete poverty

**Scrooge.** Are there no prisons?

**Portly Man.** Plenty of prisons.

**Scrooge.** And aren't the Union workhouses still in operation?

**Thin Man.** They are. Still. I wish that I could say that they are not.

**Scrooge.** The Treadmill[9] and the Poor Law[10] are in full vigor, then?

**Thin Man.** Both very busy, sir.

**Scrooge.** Ohhh, I see. I was afraid, from what you said at

**Comprehension**
Who do the thin man and the portly man want to help?

---

8. **liberality** (lib′ ər al′ i tē) generosity.
9. **the Treadmill** (tred′ mil′) kind of mill wheel turned by the weight of people treading steps arranged around it; this device was used to punish prisoners.
10. **the Poor Law** the original 16th-century Poor Laws called for overseers of the poor in each neighborhood to provide relief for the needy. The New Poor Law of 1834 made the workhouses in which the poor sometimes lived and worked extremely hard and unattractive.

LITERATURE IN CONTEXT

## Social Studies Connection

### Union Workhouses

In Victorian England, many people who were poverty-stricken, orphaned, old, or sick lived in workhouses. On a typical day, workers woke at 5 A.M. and spent ten hours doing physical labor, such as crushing stones, sewing, cleaning, and milling corn. Bedtime was 8 P.M. There was not enough food to eat. Typically, breakfast was a piece of bread; dinner was a piece of bacon and a piece of bread or a potato; supper was a piece of bread and a piece of cheese.

**Connect to the Literature**

Why does Scrooge think the workhouses are adequate?

first, that something had occurred to stop them from their useful course. [*Pauses*] I'm glad to hear it.

**Portly Man.** Under the impression that they scarcely furnish Christian cheer of mind or body to the multitude, a few of us are endeavoring to raise a fund to buy the Poor some meat and drink, and means of warmth. We choose this time, because it is a time, of all others, when Want is keenly felt, and Abundance rejoices. [*Pen in hand; as well as notepad*] What shall I put you down for, sir?

**Scrooge.** Nothing!

**Portly Man.** You wish to be left anonymous?

**Scrooge.** I wish to be left alone! [*Pauses; turns away; turns back to them*] Since you ask me what I wish, gentlemen, that is my answer. I help to support the establishments that I have mentioned: they cost enough: and those who are badly off must go there.

**Thin Man.** Many can't go there; and many would rather die.

**Scrooge.** If they would rather die, they had better do it, and decrease the surplus population. Besides—excuse me—I don't know that.

**Thin Man.** But you might know it!

**Scrooge.** It's not my business. It's enough for a man to understand his own business, and not to interfere with other people's. Mine occupies me constantly. Good afternoon, gentlemen!
[Scrooge *turns his back on the gentlemen and returns to his desk.*]

**Portly Man.** But, sir, Mr. Scrooge . . . think of the poor.

**Scrooge.** [*Turns suddenly to them. Pauses*] Take your leave of my offices, sirs, while I am still smiling.

[*The* Thin Man *looks at the* Portly Man. *They are undone. They shrug. They move to the door.* Cratchit *hops up to open it for them.*]

**Thin Man.** Good day, sir . . . [*To* Cratchit] A merry Christmas to you, sir . . .

**Cratchit.** Yes. A Merry Christmas to both of you . . .

**Portly Man.** Merry Christmas . . .

[Cratchit *silently squeezes something into the hand of the* thin man.]

**Thin Man.** What's this?

**Cratchit.** Shhhh . . .

[Cratchit *opens the door; wind and snow whistle into the room.*]

**Thin Man.** Thank you, sir, thank you.

[Cratchit *closes the door and returns to his workplace.* Scrooge *is at his own counting table. He talks to* Cratchit *without looking up.*]

**Scrooge.** It's less of a time of year for being merry, and more a time of year for being loony . . . if you ask me.

**Cratchit.** Well, I don't know, sir . . . [*The clock's bell strikes six o'clock.*] Well, there it is, eh, six?

**Scrooge.** Saved by six bells, are you?

**Cratchit.** I must be going home . . . [*He snuffs out his candle and puts on his hat.*] I hope you have a . . . very very lovely day tomorrow, sir . . .

**Scrooge.** Hmmm. Oh, you'll be wanting the whole day tomorrow, I suppose?

▼ **Critical Viewing**
How does this portrayal of Cratchit compare to your idea of how Cratchit would look?

**Cratchit.** If quite convenient, sir.

**Scrooge.** It's not convenient, and it's not fair. If I was to stop half-a-crown for it, you'd think yourself ill-used, I'll be bound?

[Cratchit *smiles faintly.*]

**Cratchit.** I don't know, sir . . .

**Scrooge.** And yet, you don't think me ill-used when I pay a day's wages for no work . . .

**Comprehension**
How does Scrooge feel about Christmas?

**Cratchit.** It's only but once a year . . .

**Scrooge.** A poor excuse for picking a man's pocket every 25th of December! But I suppose you must have the whole day. Be here all the earlier the next morning!

**Cratchit.** Oh, I will, sir. I will. I promise you. And, sir . . .

**Scrooge.** Don't say it, Cratchit.

**Cratchit.** But let me wish you a . . .

**Scrooge.** Don't say it, Cratchit. I warn you . . .

**Cratchit.** Sir!

**Scrooge.** Cratchit!

[Cratchit *opens the door.*]

**Cratchit.** All right, then, sir . . . well . . . [*Suddenly*] Merry Christmas, Mr. Scrooge!

[*And he runs out the door, shutting same behind him.* Scrooge *moves to his desk; gathering his coat, hat, etc. A* Boy *appears at his window. . . .*]

**Boy.** [*Singing*] "Away in a manger . . ."

[Scrooge *seizes his ruler and whacks at the image of the* Boy *outside. The* Boy *leaves.*]

**Scrooge.** Bah! Humbug! Christmas! Bah! Humbug! [*He shuts out the light.*]

*A note on the crossover, following Scene 2:*

[Scrooge *will walk alone to his rooms from his offices. As he makes a long slow cross of the stage, the scenery should change. Christmas music will be heard, various people will cross by* Scrooge, *often smiling happily.*

*There will be occasional pleasant greetings tossed at him.*

Scrooge, *in contrast to all, will grump and mumble. He will snap at passing boys, as might a horrid old hound.*

*In short,* Scrooge's *sounds and movements will define him in contrast from all other people who cross the stage: he is the misanthrope,*[11] *the malcontent, the miser. He is* Scrooge.

▶ **Critical Viewing**
How does the image on the facing page compare with the scene you pictured after reading the stage directions describing Scrooge's walk home?

---

**11. misanthrope** (mis′ ən thrōp′) *n.* person who hates or distrusts everyone.

*This statement of* SCROOGE'S *character, by contrast to all other characters, should seem comical to the audience.*

*During* SCROOGE'S *crossover to his rooms, snow should begin to fall. All passers-by will hold their faces to the sky, smiling, allowing snow to shower them lightly.* SCROOGE, *by contrast, will bat at the flakes with his walking-stick, as might an insomniac swat at a sleep-stopping, middle-of-the-night swarm of mosquitoes. He will comment on the blackness of the night, and, finally, reach his rooms and his encounter with the magical specter:*[12] MARLEY, *his eternal mate.*]

**Dialogue**
What do you learn about Scrooge through his words as he shuts out the light?

**Comprehension**
Why is Cratchit taking a day off?

12. **specter** (spek´ tər) *n.* ghost.

## Scene 3

**Scrooge.** No light at all . . . no moon . . . *that* is what is at the center of a Christmas Eve: dead black: **void** . . .

Vocabulary ▶
**void** (void) *n.* emptiness

[Scrooge *puts his key in the door's keyhole. He has reached his rooms now. The door knocker changes and is now* Marley's *face. A musical sound; quickly: ghostly.* Marley's *image is not at all angry, but looks at* Scrooge *as did the old* Marley *look at* Scrooge. *The hair is curiously stirred; eyes wide open, dead: absent of focus.* Scrooge *stares wordlessly here. The face, before his very eyes, does deliquesce.*[13] *It is a knocker again.* Scrooge *opens the door and checks the back of same, probably for* Marley's *pigtail. Seeing nothing but screws and nuts,* Scrooge *refuses the memory.*]

Pooh, pooh!

[*The sound of the door closing resounds throughout the house as thunder. Every room echoes the sound.* Scrooge *fastens the door and walks across the hall to the stairs, trimming his candle as he goes; and then he goes slowly up the staircase. He checks each room: sitting room, bedrooms, lumber-room. He looks under the sofa, under the table: nobody there. He fixes his evening gruel on the hob,*[14] *changes his jacket.* Scrooge *sits near the tiny low-flamed fire, sipping his gruel. There are various pictures on the walls: all of them now show likenesses of* Marley. Scrooge *blinks his eyes.*]

**Purpose for Reading**
Preview Scene 3. If your purpose were to find out what happens to Scrooge next, what details would you look for in the scene?

Bah! Humbug!

[Scrooge *walks in a circle about the room. The pictures change back into their natural images. He sits down at the table in front of the fire. A bell hangs overhead. It begins to ring, of its own accord. Slowly, surely, begins the ringing of every bell in the house. They continue ringing for nearly half a minute.* Scrooge *is stunned by the phenomenon. The bells cease their ringing all at once. Deep below* Scrooge, *in the basement of the house, there is the sound of clanking, of some enormous chain being dragged across the floors; and now up the stairs. We hear doors flying open.*]

---

13. **deliquesce** (del′ i kwes′) *v.* melt away.
14. **gruel** (grōō′ əl) **on the hob** (häb) thin broth warming on a ledge at the back or side of the fireplace.

Bah still! Humbug still! This is not happening! I won't believe it!

[MARLEY'S GHOST *enters the room. He is horrible to look at: pigtail, vest, suit as usual, but he drags an enormous chain now, to which is fastened cash-boxes, keys, padlocks, ledgers, deeds, and heavy purses fashioned of steel. He is transparent.* MARLEY *stands opposite the stricken* SCROOGE.]

How now! What do you want of me?

**MARLEY.** Much!

**SCROOGE.** Who are you?

**MARLEY.** Ask me who I was.

**SCROOGE.** Who were you then?

**MARLEY.** In life, I was your business partner: Jacob Marley.

**SCROOGE.** I see . . . can you sit down?

**MARLEY.** I can.

**SCROOGE.** Do it then.

**MARLEY.** I shall. [MARLEY *sits opposite* SCROOGE, *in the chair across the table, at the front of the fireplace.*] You don't believe in me.

**SCROOGE.** I don't.

**MARLEY.** Why do you doubt your senses?

**SCROOGE.** Because every little thing affects them. A slight disorder of the stomach makes them cheat. You may be an undigested bit of beef, a blot of mustard, a crumb of cheese, a fragment of an underdone potato. There's more of gravy than of grave about you, whatever you are!

[*There is a silence between them.* SCROOGE *is made nervous by it. He picks up a toothpick.*]

Humbug! I tell you: humbug!

[MARLEY *opens his mouth and screams a ghosty, fearful scream. The scream echoes about each room of the house. Bats fly, cats screech, lightning flashes.* SCROOGE *stands and walks backwards against the wall.* MARLEY *stands and screams again. This time, he takes his head and lifts it*

**Dialogue**
Based on this dialogue, what is Scrooge's attitude toward Marley's Ghost?

**Comprehension**
What does Scrooge see in the door knocker?

*from his shoulders. His head continues to scream.* MARLEY'S *face again appears on every picture in the room: all screaming.* SCROOGE, *on his knees before* MARLEY.]

Mercy! Dreadful apparition,[15] mercy! Why, O! why do you trouble me so?

**MARLEY.** Man of the worldly mind, do you believe in me, or not?

**Purpose for Reading**
What purpose for reading might Scrooge's question suggest to readers?

**SCROOGE.** I do. I must. But why do spirits such as you walk the earth? And why do they come to me?

**MARLEY.** It is required of every man that the spirit within him should walk abroad among his fellow-men, and travel far and wide; and if that spirit goes not forth in life, it is condemned to do so after death. [MARLEY *screams again; a tragic scream; from his ghosty bones.*] I wear the chain I forged in life. I made it link by link, and yard by yard. Is its pattern strange to *you?* Or would you know, you, Scrooge, the weight and length of the strong coil you bear yourself? It was full as heavy and long as this, seven Christmas Eves ago. You have labored on it, since. It is a ponderous chain.

[*Terrified that a chain will appear about his body,* SCROOGE *spins and waves the unwanted chain away. None, of course, appears. Sees* MARLEY *watching him dance about the room.* MARLEY *watches* SCROOGE; *silently.*]

**SCROOGE.** Jacob. Old Jacob Marley, tell me more. Speak comfort to me, Jacob . . .

**Vocabulary ▶**
**conveyed** (kən vād′) *v.* made known; expressed

**MARLEY.** I have none to give. Comfort comes from other regions, Ebenezer Scrooge, and is **conveyed** by other ministers, to other kinds of men. A very little more, is all that is permitted to me. I cannot rest, I cannot stay, I cannot linger anywhere . . . [*He moans again.*] my spirit never walked beyond our counting-house—mark me!—in life my spirit never roved beyond the narrow limits of our money-changing hole; and weary journeys lie before me!

**SCROOGE.** But you were always a good man of business, Jacob.

**MARLEY.** [*Screams word "business"; a flash-pot explodes with him.*] *BUSINESS!!!* Mankind was my business. The

15. **apparition** (ap′ ə rish′ ən) *n.* ghost.

common welfare was my business; charity, mercy, forbearance, benevolence, were, all, my business. [SCROOGE *is quaking.*] Hear me, Ebenezer Scrooge! My time is nearly gone.

**SCROOGE.** I will, but don't be hard upon me. And don't be flowery, Jacob! Pray!

**MARLEY.** How is it that I appear before you in a shape that you can see, I may not tell. I have sat invisible beside you many and many a day. That is no light part of my penance. I am here tonight to warn you that you have yet a chance and hope of escaping my fate. A chance and hope of my procuring, Ebenezer.

**SCROOGE.** You were always a good friend to me. Thank'ee!

**MARLEY.** You will be haunted by Three Spirits.

**SCROOGE.** Would that be the chance and hope you mentioned, Jacob?

**MARLEY.** It is.

**SCROOGE.** I think I'd rather not.

**MARLEY.** Without their visits, you cannot hope to shun the path I tread. Expect the first one tomorrow, when the bell tolls one.

**SCROOGE.** Couldn't I take 'em all at once, and get it over, Jacob?

**MARLEY.** Expect the second on the next night at the same hour. The third upon the next night when the last stroke of twelve has ceased to vibrate. Look to see me no more. Others may, but you may not. And look that, for your own sake, you remember what has passed between us!

**▲ Critical Viewing**
How do the characters' gestures and positions reinforce the emotion of the scene?

**Comprehension**
Why does Marley visit Scrooge?

*MARLEY places his head back upon his shoulders. He approaches the window and beckons to SCROOGE to watch. Outside the window, specters fly by, carrying money-boxes and chains. They make a confused sound of lamentation. MARLEY, after listening a moment, joins into their mournful dirge. He leans to the window and floats out into the bleak, dark night. He is gone.*]

**SCROOGE.** [*Rushing to the window*] Jacob! No, Jacob! Don't leave me! I'm frightened! [*He sees that MARLEY has gone. He looks outside. He pulls the shutter closed, so that the scene is blocked from his view. All sound stops. After a pause, he re-opens the shutter and all is quiet, as it should be on Christmas Eve. Carolers carol out of doors, in the distance. SCROOGE closes the shutter and walks down the stairs. He examines the door by which MARLEY first entered.*] No one here at all! Did I imagine all that? Humbug! [*He looks about the room.*] I did imagine it. It only happened in my foulest dream-mind, didn't it? An undigested bit of . . . [*Thunder and lightning in the room; suddenly*] Sorry! Sorry!

**Purpose for Reading**
What questions do you have about what will happen to Scrooge? Read on to answer your questions.

[*There is silence again. The lights fade out.*]

## SCENE 4

[*Christmas music, choral, "Hark the Herald Angels Sing," sung by an onstage choir of children, spotlighted, D.C. Above, SCROOGE in his bed, dead to the world, asleep, in his darkened room. It should appear that the choir is singing somewhere outside of the house, of course, and a use of scrim*[16] *is thus suggested. When the singing is ended, the choir should fade out of view and MARLEY should fade into view, in their place.*]

**MARLEY.** [*Directly to audience*] From this point forth . . . I shall be quite visible to you, but invisible to him. [*Smiles*] He will feel my presence, nevertheless, for, unless my senses fail me completely, we are—you and I—witness to the changing of a miser: that one, my partner in life, in business, and in eternity: that one: Scrooge. [*Moves to staircase, below SCROOGE*] See him now. He endeavors to pierce the

16. **scrim** (skrim) *n.* see-through fabric used to create special effects in the theater.

darkness with his ferret eyes.[17] [*To audience*] See him, now. He listens for the hour.

[*The bells toll.* SCROOGE *is awakened and quakes as the hour approaches one o'clock, but the bells stop their sound at the hour of twelve.*]

**SCROOGE.** [*Astonished*] Midnight! Why this isn't possible. It was past two when I went to bed. An icicle must have gotten into the clock's works! I couldn't have slept through the whole day and far into another night. It isn't possible that anything has happened to the sun, and this is twelve at noon! [*He runs to window; unshutters same; it is night.*] Night, still. Quiet, normal for the season, cold. It is certainly not noon. I cannot in any way afford to lose my days. Securities come due, promissory notes,[18] interest on investments: these are things that happen in the daylight! [*He returns to his bed.*] Was this a dream?

[MARLEY *appears in his room. He speaks to the audience.*]

**MARLEY.** You see? He does not, with faith, believe in me fully, even still! Whatever will it take to turn the faith of a miser from money to men?

**SCROOGE.** Another quarter and it'll be one and Marley's ghosty friends will come. [*Pauses; listens*] Where's the chime for one? [*Ding, dong*] A quarter past [*Repeats*] Half-past! [*Repeats*] A quarter to it! But where's the heavy bell of the hour one? This is a game in which I lose my senses! Perhaps, if I allowed myself another short doze . . .

**MARLEY.** . . . Doze, Ebenezer, doze.

[*A heavy bell thuds its one ring; dull and definitely one o'clock. There is a flash of light.* SCROOGE *sits up, in a sudden. A hand draws back the curtains by his bed. He sees it.*]

**SCROOGE.** A hand! Who owns it! Hello!

[*Ghosty music again, but of a new nature to the play. A strange figure stands before* SCROOGE*—like a child, yet at the same time like an old man: white hair, but unwrinkled skin, long, muscular arms, but delicate legs and feet. Wears*

**Dialogue**
What important information in Marley's opening speech will influence the rest of the play?

**Spiral Review**
**CONFLICT** How do details about the setting work together to increase the tension?

**Comprehension**
Why is Scrooge confused when he wakes up?

---

17. **ferret eyes** a ferret is a small, weasel-like animal used for hunting rabbits; this expression means to stare continuously, the way a ferret hunts.
18. **promissory** (präm´ i sôr´ ē) **notes** written promises to pay someone a certain sum of money.

*white tunic; lustrous belt cinches waist. Branch of fresh green holly in its hand, but has its dress trimmed with fresh summer flowers. Clear jets of light spring from the crown of its head. Holds cap in hand. The Spirit is called* PAST.]

Are you the Spirit, sir, whose coming was foretold to me?

**PAST.** I am.

**MARLEY.** Does he take this to be a vision of his green grocer?

**SCROOGE.** Who, and what are you?

**PAST.** I am the Ghost of Christmas Past.

**SCROOGE.** Long past?

**PAST.** Your past.

**SCROOGE.** May I ask, please, sir, what business you have here with me?

**PAST.** Your welfare.

**SCROOGE.** Not to sound ungrateful, sir, and really, please do understand that I am plenty obliged for your concern, but, really, kind spirit, it would have done all the better for my welfare to have been left alone altogether, to have slept peacefully through this night.

**PAST.** Your reclamation, then. Take heed!

**SCROOGE.** My what?

**PAST.** [*Motioning to* SCROOGE *and taking his arm*] Rise! Fly with me! [*He leads* SCROOGE *to the window.*]

**SCROOGE.** [*Panicked*] Fly, but I am a mortal and cannot fly!

**PAST.** [*Pointing to his heart*] Bear but a touch of my hand here and you shall be upheld in more than this!

[SCROOGE *touches the spirit's heart and the lights dissolve into sparkly flickers. Lovely crystals of music are heard. The scene dissolves into another. Christmas music again*]

**Dialogue**
Based on this dialogue, how has Scrooge been affected by what has happened to him so far?

# Scene 5

[SCROOGE *and the* GHOST OF CHRISTMAS PAST *walk together across an open stage. In the background, we see a field that is open; covered by a soft, downy snow: a country road.*]

**SCROOGE.** Good Heaven! I was bred in this place. I was a boy here!

[SCROOGE *freezes, staring at the field beyond.* MARLEY'S *ghost appears beside him; takes* SCROOGE'S *face in his hands, and turns his face to the audience.*]

**MARLEY.** You see this Scrooge: stricken by feeling. Conscious of a thousand odors floating in the air, each one connected with a thousand thoughts, and hopes, and joys, and care long, long forgotten. [*Pause*] This one—this Scrooge—before your very eyes, returns to life, among the living. [*To audience, sternly*] You'd best pay your most careful attention. I would suggest rapt.[19]

[*There is a small flash and puff of smoke and* MARLEY *is gone again.*]

**PAST.** Your lip is trembling, Mr. Scrooge. And what is that upon your cheek?

**SCROOGE.** Upon my cheek? Nothing . . . a blemish on the skin from the eating of overmuch grease . . . nothing . . . [*Suddenly*] Kind Spirit of Christmas Past, lead me where you will, but quickly! To be stagnant in this place is, for me, unbearable!

**PAST.** You recollect the way?

**SCROOGE.** Remember it! I would know it blindfolded! My bridge, my church, my winding river! [*Staggers about, trying to see it all at once. He weeps again.*]

**PAST.** These are but shadows of things that have been. They have no consciousness of us.

[*Four jocund travelers enter, singing a Christmas song in four-part harmony—"God Rest Ye Merry Gentlemen."*]

**SCROOGE.** Listen! I know these men! I know them! I remember the beauty of their song!

**Comprehension**
Who appears to Scrooge during Scene 4?

---

**19. rapt** (rapt) *adj.* giving complete attention; totally carried away by something.

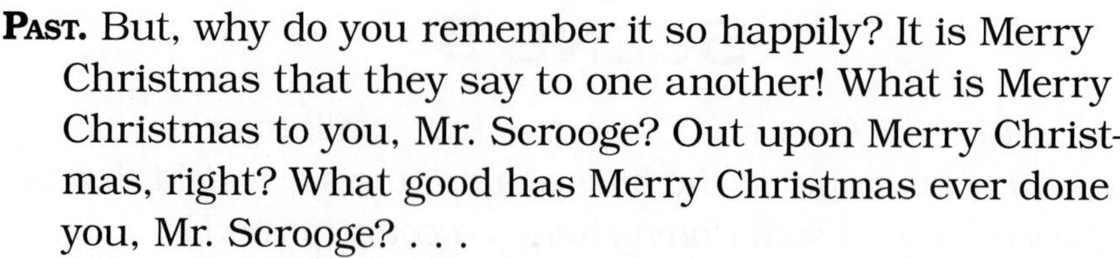

**Past.** But, why do you remember it so happily? It is Merry Christmas that they say to one another! What is Merry Christmas to you, Mr. Scrooge? Out upon Merry Christmas, right? What good has Merry Christmas ever done you, Mr. Scrooge? . . .

**Scrooge.** [*After a long pause*] None. No good. None . . . [*He bows his head.*]

**Past.** Look, you, sir, a school ahead. The schoolroom is not quite deserted. A solitary child, neglected by his friends, is left there still.

[Scrooge *falls to the ground; sobbing as he sees, and we see, a small boy, the young* Scrooge, *sitting and weeping, bravely, alone at his desk: alone in a vast space, a void.*]

**Scrooge.** I cannot look on him!

**Past.** You must, Mr. Scrooge, you must.

**Scrooge.** It's me. [*Pauses; weeps*] Poor boy. He lived inside his head . . . alone . . . [*Pauses; weeps*] poor boy. [*Pauses; stops his weeping*] I wish . . . [*Dries his eyes on his cuff*] ah! it's too late!

**Past.** What is the matter?

**Scrooge.** There was a boy singing a Christmas Carol outside my door last night. I should like to have given him something: that's all.

**Past.** [*Smiles; waves his hand to* Scrooge] Come. Let us see another Christmas.

[*Lights out on little boy. A flash of light. A puff of smoke. Lights up on older boy*]

**Dialogue**
How do these lines reveal that a change is taking place in Scrooge?

**Scrooge.** Look! Me, again! Older now! [*Realizes*] Oh, yes . . . still alone.

[*The boy—a slightly older* Scrooge *—sits alone in a chair, reading. The door to the room opens and a young girl enters. She is much, much younger than this slightly older* Scrooge. *She is, say, six, and he is, say, twelve. Elder* Scrooge *and the* Ghost of Christmas Past *stand watching the scene, unseen.*]

**Fan.** Dear, dear brother, I have come to bring you home.

**Boy.** Home, little Fan?

**Fan.** Yes! Home, for good and all! Father is so much kinder than he ever used to be, and home's like heaven! He spoke so gently to me one dear night when I was going to bed that I was not afraid to ask him once more if you might come home; and he said "yes" . . . you should; and sent me in a coach to bring you. And you're to be a man and are never to come back here, but first, we're to be together all the Christmas long, and have the merriest time in the world.

**Purpose for Reading**
What questions do you have about Scrooge's family? Read on to see if they are answered.

**Boy.** You are quite a woman, little Fan!

[*Laughing; she drags at boy, causing him to stumble to the door with her. Suddenly we hear a mean and terrible voice in the hallway, Off. It is the* Schoolmaster.]

**Schoolmaster.** Bring down Master Scrooge's travel box at once! He is to travel!

**Fan.** Who is that, Ebenezer?

**Boy.** O! Quiet, Fan. It is the Schoolmaster, himself!

[*The door bursts open and into the room bursts with it the* Schoolmaster.]

**Schoolmaster.** Master Scrooge?

**Boy.** Oh, Schoolmaster. I'd like you to meet my little sister, Fan, sir . . .

[*Two boys struggle on with* Scrooge's *trunk.*]

**Fan.** Pleased, sir . . . [*She curtsies.*]

**Schoolmaster.** You are to travel, Master Scrooge.

**Scrooge.** Yes, sir. I know sir . . .

[*All start to exit, but* Fan *grabs the coattail of the mean old* Schoolmaster.]

**Boy.** Fan!

**Schoolmaster.** What's this?

**Fan.** Pardon, sir, but I believe that you've forgotten to say your goodbye to my brother, Ebenezer, who stands still now

**Comprehension**
Where is Scrooge when his sister arrives to take him home?

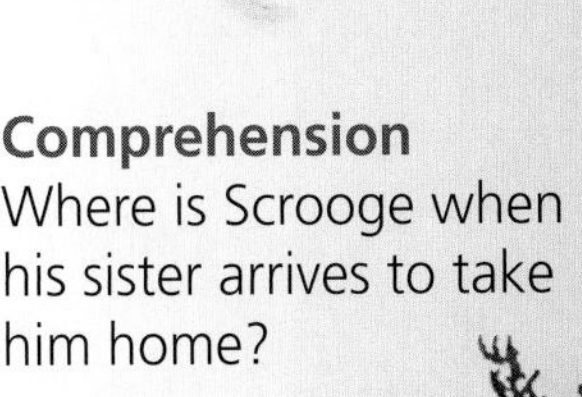

awaiting it . . . [*She smiles, curtsies, lowers her eyes.*] pardon, sir.

**Schoolmaster.** [*Amazed*] I . . . uh . . . harumph . . . uhh . . . well, then . . . [*Outstretches hand*] Goodbye, Scrooge.

**Boy.** Uh, well, goodbye, Schoolmaster . . .

[*Lights fade out on all but* Boy *looking at* FAN*; and* Scrooge *and* Past *looking at them.*]

**Scrooge.** Oh, my dear, dear little sister, Fan . . . how I loved her.

**Past.** Always a delicate creature, whom a breath might have withered, but she had a large heart . . .

**Scrooge.** So she had.

**Past.** She died a woman, and had, as I think, children.

**Scrooge.** One child.

**Past.** True. Your nephew.

**Scrooge.** Yes.

**Dialogue**
What surprising aspect of Scrooge's character does this scene reveal?

**Past.** Fine, then. We move on, Mr. Scrooge. That warehouse, there? Do you know it?

**Scrooge.** Know it? Wasn't I apprenticed[20] there?

**Past.** We'll have a look.

[*They enter the warehouse. The lights crossfade with them, coming up on an old man in Welsh wig:* Fezziwig.]

**Scrooge.** Why, it's old Fezziwig! Bless his heart; it's Fezziwig, alive again!

[Fezziwig *sits behind a large, high desk, counting. He lays down his pen; looks at the clock: seven bells sound.*]

*Quittin' time . . .*

**Fezziwig.** Quittin' time . . . [*He takes off his waistcoat and laughs; calls off*] Yo ho, Ebenezer! Dick!

[Dick Wilkins *and* Ebenezer Scrooge*—a young man version—enter the room.* Dick *and* Ebenezer *are* Fezziwig's *apprentices.*]

20. **apprenticed** (ə prenˊ tist) *v.* receiving instruction in a trade as well as food and housing or wages in return for work.

▼ **Critical Viewing**
Based on this painting, what kind of a man is Fezziwig?

**Scrooge.** Dick Wilkins, to be sure! My fellow-'prentice! Bless my soul, yes. There he is. He was very much attached to me, was Dick. Poor Dick! Dear, dear!

**Fezziwig.** Yo ho, my boys. No more work tonight. Christmas Eve, Dick. Christmas, Ebenezer!
*[They stand at attention in front of* Fezziwig; *laughing]*
Hilli-ho! Clear away, and let's have lots of room here! Hilli-ho, Dick! Chirrup, Ebenezer!
*[The young men clear the room, sweep the floor, straighten the pictures, trim the lamps, etc. The space is clear now. A fiddler enters, fiddling.]*
Hi-ho, Matthew! Fiddle away . . . where are my daughters?

*[The fiddler plays. Three young daughters of* Fezziwig *enter followed by six young male suitors. They are dancing to the music. All employees come in: workers, clerks, housemaids, cousins, the baker, etc. All dance. Full number wanted here. Throughout the dance, food is brought into the feast. It is "eaten" in dance, by the dancers.* Ebenezer *dances with all three of the daughters, as does* Dick. *They compete for the*

**Comprehension**
Who is Fezziwig?

*daughters, happily, in the dance.* Fezziwig *dances with his daughters.* Fezziwig *dances with* Dick *and* Ebenezer. *The music changes:* Mrs. Fezziwig *enters. She lovingly scolds her husband. They dance. She dances with* Ebenezer, *lifting him and throwing him about. She is enormously fat. When the dance is ended, they all dance off, floating away, as does the music.* Scrooge *and the* Ghost of Christmas Past *stand alone now. The music is gone.*]

Vocabulary ▶
**gratitude** (grat′ i to͞od′)
*n.* thankful appreciation

**Past.** It was a small matter, that Fezziwig made those silly folks so full of **gratitude**.

**Scrooge.** Small!

**Past.** Shhh!

[*Lights up on* Dick *and* Ebenezer]

**Dick.** We are blessed, Ebenezer, truly, to have such a master as Mr. Fezziwig!

**Dialogue**
What does this dialogue reveal about Scrooge's feelings for Fezziwig?

**Young Scrooge.** He is the best, best, the very and absolute best! If ever I own a firm of my own, I shall treat my apprentices with the same dignity and the same grace. We have learned a wonderful lesson from the master, Dick!

**Dick.** Ah, that's a fact, Ebenezer. That's a fact!

**Past.** Was it not a small matter, really? He spent but a few pounds[21] of his mortal money on your small party. Three or four pounds, perhaps. Is that so much that he deserves such praise as you and Dick so lavish now?

**Scrooge.** It isn't that! It isn't that, Spirit. Fezziwig had the power to make us happy or unhappy; to make our service light or burdensome; a pleasure or a toil. The happiness he gave is quite as great as if it cost him a fortune.

**Past.** What is the matter?

**Scrooge.** Nothing particular.

**Past.** Something, I think.

**Scrooge.** No, no. I should like to be able to say a word or two to my clerk just now! That's all!

---

**21. pounds** (poundz) *n.* common type of money used in Great Britain.

[EBENEZER *enters the room and shuts down all the lamps. He stretches and yawns. The* GHOST OF CHRISTMAS PAST *turns to* SCROOGE *all of a sudden.*]

**PAST.** My time grows short! Quick!

[*In a flash of light,* EBENEZER *is gone, and in his place stands an* OLDER SCROOGE, *this one a man in the prime of his life.*
*Beside him stands a young woman in a mourning dress. She is crying. She speaks to the man, with hostility.*]

**WOMAN.** It matters little . . . to you, very little. Another idol has displaced me.

**MAN.** What idol has displaced you?

**WOMAN.** A golden one.

**MAN.** This is an even-handed dealing of the world. There is nothing on which it is so hard as poverty; and there is nothing it professes to condemn with such severity as the pursuit of wealth!

**WOMAN.** You fear the world too much. Have I not seen your nobler aspirations fall off one by one, until the master-passion, Gain, engrosses you? Have I not?

**SCROOGE.** No!

**MAN.** What then? Even if I have grown so much wiser, what then? Have I changed towards you?

**WOMAN.** No . . .

**MAN.** Am I?

**WOMAN.** Our contract is an old one. It was made when we were both poor and content to be so. You are changed. When it was made, you were another man.

**MAN.** I was not another man: I was a boy.

**WOMAN.** Your own feeling tells you that you were not what you are. I am. That which promised happiness when we were one in heart is fraught with misery now that we are two . . .

**Dialogue**
What personal change in Scrooge does this dialogue show?

**Comprehension**
What does the woman tell Scrooge about himself?

**Scrooge.** No!

**Woman.** How often and how keenly I have thought of this, I will not say. It is enough that I have thought of it, and can release you . . .

**Scrooge.** [*Quietly*] Don't release me, madame . . .

**Man.** Have I ever sought release?

**Woman.** In words. No. Never.

**Man.** In what then?

**Woman.** In a changed nature; in an altered spirit. In everything that made my love of any worth or value in your sight. If this has never been between us, tell me, would you seek me out and try to win me now? Ah, no!

**Scrooge.** Ah, yes!

**Man.** You think not?

**Woman.** I would gladly think otherwise if I could, heaven knows! But if you were free today, tomorrow, yesterday, can even I believe that you would choose a dowerless girl[22]—you who in your very confidence with her weigh everything by Gain; or, choosing her, do I not know that your repentance and regret would surely follow? I do; and I release you. With a full heart, for the love of him you once were.

**Scrooge.** Please, I . . . I . . .

**Man.** Please, I . . . I . . .

**Woman.** Please. You may—the memory of what is past half makes me hope you will—have pain in this. A very, very brief time, and you will dismiss the memory of it, as an unprofitable dream, from which it happened well that you awoke. May you be happy in the life that you have chosen for yourself . . .

---

22. **a dowerless** (dou´ ər les) **girl** a girl without a dowry, the property or wealth a woman brought to her husband in marriage.

**Scrooge.** No!

**Woman.** Yourself . . . alone . . .

**Scrooge.** No!

**Woman.** Goodbye, Ebenezer . . .

**Scrooge.** Don't let her go!

**Man.** Goodbye.

**Scrooge.** No!
[*She exits.* SCROOGE *goes to younger man: himself.*]
You fool! Mindless loon! You fool!

**Man.** [*To exited woman*] Fool. Mindless loon. Fool . . .

**Scrooge.** Don't say that! Spirit, remove me from this place.

**Past.** I have told you these were shadows of the things that have been. They are what they are. Do not blame me, Mr. Scrooge.

**Scrooge.** Remove me! I cannot bear it!
[*The faces of all who appeared in this scene are now projected for a moment around the stage: enormous, flimsy, silent.*]
Leave me! Take me back! Haunt me no longer!

[*There is a sudden flash of light: a flare. The* Ghost of Christmas Past *is gone.* Scrooge *is, for the moment, alone onstage. His bed is turned down, across the stage. A small candle burns now in* Scrooge's *hand. There is a child's cap in his other hand. He slowly crosses the stage to his bed, to sleep.* Marley *appears behind* Scrooge, *who continues his long, elderly cross to bed.* Marley *speaks directly to the audience.*]

**Marley.** Scrooge must sleep now. He must surrender to the irresistible drowsiness caused by the recognition of what was. [*Pauses*] The cap he carries is from ten lives past: his boyhood cap . . . donned atop a hopeful hairy head . . . askew, perhaps, or at a rakish angle. Doffed now in honor of regret.[23] Perhaps even too heavy to carry in his present state of weak remorse . . .

**Dialogue**
What do you learn about Scrooge's past from the dialogue here?

**Comprehension**
Why does the woman leave Scrooge?

---

**23. donned . . . regret** To *don* and *doff* a hat means to put it on and take it off, *askew* means "crooked," and *at a rakish angle* means "having a dashing or jaunty look."

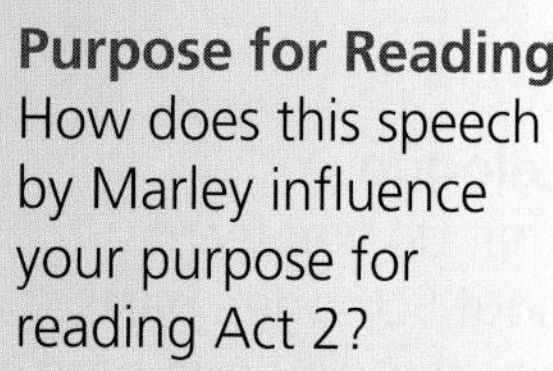

**Purpose for Reading** How does this speech by Marley influence your purpose for reading Act 2?

[SCROOGE *DROPS THE CAP. He lies atop his bed. He sleeps. To audience*]
He sleeps. For him, there's even more trouble ahead. [*Smiles*] For you? The play house tells me there's hot cider, as should be your anticipation for the specter Christmas Present and Future, for I promise you both. [*Smiles again*] So, I pray you hurry back to your seats refreshed and ready for a miser—to turn his coat of gray into a blazen Christmas holly-red. [*A flash of lightning. A clap of thunder. Bats fly. Ghosty music.* MARLEY *is gone.*]

## Language Study

**Vocabulary** Rewrite the numbered sentences so that each includes one of the vocabulary words listed below and also retains the same basic meaning.

**implored** **morose** **destitute** **void** **conveyed**

1. Jack's gloomy expression showed that he had lost the game.
2. Her sudden inheritance meant that she would no longer live among the poor.
3. The party helped to ease the emptiness I was feeling.
4. The grin on Dr. Jackson's face expressed his relief.
5. We begged the guard not to close the gate.

**WORD STUDY**
The **Latin root *-grat-*** means "thankful" or "pleasing." In this play, Bob Cratchit expresses his **gratitude**, or thankfulness, for a day off from work on Christmas.

### Word Study

**Part A** Explain how the **Latin root *-grat-*** contributes to the meanings of the words *gratuity, ingrate*, and *gratification*. Consult a dictionary if necessary.

**Part B** Use the context of the sentences and what you know about the Latin root *-grat-* to explain your answer to each question.

1. If a friend helped you out of a difficult situation, would you feel *grateful*?
2. Would *congratulations* be in order if you failed an exam?

# Close Reading Activities

## Literary Analysis

### Key Ideas and Details

1. **Purpose for Reading** What clues in the title helped you preview the content of the play?
2. **Purpose for Reading (a)** What is your purpose for reading this play? **(b)** How might your purpose be different if you were reading a nonfiction play about life in the workhouses of Victorian England?
3. **(a)** What scenes from his past does Scrooge visit? **(b) Draw Conclusions:** How does each event contribute to his current attitude and personality?
4. **(a) Deduce:** What does Scrooge value in life? Support your answer with examples and quotations from the text. **(b) Draw Conclusions:** Do his values make Scrooge a happy man? Explain.

### Craft and Structure

5. **Dialogue** Complete a chart like the one on the right by identifying important examples of dialogue. **(a)** For each line of dialogue in the first row, use the second row to tell what it means. **(b)** In the third row, tell why this dialogue is important for advancing the action of the play or developing characters.

| What Does It Say? |
|---|
| |
| **What Does It Mean?** |
| |
| **Why Is It Important?** |
| |

### Integration of Knowledge and Ideas

6. **(a) Connect:** What hints in the text suggest to you that Scrooge may change for the better? **(b) Speculate:** In the future, how might Scrooge's interactions with others differ from his interactions in the present? **(c) Predict:** Do you think you will see examples of Scrooge's changed behavior in the second act of the play? Why or why not?
7. **(a) Deduce:** What effects have Scrooge's past experiences had on the person he has become? **(b) Evaluate:** Based on Scrooge's past experiences, do you think he should be excused for his current attitudes and behavior? Explain.
8. **Speculate:** What do you think would have happened to Scrooge if he had not been visited by Marley's Ghost and the Ghost of Christmas Past? Support your ideas with details from the text.

9. THE BIG ? **Do others see us more clearly than we see ourselves?** How do the people in Scrooge's past reveal his own behavior to him?

**ACADEMIC VOCABULARY**

As you write and speak about *A Christmas Carol: Scrooge and Marley*, Act I, use the words related to self-perception that you explored on p. 447 of this textbook.

## Conventions: Prepositions and Prepositional Phrases

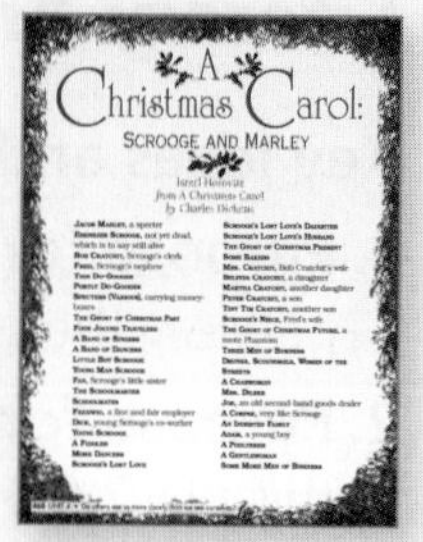

A **preposition** relates a noun or a pronoun that follows it to another word in the sentence. In the sentence *The book is on the table*, the preposition *on* relates the noun *table* to another word in the sentence, *book*.

A **prepositional phrase** begins with a preposition and ends with a noun or pronoun—called the **object of the preposition**. In the prepositional phrase *on the table*, the preposition is *on*, and the object of the preposition is *table*.

| Commonly Used Prepositions | | | |
|---|---|---|---|
| above | below | in | over |
| across | beneath | into | through |
| after | between | near | to |
| against | by | of | toward |
| along | down | on | under |
| at | during | onto | until |
| before | for | out | up |
| behind | from | outside | with |

### Practice A

Identify the prepositional phrase in each sentence. Then, identify the preposition and the object of the preposition.

1. Scroogeis sitting in his countinghouse.
2. Marley points at Scrooge's window.
3. Marley describes visits from three spirits.
4. Scrooge is weak with fear.

**Reading Application** In *A Christmas Carol: Scrooge and Marley*, Act I, find three sentences with prepositional phrases and identify the prepositions.

### Practice B

Identify the preposition and the object of the preposition in each prepositional phrase. Then, use each prepositional phrase to write a sentence about Scrooge's past.

1. by his friends
2. near a chair
3. in Fezziwig's warehouse
4. of gratitude

**Writing Application** Choose three prepositions from the drama and use them in a paragraph describing a time you were persuaded to change.

## Writing to Sources

**Argument** Write a **letter** to Scrooge, telling him what he is missing in life by being cranky and negative toward the people around him. Begin your letter with a salutation, or greeting. Then, support the main points of your argument with clear reasons and evidence. Conclude with a closing and your signature.

- Present a balanced argument by carefully organizing the body of your letter. Fully support each claim with logical reasons and relevant evidence from the text. Use transitional phrases like "another issue is . . ." or "in addition" to help unify the main argument—that there are many things Scrooge is missing.
- If you handwrite your letter, write legibly. (For a model of a friendly-letter format, refer to the Writing Handbook at the back of this book.)

**Grammar Application** Check your writing to be sure you have used prepositions and prepositional phrases correctly.

## Research and Technology

**Build and Present Knowledge** Prepare **costume plans** for this play. With a small group, research the clothing that was worn during the Victorian era in England.

- Use the Internet and library resources to gather information, photos, sketches, and descriptions.
- Review *A Christmas Carol* and note the social positions of the characters. Based on their social positions, determine what types of clothing different characters would have worn. Be sure the costumes reflect the season in which the play is set. Also, find out about the fabrics and materials that were available during the time period.
- Use the information you find to plan costumes for two different characters. In your plan, show or describe the types of clothing, including the colors and fabrics. Include pictures or sketches with your descriptions.
- Ask your classmates for feedback as to whether or not your costume plans reflect what they imagined as they read Act I. Feedback should be supported with specific textual details.

## Do others see us more clearly than we see ourselves?

Think about the Big Question as you read *A Christmas Carol: Scrooge and Marley*, Act II. Take notes on the ways in which Scrooge gains insights about himself.

## CLOSE READING FOCUS

### Key Ideas and Details: **Purpose for Reading**

Your **purpose for reading** affects the way you read and the speed of your reading. Adjust your reading rate to suit your purpose.

- As you read drama, slow down to read stage directions carefully. They may reveal action that is not shown in the dialogue.
- Speed up to read short lines of dialogue quickly to create the feeling of conversation.
- Slow down to read longer speeches by a single character so that you can reflect on the character's words.
- If one of your purposes is to appreciate an *author's style*, or unique way of writing, slow your pace as you read.

### Craft and Structure: **Stage Directions**

The **script** is the written text of a play. **Stage directions**, a part of the script, instruct actors on how to move and speak or describe what the stage should sound and look like. If you are reading a play instead of watching a performance, you get certain information only from the stage directions. Stage directions are usually written in italic type and set off by brackets or parentheses, as in this example:

*[Jen bursts through the door, stage left. There is a crack of thunder. Then, the lights go dark.]*

## Vocabulary

Copy the words from the drama into your notebook. Write a synonym for each word you know.

| | | |
|---|---|---|
| **astonish** | **compulsion** | **severe** |
| **meager** | **audible** | **intercedes** |

## CLOSE READING MODEL

The passage below is from Israel Horvitz's play *A Christmas Carol: Scrooge and Marley*, Act II. The annotations to the right of the passage show ways in which you can use close reading skills to set a purpose for reading and to analyze stage directions.

### from *A Christmas Carol: Scrooge and Marley,* Act II

*[Winter music. Choral group behind scrim, sings. When the song is done and the stage is re-set, the lights will fade up on a row of shops, behind the singers. The choral group will hum the song they have just completed now and mill about the streets, carrying their dinners to the bakers' shops and restaurants. They will, perhaps, sing about being poor at Christmastime, whatever.]*[1]

**Present.** These revelers, Mr. Scrooge, carry their own dinners to their jobs, where they will work to bake the meals the rich men and women of this city will eat as their Christmas dinners. Generous people these . . . to care for the others, so . . .

*[*Present *walks among the choral group and a sparkling incense falls from his torch on to their baskets, as he pulls the covers off of the baskets. Some of the choral group become angry with each other.]*[2]

**Man #1.** Hey, you, watch where you're going.

**Man #2.** Watch it yourself, mate!

*[*Present *sprinkles them directly, they change.]*[3]

**Man #1.** I pray go in ahead of me. It's Christmas. You be first!

**Man #2.** No, no, I must insist that YOU be first!

**Man #1.** All right, I shall be, and gratefully so.

**Man #2.** The pleasure is equally mine, for being able to watch you pass, smiling.[4]

**Stage Directions**
**1** These stage directions help you picture the scene by describing actions, sounds, and lighting effects.

**Purpose for Reading**
**2** Stage directions may reveal details not shown in the dialogue. Read them slowly so you do not overlook important information or actions.

**Stage Directions**
**3** These stage directions are brief but they convey an important detail. When Present sprinkles incense on the people, "they change." Without this information, you, as a reader, might not understand why the angry people suddenly become friendly.

**Purpose for Reading**
**4** Speed up your reading rate to read short lines of dialogue like these. Doing so will help you "hear" the conversational nature of the characters' exchange.

# A Christmas Carol:

## SCROOGE AND MARLEY

Israel Horovitz
*from* A Christmas Carol
*by* Charles Dickens

## ACT II

### SCENE 1

[*Lights. Choral music is sung. Curtain.* Scrooge, *in bed, sleeping, in spotlight. We cannot yet see the interior of his room.* Marley, *opposite, in spotlight equal to* Scrooge's. Marley *laughs. He tosses his hand in the air and a flame shoots from it, magically, into the air. There is a thunder clap, and then another; a lightning flash, and then another. Ghostly music plays under. Colors change.* Marley's *spotlight has gone out and now reappears, with* Marley *in it, standing next to the bed and the sleeping* Scrooge. Marley *addresses the audience directly.*]

**Marley.** Hear this snoring Scrooge! Sleeping to escape the nightmare that is his waking day. What shall I bring to him now? I'm afraid nothing would astonish old Scrooge now. Not after what he's seen. Not a baby boy, not a rhinoceros, nor anything in between would **astonish** Ebenezer Scrooge just now. I can think of nothing . . . [*Suddenly*] that's it! Nothing! [*He speaks confidentially.*] I'll have the

**Stage Directions**
What sounds establish this as a scary scene?

**◀ Vocabulary**
**astonish** (ə stän′ ish) *v.* amaze

**Comprehension**
What is Marley trying to figure out?

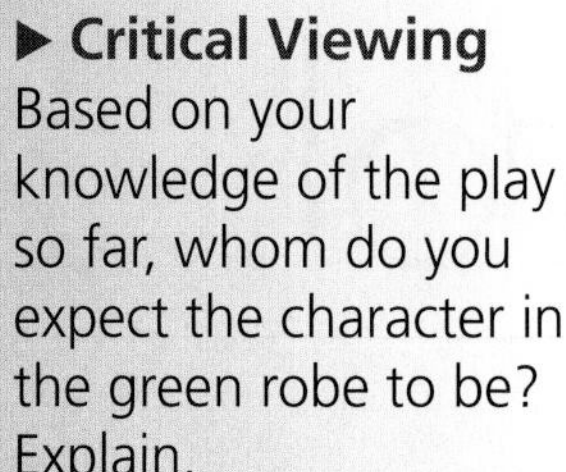

**▶ Critical Viewing**
Based on your knowledge of the play so far, whom do you expect the character in the green robe to be? Explain.

clock strike one and, when he awakes expecting my second messenger, there will be no one . . . nothing. Then I'll have the bell strike twelve. And then one again . . . and then nothing. Nothing . . . [*Laughs*] nothing will . . . astonish him. I think it will work.

[*The bell tolls one.* SCROOGE *leaps awake.*]

**SCROOGE.** One! One! This is it: time! [*Looks about the room*] Nothing!

[*The bell tolls midnight.*]

Midnight! How can this be? I'm sleeping backwards.

[*One again*]

Good heavens! One again! I'm sleeping back and forth! [*A pause.* SCROOGE *looks about.*] Nothing! Absolutely nothing!

[*Suddenly, thunder and lightning.* MARLEY *laughs and disappears. The room shakes and glows. There is suddenly springlike music.* SCROOGE *makes a run for the door.*]

**MARLEY.** Scrooge!

**SCROOGE.** What?

**MARLEY.** Stay you put!

**SCROOGE.** Just checking to see if anyone is in here.

**Purpose for Reading**
At what rate would you read these stage directions? Why?

[*Lights and thunder again: more music.* MARLEY *is of a sudden gone. In his place sits the* GHOST OF CHRISTMAS PRESENT*—to be called in the stage directions of the play,* PRESENT*—center of room. Heaped up on the floor, to form a kind of throne, are turkeys, geese, game, poultry, brawn, great joints of meat, suckling pigs, long wreaths of sausages, mince-pies, plum puddings, barrels of oysters, red hot chestnuts, cherry-cheeked apples, juicy oranges, luscious pears, immense twelfth cakes, and seething bowls of punch, that make the chamber dim with their delicious steam. Upon this throne sits* PRESENT, *glorious to see. He bears a torch, shaped as a Horn of Plenty.*[1] SCROOGE *hops out of the door, and then peeks back again into his bedroom.* PRESENT *calls to* SCROOGE.]

1. **Horn of Plenty** a horn overflowing with fruits, flowers, and grain, representing wealth and abundance.

**PRESENT.** Ebenezer Scrooge. Come in, come in! Come in and know me better!

**SCROOGE.** Hello. How should I call you?

**PRESENT.** I am the Ghost of Christmas Present. Look upon me.

[PRESENT *is wearing a simple green robe. The walls around the room are now covered in greenery, as well. The room seems to be a perfect grove now: leaves of holly, mistletoe and ivy reflect the stage lights. Suddenly, there is a mighty roar of flame in the fireplace and now the hearth burns with a lavish, warming fire. There is an ancient scabbard girdling the* GHOST'S *middle, but without sword. The sheath is gone to rust.*]

You have never seen the like of me before?

**SCROOGE.** Never.

**PRESENT.** You have never walked forth with younger members of my family; my elder brothers born on Christmases past.

**SCROOGE.** I don't think I have. I'm afraid I've not. Have you had many brothers, Spirit?

**PRESENT.** More than eighteen hundred.

**SCROOGE.** A tremendous family to provide for! [PRESENT *stands*] Spirit, conduct me where you will. I went forth last night on **compulsion**, and learnt a lesson which is working now. Tonight, if you have aught to teach me, let me profit by it.

**PRESENT.** Touch my robe.

[SCROOGE *walks cautiously to* PRESENT *and touches his robe. When he does, lightning flashes, thunder claps, music plays. Blackout*]

◀ **Vocabulary**
**compulsion** (kəm pulʹ shən) *n.* driving, irresistible force

**Comprehension**
Who visits Scrooge in Scene 1?

# Scene 2

[*PROLOGUE:* Marley *stands spotlit,* L. *He speaks directly to the audience.*]

**Marley.** My ghostly friend now leads my living partner through the city's streets.

[*Lights up on* Scrooge *and* Present]

See them there and hear the music people make when the weather is **severe**, as it is now.

Vocabulary ▶
**severe** (sə vir′) *adj.* harsh

[*Winter music. Choral group behind scrim, sings. When the song is done and the stage is re-set, the lights will fade up on a row of shops, behind the singers. The choral group will hum the song they have just completed now and mill about the streets,*[2] *carrying their dinners to the bakers' shops and restaurants. They will, perhaps, sing about being poor at Christmastime, whatever.*]

**Present.** These revelers, Mr. Scrooge, carry their own dinners to their jobs, where they will work to bake the meals the rich men and women of this city will eat as their Christmas dinners. Generous people these . . . to care for the others, so . . .

[Present *walks among the choral group and a sparkling incense*[3] *falls from his torch on to their baskets, as he pulls the covers off of the baskets. Some of the choral group become angry with each other.*]

**Purpose for Reading**
At what rate would you read dialogue such as this? Why?

**Man #1.** Hey, you, watch where you're going.

**Man #2.** Watch it yourself, mate!

[Present *sprinkles them directly, they change.*]

**Man #1.** I pray go in ahead of me. It's Christmas. You be first!

**Man #2.** No, no, I must insist that YOU be first!

**Man #1.** All right, I shall be, and gratefully so.

**Man #2.** The pleasure is equally mine, for being able to watch you pass, smiling.

**Man #1.** I would find it a shame to quarrel on Christmas Day . . .

---

2. **mill about the streets** walk around aimlessly.
3. **incense** (in′ sens) *n.* any of various substances that produce a pleasant odor when burned.

**Man #2.** As would I.

**Man #1.** Merry Christmas then, friend!

**Man #2.** And a Merry Christmas straight back to you!

[*Church bells toll. The choral group enter the buildings: the shops and restaurants; they exit the stage, shutting their doors closed behind them. All sound stops.* Scrooge *and* Present *are alone again.*]

**Stage Directions** What information in these stage directions adds to the effectiveness of the scene?

**Scrooge.** What is it you sprinkle from your torch?

**Present.** Kindness.

**Scrooge.** Do you sprinkle your kindness on any particular people or on all people?

**Present.** To any person kindly given. And to the very poor most of all.

**Scrooge.** Why to the very poor most?

**PRESENT.** Because the very poor need it most. Touch my heart . . . here, Mr. Scrooge. We have another journey.

[Scrooge *touches the* Ghost's *heart and music plays, lights change color, lightning flashes, thunder claps. A choral group appears on the street, singing Christmas carols.*]

## Scene 3

[Marley *stands spotlit in front of a scrim on which is painted the exterior of* Cratchit's *four-roomed house. There is a flash and a clap and* Marley *is gone. The lights shift color again, the scrim flies away, and we are in the interior of the* Cratchit *family home.* Scrooge *is there, with the* spirit (Present), *watching* Mrs. Cratchit *set the table, with the help of* Belinda Cratchit *and* Peter Cratchit, *a baby, pokes a fork into the mashed potatoes on his highchair's tray. He also chews on his shirt collar.*]

**Scrooge.** What is this place, Spirit?

**Present.** This is the home of your employee, Mr. Scrooge. Don't you know it?

**Comprehension** What does the Ghost of Christmas Present show Scrooge?

**Scrooge.** Do you mean Cratchit, Spirit? Do you mean this is Cratchit's home?

**Present.** None other.

**Scrooge.** These children are his?

**Present.** There are more to come presently.

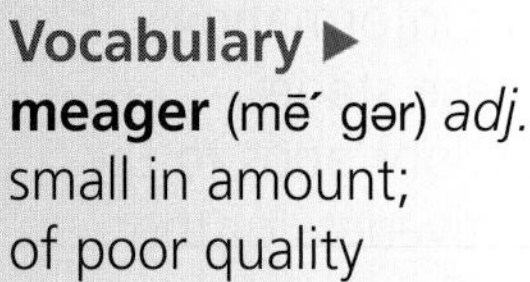

**Vocabulary ▶**
**meager** (mē´ gər) *adj.* small in amount; of poor quality

**Scrooge.** On his **meager** earnings! What foolishness!

**Present.** Foolishness, is it?

**Scrooge.** Wouldn't you say so? Fifteen shillings[4] a week's what he gets!

**Present.** I would say that he gets the pleasure of his family, fifteen times a week times the number of hours a day! Wait, Mr. Scrooge. Wait, listen and watch. You might actually learn something . . .

**Mrs. Cratchit.** What has ever got your precious father then? And your brother, Tiny Tim? And Martha warn't as late last Christmas by half an hour!

[Martha *opens the door, speaking to her mother as she does.*]

**Martha.** Here's Martha, now, Mother! [*She laughs. The* Cratchit Children *squeal with delight.*]

**Belinda.** It's Martha, Mother! Here's Martha!

**Peter.** Marthmama, Marthmama! Hullo!

**Belinda.** Hurrah! Martha! Martha! There's such an enormous goose for us, Martha!

**Mrs. Cratchit.** Why, bless your heart alive, my dear, how late you are!

**Martha.** We'd a great deal of work to finish up last night, and had to clear away this morning, Mother.

**Purpose for Reading**
How does Mrs. Cratchit's use of language affect your reading rate? Explain.

**Mrs. Cratchit.** Well, never mind so long as you are come. Sit ye down before the fire, my dear, and have a warm, Lord bless ye!

**Belinda.** No, no! There's Father coming. Hide, Martha, hide!

[Martha *giggles and hides herself.*]

**Martha.** Where? Here?

**Peter.** Hide, hide!

---

4. **Fifteen shillings** a small amount of money for a week's work.

**Belinda.** Not there! *THERE!*

Martha *is hidden.* Bob Cratchit *enters, carrying* Tiny Tim *atop his shoulder. He wears a threadbare and fringeless comforter hanging down in front of him.* Tiny Tim *carries small crutches and his small legs are bound in an iron frame brace.]*

**Bob and Tiny Tim.** Merry Christmas.

**Bob.** Merry Christmas my love, Merry Christmas Peter, Merry Christmas Belinda. Why, where is Martha?

**Mrs. Cratchit.** Not coming.

**Bob.** Not coming: Not coming upon Christmas Day?

**Martha.** [*Pokes head out*] Ohhh, poor Father. Don't be disappointed.

**Bob.** What's this?

**Martha.** 'Tis I!

**Bob.** Martha! [*They embrace.*]

**Tiny Tim.** Martha! Martha!

**Martha.** Tiny Tim!

[Tiny Tim *is placed in* Martha's *arms.* Belinda *and* Peter *rush him offstage.*]

**Belinda.** Come, brother! You must come hear the pudding singing in the copper.

**Tiny Tim.** The pudding? What flavor have we?

**Peter.** Plum! Plum!

**Tiny Tim.** Oh, Mother! I love plum!

[*The children exit the stage, giggling.*]

**Mrs. Cratchit.** And how did little Tim behave?

**Bob.** As good as gold, and even better. Somehow he gets thoughtful sitting by himself so much, and thinks the

**▲ Critical Viewing**
How do you think seeing the happy Cratchit family will affect Scrooge's attitude?

**Comprehension**
Why does Martha hide?

strangest things you ever heard. He told me, coming home, that he hoped people saw him in the church, because he was a cripple, and it might be pleasant to them to remember upon Christmas Day, who made lame beggars walk and blind men see. [*Pauses*] He has the oddest ideas sometimes, but he seems all the while to be growing stronger and more hearty . . . one would never know. [*Hears* TIM'S *crutch on floor outside door*]

**Stage Directions**
Why is the pause in Bob's speech important here?

**PETER.** The goose has arrived to be eaten!

**BELINDA.** Oh, mama, mama, it's beautiful.

**MARTHA.** It's a perfect goose, Mother!

**TINY TIM.** To this Christmas goose, Mother and Father I say . . . [*Yells*] Hurrah! Hurrah!

**OTHER CHILDREN.** [*Copying* TIM] Hurrah! Hurrah!

[*The family sits round the table.* BOB *and* MRS. CRATCHIT *serve the trimmings, quickly. All sit; all bow heads; all pray.*]

**BOB.** Thank you, dear Lord, for your many gifts . . . our dear children; our wonderful meal; our love for one another; and the warmth of our small fire—[*Looks up at all*] A merry Christmas to us, my dear. God bless us!

**ALL.** [*Except* TIM] Merry Christmas! God bless us!

**TINY TIM.** [*In a short silence*] God bless us every one.

*All freeze. Spotlight on* PRESENT *and* SCROOGE]

**SCROOGE.** Spirit, tell me if Tiny Tim will live.

**PRESENT.** I see a vacant seat . . . in the poor chimney corner, and a crutch without an owner, carefully preserved. If these shadows remain unaltered by the future, the child will die.

**SCROOGE.** No, no, kind Spirit! Say he will be spared!

**PRESENT.** If these shadows remain unaltered by the future, none other of my race will find him here. What then? If he be like to die, he had better do it, and decrease the surplus population.

[SCROOGE *bows his head. We hear* BOB'S *voice speak* SCROOGE'S *name.*]

**Bob.** Mr. Scrooge . . .

Scrooge. Huh? What's that? Who calls?

Bob. [*His glass raised in a toast*] I'll give you Mr. Scrooge, the Founder of the Feast!

**Scrooge.** Me, Bob? You toast *me?*

**Present.** Save your breath, Mr. Scrooge. You can't be seen or heard.

**Mrs. Cratchit.** The Founder of the Feast, indeed! I wish I had him here, that miser Scrooge. I'd give him a piece of my mind to feast upon, and I hope he'd have a good appetite for it!

**Bob.** My dear! Christmas Day!

**Mrs. Cratchit.** It should be Christmas Day, I am sure, on which one drinks the health of such an odious, stingy, unfeeling man as Mr. Scrooge . . .

**Comprehension**
What is wrong with Tiny Tim?

**Scrooge.** Oh, Spirit, must I? . . .

**Mrs. Cratchit.** You know he is, Robert! Nobody knows it better than you do, poor fellow!

**Bob.** This is Christmas Day, and I should like to drink to the health of the man who employs me and allows me to earn my living and our support and that man is Ebenezer Scrooge . . .

**Mrs. Cratchit.** I'll drink to his health for your sake and the day's, but not for his sake . . . a Merry Christmas and a Happy New Year to you, Mr. Scrooge, wherever you may be this day!

**Scrooge.** Just here, kind madam . . . out of sight, out of sight . . .

**Bob.** Thank you, my dear. Thank you.

**Scrooge.** Thank you, Bob . . . and Mrs. Cratchit, too. No one else is toasting me, . . . not now . . . not ever. Of that I am sure . . .

**Bob.** Children . . .

**All.** Merry Christmas to Mr. Scrooge.

**Bob.** I'll pay you sixpence, Tim, for my favorite song.

**Tiny Tim.** Oh, Father, I'd so love to sing it, but not for pay. This Christmas goose—this feast—you and Mother, my brother and sisters close with me: that's my pay—

**Bob.** Martha, will you play the notes on the lute, for Tiny Tim's song.

**Belinda.** May I sing, too, Father?

**Bob.** We'll all sing.

[*They sing a song about a tiny child lost in the snow—probably from Wordsworth's poem.* Tim *sings the lead vocal; all chime in for the chorus. Their song fades under, as the* Ghost of Christmas Present *speaks.*]

**▼ Critical Viewing**
Martha plays a lute like this one while her family sings. If this play were set in modern times, what instrument would Martha probably play?

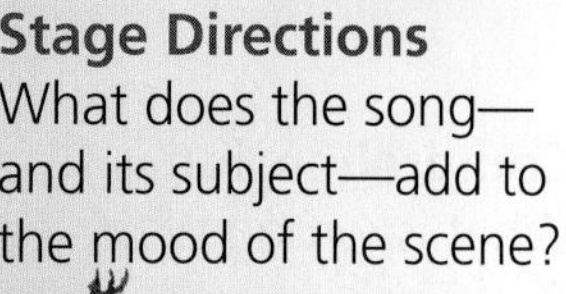

**Stage Directions**
What does the song—and its subject—add to the mood of the scene?

**PRESENT.** Mark my words, Ebenezer Scrooge. I do not present the Cratchits to you because they are a handsome, or brilliant family. They are not handsome. They are not brilliant. They are not well-dressed, or tasteful to the times. Their shoes are not even waterproofed by virtue of money or cleverness spent. So when the pavement is wet, so are the insides of their shoes and the tops of their toes. These are the Cratchits, Mr. Scrooge. They are not highly special. They are happy, grateful, pleased with one another, contented with the time and how it passes. They don't sing very well, do they? But, nonetheless, they do sing . . . [*Pauses*] think of that, Scrooge. Fifteen shillings a week and they do sing . . . hear their song until its end.

**Spiral Review**
**CHARACTER** What point is the Ghost of Christmas Present trying to impress upon Scrooge as he describes the Cratchits?

**SCROOGE.** I am listening. [*The chorus sings full volume now, until . . . the song ends here.*] Spirit, it must be time for us to take our leave. I feel in my heart that it is . . . that I must think on that which I have seen here . . .

**PRESENT.** Touch my robe again . . .

[SCROOGE *touches* PRESENT'S *robe. The lights fade out on the* CRATCHITS, *who sit, frozen, at the table.* SCROOGE *and* PRESENT *in a spotlight now. Thunder, lightning, smoke. They are gone.*]

## SCENE 4

[MARLEY *appears* D.L. *in single spotlight. A storm brews. Thunder and lightning.* SCROOGE *and* PRESENT *"fly" past,* U. *The storm continues, furiously, and, now and again,* SCROOGE *and* PRESENT *will zip past in their travels.* MARLEY *will speak straight out to the audience.*]

**MARLEY.** The Ghost of Christmas Present, my co-worker in this attempt to turn a miser, flies about now with that very miser, Scrooge, from street to street, and he points out partygoers on their way to Christmas parties. If one were to judge from the numbers of people on their way to friendly gatherings, one might think that no one was left at home to give anyone welcome . . . but that's not the case, is it? Every home is expecting company and . . . [*He laughs.*] Scrooge is amazed.

**Comprehension**
What does Scrooge observe the Cratchits doing?

[SCROOGE *and* PRESENT *zip past again. The lights fade up around them. We are in the* NEPHEW'S *home, in the living room.* PRESENT *and* SCROOGE *stand watching the* NEPHEW: FRED *and his wife, fixing the fire.*]

**Purpose for Reading**
Why is it important to read the change of scene described in the stage directions carefully?

**SCROOGE.** What is this place? We've moved from the mines!

**PRESENT.** You do not recognize them?

**SCROOGE.** It is my nephew! . . . and the one he married . . .

[MARLEY *waves his hand and there is a lightning flash. He disappears.*]

**FRED.** It strikes me as sooooo funny, to think of what he said . . . that Christmas was a humbug, as I live! He believed it!

**WIFE.** More shame for him, Fred!

**FRED.** Well, he's a comical old fellow, that's the truth.

**WIFE.** I have no patience with him.

**FRED.** Oh, I have! I am sorry for him; I couldn't be angry with him if I tried. Who suffers by his ill whims? Himself, always . . .

**SCROOGE.** It's me they talk of, isn't it, Spirit?

**FRED.** Here, wife, consider this. Uncle Scrooge takes it into his head to dislike us, and he won't come and dine with us. What's the consequence?

**WIFE.** Oh . . . you're sweet to say what I think you're about to say, too, Fred . . .

**FRED.** What's the consequence? He don't lose much of a dinner by it, I can tell you that!

**WIFE.** Ooooooo, Fred! Indeed, I think he loses a very good dinner . . . ask my sisters, or your bachelor friend, Topper . . . ask any of them. They'll tell you what old Scrooge, your uncle, missed: a dandy meal!

**FRED.** Well, that's something of a relief, wife. Glad to hear it! [*He hugs his wife. They laugh. They kiss.*] The truth is, he misses much yet. I mean to give him the same chance every year, whether he likes it or not, for I pity him. Nay, he is my only uncle and I feel for the old miser . . . but, I tell you, wife: I see my dear and perfect mother's face on his own wizened cheeks and brow: brother and sister they were, and I cannot erase that from each view of him I take . . .

**Wife.** I understand what you say, Fred, and I am with you in your yearly asking. But he never will accept, you know. He never will.

**Fred.** Well, true, wife. Uncle may rail at Christmas till he dies. I think I shook him some with my visit yesterday . . . [*Laughing*] I refused to grow angry . . . no matter how nasty he became . . . [*Whoops*] It was HE who grew angry, wife! [*They both laugh now.*]

**Scrooge.** What he says is true, Spirit . . .

**Fred and Wife.** Bah, humbug!

**Fred.** [*Embracing his wife*] There is much laughter in our marriage, wife. It pleases me. You please me . . .

**Wife.** And you please me, Fred. You are a good man . . . [*They embrace.*] Come now. We must have a look at the meal . . . our guests will soon arrive . . . my sisters, Topper . . .

**Fred.** A toast first . . . [*He hands her a glass.*] A toast to Uncle Scrooge . . . [*Fills their glasses*]

**Wife.** A toast to him?

**Fred.** Uncle Scrooge has given us plenty of merriment, I am sure, and it would be ungrateful not to drink to his health. And I say . . . *Uncle Scrooge!*

**Wife.** [*Laughing*] You're a proper loon,[5] Fred . . . and I'm a

**Comprehension**
What scenes does the Ghost of Christmas Present show Scrooge?

5. **a proper loon** a silly person.

proper wife to you . . . [*She raises her glass.*] Uncle Scrooge! [*They drink. They embrace. They kiss.*]

**Vocabulary ▶**
**audible** (ô´ də bəl) *adj.* loud enough to be heard

**Scrooge.** Spirit, please, make me visible! Make me **audible**! I want to talk with my nephew and my niece!

[*Calls out to them. The lights that light the room and* Fred *and wife fade out.* Scrooge *and* Present *are alone, spotlit.*]

**Present.** These shadows are gone to you now, Mr. Scrooge. You may return to them later tonight in your dreams. [*Pauses*] My time grows short, Ebenezer Scrooge. Look you on me! Do you see how I've aged?

**Scrooge.** Your hair has gone gray! Your skin, wrinkled! Are spirits' lives so short?

**Present.** My stay upon this globe is very brief. It ends tonight.

**Scrooge.** Tonight?

**Present.** At midnight. The time is drawing near!

[*Clock strikes 11:45.*]

**Stage Directions**
Why is the clock on stage important to the action?

Hear those chimes? In a quarter hour, my life will have been spent! Look, Scrooge, man. Look you here.

[*Two gnarled baby dolls are taken from* Present's *skirts.*]

**Scrooge.** Who are they?

**Present.** They are Man's children, and they cling to me, appealing from their fathers. The boy is Ignorance; the girl is Want. Beware them both, and all of their degree, but most of all beware this boy, for I see that written on his brow which is doom, unless the writing be erased. [*He stretches out his arm. His voice is now amplified: loudly and oddly.*]

**Scrooge.** Have they no refuge or resource?

**Present.** Are there no prisons? Are there no workhouses? [*Twelve chimes*] Are there no prisons? Are there no workhouses?

[A Phantom, *hooded, appears in dim light,* D., *opposite.*] Are there no prisons? Are there no workhouses?

[Present *begins to deliquesce.* Scrooge *calls after him.*]

**Scrooge.** Spirit, I'm frightened! Don't leave me! Spirit!

**Present.** Prisons? Workhouses? Prisons? Workhouses . . .

[*He is gone.* Scrooge *is alone now with the* Phantom, *who is, of course, the* Ghost of Christmas Future. *The* Phantom *is shrouded in black. Only its outstretched hand is visible from under his ghostly garment.*]

**Scrooge.** Who are you, Phantom? Oh, yes, I think I know you! You are, are you not, the Spirit of Christmas Yet to Come? [*No reply*] And you are about to show me the shadows of the things that have not yet happened, but will happen in time before us. Is that not so, Spirit? [*The* Phantom *allows* Scrooge *a look at his face. No other reply wanted here. A nervous giggle here.*] Oh, Ghost of the Future, I fear you more than any Specter I have seen! But, as I know that your purpose is to do me good and as I hope to live to be another man from what I was, I am prepared to bear you company. [Future *does not reply, but for a stiff arm, hand and finger set, pointing forward.*] Lead on, then, lead on. The night is waning fast, and it is precious time to me. Lead on, Spirit!

[Future *moves away from* Scrooge *in the same rhythm and motion employed at its arrival.* Scrooge *falls into the same pattern, a considerable space apart from the* Spirit. *In the space between them,* Marley *appears. He looks to* Future *and then to* Scrooge. *He claps his hands. Thunder and lightning. Three* Businessmen *appear, spotlighted singularly: One is* D.L.; *one is* D.R.; *one is* U.C. *Thus, six points of the stage should now be spotted in light.* Marley *will watch this scene from his position,* C. Scrooge *and* Future *are* R. *and* L. *of* C.]

**First Businessman.** Oh, no, I don't know much about it either way, I only know he's dead.

**Second Businessman.** When did he die?

**First Businessman.** Last night, I believe.

**Second Businessman.** Why, what was the matter with him? I thought he'd never die, really . . .

**First Businessman.** [*Yawning*] Goodness knows, goodness knows . . .

**Stage Directions** The stage direction calls for Future to stretch out his hand. How does this action add to the drama of the scene?

**Spiral Review**
**CHARACTER** What valuable information does Scrooge reveal about himself?

**Comprehension** What warning does the Ghost of Christmas Present give Scrooge?

**Third Businessman.** What has he done with his money?

**Second Businessman.** I haven't heard. Have you?

**First Businessman.** Left it to his Company, perhaps. Money to money; you know the expression . . .

**Third Businessman.** He hasn't left it to *me.* That's all I know . . .

**First Businessman.** [*Laughing*] Nor to me . . . [*Looks at* Second Businessman] You, then? You got his money???

**Second Businessman.** [*Laughing*] Me, me, his money? Nooooo!

[*They all laugh.*]

**Third Businessman.** It's likely to be a cheap funeral, for upon my life, I don't know of a living soul who'd care to venture to it. Suppose we make up a party and volunteer?

**Second Businessman.** I don't mind going if a lunch is provided, but I must be fed, if I make one.

**First Businessman.** Well, I am the most disinterested among you, for I never wear black gloves, and I never eat lunch. But I'll offer to go, if anybody else will. When I come to think of it, I'm not all sure that I wasn't his most particular friend; for we used to stop and speak whenever we met. Well, then . . . bye, bye!

**Second Businessman.** Bye, bye . . .

**Third Businessman.** Bye, bye . . .

[*They glide offstage in three separate directions. Their lights follow them.*]

**Scrooge.** Spirit, why did you show me this? Why do you show me businessmen from my streets as they take the death of Jacob Marley? That is a thing past. You are *future!*

[Jacob Marley *laughs a long, deep laugh. There is a thunder clap and lightning flash, and he is gone.* Scrooge *faces* Future, *alone on stage now.* Future *wordlessly stretches*

**▲ Critical Viewing**
How does the Ghost of Christmas Future differ from the other ghosts?

*out his arm-hand-and-finger-set, pointing into the distance, U. There, above them, scoundrels "fly" by, half-dressed and slovenly. When this scene has passed, a woman enters the playing area. She is almost at once followed by a second woman; and then a man in faded black; and then, suddenly, an old man, who smokes a pipe. The old man scares the other three. They laugh, anxious.*]

**Stage Directions**
If you were staging this play, how could you make people appear to "fly" by?

**First Woman.** Look here, old Joe, here's a chance! If we haven't all three met here without meaning it!

**Old Joe.** You couldn't have met in a better place. Come into the parlor. You were made free of it long ago, you know; and the other two ain't strangers [*He stands; shuts a door. Shrieking*] We're all suitable to our calling. We're well matched. Come into the parlor. Come into the parlor . . . [*They follow him* D. Scrooge *and* Future *are now in their midst, watching; silent. A truck comes in on which is set a small wall with fireplace and a screen of rags, etc. All props for the scene.*] Let me just rake this fire over a bit . . .

[*He does. He trims his lamp with the stem of his pipe. The* First Woman *throws a large bundle on to the floor. She sits beside it, crosslegged, defiantly.*]

**First Woman.** What odds then? What odds, Mrs. Dilber? Every person has a right to take care of themselves. HE always did!

**Mrs. Dilber.** That's true indeed! No man more so!

**First Woman.** Why, then, don't stand staring as if you was afraid, woman! Who's the wiser? We're not going to pick holes in each other's coats, I suppose?

**Mrs. Dilber.** No, indeed! We should hope not!

**First Woman.** Very well, then! That's enough. Who's the worse for the loss of a few things like these? Not a dead man, I suppose?

**Mrs. Dilber.** [*Laughing*] No, indeed!

**First Woman.** If he wanted to keep 'em after he was dead, the wicked old screw, why wasn't he natural in his lifetime? If he had been, he'd have had somebody to look after him

**Comprehension**
What does Scrooge think the spirit is showing him?

when he was struck with Death, instead of lying gasping out his last there, alone by himself.

**Purpose for Reading**
What question about the characters directs your purpose for reading this dialogue?

**Mrs. Dilber.** It's the truest word that was ever spoke. It's a judgment on him.

**First Woman.** I wish it were a heavier one, and it should have been, you may depend on it, if I could have laid my hands on anything else. Open that bundle, old Joe, and let me know the value of it. Speak out plain. I'm not afraid to be the first, nor afraid for them to see it. We knew pretty well that we were helping ourselves, before we met here, I believe. It's no sin. Open the bundle, Joe.

**First Man.** No, no, my dear! I won't think of letting you being the first to show what you've . . . earned . . . earned from this. I throw in mine.

[*He takes a bundle from his shoulder, turns it upside down, and empties its contents out on to the floor.*]

It's not very extensive, see . . . seals . . . a pencil case . . . sleeve buttons . . .

**First Woman.** Nice sleeve buttons, though . . .

**First Man.** Not bad, not bad . . . a brooch there . . .

**Old Joe.** Not really valuable, I'm afraid . . .

**First Man.** How much, old Joe?

**Old Joe.** [*Writing on the wall with chalk*] A pitiful lot, really. Ten and six and not a sixpence more!

**First Man.** You're not serious!

**Old Joe.** That's your account and I wouldn't give another sixpence if I was to be boiled for not doing it. Who's next?

**Mrs. Dilber.** Me! [*Dumps out contents of her bundle*] Sheets, towels, silver spoons, silver sugar-tongs . . . some boots . . .

**Old Joe.** [*Writing on wall*] I always give too much to the ladies. It's a weakness of mine and that's the way I ruin myself. Here's your total comin' up . . . two pounds-ten . . . if you asked me for another penny, and made it an open question, I'd repent of being so liberal and knock off half-a-crown.

**First Woman.** And now do MY bundle, Joe.

**Old Joe.** [*Kneeling to open knots on her bundle*] So many knots, madam . . . [*He drags out large curtains; dark*] What do you call this? Bed curtains!

**First Woman.** [*Laughing*] Ah, yes, bed curtains!

**Old Joe.** You don't mean to say you took 'em down, rings and all, with him lying there?

**First Woman.** Yes, I did, why not?

**Old Joe.** You were born to make your fortune and you'll certainly do it.

**First Woman.** I certainly shan't hold my hand, when I can get anything in it by reaching it out, for the sake of such a man as he was, I promise you, Joe. Don't drop that lamp oil on those blankets, now!

**Old Joe.** His blankets?

**First Woman.** Whose else's do you think? He isn't likely to catch cold without 'em, I daresay.

**Old Joe.** I hope that he didn't die of anything catching? Eh?

**First Woman.** Don't you be afraid of that. I ain't so fond of his company that I'd loiter about him for such things if he did. Ah! You may look through that shirt till your eyes ache, but you won't find a hole in it, nor a threadbare place. It's the best he had, and a fine one, too. They'd have wasted it, if it hadn't been for me.

**Old Joe.** What do you mean "They'd have wasted it?"

**First Woman.** Putting it on him to be buried in, to be sure. Somebody was fool enough to do it, but I took it off again . . .

[*She laughs, as do they all, nervously.*]

If calico[6] ain't good enough for such a purpose, it isn't good enough then for anything. It's quite as becoming to the body. He can't look uglier than he did in that one!

**Scrooge.** [*A low-pitched moan emits from his mouth; from the bones.*] *OOOOOOoooooOOOOOoooooOOOOOOO oooooOOOOOOoooooOO!*

**Stage Directions**
How do the stage directions help you picture the action in this scene?

**Comprehension**
Whose possessions are these people selling?

---

6. **calico** (kal′ i kō) *n.* coarse and cheap cloth.

**Old Joe.** One pound six for the lot. [*He produces a small flannel bag filled with money. He divvies it out. He continues to pass around the money as he speaks. All are laughing.*] That's the end of it, you see! He frightened every one away from him while he was alive, to profit us when he was dead! Hah ha ha!

**All.** HAHAHAHAhahahahahahah!

**Scrooge.** *OOOoooOOOoooOOOoooOOOooo OOoooOOoooOOOooo!* [*He screams at them.*] Obscene demons! Why not market the corpse itself, as sell its trimming??? [*Suddenly*] Oh, Spirit, I see it, I see it! This unhappy man—this stripped-bare corpse . . . could very well be my own. My life holds parallel! My life ends that way now!

**Stage Directions**
What is the effect of the spirit's silence?

[Scrooge *backs into something in the dark behind his spotlight.* Scrooge *looks at* Future, *who points to the corpse.* Scrooge *pulls back the blanket. The corpse is, of course,* Scrooge, *who screams. He falls aside the bed; weeping.*]

Spirit, this is a fearful place. In leaving it, I shall not leave its lesson, trust me. Let us go!

[Future *points to the corpse.*]

Spirit, let me see some tenderness connected with a death, or that dark chamber, which we just left now, Spirit, will be forever present to me.

[Future *spreads his robes again. Thunder and lightning. Lights up, U., in the* Cratchit *home setting.* Mrs. Cratchit *and her daughters, sewing*]

**▶ Critical Viewing**
How does this portrayal of the Cratchit family compare with the picture on page 511?

**Tiny Tim's Voice.** [*Off*] And He took a child and set him in the midst of them.

**Scrooge.** [*Looking about the room; to* Future] Huh? Who spoke? Who said that?

**Mrs. Cratchit.** [*Puts down her sewing*] The color hurts my eyes. [*Rubs her eyes*] That's better. My eyes grow weak sewing by candlelight. I shouldn't want to show your father weak eyes when he comes home . . . not for the world! It must be near his time . . .

**Peter.** [*In corner, reading. Looks up from book*] Past it, rather. But I think he's been walking a bit slower than usual these last few evenings, Mother.

**Mrs. Cratchit** I have known him walk with . . . [*Pauses*] I have know him walk with Tiny Tim upon his shoulder and very fast indeed.

**Peter.** So have I, Mother! Often!

**Daughter.** So have I.

**Mrs. Cratchit.** But he was very light to carry and his father loved him so, that it was not trouble—no trouble. [Bob, *at door*]
And there is your father at the door.

[Bob Cratchit *enters. He wears a comforter. He is cold, forlorn.*]

**Peter.** Father!

**Bob.** Hello, wife, children . . .

[*The daughter weeps; turns away from* Cratchit.]

Children! How good to see you all! And you, wife. And look at this sewing! I've no doubt, with all your industry,

**Comprehension**
Whose corpse does Scrooge see?

we'll have a quilt to set down upon our knees in church on Sunday!

**Mrs. Cratchit.** You made the arrangements today, then, Robert, for the . . . service . . . to be on Sunday.

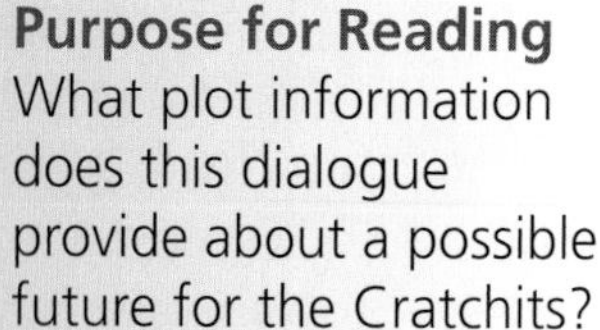

**Purpose for Reading**
What plot information does this dialogue provide about a possible future for the Cratchits?

**Bob.** The funeral. Oh, well, yes, yes, I did. I wish you could have gone. It would have done you good to see how green a place it is. But you'll see it often. I promised him that I would walk there on Sunday, after the service. [*Suddenly*] My little, little child! My little child!

**All Children.** [*Hugging him*] Oh, Father . . .

**Bob.** [*He stands*] Forgive me. I saw Mr. Scrooge's nephew, who you know I'd just met once before, and he was so wonderful to me, wife . . . he is the most pleasant-spoken gentleman I've ever met . . . he said "I am heartily sorry for it and heartily sorry for your good wife. If I can be of service to you in any way, here's where I live." And he gave me this card.

**Peter.** Let me see it!

**Bob.** And he looked me straight in the eye, wife, and said, meaningfully, "I pray you'll come to me, Mr. Cratchit, if you need some help. I pray you do." Now it wasn't for the sake of anything that he might be able to do for us, so much as for his kind way. It seemed as if he had known our Tiny Tim and felt with us.

**Mrs. Cratchit.** I'm sure that he's a good soul.

**Bob.** You would be surer of it, my dear, if you saw and spoke to him. I shouldn't be at all surprised, if he got Peter a situation.

**Mrs. Cratchit.** Only hear that, Peter!

**Martha.** And then, Peter will be keeping company with someone and setting up for himself!

**Peter.** Get along with you!

**Bob.** It's just as likely as not, one of these days, though there's plenty of time for that, my dear. But however and whenever we part from one another, I am sure we shall none of us forget poor Tiny Tim—shall we?—or this first parting that was among us?

**All Children.** Never, Father, never!

**Bob.** And when we recollect how patient and mild he was, we shall not quarrel easily among ourselves, and forget poor Tiny Tim in doing it.

**All Children.** No, Father, never!

**Little Bob.** I am very happy, I am, I am, I am very happy.

[Bob *kisses his little son, as does* Mrs. Cratchit, *as do the other children. The family is set now in one sculptural embrace. The lighting fades to a gentle pool of light, tight on them.*]

**Scrooge.** Specter, something informs me that our parting moment is at hand. I know it, but I know not how I know it.

[Future *points to the other side of the stage. Lights out on* Cratchits. Future *moves slowing, gliding.* Scrooge *follows.* Future *points opposite.* Future *leads* Scrooge *to a wall and a tombstone. He points to the stone.*]

Am I that man those ghoulish parasites[7] so gloated over? [*Pauses*] Before I draw nearer to that stone to which you point, answer me one question. Are these the shadows of things that will be, or the shadows of things that MAY be, only?

**▼ Critical Viewing**
What emotions do you think Scrooge might be feeling in this scene?

**Comprehension**
What has happened to Tiny Tim?

7. **ghoulish parasites** (go͞ol′ ish par′ ə sīts) man and women who stole and divided Scrooge's goods after he died.

[FUTURE *points to the gravestone.* MARLEY *appears in light well U. He points to grave as well. Gravestone turns front and grows to ten feet high. Words upon it:* EBENEZER SCROOGE: *Much smoke billows now from the grave. Choral music here.* SCROOGE *stands looking up at gravestone.* FUTURE *does not at all reply in mortals' words, but points once more to the gravestone. The stone undulates and glows. Music plays, beckoning* SCROOGE. SCROOGE *reeling in terror*]

Oh, no. Spirit! Oh, no, no!

[FUTURE'S *finger still pointing*]

Spirit! Hear me! I am not the man I was. I will not be the man I would have been but for this intercourse. Why show me this, if I am past all hope?

[FUTURE *considers* SCROOGE'S *logic. His hand wavers.*]

Oh, Good Spirit, I see by your wavering hand that your good nature **intercedes** for me and pities me. Assure me that I yet may change these shadows that you have shown me by an altered life!

**Vocabulary ▶**
**intercedes** (in´tər sēdz´) *v.* makes a request on behalf of another

[FUTURE'S *hand trembles; pointing has stopped.*]

I will honor Christmas in my heart and try to keep it all the year. I will live in the Past, the Present, and the Future. The Spirits of all Three shall strive within me. I will not shut out the lessons that they teach. Oh, tell me that I may sponge away the writing that is upon this stone!

**Stage Directions**
What action described in the stage directions gives Scrooge hope that he may change the future?

[SCROOGE *makes a desperate stab at grabbing* FUTURE'S *hand. He holds firm for a moment, but* FUTURE, *stronger than* SCROOGE, *pulls away.* SCROOGE *is on his knees, praying.*]

Spirit, dear Spirit, I am praying before you. Give me a sign that all is possible. Give me a sign that all hope for me is not lost. Oh, Spirit, kind Spirit, I beseech thee: give me a sign . . .

[FUTURE *deliquesces, slowly, gently. The* PHANTOM'S *hood and robe drop gracefully to the ground in a small heap. Music in. There is nothing in them. They are mortal cloth. The* SPIRIT *is elsewhere.* SCROOGE *has his sign. Scrooge is alone. Tableau. The lights fade to black.*]

## Scene 5

[*The end of it.* Marley, *spotlighted, opposite* Scrooge, *in his bed, spotlighted.* Marley *speaks to audience, directly.*]

**Marley.** [*He smiles at* Scrooge.] The firm of Scrooge and Marley is doubly blessed; two misers turned; one, alas, in Death, too late; but the other miser turned in Time's penultimate nick.[8] Look you on my friend, Ebenezer Scrooge . . .

**Scrooge.** [*Scrambling out of bed; reeling in delight*] I will live in the Past, in the Present, and in the Future! The Spirits of all Three shall strive within me!

**Marley.** [*He points and moves closer to* Scrooge's *bed.*] Yes, Ebenezer, the bedpost is your own. Believe it! Yes, Ebenezer, the room is your own. Believe it!

**Scrooge.** Oh, Jacob Marley! Wherever you are, Jacob, know ye that I praise you for this! I praise you . . . and heaven . . . and Christmastime! [*Kneels facing away from* Marley] I say it to ye on my knees, old Jacob, on my knees! [*He touches his bed curtains.*] Not torn down. My bed curtains are not at all torn down! Rings and all, here they are! They are here: I am here: the shadows of things that would have been, may now be dispelled. They will be, Jacob! I know they will be!

[*He chooses clothing for the day. He tries different pieces of clothing and settles, perhaps, on a dress suit, plus a cape of the bed clothing: something of color.*]

I am light as a feather, I am happy as an angel, I am as merry as a schoolboy. [*Yells out window and then out to audience*] Merry Christmas to everybody! Merry Christmas to everybody! A Happy New Year to all the world! Hallo here! Whoop! Whoop! Hallo! Hallo! I don't know what day of the month it is! I don't care! I don't know anything! I'm quite a baby! I don't care! I don't care a fig! I'd much rather be a baby than be an old wreck like me or Marley! (Sorry, Jacob, wherever ye be!) Hallo! Hallo there!

[*Church bells chime in Christmas Day. A small boy, named* Adam, *is seen now* D.R., *as a light fades up on him.*]

**Purpose for Reading**
Why might you read this speech by Scrooge quickly?

**Comprehension**
What promises does Scrooge make?

8. **in Time's penultimate nick** just at the last moment.

## LITERATURE IN CONTEXT

### Media Connection

**The Many Faces of Scrooge**
The part of Ebenezer Scrooge has been played by many different actors over the years.

**1983** Scrooge McDuck

**1938** Reginald Owen

**1951** Alistair Sim

**1962** Mister Magoo

**1992** Michael Caine

**Connect to the Literature**

Which of these actors best portrays Scrooge as you imagine him from your reading? Explain.

Hey, you boy! What's today? What day of the year is it?

**ADAM.** Today, sir? Why, it's Christmas Day!

**SCROOGE.** It's Christmas Day, is it? Whoop! Well, I haven't missed it after all, have I? The Spirits did all they did in one night. They can do anything they like, right? Of course they can! Of course they can!

**ADAM.** Excuse me, sir?

**SCROOGE.** Huh? Oh, yes, of course, what's your name, lad?

[SCROOGE *and* ADAM *will play their scene from their own spotlights.*]

**ADAM.** Adam, sir.

**Scrooge.** Adam! What a fine, strong name! Do you know the poulterer's[9] in the next street but one, at the corner?

**Adam.** I certainly should hope I know him, sir!

**Scrooge.** A remarkable boy! An intelligent boy! Do you know whether the poulterer's have sold the prize turkey that was hanging up there? I don't mean the little prize turkey, Adam. I mean the big one!

**Adam.** What, do you mean the one they've got that's as big as me?

**Scrooge.** I mean, the turkey the size of Adam: that's the bird!

**Adam.** It's hanging there now, sir.

**Scrooge.** It is? Go and buy it! No, no, I am absolutely in earnest. Go and buy it and tell 'em to bring it here, so that I may give them the directions to where I want it delivered, as a gift. Come back here with the man, Adam, and I'll give you a shilling. Come back here with him in less than five minutes, and I'll give you half-a-crown!

**Adam.** Oh, my sir! Don't let my brother in on this.

[Adam *runs offstage.* Marley *smiles.*]

**Marley.** An act of kindness is like the first green grape of summer: one leads to another and another and another. It would take a queer man indeed to not follow an act of kindness with an act of kindness. One simply whets the tongue for more . . . the taste of kindness is too too sweet. Gifts—goods—are lifeless. But the gift of goodness one feels in the giving is full of life. It . . . is . . . a . . . wonder.

[*Pauses; moves closer to* Scrooge, *who is totally occupied with his dressing and arranging of his room and his day. He is making lists, etc.* Marley *reaches out to* Scrooge.]

**Adam.** [*Calling, off*] I'm here! I'm here!

[Adam *runs on with a man, who carries an enormous turkey.*]

Here I am, sir. Three minutes flat! A world record! I've got the poultryman and he's got the poultry! [*He pants, out of breath.*] I have earned my prize, sir, if I live . . .

**Stage Directions**
Why does having a spotlight on both Scrooge and Adam add drama to the scene?

**Comprehension**
What does Scrooge instruct Adam to do?

9. **poulterer's** (pōl′ tər ərz) *n.* British word for a store that sells poultry.

[*He holds his heart, playacting.* SCROOGE *goes to him and embraces him.*]

**SCROOGE.** You are truly a champion, Adam . . .

**MAN.** Here's the bird you ordered, sir . . .

**SCROOGE.** *Oh, my, MY!!!* Look at the size of that turkey, will you! He never could have stood upon his legs, that bird! He would have snapped them off in a minute, like sticks of sealingwax! Why you'll never be able to carry that bird to Camden-Town. I'll give you money for a cab . . .

**MAN.** Camden-Town's where it's goin', sir?

**SCROOGE.** Oh, I didn't tell you? Yes, I've written the precise address down just here on this . . . [*Hands paper to him*] Bob Cratchit's house. Now he's not to know who sends him this. Do you understand me? Not a word . . . [*Handing out money and chuckling*]

**MAN.** I understand, sir, not a word.

**SCROOGE.** Good. There you go then . . . this is for the turkey . . . [*Chuckle*] and this is for the taxi. [*Chuckle*] . . . and this is for your world-record run, Adam . . .

**ADAM.** But I don't have change for that, sir.

**SCROOGE.** Then keep it, my lad. It's Christmas!

**Purpose for Reading**
The positive change in Scrooge is becoming more noticeable. Will your reading rate change from here until the end of the act? Why or why not?

**ADAM.** [*He kisses* SCROOGE'S *cheek, quickly.*] Thank you, sir. Merry, Merry Christmas! [*He runs off.*]

**MAN.** And you've given me a bit overmuch here, too, sir . . .

**SCROOGE.** Of course I have, sir. It's Christmas!

**MAN.** Oh, well, thanking you, sir. I'll have this bird to Mr. Cratchit and his family in no time, sir. Don't you worry none about that. Merry Christmas to you, sir, and a very happy New Year, too . . .

[*The man exits.* SCROOGE *walks in a large circle about the stage, which is now gently lit. A chorus sings Christmas music far in the distance. Bells chime as well, far in the distance. A gentlewoman enters and passes.* SCROOGE *is on the streets now.*]

**SCROOGE.** Merry Christmas, madam . . .

**WOMAN.** Merry Christmas, sir . . .

[*The portly businessman from the first act enters.*]

**SCROOGE.** Merry Christmas, sir.

**PORTLY MAN.** Merry Christmas, sir.

**SCROOGE.** Oh, you! My dear sir! How do you do? I do hope that you succeeded yesterday! It was very kind of you. A Merry Christmas.

**PORTLY MAN.** Mr. Scrooge?

**SCROOGE.** Yes, Scrooge is my name though I'm afraid you may not find it very pleasant. Allow me to ask your pardon. And will you have the goodness to—[*He whispers into the man's ear.*]

**PORTLY MAN.** Lord bless me! My dear Mr. Scrooge, are you *serious!?!*

**Comprehension**
Where does Scrooge want the turkey delivered?

**Scrooge.** If you please. Not a farthing[10] less. A great many back payments are included in it, I assure you. Will you do me that favor?

**Portly Man.** My dear sir, I don't know what to say to such munifi—

**Scrooge.** [*Cutting him off*] Don't say anything, please. Come and see me. Will you?

**Portly Man.** I will! I will! Oh I will, Mr. Scrooge! It will be my pleasure!

**Scrooge.** Thank'ee, I am much obliged to you. I thank you fifty times. Bless you!

[*Portly man passes offstage, perhaps by moving backwards.* Scrooge *now comes to the room of his* Nephew *and* Niece. *He stops at the door, begins to knock on it, loses his courage, tries again, loses his courage again, tries again, fails again, and then backs off and runs at the door, causing a tremendous bump against it. The* Nephew *and* Niece *are startled.* Scrooge, *poking head into room*]

Fred!

**Nephew.** Why, bless my soul! Who's that?

**Stage Directions** What do Scrooge's actions tell you about his feelings at this point?

**Nephew and Niece.** [*Together*] How now? Who goes?

**Scrooge.** It's I. Your Uncle Scrooge.

**Niece.** Dear heart alive!

**Scrooge.** I have come to dinner. May I come in, Fred?

**Nephew.** *May you come in???!!!* With such pleasure for me you may, Uncle!!! What a treat!

**Niece.** What a treat, Uncle Scrooge! Come in, come in!

[*They embrace a shocked and delighted* Scrooge: Fred *calls into the other room.*]

**Stage Directions** How could lighting be used to show the passage of time?

**Nephew.** Come in here, everybody, and meet my Uncle Scrooge! He's come for our Christmas party!

[*Music in. Lighting here indicates that day has gone to night and gone to day again. It is early, early morning.* Scrooge *walks alone from the party, exhausted, to his offices, opposite*

10. **farthing** (fär′ *th*iŋ) *n.* small British coin.

*side of the stage. He opens his offices. The offices are as they were at the start of the play. Scrooge seats himself with his door wide open so that he can see into the tank, as he awaits* CRATCHIT, *who enters, head down, full of guilt.* CRATCHIT, *starts writing almost before he sits.*]

**SCROOGE.** What do you mean by coming in here at this time of day, a full eighteen minutes late, Mr. Cratchit? Hallo, sir? Do you hear me?

**BOB.** I am very sorry, sir. I *am* behind my time.

**SCROOGE.** You are? Yes, I certainly think you are. Step this way, sir, if you please . . .

**BOB.** It's only but once a year, sir . . . it shall not be repeated. I was making rather merry yesterday and into the night . . .

**SCROOGE.** Now, I'll tell you what, Cratchit. I am not going to stand this sort of thing any longer. And therefore . . .

[*He stands and pokes his finger into* BOB'S *chest.*]

I am . . . about . . . to . . . raise . . . your salary.

**BOB.** Oh, no, sir, I . . . [*Realizes*] what did you say, sir?

**SCROOGE.** A Merry Christmas, Bob . . . [*He claps* BOB'S *back.*] A merrier Christmas, Bob, my good fellow! than I have given you for many a year. I'll raise your salary and endeavor to assist your struggling family and we will discuss your affairs this very afternoon over a bowl of smoking bishop.[11] Bob! Make up the fires and buy another coal scuttle before you dot another i, Bob. It's too cold in this place! We need warmth and cheer, Bob Cratchit! Do you hear me? DO . . . YOU . . . HEAR . . . ME?

[BOB CRATCHIT *stands, smiles at* SCROOGE*:* BOB CRATCHIT *faints. Blackout. As the main lights black out, a spotlight appears on* SCROOGE*: C. Another on* MARLEY*: He talks directly to the audience.*]

**MARLEY.** Scrooge was better than his word. He did it all and infinitely more; and to Tiny Tim, who did NOT die, he was a second father. He became as good a friend, as good a master, as good a man, as the good old city knew, or any other good old city, town, or borough in the good old world.

**Stage Directions**
What information in the stage directions might be funny to audiences? Why?

**Comprehension**
What has Scrooge promised to give Bob?

11. **smoking bishop** hot sweet orange-flavored drink.

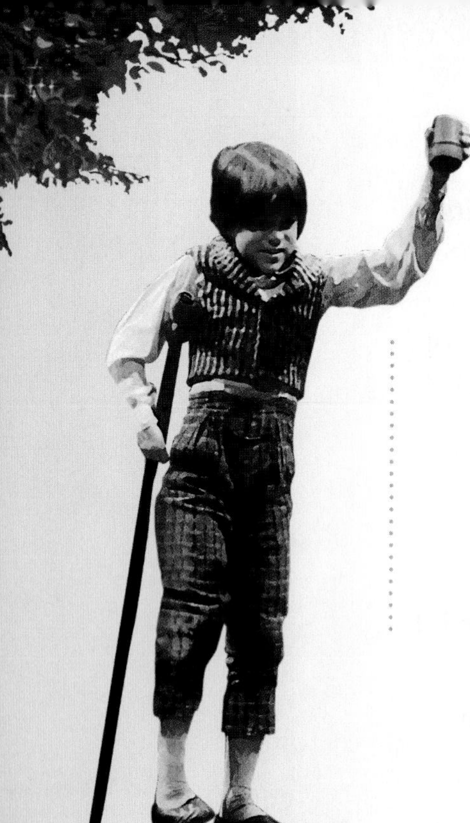

And it was always said of him that he knew how to keep Christmas well, if any man alive possessed the knowledge. [*Pauses*] May that be truly said of us, and all of us. And so, as Tiny Tim observed . . .

**TINY TIM.** [*Atop* SCROOGE'S *shoulder*] God Bless Us, Every One . . .

[*Lights up on chorus, singing final Christmas Song.* SCROOGE *and* MARLEY *and all spirits and other characters of the play join in. When the song is over, the lights fade to black.*]

## Language Study

**Vocabulary** The words listed below appear in *A Christmas Carol: Scrooge and Marley,* Act II. Answer each question, then explain your answer.

**astonish** **compulsion** **severe** **meager** **audible**

1. When you speak, do you want your voice to be *audible*?
2. Would it *astonish* you if an elephant sang?
3. Would you take cover if a *severe* storm were approaching?
4. Can a family with a *meager* income build a large, fancy house?
5. Would a person with a *compulsion* to save money give away a million dollars?

**WORD STUDY**

The **Latin prefix *inter-*** means "between" or "among." In this act, the Ghost of Christmas Future **intercedes** on behalf of Scrooge by going between him and a terrible future to protect Scrooge from what might be.

### Word Study

**Part A** Explain how the **Latin prefix *inter-*** contributes to the meanings of the words *interplanetary, interpersonal,* and *interject.* Consult a dictionary if necessary.

**Part B** Use the context of the sentences and what you know about the Latin prefix *inter-* to explain your answers.

1. Would you make an *international* phone call to the person next door?
2. Does an *intermission* usually occur at the start of a play?

# Close Reading Activities

## Literary Analysis

### Key Ideas and Details

1. **Purpose for Reading** Which did you read more quickly: the dialogue or the stage directions? In your answer, explain how your purpose affected your reading rate.
2. **Purpose for Reading** When you read long speeches that contain difficult words, what happens to your reading rate? Explain, giving a specific example from the text.
3. **(a)** In Scene 3, what does Scrooge learn about the Cratchit family? **(b) Analyze:** Why does Scrooge care about the fate of Tiny Tim? **(c) Draw Conclusions:** In what way is Scrooge changing? Support your answer with a quotation from the play.
4. **(a)** In Scene 4, what happens to Scrooge's belongings in Christmas future? **(b) Draw Conclusions:** What does Scrooge learn from this experience?

### Craft and Structure

5. **Stage Directions** Reread the stage directions at the beginning of Scene 1. Then, complete a chart like the one on the right to record the information the directions reveal.
6. **Stage Directions (a)** Which stage direction in Scene 4 is especially effective in making the scene mysterious? **(b)** What specific details contribute to the mysterious feeling?

| Characters on Stage |
| --- |
| |
| **Movement of Characters** |
| |
| **Description of Lighting** |
| |
| **Description of Sound** |
| |
| **Other Special Effects** |
| |

### Integration of Knowledge and Ideas

7. **(a) Analyze:** Why is Scrooge happy at the end of the play? **(b) Predict:** How well do you think Scrooge will live up to his promise to learn his "lessons"? **(c) Support:** What details in the play support your prediction?
8. **Take a Position:** Do you think Cratchit and Scrooge's nephew do the right thing by forgiving Scrooge immediately? Explain, using details from the play to support your answer.

9. THE BIG ? **Do others see us more clearly than we see ourselves?** Discuss the following questions with a small group. **(a)** What does Scrooge learn from the experience of watching his own life? **(b)** How does he change his behavior to reflect his new insight?

**ACADEMIC VOCABULARY**

As you write and speak about *A Christmas Carol: Scrooge and Marley,* Act II, use the words related to self-perception that you explored on p. 447 of this textbook.

## Conventions: **Appositives and Appositive Phrases**

An **appositive** is a noun or pronoun placed after another noun or pronoun to identify, rename, or explain it.

An **appositive phrase** is a noun or pronoun with modifiers. It stands next to a noun or pronoun and adds information that identifies, renames, or explains it.

| Appositive | Appositive Phrase |
|---|---|
| Our cat, Midnight, likes to sleep on my bed. | Karina—a talented violinist—played a solo. |

- If the information in an appositive or appositive phrase is essential to understanding the sentence, *do not* set it off with commas or dashes.
  **Example:** Do you watch the TV show <u>*Nature*</u>?
- If the sentence is clear without the information, *do* use commas or dashes to set off the appositive or appositive phrase.
  **Example:** My boss, <u>Ms. Parks</u>, works late every night.

### Practice A

Identify the appositive or appositive phrase in each sentence and indicate which noun or pronoun it identifies, renames, or explains.

1. The play *A Christmas Carol* is a story about how a man is changed by the spirit of Christmas.
2. Ebenezer Scrooge, one of the richest men in London, was a miserly man.
3. He collected high rents from his tenants—mostly poor people—without mercy.

**Reading Application** Find an appositive phrase in *A Christmas Carol: Scrooge and Marley,* Act II. Note whether or not it is set off by commas or dashes and explain why.

### Practice B

Identify the appositive or appositive phrase in each sentence. Then, write a new sentence about the play, using the same appositive or appositive phrase.

1. Bob Cratchit's daughter Martha hid in the closet.
2. The second spirit, the Ghost of Christmas Present, visits Scrooge at midnight.
3. The crook Old Joe was eager to see the bed curtains.

**Writing Application** Use appositive phrases in three original sentences about *A Christmas Carol*. Set off nonessential appositives with commas or dashes.

## Writing to Sources

**Argument** Respond to the play by writing a **tribute**, or expression of admiration, to the changed Scrooge. In your tribute, share examples from the drama that show how Scrooge has transformed his life, and reflect on the events or experiences that caused Scrooge to change. As you draft, identify the new traits that make Scrooge worthy of a tribute, and include evidence from the play to support your analysis. Conclude by stating your opinion of the play and providing your own insights about whether there is a lesson that everyone can learn from Scrooge's story. Support your opinion and insights with details from the play.

**Grammar Application** Check your writing to be sure that you have used and punctuated appositives and appositive phrases correctly.

## Speaking and Listening

**Presentation of Ideas** Review the sections of Act II where Scrooge encounters the ghosts. Then, choose one section to be the focus of a **dramatic monologue** in which you share Scrooge's thoughts.

- As you draft your monologue, write as Scrooge from the first-person point of view, using the word *I*.
- Include stage directions to indicate gestures and emotions.
- Punctuate your monologue correctly. Use a period after the speaker's name and brackets to set off stage directions.

As you prepare to present your monologue, consider these tips:

- Project your voice so that everyone can hear you.
- Follow stage directions that tell how to move or speak.
- As you rehearse, refer to the play to determine how Scrooge might have read the monologue. Try pausing at appropriate moments, speaking at different speeds where a tempo change makes sense, and raising and lowering your voice for effect. After reading your monologue in several different ways, decide which techniques work best and use these in your final presentation.

# ANALYZING ARGUMENTATIVE TEXTS

EDITORIAL

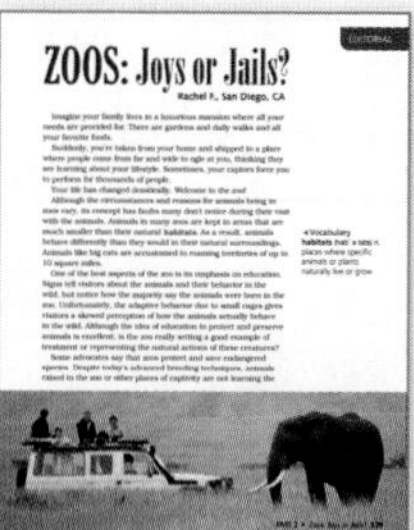
ZOOS: Joys or Jails?
Rachel F., San Diego, CA

EDITORIAL

Kid Territory:
WHY DO WE NEED ZOOS?

## Reading Skill: **Analyze Point of View**

Editorials reflect a writer's **point of view,** or opinion, on an issue. An editorial writer develops his or her point of view by clearly stating a claim and supporting it with specific evidence and persuasive language. When writers with differing points of view write about the same subject, each may focus only on evidence that supports his or her own argument. Use the chart to help you **analyze the authors' point of view** in the editorials that follow.

| Techniques for Developing Point of View | Example |
|---|---|
| A clearly stated claim | "School dress codes promote a sense of unity." |
| Supporting statistics, facts, and examples | "Students are more focused when distractions such as fashion choices are eliminated." |
| Persuasive techniques and language | "The self-confident manner of uniformed students makes a positive impression on visitors." |
| Arguments that address opposing views | "Some people believe that dress codes discourage individuality, yet there are many other creative outlets." |
| A concluding statement that reinforces the author's point of view | "Schools with dress codes shift the focus from fashion to education, which is exactly where it should be." |

### Content-Area Vocabulary

These words appear in the selections that follow. You may also encounter them in other content-area texts.

- **habitats**
- **vulnerable**
- **resources**

# ZOOS: Joys or Jails?

Rachel F., San Diego, CA

Imagine your family lives in a luxurious mansion where all your needs are provided for. There are gardens and daily walks and all your favorite foods.

Suddenly, you're taken from your home and shipped to a place where people come from far and wide to ogle at you, thinking they are learning about your lifestyle. Sometimes, your captors force you to perform for thousands of people.

Your life has changed drastically. Welcome to the zoo!

Although the circumstances and reasons for animals being in zoos vary, its concept has faults many don't notice during their visit with the animals. Animals in many zoos are kept in areas that are much smaller than their natural **habitats**. As a result, animals behave differently than they would in their natural surroundings. Animals like big cats are accustomed to roaming territories of up to 10 square miles.

◀ **Vocabulary**
**habitats** (hab´ ə tats) *n.* places where specific animals or plants naturally live or grow

One of the best aspects of the zoo is its emphasis on education. Signs tell visitors about the animals and their behavior in the wild, but notice how the majority say the animals were born in the zoo. Unfortunately, the adaptive behavior due to small cages gives visitors a skewed perception of how the animals actually behave in the wild. Although the idea of education to protect and preserve animals is excellent, is the zoo really setting a good example of treatment or representing the natural actions of these creatures?

Some advocates say that zoos protect and save endangered species. Despite today's advanced breeding techniques, animals raised in the zoo or other places of captivity are not learning the

survival techniques they would in the wild. These animals would be very **vulnerable** if released and would encounter difficulties coping. Would it not be more beneficial to raise them in their natural habitat?

**Vocabulary ▶**
**vulnerable** (vul′ nər ə bəl) *adj.* open to attack

In this way scientists wouldn't face as many risks in reintroducing captive animals raised into the wild.

Helping endangered species in the wild gives them a better chance for survival and reproduction. Scientists should only revert to the zoo if the necessary funding or habitat for breeding is not available.

Animals are not just brought to the zoo to protect their species, but also to provide entertainment. Many animals' lives will include performing for visitors. Four shows are performed every day at the San Diego Zoo. The zoo should be reserved for education and protecting endangered species, not an amusement park where animals are trained to perform.

Although the zoo is trying to be helpful in providing shows about the animals, it is harming those it intends to protect. The zoo has good intentions in its educational purposes, and in breeding endangered species, but animals shouldn't perform or be treated in a manner that could change their behaviors from how they act in the wild.

Though zoos are meant to be a joy to viewers and teach lessons about our earth, the zoo jails its inhabitants and passes on faulty knowledge. The wild animals in our world are a wonder, and they must be preserved. At the zoo they are treated with care, but they should be treated with reverence.

Next time you visit a zoo, look at the enclosure of the tigers and watch the seals balance a ball on their noses, and then think about what you are really learning from your day at the zoo.

# Kid Territory: WHY DO WE NEED ZOOS?

*San Diego Zoo Staff*

It's an interesting question that many people wonder about. Why have people created zoos, and why are they important now?

The idea of a zoo actually started a long time ago, in the ancient cultures of China, the Middle East, and then the Roman Empire. As people started to travel more, for longer distances to explore the unknown, they began to discover animals and plants that they had never seen or heard of before. They were fascinated by these amazing creatures. Travelers reported back to their communities and their leaders what they had seen. Rulers like emperors, sultans, and kings often wanted to prove how wealthy and powerful they were, to each other and to their subjects. One way to do that was to "collect" some of these animals, and allow people to come and see them. These collections were called menageries, and usually only the rich and powerful had them.

But that changed as time went on, and eventually it was countries and then individual cities that had collections of exotic animals for people to come and see, and they were no longer reserved only for wealthy rulers. Zoology is the study of animals, so these became zoological collections. You guessed it—that was then shortened to the word we use now: zoos.

## Zoos open to the public

At first most zoos only had a limited number of animals, usually the ones people had heard about but never seen in person, like lions, bears, giraffes, hippos, and other big and impressive species. Then as zoos became more popular, and traveling to get animals became more possible, zoos started to represent animals from particular countries and parts of the world. Zoologists studied these animals to find out more about them: what they ate, how they grew, how they had young, and how they behaved, among other things. But zoos were open to the general public, too, so everyone could find out about animals.

## Connecting with critters

Zoos today still serve that important purpose: they allow us to study and find out more about animals that we would not understand otherwise.

People are curious and want to know about the world around them, and that especially includes the animals and plants with which we share the Earth. In addition to studying animals in zoos, scientists are also able to go out to the countries where animals live and study them in the field, or their habitat. But most people cannot do that, so zoos allow them to see and connect with what would otherwise be unavailable to them.

## Helping wildlife

These days we also have cable TV, though, and there are lots of wild animal shows that we can watch. So why still have zoos? One of the most important reasons is conservation. Humans are destroying the Earth's habitats at a very fast pace, in order to make space, food, and products for ourselves. But that leaves less and less room for animals and plants. Zoos and wildlife parks are places where we can protect species that are in trouble, so they don't disappear from the Earth completely.

People do have different opinions about that, though. Some people think that animals should not be kept by humans for any reason, and that if they go extinct, then that's the way it should be. Other people think that animals are precious **resources**, an important part of the Earth, and that we should do everything we can to protect them, especially since we are the ones putting them in danger in the first place. Some people feel that there is lots of wild space and that animals should only live there. Other people feel that there is very little wild space left, that animals are contained by humans in some way no matter where they are, and it is up to us to take care of them the best we can. It's a discussion that will probably go on for a long time, especially as more and more species become endangered.

**Vocabulary ▶**
**resources** (rē´ sôrs´ əz) *n.* natural features that enhance the quality of human life

There is another thing that zoos accomplish, which could be one of the most important of all. Zoos give people the opportunity to see animals in person, often up close, to watch them, realize how alike we are in many ways, to understand them, and to appreciate them. It's amazing to come almost face to face with an elephant or tiger, for example, to see how big it is, to feel its power, to look in its eyes; or to see an orangutan or gorilla amble right by you, holding its baby or playing chase with its brother or sister. It is said that people only love what they understand, and they only protect what they love. Zoos may be the last stand for wild species, the place where humans can grow to love them, and then work to protect them.

## Comparing Argumentative Texts

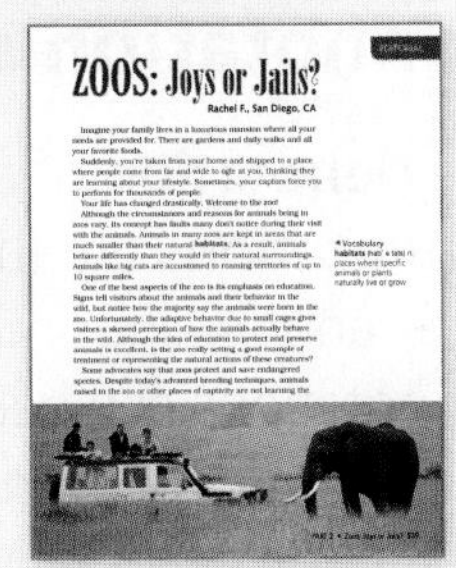
EDITORIAL

ZOOS: Joys or Jails?

Rachel F., San Diego, CA

1. Identify the two strongest points each author makes to support the point of view presented in his or her article.
2. Compare the arguments to determine which author makes the strongest case. Explain your reasoning, citing details from the texts.

### Content-Area Vocabulary

EDITORIAL

Kid Territory:
WHY DO WE NEED ZOOS?

San Diego Zoo Staff

Zoos open to the public

Connecting with critters

3. Use the words *habitats, vulnerable,* and *resources* in a paragraph in which you explain whether or not you think zoos are a good idea.

## Timed Writing

### Argument: Editorial

Write a brief editorial for a school newspaper about an issue that affects your community or the nation—for example, building affordable housing or protecting animal habitats. Use supporting details to develop your argument. **(35 minutes)**

### 5-Minute Planner

Complete these steps to write your editorial:

1. Jot down two or three issues currently affecting your community or the nation. Review your list. Choose the issue you feel most strongly about as the topic for your editorial.
2. Write a sentence that clearly states your point of view and claim about your topic.
3. Make notes that give reasons, facts, descriptions, and examples that support your claims.
   **TIP:** You can sway your readers by including language that evokes positive or negative emotions.
4. Review the two editorials to see how the authors developed their arguments and structured their writing. Finalize your organizational plan.
5. Consult your notes as you write your editorial.

# Language Study

## Connotation and Denotation

The **denotation** of a word is its dictionary meaning. A word's **connotations** are the ideas associated with that word. Those ideas and feelings might be positive or negative. Understanding connotations can help you to choose the right words in your writing. The following chart shows an example of three words with the same denotation and different connotations. Notice the various shades of meaning among the three words.

| Word | Denotation | Connotation | Example Sentence |
|---|---|---|---|
| postpone | to put off until a later time | to reschedule, usually due to something out of one's control | We had to *postpone* the party because the hostess became ill. |
| delay | | to hold off on something for a short amount of time | The heavy morning traffic will *delay* the city's buses. |
| procrastinate | | to put something off that is undesirable by doing another thing | I *procrastinate* every day by watching television before doing my homework. |

### Practice A

Each of the following words has a positive, neutral, or negative connotation. For each word pair, identify which word has a more positive connotation. If necessary, use a dictionary to check each word's denotation.

1. noise, sound
2. screech, holler
3. grab, obtain
4. discontinue, quit
5. brainy, intelligent
6. aware, alert

### Practice B

Sometimes, the connotations of words can help you see degrees of meaning. For example, the words *large* and *enormous* have the same basic meaning, but *enormous* implies greater size than *large*. Rewrite each of the following sentences by replacing the italicized word. The new word should have the same denotation but a connotation that implies a greater degree of the original word. If necessary, use a dictionary or a thesaurus to help you.

1. The coach was *angry* after the team's poor performance.
2. My little sister loves to *bother* me when I have friends over.
3. We *eat* our lunch as soon as we sit down at the table.
4. The marching band from Southern California was *good*.
5. My mother was *happy* when I told her my grade on the test.
6. The weather in the desert is *hot*.
7. The rides at the amusement park were *fun*.
8. My cousin from Georgia is *nice*.
9. I drank a *large* glass of water after the race.
10. After playing a game of "fetch," my dog was *tired*.

**Activity** Each of the following words has neutral connotations. Use a thesaurus to find synonyms, or words with a similar meaning, for each word. Find at least one synonym with positive connotations and one synonym with negative connotations. Use a graphic organizer like the one shown to organize your synonyms. The first one has been completed as an example.

difficult aged calm brave humble

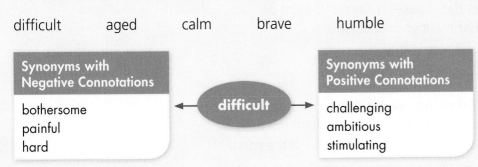

| Synonyms with Negative Connotations | | Synonyms with Positive Connotations |
|---|---|---|
| bothersome<br>painful<br>hard | ← **difficult** → | challenging<br>ambitious<br>stimulating |

## Comprehension and Collaboration

Work with a partner to write two separate paragraphs about a fictional inventor. One partner's paragraph should describe the inventor as a visionary. The other's should describe the inventor as a dreamer. When you have finished writing, exchange paragraphs and discuss how the connotations of the words *visionary* and *dreamer* influenced your descriptions of the inventor.

## Conducting an Interview

When you research a topic, you may sometimes find it necessary to interview someone in order to get the information you need. Follow these steps to conduct a successful interview.

### Learn the Skills

An interview is a conversation that is powered by questions and answers. Before the interview, have a list of probing questions that will elicit the information you need.

**Identify your purpose.** It is important that you know what kind of information you would like to get from the interview. Conduct background research on your topic to focus your questions.

**Create probing questions.** Use your research notes to help you generate a list of questions. You will use this list at the interview, but you can also ask other questions that come to mind as you listen. You may need to ask follow-up questions to clarify points and get examples.

**Listen carefully.** Listening is more than just hearing. Sometimes you think you know what someone is going to say, so you do not really hear what they *are* saying. Break this habit by rephrasing what the speaker said, or by asking for clarification before moving on. If you are listening to acquire new information or to evaluate a point of view, pay close attention to both main points and details. Here are some tips for listening effectively:

- Do not look around. Focus your eyes and ears on the speaker.
- Concentrate on what the speaker is saying. Do not be distracted by his or her manner of speaking.
- Put away anything that may distract you.
- Keep a pencil and paper handy to take notes.

**Eliminate barriers to listening.** Avoid distractions when listening. Sit close to the speaker and stay focused on what he or she is saying, not on other things that are going on in the room.

**Take notes.** Taking notes will help you remember what a speaker says. Do not write down every word. Instead, try to capture the speaker's main points and a few supporting details. Later, review your notes to be sure you understand them.

## Practice the Skills

**Presentation of Knowledge and Ideas** Use what you have learned in this workshop to complete the following activity.

### ACTIVITY: **Conduct an Interview**

Interview a community member, friend, or relative on a subject about which he or she is knowledgeable. If possible, ask a partner to videotape your interview. Follow the steps below.

- Before the interview, do background research on your topic.
- Make a list of focused questions that are based on your research.
- Listen carefully, analyze main ideas and details, rephrase what the speaker says, and ask for clarification as needed.
- Focus on what the speaker is saying, and block out distractions.
- Take notes to capture the main ideas and details.

Refer to the Interview Checklist as you prepare for your interview. If it is possible for you and your classmates to videotape your interviews, use the checklist to give each other feedback.

### Interview Checklist

**Preparing for the Interview**

Does the preparation meet all of the requirements of the activity? Check all that apply.

- ❑ The purpose of the interview is clear.
- ❑ The interviewer has performed background research on the topic.
- ❑ The list of questions is designed to draw out interesting answers.
- ❑ The questions are focused and clear.

**Conducting the Interview**

Did the interviewer follow rules for listening? Check all that apply.

- ❑ The interviewer concentrated on what the speaker said.
- ❑ The interviewer rephrased main ideas and details and asked for clarifications.
- ❑ The interviewer sat close to the speaker and avoided distractions.
- ❑ The interviewer took notes.

**Comprehension and Collaboration** With your classmates, review the completed Interview Checklists. As a group, discuss which aspects of the interview process were most challenging and which were most rewarding.

# Write an Argument

## Response to Literature: Review of a Short Story

**Defining the Form** In a **response to literature,** the writer develops an argument that addresses one or more aspects of a literary work. You might use elements of a literary response in a letter to an author, or in a book or movie review.

**Assignment** Write a review of a short story you have read. A review is a kind of argument, so it should rely on reasons and evidence. Include these elements in your response:

- ✓ a *clearly stated claim* about the impact of the story
- ✓ a logical and consistent *organization*
- ✓ *relevant evidence from the text* to support your analysis
- ✓ use of words, phrases, and clauses that *clarify the relationships* between claims and the reasons that support them
- ✓ a *formal style* and tone
- ✓ a clear understanding of the distinctions between the *denotations and connotations* of words
- ✓ error-free writing, including *correct use of participles* to combine sentences smoothly

To preview the criteria on which your oral response may be judged, see the rubric on page 555.

### FOCUS ON RESEARCH

When you write a response to literature, you must use strong evidence from the text to support your position.

- Reread the story closely to identify the key elements that shape your response.
- Take notes on important aspects of character, plot, setting, and theme.
- Find passages that support your claims about the author's use of language.

## Prewriting/Planning Strategies

**Choose a story to review.** Make a list of stories you have read recently. Put a star next to the ones that elicited a strong response in you—either positive or negative. To evaluate the stories, ask yourself questions such as these:

- Do I identify strongly with a character or situation in the story?
- Does the story seem believable?
- Are there passages in the story that are especially moving or exciting?
- What is special or unusual about the author's use of language?
- Did the story's ending surprise me?

**Find connections.** After you have decided on a story, reread it carefully to find a topic for your review. To help you narrow your focus, complete a chart like the one shown. Fill in each column by answering the leading question. Look over what you have written and highlight details that connect in ways that interest you. To create a focused topic, sum up the highlighted details in a sentence.

| Story Element | Leading Questions | Interesting Details |
|---|---|---|
| **Characters** | Who did the action? | |
| **Settings** | When or where was it done? | |
| **Actions** | What was done? | |
| **Motivations** | Why was it done? | |

**Find supporting evidence.** To write an effective short story review, you must provide evidence to support your claims. Review the story to find details that support your response. Think of the incidents of the plot, the characters' actions and words, and the author's descriptions of the characters and setting. Record these details on notecards with a heading that indicates how each is connected to your topic. If you wish to quote directly from the story, be sure to copy the words accurately.

## Drafting Strategies

**Define and develop your focus.** Review your prewriting notes to find a main idea or focus for your response. The focus statement, or thesis, sums up your reaction to one aspect of the story. Answer questions like the ones shown. Then, write one good sentence that states the focus and references a literary element. Include this sentence in your introduction, and elaborate on it in the body of your review.

| 1. My Response | 2. What Causes It | 3. My Focus |
|---|---|---|
| What is my main response to my topic?<br>I thoroughly enjoyed the story. | What features of the story cause my reaction?<br>• the suspense<br>• the believability of the characters | What conclusion can I draw about the story's features?<br>The author creates suspense and believ-able characters, producing a realistic story. |

**Organize your review.** Your review should have three parts: an introduction, a body, and a conclusion.

- In the **introduction,** identify the author and title of the story and present a brief summary. Present your thesis, a single sentence that states the focus of your response.
- In the **body** of your review, present the evidence that supports your response. You might decide to organize each paragraph to focus on the analysis of a different story element, such as characters, plot, and word choice.
- In the **conclusion,** tie your review together by restating your thesis. Then, go a step further by making a final point or presenting a final insight.

**Use examples to provide support.** Rely on examples from the story to help you support your main arguments and claims. Refer to specific scenes, characters, images, and actions. Justify your interpretations with direct quotations from the text. However, avoid simply retelling the story. It is important that you share your responses to various aspects of the text.

## Finding the Perfect Word

**Word choice** is the specific language a writer selects in order to create a strong impression. Critics choose memorable words and phrases to emphasize their arguments and to grab readers' attention. Follow these tips as you write your review.

**Developing Tone** The tone of your writing reveals your attitude toward your audience or subject. Ask yourself:

- How did the plot of this short story make me feel?
- Did I like the characters or dislike them? Why?
- How effective was the author's use of literary elements such as pacing and description?
- Would I recommend this story to others?

Write your answers to these questions in complete sentences. Then use your responses as you draft your review, using a formal style that is appropriate for a review.

**Choosing Language** As you write, use language that helps you develop your arguments and that accurately captures your feelings about an aspect of the story. Include colorful words, phrases, and comparisons. Consider the **connotations** of words, or the feelings and associations they convey, as well as their **denotations,** or meanings. For example, if you liked the climax of a story, you might describe it as *dramatic*. If you did not like it, you might describe it as *exaggerated*. Add examples and quotations to support your descriptions. The chart shows descriptive words that you might use.

| Plot | Characters | Dialogue | Description |
|---|---|---|---|
| suspenseful<br>predictable<br>confusing | hideous<br>flat<br>intriguing | unrealistic<br>engaging<br>humorous | unique<br>extensive<br>uninteresting |

**Supporting Claims With Reasons** Choose words that support your claims. For example, if you claim that a character is overly dramatic, you might use words that emphasize the character's hysterical reactions to an ordinary event.

**Checking Language** With a partner, review your word choices for fairness, accuracy, and consistency.

## Revising Strategies

**Revise to organize around your strongest idea.** Review your draft with a partner to find places to support your main point. Follow these steps:

1. Circle your strongest point—your most profound insight or the quotation that pulls your review together. Consider moving this point to the end, just before your concluding statement.
2. If you move your strongest point to the end, revise your last paragraph to add a transition sentence that clearly explains the connection between this point and your other ideas.
3. Go back to other paragraphs to link each paragraph to your concluding point. For example, use connecting language like this: *Another example that shows the story's humor is . . .*

**Show relationships clearly.** Read the final sentence of each paragraph. Then, read the opening sentence of the next paragraph. If one or both sentences clearly show the relationship between paragraphs, underline them. If you do not find a relationship, add a transitional word, phrase, or sentence to link them together. Use these tips as you revise.

| Using Effective Transitions | |
|---|---|
| **To add to an idea or show sequence** | also, next, equally important, furthermore, first, second, third, likewise, still, too, another, besides |
| **To contrast ideas** | alternatively, despite, although, yet, conversely, instead, on the other hand, however, otherwise, regardless |
| **To give examples or clarify ideas** | after all, in other words, certainly, for example, such as |
| **To show cause and effect** | after all, in other words, certainly, for example, such as |

### Peer Review

Review your draft with a partner to find places where you can add stronger support for your thesis. In addition, ask your partner to identify any grammatical or spelling errors in your review. If necessary, refer to a grammar handbook or dictionary for help with correcting the errors.

## Revising Sentences Using Participles

To make your writing flow smoothly, combine sentences using participles and participial phrases. A **participle** is a verb form that acts as an adjective, modifying a noun or pronoun. **Present participles** end in *-ing*. **Past participles** usually end in *-ed,* but may have an irregular ending, such as the *-en* in *spoken*.

**past participle** → **noun**

She banged her fist against the closed windows.

A **participial phrase** includes a participle and other words, such as modifiers. A **misplaced modifier** is placed far away from the word it describes.

**Misplaced modifier:** I heard her voice listening to the song.

**Solution:** Listening to the song, I heard her voice.

A **dangling modifier** is not logically connected to any word in the sentence.

**Dangling modifier:** Raising the flag, the wind felt strong.

**Solution:** Raising the flag, the sailors felt the strong wind.

**Fixing Choppy Passages Using Participles** To fix a choppy passage, identify sentences that can be combined. Then rewrite the passage using one or more of the following methods:

1. **Combine sentences using a present participle.**
   ▶ **Example:** We arranged a tour. We would walk the grounds.
   We arranged a walking tour of the grounds.
2. **Combine sentences using a past participle.**
   ▶ **Example:** The food is cooked. It will not spoil.
   The cooked food will not spoil.
3. **Combine sentences using a participial phrase.**
   ▶ **Example:** Marissa ate her food quickly. She was running late.
   Running late, Marissa ate her food quickly.

### Grammar in Your Writing

Choose three paragraphs in your draft. Read the paragraphs aloud, highlighting any passages that sound choppy. Using one of the methods above, fix the choppy passages by combining sentences.

STUDENT MODEL: **Tyler Blair, Somerset, KY**

## The Lesson of "Rikki-tikki-tavi"

The short story "Rikki-tikki-tavi" is a well-known short story written by Rudyard Kipling, who also wrote many novels, such as *Kim* and *Captains Courageous*. "Rikki-tikki-tavi" is a story about two natural enemies: a mongoose and a cobra. The message of the story is that although you may be small, you can still overcome major enemies. This story is enjoyable because it can teach you helpful morals while keeping you entertained at the same time.

Tyler focuses on the message, or theme, of the story.

The beginning of this story is heavyhearted and dramatic. A small boy named Teddy thinks that the mongoose is dead following a bout with its first enemy—a flood that swept him away from his burrow. The mood of the story changes when the boy realizes that the mongoose is still alive, but weak. He decides to keep it, and takes care of it much like a pet, feeding it and naming it Rikki-tikki-tavi.

When Rikki-tikki goes outside into the little boy's garden to explore his surroundings, he comes upon a bird, which he confronts. The story switches back to a gloomy mood when the mongoose discovers that Nag, a cobra, ate one of the bird's eggs. When Rikki-tikki hears this, Nag comes out of the tall grass behind him.

Tyler summarizes the most important plot events in the story in the order in which they occur.

This is when the story gets scary because Rikki faces another enemy. Nag quickly spreads his hood to intimidate the small mongoose. Then, Nagaina, Nag's wife, pulls a surprise attack on Rikki-tikki and nearly eats him. Because Rikki-tikki is young and dodges the cobra's blow from behind, he gains plenty of confidence. Readers wonder whether the mongoose will stay safe.

As the story progresses, Rikki meets Karait, another snake, and this builds excitement and tension. This snake isn't after the mongoose, although he is after the family. When Teddy runs out to pet Rikki-tikki, the snake strikes at the boy, but Rikki-tikki lunges at the snake and paralyzes it by biting it before it can bite Teddy.

Later, after Rikki-tikki discovers that the cobras are going to go after his owners, he is filled with rage and he takes on the challenge. The moment the reader is waiting for arrives. The mongoose and the cobra fight to kill. At one point Rikki-tikki has his teeth in Nag as Nag flings himself about. Readers may think that Rikki-tikki will surely die from the beating that he is taking, but he holds on and, thankfully, Teddy's dad hears the fighting and shoots Nag behind the hood with a shotgun, easily ending the brutal battle, which leaves Nag dead and Rikki-tikki dizzy, but alive.

Tyler supports his ideas about the story by giving examples of how Rikki-tikki fights several enemies even though he is small.

This story is exciting and thought provoking. It ends, leaving me and other readers to think about its real meaning. Most people can relate to a time when they have faced a challenge in their life but have felt that they were unable to overcome it. However, when they kept trying and put their minds to it, they eventually ended with success, as Rikki-tikki did.

Tyler explains what message readers can take away from the story.

## Editing and Proofreading

**Spell tricky syllables correctly.** The syllables in some words are barely heard. Because of this, letters are often left out in spelling. Double-check the spellings of words such as *different, average,* and *restaurant* in a dictionary. Notice how each word is broken into syllables. Say the word aloud while you look at it, and exaggerate your pronunciation of the sounds and syllables.

**Focus on quotations.** A response to a literary work should include a number of quotations from the work. Pay careful attention to the punctuation, indentation, and capitalization of quotations. Use quotation marks to set off short quotations. Longer quotations of four or more lines should begin on a new line, be indented, and appear without quotation marks.

**Spiral Review**
Earlier in the unit, you learned about **prepositional phrases** (p. 498) and **appositive phrases** (p. 536). Review your essay to be sure that you have used these types of phrases correctly.

## Publishing and Presenting

Consider these ideas to share your writing with a larger audience:

**Share your review.** Discuss your response with a group of classmates. Invite classmates to respond with their opinions and reactions.

**Build a collection.** Work with your classmates to assemble a book of responses to literature for your school or local library.

## Reflecting on Your Writing

**Writer's Journal** Jot down your answer to this question:
*How did writing about the work help you to understand it?*

### Rubric for Self-Assessment

Find evidence in your writing to address each category. Then, use the rating scale to grade your work.

| Criteria | Rating Scale | | | |
|---|---|---|---|---|
| | *not very* | | | *very* |
| **Purpose/Focus** Introduces the topic and make a clear claim | 1 | 2 | 3 | 4 |
| **Organization** Organizes reasons and evidence clearly and logically; provides a concluding section that follows from the argument presented | 1 | 2 | 3 | 4 |
| **Development of Ideas/Elaboration** Supports the claim with clear reasons and relevant evidence; draws evidence from the text to support analysis; establishes and maintains a formal style | 1 | 2 | 3 | 4 |
| **Language** Uses words, phrases, and clauses to clarify the relationships among claims and reasons; shows awareness of the denotations and connotations of words | 1 | 2 | 3 | 4 |
| **Conventions** Uses participles and participial phrases effectively to create smooth sentences | 1 | 2 | 3 | 4 |

# Assessment: Skills

## SELECTED RESPONSE

### I. Reading Literature

**Directions:** *Read the excerpt from the dramatization of "Alice in Wonderland" by Alice Gerstenberg. Then, answer each question that follows.*

*[A soft radiance follows the characters mysteriously. As the curtain rises ALICE comes through the looking glass; steps down, looks about in wonderment and goes to see if there is a "fire." The RED QUEEN rises out of the grate and faces her haughtily.]*

**ALICE:** Why, you're the Red Queen!

**RED QUEEN:** Of course I am! Where do you come from? And where are you going? Look up, speak nicely, and don't twiddle your fingers!

**ALICE:** I only wanted to see what the looking glass was like. Perhaps I've lost my way.

**RED QUEEN:** I don't know what you mean by *your* way; all the ways about here belong to *me*. Curtsey while you're thinking what to say. It saves time.

**ALICE:** I'll try it when I go home; the next time I'm a little late for dinner.

**RED QUEEN:** It's time for you to answer now; open your mouth a *little* wider when you speak, and always say, "Your Majesty." I suppose you don't want to lose your name?

**ALICE:** No, indeed.

**RED QUEEN:** And yet I don't know, only think how convenient it would be if you could manage to go home without it! For instance, if the governess wanted to call you to your lessons, she would call out "come here," and there she would have to leave off, because there wouldn't be any name for her to call, and of course you wouldn't have to go, you know.

**ALICE:** That would never do, I'm sure; the governess would never think of excusing me from lessons for that. If she couldn't remember my name, she'd call me "Miss," as the servants do.

**RED QUEEN:** Well, if she said "Miss," and didn't say anything more, of course you'd miss your lessons. I dare say you can't even read this book.

**ALICE:** It's all in some language I don't know. Why, it's a looking-glass book, of course! And if I hold it up to a glass, the words will all go the right way again.

**JABBERWOCKY**

'Twas brillig, and the slithy toves
  Did gyre and gimble in the wabe;
All mimsy were the borogoves,
  And the mome raths outgrabe.

It seems very pretty, but it's *rather* hard to understand; somehow it seems to fill my head with ideas, only I don't exactly know what they are.

1. Which answer choice best describes this **drama** excerpt?
   A. dialogue
   B. monologue
   C. act
   D. set

2. What do the following lines reveal about the Red Queen's **character?**

   It's time for you to answer now; open your mouth a *little* wider when you speak, and always say, "Your Majesty."

   A. The Red Queen is hard of hearing.
   B. The Red Queen is silly and entertaining.
   C. The Red Queen is ill at ease.
   D. The Red Queen is bossy and self-important.

3. **Part A** Which answer choice best describes Alice in the drama excerpt?
   A. She is cold.
   B. She is confused.
   C. She is late for her lessons.
   D. She does not know the Red Queen.

   **Part B** Which lines from the drama best support the answer to Part A?
   A. "I only wanted to see what the looking glass was like."
   B. "I'll try it when I get home; the next time I'm a little late for dinner."
   C. ". . . the governess would never think of excusing me from lessons for that."
   D. ". . . somehow it seems to fill my head with ideas, only I don't exactly know what they are."

4. How do the **stage directions** contribute to the drama excerpt?
   A. They tell which character is speaking and present his or her exact words.
   B. They tell the audience where to look.
   C. They give readers information about the characters and action.
   D. They tell readers where the play has been performed.

5. Which answer choice best explains the appropriate **reading rate** for reading stage directions?
   A. You should read stage directions slowly and carefully because they may reveal action that is not shown in the dialogue.
   B. You should read stage directions slowly in order to appreciate the playwright's style of writing.
   C. You should read stage directions quickly, or you may forget what the characters are saying and doing.
   D. You should skim stage directions because the information they contain may not be important.

6. Which event in the drama's **plot** happens first?
   A. The Red Queen reads a book.
   B. The Red Queen sees Alice.
   C. Alice misses her lessons.
   D. Alice is asked to curtsey.

7. Which answer choice is the best definition of the underlined word *haughtily?*
   A. sadly
   B. directly
   C. proudly
   D. with caution

## Timed Writing

8. In a short essay, explain how the playwright develops **characters** through the use of **dialogue.** Support your answer with details from the text.

GO ON

## II. Reading Informational Text

**Directions:** *Read the passage. Then, answer each question that follows.*

Would you like to sleep an extra hour each morning? If so, you are not alone. Most American teenagers get about seven hours of sleep each night. However, sleep researchers say adolescents and young teens actually need 9.2 hours of sleep. That is more than adults and young children need.

Stumbling through the day like a zombie can be dangerous. For example, the National Highway Traffic Safety Administration says young, sleepy drivers are involved in about 50,000 accidents each year. Lack of sleep can also result in poor grades for teenagers.

Some adults think teenagers who sleep late are lazy. However, Professor Mary Carskadon, a sleep researcher at Brown University, says sleeping late can be healthy. She thinks schools should start later. Most high schools in the United States start classes at 7 A.M. Carskadon says 8:00, or 8:30, would be a better time.

Not only do teenagers need more sleep, but they need it at different times than other people do. Melatonin is a hormone produced daily by the human brain. It tells you that you are sleepy. Research shows that teenagers produce melatonin later at night than other people do. The result is that teenagers are often wide awake when their parents want them to go to sleep. Teenagers' melatonin levels remain high in the early morning. That means they may still be sleepy, even after school has started.

1. **Part A** What is the author's main argument?
   - **A.** Schools should start classes later.
   - **B.** Mary Carskadon is the expert on sleep.
   - **C.** Teenagers should sleep more at night.
   - **D.** Teenagers need more sleep in the morning.

   **Part B** Which of the following claims supports the argument you identified in Part A?
   - **A.** Teenagers produce melatonin later at night than other people.
   - **B.** Schools should begin at 8 or 8:30.
   - **C.** Most teenagers are lazy because they do not get enough sleep.
   - **D.** Teenagers are forced to go to bed when they are wide awake.

2. Which piece of evidence supports Professor Carskadon's assertion that it is healthy for teenagers to sleep late?
   - **A.** Teenagers produce more melatonin than older and younger people produce.
   - **B.** Teenagers' melatonin levels remain high in the morning.
   - **C.** Teenagers are often sleepy even after school has started.
   - **D.** Sleepy drivers are involved in car accidents.

## III. Writing and Language Conventions

**Directions:** *Read the passage. Then, answer each question that follows.*

(1) Many students, including me, depend on our cell phones to talk with our parents. (2) Every day I hear about my mother what time she will pick me up. (3) The problem is that Mr. Galindo wants to ban cell phones from school. (4) The solution is simple. (5) We should be allowed to bring our cell phones to school, but we will only use them when school is over. (6) Calls will be missed. (7) They can be returned after school. (8) This way everyone—teachers, parents, and students—wins.

**1.** Which of the following revisions *best* corrects the use of a **preposition** in sentence 2?

**A.** Change *about* to *from*.
**B.** Change *about* to *through*.
**C.** Change *about* to *of*.
**D.** Leave as is.

**2.** Which revision to sentence 4 would include a more informative **prepositional phrase?**

**A.** The solution is simple and useful.
**B.** The solution simply depends on our cell phones.
**C.** The solution is simple and makes sense.
**D.** The solution to the problem is simple.

**3.** Which revision combines sentence 6 and sentence 7 with a **past participle?**

**A.** Missing calls will mean returning them after school.
**B.** Students can return calls after school.
**C.** Missed calls can be returned after school.
**D.** After school, you can return your calls.

**4.** Which sentence includes an **appositive phrase?**

**A.** sentence 1
**B.** sentence 5
**C.** sentence 6
**D.** sentence 8

**5.** Which sentence adds more information to sentence 3 by using an **appositive?**

**A.** The problem, declared today, is that Mr. Galindo wants to ban cell phones from school.
**B.** The problem is that Principal Galindo wants to ban cell phones from school.
**C.** The problem is that Mr. Galindo, our principal, wants to ban cell phones from school.
**D.** The problem is that Mr. Galindo wants to ban cell phones from Arthur High School.

# CONSTRUCTED RESPONSE

**Directions:** *Follow the instructions to complete the tasks below as required by your teacher.*

*As you work on each task, incorporate both general academic vocabulary and literary terms you learned in Parts 1 and 2.*

## Writing

**TASK 1 Literature**

### Analyze Setting

*Write an essay in which you analyze how the setting of* A Christmas Carol: Scrooge and Marley *shapes the characters and plot.*

- Identify details from the play that reveal the time period as nineteenth-century England.
- Explain how the playwright uses dialogue to move the plot forward.
- Discuss how the playwright used the historical time to support the major points in the play. Point out the kinds of work people did and the ways in which they socialized. Discuss differences between the wealthy and the poor, and analyze why these class differences existed.
- Develop your analysis with relevant details, information, and specific examples from the play.
- Use appropriate transitions to show relationships between or among your ideas. Show comparisons with transitions such as *likewise, similarly,* and *in addition to.* Show contrasts with transitions such as *on the other hand* or *in contrast.*

**TASK 2 Literature**

### Analyze Dramatic Structure

*Write an essay in which you analyze how a drama's structure adds to its meaning.*

- Analyze the parts of *A Christmas Carol: Scrooge and Marley,* including its division into acts and scenes and its dialogue and stage directions. Explain how each part of the drama contributes to characterization, setting, mood, and tone.
- Develop your analysis with examples from the drama. Use transitions to clarify the relationships between or among ideas.

**TASK 3 Literature**

### Analyze Characters' Motives

*Write an essay in which you analyze the motives of various characters in* A Christmas Carol: Scrooge and Marley.

**Part 1**

- Select at least two characters from the play upon which to base your essay.
- Cite several examples of dialogue that reveal each character's reasons for taking an action. Remember that information contained in stage directions might provide clues to a character's motives.

**Part 2**

- Write an essay in which you explain the connections between each characters' actions and specific events in the plot. Cite evidence from the play to support your response.
- Use a strategy such as comparison-and-contrast organization to organize your ideas logically. Use transitions and transitional phrases to connect your sentences and paragraphs smoothly.
- Provide a concluding statement that follows logically from the information in your essay.

## Speaking and Listening

TASK 4 **Literature**

### Analyze Techniques in Different Media

*Give a multimedia presentation in which you compare and contrast the script for* A Christmas Carol: Scrooge and Marley *to its film or stage version.*

- Reread *A Christmas Carol: Scrooge and Marley,* noting how you visualize the drama as you read. Then, view a film or stage version of the same play.
- Compare and contrast the written drama with its film or stage version. Analyze the effects of techniques that are unique to each medium. For example, consider the effects of lighting, sound, color, and camera angles in a film.
- In your presentation, include multimedia components, such as film clips, tape recordings, or visual displays to clarify your claims about the different techniques used in the formats and to emphasize your main points.
- Choose words and phrases for your intended effect and eliminate wordiness or repeated ideas in your presentation.

TASK 5 **Literature**

### Analyze Dialogue

*Give an oral presentation in which you analyze the dialogue in* A Christmas Carol: Scrooge and Marley.

- Analyze examples of dialogue in the play that provide key information about a character. Discuss the character's word choice, syntax, and possibly dialect.
- Cite specific passages of dialogue to support your analysis of the character. In addition, explain how the dialogue advances the plot and develops the conflict in the play.
- As you give your oral presentation, use appropriate eye contact, adequate volume, and clear pronunciation.
- If necessary, consult a digital dictionary to find the pronunciations of unknown words from the text.

## Research

TASK 6 **Literature**

### Do others see us more clearly than we see ourselves?

In Part 2, you have read literature about ways people form impressions about each other. Now, you will conduct a short research project on a person who was judged for his or her appearance, beliefs, or treatment of others.

Use both the literature you have read and your research to reflect on this unit's Big Question. Review the following guidelines before you begin your research:

- Focus your research on one person.
- Gather relevant information from at least two reliable print or digital sources.
- Take notes as you research the person you chose to write about.
- Cite your sources.

When you have completed your research, write a response to the Big Question. Discuss how your initial ideas have been either changed or reinforced. Support your response with an example from literature and an example from your research.

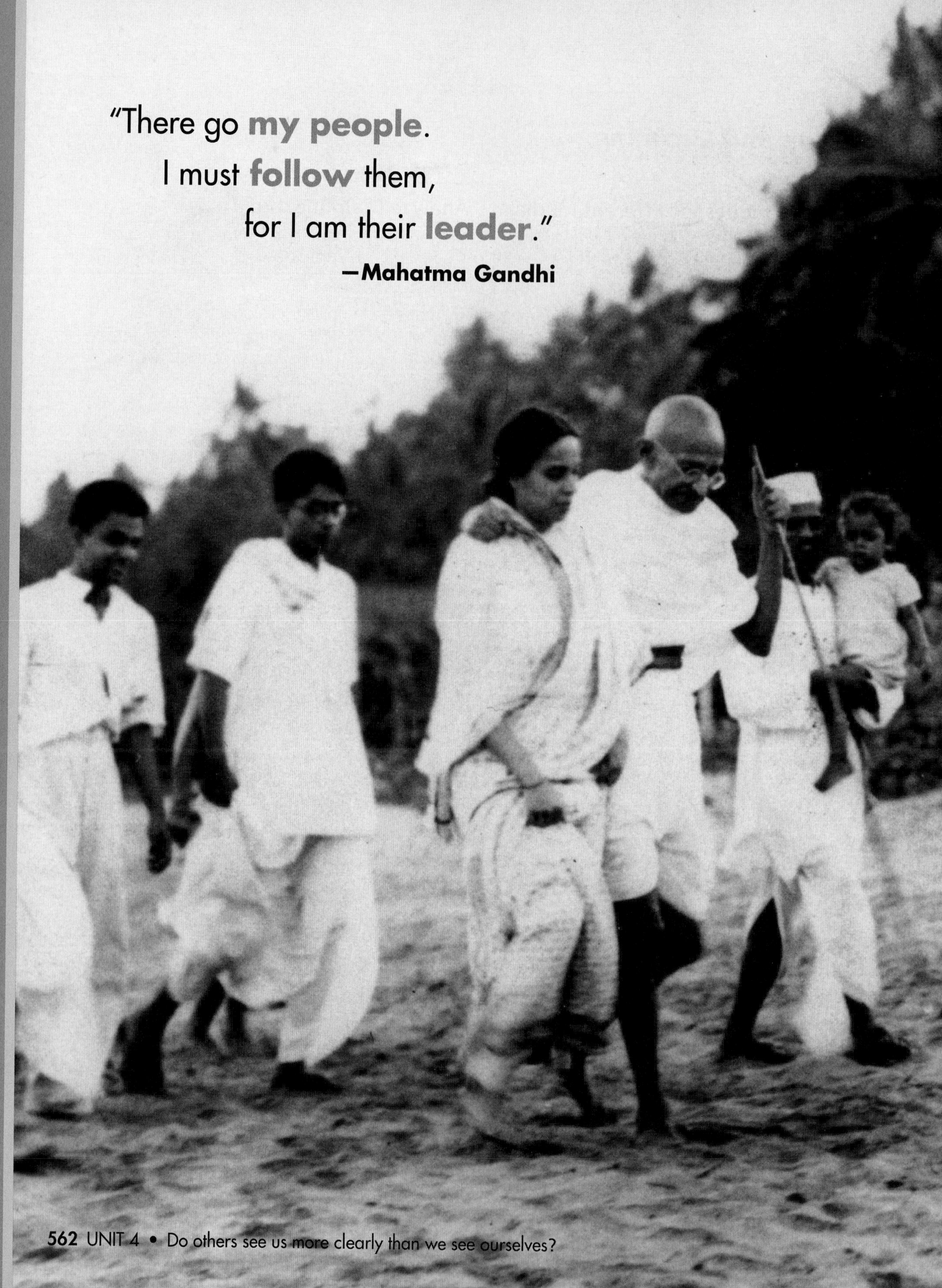
"There go **my people**.
I must **follow** them,
for I am their **leader**."
—Mahatma Gandhi

PART 3

## **TEXT SET** DEVELOPING INSIGHT

# LEADERS AND FOLLOWERS

The selections in this unit all deal with the Big Question: **Do others see us more clearly than we see ourselves?** As you read the texts in this section, think about the characteristics that make someone a leader. Also, consider the different reasons people have for following others. You may find that our ideas about leaders and followers are influenced by our own self-perception.

◀ CRITICAL VIEWING What does the quotation on the opposite page reveal about Gandhi's ideas regarding leadership? Does the photograph reinforce those ideas? Why or why not?

### READINGS IN PART 3



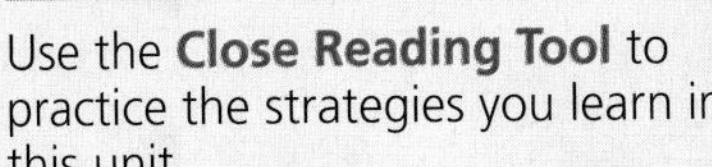

**CLOSE READING TOOL**

Use the **Close Reading Tool** to practice the strategies you learn in this unit.

# THE MONSTERS ARE DUE ON MAPLE STREET

Rod Serling

## CHARACTERS

Narrator | Figure One | Figure Two

### RESIDENTS OF MAPLE STREET

Steve Brand
Charlie's Wife
Mrs. Goodman
Mrs. Brand
Woman
Don Martin
Sally (Tommy's Mother)
Les Goodman
Man One
Man Two
Pete Van Horn
Charlie
Tommy

# ACT I

*[Fade in on a shot of the night sky. The various nebulae and planet bodies stand out in sharp, sparkling relief, and the camera begins a slow pan across the Heavens.]*

**Narrator's Voice.** There is a fifth dimension beyond that which is known to man. It is a dimension as vast as space, and as timeless as infinity. It is the middle ground between light and shadow—between science and superstition. And it lies between the pit of man's fears and the summit of his knowledge. This is the dimension of imagination. It is an area which we call The Twilight Zone.

*[The camera has begun to pan down until it passes the horizon and is on a sign which reads "Maple Street." Pan down until we are shooting down at an angle toward the street below. It's a tree-lined, quiet residential American street, very typical of the small town. The houses have front porches on which people sit and swing on gliders, conversing across from house to house.* Steve Brand *polishes his car parked in front of his house. His neighbor,* Don Martin, *leans against the fender watching him. A Good Humor man rides a bicycle and is just in the process of stopping to sell some ice cream to a couple of kids. Two women gossip on the front lawn. Another man waters his lawn.]*

**Narrator's Voice.** Maple Street, U.S.A., late summer. A tree-lined little world of front porch gliders, hop scotch, the laughter of children, and the bell of an ice cream vendor.

[*There is a pause and the camera moves over to a shot of the Good Humor man and two small boys who are standing alongside, just buying ice cream.*]

**Narrator's Voice.** At the sound of the roar and the flash of light it will be precisely 6:43 P.M. on Maple Street.

[*At this moment one of the little boys,* Tommy, *looks up to listen to a sound of a tremendous screeching roar from overhead. A flash of light plays on both their faces and then it moves down the street past lawns and porches and rooftops and then disappears.*

*Various people leave their porches and stop what they're doing to stare up at the sky.* Steve Brand, *the man who's been polishing his car, now stands there* transfixed, *staring upwards. He looks at DON MARTIN, his neighbor from across the street*]

**Steve.** What was that? A meteor?

**Don.** [*Nods*] That's what it looked like. I didn't hear any crash though, did you?

**Steve.** [*Shakes his head*] Nope. I didn't hear anything except a roar.

**Mrs. Brand.** [*From her porch*] Steve? What was that?

**Steve.** [*Raising his voice and looking toward porch*] Guess it was a meteor, honey. Came awful close, didn't it?

**Mrs. Brand.** Too close for my money! Much too close.

[*The camera pans across the various porches to people who stand there watching and talking in low tones.*]

**Narrator's Voice.** Maple Street. Six-forty-four P.M. on a late September evening. [*A pause*] Maple Street in the last calm and reflective moment . . . before the monsters came!

[*The camera slowly pans across the porches again. We see a man screwing a light bulb on a front porch, then getting down off the stool to flick the switch and finding that nothing happens.*

*Another man is working on an electric power mower. He plugs in the plug, flicks on the switch of the power mower, off and on, with nothing happening.*

*Through the window of a front porch, we see a woman pushing her finger back and forth on the dial hook. Her voice is indistinct and distant, but intelligible and repetitive.*]

**Woman.** Operator, operator, something's wrong on the phone, operator!

[Mrs. Brand *comes out on the porch and calls to* Steve.]

**Mrs. Brand.** [*Calling*] Steve, the power's off. I had the soup on the stove and the stove just stopped working.

**Woman.** Same thing over here. I can't get anybody on the phone either. The phone seems to be dead.

[*We look down on the street as we hear the voices creep up from below, small, mildly disturbed voices highlighting these kinds of phrases:*]

**Voices.**

Electricity's off.

Phone won't work.

Can't get a thing on the radio.

My power mower won't move, won't work at all.

Radio's gone dead!

[Pete Van Horn, *a tall, thin man, is seen standing in front of his house.*]

**Van Horn.** I'll cut through the back yard . . . See if the power's still on on Floral Street. I'll be right back!

[*He walks past the side of his house and disappears into the back yard.*

*The camera pans down slowly until we're looking at ten or eleven people standing around the street and overflowing to the curb and sidewalk. In the background is* Steve Brand's *car.*]

**Steve.** Doesn't make sense. Why should the power go off all of a sudden, and the phone line?

**Don.** Maybe some sort of an electrical storm or something.

**Charlie.** That don't seem likely. Sky's just as blue as anything. Not a cloud. No lightning. No thunder. No nothing. How could it be a storm?

**Woman.** I can't get a thing on the radio. Not even the portable.

[*The people again murmur softly in wonderment and question.*]

**flustered** ▶
(flus´ tərd) *adj.*
nervous; confused

**CHARLIE.** Well, why don't you go downtown and check with the police, though they'll probably think we're crazy or something. A little power failure and right away we get all **flustered** and everything.

**STEVE.** It isn't just the power failure, Charlie. If it was, we'd still be able to get a broadcast on the portable.

[*There's a murmur of reaction to this.* STEVE *looks from face to face and then over to his car.*]

**STEVE.** I'll run downtown. We'll get this all straightened out.

[*He walks over to the car, gets in it, turns the key. Looking through the open car door, we see the crowd watching him from the other side.* STEVE *starts the engine. It turns over* sluggishly *and then just stops dead. He tries it again and this time he can't get it to turn over. Then, very slowly and reflectively, he turns the key back to "off" and slowly gets out of the car.*

*The people stare at* STEVE. *He stands for a moment by the car, then walks toward the group.*]

**STEVE.** I don't understand it. It was working fine before . . .

**DON.** Out of gas?

**STEVE.** [*Shakes his head*] I just had it filled up.

**WOMAN.** What's it mean?

**CHARLIE.** It's just as if . . . as if everything had stopped. [*Then he turns toward* STEVE.] We'd better walk downtown.

[*Another murmur of assent at this.*]

**STEVE.** The two of us can go, Charlie. [*He turns to look back at the car.*] It couldn't be the meteor. A meteor couldn't do *this.*

[*He and* CHARLIE *exchange a look, then they start to walk away from the group.*

*We see* TOMMY, *a serious-faced fourteen-year-old in spectacles who stands a few feet away from the group. He is halfway between them and the two men, who start to walk down the sidewalk.*]

**TOMMY.** Mr. Brand . . . you better not!

**STEVE.** Why not?

**TOMMY.** They don't want you to.

[STEVE *and* CHARLIE *exchange a grin, and* STEVE *looks back toward the boy.*]

**Steve.** Who doesn't want us to?

**Tommy.** [*Jerks his head in the general direction of the distant horizon*] Them!

**Steve.** Them?

**Charlie.** Who are them?

**Tommy.** [*Very intently*] Whoever was in that thing that came by overhead.

[Steve *knits his brows for a moment, cocking his head questioningly. His voice is intense.*]

**Steve.** What?

**Tommy.** Whoever was in that thing that came over. I don't think they want us to leave here.

[Steve *leaves* Charlie *and walks over to the boy. He kneels down in front of him. He forces his voice to remain gentle. He reaches out and holds the boy.*]

**Steve.** What do you mean? What are you talking about?

**Tommy.** They don't want us to leave. That's why they shut everything off.

**Steve.** What makes you say that? Whatever gave you that idea?

**Woman.** [*From the crowd*] Now isn't that the craziest thing you ever heard?

**persistently** ▶
(pər sist´ ənt lē) *adv.*
firmly and steadily

**TOMMY.** [*Persistently but a little intimidated by the crowd*] It's always that way, in every story I ever read about a ship landing from outer space.

**WOMAN.** [*To the boy's mother,* SALLY, *who stands on the fringe of the crowd*] From outer space, yet! Sally, you better get that boy of yours up to bed. He's been reading too many comic books or seeing too many movies or something.

**SALLY.** Tommy, come over here and stop that kind of talk.

**STEVE.** Go ahead, Tommy. We'll be right back. And you'll see. That wasn't any ship or anything like it. That was just a . . . a meteor or something. Likely as not—[*He turns to the group, now trying to weight his words with an optimism he obviously doesn't feel but is desperately trying to instill in himself as well as the others.*] No doubt it did have something to do with all this power failure and the rest of it. Meteors can do some crazy things. Like sunspots.

**DON.** [*Picking up the cue*] Sure. That's the kind of thing—like sunspots. They raise Cain[1] with radio reception all over the world. And this thing being so close—why, there's no telling the sort of stuff it can do. [*He wets his lips, smiles nervously.*] Go ahead, Charlie. You and Steve go into town and see if that isn't what's causing it all.

[STEVE *and* CHARLIE *again walk away from the group down the sidewalk. The people watch silently.*

TOMMY *stares at them, biting his lips, and finally calling out again.*]

**TOMMY.** *Mr. Brand!*

[*The two men stop again.* TOMMY *takes a step toward them.*]

**TOMMY.** Mr. Brand . . . please don't leave here.

[STEVE *and* CHARLIE *stop once again and turn toward the boy. There's a murmur in the crowd, a murmur of irritation and concern as if the boy were bringing up fears that shouldn't be brought up; words which carried with them a strange kind of validity that came without logic but nonetheless registered and had meaning and effect. Again we hear a murmur of reaction from the crowd.*

TOMMY *is partly frightened and partly* ***defiant*** *as well.*]

**defiant** ▶
(dē fī´ ənt) *adj.*
boldly resisting

**TOMMY.** You might not even be able to get to town. It was that way in the story. Nobody could leave. Nobody except—

1. **raise Cain** badly disturb.

**Steve.** Except who?

**Tommy.** Except the people they'd sent down ahead of them. They looked just like humans. And it wasn't until the ship landed that—

[*The boy suddenly stops again, conscious of the parents staring at them and of the sudden hush of the crowd.*]

**Sally.** [*In a whisper, sensing the antagonism of the crowd*] Tommy, please son . . . honey, don't talk that way—

**Man One.** That kid shouldn't talk that way . . . and we shouldn't stand here listening to him. Why this is the craziest thing I ever heard of. The kid tells us a comic book plot and here we stand listening—

[Steve *walks toward the camera, stops by the boy.*]

**Steve.** Go ahead, Tommy. What kind of story was this? What about the people that they sent out ahead?

**Tommy.** That was the way they prepared things for the landing. They sent four people. A mother and a father and two kids who looked just like humans . . . but they weren't.

[*There's another silence as* Steve *looks toward the crowd and then toward* Tommy. *He wears a tight grin.*]

**Steve.** Well, I guess what we'd better do then is to run a check on the neighborhood and see which ones of us are really human.

[*There's laughter at this, but it's a laughter that comes from a desperate attempt to lighten the atmosphere. It's a release kind of laugh. The people look at one another in the middle of their laughter.*]

**Charlie.** There must be somethin' better to do than stand around makin' bum jokes about it.

[*Rubs his jaw nervously*] I wonder if Floral Street's got the same deal we got. [*He looks past the houses.*] Where is Pete Van Horn anyway? Didn't he get back yet?

[*Suddenly there's the sound of a car's engine starting to turn over. We look across the street toward the driveway of* Les Goodman's *house. He's at the wheel trying to start the car.*]

**Sally.** Can you get it started, Les? [*He gets out of the car, shaking his head.*]

**Goodman.** No dice.

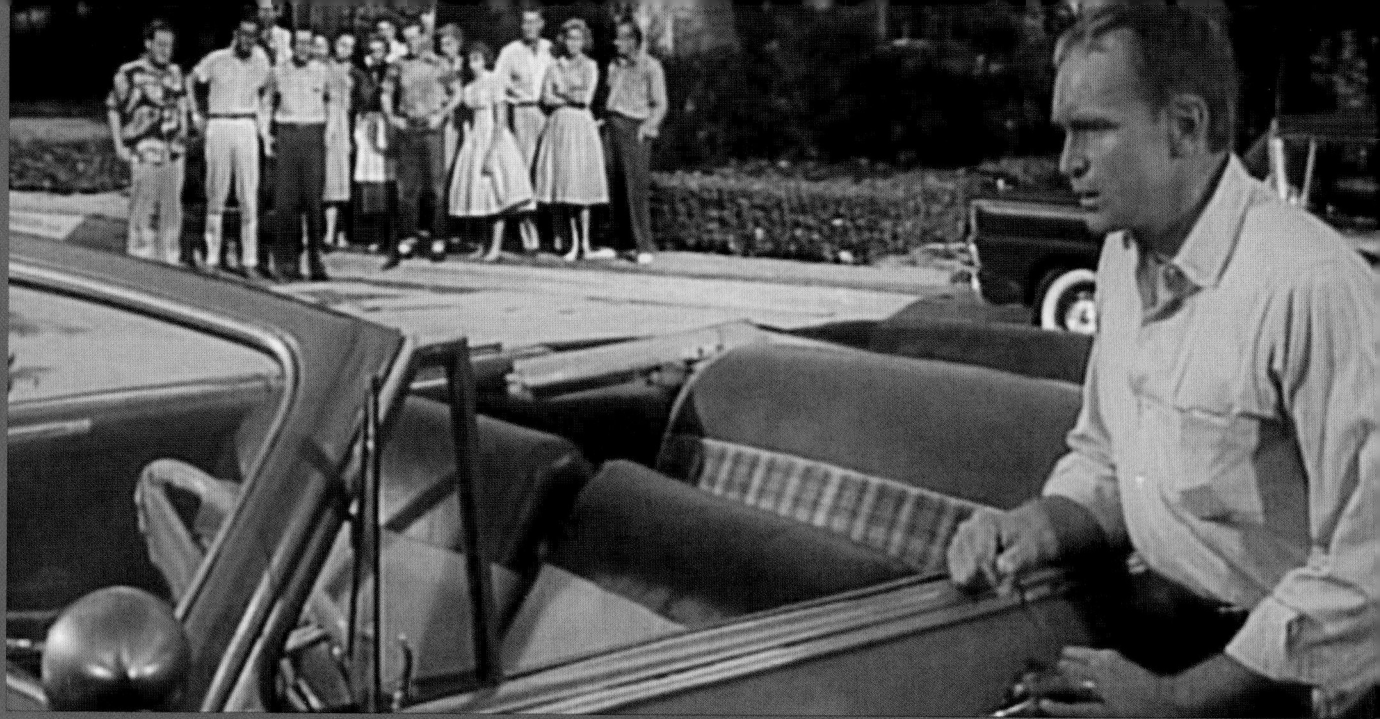

[*He walks toward the group. He stops suddenly as behind him, inexplicably and with a noise that inserts itself into the silence, the car engine starts up all by itself.* GOODMAN *whirls around to stare toward it.*

*The car idles roughly, smoke coming from the exhaust, the frame shaking gently.*

GOODMAN'S *eyes go wide, and he runs over to his car.*

*The people stare toward the car.*]

**MAN ONE.** He got the car started somehow. He got his car started!

[*The camera pans along the faces of the people as they stare, somehow caught up by this revelation and somehow, illogically, wildly, frightened.*]

**WOMAN.** How come his car just up and started like that?

**SALLY.** All by itself. He wasn't anywheres near it. It started all by itself.

[DON *approaches the group, stops a few feet away to look toward* GOODMAN'S *car and then back toward the group.*]

**DON.** And he never did come out to look at that thing that flew overhead. He wasn't even interested. [*He turns to the faces in the group, his face taut and serious.*] Why? Why didn't he come out with the rest of us to look?

**CHARLIE.** He always was an oddball. Him and his whole family. Real oddball.

**DON.** What do you say we ask him?

[*The group suddenly starts toward the house. In this brief fraction of a moment they take the first step toward performing a metamorphosis that changes people from a group into a mob. They begin to head purposefully across the street toward the house at the end.* STEVE *stands in front of them. For a moment their fear almost turns their walk into a wild stampede, but* STEVE'S *voice, loud, incisive, and commanding, makes them stop.*]

**STEVE.** Wait a minute . . . wait a minute! Let's not be a mob!

[*The people stop as a group, seem to pause for a moment, and then much more quietly and slowly start to walk across the street.* GOODMAN *stands alone facing the people.*]

**GOODMAN.** I just don't understand it. I tried to start it and it wouldn't start. You saw me. All of you saw me.

[*And now, just as suddenly as the engine started, it stops and there's a long silence that is gradually intruded upon by the frightened murmuring of the people.*]

**GOODMAN.** I don't understand. I swear . . . I don't understand. What's happening?

**DON.** Maybe you better tell us. Nothing's working on this street. Nothing. No lights, no power, no radio. [*And then meaningfully*] Nothing except one car—yours!

[*The people pick this up and now their murmuring becomes a loud chant filling the air with accusations and demands for action. Two of the men pass* DON *and head toward* GOODMAN, *who backs away, backing into his car and now at bay.*]

**GOODMAN.** Wait a minute now. You keep your distance—all of you. So I've got a car that starts by itself—well, that's a freak thing, I admit it. But does that make me some kind of a criminal or something? I don't know why the car works—it just does!

[*This stops the crowd momentarily and now* GOODMAN, *still backing away, goes toward his front porch. He goes up the steps and then stops to stand facing the mob.*

*We see a long shot of* STEVE *as he comes through the crowd.*]

**STEVE.** [*Quietly*] We're all on a monster kick, Les. Seems that the general impression holds that maybe one family isn't what we think they are. Monsters from outer space or something. Different than us. Fifth columnists[2] from the vast beyond. [*He chuckles.*] You know anybody that might fit that description around here on Maple Street?

**Goodman.** What is this, a gag or something? This a practical joke or something?

[*We see a close-up of the porch light as it suddenly goes out. There's a murmur from the group.*]

**Goodman.** Now I suppose that's supposed to incriminate me! The light goes on and off. That really does it, doesn't it? [*He looks around the faces of the people.*] I just don't understand this— [*He wets his lips, looking from face to face.*] Look, you all know me. We've lived here five years. Right in this house. We're no different from any of the rest of you! We're no different at all. Really . . . this whole thing is just . . . just weird—

**Woman.** Well, if that's the case, Les Goodman, explain why—

[*She stops suddenly, clamping her mouth shut.*]

**Goodman.** [*Softly*] Explain what?

**Steve.** [*Interjecting*] Look, let's forget this—

**Charlie.** [*Overlapping him*] Go ahead, let her talk. What about it? Explain what?

**Woman.** [*A little reluctantly*] Well . . . sometimes I go to bed late at night. A couple of times . . . a couple of times I'd come out on the porch and I'd see Mr. Goodman here in the wee hours of the morning standing out in front of his house . . . looking up at the sky. [*She looks around the circle of faces.*] That's right, looking up at the sky as if . . . as if he were waiting for something. [*A pause*] As if he were looking for something.

[*There's a murmur of reaction from the crowd again.*

*We cut suddenly to a group shot. As* Goodman *starts toward them, they back away frightened.*]

**Goodman.** You know really . . . this is for laughs. You know what I'm guilty of? [*He laughs.*] I'm guilty of insomnia. Now what's the penalty for insomnia? [*At this point the laugh, the humor, leaves his voice.*] Did you hear what I said? I said it was insomnia. [*A pause as he looks around, then shouts.*]

2. **Fifth columnists** people who help an invading enemy from within their own country.

I said it was insomnia! You fools. You scared, frightened rabbits, you. You're sick people, do you know that? You're sick people—all of you! And you don't even know what you're starting because let me tell you . . . let me tell you—this thing you're starting—that should frighten you. As God is my witness . . . you're letting something begin here that's a nightmare!

# ACT II

[*We see a medium shot of the* Goodman *entry hall at night. On the side table rests an unlit candle.* Mrs. Goodman *walks into the scene, a glass of milk in hand. She sets the milk down on the table, lights the candle with a match from a box on the table, picks up the glass of milk, and starts out of scene.*

Mrs. Goodman *comes through her porch door, glass of milk in hand. The entry hall, with table and lit candle, can be seen behind her.*

*Outside, the camera slowly pans down the sidewalk, taking in little knots of people who stand around talking in low voices. At the end of each conversation they look toward* Les Goodman's *house. From the various houses we can see candlelight but no electricity, and there's an all-pervading quiet that blankets the whole area, disturbed only by the almost whispered voices of the people as they stand around. The camera pans over to one group where* Charlie *stands. He stares across at* Goodman's *house.*

*We see a long shot of the house. Two men stand across the street in almost sentry-like poses. Then we see a medium shot of a group of people.*]

**Sally.** [*A little timorously*] It just doesn't seem right, though, keeping watch on them. Why . . . he was right when he said he was one of our neighbors. Why, I've known Ethel Goodman ever since they moved in. We've been good friends—

**Charlie.** That don't prove a thing. Any guy who'd spend his time lookin' up at the sky early in the morning—well, there's something wrong with that kind of person. There's something that ain't legitimate. Maybe under normal circumstances we could let it go by, but these aren't normal circumstances. Why, look at this street! Nothin' but candles. Why, it's like goin' back into the dark ages or somethin'!

[STEVE *walks down the steps of his porch, walks down the street over to* LES GOODMAN'S *house, and then stops at the foot of the steps.* GOODMAN *stands there, his wife behind him, very frightened.*]

**GOODMAN.** Just stay right where you are, Steve. We don't want any trouble, but this time if anybody sets foot on my porch, that's what they're going to get—trouble!

**STEVE.** Look, Les—

**GOODMAN.** I've already explained to you people. I don't sleep very well at night sometimes. I get up and I take a walk and I look up at the sky. I look at the stars!

**MRS. GOODMAN** That's exactly what he does. Why this whole thing, it's . . . it's some kind of madness or something.

**STEVE.** [*Nods grimly*] That's exactly what it is—some kind of madness.

**CHARLIE'S VOICE.** [*Shrill, from across the street*] You best watch who you're seen with, Steve! Until we get this all straightened out, you ain't exactly above suspicion yourself.

**STEVE.** [*Whirling around toward him*] Or you, Charlie. Or any of us, it seems. From age eight on up!

**WOMAN.** What I'd like to know is—what are we gonna do? Just stand around here all night?

**CHARLIE.** There's nothin' else we can do! [*He turns back looking toward* STEVE *and* GOODMAN *again.*] One of 'em'll tip their hand. They got to.

**STEVE.** [*Raising his voice*] There's something you can do, Charlie. You could go home and keep your mouth shut. You could quit strutting around like a self-appointed hanging judge and just climb into bed and forget it.

**CHARLIE.** You sound real anxious to have that happen, Steve. I think we better keep our eye on you too!

**DON.** [*As if he were taking the bit in his teeth, takes a hesitant step to the front*] I think everything might as well come out now. [*He turns toward* STEVE.] Your wife's done plenty of talking, Steve, about how odd you are!

**CHARLIE.** [*Picking this up, his eyes widening*] Go ahead, tell us what she's said.

[*We see a long shot of* STEVE *as he walks toward them from across the street.*]

**STEVE.** Go ahead, what's my wife said? Let's get it all out. Let's pick out every idiosyncrasy of every single man, woman, and child on the street. And then we might as well set up some kind of kangaroo court.[3] How about a firing squad at dawn, Charlie, so we can get rid of all the suspects? Narrow them down. Make it easier for you.

**DON.** There's no need gettin' so upset, Steve. It's just that . . . well . . . Myra's talked about how there's been plenty of nights you spent hours down in your basement workin' on some kind of radio or something. Well, none of us have ever seen that radio—

[*By this time* STEVE *has reached the group. He stands there defiantly close to them.*]

**CHARLIE.** Go ahead, Steve. What kind of "radio set" you workin' on? I never seen it. Neither has anyone else. Who you talk to on that radio set? And who talks to you?

**STEVE.** I'm surprised at you, Charlie. How come you're so dense all of a sudden? [*A pause*] Who do I talk to? I talk to monsters from outer space. I talk to three-headed green men who fly over here in what look like meteors.

[STEVE'S *wife steps down from the porch, bites her lip, calls out.*]

**MRS. BRAND.** Steve! Steve, please. [*Then looking around, frightened, she walks toward the group.*] It's just a ham radio set, that's all. I bought him a book on it myself. It's just a ham radio set. A lot of people have them. I can show it to you. It's right down in the basement.

**STEVE.** [*Whirls around toward her*] Show them nothing! If they want to look inside our house—let them get a search warrant.

**CHARLIE.** Look, buddy, you can't afford to—

**STEVE.** [*Interrupting*] Charlie, don't tell me what I can afford! And stop telling me who's dangerous and who isn't and who's safe and who's a menace. [*He turns to the group and shouts.*] And you're with him, too—all of you!

---

3. **kangaroo court** unofficial court that does not follow normal rules.

You're standing here all set to crucify—all set to find a scapegoat[4]—all desperate to point some kind of a finger at a neighbor! Well now look, friends, the only thing that's gonna happen is that we'll eat each other up alive—

[*He stops abruptly as* CHARLIE *suddenly grabs his arm.*]

**CHARLIE.** [*In a hushed voice*] That's not the only thing that can happen to us.

[*Cut to a long shot looking down the street. A figure has suddenly materialized in the gloom and in the silence we can hear the clickety-clack of slow, measured footsteps on concrete as the figure walks slowly toward them. One of the women lets out a stifled cry. The young mother grabs her boy as do a couple of others.*]

**TOMMY.** [*Shouting, frightened*] It's the monster! It's the monster!

[*Another woman lets out a wail and the people fall back in a group, staring toward the darkness and the approaching figure.*

*We see a medium group shot of the people as they stand in the shadows watching.* DON MARTIN *joins them, carrying a shotgun. He holds it up.*]

**DON.** We may need this.

**STEVE.** A shotgun? [*He pulls it out of Don's hand.*] Good Lord—will anybody think a thought around here? Will you people wise up? What good would a shotgun do against—

[*Now* CHARLIE *pulls the gun from* STEVE'S *hand.*]

**CHARLIE.** No more talk, Steve. You're going to talk us into a grave! You'd let whatever's out there walk right over us, wouldn't yuh? Well, some of us won't!

[*He swings the gun around to point it toward the sidewalk. The dark figure continues to walk toward them.*

*The group stands there, fearful, apprehensive, mothers clutching children, men standing in front of wives.* CHARLIE *slowly raises the gun. As the figure gets closer and closer he suddenly pulls the trigger. The sound of it explodes in the stillness. There is a long angle shot looking down at the figure, who suddenly lets out a small cry, stumbles forward onto his knees and then falls forward on his face.* DON, CHARLIE, *and* STEVE *race forward*

---

4. **scapegoat** person or group blamed for the mistakes or crimes of others.

*over to him.* STEVE *is there first and turns the man over. Now the crowd gathers around them.*]

**STEVE.** [*Slowly looks up*] It's Pete Van Horn.

**DON.** [*In a hushed voice*] Pete Van Horn! He was just gonna go over to the next block to see if the power was on—

**WOMAN.** You killed him, Charlie. You shot him dead!

**CHARLIE.** [*Looks around at the circle of faces, his eyes frightened, his face contorted*] But . . . but I didn't know who he was. I certainly didn't know who he was. He comes walkin' out of the darkness—how am I supposed to know who he was? [*He grabs* STEVE.] Steve—you know why I shot! How was I supposed to know he wasn't a monster or something? [*He grabs* DON *now.*] We're all scared of the same thing. I was just tryin' to . . . tryin' to protect my home, that's all! Look, all of you, that's all I was tryin' to do. [*He looks down wildly at the body.*] I didn't know it was somebody we knew! I didn't know—

[*There's a sudden hush and then an intake of breath. We see a medium shot of the living room window of* CHARLIE'S *house. The window is not lit, but suddenly the house lights come on behind it.*]

**WOMAN.** [*In a very hushed voice*] Charlie . . . Charlie . . . the lights just went on in your house. Why did the lights just go on?

**DON.** What about it, Charlie? How come you're the only one with lights now?

**GOODMAN.** That's what I'd like to know.

[*A pause as they all stare toward* CHARLIE.]

**GOODMAN.** You were so quick to kill, Charlie, and you were so quick to tell us who we had to be careful of. Well, maybe you had to kill. Maybe Peter there was trying to tell us something. Maybe he'd found out something and came back to tell us who there was amongst us we should watch out for—

[CHARLIE *backs away from the group, his eyes wide with fright.*]

**CHARLIE.** No . . . no . . . it's nothing of the sort! I don't know why the lights are on. I swear I don't. Somebody's pulling a gag or something.

[*He bumps against* STEVE, *who grabs him and whirls him around.*]

**STEVE.** *A gag?* A gag? Charlie, there's a dead man on the sidewalk and you killed him! Does this thing look like a gag to you?

[CHARLIE *breaks away and screams as he runs toward his house.*]

**CHARLIE.** No! No! Please!

[*A man breaks away from the crowd to chase* CHARLIE.

*We see a long angle shot looking down as the man tackles* CHARLIE *and lands on top of him. The other people start to run toward them.* CHARLIE *is up on his feet, breaks away from the other man's grasp, lands a couple of desperate punches that push the man aside. Then he forces his way, fighting, through the crowd to once again break free, jumps up on his front porch. A rock thrown from the group smashes a window alongside of him, the broken glass flying past him. A couple of pieces cut him. He stands there perspiring, rumpled, blood running down from a cut on the cheek. His wife breaks away from the group to throw herself into his arms. He buries his face against her. We can see the crowd converging on the porch now.*]

**VOICES.**

It must have been him.

He's the one.

We got to get Charlie.

[*Another rock lands on the porch. Now* CHARLIE *pushes his wife behind him, facing the group.*]

**CHARLIE.** Look, look I swear to you . . . it isn't me . . . but I do know who it is . . . I swear to you, I do know who it is. I know who the monster is here. I know who it is that doesn't belong. I swear to you I know.

**GOODMAN.** [*Shouting*] What are you waiting for?

**WOMAN.** [*Shouting*] Come on, Charlie, come on.

**MAN ONE.** [*Shouting*] Who is it, Charlie, tell us!

**Don.** [*Pushing his way to the front of the crowd*] All right, Charlie, let's hear it!

[Charlie's *eyes dart around wildly.*]

**Charlie.** It's . . . it's . . .

**Man Two.** [*Screaming*] Go ahead, Charlie, tell us.

**Charlie.** It's . . . it's the kid. It's Tommy. He's the one!

[*There's a gasp from the crowd as we cut to a shot of* Sally *holding her son* Tommy. *The boy at first doesn't understand and then, realizing the eyes are all on him, buries his face against his mother.*]

**Sally.** [*Backs away*] That's crazy! That's crazy! He's a little boy.

**Woman.** But he knew! He was the only one who knew! He told us all about it. Well, how did he know? How could he have known?

[*The various people take this up and repeat the question aloud.*]

**Voices.**

How could he know?

Who told him?

Make the kid answer.

**Don.** It was Charlie who killed old man Van Horn.

**Woman.** But it was the kid here who knew what was going to happen all the time. He was the one who knew!

[*We see a close-up of* Steve.]

**Steve.** Are you all gone crazy? [*Pause as he looks about*] Stop.

[*A fist crashes at* Steve's *face, staggering him back out of the frame of the picture.*

*There are several close camera shots suggesting the coming of violence. A hand fires a rifle. A fist clenches. A hand grabs the hammer from* Van Horn's *body, etc. Meanwhile, we hear the following lines.*]

**Don.** Charlie has to be the one—Where's my rifle—

**Woman.** Les Goodman's the one. His car started! Let's wreck it.

**Mrs. Goodman.** What about Steve's radio—He's the one that called them—

**Mr. Goodman.** Smash the radio. Get me a hammer. Get me something.

**Steve.** Stop—Stop—

**Charlie.** Where's that kid—Let's get him.

**Man One.** Get Steve—Get Charlie—They're working together.

[*The crowd starts to converge around the mother, who grabs the child and starts to run with him. The crowd starts to follow, at first walking fast, and then running after him.*

*We see a full shot of the street as suddenly* Charlie's *lights go off and the lights in another house go on. They stay on for a moment, then from across the street other lights go on and then off again.*]

**Man One.** [*Shouting*] It isn't the kid . . . it's Bob Weaver's house.

**Woman.** It isn't Bob Weaver's house. It's Don Martin's place.

**Charlie.** I tell you it's the kid.

**Don.** It's Charlie. He's the one.

[*We move into a series of close-ups of various people as they shout, accuse, scream, interspersing these shots with shots of houses as the lights go on and off, and then slowly in the middle of this nightmarish morass of sight and sound the camera starts to pull away, until once again we've reached the opening shot looking at the Maple Street sign from high above.*

*The camera continues to move away until we dissolve to a shot looking toward the metal side of a space craft, which sits shrouded in darkness. An open door throws out a beam of light from the illuminated interior. Two figures silhouetted against the bright lights appear. We get only a vague feeling of form, but nothing more explicit than that.*]

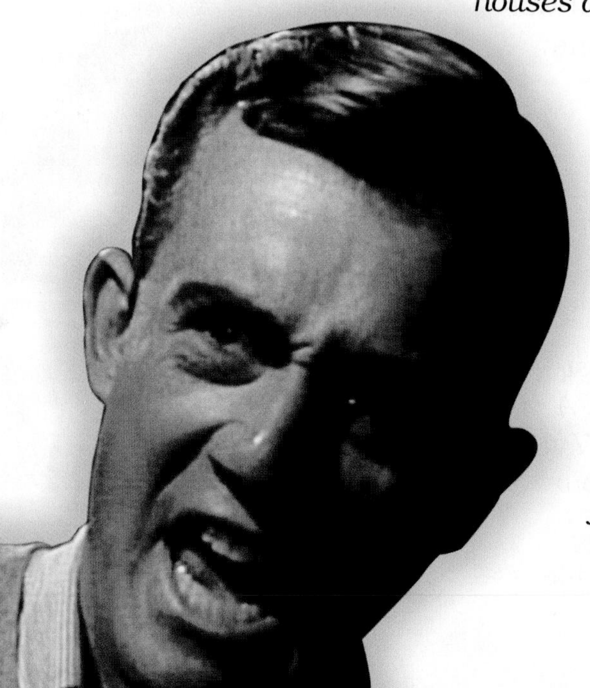

**Figure One.** Understand the procedure now? Just stop a few of their machines and radios and telephones and lawn mowers . . . throw them into darkness for a few hours, and then you just sit back and watch the pattern.

**Figure Two.** And this pattern is always the same?

**Figure One.** With few variations. They pick the most dangerous enemy they can find . . . and it's themselves. And all we need do is sit back . . . and watch.

**Figure Two.** Then I take it this place . . . this Maple Street . . . is not unique.

**Figure One.** [*Shaking his head*] By no means. Their world is full of Maple Streets. And we'll go from one to the other and let them destroy themselves. One to the other . . . one to the other . . . one to the other—

[*Now the camera pans up for a shot of the starry sky and over this we hear the narrator's voice.*]

**Narrator's Voice.** The tools of conquest do not necessarily come with bombs and explosions and fallout. There are weapons that are simply thoughts, attitudes, prejudices—to be found only in the minds of men. For the record, prejudices can kill and suspicion can destroy and a thoughtless frightened search for a scapegoat has a fallout all its own for the children . . . and the children yet unborn. [*A pause*] And the pity of it is . . . that these things cannot be confined to . . . The Twilight Zone!

## ABOUT THE AUTHOR

### Rod Serling (1924–1975)

Rod Serling once said that he did not have much imagination. This is an odd statement from a man who wrote more than 200 television scripts.

Serling did not become serious about writing until he was in college. Driven by a love for radio drama, he earned second place in a national script contest. Soon after, he landed his first staff job as a radio writer. Serling branched out into writing for a new medium—television—and rocketed to fame with his weekly television series, *The Twilight Zone.*

# Close Reading Activities

## READ

### Comprehension

Reread all or part of the text to help you answer the following questions.

1. What strange event occurs just before Maple Street loses electricity?
2. Why does Tommy try to stop Steve Brand from leaving Maple Street?
3. Why does Steve try to stop people heading for Les Goodman's house?
4. What is the surprise at the end of the teleplay?

**Research: Clarify Details** This teleplay may include references that are unfamiliar to you. Choose at least one unfamiliar detail and briefly research it. Then, explain how the information you learned from research sheds light on an aspect of the drama.

**Summarize** Write an objective summary of *The Monsters Are Due on Maple Street*. Do not include opinions or evaluations.

### Language Study

**Selection Vocabulary** Define each boldfaced word, and then use the word in a sentence of your own.

- A little power failure and right away we get all **flustered** and everything.
- [***Persistently*** *but a little intimidated by the crowd*]
- [ … TOMMY *is partly frightened and partly* ***defiant*** *as well.*]

**Diction and Style** Study the passage from the teleplay. Answer the questions that follow.

> [*This stops the crowd momentarily and now* GOODMAN, *still backing away, goes toward his front porch. He goes up the steps and then stops to stand facing the mob* … ]

1. **(a)** What is the meaning of *crowd* in the first sentence? **(b)** What does *mob* mean in the second sentence?
2. **(a)** How are meanings of *crowd* and *mob* similar? How are they different? **(b)** Which word—*crowd* or *mob*—has a stronger connotation? Explain.

**Conventions** Identify the prepositions and prepositional phrases in this passage. Then, explain how the prepositional phrases enhance the description.

> [*We see a medium shot of the* GOODMAN *entry hall at night. On the side table rests an unlit candle.* MRS. GOODMAN *walks into the scene, a glass of milk in hand. She sets the milk down on the table, lights the candle with a match from a box on the table, picks up the glass of milk, and starts out of scene.*]

### Academic Vocabulary

The following words appear in blue in the instructions and questions on the facing page.

**affect** **identify** **convince**

Categorize the words into words you know, know a little, or do not know at all. Then, use a dictionary to look up the definitions.

## Literary Analysis

Reread the identified passages. Then, respond to the questions that follow.

**Focus Passage 1** *(p. 566)*

**Narrator's Voice.** Maple Street, U.S.A., late summer … What was that? A meteor?

### Key Ideas and Details

1. **Draw Conclusions:** At the beginning of the teleplay, what type of place is Maple Street? Support your answer with details from the text.
2. **(a) Interpret:** What does the flash of light represent? **(b)** How do people react to the flash of light?

### Craft and Structure

3. **(a)** What information does the narrator convey to the audience? **(b) Analyze:** Why might a writer use an outside narrator to describe events in a drama?

### Integration of Knowledge and Ideas

4. **Compare and Contrast:** How do the events in this passage **affect** Maple Street's "little world"?

**Focus Passage 2** *(pp. 580–581)*

**Charlie.** Look, look I swear to you … It's Tommy. He's the one!

### Key Ideas and Details

1. **(a) Deduce:** Why does Charlie claim he knows who the monster is? **(b) Support:** What details show that Charlie finds it hard to **identify** the person to blame?
2. **Infer:** Why does Goodman ask what Charlie is waiting for?

### Craft and Structure

3. **Analyze:** How does dialogue create suspense in the passage?
4. **Interpret:** What information do the stage directions convey?

### Integration of Knowledge and Ideas

5. **(a) Infer:** Does Charlie really know who the monster is? Explain. **(b) Analyze Cause and Effect:** Why does Charlie say Tommy is "the one"?

## Characters' Motives

**Motives** are the reasons behind a character's actions. Reread the teleplay, taking notes on the ways that Rod Serling conveys the characters' motives.

1. **(a)** Why is Tommy determined that no one leave Maple Street? **(b)** Why is Tommy's mother concerned about the crowd's response to her son?
2. Why does Les Goodman first laugh and then shout as he tries to **convince** the crowd he has insomnia?
3. **Leaders and Followers (a)** Why does Charlie shoot Pete Van Horn? **(b)** Is he acting as the group's leader at this point? Explain. **(c)** What motivates most of the characters to be followers, and who are they following?

## DISCUSS

### From Text to Topic **Panel Discussion**

*The Monsters Are Due on Maple Street* is an episode of the television show *The Twilight Zone,* which ran from 1959 to 1964. Locate and watch the television episode with a small group of classmates. As you watch, take notes on the ways in which lighting, sound, and camera effects contribute to the television production. After viewing, hold a panel discussion in which you compare and contrast the written teleplay with the television episode. Analyze the techniques that are unique to each medium—film and print—and support your key points with evidence from both the television episode and the text.

**QUESTIONS FOR DISCUSSION**

1. Which medium is more effective in portraying the mob mentality?
2. What specific techniques made the portrayal more effective?

## WRITE

### Writing to Sources **Argument**

**Assignment**

Write an **argumentative essay** in which you make a claim about individuals who stand up to the crowd or individuals who follow others. Support your claim with details about characters in *The Monsters Are Due on Maple Street.*

**Prewriting and Planning** Reread the drama, looking for characters whose actions show them to be leaders or followers. Record your notes in web organizers that link characters and their actions.

**Drafting** Most argumentative writing includes the following:

- **Claim:** The writer's position on the issue
- **Evidence:** Relevant examples that support the claim and follow logical reasoning
- **Responses to Counterclaims:** Acknowledgement of opposing viewpoints
- **Conclusion:** A strong, concluding statement

In your draft, cite examples from the teleplay to support your points.

**Revising** Reread your essay, making sure you have clearly shown the relationships between claims and evidence.

**Editing and Proofreading** A sentence fragment is a group of words that is incorrectly punctuated as a sentence. A fragment is missing a subject, a predicate, or both. Proofread your essay to make sure all sentences are complete.

**CONVENTIONS**

When you write sentences, use the correct end punctuation. A period follows a statement, a question mark follows a question, and an exclamation point follows an exclamation.

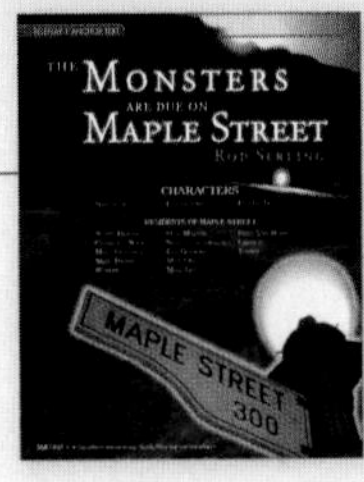

# RESEARCH

## Research **Investigate the Topic**

**Crowds and Their Actions** Many individuals will follow a crowd's actions. For example, when spectators at a sports event start chanting, others join in. Mob behavior may occur when people are unsure of what "should" be done in a difficult situation. Because the members of a crowd are anonymous, it can be hard to tell who is responsible for the crowd's actions.

**Assignment**

Conduct research to learn about the factors that can influence people to act as a mob. Search online library databases using the keywords *crowd* and *mob*. Take clear notes and carefully identify your sources. Share your findings in an **oral presentation** for the class.

**PREPARATION FOR ESSAY**

You may use the knowledge you gain during this research assignment to support your claims in an essay you will write at the end of this section.

**Gather Sources** Locate authoritative sources. Primary sources, such as psychological research studies, provide firsthand information. You may also want to consult secondary sources, such as encyclopedias of the social sciences. Look for sources that feature expert authors and up-to-date information.

**Take Notes** Record notes on each of your sources, either electronically or on notecards. Use an organized note-taking strategy.

- Write a separate note for each source.
- Use quotation marks when you record exact wording.
- Do not try to note every detail from a source. Summarize the main points and most important details.

**Synthesize Multiple Sources** Assemble data from your sources and organize it into a cohesive presentation. Use what you learned to draw conclusions about the relationship between mobs and the actions of leaders and followers. Use your notes to construct an outline for your presentation. Follow accepted conventions to cite all sources you use in your presentation. See the Citing Sources pages in the Introductory Unit of this textbook for additional guidance.

**Organize and Present Ideas** Review your outline and practice delivering your presentation. Be prepared to answer questions from your audience.

Ray Bradbury

# All Summer in a Day

# "Ready?" "Ready." "Now?" "Soon."

"Do the scientists really know? Will it happen today, will it?"

"Look, look; see for yourself!"

The children pressed to each other like so many roses, so many weeds, intermixed, peering out for a look at the hidden sun.

It rained.

It had been raining for seven years; thousands upon thousands of days compounded and filled from one end to the other with rain, with the drum and gush of water, with the sweet crystal fall of showers and the concussion of storms so heavy they were tidal waves come over the islands. A thousand forests had been crushed under the rain and grown up a thousand times to be crushed again. And this was the way life was forever on the planet Venus and this was the schoolroom of the children of the rocket men and women who had come to a raining world to set up civilization and live out their lives.

"It's stopping, it's stopping!"

"Yes, yes!"

Margot stood apart from them, from these children who could never remember a time when there wasn't rain and rain and rain. They were all nine years old, and if there had been a day, seven years ago, when the sun came out for an hour and showed its face to the stunned world, they could not recall. Sometimes, at night, she heard them stir, in remembrance, and she knew they were dreaming and remembering gold or a yellow crayon or a coin large enough to buy the world with. She knew they thought they remembered a warmness, like a blushing in the face, in the body, in the arms and legs and trembling hands. But then they always awoke to the tatting drum, the endless shaking down of clear bead necklaces upon the roof, the walk, the gardens, the forests, and their dreams were gone.

All day yesterday they had read in class about the sun. About how like a lemon it was, and how hot. And they had written small stories or essays or poems about it:

I think the sun is a flower,
That blooms for just one hour.

That was Margot's poem, read in a quiet voice in the still classroom while the rain was falling outside.

"Aw, you didn't write that!" protested one of the boys.

"I did," said Margot. "I did."

"William!" said the teacher.

**slackening ▶** (slak´ ən iŋ) *adj.* easing; becoming less active

But that was yesterday. Now the rain was **slackening**, and the children were crushed in the great thick windows.

"Where's teacher?"

"She'll be back."

"She'd better hurry, we'll miss it!"

They turned on themselves, like a feverish wheel, all fumbling spokes.

Margot stood alone. She was a very frail girl who looked as if she had been lost in the rain for years and the rain had washed out the blue from her eyes and the red from her mouth and the yellow from her hair. She was an old photograph dusted from an album, whitened away, and if she spoke at all her voice would be a ghost. Now she stood, separate, staring at the rain and the loud wet world beyond the huge glass.

"What're you looking at?" said William.

Margot said nothing.

"Speak when you're spoken to." He gave her a shove. But she did not move; rather she let herself be moved only by him and nothing else.

They edged away from her, they would not look at her. She felt them go away. And this was because she would play no games with them in the echoing tunnels of the underground city. If they tagged her and ran, she stood blinking after them and did not follow. When the class sang songs about happiness and life and games her lips barely moved. Only when they sang about the sun and the summer did her lips move as she watched the drenched windows.

And then, of course, the biggest crime of all was that she had come here only five years ago from Earth, and she remembered the sun and the way the sun was and the sky was when she was four in Ohio. And they, they had been on Venus all their lives, and they had been only two years old when last the sun came out and had long since forgotten the color and heat of it and the way it really was. But Margot remembered.

"It's like a penny," she said once, eyes closed.

"No, it's not!" the children cried.

"It's like a fire," she said, "in the stove."

"You're lying, you don't remember!" cried the children.

But she remembered and stood quietly apart from all of them and watched the patterning windows. And once, a month ago, she had refused to shower in the school shower rooms, had clutched her hands to her ears and over her head, screaming the water mustn't touch her head. So after that, dimly, dimly, she sensed it, she was different and they knew her difference and kept away.

There was talk that her father and mother were taking her back to Earth next year; it seemed **vital** to her that they do so, though it would mean the loss of thousands of dollars to her family. And so, the children hated her for all these reasons of big and little consequence. They hated her pale snow face, her waiting silence, her thinness, and her possible future.

◀ **vital**
(vīt′ 'l) *adj.*
extremely important or necessary

"Get away!" The boy gave her another push. "What're you waiting for?"

Then, for the first time, she turned and looked at him. And what she was waiting for was in her eyes.

"Well, don't wait around here!" cried the boy savagely. "You won't see nothing!"

Her lips moved.

"Nothing!" he cried. "It was all a joke, wasn't it?" He turned to the other children. "Nothing's happening today. Is it?"

They all blinked at him and then, understanding, laughed and shook their heads. "Nothing, nothing!"

"Oh, but," Margot whispered, her eyes helpless. "But this is the day, the scientists predict, they say, they know, the sun . . ."

"All a joke!" said the boy, and seized her roughly. "Hey, everyone, let's put her in a closet before teacher comes!"

"No," said Margot, falling back.

They surged[1] about her, caught her up and bore her, protesting, and then pleading, and then crying, back into a tunnel, a room, a closet, where they slammed and locked the door. They stood looking at the door and saw it tremble from her beating and throwing herself against it. They heard her muffled cries. Then, smiling, they turned and went out and back down the tunnel, just as the teacher arrived.

"Ready, children?" She glanced at her watch.

"Yes!" said everyone.

"Are we all here?"

"Yes!"

The rain slackened still more.

They crowded to the huge door.

The rain stopped.

It was as if, in the midst of a film concerning an avalanche, a tornado, a hurricane, a volcanic eruption, something had, first, gone wrong with the sound apparatus, thus muffling and finally cutting off all noise, all of the blasts and repercussions and thunders, and then, second, ripped the film from the projector and inserted in its place a peaceful tropical slide which did not move or tremor. The world ground to a standstill. The silence was so immense and unbelievable that you felt your ears had been stuffed or you had lost your hearing altogether. The children put their hands to their ears. They stood apart. The door slid back and the smell of the silent, waiting world came in to them.

The sun came out.

It was the color of flaming bronze and it was very large. And the sky around it was a blazing blue tile color. And the jungle burned with sunlight as the children, released from their spell, rushed out, yelling, into the springtime.

"Now, don't go too far," called the teacher after them. "You've only two hours, you know. You wouldn't want to get caught out!"

But they were running and turning their faces up to the sky and feeling the sun on their cheeks like a warm iron; they were taking off their jackets and letting the sun burn their arms.

"Oh, it's better than the sun lamps, isn't it?"

"Much, much better!"

They stopped running and stood in the great jungle that covered Venus, that grew and never stopped growing, tumultuously, even as you watched it. It was a nest of octopi, clustering up great arms of fleshlike weed, wavering, flowering

---

1. **surged** (surjd) *v.* moved in a violent swelling motion.

in this brief spring. It was the color of rubber and ash, this jungle, from the many years without sun. It was the color of stones and white cheeses and ink, and it was the color of the moon.

The children lay out, laughing, on the jungle mattress, and heard it sigh and squeak under them, **resilient** and alive. They ran among the trees, they slipped and fell, they pushed each other, they played hide-and-seek and tag, but most of all they squinted at the sun until tears ran down their faces, they put their hands up to that yellowness and that amazing blueness and they breathed of the fresh, fresh air and listened and listened to the silence which suspended them in a blessed sea of no sound and no motion. They looked at everything and savored everything. Then, wildly, like animals escaped from their caves, they ran and ran in shouting circles.

◂ **resilient** (ri zil′ yənt) *adj.* able to spring back into shape

They ran for an hour and did not stop running.

And then—

In the midst of their running one of the girls wailed.

Everyone stopped.

The girl, standing in the open, held out her hand.

"Oh, look, look," she said, trembling.

They came slowly to look at her opened palm.

In the center of it, cupped and huge, was a single raindrop.

She began to cry, looking at it.

They glanced quietly at the sky.

"Oh, Oh."

A few cold drops fell on their noses and their cheeks and their mouths. The sun faded behind a stir of mist. A wind blew cool around them. They turned and started to walk back toward the underground house, their hands at their sides, their smiles vanishing away.

A boom of thunder startled them and like leaves before a new hurricane, they tumbled upon each other and ran. Lightning struck ten miles away, five miles away, a mile, a half mile. The sky darkened into midnight in a flash.

They stood in the doorway of the underground for a moment until it was raining hard. Then they closed the door and heard the gigantic sound of the rain falling in tons and avalanches, everywhere and forever.

"Will it be seven more years?"

"Yes. Seven."

Then one of them gave a little cry.

"Margot!"

"What?"

"She's still in the closet where we locked her."

"Margot."

They stood as if someone had driven them, like so many stakes, into the floor. They looked at each other and then looked away. They glanced out at the world that was raining now and raining and raining steadily. They could not meet each other's glances. Their faces were solemn and pale. They looked at their hands and feet, their faces down.

"Margot."

One of the girls said, "Well . . .?"

No one moved.

"Go on," whispered the girl.

They walked slowly down the hall in the sound of cold rain. They turned through the doorway to the room in the sound of the storm and thunder, lightning on their faces, blue and terrible. They walked over to the closet door slowly and stood by it.

Behind the closet door was only silence.

They unlocked the door, even more slowly, and let Margot out.

## ABOUT THE AUTHOR

### Ray Bradbury (1920–2012)

As a boy, Ray Bradbury loved magicians, circuses, and science fiction stories. At the age of twelve, he began writing his own imaginative tales, and his first story appeared in a magazine when he was in his teens.

*The Martian Chronicles*, a collection of Bradbury's stories about Earth's colonization of Mars, was published 1950. The book was highly praised at the time and is considered a classic today. *The Martian Chronicles* has been adapted into a movie, a stage play, a television miniseries, and even an interactive computer game.

# Close Reading Activities

## READ

### Comprehension

Answer the following questions.

1. How do the other children feel about Margot?
2. How do the children react when they realize that Margot missed the sun because of their prank?

**Research: Clarify Details** Choose at least one unfamiliar detail from the story and briefly research it.

**Summarize** Write an objective summary of the story that is free from opinion and evaluation.

### Language Study

**Selection Vocabulary** Create a word map with at least one synonym and one antonym for each boldfaced word. Then, use each word in a sentence of your own.

- Now the rain was **slackening**, and the children were crushed in the great thick windows.
- … it seemed **vital** to her that they do so, though it would mean the loss of thousands of dollars to her family.
- The children lay out, laughing, on the jungle mattress, and heard it sigh and squeak under them, **resilient** and alive.

### Literary Analysis

Reread the identified passage.

**Focus Passage** *(pp. 589–590)*

Margot stood apart from them, … and their dreams were gone.

#### Key Ideas and Details

1. **(a) Interpret:** How has seven years of constant rain affected the children? **(b) Interpret:** How much do the children know about the sun?
2. How well does Margot fit in with the class? Explain.

#### Craft and Structure

3. **(a)** To what does the author compare the sun in this passage? **(b) Analyze:** What are the effects of these metaphors?

#### Integration of Knowledge and Ideas

4. **Generalize:** What does the sun represent? Cite details in the story to support your answer.

### Setting

The **setting** is the time and place of a story's action. Reread the story, and take notes on ways the author uses setting.

1. How was Margot's environment on Earth different from the **environment** of Venus?
2. How do the children act when the sun comes out?
3. How does the children's behavior change when the rain begins to fall again?

# DISCUSS • RESEARCH • WRITE

## From Text to Topic **Partner Discussion**

Discuss the following passage from page 592 with a partner. Contribute your own ideas, and support them with examples from the story.

> They surged about her, caught her up and bore her, protesting, and then pleading, and then crying, back into a tunnel, a room, a closet, where they slammed and locked the door …
>
> "Ready, children?" She glanced at her watch.
>
> "Yes!" said everyone.
>
> "Are we all here?"
>
> "Yes!"

### QUESTIONS FOR DISCUSSION

1. Would you describe the children as leaders or followers? Why?
2. What lesson might Ray Bradbury have wanted to teach with this story?

## Research **Investigate the Topic**

**Bullying** To *bully* means to frighten someone by using force. Margot's classmates bully her by locking her in a closet.

**Assignment**

Conduct research to find out why people may follow a bully and to learn what is being done to develop **awareness** of this problem. Take clear notes and carefully identify your sources. Share your findings in a **research report**.

### PREPARATION FOR ESSAY

You may use the results of your research to support your ideas in the essay you will write at the end of this section.

### ACADEMIC VOCABULARY

Academic terms appear in blue on these pages. If these words are not familiar to you, use a dictionary to find their definitions. Then, use the words as you speak and write about the text.

## Writing to Sources **Informative Text**

"All Summer in a Day" describes a major event in a fictional world.

**Assignment**

Write a **news report** based on "All Summer in a Day" in which you explain the events that occurred on the day the sun appeared on Venus. Mention the **incident** between Margot and her classmates, describing who acted as leaders and who acted as followers.

- First, list answers to the questions, *Who? What? Where? When? Why,* and *How?* Base your answers on details from the story.
- Write an engaging *lead,* or opening sentence, and present the most important information in your first paragraph.
- Include quotations from people who were on the scene.

# Joseph R. McCarthy

## *from* Prentice Hall United States History

**unscrupulous** ▶ (unskrōō′pyə ləs) *adj.* not held back by ideas of right and wrong; untrustworthy

The early Cold War[1] years saw one ominous event after another. The fall of China, Soviet nuclear bombs, and the exposure of Soviet agents in the United States all undermined American confidence. At that time, as Americans worried about the nation's security, a clever and **unscrupulous** man began to take advantage of this sense of fear and helplessness. He suggested that these setbacks were really caused by the work of traitors inside the United States.

*Joseph McCarthy during the televised Army-McCarthy hearings*

1. **Cold War** a period of conflict, without physical war, between the U.S. and the communist Soviet Union (1945–1991).

**Primary Source** "The reason why we find ourselves in a position of [weakness] is not because the enemy has sent men to invade our shores, but rather because of the traitorous actions of those who have had all the benefits that the wealthiest nation on earth has had to offer—the finest homes, the finest college educations, and the finest jobs in Government we can give. . . .I have here in my hand a list of 205 [individuals] that were known to the Secretary of State as being members of the Communist Party and who nevertheless are still working and shaping the policy of the State Department."

—Joseph McCarthy, February 9, 1950

### McCarthy Makes Accusations

In February 1950, a little-known senator from Wisconsin made a speech in Wheeling, West Virginia. The senator, **Joseph R. McCarthy,** charged that the State Department was infested with communist agents. He waved a piece of paper, which, he said, contained the names of State Department employees who were secretly communists.

The charge provoked a **furor**. When challenged to give specific names, McCarthy said he had meant that there were "205 bad security risks" in the department. Then, he claimed that 57 employees were communists. Over the next months, the numbers on his list changed. McCarthy never did produce the list of communists. Still, with the outbreak of the Korean War in June 1950, McCarthy's accusations grabbed the attention of the American public.

◀ **furor** (fyoor′ôr′) *n.* outburst of public anger or excitement

At the time of the above speech, McCarthy was finishing his first term in the Senate. He had accomplished very little in that term and was looking for a popular issue on which to focus his 1952 reelection campaign. Anticommunism seemed to be just the issue. McCarthy was easily reelected to a second term.

## McCarthy's Power Increases

In the following four years, McCarthy put forward his own brand of anticommunism—so much so that the term **McCarthyism** became a catchword for extreme, reckless charges. By making irresponsible allegations, McCarthy did more to discredit legitimate concerns about domestic communism than any other single American.

Between 1950 and 1954, McCarthy was perhaps the most powerful politician in the United States. Piling baseless accusations on top of charges that could not be proved, McCarthy became chairman of an investigations subcommittee. Merely being accused by McCarthy caused people to lose their jobs and destroyed their reputations. He attacked ruthlessly. When caught in a lie, he told another. When one case faded, he introduced a new one.

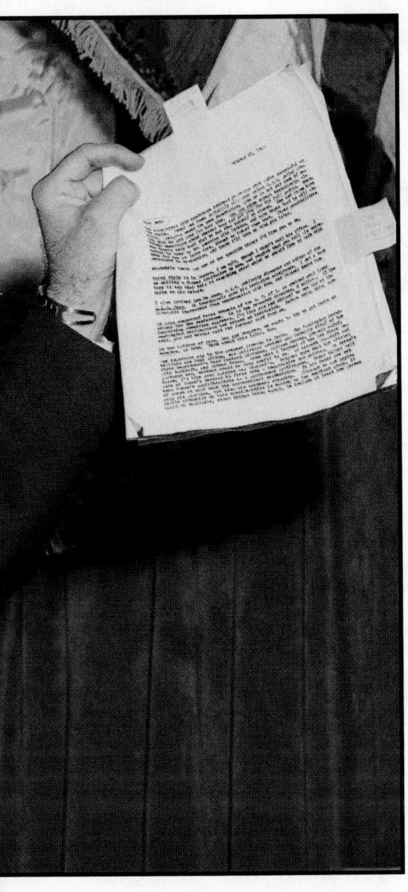

*Joseph McCarthy delivers a "report" that accuses Democratic presidential candidate Adlai Stevenson of associating with alleged subversive groups.*

Confident because of his increasing power, McCarthy took on larger targets. He attacked former Secretary of State George Marshall, a national hero and author of the Marshall Plan.[2] Even other senators came to fear McCarthy. They worried that he would brand them as communist sympathizers.

## McCarthy Falls From Power

In 1954, McCarthy went after the United States Army, claiming that it, too, was full of communists. Army leaders responded that McCarthy's attacks were personally motivated. Finally, the Senate decided to hold televised hearings to sort out the allegations. For weeks, Americans were **riveted** to their television sets. Most were horrified by McCarthy's bullying tactics. For the first time, the public saw McCarthy badger witnesses, twist the truth, and snicker at the suffering of others. It was an upsetting sight for many Americans.

◀ **riveted**
(riv′ it id) *v.* anchored; completely absorbed by

By the time the hearings ended in mid-June, the senator had lost many of his strongest supporters. The Senate formally censured, or condemned, him for his reckless accusations. Although McCarthy continued to serve in the Senate, he had lost virtually all of his power and influence.

The end of the Korean War in 1953 and McCarthy's downfall in 1954 signaled the decline of the Red Scare.[3] The nation had been damaged by the suppression of free speech and by the lack of open, honest debate. However, Americans had come to realize how important their democratic institutions were and how critical it was to preserve them.

---

2. **Marshall Plan** (officially known as the European Recovery Program, ERP) a U.S. program that provided financial aid for rebuilding European economies after World War II in an effort to prevent the spread of Soviet communism.
3. **Red Scare** a term that refers to the promotion of widespread public fear of the possible rise of communism.

# Close Reading Activities

## READ

### Comprehension

Reread as needed to answer these questions.

1. Who was Joseph McCarthy?
2. Why did many Americans believe McCarthy at first?
3. What happened when the Army-McCarthy hearings were broadcast on television?

**Research: Clarify Details** Research an unfamiliar detail in the selection. Explain how your research helps you understand the text.

**Summarize** Write an objective summary of the textbook article. Omit your opinions and **evaluations**.

### Language Study

**Selection Vocabulary** Define each boldfaced word below and use it in an original sentence.

- . . . a clever and **unscrupulous** man began to take advantage of this sense of fear . . .
- The charge provoked a **furor**.
- For weeks, Americans were **riveted** to their television sets.

### Literary Analysis

Reread the passage and answer the following questions.

> **Focus Passage** *(pp. 600–601)*
>
> **McCarthy's Power Increases** . . . he would brand them communist sympathizers.

**Key Ideas and Details**

1. How did McCarthy become very powerful in the early 1950s?

**Craft and Structure**

2. **Analyze:** According to the textbook article, McCarthy made "irresponsible allegations" and "baseless accusations", and "attacked ruthlessly." What picture do these descriptions paint of McCarthy?
3. **(a)** Identify two examples that show cause and effect in the passage. **(b) Evaluate:** Why is cause-and-effect organization useful in a textbook article?

**Integration of Knowledge and Ideas**

4. **Connect:** Review word choice in this passage, including the examples in question 2. How do vivid details and descriptions help you understand a particular period in U.S. history?

### Main Idea

The **main idea** of a text or passage is the most important idea that it presents.

1. **(a)** What is the main idea of the first paragraph? **(b)** What sentence best supports the main idea?
2. **Leaders and Followers (a)** How did support for McCarthy change in1954? **(b)** Identify three key details that support this main idea.

# DISCUSS • RESEARCH • WRITE

## From Text to Topic **Debate**

Use the following passage to prepare for a **debate**. With a team of classmates, choose a position based on one of the discussion questions, and then prepare your argument. Take notes and respond to the points raised by a team with an opposing viewpoint. Cite evidence from the text in your discussion.

**McCarthy Falls From Power** . . . It was an upsetting sight for many Americans. (p. 601)

### QUESTIONS FOR DISCUSSION

1. Is it ever right to pursue accusations based on a strong belief but no concrete proof? Explain.
2. Should cameras be allowed in Senate hearings and other court proceedings? Explain.

## Research **Investigate the Topic**

**McCarthyism** *McCarthyism* is the term that describes the **investigations** of suspected Communist activities in the United States during the 1950s.

**Assignment**

Conduct research to find out about the U.S. Senate investigation of communism and its followers during the 1950s. Use multiple print and digital sources to gather relevant information. Take detailed notes and carefully identify your sources. Share your findings in an **outline**.

### PREPARATION FOR ESSAY

You may use the results of your research to support your ideas in the essay you will write at the end of this section.

## Writing to Sources **Argument**

"Joseph R. McCarthy" describes the fall of Senator McCarthy following televised hearings in the Senate.

**Assignment**

Write an **argument** in which you take a position on the value of the rapid communication of information to the public. Is it right to broadcast information before all the facts are known, or can this practice lead to miscommunication? Cite evidence from the selection in your argument. Follow these steps:

- Choose your position on the issue and state your claim.
- Support your claim with evidence from "Joseph R. McCarthy."
- Anticipate and address counterarguments.
- Maintain a formal style in your argument.
- Provide a concluding statement that summarizes your position.

### ACADEMIC VOCABULARY

Academic terms appear in blue on these pages. If these words are not familiar to you, use a dictionary to find their definitions. Then, use the words as you speak and write about the text.

WEB ARTICLE

# The Salem Witch Trials of 1692

The Salem Witch Museum

In January of 1692, the daughter and niece of Reverend Samuel Parris of Salem Village became ill. When they failed to improve, the village doctor, William Griggs, was called in. His diagnosis of bewitchment put into motion the forces that would ultimately result in the death by hanging of nineteen men and women. In addition, one man was crushed to death; seven others died in prison, and the lives of many were irrevocably[1] changed.

1. **irrevocably** (i rev′ə kə blē) *adv.* permanently; unable to be undone.

To understand the events of the Salem witch trials, it is necessary to examine the times in which **accusations** of witchcraft occurred. There were the ordinary stresses of 17th-century life in Massachusetts Bay Colony. A strong belief in the devil, factions among Salem Village fanatics and rivalry with nearby Salem Town, a recent small pox epidemic and the threat of attack by warring tribes created a fertile ground for fear and suspicion. Soon prisons were filled with more than 150 men and women from towns surrounding Salem. Their names had been "cried out" by tormented young girls as the cause of their pain. All would await trial for a crime punishable by death in 17th-century New England, the practice of witchcraft.

◀ **accusations** (ak′yo͞o zā′shənz) *n.* charges made against a person for doing something wrong

In June of 1692, the special Court of Oyer (to hear) and Terminer (to decide) sat in Salem to hear the cases of witchcraft. Presided over by Chief Justice William Stoughton, the court was made up of magistrates[2] and jurors. The first to be tried was Bridget Bishop of Salem who was found guilty and was hanged on June 10. Thirteen women and five men from all stations of life followed her to the gallows on three **successive** hanging days before the court was **disbanded** by Governor William Phipps in October of that year. The Superior Court of Judicature, formed to replace the "witchcraft" court, did not allow spectral evidence. This belief in the power of the accused to use their invisible shapes or specters to torture their victims had sealed the fates of those tried by the Court of Oyer and Terminer. The new court released those awaiting trial and pardoned those awaiting execution. In effect, the Salem witch trials were over.

◀ **successive** (sək ses′iv) *adj.* following, in order

◀ **disbanded** (dis band′ əd) *v.* broken up; dismissed

As years passed, apologies were offered, and restitution[3] was made to the victims' families. Historians and sociologists have examined this most complex episode in our history so that we may understand the issues of that time and apply our understanding to our own society. The parallels between the Salem witch trials and more modern examples of "witch hunting" like the McCarthy hearings of the 1950's, are remarkable.

2. **magistrates** (maj′is trāt′s) *n.* civil officers in charge of enforcing the law.
3. **restitution** (res′tə to͞o′shən) *n.* payment made for losses or damage.

# Close Reading Activities

## READ

### Comprehension

Reread as needed to answer these questions.

1. What made life stressful during the time of the Salem witch trials?
2. Who were the accusers?
3. What happened to end the trials?

**Research: Clarify Details** Research an unfamiliar reference from the Web article. Explain how your findings help you better understand the article.

**Summarize** Write an objective summary of the article. Remember to leave out your opinions and evaluations.

### Language Study

**Selection Vocabulary** Define each boldfaced word. Then, identify related words for each one. Use a dictionary, if necessary.

- To understand the events of the Salem witch trials, it is necessary to examine the times in which **accusations** of witchcraft occurred.
- Thirteen women and five men from all stations of life followed her to the gallows on three **successive** hanging days before the court was **disbanded** by Governor William Phipps in October of that year.

### Literary Analysis

Reread the passage and answer the questions.

**Focus Passage** *(p. 604)*

In January of 1692, … were irrevocably changed.

**Key Ideas and Details**

1. Where and when did the events that resulted in the Salem witch trials begin?
2. **Analyze Causes and Effects:** What was the outcome of these events?

**Craft and Structure**

3. **Generalize:** Describe the mood that is **established** through the use of the words *death, hanging,* and *prison*.

**Integration of Knowledge and Ideas**

4. **Hypothesize:** Why might the people of Salem have believed that William Griggs was correct in his **determination** of what was ailing Samuel Parris's daughter and niece?

### Tone

**Tone** is the writer's attitude toward his or her audience and subject. For example, the tone might be **formal** or informal, serious or playful. Reread the article, noting the tone.

1. How does the writer's word choice establish tone? Cite examples from the text.
2. **Leaders and Followers** Why does the writer compare the Salem witch trials to the McCarthy hearings?

# DISCUSS • RESEARCH • WRITE

## From Text to Topic **Group Discussion**

Discuss the following passage with a group of classmates. Take notes during the discussion. Contribute your own ideas, and support them with examples from the text.

> As years passed, apologies were offered, and restitution was made to the victims' families. Historians and sociologists have examined this most complex episode in our history so that we may understand the issues of that time and apply our understanding to our own society.

### QUESTIONS FOR DISCUSSION

1. Why is it important to study events that took place more than three hundred years ago?
2. What can we learn from the Salem Witch Trials?

## Research **Investigate the Topic**

**Mass Hysteria** Mass hysteria is a situation in which a group of people **simultaneously** experience anxiety, irrational behavior, or symptoms of an illness that cannot be explained.

**Assignment**

Conduct research to learn more about mass hysteria and how it relates to the the concept of leaders and followers. Gather relevant information from a variety of print and digital sources, making sure that all sources are accurate and credible. Take detailed notes and carefully identify your sources. Share your findings in a **visual presentation**.

### PREPARATION FOR ESSAY

You may use the results of your research to support your ideas in the essay you will write at the end of this section.

## Writing to Sources **Explanatory Text**

"The Salem Witch Trials of 1692" describes the events that followed a diagnosis of bewitchment in two young girls.

**Assignment**

Write a **comparison-and-contrast essay** in which you analyze the similarities and differences between "The Salem Witch Trials of 1692" and a fictional portrayal of the Salem witch trials.

- Find and read a fictional account of the Salem witch trials.
- Organize your essay using the point-by-point or block method.
- Note the similarities and differences between each work's depiction of the time period, setting, characters, and events.
- Conclude your essay by assessing how the author of the fictional account uses or alters history.

### ACADEMIC VOCABULARY

Academic terms appear in blue on these pages. If these words are not familiar to you, use a dictionary to find their definitions. Then, use the words as you speak and write about the text.

# Herd Mentality? The Freakonomics[1] of Boarding a Bus

## Stephen J. Dubner

A few days a week, I bring my daughter to nursery school on the East Side of Manhattan. (On the other days, I bring my son to kindergarten; next year, they will blessedly attend the same school.) We live on the West Side, and usually take the bus across town. It is a busy time of day. At the bus stop closest to our apartment (we'll call this Point A), there are often 40 or 50 people waiting for the bus. This is largely because there is a subway stop right there; a lot of people take the train from uptown or downtown, then go aboveground to catch the crosstown bus.

I don't like crowds much in general (I know: what am I doing living in New York?), and I especially don't like fighting a crowd when I'm trying to cram onto a bus with my five-year-old daughter. Because there are so many people waiting for a

1. **Freakonomics** Stephen J. Dubner co-wrote the bestsellers *Freakonomics* and *SuperFreakonomics* with economist Steven D. Levitt. The authors also have a popular blog called *Freakonomics*.

bus at Point A, we have perhaps a 30% chance of getting aboard the first bus that stops there, and probably an 80% chance of getting aboard one of the first *two* buses that stop at Point A. (The first bus to come along after a very crowded bus is usually less crowded, but not always.)

As for getting a seat on the bus, I'd say we have perhaps a 10% chance of sitting down on either of the first two buses at Point A. It's not such a long ride across town, maybe 15 minutes, but standing on a crowded bus in winter gear, my daughter's lunch getting smushed in her backpack, isn't the ideal way to start the day. Point A is so crowded that when eastbound passengers get *off* the bus at Point A, using the bus's back door, a surge of people rush *onto* the bus via the back door, which means that a) they don't pay, since the paybox is up front and b) they take room away from the people who are legitimately waiting at the head of the crowd to get on the bus.

So a while ago, we started walking a block west to catch the bus at what we'll call Point B. Point B is perhaps 250 yards west of—that is, further from our East Side destination—than Point A. But at Point B, the lines are considerably shorter, and the buses arrive less crowded. At Point B, we have a 90% chance of getting aboard the first bus that arrives, and perhaps a 40% chance of getting a seat. To me, this seems well worth the effort and time of walking 250 yards.

Once we hit upon this solution, we haven't boarded a single bus at Point A. We get to sit; we get to listen to the iPod together; … we don't arrive with a smushed lunch.

But what I can't figure out is why no other bus passengers at Point A do what we do. To anyone standing at Point A morning after morning, the conditions there are plainly bad. The conditions at Point B are clearly better since a) Point B is close enough to see with the naked eye and b) the buses that arrive at Point A from Point B often have room on them, although only for the first 10 or 20 passengers trying to board at Point A.

**As for getting a seat on the bus, I'd say we have perhaps a 10% chance of sitting down on either of the first two buses at Point A.**

**At Point B, we have a 90% chance of getting aboard the first bus that arrives, and perhaps a 40% chance of getting a seat.**

Personally, I am happy that more people at Point A *don't* go to Point B (which would make me have to consider boarding at Point C), but I don't understand why this is so. Here are a few possibilities:

1. Walking 250 yards doesn't seem like a worthwhile **investment** to improve a short, if miserable, experience.

2. Having just gotten off the subway, the Point A passengers are already broken in spirit and can't **muster** the energy to improve their commuting lot.

3. Perhaps some Point A passengers simply never think about the existence of a Point B, or at least the conditions thereof.

4. There is a herd at Point A; people may not *like* being part of a herd, but psychologically they are somehow comforted by it; they **succumb** to "herd mentality" and unthinkingly tag along—because if everyone else is doing it, it must be the thing to do.

Personally, I am persuaded that all four points may be valid in varying measures, and there are undoubtedly additional points to be made. But if I had to pick an outright winner, I'd say No. 4: the herd mentality.

What do you think? And what are some other examples of herd mentality that you have encountered?

◂ **succumb** (sə kum´) *v.* give way to; submit to

◂ **investment** (in vest´mənt) *n.* act of devoting time or effort to a particular undertaking with the expectation of a worthwhile result

◂ **muster** (mus´tər) *v.* gather together or summon

MEET THE AUTHOR

## Stephen J. Dubner (b. 1963)

Stephen J. Dubner is an award-winning writer. His first published work appeared in the magazine *Highlights for Children* when he was eleven years old. More recently, Dubner co-wrote the popular books *Freakonomics* and *SuperFreakonomics* with economist Steven D. Levitt. Both books explore the topic of human behavior. Dubner regularly contributes articles to periodicals such as *Time* and *The New Yorker.* He lives in New York City with his wife, who is a photographer, and their two children.

# Close Reading Activities

## READ

### Comprehension

Reread as needed to answer these questions.

1. For Dubner and his daughter, what makes the bus ride from Point A unpleasant?
2. What is the disadvantage of boarding the bus at Point B?
3. What is the meaning of "herd mentality"?

**Research: Clarify Details** Choose an unfamiliar detail from the blog post and research it. Then, explain how your findings clarify an aspect of the blog post.

**Summarize** Write an objective summary of the blog post. Remember to leave out your opinions and evaluations.

### Language Study

**Selection Vocabulary** Define each boldfaced word below, and then use the word in a sentence of your own.

- Walking 250 yards doesn't seem like a worthwhile **investment** to improve a short, if miserable, experience.
- Having just gotten off the subway, the Point A passengers are already broken in spirit and can't **muster** the energy to improve their commuting lot.
- … they **succumb** to "herd mentality" and unthinkingly tag along …

### Literary Analysis

Reread the indicated passage.

**Focus Passage** *(p. 610)*
So a while ago … board at point A.

#### Key Ideas and Details

1. **(a) Analyze:** Why is Point B a good place to board the bus? **(b) Connect:** Why does Dubner choose not to go back to boarding at Point A?
2. **Interpret:** What puzzles Dubner about the other bus riders' **behavior**?

#### Craft and Structure

3. **(a)** What types of numerical details does Dubner use in this passage? **(b) Analyze:** How does the use of these details **contribute** to Dubner's message?

#### Integration of Knowledge and Ideas

4. **Synthesize:** What details in the passage support the idea that Dubner is interested in human behavior?

### Author's Argument

An **author's argument** is his or her position on a topic. Reread the blog post, and take notes on the author's argument.

1. What are Dubner's **assumptions** about boarding the bus at Point B?
2. **Leaders and Followers (a)** What format does Dubner use to present the possible reasons that other bus riders do not follow his example? **(b)** Which reason most clearly relates to leaders and followers?

# DISCUSS • RESEARCH • WRITE

## From Text to Topic **Partner Discussion**

Discuss the following passage with a partner. Take notes during the discussion. Contribute your own ideas, and support them with examples from the text.

> There is a herd at Point A; people may not *like* being part of a herd, but psychologically they are somehow comforted by it; they succumb to "herd mentality" and unthinkingly tag along—because if everyone else is doing it, it must be the thing to do.

### QUESTIONS FOR DISCUSSION

1. Why do people go along with the crowd?
2. What evidence in the blog post shows that not everyone will follow a crowd?

## Research **Investigate the Topic**

**Herd Mentality** The term "herd mentality" describes the behavior that results when people follow the crowd rather than thinking and acting for themselves.

**Assignment**

Conduct research to learn more about herd mentality. Consult the Internet to find sources, and make sure each source you find is accurate and credible. Take careful notes and identify your sources. Share your findings in an **informal speech** for the class.

### PREPARATION FOR ESSAY

You may use the results of your research to support your ideas in the essay you will write at the end of this section.

## Writing to Sources **Narrative**

"Herd Mentality? The Freakonomics of Boarding a Bus" focuses on the author's observations that people are likely to follow what the group does, even when there is a better solution to a problem.

**Assignment**

Write an **autobiographical narrative** in which you describe a time when you went along with the crowd or observed others doing so. Explain the situation, describe the group's behavior, and identify other options that might have been possible. Follow these steps:

- Establish the situation and the people involved.
- Use narrative techniques such as description, pacing, and dialogue. Consider using some of the techniques Dubner uses in his blog post.
- Compare your experience to Dubner's experience.
- Bring the narrative to a satisfying conclusion.

### ACADEMIC VOCABULARY

Academic terms appear in blue on these pages. If these words are not familiar to you, use a dictionary to find their definitions. Then, use the words as you speak and write about the text.

# *Follow the Leader:* Democracy in Herd Mentality

Michael Schirber

Bees do it. Birds do it. So do fish and wildebeests. They are all able to gracefully flock or swarm in a particular direction even though not every member of the group knows where they are going.

Even human beings will tend to follow each other with a herd mentality—say, out of a crowded theater. New research provides some surprising insight into what's going on, including a group penchant for democratic decisions.

*Even human beings will tend to follow each other with a herd mentality. . .*

"Groups of animals move purposefully, yet often only relatively few individuals have **pertinent** information as to where to travel," said Iain Couzin of the University of Oxford.

Biologists have often wondered if there is some complex communication that goes on between the informed and the uninformed. But Couzin and his collaborators have shown in simulations that a simple set of behavioral rules can control a group.

"There's no **explicit** signaling in our model," Couzin told *LiveScience*. "No one is saying, 'I know something—come follow me.'"

The only requirement seems to be a balance between a need to stay in the group and a desire on the part of some to go off in their own preferred direction. These goal-oriented individuals look just like their naïve colleagues.

"No **inherent** differences, genetic or otherwise, such as dominance or body size, need to be invoked to explain leadership," Couzin said.

The fact that the followers in the simulation have no way to recognize who is leading them may explain how animals efficiently move in crowded environments, where they can only see their nearest neighbors.

"[This study] demonstrates the power of the little guy," said Daniel Rubenstein of Princeton University, who did not participate in the study. "You don't need avowed[1] leaders, you don't need complex signaling."

The results, published in the Feb. 3 issue of the journal *Nature*, might be useful in developing swarms of robots for exploring the oceans or other planets.

◀ **pertinent** (purt′'n ənt) *adj.* connected or related to the topic

◀ **explicit** (eks plis′it) *adj.* clearly stated; readily seen

◀ **inherent** (in hir′ ənt) *adj.* natural, basic, or inborn

### Follow the virtual leader

In computer simulations, Couzin and his colleagues programmed virtual animals with the instinct to stay near others—an important survival trait in many species. The researchers then endowed some members in the flock with a preferred direction—be it toward a food source or a new nesting site.

They then determined how close the group would come to arriving at this goal.

---

1. **avowed** (ə voud′) *adj.* openly declared.

Accuracy increased as more of the members knew where to go. But at a certain point, adding more informed individuals did not increase the accuracy by very much. To give an example, a group of 10 gets about the same advantage from having five leaders as having six.

The minimum percentage of informed individuals needed to achieve a certain level of accuracy depended on the size of the group. If 10 virtual buffaloes need 50 percent of the herd to know where the watering hole is, a group of 200 can get by with only 5 percent.

In nature, it is likely that the number of leaders is kept as low as possible. Couzin gave the example of bees, for which scouting out a new nest site is dangerous, as well as time-consuming. Studies have shown that only five percent of a hive's population gets involved with scouting.

### Democratic principles

As is the case in human interactions, there will sometimes be a disagreement between those who are in the know.

For instance, there may be five individuals who know of a food supply to the east, but four others who have spotted food to the north. The researchers found that the entire group will tend to settle on the direction with the greater number of informed individuals.

"In the real world, you do have individuals with different information, needs and preferences," Couzin explained. "What we show is that—using very simple rules—the group will choose the majority. It's almost like a democratic decision."

To test whether these simple rules actually apply in real animals, Couzin's team has begun experiments in which certain fish are trained to associate one direction with a reward. These informed individuals will then be mixed with untrained fish to see if the group can be led.

### Informed humans and robots

The scientists also plan to look at human crowds. Couzin thinks there may be a similar sort of mechanism to explain, say, how we walk along a busy street.

"We do it more or less on autopilot," he said.

Perhaps we are subconsciously reconciling two simple commands: get to work on time and avoid stepping on anyone's shoes.

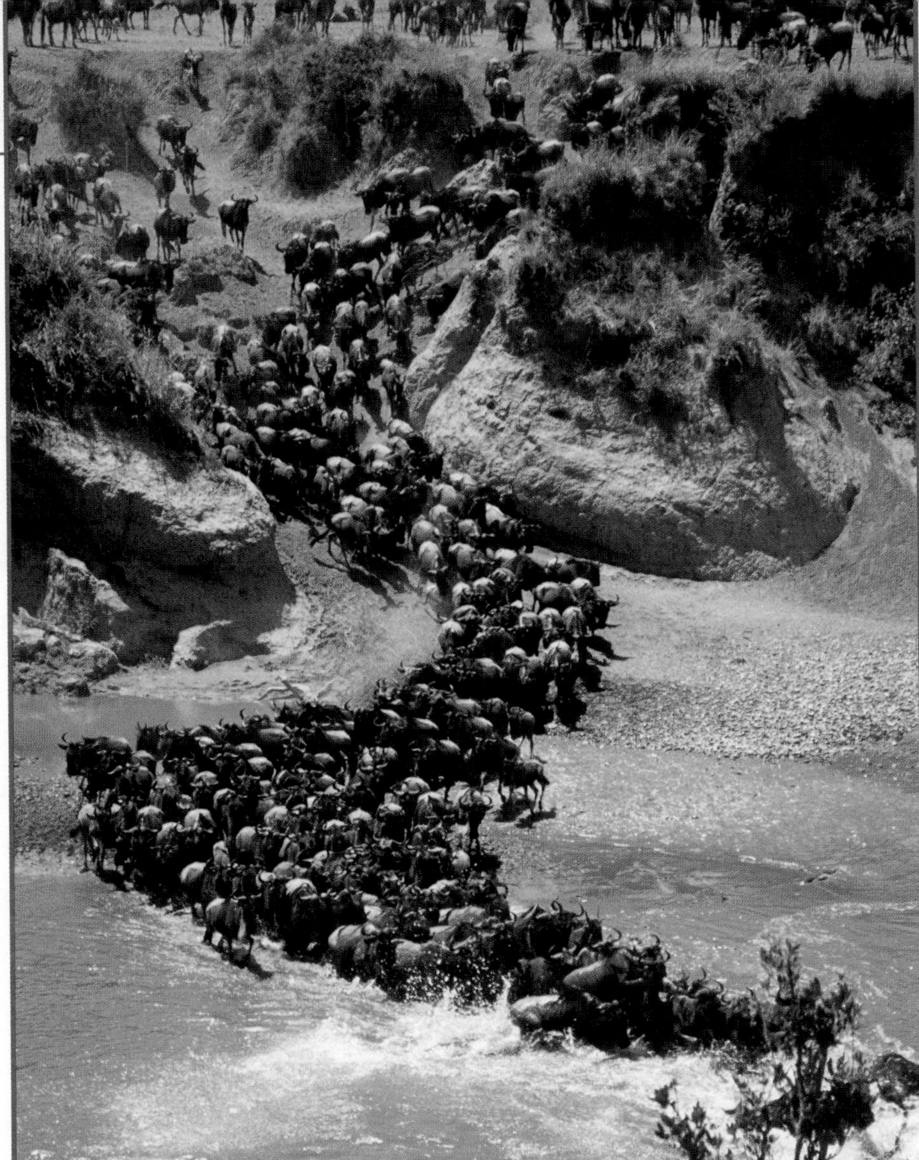

Migrating wildebeest cross the Mara River in Africa

"The mechanism of coordination we propose is very simple and requires only limited cognitive ability," Couzin said. "This simplicity, generality and the effectiveness of the mechanism lend support to its being selected for in populations."

The simple network of commands may also be an efficient way to program teams of robots. Couzin has previously worked with researchers at Princeton University, who are designing underwater robots that can act autonomously.[2]

Robots that learn the location of a certain target could lead other robots to it without any human supervision.

---

2. **autonomously** (ô tän′ ə məs lē) *adv.* independently; without being controlled by others.

# Close Reading Activities

## READ

### Comprehension

Answer the following questions.

1. Why did Iain Couzin study groups of animals?
2. According to Couzin, what happens when two parts of the same group want to go in different directions to access a food supply?
3. How might the research described in this article be useful in the future?

**Research: Clarify Details** Conduct research on an unfamiliar detail in the article. Explain how your findings help clarify the article.

**Summarize** Write an objective summary of the article. Remember to leave out your opinions and evaluations.

### Language Study

**Selection Vocabulary** Define each boldfaced term. Then, identify at least one synonym for each word.

- ... relatively few individuals have **pertinent** information as to where to travel ... .
- "There's no **explicit** signaling in our model ... ."
- "No **inherent** differences, genetic or otherwise ... need to be invoked to explain leadership ... ."

### Literary Analysis

Reread the passage and answer the questions.

**Focus Passage** *(p. 615)*

"Groups of animals move purposefully ... just like their naïve colleagues.

#### Key Ideas and Details

1. **Distinguish:** What is the difference between "informed" and "uninformed" members of a group of animals?
2. What question about **transmitting** signals did biologists want to answer?

#### Craft and Structure

3. **(a)** Which animals are the "goal-oriented individuals"? Which animals are the "naïve colleagues"? **(b) Interpret:** What ideas about the animals do these terms convey?

#### Integration of Knowledge and Ideas

4. **Synthesize:** What distinguishes leaders from followers in a group of animals?

### Expository Writing

In a piece of **expository writing,** the author provides explanations and information on a topic. Reread the article, and note how the author explains how groups of animals move.

1. **(a)** What behavior does the article explain? **(b)** Based on the research, is this behavior simple or **complex**?
2. **Leaders and Followers** In what ways is the behavior of humans similar to the behavior of animals?

# DISCUSS • RESEARCH • WRITE

## From Text to Topic Group Discussion

Discuss the following passage with a group of classmates. Take notes during the discussion. Contribute your own ideas, and support them with examples from the text.

> "In the real world, you do have individuals with different information, needs and preferences," Couzin explained. "What we show is that—using very simple rules—the group will choose the majority. It's almost like a democratic decision."

### QUESTIONS FOR DISCUSSION

1. Are leaders always in the majority? Explain, using examples to support your answer.
2. For humans, is it usually a good decision to follow the majority? Explain.

## Research Investigate the Topic

**Wisdom of the Crowd** According to some studies, a group that acts as a whole can make smarter decisions than an individual who acts alone. This concept is referred to as "the wisdom of the crowd."

**Assignment**

Conduct research to learn more about the concept of "the wisdom of the crowd." Consult multiple print and Internet sources. Take detailed notes and carefully identify your sources so that you can easily access the information later. Share your findings with the class in an **informal presentation**.

### PREPARATION FOR ESSAY

You may use the results of your research to support your ideas in the essay you will write at the end of this section.

### ACADEMIC VOCABULARY

Academic terms appear in blue on these pages. If these words are not familiar to you, use a dictionary to find their definitions. Then, use the words as you speak and write about the text.

## Writing to Sources Argument

"Follow the Leader: Democracy in Herd Mentality" implies that leaders are motivated to change while followers are motivated to go along with the majority. Consider how this idea relates to the concept of "the wisdom of the crowd."

**Assignment**

Write an **argument** in which you agree or disagree that decisions made democratically, with each person having a say, are better than decisions made by one expert individual. Follow these steps:

- State your claim about democratic decisions versus expert decisions.
- Support your position. Provide logical reasons and relevant evidence from your own research and from the article.
- Address and **refute** counterarguments.
- Provide a concluding statement that supports your argument.

# Martin Luther King, Jr., Memorial

Washington, D.C.

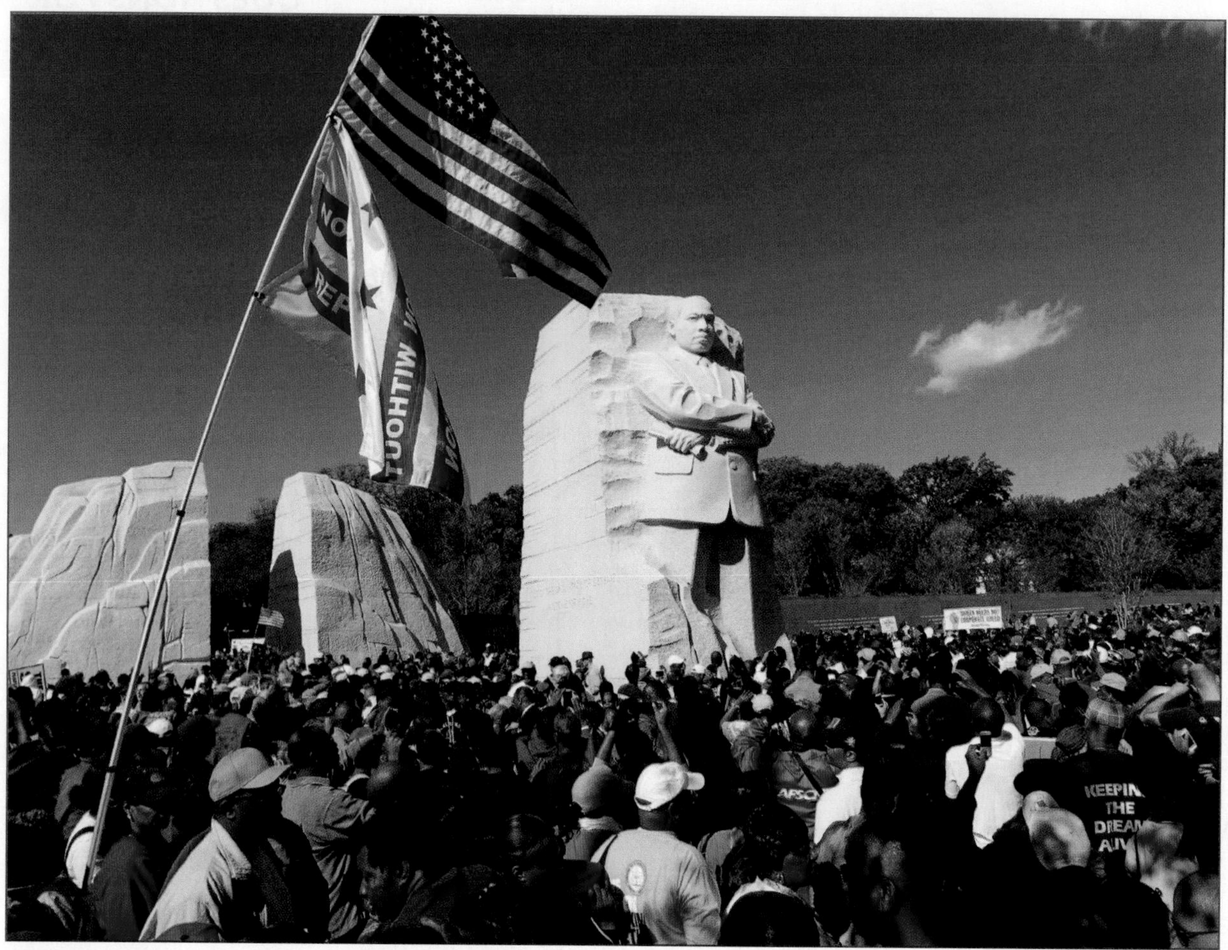

Dedication ceremony, October 16, 2011

## VIEW • RESEARCH • WRITE

### Comprehension

View the photograph again to help you answer the following questions.

1. Examine the photograph closely and describe the memorial.
2. What is the general purpose of a memorial?
3. Why is Washington, D.C., an appropriate setting for this memorial?

### Critical Analysis

**Key Ideas and Details**

1. **(a) Infer:** What can you tell about the setting from this photograph? **(b) Interpret:** What does the photograph show about the size of the memorial?

**Craft and Structure**

2. **Analyze:** Carved into the memorial are the words, "Out of the mountain of despair, a stone of hope." These lines come from King's "I Have a Dream" speech. How do these words help you **understand** the design of the memorial?

**Integration of Knowledge and Ideas**

3. How do you think the sculptor wanted to portray King? What features of the memorial led you to your answer?

### Research **Investigate the Topic**

**Memorial to a Leader** Use credible Internet sources to learn how the creator of the memorial, Lei Yixin, was chosen and what inspired him. Learn more about the memorial itself, such as the **materials** used to build it, its location in Washington, D.C., and the significance of the rolled-up paper in King's hand. Share your findings in an **oral presentation** to the class.

### Writing to Sources **Argument**

Write a brief **argument** in which you state your position on how effectively the photograph shows the memorial. Based on what you learned from your research, evaluate how well this photograph captures the memorial's **significance**. Remember to support your claim with reasons and evidence.

**ACADEMIC VOCABULARY**

Academic terms appear in blue on these pages. If these words are not familiar to you, use a dictionary to find their definitions. Then, use the words as you speak and write about the text.

# Assessment: Synthesis

## Speaking and Listening: **Group Discussion**

**Leaders and Followers** The texts in this section vary in genre, length, style, and perspective. However, all of the texts bring up issues that relate to group behavior. The insights we can gain from literature, history, and research about people's tendency to follow the crowd relate to the Big Question this unit addresses: **Do others see us more clearly than we see ourselves?**

### Assignment

**Conduct discussions.** With a small group of classmates, conduct a discussion about issues of leadership, following the crowd, and seeing ourselves as others do. Refer to the texts in this section, other texts you have read, and your personal experience and knowledge to support your ideas. Begin your discussion by addressing the following questions:

- What traits do leaders have?
- What motivates individuals to follow the crowd?
- How can others help us understand our own behavior?
- When is it good to follow what others are doing? When is it bad to be a follower?

**Summarize and present your ideas.** After you have fully explored the topic, summarize your discussion and present your findings to the class as a whole.

▲ Refer to the selections you read in Part 3 as you complete the activities on this assessment.

## Criteria for Success

✓ **Organizes the group effectively**
Appoint a group leader and a timekeeper. The group leader should present the discussion questions. The timekeeper should make sure the discussion takes no longer than 20 minutes.

✓ **Maintains focus of discussion**
As a group, stay on topic and avoid straying into other subject areas.

✓ **Involves all participants equally and fully**
No one person should monopolize the conversation. Everyone should take turns speaking and contributing ideas.

✓ **Follows the rules for collegial discussion**
As each group member speaks, others should listen carefully. Build on one another's ideas and support viewpoints and opinions with sound reasoning and evidence. Express disagreement respectfully.

### USE NEW VOCABULARY

As you speak and share ideas, work to use the vocabulary words you have learned in this unit. The more you use new words, the more you will "own" them.

## Writing: **Narrative**

**Leaders and Followers** Many authors of both fiction and nonfiction want to help us see ourselves more clearly. We can better understand our own behavior—and how our behaviour relates to social forces at work in groups—by reading about leaders and followers.

> **Assignment**
> Write an **autobiographical narrative**, a true story about your own life, in which you describe an experience you had as a member of a group. Did you follow the crowd, or did you go your own way? Explain the factors that influenced your actions. Remember that an effective autobiographical narrative explores the significance of an event in the writer's life.

### Criteria for Success

**Purpose/Focus**

✓ **Connects specific incidents with larger ideas**
Make meaningful connections between your experiences and the texts you have read in this section.

✓ **Clearly conveys the significance of the story**
Provide a conclusion in which you reflect on what you experienced.

**Organization**

✓ **Sequences events logically**
Structure your narrative so that individual events build on one another to create a coherent whole.

**Development of Ideas/Elaboration**

✓ **Supports insights**
Include both personal examples and details from the texts you have read in this section.

✓ **Uses narrative techniques effectively**
Even though an autobiographical narrative is nonfiction, it may include storytelling elements like those found in fiction. Consider using dialogue to help readers "hear" how characters sound.

**Language**

✓ **Uses description effectively**
Use vivid details to help readers understand the significance of your experience.

**Conventions**

✓ **Does not have errors**
Check your narrative to eliminate errors in grammar, spelling, and punctuation.

**WRITE TO EXPLORE**

Writing is a way to clarify what you feel and think. This means that you may change your mind or get new ideas as you work. Allowing for this will improve your final draft.

## Writing to Sources: Argument

**Leaders and Followers** The related readings in this section present a range of ideas about leaders and followers. They raise questions, such as the following, about individual and group behavior.

- What conflicts can arise between leaders and followers? How can these conflicts be resolved?
- What can a person learn by being a leader? What can a person learn by being a follower?
- Can someone be both a leader and a follower?
- Can historical events have meaning for human behavior today?
- How does research on animals help us understand human behavior? Is it ever wrong to make generalizations about humans based on research on animals?

### Assignment

Write an **argumentative essay** in which you state and defend a claim about the issues surrounding leadership and the factors that motivate people to follow a group. Build evidence for your claim by analyzing the presentation of leaders and followers in two or more texts from this section. Clearly present, develop, and support your ideas with examples and details from the texts.

**INCORPORATE RESEARCH**

In your essay, use information you gathered as you completed the brief research assignments related to the selections in this section.

### Prewriting and Planning

**Choose texts.** Review the texts in the section to determine which ones you will cite in your essay. Select at least two that will provide strong material to support your argument.

**Gather details and craft a working thesis, or claim.** Use a chart like the one shown to develop your claim.

**Focus Question: How are group conflicts best resolved?**

| Text | Passage | Notes |
|---|---|---|
| *The Monsters Are Due on Maple Street* | STEVE. Wait a minute … wait a minute! Let's not be a mob! | Steve tries to stop the group before it gets out of control. |
| "Follow the Leader" | … they succumb to "herd mentality" and unthinkingly tag along—because if everyone else is doing it, it must be the thing to do. | "Herd mentality"; people follow group because others are going along |
| **Example Claim:** It takes more courage to be a leader in an attempt to stop a group from acting wrongly than it takes to be a follower. | | |

## Drafting

**Structure your ideas and evidence.** Create an informal outline or list of ideas you want to present. Decide where you will include evidence and which evidence you will use to support each point.

**Address counterclaims.** Strong argumentation takes differing ideas into account and addresses those ideas directly. As you organize your draft, build in sections in which you present opposing opinions or differing interpretations. Then, write a reasoned, well-supported response to those counterclaims.

**Add interest to your writing.** Write an introduction that will capture your readers' attention. Consider beginning with a compelling quotation or a startling fact. Use precise, vivid language to make your ideas clear and interesting.

**CITE RESEARCH CORRECTLY**

When you quote from a source directly, use quotation marks to indicate that the words are not your own.

## Revising and Editing

**Review content.** Make sure that your claim is clearly stated and that you have supported it with convincing evidence from the texts. Underline main ideas in your paper and confirm that each one is supported. Add additional support as needed.

**Review style.** Revise to shorten passages that are unnecessarily wordy. Check that you have found the clearest, simplest way to communicate your ideas.

### Self-Evaluation Rubric

Use the following criteria to evaluate the effectiveness of your essay.

| Criteria | Rating Scale |
|---|---|
| **Purpose/Focus** Introduces a precise claim and distinguishes the claim from (implied) alternate or opposing claims; provides a concluding section that follows from and supports the argument presented | *not very ............ very*<br>1 2 3 4 |
| **Organization** Establishes a logical organization; uses words, phrases, and clauses to link the major sections of the text, create cohesion, and clarify relationships among claims, reasons, and evidence, and between claims and counterclaims | 1 2 3 4 |
| **Development of Ideas/Elaboration** Develops the claim and counterclaims fairly, supplying evidence for each while pointing out the strengths and limitations of both | 1 2 3 4 |
| **Language** Establishes and maintains a formal style and objective tone | 1 2 3 4 |
| **Conventions** Uses correct conventions of grammar, spelling, and punctuation | 1 2 3 4 |

# Independent Reading

## Titles for Extended Reading

In this unit, you have read texts in a variety of genres. Continue to read on your own. Select works that you enjoy, but challenge yourself to explore new authors and works of increasing depth and complexity. The titles suggested below will help you get started.

### INFORMATIONAL TEXT

**Creating the X-Men: How Comic Books Come to Life**
by James Buckley, Jr.

In this **nonfiction** text, comic book creators take readers behind the scenes to show how they use character, dialogue, plot, and design to bring their popular superheroes to life.

**Gandhi: A Photographic Story of a Life**
by Amy Pastan

Gandhi proved that nonviolent, peaceful movements can succeed in creating powerful changes. His **biography** shows the impact one person can have, even when confronting a mighty empire.

**A Night to Remember** EXEMPLAR TEXT
by Walter Lord

This work of **historical nonfiction,** based on true accounts by survivors of the *Titanic,* details the sinking of the famous ship.

### LITERATURE

**Roald Dahl's Charlie and the Chocolate Factory: A Play**
Adapted by Richard R. George

In this **play,** adapted from Dahl's novel, poor Charlie Bucket wins one of five golden tickets to tour Willy Wonka's chocolate factory. As his spoiled competitors start disappearing, the question remains: Can Charlie outlast the others in Wonka's fun-house world of chocolate rivers and everlasting chewing gum?

**Eight Science Fiction Plays**

In this wide-ranging science fiction collection, you will find **plays** such as *Only Slightly Different* by Bruce Goldstone and *A Clash of Wills* by Mary Canrobert.

**Sorry, Wrong Number *and* The Hitchhiker**
by Lucille Fletcher EXEMPLAR TEXT
Dramatists Play Service, Inc., 1998

In the first of these two suspenseful **plays,** a woman overhears a murder plot. In the second, a man on a cross-country trip is followed by a ghostly hitchhiker.

**Dragonwings** EXEMPLAR TEXT
by Laurence Yep
Dramatists Play Service, Inc., 1998

In this **play,** set in the early twentieth century, eight-year-old Moon Shadow sails from China to San Francisco to live with his father, whom he has never met. He quickly comes to admire his fascinating father, Windrider, who dreams of building a flying machine and is willing to endure scorn, hardship, and prejudice to make his dream come true.

### ONLINE TEXT SET

POEM
**Loo Wit** Wendy Rose

QUESTION AND ANSWER ARTICLE
**What Gives the Sunrise and Sunset its Orange Glow?** GantDaily

AFRICAN AMERICAN FOLK TALE
**How the Snake Got Poison** Zora Neale Hurston

## Preparing to Read Complex Texts

**Attentive Reading** As you read on your own, ask yourself questions like these to enrich your reading experience.

**When reading drama, ask yourself...**

### Comprehension: **Key Ideas and Details**

- Who is the main character? What struggles does this character face?
- What other characters are important? How do these characters relate to the main character?
- Where and when does the play take place? Do the time and place of the setting affect the characters? If so, how?
- Do the characters, settings, and events seem real? Why or why not?
- How does the play end? How does the ending make me feel?

### Text Analysis: **Craft and Structure**

- Does the play have a narrator? If so, what information does the narrator provide?
- How many acts are in this play? What happens in each act?
- Does the dialogue sound like real speech? Are there specific passages that seem especially real? Are there any that seem false?
- What do the stage directions tell me about the ways characters move, speak, and feel? In what other ways do I learn about the characters?
- At what point in the play do I feel the most suspense? Why?
- What speech or passage in the play do I like the most? Why?
- Does the playwright seem to have a positive or a negative point of view? How do I think the playwright's point of view affects the story?
- Do I agree with the playwright's point of view? Why or why not?

### Connections: **Integration of Knowledge and Ideas**

- Does the play remind me of others I have read or seen? If so, how?
- In what ways is the play different from others I have read or seen?
- What new information or ideas have I gained from reading this play?
- What actors would I choose to play each role in this play?
- If I were to be in this play, what role would I want?
- Would I recommend this play to others? Why or why not?

# UNIT 5

THE BIG ?

# Community or individual—which is more important?

## UNIT PATHWAY

**PART 1**
**SETTING EXPECTATIONS**

- INTRODUCING THE BIG QUESTION
- CLOSE READING WORKSHOP

**PART 2**
**TEXT ANALYSIS**
GUIDED EXPLORATION

EXPLAINING THE WORLD

**PART 3**
**TEXT SET**
DEVELOPING INSIGHT

BECOMING AMERICAN

**PART 4**
**DEMONSTRATING INDEPENDENCE**

- INDEPENDENT READING
- ONLINE TEXT SET

**CLOSE READING TOOL**

Use this tool to practice the close reading strategies you learn.

**STUDENT eTEXT**

Bring learning to life with audio, video, and interactive tools.

**ONLINE WRITER'S NOTEBOOK**

Easily capture notes and complete assignments online.

Find all Digital Resources at **pearsonrealize.com.**

# Introducing the Big Question

## Community or individual—which is more important?

In many parts of our lives, we celebrate the individual—encouraging people to reach their personal best and to pursue their own dreams. Each individual has unique qualities and beliefs. However, an individual may also be part of a family or group that shares common cultural beliefs, traditions, or customs. Even these families and groups are part of a larger community.

Communities help individuals by providing services, support, and opportunities. Yet, sometimes the rights or desires of an individual may conflict with those of his or her community. In these cases, it can be difficult to find a fair solution.

## Exploring the Big Question

**Collaboration: One-on-One Discussion** Start thinking about the Big Question by making a list of conflicts between individuals and their communities. Describe one specific example of each of the following situations:

- A school rule that students do not believe is fair
- A situation in which one family member does not want to do what the rest of the family is doing
- A sacrifice that one person is asked to make in order to help many others
- A decision made by someone in power that affects a large group of people

Share your examples with a partner. For each example, discuss whether the interests of the community or the individual seem more important. Use the vocabulary words on the next page in your discussion.

**Connecting to the Literature** Each reading in this unit will give you additional insight into the Big Question.

## Vocabulary

**Acquire and Use Academic Vocabulary** The term "academic vocabulary" refers to words you typically encounter in scholarly and literary texts and in technical and business writing. Review the definitions of these academic vocabulary words.

**common** (käm´ ən) *adj.* shared; public

**community** (kə myo͞o´ nə tē) *n.* group of people who share an interest or who live near each other

**culture** (kul´ chər) *n.* customs of a group or community

**diversity** (də vʉr´ sə tē) *n.* variety, as of groups or cultures

**duty** (do͞ot´ ē) *n.* responsibility

**environment** (en vī´ rən mənt) *n.* surroundings; the natural world

**individual** (in´də vij´ o͞o əl) *n.* single person or thing

**team** (tēm) *n.* group with a common goal

**tradition** (trə dish´ ən) *n.* customs, as of a social group or culture

**unify** (yo͞o´ nə fī´) *v.* bring together as one

**unique** (yo͞o nēk´) *adj.* one of a kind

**Gather Vocabulary Knowledge** Additional words related to community and the individual are listed below. Categorize the words by deciding whether you know each one well, know it a little bit, or do not know it at all.

**custom** **family** **group**
**ethnicity**

Then, do the following:

1. Discuss the meaning of each word with a partner. Then, verify each meaning using a dictionary.
2. Next, use each word in an original paragraph that gives examples of what community and individuality mean to you. Provide context clues for every vocabulary word you use.
3. Remember that context clues might be definitions, synonyms, antonyms, examples, or explanations.
4. Finally, take turns reading your paragraph with a partner. If, during the readings, the meaning of any vocabulary word is still unclear, work with your partner to clarify it.

# Close Reading Workshop

In this workshop you will learn an approach to reading that will deepen your understanding of literature and will help you better appreciate the author's craft. The workshop includes models for close reading, discussion, research, and writing. After you have reviewed the strategies and models, practice your skills with the Independent Practice selection.

## CLOSE READING: THE ORAL TRADITION

Use these strategies as you read the texts in Part 2.

### Comprehension: **Key Ideas and Details**

- Use context clues to help you determine the meanings of unfamiliar words.
- Identify unfamiliar details that you might need to clarify through research.
- Distinguish between what is stated directly and what must be inferred.

**Ask yourself questions such as these:**

- What unique qualities do the characters exhibit?
- What motivates the characters to act as they do?
- What conflicts do the characters encounter?

### Text Analysis: **Craft and Structure**

- Think about the genre of the work and how the author presents ideas.
- Analyze how the setting influences characters and story events.
- Identify elements of folk literature, including the use of fantasy, exaggeration, and repeated patterns.

**Ask yourself questions such as these:**

- How does the author's purpose determine the form of folk literature?
- What details in the story reflect the background, customs, and beliefs of the culture from which the story comes?
- What insight does the story present?

### Connections: **Integration of Knowledge and Ideas**

- Look for relationships among key ideas.
- Look for repeated patterns or ideas and analyze their deeper meaning. Then, synthesize to determine the theme or central insight conveyed by the author.

**Ask yourself questions such as these:**

- How has this work increased my knowledge of a culture, an author, or the genre of folk literature?
- What is the moral of this story?
- What theme, or insight about life, does this work express?

## Read

As you read this fable, take note of the annotations that model ways to closely read the text.

### Reading Model

### "The Travelers and the Bear" from *Aesop's Fables* retold by Jerry Pinkney

Two men were traveling through the forest together on a lonely trail. Soon they heard a sound up ahead as if heavy feet were trampling through the underbrush.[1]

"It could be a bear!" one whispered with alarm, and quickly as he could, he scrambled up a tall tree. He had barely reached the first branch when a huge brown bear thrust aside the bushes and stepped out onto the path.[2]

Hugging the trunk with both arms, the first traveler refused to lend a hand to his terrified companion,[3] who threw himself on the ground and prepared for death.

The bear lowered its great head and sniffed at the man, ruffling his hair with its nose. Then, to the amazement of both men, the fierce beast walked away.

The first traveler slid down from his tree. "Why, it almost looked as if the bear whispered something in your ear," he marveled.

"It did," said the second traveler.[4] "It told me to choose a better companion for my next journey."

*Misfortune is the true test of friendship.*[5]

**Craft and Structure**

**1** The forest is a typical threatening setting in folk literature. The words *lonely* and *heavy* suggest that the travelers may encounter something dangerous.

**Key Ideas and Details**

**2** You may sense that the threatening appearance of the bear will propel the story's action forward.

**Craft and Structure**

**3** Folk literature often features *flat,* or one-sided, characters who display one main trait, such as the first traveler's selfish lack of concern for his companion.

**Craft and Structure**

**4** The bear "whispered" to the second traveler. In folk literature, animal characters often behave like humans.

**Integration of Knowledge and Ideas**

**5** As is often the case in fables, the author directly states the moral, or lesson, in the last line. This technique makes the theme of the story very clear to readers.

## Discuss

Sharing your own ideas and listening to the ideas of others can deepen your understanding of a text and help you look at a topic in a whole new way. As you participate in collaborative discussions, work to have a genuine exchange in which classmates build upon one another's ideas. Support your points with evidence and ask meaningful questions.

### Discussion Model

**Student 1:** I was really surprised when the bear walked away. I was sure it would attack the second traveler.

**Student 2:** I thought it was more surprising that the bear whispered to the man. I wonder why the author gave the bear the human ability to speak. Maybe this contributes to the fable's meaning and theme.

**Student 3:** I think the bear's ability to speak is crucial to the theme. The author ends with a moral: "Misfortune is the true test of friendship." If the bear couldn't speak, this lesson might be lost.

**Student 4:** I agree. Jerry Pinkney probably decided to retell this fable because its message still has meaning today.

## Research

Targeted research can clarify unfamiliar details and shed light on various aspects of a text. Consider questions that arise in your mind as you read, and use those questions as the basis for research.

### Research Model

**Question:** *Why does Jerry Pinkney's retelling of Aesop's fable have meaning today?*

**Key Words for Internet Search:** Pinkney AND fable

**Result:** *The New York Times,* "The Same Old Stories," a book review by Rosemary Wells

**What I Learned:** In a review of three books of fables, Rosemary Wells refers to the universal appeal of fables today. She attributes this appeal to the fact that fables provide valuable, timeless lessons in brief, action-packed stories. She praises Pinkney's retelling and attributes his understanding of the fables to the important role they played in his childhood view of the world.

## Write

Writing about a text will deepen your understanding of it and will also allow you to share your ideas more formally with others. The following model essay evaluates the universal appeal of Aesop's fables and cites evidence to support the main ideas.

### Writing Model: Informative Text

### The Universal Appeal of Fables

According to *New York Times* book reviewer Rosemary Wells, fables have universal appeal. Jerry Pinkney's retelling of Aesop's "The Travelers and the Bear" is an example that shows how a fable can effectively convey a universal message with a brief story. Through the short, eventful story, Pinkney demonstrates the basic wisdom that characterizes a long tradition of fables.

Introducing the focus of the essay in the first paragraph is an effective way to begin a short response assignment.

One appeal of Aesop's fables is that the stories are usually short and to the point. Wells writes, "The fables are compact, action-filled—the reader, or listener, must charge into the story's full-blown drama in the first sentence." In "The Travelers and the Bear," Pinkney retells Aesop's fable in under 200 words. In the first two sentences, he sets the scene. He introduces characters, describes the setting, and advances the action of the story all within the first paragraph. Despite the short length of the introduction, the author is able to create a sense of danger and mystery, "Soon they heard a sound up ahead as if heavy feet were trampling through the underbrush."

The writer introduces the first claim with a clear topic sentence.

The writer concludes this paragraph by supporting the claim with a quotation from the selection.

Another reason Aesop's fables have universal appeal is the clarity of the lesson or moral, which is traditionally summarized in one sentence at the end of the story. Wells is critical of renditions of Aesop's fables that neglect to include these summarizing sentences, which she calls "part and parcel of Aesop." In "The Travelers and the Bear," Pinkney maintains this tradition, by directly stating the moral: "Misfortune is the true test of friendship." The clarity of the moral in Aesop's fables makes the fables accessible to readers and listeners of all ages. Wells explains, "Without it, children must draw their own conclusions about the story's meaning."

Evidence from research effectively supports the claim introduced in the third paragraph.

Aesop's fables have been an important part of the oral tradition for centuries. They have been retold by different cultures all over the world. Despite originating more than 2,000 years ago, Aesop's fables have endured and continue to have universal appeal for modern listeners and readers of all ages.

The essay ends with a strong concluding statement that restates and clarifies the main idea.

As you read the following selections, apply the close reading strategies you have learned. You may need to read the stories multiple times.

*Meet the Author*

Before he wrote books, **Jon Scieszka** (SHEH ska) (b. 1954) worked as a house painter, a lifeguard, and a teacher. One of his favorite books is also one of the first books he ever read—Dr. Seuss's *Green Eggs and Ham.* It showed Scieszka "that books could be goofy."

**CLOSE READING TOOL**

Read and respond to this selection online using the **Close Reading Tool.**

# "Grasshopper Logic" from *Squids Will Be Squids*

by Jon Scieszka and Lane Smith

One bright and sunny day, Grasshopper came home from school, dropped his backpack, and was just about to run outside to meet his friends.

"Where are you going?" asked his mom.

"Out to meet some friends," said Grasshopper.

"Do you have any homework due tomorrow?" asked his mom.

"Just one small thing for History. I did the rest in class."

"Okay" said Mom Grasshopper. "Be back at six for dinner."

Grasshopper hung out with his friends, came home promptly at six, ate his dinner, then took out his History homework.

His mom read the assignment and freaked out.

"Rewrite twelve Greek myths as Broadway musicals. Write music for songs. Design and build all sets. Sew original costumes for each production."

"How long have you known about this assignment?" asked Mom Grasshopper, trying not to scream.

"I don't know," said Grasshopper.

**Moral**

*There are plenty of things to say to calm a hopping mad Grasshopper mom. "I don't know" is not one.*

# "The Other Frog Prince" from *The Stinky Cheese Man and Other Fairly Stupid Tales*

by Jon Scieszka and Lane Smith

Once upon a time there was a frog. One day when he was sitting on his lily pad, he saw a beautiful princess sitting by the pond. He hopped in the water, swam over to her, and poked his head out of the weeds.

"Pardon me, O beautiful princess," he said in his most sad and pathetic voice. "I wonder if you could help me."

The princess was about to jump up and run, but she felt sorry for the frog with the sad and pathetic voice.

So she asked, "What can I do to help you, little frog?"

"Well," said the frog. "I'm not really a frog, but a handsome prince who was turned into a frog by a wicked witch's spell. And the spell can only be broken by the kiss of a beautiful princess."

The princess thought about this for a second, then lifted the frog from the pond and kissed him.

"I was just kidding," said the frog. He jumped back into the pond and the princess wiped the frog slime off her lips.

The End.

# "Duckbilled Platypus vs. BeefSnakStik®" from *Squids Will Be Squids*

by Jon Scieszka and Lane Smith

"I have a bill like a duck and a tail like a beaver," bragged Duckbilled Platypus.

"So what?" said BeefSnakStik®. "I have beef, soy protein concentrate, and dextrose."

"I also have webbed feet and fur," said Duckbilled Platypus.

"Who cares?" said BeefSnakStik®. "I also have smoke flavoring, sodium erythorbate, and sodium nitrite."

"I am one of only two mammals in the world that lay eggs," said Duckbilled Platypus.

"Big deal," said BeefSnakStik®. "I have beef lips."

**Moral**

*Just because you have a lot of stuff, don't think you're so special.*

# Close Reading Activities

## Read

### Comprehension: **Key Ideas and Details**

1. **(a) Summarize:** Summarize the plot of each story, making sure not to include your own opinions or judgments. **(b) Analyze:** Which of the stories has a surprise ending?
2. **(a) Infer:** Why does Grasshopper call his History assignment "small"? **(b) Generalize:** What makes the details of the assignment funny? Cite an example from the text.
3. **(a) Describe:** What is the argument between Duckbilled Platypus and BeefSnakStik® about? **(b) Draw Conclusions:** Why is neither of these characters likely to win the argument?

### Text Analysis: **Craft and Structure**

4. **(a) Analyze:** How does the author make the moral of each tale funny? **(b) Evaluate:** In your opinion, which story is the funniest, and why?
5. **(a) Describe:** What tone of voice does the frog use with the princess? **(b) Compare:** Does the frog have the same attitude or tone of voice as BeefSnakStik®? **(c)** What makes these characters funny?
6. **(a) Interpret:** Explain the attitude toward life and literature that the fables reflect. **(b) Apply:** Is one type of reader more likely than other types to appreciate this attitude? Explain.

### Connections: **Integration of Knowledge and Ideas**

#### Discuss

Conduct a **small group discussion** about the ways the three Scieszka stories reflect common elements of traditional folk literature. For example, consider surprise endings, animals that talk and act like people, and the way the author conveys themes. Use textual examples to support your points.

#### Research

Fables and fairy tales are two common types of folk literature. Briefly research the similarities and differences between these two types of stories. Consider these elements:

**a.** stylistic elements

**b.** common character types

**c.** types of themes or morals

Take notes as you research. Then, write a brief **comparison** of fables and fairy tales.

#### Write

Writers often use unexpected combinations of reality and fantasy to create humor. Write an **essay** in which you analyze the humorous elements in Scieszka's stories and explain the techniques the author uses to create humor. Use details from the texts to support your analysis.

**Community or individual—which is more important?**

Are the morals in Scieszka's stories more useful to an individual or to a community as a whole? Explain.

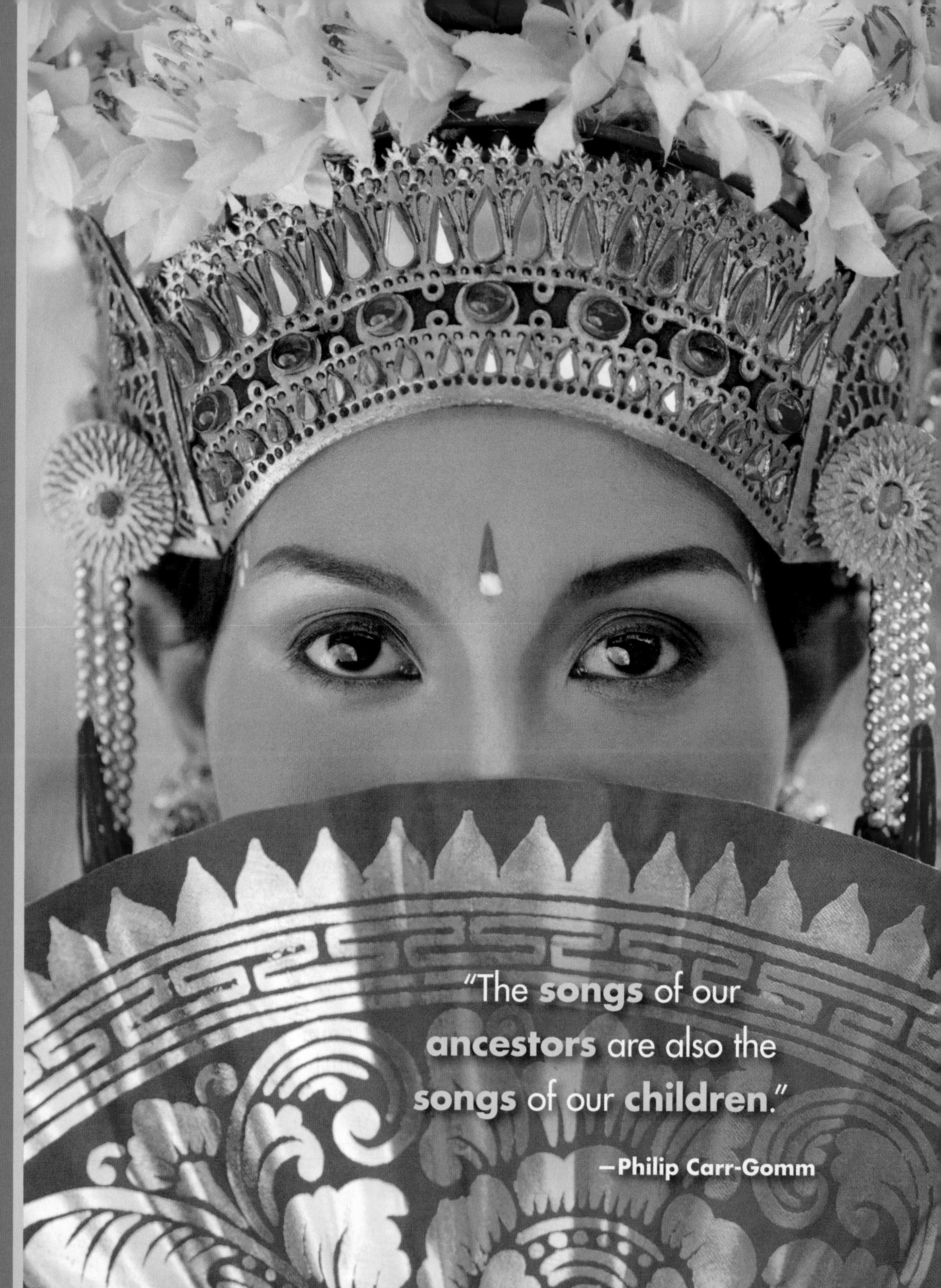
"The **songs** of our **ancestors** are also the **songs** of our **children**."
—Philip Carr-Gomm

PART 2

## TEXT ANALYSIS GUIDED EXPLORATION

# EXPLAINING THE WORLD

As you read the selections in this section, analyze the insights about life and human nature that the authors present through various forms of folk literature. The quotation on the opposite page will help you start to think about the ways in which the traditional tales of our ancestors can still guide us in explaining and celebrating the world around us.

◀ **CRITICAL VIEWING** People pass down traditions through stories, celebrations, and clothing, such as that worn by the woman in this photograph. What is the value of preserving cultural traditions?

### READINGS IN PART 2

**CLOSE READING TOOL**

Use the **Close Reading Tool** to practice the strategies you learn in this unit.

## Elements of Folk Literature

Folk literature is a genre of writing that has its roots in the oral tradition.

**The Oral Tradition** Stories were told long before reading and writing began. These stories were handed down through the ages by word of mouth. The sharing of stories by word of mouth is called the **oral tradition.**

Folk literature is a genre of writing that originated in the oral tradition. Once writing and books were invented, the stories were collected and retold in print. Myths, legends, folk tales, and fables are all forms of folk literature.

**The Importance of the Storyteller** Stories in the oral tradition were created thousands of years ago. No one knows for sure who the first storytellers were. As stories were passed down, new storytellers added and changed details. These details reflected the storyteller's roots and **cultural perspective,** or view of the world. That viewpoint was shaped by the storyteller's background and experiences.

**Theme** is the central idea, message, or insight about life that a story conveys.

Some works of folk literature have **universal themes**—themes that are repeated across many cultures and over many time periods. They express insights into life and human nature that many people understand and find important. The struggle of good against evil is an example of a universal theme.

Other works of folk literature—especially fables—present their theme in the form of a **moral.** A moral is a lesson about life that is stated directly, usually at the very end of the work.

**Purposes of Folk Literature** The **purpose** of a piece of literature is the reason it was written. The purpose of some forms of folk literature may be to explain or teach. For example, a myth may explain a natural phenomenon, and a fable may teach a lesson about life. Other types of folk literature may have the simple purpose of entertaining readers.

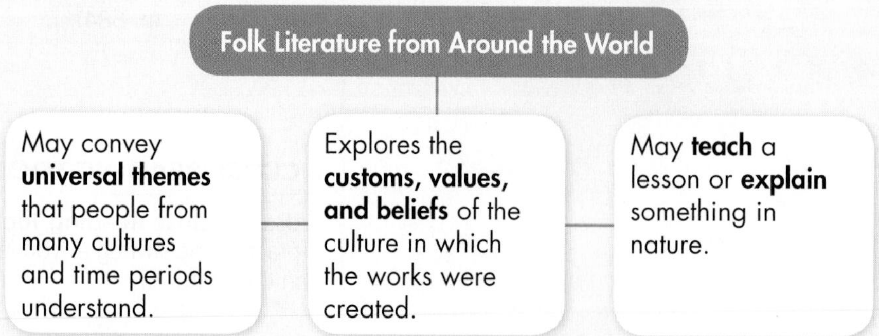

Folk Literature from Around the World
May convey **universal themes** that people from many cultures and time periods understand.
Explores the **customs, values, and beliefs** of the culture in which the works were created.
May **teach** a lesson or **explain** something in nature.

## Forms of Folk Literature

**Myths** are tales that relate the actions of gods, goddesses, and the heroes who interact with them. Many cultures have their own collections of myths, or **mythology.**

**Legends** are traditional stories based on real-life events. As these stories are told and retold, fact often changes to fiction, and the characters often become larger than life.

**Tall tales** often focus on a central hero who performs impossible feats.

**Folk tales** may deal with real people or magical characters. They reflect the values and beliefs of the culture in which they were created.

**Fables** are brief stories or poems that often feature animal characters who act and speak like humans. They usually end with a moral that is directly stated.

**Epics** are long narrative poems important to the history of a nation or culture. They tell of a larger-than-life hero who goes on a dangerous journey, or **quest.**

## Characteristics of Folk Literature

Here are some common characteristics you will see as you read folk literature.

| Characteristic | Definition | Often Featured In... |
|---|---|---|
| **Heroes and heroines** | Larger-than-life figures who overcome obstacles or participate in exciting adventures | Myths<br>Legends<br>Epics |
| **Trickster** | A clever character who can fool others but often gets into trouble | Folk tales<br>Fables |
| **Personification** | A type of figurative language in which nonhuman subjects are given human qualities | Myths<br>Fables |
| **Hyperbole** | A type of figurative language that uses exaggeration, either for comic effect or to express strong emotion | Tall tales<br>Myths<br>Epics |
| **Dialect** | Language spoken by people in a particular region or group | Tall tales<br>Folk tales |

## Analyzing Structure and Theme in Folk Literature

The **structural elements** of a work of folk literature contribute to its **theme**, or insight about life and human nature.

Folk literature is rich with humor, adventure, romance, suspense, and drama. At the same time, it is the themes of these stories that have made them meaningful to readers of many generations and cultures.

**Stated Themes** Themes in folk literature take different forms. Sometimes, the theme is directly stated at the end of the story as a moral, or lesson. For example, look at the retelling of Aesop's fable, "The Lion and the Mouse."

**Example: The Lion and the Mouse**

A tiny mouse accidentally crossed paths with a ferocious lion. The lion was about to eat the mouse, when the mouse pleaded with the lion to let him go. "If you do, I promise to help you one day," the mouse said. The mighty lion doubted he would ever need the help of a tiny mouse, but he let the mouse go. One day, the lion became trapped in a hunter's net. The little mouse heard the lion's roars and came to his aid. In a few minutes, the mouse had gnawed his way through the net, setting the lion free.

**Moral:** *One act of kindness often leads to another.*

**Implied Themes** As in other literary genres, themes in folk literature are sometimes implied, or suggested, rather than stated. Clues to these themes lie in the details that describe setting, characters, and plot. Stories with implied themes require the reader to analyze the details to see what they reveal about the deeper meaning of the story.

**Universal Themes** A universal theme is an insight or lesson that appears in literature across cultures and throughout different periods in history. These themes are "universal" because they express ideas that are meaningful to most people. Here are a few universal themes that are commonly found in folk literature. They reflect ideas that have been understood for many generations.

- Goodness is eventually rewarded.
- Inner beauty is more important than outward appearance.
- Those who always want more are never satisfied.
- Cleverness and courage can overcome brute strength.

Folk literature of various types contains structural elements that contribute to the development of theme. As you read, look for these elements.

**Repetition** Folk literature often features the repetition of events, dialogue, descriptions, and sound patterns. Repetition adds rhythm to the text. It can also help build suspense and emphasize main ideas. For example, in the well-known tale of "The Three Little Pigs," the following lines of dialogue are repeated three times.

**Example: Repetition**

"Little pig, little pig, let me come in."
"Not by the hair of my chinny chin chin."
"Then I'll huff, and I'll puff, and I'll blow your house in."

**Patterns** Many works of folk literature share a common pattern, or repeated element. For example, many stories begin and end with such familiar phrases as "Once upon a time" and "They lived happily ever after." Another common structural element found in folk literature is the pattern of three. Many stories feature three important characters, three wishes, or three tasks.

**Archetypes** An archetype is an element that occurs regularly in literature from around the world and throughout history. Oral storytellers have used archetypes to convey such universal themes as the power of love or the importance of bravery. Here are some common archetypes found in folk literature:

| | |
|---|---|
| **Plot** | • a dangerous journey<br>• a struggle between a good character and an evil one<br>• an explanation of how something came to be |
| **Characters** | • a brave hero<br>• trickster, or wise fool<br>• talking animals |
| **Ideas** | • magic in the normal world<br>• hero or heroine helped by supernatural forces<br>• evil disguised as good |

**Flat Characters** Folk literature often features characters who seem to have only one main trait, such as kindness, cruelty, wisdom, or foolishness. Such characters are **flat,** or one-sided. They are not like real people, who usually have many different sides to their personalities. Flat characters can help storytellers express important themes. For example, in "Snow White," the evil queen remains evil throughout the tale, while Snow White herself remains kind and good. Together, these opposing characters help develop the theme that kindness is stronger than cruelty.

# Building Knowledge

## Community or individual—which is more important?

Think about the Big Question as you read "Demeter and Persephone." Take notes on the ways in which the myth explores the concepts of community and the individual.

### *Meet the Author*

**Anne Terry White** (1896–1980) was born in Ukraine, which was then part of Russia. She was one of the leading writers of nonfiction for children. White's first two books were *Heroes of the Five Books,* a look at figures of the Old Testament, and *Three Children and Shakespeare,* a family discussion of four of Shakespeare's plays. She wrote these books to introduce her own children to great works of literature. In addition to being a writer, White was an editor, a translator, and an authority on ancient Greece.

## CLOSE READING FOCUS

### Key Ideas and Details: **Cause and Effect**

A **cause** is an event, action, or feeling that produces a result. That result is called an **effect**. In some literary works, multiple causes result in a single effect. In other works, a single cause results in multiple effects. Effects can also become causes for events that follow. In a narrative, this linking of causes and effects propels the action forward. To analyze cause-and-effect relationships, ask yourself questions, such as *What happened? Why?* and *What will happen as a result of this?*

### Craft and Structure: **Myth**

Since time began, people have tried to understand the world around them. Ancient peoples created **myths**—stories that explain natural occurrences and express beliefs about right and wrong. Most myths were composed orally and then passed from generation to generation by word of mouth. Every ancient culture has its own mythology, or collection of myths. Greek and Roman myths are known collectively as *classical mythology.*

In many myths, gods and goddesses have human traits, while human heroes possess superhuman traits. As you read, notice the ways that myths explain the world and explore universal themes.

## Vocabulary

You will encounter the following words in this myth. Copy the words into your notebook. Circle the words that you think relate to ruling or governing a community of people.

| | | |
|---|---|---|
| **defies** | **monarch** | **dominions** |
| **intervene** | **realm** | **abode** |

## CLOSE READING MODEL

The passage below is from Anne Terry White's myth "Demeter and Persephone." The annotations to the right of the passage show ways in which you can use close reading skills to analyze cause-and-effect relationships and explore the elements of a myth.

### *from* "Demeter and Persephone"

Now the goddess of love and beauty, fair Aphrodite, was sitting on a mountainside playing with her son, Eros.[1] She saw Pluto as he drove around with his coal-black horses and she said:

"My son, there is one who defies your power and mine. Quick! Take up your darts! Send an arrow into the breast of that dark monarch. Let him, too, feel the pangs of love. Why should he alone escape them?"[2]

At his mother's words, Eros leaped lightly to his feet. He chose from his quiver his sharpest and truest arrow, fitted it to his bow, drew the string, and shot straight into Pluto's heart.

The grim King had seen fair maids enough in the gloomy underworld over which he ruled. But never had his heart been touched. Now an unaccustomed warmth stole through his veins. His stern eyes softened.[3] Before him was a blossoming valley, and along its edge a charming girl was gathering flowers. She was Persephone, daughter of Demeter, goddess of the harvest.[4] She had strayed from her companions, and now that her basket overflowed with blossoms, she was filling her apron with lilies and violets. The god looked at Persephone and loved her at once.

**Myth**

**1** The reference to Aphrodite as the "goddess of love and beauty" gives you a clue that this story is a myth. Like Aphrodite and Eros, mythical gods often possess human traits and exhibit human behavior.

**Cause and Effect**

**2** Aphrodite resents Pluto because he "defies" her power—the power of love. As a result, she orders Eros to shoot Pluto with an arrow that will cause him to feel love. Note the effects of this action as you read on.

**Cause and Effect**

**3** This sentence shows the immediate effect caused by Eros's arrow. You may guess that this event will cause other effects that will propel the action forward.

**Myth**

**4** Mythical gods often rule over important aspects of human life. This detail about Demeter may help you infer that the harvest was important to the ancient Greeks, who first told this myth.

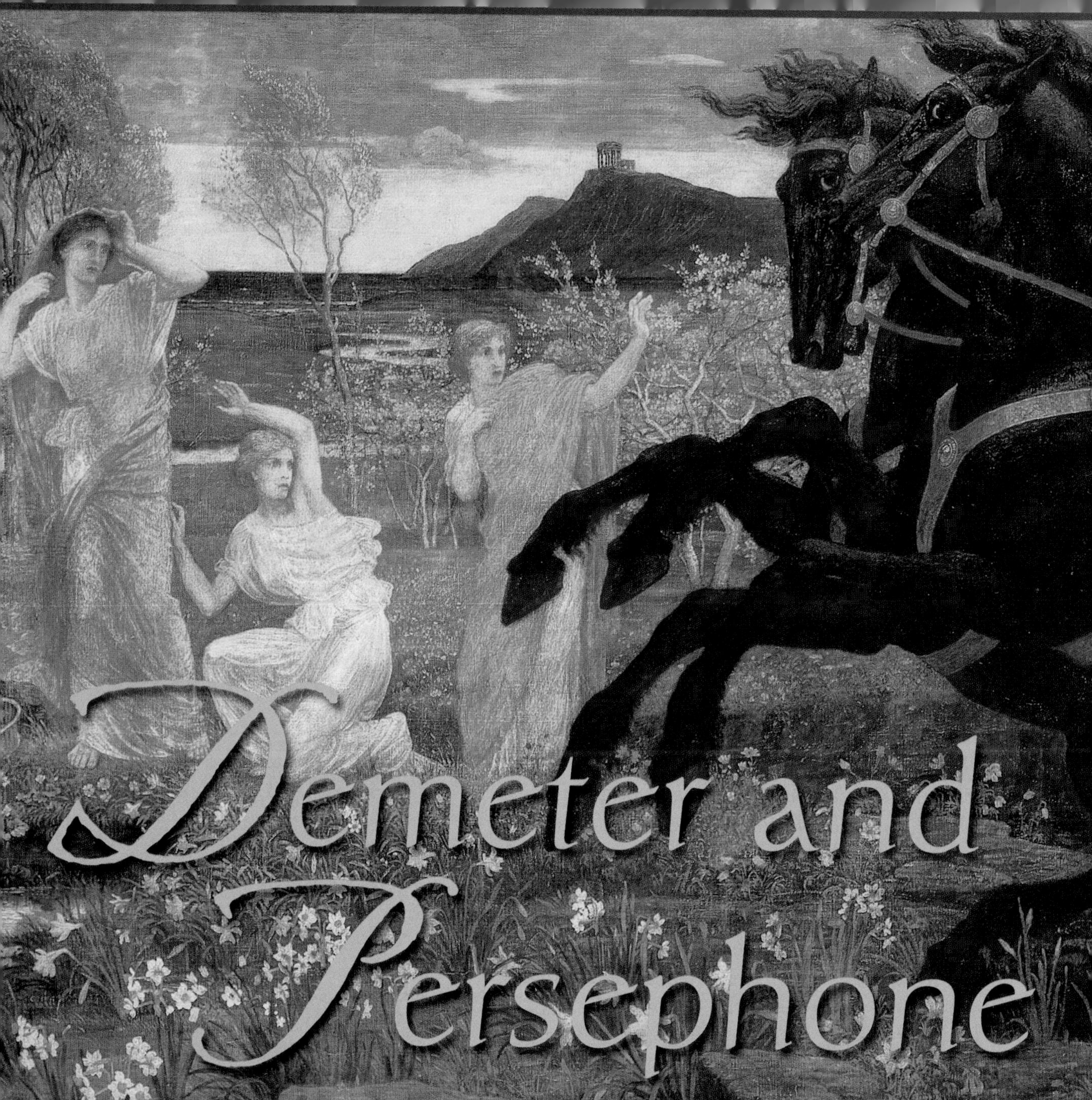

# Demeter and Persephone

Anne Terry White

Deep under Mt. Aetna, the gods had buried alive a number of fearful, fire-breathing giants. The monsters heaved and struggled to get free. And so mightily did they shake the earth that Pluto, the king of the underworld, was alarmed.

"They may tear the rocks asunder and leave the realm of the dead open to the light of day," he thought. And mounting his golden chariot, he went up to see what damage had been done.

Now the goddess of love and beauty, fair Aphrodite (af′ rə dīt′ ē), was sitting on a mountainside playing with her son, Eros.[1] She saw Pluto as he drove around with his coal-black horses and she said:

**Vocabulary ▶**
**defies** (dē fīz′) *v.* boldly resists or opposes
**monarch** (män′ ərk) *n.* ruler, such as a king or queen

"My son, there is one who **defies** your power and mine. Quick! Take up your darts! Send an arrow into the breast of that dark **monarch**. Let him, too, feel the pangs of love. Why should he alone escape them?"

At his mother's words, Eros leaped lightly to his feet. He chose from his quiver[2] his sharpest and truest arrow, fitted it to his bow, drew the string, and shot straight into Pluto's heart.

The grim King had seen fair maids enough in the gloomy underworld over which he ruled. But never had his heart been touched. Now an unaccustomed warmth stole through his veins. His stern eyes softened. Before him was a blossoming valley, and along its edge a charming girl was gathering flowers. She was Persephone (pər sef′ ə nē), daughter of Demeter (di mēt′ ər), goddess of the harvest. She had strayed from her companions, and now that her basket overflowed with blossoms, she was filling her apron with lilies and violets. The god looked at Persephone and loved her at once. With one sweep of his arm he caught her up and drove swiftly away.

*She saw Pluto as he drove around with his coal-black horses...*

"Mother!" she screamed, while the flowers fell from her apron and strewed the ground. "Mother!"

And she called on her companions by name. But already they were out of sight, so fast did Pluto urge the horses on.

---

1. **Eros** (er′ äs) in Greek mythology, the god of love; identified by the Romans as Cupid.
2. **quiver** (kwiv′ ər) case for arrows.

In a few moments they were at the River Cyane.[3] Persephone struggled, her loosened girdle[4] fell to the ground, but the god held her tight. He struck the bank with his trident.[5] The earth opened, and darkness swallowed them all—horses, chariot, Pluto, and weeping Persephone.

From end to end of the earth Demeter sought her daughter. But none could tell her where Persephone was. At last, worn out and despairing, the goddess returned to Sicily. She stood by the River Cyane, where Pluto had cleft the earth and gone down into his own **dominions**.

Now a river nymph[6] had seen him carry off his prize. She wanted to tell Demeter where her daughter was, but fear of Pluto kept her dumb. Yet she had picked up the girdle Persephone had dropped, and this the nymph wafted[7] on the waves to the feet of Demeter.

The goddess knew then that her daughter was gone indeed, but she did not suspect Pluto of carrying her off. She laid the blame on the innocent land.

"Ungrateful soil!" she said. "I made you fertile. I clothed you in grass and nourishing grain, and this is how you reward me. No more shall you enjoy my favors!"

That year was the most cruel mankind had ever known. Nothing prospered, nothing grew. The cattle died, the seed would not come up, men and oxen toiled in vain. There was too much sun. There was too much rain. Thistles[8] and weeds were the only things that grew. It seemed that all mankind would die of hunger.

"This cannot go on," said mighty Zeus. "I see that I must **intervene**." And one by one he sent the gods and goddesses to plead with Demeter.

**Myth**
What details in this paragraph reveal that the story is a myth?

◀ **Vocabulary**
**dominions** (də min′ yəns) *n.* governed countries or territories

**intervene** (in tər vēn′) *v.* come between in an effort to influence or help settle an action or argument

**Comprehension**
Who is Pluto?

3. **River Cyane** (sī an) a river in Sicily, an island just south of Italy.
4. **girdle** (gurd′ əl) *n.* belt or sash for the waist.
5. **trident** (trīd′ ənt) *n.* spear with three points.
6. **river nymph** (nimf) *n.* goddess living in a river.
7. **wafted** (wäft′ əd) *n.* carried.
8. **thistles** (this′ əlz) *n.* stubborn, weedy plants with sharp leaves and usually purplish flowers.

But she had the same answer for all: "Not till I see my daughter shall the earth bear fruit again."

Zeus, of course, knew well where Persephone was. He did not like to take from his brother the one joyful thing in his life, but he saw that he must if the race of man was to be preserved. So he called Hermes[9] to him and said:

"Descend to the underworld, my son. Bid Pluto release his bride. Provided she has not tasted food in the **realm** of the dead, she may return to her mother forever."

Down sped Hermes on his winged feet, and there in the dim palace of the king, he found Persephone by Pluto's side. She was pale and joyless. Not all the glittering treasures of the underworld could bring a smile to her lips.

**Vocabulary ▶**
**realm** (relm)
*n.* kingdom

"You have no flowers here," she would say to her husband when he pressed gems upon her. "Jewels have no fragrance. I do not want them."

When she saw Hermes and heard his message, her heart leaped within her. Her cheeks grew rosy and her eyes

9. **Hermes** (hur´ mēz) a god who served as a messenger.

## LITERATURE IN CONTEXT

### Mythology Connection

**Gods and Goddesses**

The ancient Greeks and Romans had different names for their gods and goddesses. In the diagram below, the Roman name for the god or goddess is given in parentheses. In their traditions, each god and goddess had control or power in a different area.

**Poseidon** (Neptune) god of the sea

**Zeus** (Jupiter) ruler of gods and men

**Hera** (Juno) goddess of marriage

**Demeter** (Ceres) goddess of agriculture

**Hades** (Pluto) god of the underworld

**Hermes** (Mercury) messenger of the gods

**Aphrodite** (Venus) goddess of beauty

**Ares** (Mars) god of war

**Athena** (Minerva) goddess of wisdom

**Persephone** (Proserpina) goddess of springtime

**Connect to the Literature** **Why do you think that ancient peoples told stories about gods and goddesses such as Demeter and Persephone?**

sparkled, for she knew that Pluto would not dare to disobey his brother's command. She sprang up, ready to go at once. Only one thing troubled her—that she could not leave the underworld forever. For she had accepted a pomegranate[10] from Pluto and sucked the sweet pulp from four of the seeds.

With a heavy heart Pluto made ready his golden car.[11] He helped Persephone in while Hermes took up the reins.

"Dear wife," said the King, and his voice trembled as he spoke, "think kindly of me, I pray you. For indeed I love you truly. It will be lonely here these eight months you are away.

**Comprehension**
What does Zeus want Pluto to do?

10. **pomegranate** (päm´ ə gran´ it) *n.* round fruit with a red leathery rind and many seeds.
11. **car** (kär) *n.* chariot.

And if you think mine is a gloomy palace to return to, at least remember that your husband is great among the immortals. So fare you well—and get your fill of flowers!"

Straight to the temple of Demeter at Eleusis, Hermes drove the black horses. The goddess heard the chariot wheels and, as a deer bounds over the hills, she ran out swiftly to meet her daughter. Persephone flew to her mother's arms. And the sad tale of each turned into joy in the telling.

So it is to this day. One third of the year Persephone spends in the gloomy **abode** of Pluto—one month for each seed that she tasted. Then Nature dies, the leaves fall, the earth stops bringing forth. In spring Persephone returns, and with her come the flowers, followed by summer's fruitfulness and the rich harvest of fall.

**Vocabulary ▶**
**abode** (ə bōd) *n.* home; residence

## Language Study

**Vocabulary** The words listed below appear in "Demeter and Persephone." For each numbered item, write a single sentence using the words indicated.

**defies** **monarch** **intervene** **realm** **abode**

**1.** realm; distant
**2.** intervene; argument
**3.** monarch; ancient
**4.** defies; stubborn
**5.** abode; family

**WORD STUDY**
The **Latin root *-dom-*** means "master" or "building." Pluto snatches Persephone and takes her to his underground **dominions,** the territories he rules.

### Word Study

**Part A** Explain how the **Latin root *-dom-*** contributes to the meaning of the words *domain, dominant,* and *predominate.* Consult a dictionary if necessary.

**Part B** Use the context of the sentences and your knowledge of the Latin root *-dom-* to explain your answer to each question.

**1.** If you are behaving in a *domineering* manner, are you being humble?

**2.** If a building *dominates* a city skyline, is it hard to see?

# Close Reading Activities

## Literary Analysis

### Key Ideas and Details

1. **Cause and Effect** Answer these questions to analyze cause-and-effect in the myth: **(a)** What happens to Persephone at the end of the myth? Why? **(b)** What happens to Demeter? Why?
2. **Cause and Effect** Describe the effect of the giants struggling to get free at the beginning of the myth.
3. **(a)** Why did Pluto take Persephone to his kingdom? **(b) Analyze:** What does Pluto's nickname, "the grim King," suggest about his emotional outlook on the world?
4. **Cause and Effect (a)** How does nature change as Persephone moves between Earth and the underworld? **(b)** How do the powerful emotions of the main characters account for the changing of the seasons?

### Craft and Structure

5. **Myth** What human qualities does Pluto possess? Use specific details from the myth to support your answers.
6. **Myth** Complete a chart like the one on the right to describe the lessons the myth teaches through the characters of Demeter, Persephone, and Pluto.

| Character: Demeter | |
|---|---|
| Lesson: | How Taught: |
| | |
| Character: Persephone | |
| | |
| Character: Pluto | |
| | |

### Integration of Knowledge and Ideas

7. **(a)** What does Demeter do when she discovers her daughter is lost? **(b) Make a Judgment:** Do you think her actions were justifiable? Why or why not? Find evidence in the text to support your opinion. **(c) Discuss:** Share your answer with a classmate. Then, evaluate how your response has changed.
8. **(a)** How is Persephone reunited with her mother? **(b) Speculate:** How might their experiences in this myth change each of the three main characters? Cite specific textual evidence to support your ideas.

9. THE BIG ? **Community or individual—which is more important? (a)** What was the consequence of Demeter's actions? **(b)** How did humankind suffer as a result of one individual's impulses? **(c)** What does this myth suggest about the effects of an individual's actions on the community as a whole?

**ACADEMIC VOCABULARY**

As you write and speak about "Demeter and Persephone," use the words related to community and the individual that you explored on page 631 of this textbook.

## Conventions: **Infinitive Phrases and Gerund Phrases**

An **infinitive** is a verb form that acts as a noun, an adjective, or an adverb. An infinitive usually begins with the word *to*. An **infinitive phrase** is an infinitive plus its own modifiers, objects, or complements.

**Noun** (functioning as subject): *To speak Spanish fluently* is my goal.
**Adjective** (modifying *one*): She is the one *to see immediately* if you need help.
**Adverb** (modifying *waited*): Everyone waited *to hear the news.*

An **gerund** is a verb form that ends in *-ing* and acts as a noun. It can function as a subject, an object, a predicate noun, or the object of a preposition. A **gerund phrase** is a gerund plus its own modifiers, objects, or complements.

**Subject:** *Remodeling the building* was a good idea.
**Direct Object:** Mischa enjoys *painting with watercolors.*
**Predicate Noun:** Her favorite sport is *cross-country skiing.*
**Object of the Preposition:** Lucille never gets tired of *singing holiday songs.*

### Practice A

Identify each infinitive and infinitive phrase or gerund and gerund phrase.

1. To get free, the monsters heaved and struggled beneath the mountain.
2. Persephone did not want to return to the underworld.
3. Spending time with Pluto is not enjoyable to Persephone.
4. Demeter wanted to see her daughter.

**Reading Application** In the myth, find a sentence that contains an infinitive phrase and a sentence that contains a gerund phrase. Explain how each functions.

### Practice B

Identify each infinitive phrase or gerund phrase. Determine the function each phrase performs in the sentence. Then, use each infinitive or gerund to write a new sentence.

1. Pluto wants to keep Persephone with him.
2. To get her daughter back is Demeter's goal.
3. Neglecting the Earth was Demeter's revenge.
4. Demeter hates waiting for Persephone to return.

**Writing Application** Choose a sentence from the myth and rewrite it to include an infinitive phrase or a gerund phrase.

## Writing to Sources

**Narrative Text** You may have wondered why leaves change colors in the fall or what causes an earthquake. Write a short **myth** that explains a natural phenomenon. Follow these steps:

- Think of a natural phenomenon and a creative explanation for its occurrence.
- Limit the number of characters in your myth to keep the story simple.
- Develop your characters by describing their personalities and actions and by showing how they relate to other characters.
- Plan the action by developing a well-structured sequence of events that unfolds naturally and logically.

Exchange your finished myth with a partner and compare your partner's myth to the myth of "Demeter and Persephone." Identify specific ways the two myths are similar and different using details from the selection.

**Grammar Application** Check your writing to be sure that you have properly used infinitive phrases and gerund phrases.

## Speaking and Listening

**Comprehension and Collaboration** With a small group, conduct a **debate** on whether or not Demeter was justified in changing the weather on Earth. Each side should prepare an argument and material to support the argument, including specific details and examples from the text.

- Appoint a leader for your debate team and choose a person to act as a moderator, or discussion leader.
- Before the debate, consider what the opposing arguments might be and prepare text-based counterarguments to address them.
- Volunteer your own relevant opinions and make contributions to your team. Cite logical evidence to support your ideas.
- Respond directly to questions, and pose your own questions in response to others' comments.
- After the debate, meet with your group to provide constructive feedback about how well speakers conveyed their ideas.

*Meet the Author*

**Juliet Piggott Wood** (1924–1996) discovered her love for learning about different cultures while living in Japan, where her grandfather was a legal advisor to Prince Ito. Wood's interest in Japan inspired her to produce several books on Japanese history and folklore. Her fascination with one culture led to research about others. She went on to co-author a book retelling famous fairy tales from around the world.

## Community or individual—which is more important?

Explore the Big Question as you read. Take notes on the ways in which the legend explores the concepts of community and the individual.

## CLOSE READING FOCUS

### Key Ideas and Details: **Cause and Effect**

A **cause** is an event or situation that produces a result. An **effect** is the result produced. In a literary work, each effect may eventually become a cause for the next event. This results in a cause-and-effect chain that propels the action forward.

If you do not clearly see the cause-and-effect relationships in a passage of text, reread to look for connections among the words and sentences. Some words that identify causes and effects are *because, due to, for this reason,* and *as a result.*

### Craft and Structure: **Legend and Fact**

A **legend** is a traditional story about the past. A **fact** is something that can be proved to be true. Before legends were written down, they were passed on orally. Legends are based on facts that have grown into fiction through many retellings over generations.

Every culture has its own legends to immortalize famous people. Most legends include these elements:

- a human who is larger than life
- fantastic elements
- roots or basis in historical facts
- events that reflect the culture that created the story

## Vocabulary

You will encounter the following words in this legend. Copy the words into your notebook. Circle the two words that share a suffix. How does this suffix contribute to the meaning of each word?

| | | |
|---|---|---|
| **shortsightedness** | **routed** | **decreed** |
| **relished** | **unanimous** | **feebleness** |

## CLOSE READING MODEL

The passage below is from Juliet Piggott Wood's Aztec legend "Popocatepetl and Ixtlaccihuatl." The annotations to the right of the passage show ways in which you can use close reading skills to analyze cause-and-effect relationships and distinguish between legend and fact.

### *from* "Popocatepetl and Ixtlaccihuatl"

There was once an Aztec Emperor in Tenochtitlan. He was very powerful. Some thought he was wise as well, whilst others doubted his wisdom. He was both a ruler and a warrior and he kept at bay those tribes living in and beyond the mountains surrounding the Valley of Mexico, with its huge lake called Texcoco in which Tenochtitlan was built.[1] His power was absolute and the splendor in which he lived was very great.

It is not known for how many years the Emperor ruled in Tenochtitlan, but it is known that he lived to a great age.[2] However, it was not until he was in his middle years that his wife gave him an heir, a girl. The Emperor and Empress loved the princess very much and she was their only child. She was a dutiful daughter and learned all she could from her father about the art of ruling, for she knew that when he died she would reign in his stead in Tenochtitlan.[3]

Her name was Ixtlaccihuatl. Her parents and her friends called her Ixtla. She had a pleasant disposition and, as a result, she had many friends.[4] The great palace where she lived with the Emperor and Empress rang with their laughter when they came to the parties her parents gave for her. As well as being a delightful companion, Ixtla was also very pretty, even beautiful.

**Legend and Fact**

**1** The Aztecs were a real civilization and Tenochtitlan was an actual place. These true historical details are the basis for this legend.

**Legend and Fact**

**2** The Emperor's absolute power, great splendor, and great age create the impression of a larger-than-life, legendary figure.

**Cause and Effect**

**3** In this sentence, the word *for* means "because." It signals a cause-and-effect relationship between the daughter's knowledge of her future duties (cause) and her current desire to learn the art of ruling (effect).

**Cause and Effect**

**4** The phrase *as a result* signals a cause-and-effect relationship: the princess had many friends because she had a pleasant disposition.

MEXICAN LEGEND

# Popocatepetl and Ixtlaccihuatl

Juliet Piggott Wood

Before the Spaniards came to Mexico and marched on the Aztec capital of Tenochtitlan[1] there were two volcanoes to the southeast of that city. The Spaniards destroyed much of Tenochtitlan and built another city in its place and called it Mexico City. It is known by that name still, and the pass through which the Spaniards came to the ancient Tenochtitlan is still there, as are the volcanoes on each side of that pass. Their names have not been changed. The one to the north is Ixtlaccihuatl [ēs´ tlä sē´ wät´ əl] and the one on the south of the pass is Popocatepetl [pô pô kä te´ pet´ əl]. Both are snowcapped and beautiful, Popocatepetl being the taller of the two. That name means Smoking Mountain. In Aztec days it gushed forth smoke and, on occasion, it does so still. It erupted too in Aztec days and has done so again since the Spaniards came. Ixtlaccihuatl means The White Woman, for its peak was, and still is, white.

Perhaps Ixtlaccihuatl and Popocatepetl were there in the highest part of the Valley of Mexico in the days when the earth was very young, in the days when the new people were just learning to eat and grow corn. The Aztecs claimed the volcanoes as their own, for they possessed a legend about them and their creation, and they believed that legend to be true.

There was once an Aztec Emperor in Tenochtitlan. He was very powerful. Some thought he was wise as well, whilst others doubted his wisdom. He was both a ruler and a warrior and he kept at bay those tribes living in and beyond the mountains surrounding the Valley of Mexico, with its huge lake called Texcoco [tā skō´ kō] in which Tenochtitlan was built. His power was absolute and the splendor in which he lived was very great.

It is not known for how many years the Emperor ruled in Tenochtitlan, but it is known that he lived to a great age. However, it was not until he was in his middle years that his wife gave him an heir, a girl. The Emperor and Empress loved the princess very much and she was their only child. She was a dutiful daughter and learned all she could from her father about the art of ruling, for she knew that when he died she would reign in his stead in Tenochtitlan.

◀ **Critical Viewing**
Why do you think volcanoes like these inspired ancient peoples?

**Comprehension**
Explain the meaning of each mountain's name.

---

1. **Tenochtitlan** (tā noch´ tēt län´) the Aztec capital, conquered by the Spanish in 1521.

Vocabulary ▶
**shortsightedness**
(short′ sīt′ id ness)
*n.* condition of not considering the future effects of something

**Cause and Effect**
What causes Ixtla to be serious?

Her name was Ixtlaccihuatl. Her parents and her friends called her Ixtla. She had a pleasant disposition and, as a result, she had many friends. The great palace where she lived with the Emperor and Empress rang with their laughter when they came to the parties her parents gave for her. As well as being a delightful companion Ixtla was also very pretty, even beautiful.

Her childhood was happy and she was content enough when she became a young woman. But by then she was fully aware of the great responsibilities which would be hers when her father died and she became serious and studious and did not enjoy parties as much as she had done when younger.

Another reason for her being so serious was that she was in love. This in itself was a joyous thing, but the Emperor forbade her to marry. He wanted her to reign and rule alone when he died, for he trusted no one, not even his wife, to rule as he did except his much loved only child, Ixtla. This was why there were some who doubted the wisdom of the Emperor for, by not allowing his heiress to marry, he showed a selfishness and **shortsightedness** towards his daughter and his empire which many considered was not truly wise. An emperor, they felt, who was not truly wise could not also be truly great. Or even truly powerful.

The man with whom Ixtla was in love was also in love with her. Had they been allowed to marry their state could have been doubly joyous. His name was Popocatepetl and Ixtla and his friends all called him Popo. He was a warrior in the service of the Emperor, tall and strong, with a capacity for gentleness, and very brave. He and Ixtla loved each other very much and while they were content and even happy when they were together, true joy was not theirs because the Emperor continued to insist that Ixtla should not be married when the time came for her to take on her father's responsibilities.

This unfortunate but moderately happy relationship between Ixtla and Popo continued for several years, the couple pleading with the Emperor at regular intervals and the Emperor remaining constantly adamant. Popo loved Ixtla no less for her father's stubbornness and she loved him no less while she studied, as her father demanded she should do, the art of ruling in preparation for her reign.

When the Emperor became very old he also became ill. In his **feebleness** he channeled all his failing energies towards instructing Ixtla in statecraft, for he was no longer able to exercise that craft himself. So it was that his enemies, the tribes who lived in the mountains and beyond, realized that the great Emperor in Tenochtitlan was great no longer, for he was only teaching his daughter to rule and not ruling himself.

The tribesmen came nearer and nearer to Tenochtitlan until the city was besieged. At last the Emperor realized himself that he was great no longer, that his power was nearly gone and that his domain was in dire peril.

Warrior though he long had been, he was now too old and too ill to lead his fighting men into battle. At last he understood that, unless his enemies were frustrated in their efforts to enter and lay waste to Tenochtitlan, not only would he no longer be Emperor but his daughter would never be Empress.

Instead of appointing one of his warriors to lead the rest into battle on his behalf, he offered a bribe to all of them. Perhaps it was that his wisdom, if wisdom he had, had forsaken him, or perhaps he acted from fear. Or perhaps he simply changed his mind. But the bribe he offered to whichever warrior succeeded in lifting the siege of Tenochtitlan and defeating the enemies in and around the Valley of Mexico was both the hand of his daughter and the equal right to reign and rule, with her, in Tenochtitlan. Furthermore, he **decreed** that directly he learned that his enemies had been defeated he would instantly cease to be Emperor himself. Ixtla would not have to wait until her father died to become Empress and, if her father should die of his illness or old age before his enemies were vanquished,

**Cause and Effect**
What is one effect of the Emperor's becoming old and ill?

**◀ Vocabulary**
**feebleness** (fē′ bəl nəs) *n.* weakness

**decreed** (di krēd′) *v.* officially ordered

**Comprehension**
What does the Emperor forbid Ixtla to do?

**Vocabulary ▶**
**relished** (rel′ isht)
*v.* enjoyed; liked

**▼ Critical Viewing**
How does this picture relate to the details of the battle in the story?

he further decreed that he who overcame the surrounding enemies should marry the princess whether he, the Emperor, lived or not.

Ixtla was fearful when she heard of her father's bribe to his warriors, for the only one whom she had any wish to marry was Popo and she wanted to marry him, and only him, very much indeed.

The warriors, however, were glad when they heard of the decree: there was not one of them who would not have been glad to have the princess as his wife and they all **relished** the chance of becoming Emperor.

And so the warriors went to war at their ruler's behest, and each fought trebly[2] hard for each was fighting not only for the safety of Tenochtitlan and the surrounding valley, but for the delightful bride and for the right to be the Emperor himself.

Even though the warriors fought with great skill and even though each one exhibited a courage he did not know he possessed, the war was a long one. The Emperor's enemies were firmly entrenched around Lake Texcoco and Tenochtitlan by the time the warriors were sent to war, and as battle followed battle the final outcome was uncertain.

The warriors took a variety of weapons with them; wooden clubs edged with sharp blades of obsidian,[3] obsidian machetes,[4] javelins which they hurled at their enemies from troughed throwing boards, bows and arrows, slings and spears set with obsidian fragments, and lances, too. Many of them carried shields woven from wicker and covered in tough hide and most wore armor made of thick quilted cotton soaked in brine.

The war was long and fierce. Most of the warriors fought together and in unison, but some fought alone. As time went on natural leaders emerged and, of these, undoubtedly Popo was the best. Finally it was he, brandishing his club and shield,

2. **trebly** (treb′ lē) *adv.* three times as much; triply.
3. **obsidian** (əb sid′ ē ən) *n.* hard, usually dark-colored or black, volcanic glass.
4. **machetes** (mə shet′ ēz) *n.* large, heavy-bladed knives.

who led the great charge of running warriors across the valley, with their enemies fleeing before them to the safety of the coastal plains and jungles beyond the mountains.

The warriors acclaimed Popo as the man most responsible for the victory and, weary though they all were, they set off for Tenochtitlan to report to the Emperor and for Popo to claim Ixtla as his wife at last.

But a few of those warriors were jealous of Popo. Since they knew none of them could rightly claim the victory for himself (the decision among the Emperor's fighting men that Popo was responsible for the victory had been **unanimous**), they wanted to spoil for him and for Ixtla the delights which the Emperor had promised.

These few men slipped away from the rest at night and made their way to Tenochtitlan ahead of all the others. They reached the capital two days later, having traveled without sleep all the way, and quickly let it be known that, although the Emperor's warriors had been successful against his enemies, the warrior Popo had been killed in battle.

It was a foolish and cruel lie which those warriors told their Emperor, and they told it for no reason other than that they were jealous of Popo.

When the Emperor heard this he demanded that Popo's body be brought to him so that he might arrange a fitting burial. He knew the man his daughter had loved would have died courageously. The jealous warriors looked at one another and said nothing. Then one of them told the Emperor that Popo had been killed on the edge of Lake Texcoco and that his body had fallen into the water and no man had been able to retrieve it. The Emperor was saddened to hear this.

After a little while he demanded to be told which of his warriors had been responsible for the victory but none of the fighting men before him dared claim the successful outcome of the war for himself, for each knew the others would refute him. So they were silent. This puzzled the Emperor and he decided to wait for the main body of his warriors to return and not to press the few who had brought the news of the victory and of Popo's death.

**Legend and Fact**
What does the account of the battle suggest about the Aztecs' attitudes toward war?

**◀ Vocabulary**
**unanimous** (yo͞o nan′ ə məs) *adj.* based on complete agreement

**Comprehension**
What is the outcome of the battle?

Then the Emperor sent for his wife and his daughter and told them their enemies had been overcome. The Empress was thoroughly excited and relieved at the news. Ixtla was only apprehensive. The Emperor, seeing her anxious face, told her quickly that Popo was dead. He went on to say that the warrior's body had been lost in the waters of Lake Texcoco, and again it was as though his wisdom had left him, for he spoke at some length of his not being able to tell Ixtla who her husband would be and who would become Emperor when the main body of warriors returned to Tenochtitlan.

But Ixtla heard nothing of what he told her, only that her beloved Popo was dead. She went to her room and lay down. Her mother followed her and saw at once she was very ill. Witch doctors were sent for, but they could not help the princess, and neither could her parents. Her illness had no name, unless it was the illness of a broken heart. Princess Ixtlaccihuatl did not wish to live if Popocatepetl was dead, and so she died herself.

The day after her death Popo returned to Tenochtitlan with all the other surviving warriors. They went straight to the palace and, with much cheering, told the Emperor that his enemies had been **routed** and that Popo was the undoubted victor of the conflict.

The Emperor praised his warriors and pronounced Popo to be the new Emperor in his place. When the young man asked first to see Ixtla, begging that they should be married at once before being jointly proclaimed Emperor and Empress, the Emperor had to tell Popo of Ixtla's death, and how it had happened.

Popo spoke not a word.

He gestured the assembled warriors to follow him and together they sought out the few jealous men who had given the false news of his death to the Emperor. With the army of warriors watching, Popo killed each one of them in single combat with

## LITERATURE IN CONTEXT

### Social Studies Connection

**Tenochtitlan** Archaeologists believe that at one time, more than 200,000 people lived in Tenochtitlan, the Aztec capital city in the middle of the giant lake Texcoco. Approximately one half of the population were farmers. Much of the farming was done on small island gardens surrounding the city. People living in Tenochtitlan depended on food the farmers grew outside the city. They also depended on water from outside the city, which was carried to the city by a system of aqueducts.

Because of its location and dependence on outside food and water, the city would have been helpless in the face of a siege. With no way to get in or out to get food, a siege would soon lead to starvation.

### Connect to the Literature

Based on the situation, do you think the rewards offered by the Emperor in this story were appropriate? Explain.

his obsidian studded club. No one tried to stop him.

That task accomplished Popo returned to the palace and, still without speaking and still wearing his stiff cotton armor, went to Ixtla's room. He gently lifted her body and carried it out of the palace and out of the city, and no one tried to stop him doing that either. All the warriors followed him in silence.

When he had walked some miles he gestured to them again and they built a huge pile of stones in the shape of a pyramid. They all worked together and they worked fast while Popo stood and watched, holding the body of the princess in his arms. By sunset the mighty edifice was finished. Popo climbed it alone, carrying Ixtla's corpse with him. There, at the very top, under a heap of stones, he buried the young woman he had loved so well and for so long, and who had died for the love of him.

That night Popo slept alone at the top of the pyramid by Ixtla's grave. In the morning he came down and spoke for the first time since the Emperor had told him the princess was dead. He told the warriors to build another pyramid, a little to the southeast of the one which held Ixtla's body and to build it higher than the other.

He told them too to tell the Emperor on his behalf that he, Popocatepetl, would never reign and rule in Tenochtitlan. He would keep watch over the grave of the Princess Ixtlaccihuatl for the rest of his life.

The messages to the Emperor were the last words Popo ever spoke. Well before the evening the second mighty pile of stones was built. Popo climbed it and stood at the top, taking a torch of resinous pine wood with him.

◀ **Vocabulary**
**routed** (rout´ əd) *v.* completely defeated

**Comprehension**
What does Popo ask the Emperor when he returns?

**Legend and Fact**
Are the volcanoes real? How do you know?

And when he reached the top he lit the torch and the warriors below saw the white smoke rise against the blue sky, and they watched as the sun began to set and the smoke turned pink and then a deep red, the color of blood.

So Popocatepetl stood there, holding the torch in memory of Ixtlaccihuatl, for the rest of his days.

**▶ Critical Viewing**
What details in this photo are similar to the description of Popo's actions in the story?

The snows came and, as the years went by, the pyramids of stone became high white-capped mountains. Even now the one called Popocatepetl emits smoke in memory of the princess whose body lies in the mountain which bears her name.

## Language Study

**Vocabulary** The words listed below appear in "Popocatepetl and Ixtlaccihuatl." Answer each question and then explain your answer.

**decreed  routed  shortsightedness  feebleness  relished**

1. If something is *decreed,* is it undecided?
2. If one's enemies have been *routed,* have the enemies won?
3. Is *shortsightedness* useful when making decisions for the future?
4. Would *feebleness* prevent a person from exercising?
5. If you *relished* the last book you read, did you enjoy it?

**WORD STUDY**

The **Latin prefix *uni-*** means "having or consisting of only one." In this legend, the Aztec warriors are **unanimous,** or sharing one opinion, about who is responsible for their victory.

### Word Study

**Part A** Explain how the **Latin prefix *uni-*** contributes to the meanings of the words *unity, unilateral,* and *uniform.* Consult a dictionary if necessary.

**Part B** Use the context of the sentences and your knowledge of the Latin prefix *uni-* to explain your answer to each question.

1. How many wheels does a *unicycle* have?
2. If two people speak in *unison,* do they speak at the same time?

# Close Reading Activities

## Literary Analysis

### Key Ideas and Details

1. **Cause and Effect** Reread the legend to find an effect for each of these causes.
   **(a)** The Emperor does not allow his daughter to marry.
   **(b)** The Emperor spends all his time teaching Ixtla statecraft.
   **(c)** The warriors lie to the Emperor about Popo's death.
   **(d)** Ixtla hears that Popo is dead.
2. **Cause and Effect** According to the legend, what causes the volcano to smoke? Cite textual evidence to support your answer.
3. **(a)** Why are Ixtla and Popo unable to marry? **(b) Analyze:** What qualities make the two well matched? Support your answer.

### Craft and Structure

4. **Legend and Fact (a)** Identify two facts in this legend. **(b)** How do you know they are facts?
5. **Legend and Fact** Use a chart like the one on the right to help you identify which events in this legend might have been based on historical events.
6. **Legend and Fact (a)** What details in the legend convey the size and magnificence of Tenochtitlan and the Aztec empire? **(b)** What elements are present in the legend that you would not find in a factual account?

| Events from Legend |
| --- |
| |
| **Possible Historic Connections** |
| |

### Integration of Knowledge and Ideas

7. **(a)** Why does Popo refuse to become emperor and rule Tenochtitlan? **(b) Draw Conclusions:** Based on this legend, what traits do you think the Aztecs admired? **(c) Relate:** Do you think these traits are still valued today? Provide examples to support your response.
8. **(a) Interpret:** What lesson does the legend suggest? **(b) Evaluate:** Can this lesson be applied in modern times? Cite details from the text and your own experience to support your answer.

9. **Community or individual—which is more important?** **(a)** Was the Emperor's decision at the legend's beginning better for the individual or the community? **(b)** Is it ever important to consider the needs of a community over the needs of an individual? Explain.

**ACADEMIC VOCABULARY**

As you write and speak about "Popocatepetl and Ixtlaccihuatl," use the words related to community and the individual that you explored on page 631 of this textbook.

## Conventions: Punctuation Marks

**Punctuation marks** are used to make the meaning of written text clearer. Each punctuation mark serves a specific function.

| Punctuation/Usage | Example |
|---|---|
| **colon (:)** A *colon* introduces information that defines, explains, or provides a list of what is referred to before. | Lily brought many toys to the beach: buckets, shovels, balls, and floats. |
| **semicolon (;)** *Semicolons* join related clauses to form compound sentences. | We spent all morning riding our bikes; then we had a picnic. |
| **hyphen (-)** A *hyphen* is used to join two or more separate words into a single word. | Billy ordered a double-scoop, bubble-gum-flavored ice cream cone. |
| **dash (—)** *Dashes* are used to set off information that interrupts a thought. | On our way to the theater—it had just opened—we stopped for gas. |
| **brackets ( [ ] )** *Brackets* are used to add clarifying information within a quotation. | Ames said, "In that year [2013] we won our first championship." |
| **parentheses ( ( ) )** *Parentheses* are used to include extra information without changing the meaning of the sentence. | My brother Raf (the shyest person in our family) declined to make a speech at the party. |

### Practice A

Identify each punctuation mark in this paragraph and explain its function.

Ixtla had many admirable qualities: grace, beauty, loyalty, and devotion. Her only love was Popo—they had met when they were both young—and he returned her love. Her father (a powerful, wealthy man) would not let Ixtla marry Popo; he wanted her to be unmarried when she took his place as ruler of Tenochtitlan.

**Reading Application** In the legend, find one sentence that contains parentheses and one that contains a hyphen.

### Practice B

Rewrite the paragraph below, using punctuation, so that each sentence makes sense.

Ixtlaccihuatl her beauty was legendary waited nervously for Popocatepetl to return from battle. She hoped they would be married the marriage was previously forbidden. Then she heard that he had died she lay down and died soon after.

**Writing Application** Write a brief paragraph about the legend using at least one hyphen, one dash, one colon, one semicolon, and one set of parentheses.

## Writing to Sources

**Informative Text** Write a short **description** of the ancient city of Tenochtitlan based on two sources: the legend "Popocatepetl and Ixtlaccihuatl" and a nonfiction article about Tenochtitlan. You might consult library or Internet resources, or you may read "Tenochtitlan: Inside the Aztec Capital," a social studies article you will find in your eText.

- As you read both the fiction and the nonfiction selection, jot down details about the time, place, and overall environment of the city as well as details about the lives of its inhabitants.
- Refer to your notes as you draft your description.
- Draw on your description to write a brief **comparison** of the selections. Identify common historical elements to which the article and the legend refer.
- Finally, explain the ways in which the legend adapts or alters historical fact.

**Grammar Application** Check your writing to be sure that you have used punctuation marks properly.

## Speaking and Listening

**Presentation of Ideas** Deliver a **persuasive speech** based on the legend. Your goal is to persuade the Emperor to allow Popo and Ixtla to marry.

- On a note card, write your position and a short statement explaining the reasons for your position.
- Use relevant evidence, including specific details and quotations from the legend, to demonstrate your understanding of the issues and to overcome opposing views.
- Jot down phrases that will remind you of your key points, rather than writing complete sentences.
- Refer to your note cards as you deliver your speech.
- While you are delivering your speech, establish eye contact, adjust the volume of your voice, when appropriate, and pronounce each word clearly.

## Community or individual—which is more important?

Explore the Big Question as you read "Sun and Moon in a Box." Take notes on the ways in which the selection explores the concepts of community and the individual.

### Meet the Authors

**Richard Erdoes** (1912–2008) was born in Vienna, Austria. He studied art and later sketched humorous portraits for daily newspapers. He moved to New York in 1940, where he worked as an illustrator for newspapers and magazines. He has written more than twenty books on the American West.

**Alfonso Ortiz** (1939–1997) was born in San Juan, a Tewa pueblo in northern New Mexico. He earned degrees in both sociology and anthropology, and spent many years of his life as a university professor. He also served as president of the Association on American Indian Affairs for fifteen years.

## CLOSE READING FOCUS

### Key Ideas and Details: **Compare and Contrast**

- A **comparison** tells how two or more things are alike.
- A **contrast** tells how two or more things are different.

Often, you can understand an unfamiliar concept by using your prior knowledge to compare and contrast. For example, you may understand an ancient culture better if you look for ways it is similar to and different from your own culture. You might also find similarities and differences between a story told long ago and one that is popular today. To compare and contrast stories, ask yourself questions about the characters, plots, settings, and themes.

### Craft and Structure: **Cultural Context**

Stories such as fables, folk tales, and myths are influenced by the **cultural context**, or the background, customs, and beliefs of the people who originally told them. Recognizing the cultural context can help you understand and appreciate a literary work. As you read, consider the impact that cultural context might have on the author's intended theme, or message about life.

## Vocabulary

You will encounter the following words in this folk tale. Decide whether you know each word well, know it a little bit, or do not know it at all. After you read the selection, see how your knowledge of each word has increased.

| | | |
|---|---|---|
| **regretted** | **reliable** | **curiosity** |
| **pestering** | **relented** | **cunning** |

## CLOSE READING MODEL

The passage below is from Richard Erdoes and Alfonso Ortiz's "Sun and Moon in a Box." The annotations to the right of the passage show ways in which you can use close reading skills to compare and contrast to increase your understanding and analyze cultural context.

### *from* "Sun and Moon in a Box"

Coyote and Eagle were hunting. Eagle caught rabbits. Coyote caught nothing but grasshoppers. Coyote said: "Friend Eagle, my chief, we make a great hunting pair."

"Good, let us stay together," said Eagle.[1]

They went toward the west. They came to a deep canyon. "Let us fly over it," said Eagle.

"My chief, I cannot fly," said Coyote. "You must carry me across."

"Yes, I see that I have to," said Eagle.[2] He took Coyote on his back and flew across the canyon. They came to a river. "Well," said Eagle, "you cannot fly, but you certainly can swim. This time I do not have to carry you."

Eagle flew over the stream, and Coyote swam across. He was a bad swimmer. He almost drowned. He coughed up a lot of water. "My chief," he said, "when we come to another river, you must carry me." Eagle regretted to have Coyote for a companion.[3]

**Cultural Context**
**1** Coyote addresses Eagle as "my chief," and the characters agree that they make "a great hunting pair." From these details, you may infer that in the Zuni culture, hunting is an important way of life, a chief is a respected member of the group, and cooperation is valued.

**Cultural Context**
**2** The conversation between Coyote and Eagle sounds similar to a conversation between two human beings. This may lead you to believe that the folk tale originates from a culture in which people greatly respect animals and feel a kinship with them.

**Compare and Contrast**
**3** A growing contrast has emerged between Eagle and Coyote. Eagle is skilled and able, while Coyote is not. Coyote has become a burden because he is needy and often requires Eagle's assistance.

ZUNI FOLK TALE

# SUN AND MOON IN A BOX

Richard Erdoes and Alfonso Ortiz

Coyote and Eagle were hunting. Eagle caught rabbits. Coyote caught nothing but grasshoppers. Coyote said: "Friend Eagle, my chief, we make a great hunting pair."

"Good, let us stay together," said Eagle.

They went toward the west. They came to a deep canyon. "Let us fly over it," said Eagle.

"My chief, I cannot fly," said Coyote. "You must carry me across."

"Yes, I see that I have to," said Eagle. He took Coyote on his back and flew across the canyon. They came to a river. "Well," said Eagle, "you cannot fly, but you certainly can swim. This time I do not have to carry you."

Eagle flew over the stream, and Coyote swam across. He was a bad swimmer. He almost drowned. He coughed up a lot of water. "My chief," he said, "when we come to another river, you must carry me." Eagle **regretted** to have Coyote for a companion.

**Spiral Review**
**THEME** In some cultures, coyotes are trickster characters. How might Eagle's willingness to listen to Coyote contribute to this folk tale's theme?

◀ **Vocabulary**
**regretted** (ri gret´ əd) *v.* felt sorry about

**Comprehension**
Why do Eagle and Coyote stay together?

They came to Kachina Pueblo.[1] The Kachinas were dancing. Now, at this time, the earth was still soft and new. There was as yet no sun and no moon. Eagle and Coyote sat down and watched the dance. They saw that the Kachinas had a square box. In it they kept the sun and the moon. Whenever they wanted light they opened the lid and let the sun peek out. Then it was day. When they wanted less light, they opened the box just a little for the moon to look out.

"This is something wonderful," Coyote whispered to Eagle.

"This must be the sun and the moon they are keeping in that box," said Eagle. "I have heard about these two wonderful beings."

"Let us steal the box," said Coyote.

"No, that would be wrong," said Eagle. "Let us just borrow it."

When the Kachinas were not looking, Eagle grabbed the box and flew off. Coyote ran after him on the ground. After a while Coyote called Eagle: "My chief, let me have the box. I am ashamed to let you do all the carrying."

"No," said Eagle, "you are not **reliable**. You might be curious and open the box and then we could lose the wonderful things we borrowed."

For some time they went on as before—Eagle flying above with the box, Coyote running below, trying to keep up. Then once again Coyote called Eagle: "My chief, I am ashamed to let you carry the box. I should do this for you. People will talk badly about me, letting you carry this burden."

"No, I don't trust you," Eagle repeated. "You won't be able to refrain from opening the box. **Curiosity** will get the better of you."

"No," cried Coyote, "do not fear, my chief, I won't even think of opening the box." Still, Eagle would not give it to

**Cultural Context**
What details show that this is a Native American story set in the Southwest?

**Vocabulary ▶**
**reliable** (ri lī´ ə bəl) *adj.* dependable

**curiosity** (kyoor´ ē äs´ ə tē) *n.* desire to learn or know

1. **Kachina Pueblo** (kə chē´ nə pweb´ lō) Native American village.

him, continuing to fly above, holding the box in his talons. But Coyote went on **pestering** Eagle: "My chief, I am really embarrassed. People will say: 'That lazy, disrespectful Coyote lets his chief do all the carrying.'"

"No, I won't give this box to you," Eagle objected. "It is too precious to entrust to somebody like you."

They continued as before, Eagle flying, Coyote running. Then Coyote begged for the fourth time: "My chief, let me carry the box for a while. My wife will scold me, and my children will no longer respect me, when they find out that I did not help you carry this load."

Then Eagle **relented**, saying: "Will you promise not to drop the box and under no circumstances to open it?"

"I promise, my chief, I promise," cried Coyote. "You can rely upon me. I shall not betray your trust."

Then Eagle allowed Coyote to carry the box. They went on as before, Eagle flying, Coyote running, carrying the box in his mouth. They came to a wooded area, full of trees and bushes. Coyote pretended to lag behind, hiding himself behind some bushes where Eagle could not see him. He could not curb his curiosity. Quickly he sat down and opened the box. In a flash, Sun came out of the box and flew away, to

**Compare and Contrast**
How do Coyote's and Eagle's feelings about responsibility differ?

◀ **Vocabulary**
**pestering** (pes´ tər iŋ) *v.* annoying; bothering
**relented** (ri lent´ əd) *v.* gave in

**Vocabulary ▶**
**cunning** (kun′ iŋ)
*adj.* sly; crafty

the very edge of the sky, and at once the world grew cold, the leaves fell from the tree branches, the grass turned brown, and icy winds made all living things shiver.

Then, before Coyote could put the lid back on the box, Moon jumped out and flew away to the outer rim of the sky, and at once snow fell down from heaven and covered the plains and the mountains.

Eagle said: "I should have known better. I should not have let you persuade me. I knew what kind of low, **cunning**, stupid creature you are. I should have remembered that you never keep a promise. Now we have winter. If you had not opened the box, then we could have kept Sun and Moon always close to us. Then there would be no winter. Then we would have summer all the time."

## Language Study

**Vocabulary** Use one of the words in blue to complete each *analogy*. An analogy shows the relationship between a pair of words or phrases. Your choice should make a word pair that matches the relationship between the first pair of words or phrases.

**regretted** **reliable** **pestering** **relented** **cunning**

1. came in : went out :: __________ : stood firm
2. insult : anger :: __________ : annoyance
3. famous : unknown :: __________ : undependable
4. felt pride : accomplishment :: __________ : mistake
5. amiable : friendly :: __________ : sly

**WORD STUDY**

The **Latin suffix *-ity*** means "state," "quality," or "condition of." This folk tale shows how too much **curiosity**, the state of feeling a strong desire to know, can lead one to make unwise choices.

### Word Study

**Part A** Explain how the **Latin suffix *-ity*** contributes to the meanings of the words *density, integrity,* and *reliability*. Consult a dictionary if necessary.

**Part B** Use the context of the sentences and what you know about the Latin suffix *-ity* to explain your answer to each question.

1. Would a supervisor appreciate a worker's *productivity*?
2. If I show *sensitivity,* am I being thoughtful?

# Close Reading Activities

## Literary Analysis

### Key Ideas and Details

1. **Compare and Contrast** Use a Venn diagram like the one on the right to compare and contrast Eagle and Coyote. Think about how they look, their abilities, and how they react to responsibility.

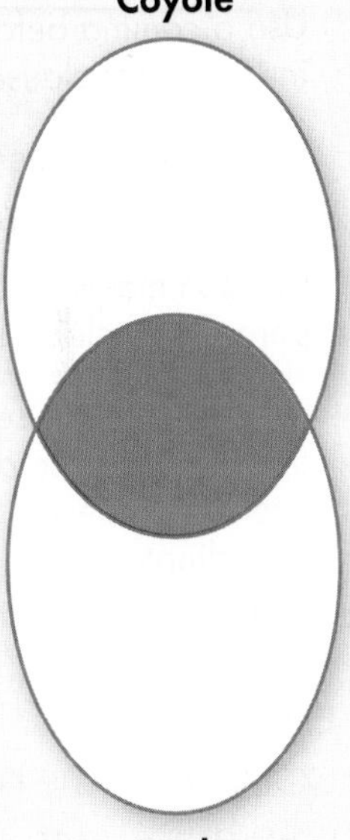


2. **(a) Support:** Make a two-column chart. In the first column, write sentences or comments from other characters or the narrator that give details about what Coyote is like. In the second column, explain what you think each detail reveals about Coyote.
   **(b) Discuss:** In a small group, discuss your lists. Then, choose the best details from each list to share with the class.
3. **(a)** What does Coyote say to Eagle when Eagle is carrying the box? **(b) Speculate:** Why do you think he says this? **(c) Infer:** Why do you think Eagle finally agrees to give the box to Coyote?

### Craft and Structure

4. **Cultural Context (a)** Describe where Coyote and Eagle are when they first see the box. **(b)** How do these details help you understand the cultural context of the story?
5. **Cultural Context** What Zuni beliefs and values are revealed in this folk tale? Identify details that support your answer.

### Integration of Knowledge and Ideas

6. **(a) Evaluate:** Compare and contrast the environment enjoyed by the Kachina tribe before and after their box with the sun and the moon was stolen. What did the Kachina lose? **(b) Make a Judgement:** Do you think they gained anything? Why or why not? Cite textual evidence to support your answer.
7. **Make a Judgment:** In your opinion, does Eagle share any responsibility for the appearance of the first winter? Why or why not? Support your answer with evidence from the folk tale.

8. THE BIG ? **Community or individual—which is more important?** **(a)** How do Coyote's ignorance and selfishness cause harm to others? **(b)** Which character bears more blame for losing the sun and moon? Why? **(c)** What does this folk tale imply about the individual's responsibility to the community?

**ACADEMIC VOCABULARY**

As you write and speak about "Sun and Moon in a Box," use the words related to community and the individual that you explored on page 631 of this textbook.

## Conventions: Commas

A **comma** signals a brief pause.

Review the chart to learn the functions of commas.

| Using Commas | Example |
|---|---|
| Use a comma before a conjunction that joins independent clauses in a compound sentence. | John thought he was late, and he rushed through the parking lot. |
| Use a comma after an introductory word, phrase, or clause. | If you go to the play, how will you get your homework finished? |
| Use commas to separate three or more words, phrases, or clauses in a series. | The café offered fruit juice, iced tea, and sparkling water. |
| Use a comma to separate coordinate adjectives. These are adjectives in a row that each separately modify the noun that follows. Coordinate adjectives can be linked smoothly together with the word *and*. | We received a warm, joyful welcome. [We received a warm *and* joyful welcome.] |

### Practice A

Explain how the comma in each sentence is used.

1. Eagle caught rabbits, but Coyote caught only grasshoppers.
2. The winter weather grew cold, wet, and dreary.
3. Eagle thought that Coyote was a cunning, stupid creature.
4. When they got to the river, Eagle flew across it.

**Reading Application** In "Sun and Moon in a Box," find three sentences that contain commas and explain the function of each comma.

### Practice B

Rewrite the following sentences, inserting commas as necessary.

1. Coyote was a very bad swimmer so he almost drowned.
2. Since Coyote could not control his curiosity he opened the box.
3. Coyote begged complained and moaned until Eagle gave him the box.
4. It was a cold dark world without the sun.

**Writing Application** Write five sentences about a folk tale with which you are familiar. At least one of the sentences should be a compound sentence, one should contain items in a series, one should use coordinate adjectives, and one should start with an introductory word, phrase, or clause.

## Writing to Sources

**Informative Text** Write a **plot summary** of "Sun and Moon in a Box."

- Review the folk tale, taking notes to describe the setting, major characters, main events, and final outcome.
- Use your notes to write your summary. Include one major event from the beginning, one from the middle, and one from the end of the story.
- Conclude your summary by stating a possible theme that is logically supported by the ideas in your summary.

Remember to remain objective. Include the folk tale's main ideas and details, but do not include personal opinions or judgments.

**Grammar Application** Check your writing to be sure that you have used commas correctly.

## Speaking and Listening

**Comprehension and Collaboration** Prepare and present a **retelling** of "Sun and Moon in a Box" from either Coyote's or Eagle's point of view. Review the folk tale, noting the traits and behaviors of the character you have chosen. Consider these details to determine how Coyote or Eagle would think and feel about the folk tale's events. Make your retelling entertaining and effective by using these strategies:

- Organize the plot of your retelling so that it unfolds naturally and is engaging and interesting.
- Include narrative techniques, such as dialogue and description to express the character's emotions and reactions to events.
- Create suspense by withholding certain details until the end of the story.
- As you present, use facial expressions and body movements to enhance and support your retelling.
- Adjust your speaking rate, volume, and tone to suit the action. Pronounce words clearly, and use appropriate expression.
- Make eye contact with your audience from time to time.
- After your presentation, have classmates critique the retelling based on their own interpretations of the folk tale.

# Building Knowledge

*Meet the Author*

**Virginia Hamilton** (1934–2002) is the author of countless novels, stories, and collections of African American folk tales. She was raised in a house of gifted storytellers. Hamilton described her childhood as ideal, saying "I heard 'tells' every day of my life from parents and relatives." Some of those stories were about slavery, and most were about the past. As a result, the past came to play an important role in Hamilton's writing. She developed a unique style, combining elements of history, myth, legend, and dream to bring her stories to life.

## Community or individual—which is more important?

Think about the Big Question as you read "The People Could Fly." Take notes on the ways in which the folk tale explores the concepts of community and the individual.

## CLOSE READING FOCUS

### Key Ideas and Details: **Compare and Contrast**

When you **compare and contrast,** you analyze similarities and differences. You can compare and contrast elements in a literary work by using a graphic organizer, such as a Venn diagram or a two-column chart, to help you keep track of character traits, situations, and ideas.

- First, reread the text to locate the details you will compare.
- Then, write the details in your graphic organizer.

Recording details in this way will help you understand the similarities and differences in a literary work.

### Craft and Structure: **Folk Tales**

A **folk tale** is a fictional story that is composed orally and then passed from person to person by word of mouth. Although they originate in this oral tradition, most folk tales are eventually collected and written down. Similar folk tales are told by different cultures throughout the world, using common character types, plot elements, and themes. Folk tales often teach a lesson about life and clearly differentiate between good and evil. As you read, notice how the different elements of a folk tale work together to give meaning to the story.

## Vocabulary

You will encounter the following words in this folk tale. Copy the words into your notebook, circling the words with multiple meanings. Then, record the different meanings you know.

| | | |
|---|---|---|
| **shed** | **scorned** | **hoed** |
| **croon** | **mystery** | **shuffle** |

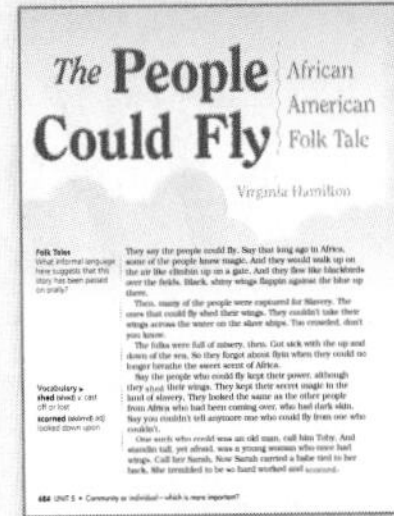

## CLOSE READING MODEL

The passage below is from Virginia Hamilton's folk tale "The People Could Fly." The annotations to the right of the passage show ways in which you can use close reading skills to compare and contrast the elements of a literary work and to understand folk tales.

### *from* "The People Could Fly"

They say the people could fly. Say that long ago in Africa, some of the people knew magic. And they would walk up on the air like climbin up on a gate. And they flew like blackbirds over the fields. Black, shiny wings flappin against the blue up there.

Then, many of the people were captured for Slavery. The ones that could fly shed their wings. They couldn't take their wings across the water on the slave ships. Too crowded, don't you know.[1]

The folks were full of misery, then. Got sick with the up and down of the sea. So they forgot about flyin when they could no longer breathe the sweet scent of Africa.[2]

Say the people who could fly kept their power, although they shed their wings. They kept their secret magic in the land of slavery.[3] They looked the same as the other people from Africa who had been coming over, who had dark skin. Say you couldn't tell anymore one who could fly from one who couldn't.

One such who could was an old man, call him Toby. And standin tall, yet afraid, was a young woman who once had wings. Call her Sarah. Now Sarah carried a babe tied to her back. She trembled to be so hard worked and scorned.

**Folk Tales**

**1** The informal language in this folk tale shows that the story was once told aloud. The author drops the final *g* in the words *climbin* and *flappin,* and uses casual expressions such as "don't you know." These details suggest spoken rather than written language.

**Compare and Contrast**

**2** After they are "captured for Slavery," the people's situation changes dramatically. You can contrast the image of the people "flyin" and breathing "the sweet scent of Africa" with the image of them feeling "full of misery" and "sick" on the slave ship.

**Folk Tales**

**3** Magic is a common element of folk tales. You may begin to wonder how the people will use their "power" and "secret magic" to overcome their terrible situation.

# The People Could Fly

## African American Folk Tale

### Virginia Hamilton

**Folk Tales**
What informal language here suggests that this story has been passed on orally?

They say the people could fly. Say that long ago in Africa, some of the people knew magic. And they would walk up on the air like climbin up on a gate. And they flew like blackbirds over the fields. Black, shiny wings flappin against the blue up there.

Then, many of the people were captured for Slavery. The ones that could fly shed their wings. They couldn't take their wings across the water on the slave ships. Too crowded, don't you know.

The folks were full of misery, then. Got sick with the up and down of the sea. So they forgot about flyin when they could no longer breathe the sweet scent of Africa.

**Vocabulary ▶**
**shed** (shed) *v.* cast off or lost
**scorned** (skôrnd) *adj.* looked down upon

Say the people who could fly kept their power, although they **shed** their wings. They kept their secret magic in the land of slavery. They looked the same as the other people from Africa who had been coming over, who had dark skin. Say you couldn't tell anymore one who could fly from one who couldn't.

One such who could was an old man, call him Toby. And standin tall, yet afraid, was a young woman who once had wings. Call her Sarah. Now Sarah carried a babe tied to her back. She trembled to be so hard worked and **scorned**.

The slaves labored in the fields from sunup to sundown. The owner of the slaves callin himself their Master. Say he was a hard lump of clay. A hard, glinty[1] coal. A hard rock pile, wouldn't be moved. His Overseer[2] on horseback pointed out the slaves who were slowin down. So the one called Driver[3] cracked his whip over the slow ones to make them move faster. That whip was a slice-open cut of pain. So they did move faster. Had to.

Sarah **hoed** and chopped the row as the babe on her back slept.

Say the child grew hungry. That babe started up bawling too loud. Sarah couldn't stop to feed it. Couldn't stop to soothe and quiet it down. She let it cry. She didn't want to. She had no heart to **croon** to it.

"Keep that thing quiet," called the Overseer. He pointed his finger at the babe. The woman scrunched low. The Driver

◀ **Vocabulary**

**hoed** (hōd) *v.* weeded or loosened soil with a metal hand tool

**croon** (kro͞on) *v.* sing or hum quietly and soothingly

**Comprehension**

What special gift do some of the people in this tale have?

1. **glinty** (glint′ ē) *adj.* shiny; reflecting light.
2. **Overseer** (ō′ vər sē′ ər) *n.* someone who watches over and directs the work of others.
3. **Driver** *n.* someone who forced (drove) the slaves to work harder.

cracked his whip across the babe anyhow. The babe hollered like any hurt child, and the woman fell to the earth.

The old man that was there, Toby, came and helped her to her feet.

"I must go soon," she told him.

"Soon," he said.

**Compare and Contrast** How does the Overseer's treatment of Sarah compare with Toby's treatment of her?

Sarah couldn't stand up straight any longer. She was too weak. The sun burned her face. The babe cried and cried, "Pity me, oh, pity me," say it sounded like. Sarah was so sad and starvin, she sat down in the row.

"Get up, you black cow," called the Overseer. He pointed his hand, and the Driver's whip snarled around Sarah's legs. Her sack dress tore into rags. Her legs bled onto the earth. She couldn't get up.

Toby was there where there was no one to help her and the babe.

"Now, before it's too late," panted Sarah. "Now, Father!"

"Yes, Daughter, the time is come," Toby answered. "Go, as you know how to go!"

He raised his arms, holding them out to her. *"Kum . . . yali, kum buba tambe,"* and more magic words, said so quickly, they sounded like whispers and sighs.

The young woman lifted one foot on the air. Then the other. She flew clumsily at first, with the child now held tightly in her arms. Then she felt the magic, the African **mystery**. Say she rose just as free as a bird. As light as a feather.

**Vocabulary ▶**
**mystery** (mis´ tə rē) *n.* something unexplained, unknown, or kept secret

The Overseer rode after her, hollerin. Sarah flew over the fences. She flew over the woods. Tall trees could not snag her. Nor could the Overseer. She flew like an eagle now, until she was gone from sight. No one dared speak about it. Couldn't believe it. But it was, because they that was there saw that it was.

Say the next day was dead hot in the fields. A young man slave fell from the heat. The Driver come and whipped him. Toby come over and spoke words to the fallen one. The words of ancient Africa once heard are never remembered completely. The young man forgot them as soon as he heard them. They went way inside him. He got up and rolled over on the air. He rode it awhile. And he flew away.

Another and another fell from the heat. Toby was there. He cried out to the fallen and reached his arms out to them. "*Kum kunka yali, kum . . . tambe!*" Whispers and sighs. And they too rose on the air. They rode the hot breezes. The ones flyin were black and shinin sticks, wheelin above the head of the Overseer. They crossed the rows, the fields, the fences, the streams, and were away.

"Seize the old man!" cried the Overseer. "I heard him say the magic *words*. Seize him!"

The one callin himself Master come runnin. The Driver got his whip ready to curl around old Toby and tie him up. The slaveowner took his hip gun from its place. He meant to kill old, black Toby.

But Toby just laughed. Say he threw back his head and said, "Hee, hee! Don't you know who I am? Don't you know some of us in this field?" He said it to their faces. "We are ones who fly!"

And he sighed the ancient words that were a dark promise. He said them all around to the others in the field under the whip,

"*. . . buba yali . . . buba tambe. . . .*"

There was a great outcryin. The bent backs straightened up. Old and young who were called slaves and could fly joined hands. Say like they would ring-sing.[4] But they didn't **shuffle** in a circle. They didn't sing. They rose on the air. They flew in a flock that was black against the heavenly blue. Black crows or black shadows. It didn't matter, they went so high. Way above the plantation, way over the slavery land. Say they flew away to *Free-dom.*

And the old man, old Toby, flew behind them, takin care of them. He wasn't cryin. He wasn't laughin. He was the seer.[5] His gaze fell on the plantation where the slaves who could not fly waited.

**▲ Critical Viewing**
What are some reasons why a person might wish to fly?

**◀ Vocabulary**
**shuffle** (shuf′ əl) *v.* walk with dragging feet

**Comprehension**
What did Sarah do to escape the Overseer?

---

4. **ring-sing** joining hands in a circle to sing and dance.
5. **seer** (sē′ ər) *n.* one who has supposed power to see the future; prophet.

**Compare and Contrast** How is Toby's position now different from his position at the beginning of the story?

*"Take us with you!"* Their looks spoke it but they were afraid to shout it. Toby couldn't take them with him. Hadn't the time to teach them to fly. They must wait for a chance to run.

"Goodie-bye!" The old man called Toby spoke to them, poor souls! And he was flyin gone.

So they say. The Overseer told it. The one called Master said it was a lie, a trick of the light. The Driver kept his mouth shut.

The slaves who could not fly told about the people who could fly to their children. When they were free. When they sat close before the fire in the free land, they told it. They did so love firelight and *Free-dom*, and tellin.

They say that the children of the ones who could not fly told their children. And now, me, I have told it to you.

## Language Study

**Vocabulary** The words listed below appear in "The People Could Fly." For each numbered item, write a single sentence correctly using the words indicated.

**shed** **scorned** **hoed** **croon** **shuffle**

1. shuffle; dance
2. scorned; opinion
3. croon; lullaby
4. shed; leaves
5. hoed; planting

**WORD STUDY**

The **Greek root *-myst-*** means "secret." This folk tale tells a story about the African **mystery**, or secret, of people who could fly.

### Word Study

**Part A** Explain how the **Greek root *-myst-*** contributes to the meanings of the words *mystique, mystical,* and *mysticism.* Consult a dictionary if necessary.

**Part B** Use the context of the sentences and what you know about the Greek root *-myst-* to explain your answer to each question.

1. Would a *mysterious* disappearance be easy to solve?
2. If I am *mystified* by your answer to my question, how might I respond?

# Close Reading Activities

## Literary Analysis

### Key Ideas and Details

1. **Compare and Contrast (a)** How are the personalities of Toby and the Overseer similar? **(b)** How are they different? Use details from the text to support your answer to each question.
2. **(a)** What happens when Toby says the "magic words"? **(b) Draw Conclusions:** What do you think "flying" really means? **(c) Support:** Cite textual evidence to support your answer.
3. **Compare and Contrast** Use a Venn diagram or two-column chart to compare and contrast "The People Could Fly" with another story you have read in this book. In your diagram, include details about the setting, the plot, and the characters.

### Craft and Structure

4. **Folk Tales** Use a chart like the one on the right to identify examples of the elements of folk tales that you find in this story and explain how they contribute to the story's meaning.
5. **Folk Tales (a)** What are the "magic words" Toby says? **(b)** Why do you think the author includes these words in the story?

| Characters |
|---|
| ______________ |
| **Plot Events** |
| ______________ |
| **Lesson** |
| ______________ |
| **Theme** |
| ______________ |

### Integration of Knowledge and Ideas

6. **(a) Describe:** What words would you use to describe the living conditions of many African Americans during the time this story originated? **(b) Support:** Describe three details from the story that help you understand these living conditions. **(c) Speculate:** How do you think these conditions impacted the community?
7. **(a)** Who is called Master? **(b) Contrast:** Who is the real "master" in the story? **(c) Evaluate:** Do you think this folk tale inspires hope? Explain.

8. THE BIG ? **Community or individual—which is more important?** Discuss the following questions with a small group of classmates. **(a) Speculate:** What effect might freedom tales, like this folk tale, have had on enslaved or otherwise oppressed people? **(b) Generalize**: How can folk tales and other stories from the oral tradition inspire and support a community?

**ACADEMIC VOCABULARY**

As you write and speak about "The People Could Fly," use the words related to community and the individual that you explored on page 631 of this textbook.

## Conventions: Capitalization

**Capital letters** signal the beginning of a sentence or quotation and identify proper nouns and proper adjectives.

**Proper nouns** include the names of people, geographical locations, specific events and time periods, organizations, languages, historical events and documents, and religions. **Proper adjectives** are derived from proper nouns, as in *French* (from *France*) and *Canadian* (from *Canada*).

**Sentence beginning:** **M**y dog ran away.

**Quotation:** I yelled, "**C**ome back!"

**Proper nouns:** **M**ichael, **Q**ueen **E**lizabeth, **U.S. C**onstitution, **F**riday

**Proper adjectives:** **M**exican, **J**effersonian, **I**rish

### Practice A

Identify the proper nouns and proper adjectives in each sentence, and tell what each names (geographic location, historical event, etc.) or describes.

1. Virginia Hamilton wrote many collections of African American folk tales.
2. Hamilton was born on March 12, 1934.
3. She was born in Yellow Springs, Ohio, and went to college in Columbus, Ohio.
4. Virginia met poet Arnold Adoff in New York City, and they were married in 1960.
5. Hamilton's novel *The House of Dies Drear* won the Edgar Allan Poe Award.

**Reading Application** In "The People Could Fly," find two sentences that contain quotations and two additional sentences that each contain a different type of capitalized word.

### Practice B

Rewrite the following sentences, correcting the capitalization.

1. hamilton's grandfather levi perry was brought to ohio as an infant via the underground railroad.
2. in 1974, virginia hamilton became the first african american to win the newbery award.
3. she received this award for her most successful novel, *m. c. higgins, the great.*
4. hamilton's daughter is named leigh, and her son is named jaime.
5. the library of congress houses a collection of hamilton's papers.

**Writing Application** Write three sentences about "The People Could Fly" or another folk tale you have read. In your sentences, use at least one quotation, one proper adjective, and two proper nouns.

## Writing to Sources

**Argument** Write a **review** of "The People Could Fly" in which you state your position on whether or not other readers will enjoy this folk tale.

- Reread the folk tale, reviewing story elements, such as characters, description, dialogue, and plot, in order to choose your position.
- State your opinion clearly, acknowledging that some readers may not agree with you. Then, support your ideas with details from the story. Organize an effective argument by giving your strongest reasons or evidence at the beginning.
- Provide a concluding paragraph that summarizes your review and supports your arguments.

Revise your word choice to use words that are precise and descriptive. For example, replace "good" with "entertaining" or "comical," or change "boring" to "simplistic" or "predictable."

**Grammar Application** Check your writing to be sure that you have used correct conventions of capitalization.

## Speaking and Listening

**Presentation of Ideas** Prepare a **television news report** that provides a clear interpretation of the events in "The People Could Fly."

- Begin by summarizing the main points of the story, starting with the most important point or event. Follow each main point with supporting ideas.
- Describe events in your own words. Tell when and where the incidents took place, using details from the folk tale.
- Include an interview with an eyewitness—someone who saw events and can provide an on-the-scene reaction. In your report, use quotations to add credibility and bring the action to life.
- Conclude your report with an insight about the meaning of the events and the characters' actions.
- Present your news report to a small group. Speak clearly and vary the tone of your voice to emphasize key points.

## Community or individual—which is more important?

Explore the Big Question as you read the following selections. Both show that travel can enrich individuals and shape their views.

## READING TO COMPARE UNIVERSAL THEMES

As you read, compare how these two authors explore universal themes, even though they are writing in different genres.

GREEK MYTH

THE VOYAGE

FROM TALES FROM THE ODYSSEY

MARY POPE OSBORNE

▲ Critical Viewing In what ways does this image reflect the description of gods and goddesses in these three paragraphs?

*In the early morning of time, there existed a mysterio…
world called Mount Olympus. Hidden behind a veil of…
this world was never swept by winds, nor washed b…
Those who lived on Mount Olympus never grew old;…
died. They were not humans. They were the might…
goddesses of ancient Greece.*

*The Olympian gods and goddesses had great p…
lives of the humans who lived on earth below. Th…
caused a man named Odysseus to wander the s…
long years, trying to find his way home.*

*Almost three thousand years ago, a Greek poet…
Homer first told the story of Odysseus' journey. S…
storytellers have told the strange and wondrous t…
again. We call that story the Odyssey.*

694 UNIT 5 • Community or individual—which is more important?

BLOG

To the Top of Everest

Samantha Larson

**Friday, March 30, 2007**
**Here we go ⟶ Kathmandu!**
Today is the day! Our bags are (nearly) packed and we're (just about) ready to go. I've got eleven hours to run around doing last minute errands before our plane takes off.

I arrived back in Long Beach from New York last Saturday, where I've been since our return from Cho Oyu. When I wasn't training by running, swimming at the pool, taking dance classes, or rock climbing, I was taking oboe lessons, French, and photography classes. Hopefully I'll be able to take some great pictures on this expedition!

It has been a very exciting week in all our general trip preparation mayhem, filled with lots of gear sorting and fedex package arrivals. But now my dad and I are pretty much all set to go.

See you in Kathmandu!

◀ Critical Viewing Which details in…

PART 2 •

### "The Voyage" *from* Tales from the Odyssey

**Mary Pope Osborne** (b. 1949)
Mary Pope Osborne has lived an adventurous life. Her father was in the military, and the family moved seven times before Mary was fifteen. As a young adult, she explored sixteen Asian countries with friends. Osborne began to write in her thirties. Today, she is best known for her series, *The Magic Tree House.* "There is no career better suited to my eccentricities, strengths, and passions than that of a children's book author," Osborne says.

### "To the Top of Everest"

**Samantha Larson** (b. 1988)
In 2007, American Samantha Larson became the youngest person to climb the "Seven Summits"—the highest mountains on each of the seven continents. Larson climbed her first, Mount Kilimanjaro in Africa, at the age of 12. She finished her quest when she successfully reached the top of Mt. Everest at age 18. Larson calls Everest "much harder, longer, and higher" than the other peaks. "It was one big challenge," she recalls, but adds, "Deep down I thought I would make it."

## Comparing Universal Themes

A **universal theme** is a message about life that is expressed repeatedly in many different cultures and time periods. Universal themes include concepts such as the value of courage and the danger of greed. You can identify the universal theme in a literary work by focusing on the main character, thinking about conflicts the character faces, and noticing the changes that the character undergoes as a result of those conflicts.

Universal themes are important ideas, so many cultures present these themes in **epics**—stories or long poems about larger-than-life heroes. In many ways, an epic can be seen as a portrait of the culture that produced it. Epics express a culture's values and its perspective on universal themes, such as bravery. Other **epic conventions**, or elements typical of epics, are listed in the chart below.

Epics and their themes are an important part of the literature of different cultures. Ancient epics were recited as entertainment and passed down from storyteller to storyteller. New generations often create works inspired by these epics. For example, it is not unusual to find an allusion, or reference, to the ancient Greek epic the *Odyssey* in a new adventure story. As you read these selections, use a chart like this to note the examples of epic conventions that help point toward a universal theme.

| Epic Conventions | "The Voyage" from *Tales from the Odyssey* | "To the Top of Everest" |
|---|---|---|
| dangerous journey | | |
| characters who help | Goddesses Ino and Athena | |
| broad setting | | |
| serious, formal style | | |

# THE VOYAGE

## *FROM* TALES FROM THE ODYSSEY

### MARY POPE OSBORNE

**▲ Critical Viewing**
In what ways does this image reflect the description of gods and goddesses in these three paragraphs?

*In the early morning of time, there existed a mysterious world called Mount Olympus. Hidden behind a veil of clouds, this world was never swept by winds, nor washed by rains. Those who lived on Mount Olympus never grew old; they never died. They were not humans. They were the mighty gods and goddesses of ancient Greece.*

*The Olympian gods and goddesses had great power over the lives of the humans who lived on earth below. Their anger once caused a man named Odysseus to wander the seas for many long years, trying to find his way home.*

*Almost three thousand years ago, a Greek poet named Homer first told the story of Odysseus' journey. Since that time, storytellers have told the strange and wondrous tale again and again. We call that story the* Odyssey.

With his hands gripping the rudder, Odysseus skillfully guided his raft over the waves. He never slept. All night, he kept his eyes fixed on the stars that Calypso had told him to watch—the Pleiades and the Bear.

Day after day and night after night, Odysseus sailed the seas. Finally, on the eighteenth day, he saw the dim outline of mountains on the horizon.

As Odysseus steered his raft toward the shore, dark clouds gathered overhead. The water began to rise. The wind began to blow, until it was roaring over the earth and sea.

*Has Poseidon discovered my raft?* Odysseus wondered anxiously. *Does he now seek his final revenge?*

For many years, Poseidon, mighty ruler of the sea, had been angry with Odysseus for blinding his son, the Cyclops. Now it seemed he was trying to destroy Odysseus once again. The wind roared from the north, south, east, and west. Daylight plunged into darkness. Odysseus feared he was about to come to a terrible, lonely end.

Suddenly an enormous wave crashed down on Odysseus' raft. Odysseus was swept overboard and pulled deep beneath the sea. He struggled wildly to raise his head above the water and breathe.

When his head finally broke the surface, Odysseus saw his raft swiftly moving away across the water. He swam as fast as he could toward the wooden craft. He grabbed the timbers and pulled himself aboard.

Then, as the wind swirled the raft across the water, Odysseus saw an astonishing sight. A sea goddess was floating like a gull on top of the waves.

Seemingly **impervious** to the great storm, she floated near his raft and climbed aboard.

"My friend," she said, "I am Ino, the White Goddess, who guides sailors in storms. I know not why Poseidon is angry with you. But I know this: for all the torture he has **inflicted** upon you, he will not kill you. But you must leave your raft at once and swim for the shore. Take my veil, for it is enchanted. You will come to no harm as long as you possess it. As soon as you reach land, you must throw it back into the sea."

◀ **Vocabulary**

**impervious** (im pur′ vē əs) *adj.* not affected by something

**inflicted** (in flikt′ əd) *v.* delivered something painful

**Comprehension**

Who climbs aboard Odysseus' raft?

With these words, the White Goddess removed her enchanted veil and gave it to Odysseus. Then she disappeared back into the wild seas.

At that moment, a huge wave crashed down on Odysseus' raft, ripping it to pieces. Clutching Ino's veil, Odysseus pulled himself onto a wooden plank and rode it as if it were a horse. Then he dove down into the sea.

**Universal Themes**
Which epic convention appears in this paragraph?

Suddenly, all the winds died down—except the north wind. Odysseus felt that Athena[1] was holding the other winds back, so he could swim safely and swiftly to some distant shore. For two days and two nights, with the north wind gently flattening the waves before him, he swam and floated on the calm sea.

On the third day, the north wind died away and the sea was completely calm. Odysseus saw land ahead. With a burst of joy, he swam toward the rocky shore.

In an instant, the wind and waves returned. With a thundering roar, sea spray rained down on him.

Odysseus struggled to keep his head above the churning water, seeking a place to go ashore.

**Spiral Review**
**THEME** What is Odysseus' relationship to the sea?

Angry waves were pounding the reefs with great force. *I'll be dashed against the rocks if I try to swim ashore now,* he thought desperately.

But once again, Odysseus felt the presence of Athena. A giant wave picked him up and carried him over the rocks toward the beach. But before Odysseus could crawl ashore to safety, another wave dragged him back into the sea and pulled him under the water.

Odysseus swam desperately, escaping the waves pounding the shore. Soon he came to a sheltered cove. He saw a riverbank free of rough stones. As he swam toward the bank, he prayed to the gods to save him from the angry attack of Poseidon.

Suddenly the waves were still. But when Odysseus tried to haul himself ashore, his body failed him. He had been defeated by the storm. It had ripped his flesh and robbed his muscles of their strength. He was passing in and out of consciousness.

1. **Athena** *n.* goddess of wisdom and protector of Odysseus.

Gasping for breath, he pulled off Ino's veil and threw it back into the sea. Then he used his last bit of strength to drag himself out of the water and throw himself into the river reeds.

*If I lie here all night, I shall die from the cold and damp,* he thought. *If I go farther ashore and pass out in a thicket, wild beasts will devour me.* No matter what evils lay ahead, he knew he had to push on. On bleeding hands and knees, he crawled to a sheltered spot under an olive tree, a tree sacred to the goddess Athena.

**Universal Themes** Based on this paragraph, what trait do you think the ancient Greeks valued in heroes?

Odysseus lay down in a pile of dead leaves. With his bloody hands, he spread leaves over his torn body. Like a farmer spreading ashes over the embers of his fire, he tried to protect the last spark of life within him.

Mercifully, the gray-eyed goddess slipped down from the heavens and appeared at his side. She closed his weary eyes and pulled him down into a sweet sleep that took away his pain and sorrow.

## Critical Thinking

1. **Key Ideas and Details (a)** How does Odysseus react to the storm at sea? **(b) Generalize:** Choose three adjectives that describe Odysseus. **(c) Speculate:** Why do you think the goddesses help Odysseus?
2. **Key Ideas and Details (a) Make a Judgment:** Do you think Odysseus will survive his injuries? **(b) Support:** Find several passages in the text that support your answer.
3. **Integration of Knowledge and Ideas** How would you describe ancient Greek culture after reading this passage based on an ancient Greek myth?
4. **Integration of Knowledge and Ideas** Odysseus struggles mightily against beings more powerful than he is. Do you think his story can teach lessons to individuals, communities, or both? Explain your answer, using details from the text. ***[Connect to the Big Question: Community or individual—which is more important?]***

# To the Top of Everest

Samantha Larson

**Friday, March 30, 2007**

Here we go ⟶ Kathmandu!

Today is the day! Our bags are (nearly) packed and we're (just about) ready to go. I've got eleven hours to run around doing last minute errands before our plane takes off.

I arrived back in Long Beach from New York last Saturday, where I've been since our return from Cho Oyu. When I wasn't training by running, swimming at the pool, taking dance classes, or rock climbing, I was taking oboe lessons, French, and photography classes. Hopefully I'll be able to take some great pictures on this expedition!

It has been a very exciting week in all our general trip preparation mayhem, filled with lots of gear sorting and fedex package arrivals. But now my dad and I are pretty much all set to go.

See you in Kathmandu!

**◄ Critical Viewing**
Which details in this photograph suggest Larson is about to go on a dangerous journey?

**Comprehension**
How did Larson train for her expedition?

**Monday, April 2, 2007**
**Kathmandu**
After nearly 24 hours of travel we finally arrived in Kathmandu yesterday afternoon. Doug, my dad, and I met up with the rest of the team (Victor, James, and Wim) at our hotel in Kathmandu. We had a group meeting where we went over the route we are going to take to base camp, and then we picked up some odds and ends at one of the dozens of local climbing stores.

**▼ Critical Viewing**
Why would a person have to be brave to attempt the climb seen here?

The team is flying to Lukla to begin the trek to base camp early tomorrow morning.

**Wednesday, April 4, 2007**
**Namche Bazar**
Yesterday after a very scenic flight and a heart-stopping landing on a small airstrip perched on the side of a mountain, we arrived in Lukla to begin the trek to base camp. Lukla was filled with excitement as porters organized their loads and trekkers began their journeys. From Lukla, we hiked for about 4 hours through the beautiful Nepalese countryside, passing through several villages until we reached the village of Monjo, where we stayed the night in the Monjo Guesthouse. I think my dad and I got the big sleep that we needed to catch up on our jetlag; around 4 in the afternoon, we decided to take a "nap" that lasted until 7 the next morning!

**Thursday, April 12, 2007**
**Base Camp**
We made it to base camp yesterday afternoon. Today we are going to practice crossing the ladders over the Khumbu Icefall. We are well and safe.

En route here we visited Lama Gesa and he blessed our journey. It was an amazing experience!

I am going to try and connect my laptop and charge it with my solar charger—we will see if that works.

More to follow.....

**Monday, April 16, 2007**

**Rest Day**

Yesterday we got an early start for our first time through the icefall. We left around 6:30 in the morning, with the idea that we would turn around 11—we did not necessarily have a destination in mind, it was more for acclimatization[1] and to get an idea of what the icefall was like. However, at 11 we were about half an hour from the top of the icefall, so we decided to just continue to the top.

It was quite fun climbing up the icefall. The ladders that we had to cross over crevasses[2] were especially exciting. I was pretty tired by the time we got back to base camp, but today was a rest day (our first), so I've had plenty of time to recover.

**▲ Critical Viewing**
Why might someone take a lot of risks to visit a place like this?

Tomorrow we are going up to camp one to spend the night. Camp one is about an hour further than we went yesterday. The next day we will go up to tag camp two and then come back down to base camp.

**Thursday, April 19, 2007**

**Puja**

The day before yesterday we all made it up to camp one to spend the night. This time we were able to get through the Khumbu Icefall an hour quicker than the last. We had a pretty good night at camp one; my dad and I both had a bit of a headache at first, but we were both able to eat and sleep well.

**Universal Themes**
How is Lama Gesa's role in this selection similar to Athena's role in "The Voyage"?

Camp one is at the start of the Western Cwm.[3] Yesterday, from camp one we continued up the Cwm to camp two. The cwm

**Comprehension**
How long did it take to travel to Kathmandu?

1. **acclimatization** (ə klī′ mə tə zā′ shən) *n.* process of allowing the body to adjust to the climate, especially at high altitude.
2. **crevasses** (krə vas′ əz) *n.* deep cracks in ice or a glacier.
3. **Western Cwm** *n.* a broad valley at the base of Mount Everest.

is infamous for being very uncomfortably hot, but yesterday it was actually really nice. It was very beautiful, and we could see the summit of Everest, which we haven't been able to see since before we got to base camp. After we tagged camp two we came all the way back down to base camp. It was a long day, and we all returned pretty tired. However, it was nice to be back in base camp, and after dinner we watched Mission Impossible III on Ben's laptop (from the London Business School team). Unfortunately the power ran out about half way through, but I have been asked to charge up my laptop so we can finish tonight.

**Spiral Review CULTURAL PERSPECTIVE** Why do you think the Sherpas organize a blessing ceremony?

Today was the Puja, which is a ceremony that the Sherpas organize. A Lama comes up and performs many chants to ask the mountain gods for permission to climb the mountain, and to ask for protection. I had my ice ax and my crampons[4] blessed in the ceremony. As part of the ceremony, they also put out long lines of prayer flags coming out from the stupa where the ceremony was performed. Afterwards, they passed out lots of yummy treats.

While we were up at camp one, the shower tent was set up here at base camp. It's just a little bucket of water with a hose attached to it, but definitely 15 minutes of heaven.

### Saturday, April 28, 2007
**Base Camp**

**Universal Themes** Which details in this entry show that Larson and her team face great dangers as they continue to climb?

We are back at base camp! We came down from camp two yesterday, and arrived just in time for lunch. We were delayed a bit in the morning because we were radioed from base camp that there was a break in the icefall, and we didn't want to leave until we knew that the "ice doctors" had fixed up the route. As we came down, we found that the break was in a flat area known as the "football field" that we had previously **designated** as a "safe" area to take a little rest. And the whole shelf just collapsed!

**Vocabulary ▶ designated** (dez′ ig nāt′ əd) *v.* identified; pointed out

Now that we have spent a night at camp three, we are done with the acclimatization process. We are going to take a few days for rest and recovery, and then we just wait for good weather to make a summit bid. We plan to go back down to Pengboche tomorrow so we can really get a good rest at lower altitude before our summit attempt.

4. **crampons** (kram′ pənz) *n.* metal plates with spikes that are attached to boots to provide greater traction.

Here is what we have been up to these past few days:

**4/23/07**

Yesterday we all made it up to camp one for the night. We were joined by Tori from the London Business School team, because she wasn't feeling 100% when her team went up the day before.

Today we all came up to camp two. It was very hot coming up the Cwm this time, and we all had heavy packs because we had to bring up what we had left at camp one the last time we stayed there. It certainly made it a lot harder work!

**4/24/07**

Despite the fact that I caused us to get a later start than planned this morning (I had a particularly hard time getting out of my warm sleeping bag into the cold air) we accomplished our goal for the day. We went up the very first pitch of the Lhotse Face, and are now back at camp two for the evening.

**4/26/07**

Yesterday we went about halfway up the Lhotse Face to camp three to spend the night. This was a new record for my dad and me, as our highest night ever! Camp three is at about 23,500 feet, and our previous highest night was at camp two on Cho Oyu, at 23,000 feet. We arrived at camp three around noon, and then had a lot of time to kill in our tents, as it wasn't really safe to go more than five feet outside the tent without putting on crampons and clipping into the fixed ropes. Thankfully, I had not yet reached a hypoxic[5] level where I couldn't enjoy my book.

Coming up the Lhotse Face was a bit windy, and some parts were pretty icy. It gets fairly steep, so I was glad to have my ascender, which slides up the rope, but not back down, so you can use it as a handhold to pull yourself up.

**Comprehension**
What did the Lama ask for during the Puja?

5. **hypoxic** (hī päk′ sik) *adj.* having too little oxygen.

**Sunday, May 6, 2007**

**Back from Holiday**

We're back at base camp from our little holiday down the mountain.

Now that we are back in base camp, we are just waiting till we can go for our summit attempt. The ropes are not yet fixed to the summit. Once the ropes are fixed, we hope there will soon be a good weather window.

**Friday, May 11, 2007**

**Base Camp**

We're still at base camp. Hopefully we'll be able to go up soon though.

We've tried to hold on to our fitness these past few days by doing some sort of activity each day. We've been ice climbing in a really neat cave near base camp, and we've also been on hikes up Pumori to Pumori base camp, and then up to camp one. Pumori is a 7145-meter mountain near Everest.

**Universal Themes**
How do you know that Larson is willing to face challenges to meet her goal?

**Vocabulary ▶**
**saturation** (sach´ ə rā´ shən) *n.* state of being completely filled

**Saturday, May 12, 2007**

**Still at Base Camp**

It looks like we're going to be able to go up soon for our summit attempt. Fingers crossed!

We've gotten our oxygen masks and tested them out. I was able to get my oxygen **saturation** back up to 100% this morning! After I turned off the oxygen, I only had a few seconds of being at pseudo sea-level before it went back down, though.

We're all getting a little restless hanging around base camp.

**Monday, May 14, 2007**

**Camp 2**

We finally started our summit push yesterday, making our way from base camp to camp two. We don't have internet access up here, but we were able to relay this information to our correspondents in New York via satellite phone. We're taking a rest day today, and plan to press on tomorrow. If all goes well, we should summit on the 17th.

**Thursday, May 17, 2007**

**Summit!**

We made it to the top! Now all we have to do is get back down...

**Wednesday, May 23, 2007**

**Back Home!**

We've been in a big rush getting back home, and I haven't been able to update for awhile, as I have not had internet access. We woke up this morning at 16,000 feet in a village called Lobuche, and this evening my dad and I arrived back at sea-level in Long Beach! The rest of the team are celebrating in Kathmandu—my dad and I skipped out on the celebration to make it back in time for my brother Ted's college graduation in New York.

**Comprehension**
How does Larson stay fit while waiting to go to the summit?

The day after we summited, we came down from the South Col (camp 4) to camp 2. I was very tired at that point, but glad that we had all made it back safely lower on the mountain. It was amazing how after being to almost 30,000 feet, 20,000-foot camp 2 felt like it was nearly at sea-level!

The day after that, we came back down to base camp, where we received lots of warm hugs and congratulations. We only had one night back at base camp, as the next day (the 20th), we packed up our bags and headed down the valley. Base camp had a strange, empty feeling—it was sad to leave my little tent that had been my home for the past 2 months! My dad, Doug, Wim, and I were hoping to get a helicopter out of Lobuche on the 21st to save a little time, but Victor and

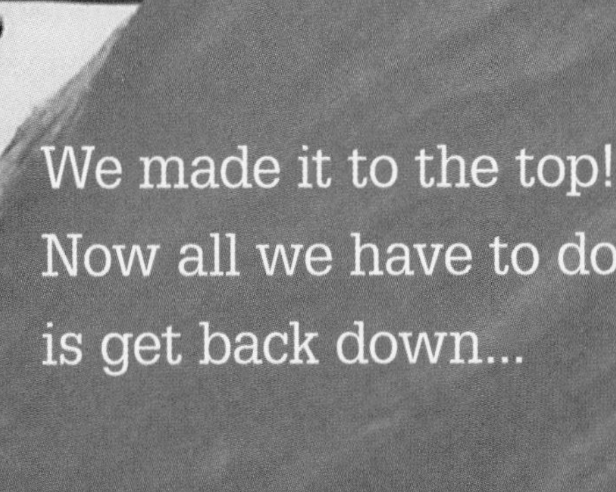
We made it to the top! Now all we have to do is get back down...

James decided to walk down to the Lukla airstrip to fly out to Kathmandu on the 23rd. However, even though we awoke on the 21st to a beautiful, clear day in Lobuche, apparently there were clouds lower down the valley, so the helicopter couldn't fly in until the 23rd either. It was kind of hard waiting those two days in Lobuche. We were just an hour away from a hot shower and a big meal, if only those clouds would clear!

**Universal Themes** What details here suggest some people consider Larson and her team heroes?

Once the helicopter landed in Kathmandu, I was greeted by a mob of journalists and cameramen. I was so surprised! After nearly 20 hours of travel, my dad and I landed at LAX[6] and were greeted by my family, and some more news people. Now we only have a few hours before we jump back on a plane to go to New York! I am very excited to see my mom and brother though.

Thank you everyone for all of your wonderful comments and your support!!!

6. **LAX** *n.* Los Angeles International Airport.

## Critical Thinking

1. **Key Ideas and Details (a)** What are some of the things Larson does to prepare for her journey before leaving home? **(b) Infer:** Why is it important for Larson to be in top physical shape? **(c) Deduce:** How might her other lessons and interests affect her trip?
2. **Key Ideas and Details (a)** How much time does Larson spend on the mountain before trying to reach the summit? **(b) Summarize:** List five things the team does with its time on the mountain before heading out for the summit. **(c) Deduce:** What prevents the team from trying to summit earlier?
3. **Integration of Knowledge and Ideas** Why might climbers of many faiths want to take part in the Puja ceremony?
4. **Integration of Knowledge and Ideas** Climbing Mt. Everest takes an incredible amount of time, effort, and money. **(a)** How might a journey like Larson's enrich her as an individual? **(b)** Do you think the community also gains from her success? Explain. ***[Connect to the Big Question: Community or individual—which is more important?]***

## Comparing Universal Themes

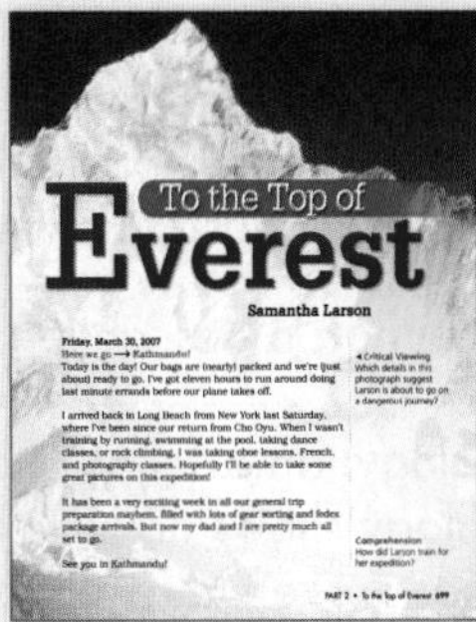

**1. Key Ideas and Details** Compare and contrast Larson's voyage with Odysseus's voyage.

| | Odysseus | Samantha Larson |
|---|---|---|
| Journey undertaken | | |
| Attitude of character | | |
| Obstacles character must overcome | | |
| Outcome | | |

**2. Craft and Structure (a)** Why might you include an allusion to the *Odyssey* if you were writing about Larson for your school paper? **(b)** Would you describe her as a "hero"? Explain.

**3. Integration of Knowledge and Ideas** One theme of the *Odyssey* is the triumph of bravery over power. Do you think "To the Top of Everest" expresses the same message? Why or why not? If not, how would you state its central idea?

## Timed Writing

### Explanatory Text: Essay

In an essay, compare and contrast the themes of the classic epic tale "The Voyage" with the modern account "To the Top of Everest." Explain how time and place influence the theme of each selection. **(40 minutes)**

### 5-Minute Planner

1. Read the prompt carefully and completely.
2. Jot down answers to these questions:
    - What is the universal theme of each selection?
    - How do the heroes overcome obstacles?
    - How do the two authors affect your response by the way they emphasize different evidence?
3. Reread the prompt, and then draft your essay.

**USE ACADEMIC VOCABULARY**

As you write, use academic language, including the following words or their related forms:

**attitude**
**challenge**
**environment**
**outcome**

For more information about academic vocabulary, see pages xlvi–l.

## Language Study

### Figurative Language

**Figurative language** is language that is not meant to be taken literally. Most types of figurative language are based on imaginative comparisons, lending ordinary things extraordinary qualities. The use of figurative language makes writing vivid and expressive. The chart below contains examples of common types of figurative language.

| Type of Figurative Language | Example |
|---|---|
| **Simile:** a figure of speech that uses *like* or *as* to make a direct comparison between two unlike ideas | The sky is like a patchwork quilt. |
| **Metaphor:** a description of one thing as if it were another | The sky is a patchwork quilt. |
| **Analogy:** an extended comparison of relationships. An analogy shows how the relationship between one pair of things is like the relationship between another pair | Walter lives like a sheet of paper blown along a windy street. He is carried this way and that way with no control of his direction. |
| **Personification:** a figure of speech in which a nonhuman subject is given human characteristics | The sea was angry that day, my friends. |
| **Paradox:** a statement, an idea, or a situation that seems contradictory but actually expresses a truth | The more things change, the more they stay the same. |
| **Idiom:** an expression whose meaning differs from the meanings of its individual words | It was raining cats and dogs last night. |

**Practice A** Identify each instance of figurative language in these sentences as a *simile* or *metaphor.*

1. Because I studied for several nights, the quiz was a breeze.
2. The winter night was so quiet that every sound was as clear as a bell.
3. My dog is the sunshine of my life.
4. After shoveling snow for several hours, I slept like a log last night.
5. A ghost of a moon shone over the fields.

**Practice B** Identify the *simile, metaphor, idiom,* or *analogy* in each sentence. Then, use context clues to explain the meaning of each.

1. Tyrone understands people very well; he reads them like a book.
2. I tried to get my friend to change his mind, but he was a mule.
3. Two peas in a pod, Simon and Jack liked exactly the same music.
4. Seeing the fascinating art in the museum sparked my interest in sculpture.
5. After she won the diving competition, Elana was as happy as a lark.
6. Learning the multiplication tables is like riding a bike; once you learn it, you never forget it.
7. After losing the concert tickets, Kevin was as mad as a hornet.
8. Her hair was a cloud of snowy white.

**Activity** With a partner, browse through some current magazines. Search through the articles to find examples of at least four types of figurative language. Use a notecard like the one shown to list the examples you have found. Then, explain the meaning of each example. Use the context clues in the article to aid your understanding.

| **Similes:** |
|---|
| |
| **Metaphors:** |
| |
| **Analogies:** |
| |
| **Personifications:** |
| |
| **Paradoxes:** |
| |
| **Idioms:** |
| |
| |

## Comprehension and Collaboration

With a partner, write a scene with dialogue between two characters, taking care to use no figurative language. Then, rewrite the dialogue, adding idioms, analogies, similes, and metaphors. Compare your scenes. Which one sounds more realistic? Why?

## Research Presentation

These guidelines will help you through the processes of conducting research, writing a report, and presenting it to an audience.

### Learn the Skills

**Generate questions.** Consider what you would like to discover about your topic. Pose relevant and concise questions to guide your research and help you to stay on topic.

**Evaluate your sources.** Prepare to use both print and electronic sources, such as databases, the Internet, and magazines. Evaluate the credibility, scope, and objectivity of each source.

- Is the source known for its correct facts?
- Does a Web site have *.edu, .gov,* or *.org* at the end of its Web address?
- Does the publication date fall within the last three years?

**Organize your information.** Take notes from each source to answer your research questions. Include only the information that is meaningful to your topic. Use your notes to develop an outline.

**Write the report.** Organize the report to include an introduction, several body paragraphs, and a conclusion. Avoid plagiarism by paraphrasing instead of copying information directly from each source. Credit your sources by citing them at the end of your report on a Bibliography or Works Cited page.

**Present your report.** Practice your presentation using the following techniques.

- Use graphics, such as charts, graphs, photographs, or a slideshow to enhance the main points in your report.
- Credit sources by using phrases like "According to . . ." and "In the book by . . . ."
- Vary your speaking rate and pitch to engage your listeners and retain their interest. Pronounce words clearly and speak loudly enough for everyone to hear.
- Use a natural but serious tone. Speak in formal English. For example, avoid using "filler" phrases, such as "as you know." Make eye contact and use hand gestures to emphasize certain points.

## Practice the Skills

**Presentation of Knowledge and Ideas** Use the skills you learned in this workshop to complete the following activity.

> ACTIVITY: **Delivering a Research Report**
>
> Prepare a research presentation by following the steps below. Then, deliver the report to your class.
>
> - Develop your major research question and additional questions that address your topic.
> - Gather research and organize your report.
> - Present your research report to your classmates.
> - Use the Research Guide to plan your report.

Use a Research Guide like the one below to develop your presentation.

**Research Guide**

**Major Research Question:**

**Brainstorm to list ideas that address the research topic:**

**Open-ended research questions:**

| | |
|---|---|
| **1.** | **3.** |
| **2.** | **4.** |

**Research plan:** Jot down notes explaining your plan for researching each question.

**Assessment of sources:** Briefly demonstrate the reliability and credibility of each source. Then, explain why one source is more useful than another.

**Synthesize the research:** Draw conclusions about and summarize or paraphrase each source to synthesize the research.
Conclusions:
Summary:

**Organize your research:** Think about your purpose and audience when you organize your presentation.
Purpose of the research:
Audience:

**Comprehension and Collaboration** At the end of your presentation, invite your audience to discuss, respond to, or ask questions about your presentation. Then, listen as your classmates present their reports. Interpret the purpose of each report by explaining the content, evaluating the delivery of the presentation, and asking questions or making comments about the evidence that supports the presenter's claims.

## Write an Explanatory Text

### Cause-and-Effect Essay

**Defining the Form** A **cause-and-effect essay** explains why something happens or what happens as a result of something else. You may use this type of writing in lab reports, historical accounts, persuasive essays, magazine articles, and speeches.

**Assignment** Write a cause-and-effect essay about a question or issue that interests you. Include the following elements in your essay:

- ✓ a *well-defined* topic that can be covered in a few pages
- ✓ information drawn from *several credible sources*
- ✓ *detailed, factual explanations* of events or situations and the *relationships among them*
- ✓ a *clear and coherent organization* with *effective transitions that show causes and effects*
- ✓ a style *appropriate to the task, purpose, and audience*
- ✓ error-free writing, including the *correct use of commas with coordinate adjectives*

To preview the criteria on which your cause-and-effect essay may be judged, see the rubric on page 719.

### FOCUS ON RESEARCH

When you conduct research to write a cause-and-effect essay, bear these points in mind:

- Some experts might emphasize one or two causes over others. Other experts might emphasize different causes. Evaluate the evidence each expert offers to determine which position makes the most sense to you.
- Experts might also differ on which effects are most serious. Again, study their evidence to see which side you support.

If a source seems extremely partial to one point of view, you might not want to rely on that source. Look for sources that are balanced. Examples include encyclopedias, news articles, and Web pages from organizations with a reputation for fairness.

**READING-WRITING CONNECTION**

To get the feel for cause-and-effect writing, read "Life Without Gravity" by Robert Zimmerman on page 194.

## Prewriting/Planning Strategies

**Choose a topic.** Use one of these strategies:

- **Brainstorming** Sometimes the best way to find a topic is to just start writing. Write for five minutes about whatever questions come to mind. Use phrases such as "What causes . . ." or "Why does . . ." to begin each question. Circle any questions that you think would make an interesting topic.
- **Imagining a Walk** Close your eyes and imagine yourself walking through a house, apartment, or other place you know well. Observe the objects, people, or activities that you "see" along the way. To find items that suggest cause-and-effect relationships, ask, "What caused this?" or "What effects does this have?" Jot down several ideas, then choose your topic from these items.

**Narrow your topic.** A topic with many causes and effects, such as the causes and effects of storms, is far too broad. Narrow a broad topic to focus on a single cause or a single effect. For example, the effects of a tornado—a single cause—would be an appropriate topic. Use a web like the one shown to narrow your topic. Write your topic in the center and surround it with subtopics. Then, note causes or effects connected to each subtopic. Consider whether any of the subtopics would make a good focus for your essay.

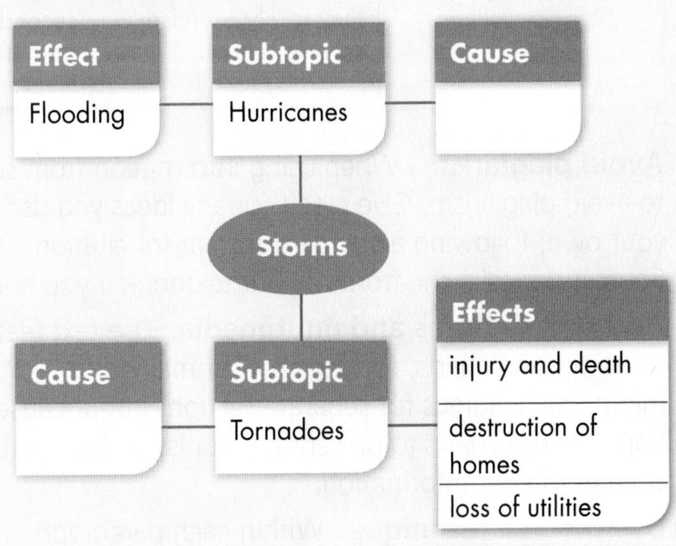


**Conduct research.** Do research to fill in any gaps in your knowledge about your topic. First write down a series of questions about your topic to guide your research. Then, use library resources and online references, or interview an expert on the topic to find answers to the questions you posed. Continue to generate focused questions for further research. Use a two-column chart to help you gather details. In one column, list the causes involved in your event or situation. In the other column, list the effects.

## Drafting Strategies

**Write a strong introduction.** Your introduction is the first thing your audience will read. Include a sentence or two that explains the importance of your topic. Then, identify the main points you will address in your essay.

**Explain causes and effects logically.** Explain the logic of each cause-and-effect relationship you present. Support your statements with specific facts, statistics, names, and dates whenever possible. Opinions and trivial, or unimportant, details are not strong support for an argument.

| Unsupported Statement | Supported Statement | Difference |
|---|---|---|
| Children watch too much TV nowadays. | Studies show that children watch an average of 15 hours of TV every week. | The first statement is an opinion. The second is a statement of fact. |
| I have a neighbor who never exercises. | In a survey of 100 teens, 32 percent said they rarely exercise outside school. | The first statement is a trivial example. The second cites evidence from a survey of many teens. |

**Avoid plagiarism.** When using information from sources, be sure to avoid plagiarism. Give credit for any ideas you use that are not your own, following a standard format for citation. See the Citing Sources pages in the front of your textbook if you need guidance.

**Add text features and multimedia.** Use text features, such as headings and charts, to support your main ideas. For example, you might use headings for separate sections about causes and effects. You may use charts to present key statistics. Be sure to credit the sources of your information.

**Use the SEE technique.** Within each paragraph, use the **SEE** technique to add depth to your essay.

- In a paragraph, first write a **S**tatement of the main idea.
- Next, write a sentence that **E**xtends that idea.
- Finally, write a sentence that **E**laborates on the extension.

## Organize Logically

Before you begin to write your essay, decide how you want to organize your details. You might try one of these suggestions:

- If you are writing about a single cause with many effects, devote a paragraph to each effect.
- If you are writing about one effect with many causes, devote one paragraph to each cause and one paragraph to the effect.
- If you are writing about a series of causes and effects, organize your paragraphs in chronological, or time, order.

The chart shows how the paragraphs of the body of the essay would be organized in these three arrangements.

| Body Paragraph | Single Cause, Many Effects | Many Causes, Single Effect | Series of Causes and Effects |
|---|---|---|---|
| 1 | **Cause**<br>Mount Saint Helens erupts | **Cause 1**<br>Increased TV watching | **Cause**<br>Growing power of computers |
| 2 | **Effect 1**<br>People, animals, and plants die | **Cause 2**<br>Increased junk-food eating | **Effect/Cause**<br>Computers have more uses |
| 3 | **Effect 2**<br>Forest fires, mudslides, floods | **Cause 3**<br>Less exercise | **Effect/Cause**<br>Computers become more popular |
| 4 | **Effect 3**<br>Loss of buildings, roads, bridges | **Effect**<br>A generation of children is gaining weight | **Effect**<br>People rely on computers in many areas of life |

**Indicate Relative Importance** Some causes or effects are more important than others. You might wish to build up from the least important to the most important point. Alternatively, you may decide to begin with your most important point. For instance, in the first example in the chart above, loss of life is listed as the first effect because the writer thinks that detail is the most important.

Whatever organization you choose, use transition words to clearly show the relationships among ideas. For example, beginning a paragraph with the words *Most important . . .* tells your readers that the effect you are about to describe is more serious than others you have mentioned.

## Revising Strategies

**State main ideas clearly.** By starting a new paragraph, you signal readers that you are introducing a new idea. Effective writers clearly state the main idea in each paragraph. To analyze the connections among your other sentences, use color-coding.

Reread each paragraph. Use two highlighters—one color to mark phrases that present causes and another color to mark phrases that indicate effects. Evaluate the connections between the two. Go back and add transitions such as *because of* and *as a result* to help readers see cause-and-effect connections.

**Model: Color-Coding Causes and Effects**

A generation of children is gaining weight. Instead of running and playing outside, many children sit in front of the TV, play video games or surf the Internet. While doing so, young children often eat junk food to pass the time. Because this time is so unstructured, they don't monitor how much food they are actually eating. In time, these young children are becoming very overweight.

**Use the appropriate verb tense.** Generally, you should use one verb tense consistently throughout your essay. However, to show the order of events, you may need to shift tenses. Review your draft to determine the tenses of most of your verbs. Circle any verbs that are in a different tense. If these verbs do not show events happening at different times or if they show a recurring event, consider changing them.

**Events at different times:**

Because I **missed** (past) my math test yesterday, I **need** (present) to take it today.

**Events that recur:**

Last week, I **missed** (past) French. Because I **leave** (present) school early on Wednesdays, I **miss** (present) one class every week.

### Peer Review

Ask a classmate to review your draft to help you determine whether you have logically and clearly stated cause-and-effect links.

## Revising Incorrect Use of Commas

A **comma** is a punctuation mark used to indicate a brief pause. The following examples illustrate some common misuses of commas. Misused commas are shown in red.

**Rule:** Commas separate **coordinate adjectives**—or two adjectives that modify the same noun—but not the adjective from the noun:

**Misused:** My favorite drink is a cool, refreshing, lemonade.

**Correct:** My favorite drink is a cool, refreshing lemonade.

**Rule:** Commas do not separate parts of a compound subject or object.

**Misused:** After dinner, my friend Annie, and her sister Emma, left.

**Correct:** After dinner, my friend Annie and her sister Emma left.

**Misused:** He made a sundae with whipped cream, and sprinkles.

**Correct:** He made a sundae with whipped cream and sprinkles.

**Rule:** Commas separate clauses that include both a subject and its verb, not parts of a compound verb.

**Misused:** The candidate looked out at the audience, and laughed.

**Correct:** The candidate looked out at the audience and laughed.

**Fixing Incorrect Use of Commas** Follow these rules:

1. **Add a comma or commas:**
   - before a conjunction that separates two independent clauses in a compound sentence.
   - to separate three or more words, phrases, or clauses in a series.
   - to separate coordinate adjectives.
   - to set off an introductory adverb clause.
2. **Eliminate the comma:**
   - if it comes directly between the subject and the verb of a sentence.
   - if it separates an adjective from the noun that follows it.
   - if it separates a compound subject, verb, or object.

### Grammar in Your Writing

Reread your cause-and-effect essay, noting coordinate adjectives and compound subjects, verbs, and objects. If necessary, fix the use of commas.

STUDENT MODEL: **Sarah Langsam, South Orange, NJ**

## The Invention of Cell Phones

Imagine our world today without cell phones. This portable way of communicating is a part of many people's everyday lives. If we did not have cell phones, moms would not be able to call from the store, more kids might have trouble staying in touch, and emergencies would be harder to report.

Sarah defines her topic in the first paragraph.

However people did, and still do, manage without them. Cell phones weren't invented that long ago. In 1973, Dr. Martin Cooper invented the first portable handset and soon after created the first prototype of a cellular phone. Four years later, cell phones became available to the public and cell phone testing began.

Sarah uses facts in her explanation.

What effect has the invention of cell phones had on the world? With everything in life there are pros and cons. Today, most teenagers own cell phones. This means there is no excuse for not letting a parent or guardian know where you are or for not having your cell phone charged. And of course the most important thing is never to lose your phone.

Sarah restates her topic and begins to support it with examples.

Cell phones have caused a change in our economy. Although the cost of cell phones has gone down greatly over the years, they are still very expensive. As a result, for families that are not very wealthy, owning a cell phone might affect their income badly. However, loads of money is coming in to phone companies every month from cell phone bills.

Many people say that cell phones cause a disturbance. You cannot go on a train or shop in a mall without constantly hearing phones ring and listening to other people's conversations. The effect of this is that more people are stressed and being disturbed by cell phones. Others are disturbed by not having cell phones. A teacher in school left her cell phone at school over the weekend. She was in the office on Monday recalling her story angrily, reporting that it was an awful experience and that she could not function without her phone.

Sarah gives examples to show how cell phones can be disturbing.

Although there are many negative aspects of cell phones, these items have also caused our world to be more secure. If you ask people why they first bought their cell phone, many will mention safety. Cell phones are very effective when people get into car accidents and can call "911" immediately. Parents can always know where their kids are.

The invention of cell phones has changed our lives immensely. There are positive and negative effects. However, despite the nuisance some cell phones present, I believe the safety issues cell phones solve can make us all feel a little more secure.

Sarah sums up the effects of cell phones in her conclusion.

## Editing and Proofreading

**Focus on spelling irregular plurals.**

- Change *y* to *i* and add *-es* to nouns that end in a consonant and *y (memory / memories)*.
- Do not change the *y*, but add *-s* to nouns that end in a vowel and *y* (*play / plays, key / keys*).
- For most nouns ending in *f* or *fe*, change the *f* or *fe* to *ve* and add *-s* (*elf / elves, wife / wives*).

Some nouns' base spelling changes in the plural form (*foot / feet*). Nouns that are not countable do not have plural forms (*cash*).

**Spiral Review**
Earlier in the unit, you learned about **punctuation marks** (p. 670) and **capitalization** (p. 690). Check your essay to be sure that you have used end marks correctly to punctuate your sentences.

## Publishing and Presenting

Consider one of the following ways to share your writing:

**Present a diagram.** On a posterboard or an overhead slide, create a diagram of the cause-and-effect chain in your essay.

**Produce a talk show.** Work with a partner, taking turns being a talk-show host and a guest expert. Answer questions about your topic.

## Reflecting on Your Writing

**Writer's Journal** Jot down your answer to this question:
*Which prewriting strategy was most useful for generating a topic?*

### Rubric for Self-Assessment

Find evidence in your writing to address each category. Then, use the rating scale to grade your work.

| Criteria | Rating Scale |
|---|---|
| **Purpose/Focus** Creates informative and explanatory text that examines a topic using a cause-and-effect strategy | *not very* ............ *very*<br>1 2 3 4 |
| **Organization** Organizes information to show causes and effects; writes clearly and coherently; uses formatting, graphics, and multimedia | 1 2 3 4 |
| **Development of Ideas/Elaboration** Provides support through relevant facts, definitions, concrete details, quotations, and examples; uses information from and cites several sources; maintains a formal style | 1 2 3 4 |
| **Language** Writes in a style appropriate to the task, purpose, and audience; uses transitions to clarify relationships among ideas | 1 2 3 4 |
| **Conventions** Demonstrates command of the conventions of standard English; uses commas to separate coordinate adjectives | 1 2 3 4 |

## SELECTED RESPONSE

### I. Reading Literature

**Directions:** *Read the excerpt from "Icarus and Daedalus" by Josephine Preston Peabody. Then, answer each question that follows.*

Among all those mortals who grew so wise that they learned the secrets of the gods, none was more cunning than Daedalus.

He once built, for King Minos of Crete, a wonderful Labyrinth of winding ways so cunningly tangled up and twisted around that, once inside, you could never find your way out again without a magic clue. But the king's favor veered with the wind, and one day he had his master architect imprisoned in a tower. Daedalus managed to escape from his cell; but it seemed impossible to leave the island, since every ship that came or went was well guarded by order of the king.

At length, watching the sea-gulls in the air—the only creatures that were sure of liberty—he thought of a plan for himself and his young son Icarus, who was captive with him.

Little by little, he gathered a store of feathers great and small. He fastened these together with thread, molded them in with wax, and so fashioned two great wings like those of a bird. When they were done, Daedalus fitted them to his own shoulders, and after one or two efforts, he found that by waving his arms he could winnow the air and cleave it, as a swimmer does the sea. He held himself aloft, wavered this way and that with the wind, and at last, like a great fledgling, he learned to fly.

Without delay, he fell to work on a pair of wings for the boy Icarus, and taught him carefully how to use them, bidding him beware of rash adventures among the stars. "Remember," said the father, "never to fly very low or very high, for the fogs about the earth would weigh you down, but the blaze of the sun will surely melt your feathers apart if you go too near."

For Icarus, these cautions went in at one ear and out by the other. Who could remember to be careful when he was to fly for the first time? Are birds careful? Not they! And not an idea remained in the boy's head but the one joy of escape.

1. **Part A** What type of story is "Icarus and Daedalus"?

   **A.** a legend
   **B.** a myth
   **C.** a folk tale
   **D.** a poem

   **Part B** Which detail from the story best supports the answer to Part A?

   **A.** "they learned the secrets of the gods"
   **B.** "like a great fledgling, he learned to fly"
   **C.** "you could never find your way out again without a magic clue"
   **D.** "but the king's favor veered with the wind"

2. Which answer choice expresses a **universal theme?**

   **A.** Mortals do not have magic powers.
   **B.** Birds fly by flapping their wings.
   **C.** Too much pride can lead to a fall.
   **D.** Crete is the largest of the Greek islands.

3. Which passage from the story expresses a **cause-and-effect** relationship?

   **A.** "He once built, for King Minos of Crete, a wonderful Labyrinth of winding ways . . ."
   **B.** "Little by little, he gathered a store of feathers great and small."
   **C.** ". . . the blaze of the sun will surely melt your feathers apart if you go too near.'"
   **D.** "And not an idea remained in the boy's head but the one joy of escape."

4. Which passage from the story expresses **comparison and contrast?**

   **A.** "Among all those mortals who grew so wise that they learned the secrets of the gods, none was more cunning than Daedalus."
   **B.** "But the king's favor veered with the wind, and one day he had his master architect imprisoned in a tower."
   **C.** "When they were done, Daedalus fitted them to his own shoulders . . ."
   **D.** "Without delay, he fell to work on a pair of wings for the boy Icarus . . ."

5. Which answer choice describes **cultural context?**

   **A.** customs and beliefs
   **B.** plot and setting
   **C.** dialogue and description
   **D.** facts and examples

6. Which answer choice states a key feature of stories such as this one that come from the **oral tradition?**

   **A.** The stories tell the true story of a real person's life.
   **B.** The stories were passed down orally from generation to generation.
   **C.** The stories are all set in ancient Greece.
   **D.** The stories have happy endings.

7. **Part A** Which is the best definition of the underlined word *wavered?*

   **A.** flew
   **B.** swayed
   **C.** followed
   **D.** fell

   **Part B** Which phrase from the story helps you understand the meaning of *wavered?*

   **A.** "as a swimmer does the sea"
   **B.** "He held himself"
   **C.** "this way and that"
   **D.** "he learned to fly"

## Timed Writing

8. Write your own ending to the excerpt from "Icarus and Daedelus." Develop your ending to follow logically from the events described in the excerpt and to express a **universal theme.**

## II. Reading Informational Text

**Directions:** *Read the passage. Then, answer each question that follows.*

Pet ownership is a wonderful way for children to learn responsibility. I didn't always think so, but then my daughter changed my mind.

Anna was four when she began asking for a dog. I always said no. Anna was the kind of child who "forgot" her homework and never made her bed. Whenever Anna asked for a dog, I'd tell her that she needed to be more responsible before I would feel comfortable putting her in charge of a living creature.

Then, one day a little dog followed Anna home. We put up signs, but nobody claimed the dog. It seemed like she was meant to be ours.

Anna was twelve when the lost dog we named Coco joined the family. I didn't expect her to take care of the dog without help, but I was pleasantly surprised. Anna used to dawdle on her way home from school, always taking the long way. Suddenly, she was running home to feed Coco and take her for a walk. Anna used to tease me for picking up garbage at the park. Now she carries a bag and a glove with her so she can pick up broken glass. She doesn't want Coco to cut her paws. More surprisingly, Anna has become more responsible about things that have nothing to do with Coco—things like getting dressed in the morning and remembering her homework. Anna isn't the only one who is happy that Coco followed her home. I'm happy too!

**1. Part A** What is the author's argument at the beginning of the passage?

**A.** Children should demonstrate responsibility before getting a pet.
**B.** Owning a pet can teach responsibility.
**C.** Twelve is too young to own a dog.
**D.** Children should do chores at home.

**Part B** Which of the following is a claim that supports the argument you identified in Part A?

**A.** Anna runs home from school to take care of Coco.
**B.** No one claimed the dog that followed Anna home.
**C.** Anna was four when she began asking for a dog.
**D.** Anna used to tease her mother for picking up garbage at the park.

**2.** In what order does the author present events in the passage?

**A.** in spatial order
**B.** in chronological order
**C.** in backwards order
**D.** in order of importance

**3.** For what purpose did the author most likely write this selection?

**A.** To entertain readers with stories about her daughter.
**B.** To inform pet owners about how to care for a dog.
**C.** To convince cat owners that dogs make good pets.
**D.** To persuade parents that it is beneficial for children to care for pets.

## III. Writing and Language Conventions

**Directions:** *Read the passage. Then, answer each question that follows.*

(1) October 3, 2015

(2) Dear Johnson Construction:

(3) The Red aces baseball team has not replaced its uniforms in five years. (4) A $200 donation would allow for purchasing new shirts for each team member. (5) To show our thanks and gratitude we will put the name of your business on each shirt. (6) Spectators will see that you support an organization that gives kids a positive healthful afterschool activity. (7) Please help support this talented Pleasantville team.

(8) Thank you,

(9) Joe Green

1. Which revision to sentence 4 includes an **infinitive phrase?**
   **A.** A $200 donation would mean we could purchase new shirts for each team member.
   **B.** A $200 donation would allow us to purchase new shirts for each team member.
   **C.** A $200 donation would allow for our purchasing new shirts for each team member.
   **D.** A $200 donation would allow new shirts for each team member.

2. Which of the following revisions correctly uses a **comma** and a **hyphen?**
   **A.** positive, healthful, after-school
   **B.** positive, healthful after-school
   **C.** positive healthful afterschool
   **D.** positive, health-ful afterschool

3. Which of the following revisions uses **capitalization** correctly?
   **A.** The Red Aces baseball team
   **B.** The Red Aces Baseball team
   **C.** the Red Aces baseball team
   **D.** The red aces Baseball Team

4. Which of the following revisions correctly uses a **comma?**
   **A.** To show our thanks, and gratitude, we will put the name of your business on each shirt.
   **B.** To show our thanks and gratitude, we will put the name of your business on each shirt.
   **C.** To show, our thanks and gratitude, we will put the name of your business on each shirt.
   **D.** To show our thanks and gratitude we will put the name of your business, on each shirt.

# CONSTRUCTED RESPONSE

**Directions:** *Follow the instructions to complete the tasks below as required by your teacher.*

*As you work on each task, incorporate both general academic vocabulary and literary terms you learned in Parts 1 and 2.*

## Writing

**TASK 1 Literature**

### Analyze the Use of Historical Fact in Fiction and Nonfiction

*Write an essay in which you compare and contrast the use of facts in a work of fiction and a work of nonfiction.*

- Explain that you will discuss similarities and differences in the use of facts in "Popocatepetl and Ixtlaccihuatl" and "Tenochtitlan: Inside the Aztec Capital," which you can find in your eText.
- Identify at least three facts in the article and three facts in the legend. Explain at least two similarities and differences in the ways each author uses these facts. Consider the purpose each fact serves.
- Explain whether the author of the legend has changed any facts. If so, identify how the fact was changed and state the likely purpose for the change.
- Write a thesis statement in which you present your key ideas.
- Support your thesis statement by citing specific details from the texts.
- Summarize your ideas in a conclusion.

**TASK 2 Literature**

### Analyze the Development of a Theme

*Analyze a theme in a literary work from Part 2, and write an objective summary of that story.*

- Choose a story from Part 2 to analyze. Identify a theme that the story expresses.
- Explain how the theme is developed through characters' actions and story events.
- To make sure you understand the development of the theme, write an objective summary of the story. Use your own words to retell main ideas and details.
- Include events from each part of the story to ensure completeness.
- Leave out minor details and avoid including your personal opinions.

**TASK 3 Literature**

### Analyze a Universal Theme

Write an essay in which you analyze a universal theme from a story in Part 2.

**Part 1**

- Identify a universal theme in a story in Part 2. Be sure that the theme contains a message about life that can be found in other cultures and eras.
- Take notes in which you connect the universal theme to specific details from the story, including character traits, settings, conflicts, and the changes or results of these conflicts.

**Part 2**

- Write an essay in which you explain how the same theme can be found in other works you have read.
- Cite examples from the story from Part 2 and from other stories that share its universal theme.

## Speaking and Listening

**TASK 4** Literature

### Analyze the Characters in a Folk Tale

*Plan a presentation in which you analyze character development in a folk tale in Part 2.*

- Choose a folk tale from Part 2 that features interesting and memorable characters. Identify specific details about the characters, including their personality traits, the conflicts they face, how the setting influences their choices, and what they learn as a result of their conflicts.
- Jot down details and quotations from the folk tale that contribute to character development. Plan to use these in your presentation.
- Extend the ideas in your presentation by discussing the ways in which the characters' behavior reflects the beliefs of the culture that produced the folk tale.
- Practice delivering your presentation. Use your notes for reference as you speak, but strive to make eye contact periodically with your audience.

**TASK 5** Literature

### Analyze and Discuss Theme

*Analyze a theme from a story in Part 2 and determine which customs and beliefs it reflects. Then, organize a discussion with a small group of classmates about the value of the story's message.*

- Determine the theme of a story in Part 2. Analyze how the theme is developed over the course of the story through plot events and characters' actions.
- List questions about customs and beliefs that arise as you analyze the theme. Explore one question in your analysis. Conduct research as needed.
- Evaluate whether the story still contains a meaningful message for today's readers. Support your arguments with clear and relevant reasons.
- Discuss your findings with a small group, using vocabulary that accurately expresses your ideas.

## Research

**TASK 6** Literature

### Community or individual—Which is more important?

In Part 2, you have read literature about conflicts between individuals and their communities. Now you will conduct a short research project about a current conflict that is happening between individuals and a community, such as a school or city. Use the literature you have read as well as your research to reflect on this unit's Big Question. Review the following guidelines before you begin your research:

- Focus your research on one conflict between individuals and a community.
- Gather relevant information from at least two reliable print or digital sources.
- Take notes as you research the conflict.
- Cite your sources.

When you have completed your research, write a response to the Big Question. Discuss how your initial ideas have been changed or reinforced. Support your response with an example from literature and an example from your research.

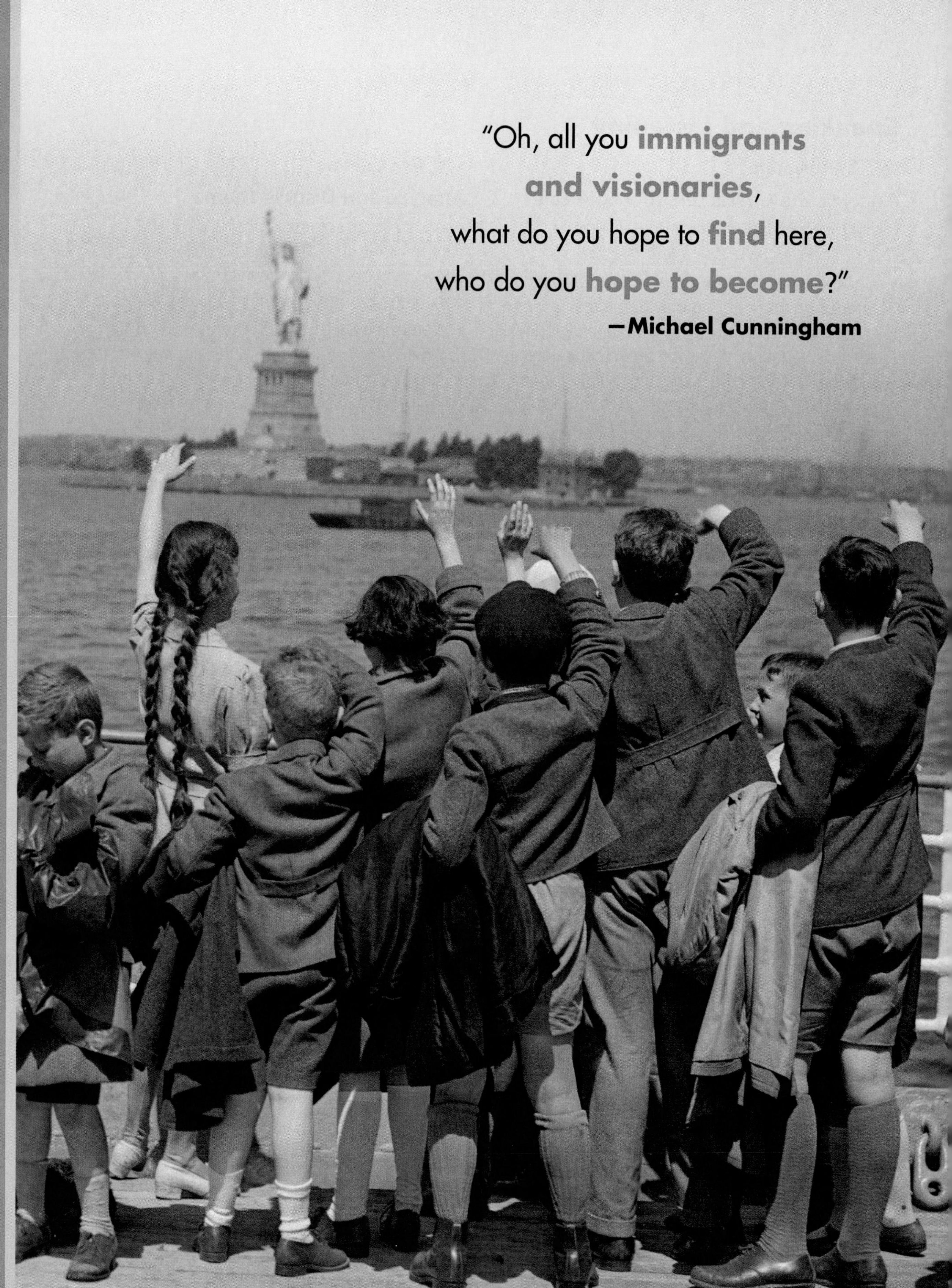
"Oh, all you immigrants
and visionaries,
what do you hope to find here,
who do you hope to become?"
—Michael Cunningham

PART 3

## TEXT SET DEVELOPING INSIGHT

# BECOMING AMERICAN

The selections in this unit all deal with the Big Question: **Community or individual—which is more important?** As you read the texts in this section, analyze the ways in which our varied backgrounds, cultures, and traditions shape our communities and help us explore what it means to become American.

◀ CRITICAL VIEWING What do you imagine are some of the hopes and dreams of the children in the photograph?

**CLOSE READING TOOL**

Use the **Close Reading Tool** to practice the strategies you learn in this unit.

## READINGS IN PART 3

# My First Free Summer

## Julia Alvarez

I never had summer—I had summer school. First grade, summer school. Second grade, summer school. Thirdgradesummerschoolfourthgradesummerschool. In fifth grade, I **vowed** I would get interested in fractions, the presidents of the United States, Mesopotamia; I would learn my English.

**vowed ▶** (voud) *v.* promised solemnly

That was the problem. English. My mother had decided to send her children to the American school so we could learn the language of the nation that would soon be liberating us. For thirty years, the Dominican Republic had endured a bloody and repressive dictatorship. From my father, who was involved in an underground plot, my mother knew that *los américanos*[1] had promised to help bring democracy to the island.

"You have to learn your English!" Mami kept scolding me.

"But why?" I'd ask. I didn't know about my father's activities. I didn't know the dictator was bad. All I knew was that my friends who were attending Dominican schools were often on holiday to honor the dictator's birthday, the dictator's saint day, the day the dictator became the dictator, the day the dictator's oldest son was born, and so on. They marched in parades and visited the palace and had their picture in the paper.

Meanwhile, I had to learn about the pilgrims with their funny witch hats, about the 50 states and where they were on the map, about Dick and Jane[2] and their tame little pets, Puff

1. **los américanos** (lōs ä meˊ rē käˊ nōs) *n.* Spanish for "the Americans."
2. **Dick and Jane** characters in a reading book commonly used by students in the 1950s.

and Spot, about freedom and liberty and justice for all—while being imprisoned in a hot classroom with a picture of a man wearing a silly wig hanging above the blackboard. And all of this learning I had to do in that impossibly difficult, rocks-in-your-mouth language of English!

Somehow, I managed to scrape by. Every June, when my prospects looked iffy, Mami and I met with the principal. I squirmed in my seat while they arranged for my special summer lessons.

"She is going to work extra hard. Aren't you, young lady?" the principal would quiz me at the end of our session.

My mother's eye on me, I'd murmur, "Yeah."

"Yes, what?" Mami coached.

"Yes." I sighed. "Sir."

It's a wonder that I just wasn't thrown out, which was what I secretly hoped for. But there were extenuating circumstances, the grounds on which the American school stood had been donated by my grandfather. In fact, it had been my grandmother who had encouraged Carol Morgan to start her school. The bulk of the student body was made up of the sons and daughters of American diplomats and business people, but a few Dominicans—most of them friends or members of my family—were allowed to attend.

"You should be grateful!" Mami scolded on the way home from our meeting. "Not every girl is lucky enough to go to the Carol Morgan School!"

In fifth grade, I straightened out. "Yes, ma'am!" I learned to say brightly. "Yes, sir!" To wave my hand in sword-wielding swoops so I could get called on with the right answer. What had changed me? Gratitude? A realization of my luckiness? No, sir! The thought of a fun summer? Yes, ma'am! I wanted to run with the pack of cousins and friends in the common yard that connected all our properties. To play on the trampoline and go off to la playa[3] and get brown as a berry. I wanted to be free. Maybe American principles had finally sunk in!

The summer of 1960 began in bliss: I did not have to go to summer school! *Attitude much improved. Her English progressing nicely. Attentive and cooperative in classroom.*

---

3. **la playa** (lä plä' yä) *n.* Spanish for "the beach."

I grinned as Mami read off the note that accompanied my report card of Bs.

But the yard replete with cousins and friends that I had dreamed about all year was deserted. Family members were leaving for the United States, using whatever connections they could drum up. The plot had unraveled. Every day there were massive arrests. The United States had closed its embassy and was advising Americans to return home.

My own parents were terrified. Every night black Volkswagens blocked our driveway and stayed there until morning. "Secret police," my older sister whispered.

"Why are they secret if they're the police?" I asked.

"Shut up!" my sister hissed. "Do you want to get us all killed?"

Day after day, I kicked a deflated beach ball around the empty yard, feeling as if I'd been tricked into good behavior by whomever God put in charge of the lives of 10-year-olds. I was bored. Even summer school would have been better than this!

One day toward the end of the summer, my mother **summoned** my sisters and me. She wore that too-bright smile she sometimes pasted on her terrified face.

**summoned ▶** (sum´ ənd) *v.* called together

"Good news, girls! Our papers and tickets came! We're leaving for the United States!"

Our mouths dropped. We hadn't been told we were going on a trip anywhere, no less to some place so far away.

I was the first to speak up, "But why?"

My mother flashed me the same look she used to give me when I'd ask why I had to learn English.

I was about to tell her that I didn't want to go to the United States, where summer school had been invented and everyone spoke English. But my mother lifted a hand for silence. "We're leaving in a few hours. I want you all to go get ready! I'll be in to pack soon." The desperate look in her eyes did not allow for **contradiction**. We raced off, wondering how to fit the contents of our Dominican lives into four small suitcases.

**contradiction ▶** (kän´ trə dik´ shən) *n.* difference between two conflicting things that means they both cannot be true

Our flight was scheduled for that afternoon, but the airplane did not appear. The terminal lined with soldiers wielding machine guns, checking papers, escorting passengers into a small interrogation room. Not everyone returned.

"It's a trap," I heard my mother whisper to my father.

This had happened before, a cat-and-mouse game the dictator liked to play. Pretend that he was letting someone go, and then at the last minute, their family and friends conveniently gathered together—wham! The secret police would haul the whole clan away.

Of course, I didn't know that this was what my parents were dreading. But as the hours ticked away, and afternoon turned into evening and evening into night and night into midnight with no plane in sight, a light came on in my head. If the light could be translated into words, instead, they would say: Freedom and liberty and justice for all . . . I knew that ours was not a trip, but an escape. We had to get to the United States.

The rest of that night is a blur. It is one, then two the next morning. A plane lands, lights flashing. We are walking on the runway, climbing up the stairs into the cabin. An American lady wearing a cap welcomes us. We sit down, ready to depart. But suddenly, soldiers come on board. They go seat by seat, looking at our faces. Finally, they leave, the door closes, and with a powerful roar we lift off and I fall asleep.

Next morning, we are standing inside a large, echoing hall as a stern American official reviews our documents. What if he doesn't let us in? What if we have to go back? I am holding my breath. My parents' terror has become mine.

He checks our faces against the passport pictures. When he is done, he asks, "You girls ready for school?" I swear he is looking at me.

"Yes, sir!" I speak up.

The man laughs. He stamps our papers and hands them to my father. Then wonderfully, a smile spreads across his face. "Welcome to the United States," he says, waving us in.

## ABOUT THE AUTHOR

### Julia Alvarez (b. 1950)

Shortly after her birth, Julia Alvarez moved from New York City to the Dominican Republic with her family. When Alvarez was ten years old, however, her family was forced to return to the United States because her father was involved in a failed rebellion against the country's dictator, Rafael L. Trujillo. Alvarez had trouble adjusting to her new home. Turning inward, she began to read books and to write. Later, she said, "I fell in love with how words can make you feel complete in a way that I hadn't felt complete since leaving the island."

# Close Reading Activities

## READ

### Comprehension

Reread all or part of the text to help you answer the following questions.

1. What is the setting of the essay?
2. What historical conflict is described in the essay?
3. How did Alvarez usually spend her summers? Why?
4. What happened in the summer after Alvarez completed fifth grade?

**Research: Clarify Details** Choose at least one unfamiliar detail or reference and briefly research it. Then, explain how the information you learned from your research helped you understand an aspect of the essay.

**Summarize** Write an objective summary of the essay. Remember that an objective summary is free from opinion and evaluation.

### Language Study

**Selection Vocabulary** The following sentences appear in "My First Free Summer." Define each boldfaced word, and then use the word in a sentence of your own.

- In fifth grade, I **vowed** I would get interested in fractions ...
- One day toward the end of the summer, my mother **summoned** my sisters and me.
- The desperate look in her eyes did not allow for **contradiction**.

**Diction and Style** Study the following sentences from the essay. Then, answer the questions that follow.

> I wanted to run with the pack of cousins and friends. ... To play on the trampoline and go off to la playa and get brown as a berry. I wanted to be free. Maybe American principles had finally sunk in!

1. What does the word *free* mean to Alvarez at age 10?
2. At this point in her life, what is Alvarez's understanding of "American principles"?

**Conventions** Read this passage from the essay. Identify and label the punctuation marks. Then, explain how the author's use of varied punctuation adds meaning to the passage.

> In fifth grade, I straightened out. "Yes, ma'am!" I learned to say brightly. "Yes, sir!" To wave my hand in sword-wielding swoops so I could get called on with the right answer. What had changed me? Gratitude? A realization of my luckiness? No, sir! The thought of a fun summer? Yes, ma'am!

### Academic Vocabulary

The following words appear in blue in the instructions and questions on the facing page.

**explain** **perspective** **strategy**

Decide whether you know each word well, know it a little bit, or do not know it at all. Then, look up the definitions of the words you do not know well or do not know at all.

## Literary Analysis

Reread the identified passages. Then, respond to the following questions.

**Focus Passage 1** *(p. 728)*
That was the problem … had their picture in the paper.

**Key Ideas and Details**

1. **(a)** Why does Alvarez's mother send her to the American school? **(b) Contrast:** How does this school differ from other schools on the island?
2. **Infer:** Why does Alvarez initially dismiss the importance of learning English?

**Craft and Structure**

3. **(a)** What information does Alvarez list in the sentence that begins, "All I knew was …" **(b) Analyze: Explain** the effect of the repeated use of the word *dictator* in this sentence.
4. **(a) Distinguish:** Does Alvarez write from the **perspective** of her young self or her adult self? **(b) Interpret:** How does this perspective add meaning to the passage?

**Integration of Knowledge and Ideas**

5. **Speculate:** Why do you think Alvarez's parents did not tell their children about their father's involvement in an underground plot?

**Focus Passage 2** *(pp. 730–731)*
This had happened before … We had to get to the United States.

**Key Ideas and Details**

1. **(a)** What do Alvarez's parents fear? **(b) Draw Conclusions:** Do they have a legitimate reason to be afraid? Use details from the text to support your answer.

**Craft and Structure**

2. **(a)** Explain the use of parallel structure in the sentence that begins, "But as the hours …" **(b) Interpret:** How does this structure add meaning to the passage?
3. **(a)** What term does Alvarez use to describe the dictator's **strategy**? **(b) Analyze:** How does this figurative language illustrate the nature of the family's situation?

**Integration of Knowledge and Ideas**

4. **(a) Hypothesize:** What might Alvarez want readers to learn from this story? **(b) Support:** What details in the essay support your answer?

## Symbolism

A **symbol** is an object or idea that represents something other than itself. For example, spring can be a symbol of hope or rebirth. Reread the essay, and take notes on how the author uses symbolism.

1. What does summer symbolize for Alvarez?
2. Why do you think Alvarez titled her essay "My First Free Summer"?
3. **Becoming American** Identify symbols in the essay that relate to the idea of becoming American.

## DISCUSS

### From Text to Topic **Group Discussion**

Discuss the following passage with a group of classmates. Take notes during the discussion. Contribute your own ideas, and support them with examples from the text.

> Meanwhile, I had to learn about the pilgrims with their funny witch hats, about the 50 states and where they were on the map, about Dick and Jane and their tame little pets, Puff and Spot, about freedom and liberty and justice for all—while being in a hot classroom with a picture of a man wearing a silly wig hanging above the blackboard. And all of this learning I had to do in that impossibly difficult, rocks-in-your-mouth language of English!

**QUESTIONS FOR DISCUSSION**

1. How do phrases such as "funny witch hats" and "silly wig" develop Alvarez's feelings about American history and culture?
2. Why is American school difficult for Alvarez?

## WRITE

### Writing to Sources **Informative Text**

**Assignment**

Write a **comparison-and-contrast essay** in which you analyze the changes Alvarez goes through during the time period she describes in "My First Free Summer." Examine similarities and differences between Alvarez's feelings, motivations, and actions at the beginning and at the end of her narrative.

**Prewriting and Planning** Reread the essay, looking for details that describe Alvarez's feelings, motivations, and actions. Record your notes in a two-column chart listing details from before her family moved to the U.S. on one side and details from after they moved on the other side.

**Drafting** Review your notes to find the main focus for your essay. Then, write a sentence that sums up your main idea. Include this sentence in your introduction, and elaborate on it in the body of your essay. As you draft, cite specific examples from the essay to support your key points.

**Revising** Reread your essay to make sure you have supported your key ideas with evidence from the text.

**Editing and Proofreading** Make sure that you have used adjectives correctly. Comparative adjectives, such as *older* and *more,* compare two things. Superlative adjectives, such as *oldest* and *most,* compare three or more things.

**CONVENTIONS**

Like adverbs, adverbial clauses modify verbs, adjectives, and adverbs. Adverbial clauses are introduced by subordinate conjunctions such as *before, since,* and *as.* An introductory adverbial phrase is usually followed by a comma.

# RESEARCH

## Research **Investigate the Topic**

**Politics and Becoming American** Alvarez's family had to flee the Dominican Republic because her father was part of a failed rebellion against the country's brutal dictator, Rafael L. Trujillo. Like Alvarez's family, many people come to the United States hoping to escape political oppression that threatens their physical safety.

**Assignment**

Conduct research to learn different reasons that people immigrate to the United States. Then, choose a past or current political situation (such as Trujillo's dictatorship) on which to focus. Consult primary, government, and historical sources. Take clear notes and carefully identify your sources so that you can easily access the information later. Share your findings in an **oral presentation** for the class.

**PREPARATION FOR ESSAY**

You may use the knowledge you gain during this research assignment to support your claims in an essay you will write at the end of this section.

**Gather Sources** Locate authoritative print and electronic sources. Primary sources, such as letters, journals, diaries, or memoirs, provide authentic firsthand information. You should also use secondary sources, such as government and historical Web sites, especially those that compile information about immigrants. Look for sources that feature expert authors and up-to-date information.

**Take Notes** Take notes on each source, either electronically or on notecards. Use an organized note-taking strategy:

- Review past and current political situations that have caused people to emigrate and choose one to use as the focus for your presentation.
- Find appropriate sources and use a separate set of notecards for each source. Record source information to use in citations.
- In your notes, use quotation marks around direct quotations from your sources to avoid accidental plagiarism.

**Synthesize Multiple Sources** Assemble data from your sources and organize it into a cohesive presentation. Use your notes to construct an outline for your presentation. Create a Works Cited list as described in the Citing Sources pages in the Introductory Unit of this textbook.

**Organize and Present Ideas** Review your outline and practice delivering your presentation. Be ready to respond to questions from your audience.

# How I Learned English

Gregory Djanikian

It was in an empty lot
Ringed by elms and fir and honeysuckle.
Bill Corson was pitching in his buckskin[1] jacket,
Chuck Keller, fat even as a boy, was on first,
His t-shirt riding up over his gut,
Ron O'Neill, Jim, Dennis, were talking it up
In the field, a blue sky above them
Tipped with cirrus.[2]
And there I was,
Just off the plane and plopped in the middle
Of Williamsport, Pa., and a neighborhood game,
Unnatural and without any moves,
My **notions** of baseball and America
Growing fuzzier each time I whiffed.[3]

**notions** ▶ (nō´shənz) *n.* general ideas

So it was not impossible that I,
Banished to the outfield and daydreaming
Of water, or a hotel in the mountains,
Would suddenly find myself in the path
Of a ball stung[4] by Joe Barone.
I watched it closing in
Clean and untouched, **transfixed**
By its easy arc before it hit
My forehead with a thud.
I fell back.

**transfixed** ▶ (trans fikst´) *adj.* rooted to the spot

1. **buckskin** *adj.* yellowish-gray leather made from the hide of a deer.
2. **cirrus** (sir´ əs) *n.* high, thin clouds.
3. **whiffed** (hwift) *v.* struck out.
4. **stung** *v.* hit hard.

Dazed, clutching my brow,
Groaning, "Oh my shin, oh my shin,"
And everybody peeled away from me
And dropped from laughter, and there we were,
All of us **writhing** on the ground for one reason
Or another.
                    Someone said "shin" again,
There was a wild stamping of hands on the ground,
A kicking of feet, and the fit
Of laughter overtook me too,
And that was important, as important
As Joe Barone asking me how I was
Through his tears, picking me up
And dusting me off with hands like swatters,
And though my head felt heavy,
I played on till dusk
Missing flies and pop-ups and grounders
And calling out in desperation things like
"Yours" and "take it," but doing all right,
Tugging at my cap in just the right way,
Crouching low, my feet set,
"Hum baby" sweetly on my lips.

◀ **writhing**
(rīth′ iŋ) *v.* squirming, often in response to pain

## ABOUT THE AUTHOR

### Gregory Djanikian (b. 1949)

Born in Alexandria, Egypt, Gregory Djanikian moved to the United States with his family when he was eight years old. Since 1983, he has been a creative writing professor, as well as the head of the Creative Writing Department, at the University of Pennsylvania in Philadelphia. Djanikian's poetry has been published in many journals and magazines, and he is the author of five books of poetry. He has received many awards and honors, including a National Endowment for the Arts fellowship. "How I Learned English" is from his 1989 poetry collection *Falling Deeply into America*.

# Close Reading Activities

## READ

### Comprehension

Reread as needed to answer the questions.

1. Where is the poem set?
2. What happens to the speaker in the outfield?
3. What happens after the boys start laughing?

**Research: Clarify Details** Choose an unfamiliar detail from the poem and research it. Then, explain how your research helped you understand the poem.

**Summarize** Write an objective summary of the poem.

### Language Study

**Selection Vocabulary** Write a synonym or an antonym for each boldfaced word.

- My **notions** of baseball and America/ Growing fuzzier each time I whiffed.
- Clean and untouched, **transfixed**/By its easy arc before it hit/My forehead with a thud.
- All of us **writhing** on the ground for one reason/Or another.

### Literary Analysis

Reread the identified passage. Then, respond to the following questions.

**Focus Passage** *(pp. 736–737)*

So it was not impossible … one reason/ Or another.

#### Key Ideas and Details

1. **(a) Infer:** Why might the speaker be "daydreaming / Of water, or a hotel in the mountains"? **(b) Interpret:** What might make it difficult for the speaker to focus on the game?
2. What happens to the speaker in this stanza?

#### Craft and Structure

3. **(a) Determine:** How is line 24 different from the other lines in the stanza?
   **(b) Analyze:** Why might the poet have presented this line in a different way?

#### Integration of Knowledge and Ideas

4. **(a) Infer:** Why does the speaker groan, "Oh my shin, oh my shin"? **(b) Analyze:** What is the effect of these words?
   **(c) Interpret:** How does the incident that is described in this stanza change the speaker's **relationship** to the other players?

### Narrative Poem

A **narrative poem** is a story told in verse. Narrative poetry includes elements of short stories.

1. **(a)** How does the poet describe the speaker? **(b)** What do these descriptions show the reader?
2. **Becoming American (a)** What is the main conflict in the poem? **(b)** How does the resolution help the speaker "become American"?

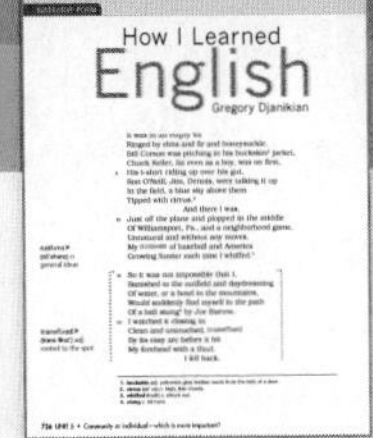

# DISCUSS • RESEARCH • WRITE

## From Text to Topic **Partner Discussion**

Discuss the following passage with a partner. Take notes during the discussion. Contribute your own ideas, and support them with examples from the text.

> Someone said "shin" again ... And dusting me off with hands like swatters, (p. 737)

### QUESTIONS FOR DISCUSSION

1. Why does the speaker think it is important that he joined in the laughter?
2. How might the outcome of the day have been different if the speaker had not been hit in the head or if he had been angered by the boys' laughter?

## Research **Investigate the Topic**

**Help in "Becoming American"** The speaker of Djanikian's poem learns some English and absorbs American culture on the baseball field. Today, recent immigrants can find help in many places in their quest to "become American."

**Assignment**

Conduct research to find resources that help recent immigrants to the United States learn about their new home. Consult the websites of government agencies and cultural organizations. Share your findings in a brief **research report.**

### PREPARATION FOR ESSAY

You may use the results of your research to support your ideas in the essay you will write at the end of this section.

## Writing to Sources **Narrative**

In "How I Learned English," the speaker describes a situation in which he felt as if he did not fit in. Everyone has felt that way at one time or another.

**Assignment**

Write an **autobiographical narrative** in which you describe a time when you felt like you did not fit in. Follow these steps:

- Introduce the time, place, and situation.
- **Explain** why you felt that you did not fit in. Then, describe how the situation turned out.
- Use the elements of a short story—plot, conflict, characterization, and dialogue—to make your experience "come alive" for the reader.
- In your conclusion, explain what you learned from the experience. Make connections between your situation and that of the poem's speaker.

### ACADEMIC VOCABULARY

Academic terms appear in blue on these pages. If these words are not familiar to you, use a dictionary to find their definitions.

# mk

Jean Fritz

I suspect for most of us MKs[1] China not only sharpened our sense of time but our sense of place. We always knew where we were in relation to the rest of the world. And we noticed. Perhaps because we knew we would be leaving China sometime (we wouldn't be MKs or even Ks forever), we developed the habit of observing our surroundings with care. We have strong memories, which explains why as an adult, walking along a beach in Maine, I suddenly found myself on the verge of tears. In front of me, pushing up from the crevice of a rock, was a wild bluebell[2] like the wild bluebells I had known in my summers at Kuling.[3] Suddenly I was a child again. I was back in China, welcoming bluebells back in my life.

For a long time it was hard for me to unscramble the strings that made up my quest. I have noticed, however, that those MKs who were born in China and stayed there through their high school years were more likely to commit their lives in some way to China. After finishing their higher education in the States, they would return to China as consuls, as teachers, as businessmen and women, as writers, as historians.

I wouldn't be staying through high school. My family planned to return to America when I had finished seventh grade, whether I was finished with China or not. Of course I knew I had to become an American, the sooner the better. So far away from America, I didn't feel like a real American. Nor would I, I thought, until I had put my feet down on American soil.

1. **MKs** (em′ kāz′) *n.* Missionary Kids; the children of missionaries.
2. **bluebell** (blo͞o′ bel′) *n.* plant with blue, bell-shaped flowers.
3. **Kuling** (ko͞ol′ iŋ) *n.* now called Lushan, a hill resort south of the Yangtze River in China.

I had just finished sixth grade at the British School in Wuhan,[4] so I would have one more year to go. Nothing would change that. I knew that there was fighting up and down the Yangtze River, but the Chinese were always fighting—warlord against warlord.[5] That had nothing to do with me. But as soon as I saw the servant from next door racing toward our house with a message for my mother, I knew something was happening. Since we had no phone, we depended on our German neighbors for emergency messages. My father had called, the servant explained. All American women and children had to catch the afternoon boat to Shanghai.[6] The army, which had done so much damage to Nanjing (just down the river), was on its way here.

As I helped my mother pack, my knees were shaking. I had only felt this once before. My mother and I had been in a ricksha on the way to the racecourse when farmers ran to the road, calling hateful words at us and throwing stones. The ricksha-pullers were fast runners, so we weren't hurt, but I told myself this was like Stephen in the Bible who was stoned to death. He just didn't have a ricksha handy. By the time we reached the boat that afternoon, my knees were normal. So was I. And I knew what our plans were. My father and other American men would work in the daytime, but for safety at night they would board one of the gunboats anchored in the river. The women and children going to Shanghai would be protected from bullets by steel barriers erected around the deck. And when we reached Shanghai, then what? I asked my mother.

---

4. **Wuhan** (wo͞o′ hän′) *n.* city in the central part of China, near the Yangtze River.
5. **warlord** (wôr′ lôrd′) *n.* military commander who exercises power by force.
6. **Shanghai** (shaŋ′ hī′) *n.* seaport in eastern China.

We would be staying with the Barretts, another missionary family, who had one son, Fletcher, who was two years younger than I and generally unlikable. Mr. Barrett met us in Shanghai and drove us to their home, where his wife was on the front porch. My mother greeted her warmly but I just held out my hand and said, "Hello, Mrs. Barrett," which I thought was adequate. She raised her eyebrows. "Have you become so grown up, Jean," she said, "that I'm no longer your 'Auntie Barrett'?"

◀ **adequate** (ad′ i kwət) *adj.* enough

I didn't say that I'd always been too grown up for the "auntie" business. I just smiled. In China all MKs called their parents' friends "auntie" or "uncle." Not me. Mrs. B. pushed Fletcher forward.

"Fletcher has been so excited about your visit, Jean," she said. "He has lots of games to show you. Now, run along, children."

Fletcher did have a lot of games. He decided what we'd play—rummy, then patience, while he talked a blue streak. I didn't pay much attention until, in the middle of an Uncle Wiggley game, he asked me a question.

"Have you ever been in love, Jean?" he asked.

What did he think I was? I was twelve years old, for heaven's sakes!

Ever since first grade I'd been in love with someone. The boys never knew it, of course.

Fletcher hadn't finished with love. "I'm in love now," he said. "I'll give you a hint. She's an MK."

"Naturally."

"And she's pretty." Then he suddenly shrieked out the answer as if he couldn't contain it a second longer. "It's you," he cried. "Y-O-U."

Well, Fletcher Barrett was even dumber than I'd thought. No one had ever called me "pretty" before. Not even my parents. Besides, this conversation was making me sick. "I'm tired," I said. "I think I'll get my book and lie down."

At the last minute I had slipped my favorite book in my suitcase. It was one my father and I had read last year—*The Courtship of Miles Standish*[7]—all about the first settlers in America. I knew them pretty well now and often visited with Priscilla Alden.

---

7. ***The Courtship of Miles Standish*** *n.* narrative poem by Henry Wadsworth Longfellow, written in 1858. One character in the poem is Priscilla Alden.

Settled on the bed in the room I'd been told was mine, I opened the book and let the Pilgrims step off the *Mayflower* into Shanghai. Priscilla was one of the first.

"You're still a long way from Plymouth," I told her, "but you'll get there. Think you'll like it?"

"I know I will," she answered promptly. "Everything will be better there."

"How do you know?"

"It's a new country. It will be whatever we make it."

"It may be hard," I warned her.

"Maybe," she admitted. "But I'll never give up. Neither will John," she added.

I was being called for supper. I waited for the Pilgrims to get back on the *Mayflower*. Then I closed the book and went downstairs.

The days that followed, I spent mostly with Fletcher, whether I liked it or not. Fletcher was fussing now that the summer was almost over and he'd have to go back to school soon.

"I thought you'd like it," I said. "After all, it's an American school and you're an American."

"So what?"

"Don't you feel like an American when you're in school?"

"What's there to feel?"

He was impossible. If he had gone to a British school, the way I had all my life, he might realize how lucky he was. The Shanghai American School was famous. Children from all over China were sent there to be boarders. Living in Shanghai, Fletcher was just a day student. But even so!

Then one day my mother got a letter from my father. The danger was mostly over, he thought, but some foreign businesses were not reopening. The British School had closed down. (Good news!)

The Yangtze River boats went back in service the next week, so my mother went downtown to buy our tickets back to Wuhan. Fletcher was back in school now, and as soon as he came home, he rushed to see me, his face full of news.

"Your mother is only buying one ticket," he informed me. "You're not going. You're going to the Shanghai American School as a boarder."

"My mother would never do that. You're crazy," I replied. "Where did you get such an idea?"

"I overheard our mothers talking. It's true, Jean."

"Yeah, like cows fly."

When my mother came back, I could see that she was upset. Fletcher did a disappearing act; I figured he didn't want to be caught in a lie.

"Oh, I'm sorry, Jean," my mother said, her eyes filling with tears. She put her arms around me. "Since the British School is closed," she said, "I've arranged for you to be a boarder at the American School. It won't be for long. We may even go back to America early. At least I'll know you're safe."

I knew my mother was worried that I'd be homesick, so I couldn't let on how I really felt. (Just think, I told myself, I'd have almost a year to practice being an American.) I buried my head on her shoulder. "I'll be okay," I said, sniffing back fake tears. Sometimes it's necessary to **deceive** your parents if you love them, and I did love mine.

◀ **deceive** (dē sēv′) *v.* make someone believe something that is not true

After my mother left on the boat, Mr. Barrett took me to the Shanghai American School (SAS for short). I guess I expected some kind of immediate transformation. I always felt a

▲ **Jean Fritz (center, in white) and her classmates.**

tingling when I saw the American flag flying over the American consulate. Surely it would be more than a tingling now; surely it would overwhelm me. But when we went through the iron gates of the school grounds, I didn't feel a thing. On the football field a group of high school girls were practicing cheerleading. They were jumping, standing on their hands, yelling rah, rah, rah. It just seemed like a lot of fuss about football. What was the matter with me?

The dormitory where I'd be living was divided in half by a swinging door. The high school girls were on one side of the door; the junior high (which included me) were on the other. On my side there were two Russian girls and two American MKs, the Johnson sisters, who had long hair braided and wound around their heads like Sunday school teachers. And there was Paula, my American roommate, who looked as though she belonged on the other side of the door. Hanging in our shared closet I noticed a black velvet dress. And a pair of high heeled shoes. She wore them to tea dances, she explained, when one of her brother's friends came to town. She was squinting her eyes as she looked at me, sizing up my straight hair and bangs.

"I happen to know you're an MK," she said, "but you don't have to look like one." The latest style in the States, she told me, was a boyish bob.[8] She'd give me one, she decided.

So that night she put a towel around my shoulders and newspaper on the floor, and she began cutting. This might make all the difference, I thought, as I watched my hair travel to the floor.

8. **bob** (bäb) *n.* woman's or child's short haircut.

It didn't. My ears might have felt more American, but not me. After being in hiding all their lives, my ears were suddenly outdoors, looking like jug handles on each side of my face. I'd get used to them, I told myself. Meanwhile I had to admit that SAS was a big improvement over the British School. Even without an American flag feeling, I enjoyed the months I was there.

What I enjoyed most were the dances, except they weren't dances. There were too many MKs in the school, and the Ms didn't approve of dancing. Instead, we had "talk parties." The girls were given what looked like dance cards and the boys were supposed to sign up for the talk sessions they wanted. Of course a girl could feel like a wallflower[9] if her card wasn't filled up, but mine usually was. These parties gave me a chance to look over the boys in case I wanted to fall in love, and actually I was almost ready to make a choice when my parents suddenly appeared. It was early spring. Just as my mother had suspected, we were going to America early.

I knew that three weeks crossing the Pacific would be different from five days on the Yangtze but I didn't know how different. My father had given me a gray-and-green plaid steamer rug that I would put over me when I was lying on my long folding deck chair. At eleven o'clock every morning a waiter would come around with a cup of "beef tea." I loved the idea of drinking beef tea under my steamer rug but it didn't happen often. The captain said this was the roughest crossing he'd ever made, and passengers spent most of their time in their cabins. If they came out for a meal, they were lucky if they could get it down before it came back up again. I had my share of seasickness, so of course I was glad to reach San Francisco.

I couldn't wait to take my first steps on American soil, but I expected the American soil to hold still for me. Instead, it swayed as if we were all still at sea, and I lurched about as I had been doing for the last three weeks. I noticed my parents were having difficulty, too. "Our heads and our legs aren't ready for land," my father explained. "It takes a little while." We spent the night in a hotel and took a train the next day for Pittsburgh where our relatives were meeting us.

It was a three-day trip across most of the continent, but it didn't seem long. Every minute America was under us and rushing past our windows—the Rocky Mountains, the

---

9. **wallflower** (wôl′ flou′ ər) *n.* person who stands against the wall and watches at a dance due to shyness or lack of popularity.

Mississippi river, flat ranch land, small towns, forests, boys dragging school bags over dusty roads. It was all of America at once splashed across where we were, where we'd been, where we were going. How could you not feel American? How could you not feel that you belonged? By the time we were settled at my grandmother's house, I felt as if I'd always been a part of this family. And wasn't it wonderful to have real aunts and uncles, a real grandmother, and yes, even a real bathroom, for heaven's sakes?

I wanted to talk to Priscilla, so I took my book outside, and when I opened it, out tumbled the Pilgrims, Priscilla first. I smiled. Here we were, all of us in America together, and it didn't matter that we came from different times. We all knew that America was still an experiment and perhaps always would be. I was one of the ones who had to try to make the experiment work.

"You'll have disappointments," Priscilla said. "But it will help if you get to know Americans who have spent their lives working on the experiment."

I wasn't sure just what she meant, but I knew it was important. "I'll try," I said.

"Try!" Priscilla scoffed. "If you want to be a real American, you'll have to do more than that." Her voice was fading. Indeed, the Pilgrims themselves were growing faint. Soon they had all slipped away.

I learned about disappointment as soon as I went to school. Of course I was no longer an MK, but I was certainly a curiosity. I was the Kid from China. "Did you live in a mud hut?" one boy asked me. "Did you eat rats and dogs? Did you eat with sticks?"

**ignorant ▶** (ig´ nə rənt) *adj.* not knowing facts or information

I decided that American children were **ignorant**. Didn't their teachers teach them anything? After a while, as soon as anyone even mentioned China, I shut up. "What was the name of your hometown?" I was asked, but I never told. I couldn't bear to have my hometown laughed at.

"Not all American children are ignorant," my mother pointed out. "Just a few who ask dumb questions."

Even in high school, however, I often got the same questions. But now we were studying about the American Revolution and George Washington. Of course I'd always known who Washington was, but knowing history and understanding it are two different things. I had never realized how much he had done to make America into America. No matter how much he was asked to do for his country, he did it, even though he could hardly wait to go back home and be a farmer again. Of course there were disappointments on the way; of course he became discouraged. "If I'd known what I was getting into," he said at the beginning of the Revolution, "I would have chosen to live in an Indian teepee all my life." He never took the easiest way. When he thought his work was over at the end of the Revolution, he agreed to work on the Constitution. When the country needed a president, he took the oath of office. When his term was over, he was persuaded to run once again. Everyone had confidence that as long as he was there, the new government would work.

Although Washington was the first, there were many more like him who were, as Priscilla would say, "real" Americans. As I went through college and read about them, I knew I wanted to write about them someday. I might not talk to them in the same way I talked to Priscilla, but I would try to make them as real as they were when they were alive.

I had the feeling that I was coming to the end of my quest. But not quite. One day when someone asked me where I was born, I found myself smiling. I was for the moment standing beside the Yangtze River. "My hometown," I said, "was Wuhan, China." I discovered that I had to take China with me wherever I went.

## ABOUT THE AUTHOR

### Jean Fritz (b. 1915)

An only child of missionary parents, Jean Fritz spent the first thirteen years of her life in China. Although she had not yet been to the United States, she read and heard from her father about American heroes, such as George Washington and Teddy Roosevelt. Her fascination with these heroes inspired her career as a writer of American history. Fritz fills her biographies with unusual but true details about her subjects, which she researches thoroughly. "History is full of gossip; it's real people and emotion," she says. The details make her books about historical figures, such as Pocahontas or Sam Adams, spring to life. Fritz has received many awards and honors over her long career. In 1983, her autobiography *Homesick: My Own Story*—from which "mk" comes—won a National Book Award and was named a Newbery Honor Book.

# Close Reading Activities

## READ

### Comprehension

Reread as needed to answer the questions.

1. What is an "MK"?
2. Why does Fritz's family move in with the Barretts?
3. What happens to Fritz when the British School closes?

**Research: Clarify Details** Choose an unfamiliar detail from the autobiography, and conduct research to learn more about it.

**Summarize** Write an objective summary of the autobiography. Remember to leave out your opinions and evaluations.

### Language Study

**Selection Vocabulary** For each boldfaced word, write its definition and list two other words in the same word family (example: *express, expressive, expression*).

- **adequate**
- **deceive**
- **ignorant**

### Literary Analysis

Reread the identified passage.

**Focus Passage** *(p. 744)*

Settled on the bed in the room I'd been told was mine, . . . . "But I'll never give up. Neither will John," she added.

#### Key Ideas and Details

1. To whom is Fritz speaking in this passage?
2. **Connect:** What does Fritz have in common with this person?

#### Craft and Structure

3. **Analyze:** Fritz writes, *I opened the book and let the Pilgrims step off the Mayflower into Shanghai.* What idea do these words **communicate**?

#### Integration of Knowledge and Ideas

4. **(a) Draw Conclusions:** What does this conversation reveal about Fritz's concerns about moving to America? **(b) Predict:** Based on this conversation, would you **predict** that Fritz will adjust well to her new home in the U.S.? Why or why not?

### Narration

**Narration** is the act or **process** of telling a story. Take notes on the narration in this autobiography.

1. **(a)** What is the point of view of the selection? **(b)** How does this point of view help readers learn about Fritz?
2. **Becoming American** The order of events is important in narration. **(a)** What is the first thing Fritz sees as she goes through the iron gates of the Shanghai American School? **(b)** Why is this information important to the story?

# DISCUSS • RESEARCH • WRITE

## From Text to Topic **Group Discussion**

Discuss the following passage with a group of classmates. Take notes during the discussion. Contribute your own ideas, and support them with examples from the text.

> I had the feeling that I was coming to the end of my quest. . . . I discovered that I had to take China with me wherever I went. (p. 749)

### QUESTIONS FOR DISCUSSION

1. Why did Fritz avoid naming her hometown in China at first?
2. Why was she finally able to name her hometown?

## Research **Investigate the Topic**

**American Literature** "The Courtship of Miles Standish" is a long narrative poem by American poet Henry Wadsworth Longfellow.

**Assignment**

Conduct research to find out why "The Courtship of Miles Standish" is important to American literature. Consult literary and historical sources. Review a plot summary, and read at least part of the poem to get a feel for the language. Consider why Fritz was attracted to this poem as an American child living in China. Write a **short research paper** in which you share your findings.

### PREPARATION FOR ESSAY

You may use the results of your research to support your ideas in the essay you will write at the end of this section.

## Writing to Sources **Explanatory Text**

In "mk," Jean Fritz describes her experiences as a "missionary kid" who does not move to America until she is thirteen years old.

**Assignment**

Write a **comparison-and-contrast essay** in which you examine Fritz's feelings about America before and after she arrives in the United States. Follow these steps:

- Review "mk" and gather story details in a two-column chart. In the first column, list details that show Fritz's thoughts and feelings about America when she was living in China. In the second column, list her thoughts and feelings when she lived in the U.S.
- First, write an engaging introduction. Then, in the body of your essay, organize the information from your chart to show clear comparisons and contrasts.
- Sum up your main idea in a strong concluding paragraph.

### ACADEMIC VOCABULARY

Academic terms appear in blue on these pages. If these words are not familiar to you, use a dictionary to find their definitions. Then, use the words as you speak and write about the text.

The Statue of Liberty - Ellis Island Foundation, Inc.

# Byron Yee: Discovering a Paper Son

Angel Island, San Francisco

For actor Byron Yee, family history provides the inspiration for his one-man show. "My name is Byron Yee. I am the second son of Bing Quai Yee. I am the son of a paper son.

"My father was an immigrant. He came to America to escape the Japanese invasion of China in 1938. He was 15 years old and he didn't know a word of English. He didn't have a penny in his pocket and he was living in a crowded apartment in New York City with relatives he had never met. I know nothing about my father's history, about his past."

**decipher ▸** (dē sī′ fər) *v.* make out the meaning of

With little to go on, Byron set out to **decipher** his father's story. He started at Angel Island, located in the middle of San Francisco Bay. "Angel Island has been called the Ellis Island of the West and for the most part, all the Chinese who came to the United States came through here, from a period of 1910 to 1940. But the rules were a little bit different. European settlers, Russian settlers were processed within an hour. The Japanese were kept for one day. But the Chinese were detained anywhere from three weeks to two years for their **interrogations**. So this was not so much the Ellis Island of the West for the Chinese; it was more like Alcatraz."

**interrogations ▸** (in ter′ ə gā′ shənz) *n.* formal examinations that involve questioning the subject

In 1882, Congress passed a law prohibiting Chinese laborers from immigrating to the United States. The Chinese Exclusion Act was the only immigration law ever based on race alone. But people found ways around the act: U.S. law states that children of American citizens are automatically granted citizenship themselves, no matter where they were born. Taking advantage of that opening, some immigrants claimed to be legitimate offspring of U.S. citizens when in fact they were not. These individuals, mostly male, were called paper sons.

Byron's next step was to find his father's immigration file. The National Archives regional office in San Bruno, California contains thousands of files related to Angel Island. While Byron did not find his father's records there, he did find those of his grandfather, Yee Wee Thing. In one of the documents in his grandfather's file, Byron found a cross reference to his father, Yee Bing Quai. To avoid the **scrutiny** of Angel Island, Byron's father had sailed through Boston. Byron found his file at the National Archives in Massachusetts.

◀ **scrutiny** (skro͞ot'ʼn ē) *n.* close, thorough inspection

"My father at 15. He is asked 197 questions: 'When did your alleged father first come to the United States?' 'Have you ever seen a photograph of your alleged father?' 'How many trips to China has your alleged father made since first coming to the United States?'" The lengthy interrogation made Byron suspect that his father was in fact a paper son. Maybe this was why he never knew his father's story.

Though Byron's mother knew very little about her husband's past, she did have an old photo, which she sent to Byron—a portrait of his father's family back in China. Byron learned that the baby on the left was his father. The boy in the middle was Yee Wee Thing, not Byron's grandfather at all, but his uncle.

"It kind of floored me because all of a sudden it made a lot of sense—why he was the way he was, why he never really talked about his past, why he was very secretive. It explained a lot about him and about his history.

"You see my story is no different from anyone else's. . . In all of our collective past, we've all had that one ancestor that had the strength to break from what was familiar to venture into the unknown. I can never thank my father and uncle enough for what they had to do so that I could be here today. One wrong answer between them and I would not be here."

# Close Reading Activities

## READ

### Comprehension

Reread the text as needed to answer the questions.

1. What was the Chinese Exclusion Act?
2. What were "paper sons"?
3. What did Byron Yee discover about Yee Wee Thing and his father?

**Research: Clarify Details** Conduct research on an unfamiliar detail from the selection. Then, explain how your research helped you understand the public document.

**Summarize** Write an objective summary of the article. Remember that an objective summary is free from opinion and evaluation.

### Language Study

**Selection Vocabulary** Define each boldfaced word, and then use the word in a sentence of your own.

- With little to go on, Byron set out to **decipher** his father's story.
- But the Chinese were detained anywhere from three weeks to two years for their **interrogations.**
- To avoid the **scrutiny** of Angel Island, Byron's father had sailed through Boston.

### Literary Analysis

Reread the identified passage. Then, respond to the following questions.

**Focus Passage** *(p. 753)*

"My father at 15 … about him and about his history.

**Key Ideas and Details**

1. **(a) Infer:** Why was Byron Yee's father asked so many questions? **(b) Interpret:** Why did the officials repeatedly use the word *alleged*?
2. **(a)** What does Byron Yee **discover** when he examines the photograph his mother sent? **(b) Draw Conclusions:** Why did it make sense that Byron Yee's father "never really talked about his past"?

**Craft and Structure**

3. **(a) Analyze:** Why does the author combine Byron Yee's own words with passages of explanatory text? **(b) Evaluate:** Would the account be as effective if it had consisted only of questions and answers? Explain.

**Integration of Knowledge and Ideas**

4. **Interpret:** How does the discovery about Yee Wee Thing change Byron Yee's attitude toward his father?

### Direct Quotation

**Direct quotations** are a person's exact words.

1. **(a)** Who is the source of all of the direct quotations? **(b)** How do the quotations **enhance** the article?
2. **Becoming American** How do the quotations help convey to readers the experience of "becoming American"?

# DISCUSS • RESEARCH • WRITE

## From Text to Topic **Partner Discussion**

Discuss the following passage with a partner. Take notes during the discussion. Contribute your own ideas, and support them with examples from the text.

> You see my story is no different from anyone else's ... In all of our collective past, we've all had that one ancestor that had the strength to break from what was familiar to venture into the unknown.

### QUESTIONS FOR DISCUSSION

1. How did Bing Quai Yee display courage in his quest to become an American citizen?
2. How is Byron Yee's story "no different from anyone else's"?

## Research **Investigate the Topic**

**The Chinese Exclusion Act** The article **cites** a law that restricted immigration to the United States: "The Chinese Exclusion Act was the only immigration law ever based on race alone." The law affected countless numbers of people, many of whom found ways around the law.

**Assignment**

Conduct research to learn why the Chinese Exclusion Act was passed, and when and why it was repealed. In addition, find out approximately how many people became "paper sons" in the U.S. as a result of the Act. Consult government and historical sources. Share your findings in an **informal speech** for the class.

### PREPARATION FOR ESSAY

You may use the results of your research to support your ideas in the essay you will write at the end of this section.

## Writing to Sources **Explanatory Text**

"Byron Yee: Discovering a Paper Son" focuses on one man's attempts to discover the truth about his father's immigration to the United States.

**Assignment**

Write an **expository essay** in which you explain how and why Byron Yee's father became a "paper son." Follow these steps:

- Write an introduction in which you provide a thesis statement.
- Introduce new paragraphs with clear transitions to explain the chain of events that preceded Bing Quai Yee's admittance into the United States.
- Provide a conclusion that summarizes the chain of events and the causes of Bing Quai Yee's actions.
- During your revision process, make sure there are no gaps in your essay's chain of events.

### ACADEMIC VOCABULARY

Academic terms appear in blue on these pages. If these words are not familiar to you, use a dictionary to find their definitions. Then, use them as you speak and write about the text.

# FROM GRANDPA AND THE STATUE

ARTHUR MILLER

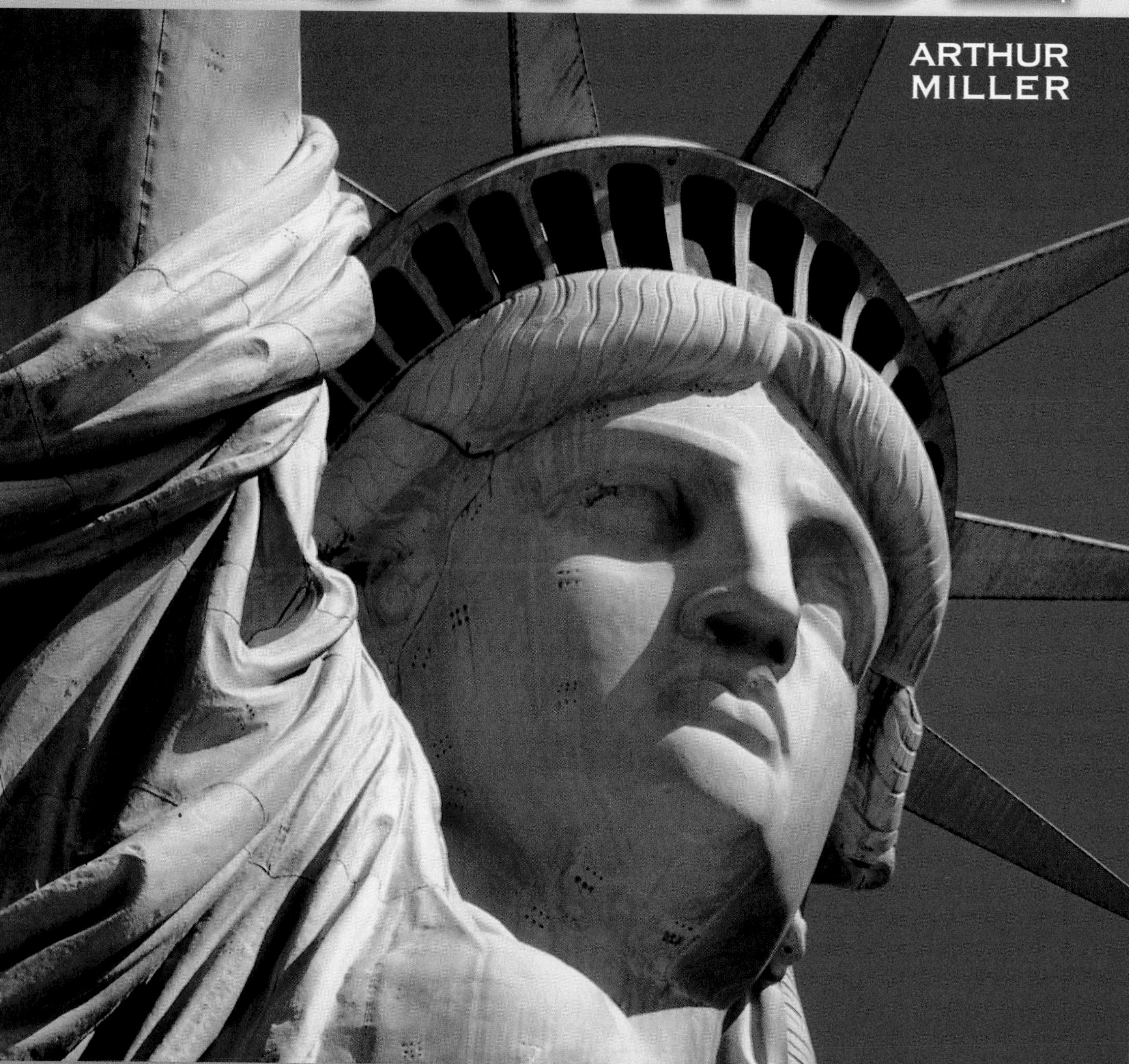

**SHEEAN.** [*Slight brogue*[1]] A good afternoon to you, Monaghan.

**MONAGHAN.** How're you, Sheean, how're ya?

**SHEEAN.** Fair, fair. And how's Mrs. Monaghan these days?

**MONAGHAN.** Warm. Same as everybody else in summer.

**SHEEAN.** I've come to talk to you about the fund, Monaghan.

**MONAGHAN.** What fund is that?

**SHEEAN.** The Statue of Liberty fund.

**MONAGHAN.** Oh, that.

**SHEEAN.** It's time we come to grips with the subject, Monaghan.

**MONAGHAN.** I'm not interested, Sheean.

**SHEEAN.** Now hold up on that a minute. Let me tell you the facts. This here Frenchman has gone and built a fine statue of Liberty. It costs who knows how many millions to build. All they're askin' us to do is contribute enough to put up a base for the statue to stand on.

**MONAGHAN.** I'm not . . . !

**SHEEAN.** Before you answer me. People all over the whole United States are puttin' in for it. Butler Street is doin' the same. We'd like to hang up a flag on the corner saying—"Butler Street, Brooklyn, is one hundred per cent behind the Statue of Liberty." And Butler Street is a hundred per cent **subscribed** except for you. Now will you give us a dime, Monaghan? One dime and we can put up the flag. Now what do you say to that?

◄ **subscribed** (səb skrībʹ əd) *v.* promised to give money in support of something

1. **brogue** (brōg) *n.* Irish accent.

**Monaghan.** I'm not throwin' me good money away for somethin' I don't even know exists.

**Sheean.** Now what do you mean by that?

**Monaghan.** Have you seen this statue?

**Sheean.** No, but it's in a warehouse. And as soon as we get the money to build the pedestal they'll take it and put it up on that island in the river, and all the boats comin' in from the old country will see it there and it'll raise the hearts of the poor immigrants to see such a fine sight on their first look at this country.

**Monaghan.** And how do I know it's in this here warehouse at all?

**Sheean.** You read your paper, don't you? It's been in all the papers for the past year.

**Monaghan.** Ha, the papers! Last year I read in the paper that they were about to pave Butler Street and take out all the holes. Turn around and look at Butler Street, Mr. Sheean.

**Sheean.** All right. I'll do this: I'll take you to the warehouse and show you the statue. Will you give me a dime then?

**Monaghan.** Well . . . I'm not sayin' I would, and I'm not sayin' I wouldn't. But I'd be more likely if I saw the thing large as life, I would.

**peeved** ▶ (pēvd) *adj.* irritated; annoyed

**Sheean.** [Peeved] All right, then. Come along.

*[Music up and down and out]*

*[Footsteps, in a warehouse . . . echo . . . they come to a halt.]*

Now then. Do you see the Statue of Liberty or don't you see it?

**Monaghan.** I see it all right, but it's all broke!

**Sheean.** *Broke!* They brought it from France on a boat. They had to take it apart, didn't they?

**Monaghan.** You got a secondhand statue, that's what you got, and I'm not payin' for new when they've shipped us something that's all smashed to pieces.

**Sheean.** Now just a minute, just a minute. Visualize what I'm about to tell you, Monaghan, get the picture of it. When

this statue is put together it's going to stand ten stories high. Could they get a thing ten stories high into a four-story building such as this is? Use your good sense, now Monaghan.

**Monaghan.** What's that over there?

**Sheean.** Where?

**Monaghan.** That tablet there in her hand. What's it say? July Eye Vee (IV) MDCCLXXVI . . . what . . . what's all that?

**Sheean.** That means July 4, 1776. It's in Roman numbers. Very high class.

**Monaghan.** What's the good of it? If they're going to put a sign on her they ought to put it: Welcome All. That's it. Welcome All.

**Sheean.** They decided July 4, 1776, and July 4, 1776, it's going to be!

**Monaghan.** All right, then let them get their dime from somebody else!

**Sheean.** Monaghan!

**Monaghan.** No, sir! I'll tell you something. I didn't think there was a statue but there is. She's all broke, it's true, but she's here and maybe they can get her together. But even if they do, will you tell me what sort of a welcome to immigrants it'll be, to have a gigantic thing like that in the middle of the river and in her hand is July Eye Vee MCDVC . . . whatever it is?

**Sheean.** That's the date the country was made!

**Monaghan.** The divil with the date! A man comin' in from the sea wants a place to stay, not a date. When I come from the old country I git off at the dock and there's a feller says to me, "Would you care for a room for the night?" "I would that," I sez, and he sez, "All right then, follow me." He takes me to a rooming house. I no sooner sign me name on the register—which I was able to do even at that time—when I look around and the feller is gone clear away and took my valise[2] in the bargain. A statue anyway can't move off so fast, but if she's going to welcome let her say welcome, not this MCDC. . . .

2. **valise** (və lēs′) *n.* small suitcase.

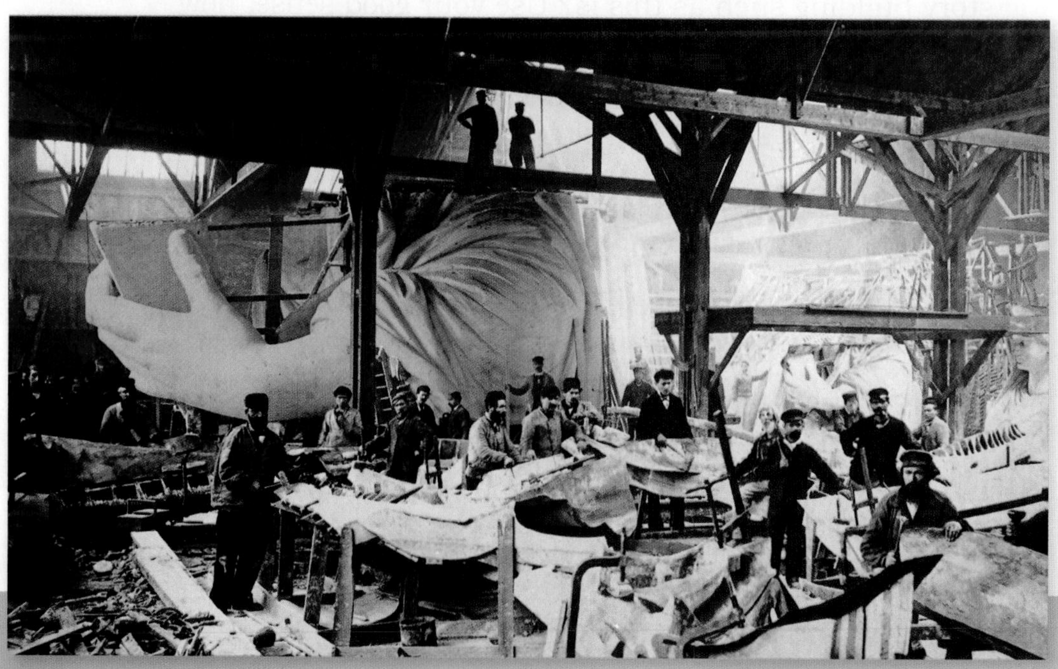

**Sheean.** All right, then, Monaghan. But all I can say is, you've laid a disgrace on the name of Butler Street. I'll put the dime in for ya.

**Monaghan.** Don't connect me with it! It's a **swindle**, is all it is. In the first place, it's broke; in the second place, if they do put it up it'll come down with the first high wind that strikes it.

◄ **swindle** (swin′dəl) *n.* act of cheating or fraud

**Sheean.** The engineers say it'll last forever!

**Monaghan.** And I say it'll topple into the river in a high wind! Look at the inside of her. She's all hollow!

**Sheean.** I've heard everything now, Monaghan. Just about everything. Good-bye.

**Monaghan.** What do you mean, good-bye? How am I to get back to Butler Street from here?

**Sheean.** You've got legs to walk.

**Monaghan.** I'll remind you that I come on the trolley.

**Sheean.** And I'll remind you that I paid your fare and I'm not repeating the kindness.

**Monaghan.** Sheean? You've stranded me!

*[Music up and down]*

## ABOUT THE AUTHOR

### Arthur Miller (1915–2005)

Arthur Miller was born in New York City in 1915. His father, who ran a small manufacturing business, went bankrupt during the Great Depression. After graduating from high school, Miller worked for two years to earn money so he could attend college. He had many jobs during this time, including one as a clerk in a warehouse. Miller began to write plays while attending college. Today, he is considered among the finest American playwrights. Most of his plays—which have won multiple Tony Awards and other honors—focus on the problems of ordinary people. One of his most famous plays, *Death of a Salesman* (1949), won a Pulitzer Prize and made him internationally famous.

# Close Reading Activities

## READ

### Comprehension

Reread as needed to answer the questions.

1. What does Sheean want from Monaghan?
2. What are two reasons Monaghan gives for his lack of participation?
3. What happens at the end of the selection?

**Research: Clarify Details** Choose one unfamiliar detail from the play and research it.

**Summarize** Write an objective summary of the play excerpt. Remember that an objective summary is free from opinion and evaluation.

### Language Study

**Selection Vocabulary** Use each boldfaced word from the play in a sentence that shows the word's meaning.

- And Butler Street is a hundred per cent **subscribed** except for you.
- SHEEAN. [**Peeved**] All right, then. Come along.
- It's a **swindle,** is all it is.

### Literary Analysis

Reread the identified passage.

**Focus Passage** *(p. 760)*

**Monaghan.** The divil with the date! . . . not this MCDC. . . .

#### Key Ideas and Details

1. **(a) Summarize:** What happened when Monaghan arrived in the United States? **(b) Speculate:** How did this experience affect his feelings toward the United States?
2. **(a)** What does Monaghan say new immigrants want? **(b) Analyze:** According to Monaghan, how does the statue fail to meet this need?

#### Craft and Structure

3. **(a) Distinguish:** How would you **characterize** Monaghan's way of speaking? Give examples from the text to support your answer. **(b) Draw Conclusions:** What does his style of speech tell you about Monaghan?

#### Integration of Knowledge and Ideas

4. **(a) Compare and Contrast:** How does Sheean's opinion of the Statue of Liberty differ from Monaghan's? **(b) Draw Conclusions:** What might be the author's purpose in having these two particular characters discuss the Statue of Liberty?

### Dialogue

A **dialogue** is a conversation between characters. Reread the excerpt from the play, taking notes on the dialogue.

1. **(a)** What characteristics of Monaghan are revealed through his dialogue? **(b)** What characteristics of Sheean are revealed through his lines?
2. **Becoming American** Based on the dialogue, which of the two men feels more comfortable in the United States? Explain.

# DISCUSS • RESEARCH • WRITE

## From Text to Topic **Debate**

**Debate** the following passage with your classmates. When it is your turn to speak, respond to the previous speaker and then add your own ideas. Support your ideas with examples from the text.

> **MONAGHAN**. That tablet there in her hand. What's it say? July Eye Vee [IV] MDCCLXXVI . . . what . . . what's all that?
> **SHEEAN**. That means July 4, 1776. It's in Roman numbers. Very high class.
> **MONAGHAN**. What's the good of it? If they're going to put a sign on her they ought to put it: Welcome All. That's it. Welcome All.

### QUESTIONS FOR DISCUSSION

1. Why does Monaghan object to the Roman numbers on the tablet?
2. What does Sheean think of the tablet?
3. What different attitudes about coming to the United States do these opinions show?

## Research **Investigate the Topic**

**"The New Colossus"** A poem titled "The New Colossus," by Emma Lazarus, is inscribed on the base of the Statue of Liberty. The poem is a spirited explanation of the American ideals that the statue represents.

**Assignment**

Find and read "The New Colossus" and conduct research to **discover** more about the poem and its meaning for people "becoming American." Consult government and historical sources. Read the poem to the class and share your findings about it in a short **research paper**.

### PREPARATION FOR ESSAY

You may use the results of your research to support your ideas in the essay you will write at the end of this section.

## Writing to Sources **Argument**

The excerpt from "Grandpa and the Statue" focuses on two differing opinions about the Statue of Liberty.

**Assignment**

Write an **argument** in which you evaluate the characters' reasons for and against contributing to the Statue of Liberty Fund. In your essay, state a claim about whose reasons are strong and supported with evidence, and whose reasons are weak. Follow these steps:

- Write a thesis statement that clearly states your claim about which character—Sheean or Monaghan—presents a better argument.
- Use evidence and quotations from the play to support your argument.
- Proofread your essay, and correct errors in grammar, spelling, and capitalization.

### ACADEMIC VOCABULARY

Academic terms appear in blue on these pages. If these words are not familiar to you, use a dictionary to find their definitions. Then, use them as you speak and write about the text.

# Melting Pot

Anna Quindlen

My children are upstairs in the house next door, having dinner with the Ecuadorian family that lives on the top floor. The father speaks some English, the mother less than that. The two daughters are **fluent** in both their native and their adopted languages, but the youngest child, a son, a close friend of my two boys, speaks almost no Spanish. His parents thought it would be better that way. This doesn't surprise me; it was the way my mother was raised, American among Italians.

**fluent** ▶ (flo͞o′ ənt) *adj.* able to write or speak easily and smoothly

I always suspected, hearing my grandfather talk about the "No Irish Need Apply" signs outside factories, hearing my mother talk about the neighborhood kids, who called her greaseball, that the American fable of the melting pot was a myth. Here in our neighborhood it exists, but like so many other things, it exists only person-to-person.

The letters in the local weekly tabloid[1] suggest that everybody hates everybody else here, and on a macro level they do. The old-timers are angry because they think the new moneyed professionals are taking over their town. The professionals are tired of being blamed for the neighborhood's rising rents, particularly since they are the ones paying them. The old immigrants are suspicious of the new ones. The new ones think the old ones are **bigots**. Nevertheless, on a micro level most of us get along. We are friendly with the Ecuadorian family, with the Yugoslavs across the street, and with the Italians next door, mainly by virtue of our children's sidewalk friendships. It took awhile. Eight years ago we were the new people on the block, filling dumpsters with old plaster and lath, . . . (sitting) on the stoop with our demolition masks hanging around our necks like goiters.[2] We thought we could feel people staring at us from behind the sheer curtains on their windows. We were right.

My first apartment in New York was in a gritty warehouse district, the kind of place that makes your parents wince. A lot of old Italians lived around me, which suited me just fine because I was the granddaughter of old Italians. Their own children and grandchildren had moved to Long Island and New Jersey. All they had was me. All I had was them.

I remember sitting on a corner with a group of half a dozen elderly men, men who had known one another since they were boys sitting together on this same corner, watching a glazier install a great spread of tiny glass panes to make one wall of a restaurant in the ground floor of an old building across

◀ **bigots**
(big′ əts)
*n.* narrow-minded, prejudiced people

1. **tabloid** (tab′ loid′) *n.* small newspaper.
2. **goiters** (goit′ ərz) *n.* swellings in the lower front of the neck caused by an enlarged thyroid gland.

the street. The men laid bets on how long the panes, and the restaurant, would last. Two years later two of the men were dead, one had moved in with his married daughter in the suburbs, and the three remaining sat and watched **dolefully** as people waited each night for a table in the restaurant. "Twenty-two dollars for a piece of veal!" one of them would say, apropos of nothing.[3] But when I ate in the restaurant they never blamed me. "You're not one of them," one of the men explained. "You're one of me." It's an argument familiar to members of almost any embattled race or class: I like you, therefore you aren't like the rest of your kind, whom I hate.

**dolefully** ▶ (dōl′fəl lē) *adv.* with sadness and sorrow

Change comes hard in America, but it comes constantly. The butcher whose old shop is now an antiques store sits day after day outside the pizzeria here like a lost child. The old people across the street cluster together and discuss what kind of money they might be offered if the person who bought their building wants to turn it into condominiums. The greengrocer stocks yellow peppers and fresh rosemary for the gourmands, plum tomatoes and broad-leaf parsley for the older Italians, mangoes for the Indians. He doesn't carry plantains, he says, because you can buy them in the bodega.[4]

Sometimes the baby slips out with the bath water. I wanted to throw confetti the day that a family of rough types who propped their speakers on

3. **apropos** (ap′ rə pō′) **of nothing** without connection.
4. **bodega** (bō dā′ gə) *n.* small, Hispanic grocery store.

their station wagon and played heavy metal music at 3:00 a.m. moved out. I stood and smiled as the seedy bar at the corner was transformed into a slick Mexican restaurant. But I liked some of the people who moved out at the same time the rough types did. And I'm not sure I have that much in common with the singles who have made the restaurant their second home.

Yet somehow now we seem to have reached a nice mix. About a third of the people in the neighborhood think of squid as calamari, about a third think of it as sushi, and about a third think of it as bait. Lots of the single people who have moved in during the last year or two are easygoing and good-tempered about all the kids. The old Italians have become philosophical about the new Hispanics, although they still think more of them should know English. The firebrand community organizer with the storefront on the block, the one who is always talking about people like us as though we stole our houses out of the open purse of a ninety-year-old blind widow, is pleasant to my boys.

Drawn in broad strokes, we live in a pressure cooker: oil and water, us and them. But if you come around at exactly the right time, you'll find members of all these groups gathered around complaining about the condition of the streets, on which everyone can agree. We melt together, then draw apart. I am the granddaughter of immigrants, a young professional—either an interloper[5] or a longtime resident, depending on your concept of time. I am one of them, and one of us.

---

5. **interloper** (in´ tər lō´ pər) *n.* one who intrudes on another.

## ABOUT THE AUTHOR

### Anna Quindlen (b. 1953)

Anna Quindlen spent five years reporting for the *New York Times,* often covering issues related to her family and her neighborhood. "Melting Pot" originally appeared in "Life in the 30s," a popular column that Quindlen wrote in the 1980s. In 1992, Quindlen won a Pulitzer Prize for her columns. Later, she left journalism to write novels. She has published several bestsellers, including *One True Thing, Black and Blue,* and *Blessings*. She has also written children's books, nonfiction books, and a memoir.

# Close Reading Activities

## READ

### Comprehension

Reread as needed to answer the questions.

1. What is the setting of this article?
2. How long has Quindlen lived in her **community**?
3. Why did Quindlen get along with the people who lived near her first apartment?

**Research: Clarify Details** Choose one unfamiliar detail from the text and research it. Then, explain how your research helped you understand the newspaper column more fully.

**Summarize** Write an objective summary of the newspaper column.

### Language Study

**Selection Vocabulary** Use each boldfaced word in a sentence that shows the word's meaning.

- The two daughters are **fluent** in both their native and their adopted languages ...
- The new ones think the old ones are **bigots.**
- ... the three remaining sat and watched **dolefully** as people waited each night for a table in the restaurant.

### Literary Analysis

Reread the identified passage. Then, respond to the following questions.

**Focus Passage** *(pp. 765–766)*
I remember sitting on a corner... your kind, whom I hate.

#### Key Ideas and Details

1. On what do the elderly men lay bets?
2. **Analyze:** Why do the men comment on the restaurant's prices?

#### Craft and Structure

3. **(a)** What words indicate a time shift in the middle of in this passage? **(b) Draw Conclusions:** What has changed? What has stayed the same?

#### Integration of Knowledge and Ideas

4. **(a) Interpret:** What does the man mean when he says, "You're not one of them. You're one of me."? **(b) Hypothesize:** How does this **attitude** show that the man is resistant to change?

### Idiom

An **idiom** is an expression with a meaning that is different from the meanings of its individual words. Review the text, and take notes on the idioms that Quindlen uses.

1. **(a)** What do you think the expression "the baby slips out with the bath water" (p. 766) means? **(b)** What idea does Quindlen express through the use of this idiom?
2. **Becoming American (a)** What is the meaning of "the melting pot"? **(b)** Why does Quindlen say that the "fable of the melting pot was a myth" when people become American?

# DISCUSS • RESEARCH • WRITE

## From Text to Topic **Write and Discuss**

Write a short response to this passage, and then share and discuss it with a small group of classmates. Take notes during the discussion. Contribute your own ideas, and support them with examples from the text.

> Drawn in broad strokes, we live in a pressure cooker:… I am one of them, and one of us. (p. 767)

### QUESTIONS FOR DISCUSSION

1. According to Quindlen, what can bring different groups of people together?
2. Why might a person feel as if he or she is part of more than just one group of people?

## Research **Investigate the Topic**

**Urban "Melting Pots"** In this newspaper column, Quindlen describes a neighborhood that is made up of people from many different countries. Many urban neighborhoods in the U.S. have large populations of immigrants.

**Assignment**

Conduct research to learn about U.S. cities with large immigrant populations. Consult government websites and other print and online sources. Choose one area on which to focus your research. Share your findings in a **visual presentation**.

### PREPARATION FOR ESSAY

You may use the results of your research to support your ideas in the essay you will write at the end of this section.

## Writing to Sources **Argument**

In "Melting Pot," Anna Quindlen writes about some of the challenges that are faced by members of a multicultural community.

**Assignment**

Write a **problem-and-solution essay** in which you propose solutions for some of the conflicts Quindlen describes in her column. Follow these steps:

- Review "Melting Pot" to identify one or more problems to address in your essay. Brainstorm for possible solutions.
- **Compose** a thesis statement in which you present an argument for the best solutions to the problems you have identified.
- Support your thesis statement with evidence from the text, and explain why the solutions you propose are better than alternative solutions.
- Proofread to ensure correct spelling, punctuation, and grammar.

### ACADEMIC VOCABULARY

Academic terms appear in blue on these pages. If these words are not familiar to you, use a dictionary to find their definitions. Then, use them as you speak and write about the text.

# United States Immigration Statistics

**Legal Permanent Resident Flow by Region and Country of Birth: Fiscal Years 2009 to 2011**

| Region and country of birth | 2011 Number | 2011 Percent | 2010 Number | 2010 Percent | 2009 Number | 2009 Percent |
|---|---|---|---|---|---|---|
| REGION | | | | | | |
| Total | 1,062,040 | 100.0 | 1,042,625 | 100.0 | 1,130,818 | 100.0 |
| Africa | 100,374 | 9.5 | 101,355 | 9.7 | 127,046 | 11.2 |
| Asia | 451,593 | 42.5 | 422,063 | 40.5 | 413,312 | 36.5 |
| Europe | 83,850 | 7.9 | 88,801 | 8.5 | 105,476 | 9.3 |
| North America | 333,902 | 31.4 | 336,553 | 32.3 | 375,180 | 33.2 |
| Caribbean | 133,680 | 12.6 | 139,951 | 13.4 | 146,071 | 12.9 |
| Central America | 43,707 | 4.1 | 43,951 | 4.2 | 47,868 | 4.2 |
| Other North America | 156,515 | 14.7 | 152,651 | 14.6 | 181,241 | 16.0 |
| Oceania | 4,980 | 0.5 | 5,345 | 0.5 | 5,578 | 0.5 |
| South America | 86,096 | 8.1 | 87,178 | 8.4 | 102,860 | 9.1 |
| Unknown | 1,245 | 0.1 | 1,330 | 0.1 | 1,366 | 0.1 |
| COUNTRY | | | | | | |
| Total | 1,062,040 | 100.0 | 1,042,625 | 100.0 | 1,130,818 | 100.0 |
| Mexico | 143,446 | 13.5 | 139,120 | 13.3 | 164,920 | 14.6 |
| China, People's Republic | 87,016 | 8.2 | 70,863 | 6.8 | 64,238 | 5.7 |
| India | 69,013 | 6.5 | 69,162 | 6.6 | 57,304 | 5.1 |
| Philippines | 57,011 | 5.4 | 58,173 | 5.6 | 60,029 | 5.3 |
| Dominican Republic | 46,109 | 4.3 | 53,870 | 5.2 | 49,414 | 4.4 |
| Cuba | 36,452 | 3.4 | 33,573 | 3.2 | 38,954 | 3.4 |
| Vietnam | 34,157 | 3.2 | 30,632 | 2.9 | 29,234 | 2.6 |
| Korea, South | 22,824 | 2.1 | 22,227 | 2.1 | 25,859 | 2.3 |
| Colombia | 22,635 | 2.1 | 22,406 | 2.1 | 27,849 | 2.5 |
| Haiti | 22,111 | 2.1 | 22,582 | 2.2 | 24,280 | 2.1 |
| Iraq | 21,133 | 2.0 | 19,855 | 1.9 | 12,110 | 1.1 |
| Jamaica | 19,662 | 1.9 | 19,825 | 1.9 | 21,783 | 1.9 |
| El Salvador | 18,667 | 1.8 | 18,806 | 1.8 | 19,909 | 1.8 |
| Bangladesh | 16,707 | 1.6 | 14,819 | 1.4 | 16,651 | 1.5 |
| Burma | 16,518 | 1.6 | 12,925 | 1.2 | 13,621 | 1.2 |
| Pakistan | 15,546 | 1.5 | 18,258 | 1.8 | 21,555 | 1.9 |
| Iran | 14,822 | 1.4 | 14,182 | 1.4 | 18,553 | 1.6 |
| Peru | 14,064 | 1.3 | 14,247 | 1.4 | 16,957 | 1.5 |
| Ethiopia | 13,793 | 1.3 | 14,266 | 1.4 | 15,462 | 1.4 |
| Canada | 12,800 | 1.2 | 13,328 | 1.3 | 16,140 | 1.4 |
| All other countries | 357,554 | 33.7 | 359,506 | 34.5 | 415,996 | 36.8 |

Source: U.S. Department of Homeland Security, Computer Linked Application Information Management System (CLAIMS),
Legal Immigrant Data, Fiscal Years 2009 to 2011.

## READ • RESEARCH • WRITE

### Comprehension

Study the infographic to help you answer the questions.

**1.** What information appears in the table?

**2. (a)** What agency released the data table? **(b)** How are **legal** permanent residents (LPRs) classified in the table?

### Critical Analysis

#### Key Ideas and Details

**1. (a) Interpret: Approximately** how many people, in total, became legal permanent residents in the United States from 2009 to 2011? **(b) Identify:** From which continent did the majority of the new LPRs come? **(c)** From which country did the most new LPRs come?

#### Craft and Structure

**2. Draw Conclusions:** Why does the table include an entry for "All other countries"?

#### Integration of Knowledge and Ideas

**3. Generalize:** Why might the information in this table be useful to immigration officials in the United States?

**ACADEMIC VOCABULARY**

Academic terms appear in blue on this page. If these words are not familiar to you, use a dictionary to find their definitions. Then, use the words as you speak and write about the text.

### Research **Investigate the Topic**

**Immigration to the United States** This table shows the number of people who became legal permanent residents of the United States from 2009 to 2011. The process of becoming a LPR is often long and difficult.

**Assignment**

Conduct research to learn about the current immigration process for people who want to move to the U.S. today. Investigate the reasons why people want to come here, and find out what they need to do in their home countries before they leave. Consult government sources for information. Share your findings in an **informal presentation.**

### Writing to Sources **Narrative**

Write a brief **short story** in which you describe the experiences of an **individual** or a family who is immigrating to the United States.

# Assessment: Synthesis

## Speaking and Listening: Group Discussion

**Becoming American** The texts in this section vary in genre, length, style, and perspective. However, all of the texts comment in some way on the experience of becoming American and on the Big Question addressed in this unit: **Community or individual—which is more important?**

### Assignment

**Conduct discussions.** With a small group of classmates, conduct a discussion connecting issues related to becoming American with the relationship between the community and the individual. Refer to the texts in this section, other texts you have read, and your personal experience and knowledge to support your ideas. Begin your discussion by addressing the following questions:

- In what ways may an individual change if he or she moves to another country? In what ways may he or she stay the same?
- What are some different types of communities to which people belong in the United States?
- Can a person who moves to the U.S. from another country bring elements of his or her community along? If so, how?
- Are the needs of an individual ever more important than the needs of a community? Explain.

**Summarize and present your ideas.** After you have fully explored the topic, summarize your discussion and present your findings to the class.

▲ Refer to the selections you read in Part 3 as you complete the activities on this assessment.

## Criteria for Success

✓ **Organizes the group effectively**
Appoint a group leader and a timekeeper. The group leader should present the discussion questions. The timekeeper should make sure the discussion takes no longer than 20 minutes.

✓ **Maintains focus of discussion**
As a group, stay on topic and avoid straying into other subject areas.

✓ **Involves all participants equally and fully**
No one person should monopolize the conversation. Rather, everyone should take turns speaking and contributing ideas.

✓ **Follows the rules for collegial discussion**
As each group member speaks, others should listen carefully. Build on one another's ideas and support viewpoints and opinions with sound reasoning and evidence. Express disagreement respectfully.

**USE NEW VOCABULARY**

As you speak and share ideas, work to use the vocabulary words you have learned in this unit. The more you use new words, the more you will "own" them.

## Writing: Narrative

**Becoming American** As Americans, we may come from different ethnic, religious, and economic backgrounds. One thing we all share, however, is the experience of navigating our way through the various communities in our lives: our families, religious institutions, neighborhoods, schools, and workplaces.

**Assignment**

Write an **autobiographical narrative**—a true story about your own life—in which you discuss an experience you have had as an individual functioning within a community. Frame your narrative around a problem or conflict that you had to address or are still addressing. For example, you might describe a conflict that resulted from the collision of one of your communities with another. In your narrative, compare your experience to the experience of someone you read about in one of the texts in this section. Explain how your experience relates to the idea of becoming, or being, American.

### Criteria for Success

#### Purpose/Focus

✓ **Connects specific incidents with larger ideas**
Make meaningful connections between your experiences and the texts you have read in this section.

✓ **Clearly conveys the significance of the story**
Provide a conclusion in which you reflect on what you experienced.

#### Organization

✓ **Sequences events logically**
Structure your narrative so that individual events build on one another to create a coherent whole.

#### Development of Ideas/Elaboration

✓ **Supports insights**
Include both personal examples and details from the texts you have read.

✓ **Uses narrative techniques effectively**
Consider using storytelling elements such as figurative language, dialogue, and symbolism.

#### Language

✓ **Uses description effectively**
Use descriptive details to engage your readers.

#### Conventions

✓ **Does not have errors**
Eliminate errors in grammar, spelling, and punctuation.

**WRITE TO EXPLORE**

Writing is a way to explore what you feel and think: You may change your mind or get new ideas as you work. As you write your autobiographical narrative, explore your ideas on becoming American and on community and the individual.

## Writing to Sources: **Explanatory Text**

**Becoming American** The related readings in this section present a range of ideas about becoming American. The selections raise questions, such as those below, about the differing experiences of individuals within communities, both in the U.S. and in other countries.

- What does it mean to be an individual?
- What happens when the needs of an individual conflict with the needs of the community?
- How does living in the United States make it easier or more difficult to belong to multiple communities?
- What actions do people take to "become American"? What is involved in the process?

Focus on the question that intrigues you the most, and then complete the following assignment.

> **Assignment**
> Write an **explanatory essay** in which you explore what it means to "become American" by comparing and contrasting characters in two or more texts from this section. Clearly present, develop, and support your ideas with examples and details from the texts.

### Prewriting and Planning

**Choose texts.** Review the texts in the section to determine which ones you will cite in your essay. Select at least two texts that will provide strong material to support your thesis statement.

**Gather details and craft a working thesis statement.** Use a chart like the one shown to develop your thesis statement.

**Focus Question: What actions does one have to take to "become American"? What is involved in the process?**

| Text | Passage | Notes |
|---|---|---|
| "My First Free Summer" | If the light could be translated into words, instead, they would say: Freedom and liberty and justice for all ... | Alvarez begins to understand the American ideals she has learned at school. |
| "Melting Pot" | I am one of them, and one of us. | Quindlen recognizes that she belongs to multiple communities. |
| **Example Thesis Statement:** In these texts, becoming American involves embracing both the principles upon which the U.S. was founded, and the different groups of people gathered together under those principles. | | |

**INCORPORATE RESEARCH**

In your essay, use the information you gathered as you completed the brief research assignments related to the selections in this section.

## Drafting

**Present a clear thesis.** Review your notes to develop a single sentence, or thesis statement, in which you clearly present the main idea of your essay. Include this sentence in your opening paragraph.

**Organize for clarity.** For clarity and readability, address one key point in each paragraph. Make sure that all of your points connect to your thesis statement.

**Use transition words and phrases.** Use transitions that help you create a smooth flow between paragraphs and between ideas. Examples of transitions include: *next, although, as a result, therefore, however, furthermore,* and *finally.*

## Revising and Editing

**Check support for your thesis.** Make sure that your thesis is clearly stated and that you have supported it with convincing textual evidence. Check your conclusion to make sure it reinforces your thesis while providing a sense of closure for your essay.

**Maintain a formal style.** Review your writing to ensure you have maintained a formal style. If necessary, revise to eliminate slang and contractions and to correct incomplete sentences and other grammatical errors.

**CITE RESEARCH CORRECTLY**

When you quote from a source directly, use quotation marks to indicate that the words are not your own.

### Self-Evaluation Rubric

Use the following criteria to evaluate the effectiveness of your essay.

| Criteria | Rating Scale |
|---|---|
| **Purpose/Focus** Introduces a clear thesis statement; provides a concluding section that follows from and supports the information or explanation presented | *not very* ............ *very*<br>1 2 3 4 |
| **Organization** Organizes complex ideas, concepts, and information to make important connections and distinctions; uses appropriate and varied transitions to link the major sections, create cohesion, and clarify relationships among ideas | 1 2 3 4 |
| **Development of Ideas/Elaboration** Develops the topic with well-chosen, relevant and sufficient facts, extended definitions, concrete details, quotations or other information and examples appropriate to the audience's knowledge of the topic | 1 2 3 4 |
| **Language** Uses precise language and domain-specific vocabulary to manage the complexity of the topic; establishes and maintains a formal style and objective tone | 1 2 3 4 |
| **Conventions** Uses correct conventions of grammar, spelling, and punctuation | 1 2 3 4 |

# Independent Reading

## Titles for Extended Reading

In this unit, you have read texts in a variety of genres. Continue to read on your own. Select works that you enjoy, but challenge yourself to explore new authors and works of increasing depth and complexity. The titles suggested below will help you get started.

### INFORMATIONAL TEXT

**Around the World in a Hundred Years**
by Jean Fritz

This entertaining **nonfiction** book describes what happened when explorers, such as Columbus and Magellan, met the inhabitants of the lands they called "the Unknown."

**The Great Fire** EXEMPLAR TEXT
by Jim Murphy

In this **nonfiction** book, Jim Murphy uses a variety of personal accounts to tell the story of the tragic Great Chicago Fire of 1871. This fascinating history tells how the fire began, how people responded to it, and how it was finally contained.

**Discoveries: Truth Is Stranger Than Fiction**

The **essays** in this book explore a variety of topics, including "The Wonders of the World," "Snakes in the Sky!," "Reel Time," and "Math Tricks."

### LITERATURE

**The People Could Fly: American Black Folktales** EXEMPLAR TEXT
by Virginia Hamilton

These twenty-four **folk tales** celebrate the strength and resourcefulness of the people who survived slavery. The collection includes the selection "The People Could Fly," which is featured in this unit.

**Trojan Horse**
by David Clement-Davies

In this modern retelling of the classic **myth,** the Greeks cleverly use a huge wooden horse to enter and destroy the city of Troy.

**The Time Warp Trio: It's All Greek to Me**
by Jon Scieszka

In this funny **novel,** Joe and his friends accidentally find themselves trapped in ancient Greece. With only a cardboard thunderbolt and a painted apple as weapons, they must outwit the gods to survive the dangers of Hades and Mount Olympus.

**Thirteen Moons on Turtle's Back**
by Joseph Bruchac

The thirteen **poems** in this collection of myths and legends represent the thirteen moon cycles that make up the year in traditional Native American folklore.

**ONLINE TEXT SET**

POEM
**Martin Luther King** Raymond R. Patterson

SHORT STORY
**The Bear Boy** Joseph Bruchac

CONTRACT
**Theater Show Contract** Crystal Springs Upland School

## Preparing to Read Complex Texts

**Attentive Reading** As you read on your own, ask yourself questions like these to enrich your reading experience.

**When reading texts from the oral tradition, ask yourself…**

### Comprehension: **Key Ideas and Details**

- From what culture does this text come? What do I know about that culture?
- What type of text am I reading? For example, is it a myth, a legend, or a tall tale? What characters and events do I expect to find in this type of text?
- What elements of the culture do I see in the text? For example, do I notice beliefs, foods, or settings that have meaning for the people of this culture?
- Does the text teach a lesson or a moral? If so, is this a valuable lesson?

### Text Analysis: **Craft and Structure**

- Who is retelling or presenting this text? Do I think the author has changed the text from the original? If so, how?
- Does the text include characters and tell a story? If so, are the characters and plot interesting?
- What do I notice about the language used in the text? Which aspects seem similar to or different from the language used in modern texts?
- Does the text include symbols? If so, do they have a special meaning in the original culture of the text? Do they also have meaning in modern life?

### Connections: **Integration of Knowledge and Ideas**

- What does this text teach me about the culture from which it comes?
- What, if anything, does this text teach me about people in general?
- Does this text seem like others I have read or heard? Why or why not?
- Do I know of any modern versions of this text? How are they similar to or different from this one?
- If I were researching this culture for a report, would I include passages from this text? If so, what would those passages show?
- Do I enjoy reading this text and others like it? Why or why not?

# Resources

# Literary Terms



**ALLITERATION** ***Alliteration*** is the repetition of initial consonant sounds. Writers use alliteration to draw attention to certain words or ideas, to imitate sounds, and to create musical effects.

**ALLUSION** An ***allusion*** is a reference to a well-known person, event, place, literary work, or work of art. Allusions allow the writer to express complex ideas without spelling them out. Understanding what a literary work is saying often depends on recognizing its allusions and the meanings they suggest.

**ANALOGY** An ***analogy*** makes a comparison between two or more things that are similar in some ways but otherwise unalike.

**ANECDOTE** An ***anecdote*** is a brief story about an interesting, amusing, or strange event. Writers tell anecdotes to entertain or to make a point.

**ANTAGONIST** An ***antagonist*** is a character or a force in conflict with a main character, or protagonist.

See ***Conflict*** and ***Protagonist.***

**ARGUMENT** See ***Persuasion.***

**ATMOSPHERE** ***Atmosphere,*** or ***mood,*** is the feeling created in the reader by a literary work or passage.

**AUTHOR'S ARGUMENT** An ***author's argument*** is the position he or she puts forward, supported by reasons.

**AUTHOR'S PURPOSE** An ***author's purpose*** is his or her main reason for writing. For example, an author may want to entertain, inform, or persuade the reader. Sometimes an author is trying to teach a moral lesson or reflect on an experience. An author may have more than one purpose for writing.

**AUTOBIOGRAPHY** An ***autobiography*** is the story of the writer's own life, told by the writer. Autobiographical writing may tell about the person's whole life or only a part of it.

Because autobiographies are about real people and events, they are a form of nonfiction. Most autobiographies are written in the first person.

See ***Biography, Nonfiction,*** and ***Point of View.***

**BIOGRAPHY** A ***biography*** is a form of nonfiction in which a writer tells the life story of another person. Most biographies are written about famous or admirable people. Although biographies are nonfiction, the most effective ones share the qualities of good narrative writing.

See ***Autobiography*** and ***Nonfiction.***

**CHARACTER** A ***character*** is a person or an animal that takes part in the action of a literary work. The main, or ***major,*** character is the most important character in a story, poem, or play. A ***minor*** character is one who takes part in the action but is not the focus of attention.

Characters are sometimes classified as flat or round. A ***flat character*** is one-sided and often stereotypical. A ***round character,*** on the other hand, is fully developed and exhibits many traits—often both faults and virtues. Characters can also be classified as dynamic or static. A ***dynamic character*** is one who changes or grows during the course of the work. A ***static character*** is one who does not change.

See ***Characterization, Hero/Heroine,*** and ***Motive.***

**CHARACTERIZATION** ***Characterization*** is the act of creating and developing a character. Authors use two major methods of characterization—***direct*** and ***indirect.*** When using direct characterization, a writer states the ***characters' traits,*** or characteristics.

When describing a character indirectly, a writer depends on the reader to draw conclusions about the character's traits. Sometimes the writer tells what other participants in the story say and think about the character.

See ***Character*** and ***Motive.***

**CLIMAX** The ***climax,*** also called the turning point, is the high point in the action of the plot. It is the moment of greatest tension, when the outcome of the plot hangs in the balance.

See ***Plot.***

**COMEDY** A ***comedy*** is a literary work, especially a play, which is light, often humorous or satirical, and ends happily. Comedies frequently depict ordinary characters faced with temporary difficulties and conflicts. Types of comedy include ***romantic comedy,*** which involves problems between lovers, and the ***comedy of manners,*** which satirically challenges social customs of a society.

**CONCRETE POEM** A ***concrete poem*** is one with a shape that suggests its subject. The poet arranges the letters, punctuation, and lines to create an image, or picture, on the page.

**CONFLICT** A ***conflict*** is a struggle between opposing forces. Conflict is one of the most important elements of stories, novels, and plays because it causes the action. There are two kinds of conflict: external and internal. An ***external conflict*** is one in which a character struggles against some outside force, such as another person. Another kind of external conflict may occur between a character and some force in nature.

An ***internal conflict*** takes place within the mind of a character. The character struggles to make a decision, take an action, or overcome a feeling.

See ***Plot.***

**CONNOTATIONS** The ***connotation*** of a word is the set of ideas associated with it in addition to its explicit meaning. The connotation of a word can be personal, based on individual experiences. More often, cultural connotations—those recognizable by most people in a group—determine a writer's word choices.

See also ***Denotation.***

**COUPLET** A ***couplet*** is two consecutive lines of verse with end rhymes. Often, a couplet functions as a stanza.

**CULTURAL CONTEXT** The ***cultural context*** of a literary work is the economic, social, and historical environment of the characters. This includes the attitudes and customs of that culture and historical period.

**DENOTATION** The ***denotation*** of a word is its dictionary meaning, independent of other associations that the word may have. The denotation of the word ***lake,*** for example, is "an inland body of water." "Vacation spot" and "place where the fishing is good" are connotations of the word ***lake.***

See also ***Connotation.***

**DESCRIPTION** A ***description*** is a portrait, in words, of a person, place, or object. Descriptive writing uses images that appeal to the five senses —sight, hearing, touch, taste, and smell.

See ***Images.***

**DEVELOPMENT** See ***Plot.***

**DIALECT** ***Dialect*** is the form of a language spoken by people in a particular region or group. Dialects differ in pronunciation, grammar, and word choice. The English language is divided into many dialects. British English differs from American English.

**DIALOGUE** A ***dialogue*** is a conversation between characters. In poems, novels, and short stories, dialogue is usually set off by quotation marks to indicate a speaker's exact words.

In a play, dialogue follows the names of the characters, and no quotation marks are used.

**DICTION** ***Diction*** is a writer's word choice and the way the writer puts those words together. Diction is part of a writer's style and may be described as formal or informal, plain or fancy, ordinary or technical, sophisticated or down-to-earth, old-fashioned or modern.

**DRAMA** A ***drama*** is a story written to be performed by actors. Although a drama is meant to be performed, one can also read the script, or written version, and imagine the action. The ***script*** of a drama is made up of dialogue and stage directions. The ***dialogue*** is the words spoken by the actors. The ***stage directions,*** usually printed in italics, tell how the actors should look, move, and speak. They also describe the setting, sound effects, and lighting.

Dramas are often divided into parts called ***acts.*** The acts are often divided into smaller parts called ***scenes.***

**DYNAMIC CHARACTER** See ***Character.***

**ESSAY** An ***essay*** is a short nonfiction work about a particular subject. Most essays have a single major focus and a clear introduction, body, and conclusion.

There are many types of essays. An ***informal essay*** uses casual, conversational language. A ***historical essay*** gives facts, explanations, and insights about historical events. An ***expository essay*** explains an idea by breaking it down. A ***narrative essay*** tells a story about a real-life experience. An ***informational essay*** explains a process. A ***persuasive essay*** offers an opinion and supports it. A ***humorous essay*** uses humor to achieve the author's purpose. A ***reflective essay*** addresses an event or experience and includes the writer's personal insights about the event's importance.

See ***Exposition, Narration,*** and ***Persuasion.***

**EXPOSITION** In the plot of a story or a drama, the ***exposition,*** or introduction, is the part of the work that introduces the characters, setting, and basic situation.

See ***Plot.***

**EXPOSITORY WRITING** ***Expository writing*** is writing that explains or informs.

**EXTENDED METAPHOR** In an ***extended metaphor,*** as in a regular metaphor, a subject is spoken or written of as though it were something else. However, extended metaphor differs from regular metaphor in that several connected comparisons are made.

See ***Metaphor.***

**EXTERNAL CONFLICT** See ***Conflict.***

**FABLE** A ***fable*** is a brief story or poem, usually with animal characters, that teaches a lesson, or moral. The moral is usually stated at the end of the fable.

See ***Irony*** and ***Moral.***

**FANTASY** A ***fantasy*** is highly imaginative writing that contains elements not found in real life. Examples of fantasy include stories that involve supernatural elements, stories that resemble fairy tales, stories that deal with imaginary places and creatures, and science-fiction stories.

See ***Science Fiction.***

**FICTION** ***Fiction*** is prose writing that tells about imaginary characters and events. Short stories and novels are works of fiction. Some writers base their fiction on actual events and people, adding invented characters, dialogue, settings, and plots. Other writers rely on imagination alone.

See ***Narration, Nonfiction,*** and ***Prose.***

**FIGURATIVE LANGUAGE** ***Figurative language*** is writing or speech that is not meant to be taken literally. The many types of figurative language are known as ***figures of speech.*** Common figures of speech include metaphor, personification, and simile. Writers use figurative language to state ideas in vivid and imaginative ways.

See ***Metaphor, Personification, Simile,*** and ***Symbol.***

**FIGURE OF SPEECH** See ***Figurative Language.***

**FLASHBACK** A ***flashback*** is a scene within a story that interrupts the sequence of events to relate events that occurred in the past.

**FLAT CHARACTER** See ***Character.***

**FOIL** A ***foil*** is a character whose behavior and attitude contrast with those of the main character.

**FOLK TALE** A ***folk tale*** is a story composed orally and then passed from person to person by word of mouth. Folk tales originated among people who could neither read nor write. These people entertained one another by telling stories aloud—often dealing with heroes, adventure, magic, or romance. Eventually, modern scholars collected these stories and wrote them down.

Folk tales reflect the cultural beliefs and environments from which they come.

See ***Fable, Legend, Myth,*** and ***Oral Tradition.***

**FOOT** See ***Meter.***

**FORESHADOWING** ***Foreshadowing*** is the author's use of clues to hint at what might happen later in the story. Writers use foreshadowing to build their readers' expectations and to create suspense.

**FREE VERSE** ***Free verse*** is poetry not written in a regular, rhythmical pattern, or meter. The poet is free to write lines of any length or with any number of stresses, or beats. Free verse is therefore less constraining than ***metrical verse,*** in which every line must have a certain length and a certain number of stresses.

See ***Meter.***

**GENRE** A ***genre*** is a division or type of literature. Literature is commonly divided into three major genres: poetry, prose, and drama. Each major genre is, in turn, divided into lesser genres, as follows:

1. ***Poetry:*** lyric poetry, concrete poetry, dramatic poetry, narrative poetry, epic poetry
2. ***Prose:*** fiction (novels and short stories) and nonfiction (biography, autobiography, letters, essays, and reports)
3. ***Drama:*** serious drama and tragedy, comic drama, melodrama, and farce

See ***Drama, Poetry,*** and ***Prose.***

**HAIKU** The ***haiku*** is a three-line Japanese verse form. The first and third lines of a haiku each have five syllables. The second line has seven syllables. A writer of haiku uses images to create a single, vivid picture, generally of a scene from nature.

**HERO/HEROINE** A ***hero*** or ***heroine*** is a character whose actions are inspiring or noble. Often heroes and heroines struggle to overcome the obstacles and problems that stand in their way. Note that the term ***hero*** was originally used only for male characters, while heroic female characters were always called ***heroines.*** However, it is now acceptable to use ***hero*** to refer to females as well as to males.

**HISTORICAL CONTEXT** The ***historical context*** of a literary work includes the actual political and social events and trends of the time. When a work takes place in the past, knowledge about that historical time period can help the reader understand its setting, background, culture, and message, as well as the attitudes and actions of its characters. A reader must also take into account the historical context in which the writer was creating the work, which may be different from the time period of the work's setting.

**HUMOR** ***Humor*** is writing intended to evoke laughter. While most humorists try to entertain, humor can also be used to convey a serious theme.

**IDIOM** An ***idiom*** is an expression that has a meaning particular to a language or region. For example, in "Seventh Grade," Gary Soto uses the idiom "making a face," which means to contort one's face in an unusual, usually unattractive way.

**IMAGERY** See ***Images.***

**IMAGES** ***Images*** are words or phrases that appeal to one or more of the five senses. Writers use images to describe how their subjects look, sound, feel, taste, and smell. Poets often paint images, or word pictures, that appeal to the senses. These pictures help you to experience the poem fully.

**INTERNAL CONFLICT** See ***Conflict.***

**IRONY** ***Irony*** is a contradiction between what happens and what is expected. There are three main types of irony. ***Situational irony*** occurs when something happens that directly contradicts the expectations of the characters or the audience. ***Verbal irony*** is something contradictory that is said. In ***dramatic irony,*** the audience is aware of something that the character or speaker is not.

**JOURNAL** A ***journal*** is a daily, or periodic, account of events and the writer's thoughts and feelings about those events. Personal journals are not normally written for publication, but sometimes they do get published later with permission from the author or the author's family.

**LEGEND** A ***legend*** is a widely told story about the past—one that may or may not have a foundation in fact. Every culture has its own legends—its familiar, traditional stories.

See ***Folk Tale, Myth,*** and ***Oral Tradition.***

**LETTERS** A ***letter*** is a written communication from one person to another. In personal letters, the writer shares information and his or her thoughts and feelings with one other person or group. Although letters are not normally written for publication, they sometimes do get published later with the permission of the author or the author's family.

**LIMERICK** A ***limerick*** is a humorous, rhyming, five-line poem with a specific meter and rhyme scheme. Most limericks have three strong stresses in lines 1, 2, and 5 and two strong stresses in lines 3 and 4. Most follow the rhyme scheme ***aabba.***

**LYRIC POEM** A ***lyric poem*** is a highly musical verse that expresses the observations and feelings of a single speaker. It creates a single, unified impression.

**MAIN CHARACTER** See ***Character.***

**MEDIA ACCOUNTS** ***Media accounts*** are reports, explanations, opinions, or descriptions written for television, radio, newspapers, and magazines. While some media accounts report only facts, others include the writer's thoughts and reflections.

**METAPHOR** A ***metaphor*** is a figure of speech in which something is described as though it were something else. A metaphor, like a simile, works by pointing out a similarity between two unlike things.

See ***Extended Metaphor*** and ***Simile.***

**METER** The ***meter*** of a poem is its rhythmical pattern. This pattern is determined by the number of ***stresses,*** or beats, in each line. To describe the meter of a poem, read it emphasizing the beats in each line. Then, mark the stressed and unstressed syllables, as follows:

M̆y fáth | ĕr wás | th̆e fírst | tŏ héar |

As you can see, each strong stress is marked with a slanted line (´) and each unstressed syllable with a horseshoe symbol (˘). The weak and strong stresses are then divided by vertical lines (|) into groups called feet.

**MINOR CHARACTER** See ***Character.***

**MOOD** See ***Atmosphere.***

**MORAL** A ***moral*** is a lesson taught by a literary work. A fable usually ends with a moral that is directly stated. A poem, novel, short story, or essay often suggests a moral that is not directly stated. The moral must be drawn by the reader, based on other elements in the work.

See ***Fable.***

**MOTIVATION** See ***Motive.***

**MOTIVE** A ***motive*** is a reason that explains or partially explains a character's thoughts, feelings, actions, or speech. Writers try to make their characters' motives, or motivations, as clear as possible. If the motives of a main character are not clear, then the character will not be believable.

Characters are often motivated by needs, such as food and shelter. They are also motivated by feelings, such as fear, love, and pride. Motives may be obvious or hidden.

**MYTH** A ***myth*** is a fictional tale that explains the actions of gods or heroes or the origins of elements of nature. Myths are part of the oral tradition. They are composed orally and then passed from generation to generation by word of mouth. Every ancient culture has its own mythology, or collection of myths. Greek and Roman myths are known collectively as ***classical mythology.***

See ***Oral Tradition.***

**NARRATION** ***Narration*** is writing that tells a story. The act of telling a story is also called narration. Each piece is a ***narrative.*** A story told in fiction, nonfiction, poetry, or even drama is called a narrative.

See ***Narrative, Narrative Poem,*** and ***Narrator.***

**NARRATIVE** A ***narrative*** is a story. A narrative can be either fiction or nonfiction. Novels and short stories are types of fictional narratives. Biographies and autobiographies are nonfiction narratives. Poems that tell stories are also narratives.

See ***Narration*** and ***Narrative Poem.***

**NARRATIVE POEM** A ***narrative poem*** is a story told in verse. Narrative poems often have all the elements of short stories, including characters, conflict, and plot.

**NARRATOR** A ***narrator*** is a speaker or a character who tells a story. The narrator's perspective is the way he or she sees things. A ***third-person narrator*** is one who stands outside the action and speaks about it. A ***first-person narrator*** is one who tells a story and participates in its action.

See ***Point of View.***

**NONFICTION** ***Nonfiction*** is prose writing that presents and explains ideas or that tells about real people, places, objects, or events. Autobiographies, biographies, essays, reports, letters, memos, and newspaper articles are all types of nonfiction.

See ***Fiction.***

**NOVEL** A ***novel*** is a long work of fiction. Novels contain such elements as characters, plot, conflict, and setting. The writer of novels, or novelist, develops these elements. In addition to its main plot, a novel may contain one or more subplots, or independent, related stories. A novel may also have several themes.

See ***Fiction*** and ***Short Story.***

**NOVELLA** A fiction work that is longer than a short story but shorter than a novel.

**ONOMATOPOEIA** ***Onomatopoeia*** is the use of words that imitate sounds. ***Crash, buzz, screech, hiss, neigh, jingle,*** and ***cluck*** are examples of onomatopoeia. ***Chickadee, towhee,*** and ***whippoorwill*** are onomatopoeic names of birds.

Onomatopoeia can help put the reader in the activity of a poem.

**ORAL TRADITION** ***Oral tradition*** is the passing of songs, stories, and poems from generation to generation by word of mouth. Folk songs, folk tales, legends, and myths all come from the oral tradition. No one knows who first created these stories and poems.

See ***Folk Tale, Legend,*** and ***Myth.***

**OXYMORON** An ***oxymoron*** (pl. ***oxymora***) is a figure of speech that links two opposite or contradictory words in order to point out an idea or situation that seems contradictory or inconsistent but on closer inspection turns out to be somehow true.

**PERSONIFICATION** ***Personification*** is a type of figurative language in which a nonhuman subject is given human characteristics.

**PERSPECTIVE** See ***Narrator*** and ***Point of View.***

**PERSUASION** ***Persuasion*** is used in writing or speech that attempts to convince the reader or listener to adopt a particular opinion or course of action. Newspaper editorials and letters to the editor use persuasion. So do advertisements and campaign speeches given by political candidates. An ***argument*** is a logical way of presenting a belief, conclusion, or stance. A good argument is supported with reasoning and evidence.

**See *Essay.***

**PLAYWRIGHT** A ***playwright*** is a person who writes plays. William Shakespeare is regarded as the greatest playwright in English literature.

**PLOT** ***Plot*** is the sequence of events in which each event results from a previous one and causes the next. In most novels, dramas, short stories, and narrative poems, the plot involves both characters and a central conflict. The plot usually begins with an ***exposition*** that introduces the setting, the characters, and the basic situation. This is followed by the ***inciting incident,*** which introduces the central conflict. The conflict then increases during the ***development*** until it reaches a high point of interest or suspense, the ***climax.*** The climax is followed by the ***falling action,*** or end, of the central conflict. Any events that occur during the ***falling action*** make up the ***resolution*** or ***denouement.***

Some plots do not have all of these parts. Some stories begin with the inciting incident and end with the resolution.

See ***Conflict.***

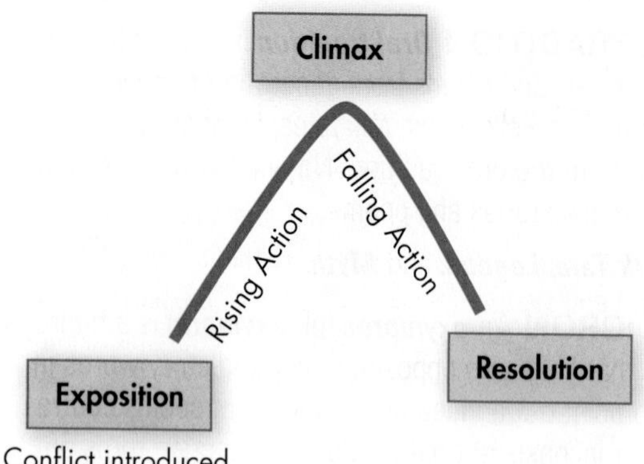


**POETRY** ***Poetry*** is one of the three major types of literature, the others being prose and drama. Most poems make use of highly concise, musical, and emotionally charged language. Many also make use of imagery, figurative language, and special devices of sound such as rhyme. Major types of poetry include ***lyric poetry, narrative poetry,*** and ***concrete poetry.***

See ***Concrete Poem, Genre, Lyric Poem,*** and ***Narrative Poem.***

**POINT OF VIEW** ***Point of view*** is the perspective, or vantage point, from which a story is told. It is either a narrator outside the story or a character in the story. ***First-person point of view*** is told by a character who uses the first-person pronoun "I."

The two kinds of ***third-person point of view,*** limited and omniscient, are called "third person" because the narrator uses third-person pronouns such as he and she to refer to the characters. There is no "I" telling the story.

In stories told from the ***omniscient third-person point of view,*** the narrator knows and tells about what each character feels and thinks.

In stories told from the ***limited third-person point of view,*** the narrator relates the inner thoughts and feelings of only one character, and everything is viewed from this character's perspective.

See ***Narrator.***

**PROBLEM** See ***Conflict.***

**PROSE** ***Prose*** is the ordinary form of written language. Most writing that is not poetry, drama, or song is considered prose. Prose is one of the major genres of literature and occurs in fiction and nonfiction.

See ***Fiction, Genre,*** and ***Nonfiction.***

**PROTAGONIST** The ***protagonist*** is the main character in a literary work. Often, the protagonist is a person, but sometimes it can be an animal.

See ***Antagonist*** and ***Character.***

**REFRAIN** A ***refrain*** is a regularly repeated line or group of lines in a poem or a song.

**REPETITION** ***Repetition*** is the use, more than once, of any element of language—a sound, word, phrase, clause, or sentence. Repetition is used in both prose and poetry.

See ***Alliteration, Meter, Plot, Rhyme,*** and ***Rhyme Scheme.***

**RESOLUTION** The ***resolution*** is the outcome of the conflict in a plot.

See ***Plot.***

**RHYME** ***Rhyme*** is the repetition of sounds at the ends of words. Poets use rhyme to lend a songlike quality to their verses and to emphasize certain words and ideas. Many traditional poems contain ***end rhymes,*** or rhyming words at the ends of lines.

Another common device is the use of ***internal rhymes,*** or rhyming words within lines. Internal rhyme also emphasizes the flowing nature of a poem.

See ***Rhyme Scheme.***

**RHYME SCHEME** A ***rhyme scheme*** is a regular pattern of rhyming words in a poem. To indicate the rhyme scheme of a poem, one uses lowercase letters. Each rhyme is assigned a different letter, as follows in the first stanza of "Dust of Snow" by Robert Frost:

The way a crow ***a***
Shook down on me ***b***
The dust of snow ***a***
From a hemlock tree ***b***

Thus, the stanza has the rhyme scheme ***abab.***

**RHYTHM** ***Rhythm*** is the pattern of stressed and unstressed syllables in spoken or written language.

See ***Meter.***

**ROUND CHARACTER** See ***Character.***

**SCENE** A ***scene*** is a section of uninterrupted action in the act of a drama.

See ***Drama.***

**SCIENCE FICTION** ***Science fiction*** combines elements of fiction and fantasy with scientific fact. Many science-fiction stories are set in the future.

**SENSORY LANGUAGE** ***Sensory language*** is writing or speech that appeals to one or more of the five senses.

See ***Images.***

**SETTING** The ***setting*** of a literary work is the time and place of the action. The setting includes all the details of a place and time—the year, the time of day, even the weather. The place may be a specific country, state, region, community, neighborhood, building, institution, or home. Details such as dialects, clothing, customs, and modes of transportation are often used to establish setting. In most stories, the setting serves as a backdrop—a context in which the characters interact. Setting can also help to create a feeling, or atmosphere.

See ***Atmosphere.***

**SHORT STORY** A ***short story*** is a brief work of fiction. Like a novel, a short story presents a sequence of events, or plot. The plot usually deals with a central conflict faced by a main character, or protagonist. The events in a short story usually communicate a message about life or human nature. This message, or central idea, is the story's theme.

See ***Conflict, Plot,*** and ***Theme.***

**SIMILE** A ***simile*** is a figure of speech that uses ***like*** or ***as*** to make a direct comparison between two unlike ideas. Everyday speech often contains similes, such as "pale as a ghost," "good as gold," "spread like wildfire," and "clever as a fox."

**SOUND DEVICES** ***Sound devices*** are techniques used by writers to give musical effects to their writing. Some of these include ***onomatopoeia, alliteration, rhyme, meter,*** and ***repetition.***

**SPEAKER** The ***speaker*** is the imaginary voice a poet uses when writing a poem. The speaker is the character who tells the poem. This character, or voice, often is not identified by name. There can be important differences between the poet and the poem's speaker.

See ***Narrator.***

**SPEECH** A ***speech*** is a work that is delivered orally to an audience. There are many kinds of speeches suiting almost every kind of public gathering. Types of speeches include ***dramatic, persuasive,*** and ***informative.***

**STAGE DIRECTIONS** ***Stage directions*** are notes included in a drama to describe how the work is to be performed or staged. Stage directions are usually printed in italics and enclosed within parentheses or brackets. Some stage directions describe the movements, costumes, emotional states, and ways of speaking of the characters.

**STAGING** ***Staging*** includes the setting, lighting, costumes, special effects, and music that go into a stage performance of a drama.

See ***Drama.***

**STANZA** A ***stanza*** is a group of lines of poetry that are usually similar in length and pattern and are separated by spaces. A stanza is like a paragraph of poetry—it states and develops a single main idea.

**STATIC CHARACTER** See ***Character.***

**SURPRISE ENDING** A ***surprise ending*** is a conclusion that is unexpected. The reader has certain expectations about the ending based on details in the story. Often, a surprise ending is ***foreshadowed,*** or subtly hinted at, in the course of the work.

See ***Foreshadowing*** and ***Plot.***

**SUSPENSE** ***Suspense*** is a feeling of anxious uncertainty about the outcome of events in a literary work. Writers create suspense by raising questions in the minds of their readers.

**SYMBOL** A ***symbol*** is anything that stands for or represents something else. Symbols are common in everyday life. A dove with an olive branch in its beak is a symbol of peace. A blindfolded woman holding a balanced scale is a symbol of justice. A crown is a symbol of a king's status and authority.

**SYMBOLISM** ***Symbolism*** is the use of symbols. Symbolism plays an important role in many different types of literature. It can highlight certain elements the author wishes to emphasize and also add levels of meaning.

**THEME** The ***theme*** is a central message in a literary work. A theme can usually be expressed as a generalization, or a general statement, about human beings or about life. The theme of a work is not a summary of its plot. The theme is the writer's central idea.

Although a theme may be stated directly in the text, it is more often presented indirectly. When the theme is stated indirectly, or implied, the reader must figure out what the theme is by looking at what the work reveals about people or life.

**TONE** The ***tone*** of a literary work is the writer's attitude toward his or her audience and subject. The tone can often be described by a single adjective, such as ***formal*** or ***informal, serious*** or ***playful, bitter*** or ***ironic.*** Factors that contribute to the tone are word choice, sentence structure, line length, rhyme, rhythm, and repetition.

**TRAGEDY** A ***tragedy*** is a work of literature, especially a play, that results in a catastrophe for the main character. In ancient Greek drama, the main character is always a significant person—a king or a hero—and the cause of the tragedy is a tragic flaw, or weakness, in his or her character. In modern drama, the main character can be an ordinary person, and the cause of the tragedy can be some evil in society itself. The purpose of tragedy is not only to arouse fear and pity in the audience, but also, in some cases, to convey a sense of the grandeur and nobility of the human spirit.

**TURNING POINT** See ***Climax.***

**UNIVERSAL THEME** A ***universal theme*** is a message about life that is expressed regularly in many different cultures and time periods. Folk tales, epics, and romances often address universal themes like the importance of courage, the power of love, or the danger of greed.

**WORD CHOICE** See ***Diction.***

# Tips for Literature Circles



As you read and study literature, discussions with other readers can help you understand and enjoy what you have read. Use the following tips.

- ## Understand the purpose of your discussion

  Your purpose when you discuss literature is to broaden your understanding of a work by testing your own ideas and hearing the ideas of others. Keep your comments focused on the literature you are discussing. Starting with one focus question will help to keep your discussion on track.

- ## Communicate effectively

  Effective communication requires thinking before speaking. Plan the points that you want to make and decide how you will express them. Organize these points in logical order and use details from the work to support your ideas. Jot down informal notes to help keep your ideas focused.

  Remember to speak clearly, pronouncing words slowly and carefully. Also, listen attentively when others are speaking, and avoid interrupting.

- ## Consider other ideas and interpretations

  A work of literature can generate a wide variety of responses in different readers. Be open to the idea that many interpretations can be valid. To support your own ideas, point to the events, descriptions, characters, or other literary elements in the work that led to your interpretation. To consider someone else's ideas, decide whether details in the work support the interpretation he or she presents. Be sure to convey your criticism of the ideas of others in a respectful and supportive manner.

- ## Ask questions

  Ask questions to clarify your understanding of another reader's ideas. You can also use questions to call attention to possible areas of confusion, to points that are open to debate, or to errors in the speaker's points. To move a discussion forward, summarize and evaluate conclusions reached by the group members.

  When you meet with a group to discuss literature, use a chart like the one shown to analyze the discussion.

| **Work Being Discussed:** | |
|---|---|
| Focus Question: | |
| Your Response: | Another Student's Response: |
| Supporting Evidence: | Supporting Evidence: |

# Tips for Improving Reading Fluency

When you were younger, you learned to read. Then, you read to expand your experiences or for pure enjoyment. Now, you are expected to read to learn. As you progress in school, you are given more and more material to read. The tips on these pages will help you improve your reading fluency, or your ability to read easily, smoothly, and expressively.

## Keeping Your Concentration

One common problem that readers face is the loss of concentration. When you are reading an assignment, you might find yourself rereading the same sentence several times without really understanding it. The first step in changing this behavior is to notice that you do it. Becoming an active, aware reader will help you get the most from your assignments. Practice using these strategies:

- Cover what you have already read with a note card as you go along. Then, you will not be able to reread without noticing that you are doing it.
- Set a purpose for reading beyond just completing the assignment. Then, read actively by pausing to ask yourself questions about the material as you read.
- Use the Reading Strategy instruction and notes that appear with each selection in this textbook.
- Stop reading after a specified period of time (for example, 5 minutes) and summarize what you have read. To help you with this strategy, use the Reading Check questions that appear with each selection in this textbook. Reread to find any answers you do not know.

## Reading Phrases

Fluent readers read phrases rather than individual words. Reading this way will speed up your reading and improve your comprehension. Here are some useful ideas:

- Experts recommend rereading as a strategy to increase fluency. Choose a passage of text that is neither too hard nor too easy. Read the same passage aloud several times until you can read it smoothly. When you can read the passage fluently, pick another passage and keep practicing.
- Read aloud into a tape recorder. Then, listen to the recording, noting your accuracy, pacing, and expression. You can also read aloud and share feedback with a partner.
- Use *Hear It!* Prentice Hall Literature Audio program CDs to hear the selections read aloud. Read along silently in your textbook, noticing how the reader uses his or her voice and emphasizes certain words and phrases.

## Understanding Key Vocabulary

If you do not understand some of the words in an assignment, you may miss out on important concepts. Therefore, it is helpful to keep a dictionary nearby when you are reading. Follow these steps:

- Before you begin reading, scan the text for unfamiliar words or terms. Find out what those words mean before you begin reading.

- Use context—the surrounding words, phrases, and sentences—to help you determine the meanings of unfamiliar words.
- If you are unable to understand the meaning through context, refer to the dictionary.

## Paying Attention to Punctuation

When you read, pay attention to punctuation. Commas, periods, exclamation points, semicolons, and colons tell you when to pause or stop. They also indicate relationships between groups of words. When you recognize these relationships you will read with greater understanding and expression. Look at the chart below.

| Punctuation Mark | Meaning |
|---|---|
| comma | brief pause |
| period | pause at the end of a thought |
| exclamation point | pause that indicates emphasis |
| semicolon | pause between related but distinct thoughts |
| colon | pause before giving explanation or examples |

## Using the Reading Fluency Checklist

Use the checklist below each time you read a selection in this textbook. In your Language Arts journal or notebook, note which skills you need to work on and chart your progress each week.

| Reading Fluency Checklist |
|---|
| ❑ Preview the text to check for difficult or unfamiliar words. |
| ❑ Practice reading aloud. |
| ❑ Read according to punctuation. |
| ❑ Break down long sentences into the subject and its meaning. |
| ❑ Read groups of words for meaning rather than reading single words. |
| ❑ Read with expression (change your tone of voice to add meaning to the word). |

Reading is a skill that can be improved with practice. The key to improving your fluency is to read. The more you read, the better your reading will become.

# Types of Writing

Good writing can be a powerful tool used for many purposes. Writing can allow you to defend something you believe in or to show how much you know about a subject. Writing can also help you share what you have experienced, imagined, thought, and felt. The three main types of writing are argument, informative/explanatory, and narrative.

## Argument

When you think of the word *argument,* you might think of a disagreement between two people, but an argument is more than that. An argument is a logical way of presenting a belief, conclusion, or stance. A good argument is supported with reasoning and evidence.

Argument writing can be used for many purposes, such as to change a reader's point of view or opinion or to bring about an action or a response from a reader.

There are three main purposes for writing a formal argument:

- to change the reader's mind
- to convince the reader to accept what is written
- to motivate the reader to take action, based on what is written

The following are some types of argument writing:

**Advertisements** An advertisement is a planned message meant to be seen, heard, or read. It attempts to persuade an audience to buy a product or service, accept an idea, or support a cause. Advertisements may appear in print, online, or in broadcast form.

Several common types of advertisements are public-service announcements, billboards, merchandise ads, service ads, and political campaign literature.

**Persuasive Essay** A persuasive essay presents a position on an issue, urges readers to accept that position, and may encourage a specific action. An effective persuasive essay

- Explores an issue of importance to the writer
- Addresses an issue that is arguable
- Uses facts, examples, statistics, or personal experiences to support a position
- Tries to influence the audience through appeals to the readers' knowledge, experiences, or emotions
- Uses clear organization to present a logical argument

Forms of persuasion include editorials, position papers, persuasive speeches, grant proposals, advertisements, and debates.

## Informative/Explanatory

Informative/explanatory writing should rely on facts to inform or explain. Informative/explanatory writing serves some closely related purposes: to increase readers' knowledge of a subject, to help readers better understand a procedure or process, or to provide readers with an enhanced comprehension of a concept. It should also feature a clear introduction, body, and conclusion. The following are some examples of informative/explanatory writing:

**Cause-and-Effect Essay** A cause-and-effect essay examines the relationship between events, explaining how one event or situation causes another. A successful cause-and-effect essay includes

- A discussion of a cause, event, or condition that produces a specific result
- An explanation of an effect, outcome, or result
- Evidence and examples to support the relationship between cause and effect
- A logical organization that makes the explanation clear

**Comparison-and-Contrast Essay** A comparison-and-contrast essay analyzes the similarities and differences between or among two or more things. An effective comparison-and-contrast essay

- Identifies a purpose for comparison and contrast
- Identifies similarities and differences between or among two or more things, people, places, or ideas
- Gives factual details about the subjects
- Uses an organizational plan suited to the topic and purpose

**Descriptive Writing** Descriptive writing creates a vivid picture of a person, place, thing, or event. Most descriptive writing includes

- Sensory details—sights, sounds, smells, tastes, and physical sensations
- Vivid, precise language

- Figurative language or comparisons
- Adjectives and adverbs that paint a word picture
- An organization suited to the subject

Types of descriptive writing include descriptions of ideas, observations, remembrances, travel brochures, physical descriptions, functional descriptions, and character sketches.

**Problem-and-Solution Essay** A problem-and-solution essay describes a problem and offers one or more solutions to it. It describes a clear set of steps to achieve a result. An effective problem-and-solution essay includes

- A clear statement of the problem, with its causes and effects summarized for the reader
- The most important aspects of the problem
- A proposal of at least one realistic solution
- Facts, statistics, data, or expert testimony to support the solution
- A clear organization that makes the relationship between problem and solution obvious

**Research Writing** Research writing is based on information gathered from outside sources. A research paper—a focused study of a topic—helps writers explore and connect ideas, make discoveries, and share their findings with an audience. An effective research paper

- Focuses on a specific, narrow topic, which is usually summarized in a thesis statement
- Presents relevant information from a wide variety of sources
- Uses a clear organization that includes an introduction, body, and conclusion
- Includes a bibliography or works-cited list that identifies the sources from which the information was drawn

Other types of writing that depend on accurate and insightful research include multimedia presentations, statistical reports, annotated bibliographies, and experiment journals.

**Workplace Writing** Workplace writing is probably the format you will use most after you finish school. In general, workplace writing is fact-based and meant to communicate specific information in a structured format. Effective workplace writing

- Communicates information concisely
- Includes details that provide necessary information and anticipate potential questions
- Is error-free and neatly presented

Common types of workplace writing include business letters, memorandums, résumés, forms, and applications.

## Narrative

Narrative writing conveys experience, either real or imaginary, and uses time to provide structure. It can be used to inform, instruct, persuade, or entertain. Whenever writers tell a of story, they are using narrative writing. Most narrative-writing types share certain elements, such as characters, a setting, a sequence of events, and, often, a theme. The following are some types of narration:

**Autobiographical Writing** Autobiographical writing tells a true story about an important period, experience, or relationship in the writer's life. Effective autobiographical writing includes

- A series of events that involve the writer as the main character
- Details, thoughts, feelings, and insights from the writer's perspective
- A conflict or an event that affects the writer
- A logical organization that tells the story clearly
- Insights that the writer gained from the experience

Types of autobiographical writing include personal narratives, autobiographical sketches, reflective essays, eyewitness accounts, and memoirs.

**Short Story** A short story is a brief, creative narrative. Most short stories include

- Details that establish the setting in time and place
- A main character who undergoes a change or learns something during the course of the story
- A conflict or a problem to be introduced, developed, and resolved
- A plot, the series of events that make up the action of the story
- A theme or message about life

Types of short stories include realistic stories, fantasies, historical narratives, mysteries, thrillers, science-fiction stories, and adventure stories.

# Writing Friendly Letters

## Writing Friendly Letters

A friendly letter is much less formal than a business letter. It is a letter to a friend, a family member, or anyone with whom the writer wants to communicate in a personal, friendly way. Most friendly letters are made up of five parts:

- ✔ the heading
- ✔ the salutation, or greeting
- ✔ the body
- ✔ the closing
- ✔ the signature

The purpose of a friendly letter is often one of the following:

- ✔ to share personal news and feelings
- ✔ to send or to answer an invitation
- ✔ to express thanks

## Model Friendly Letter

In this friendly letter, Betsy thanks her grandparents for a birthday present and gives them some news about her life.

11 Old Farm Road
Topsham, Maine 04011

April 14, 20—

Dear Grandma and Grandpa,

Thank you for the sweater you sent me for my birthday. It fits perfectly, and I love the color. I wore my new sweater to the carnival at school last weekend and got lots of compliments.

The weather here has been cool but sunny. Mom thinks that "real" spring will never come. I can't wait until it's warm enough to go swimming.

School is going fairly well. I really like my Social Studies class. We are learning about the U.S. Constitution, and I think it's very interesting. Maybe I will be a lawyer when I grow up.

When are you coming out to visit us? We haven't seen you since Thanksgiving. You can stay in my room when you come. I'll be happy to sleep on the couch. (The TV is in that room!!)

Well, thanks again and hope all is well with you.

Love,

Betsy

The **heading** includes the writer's address and the date on which he or she wrote the letter.

The **body** is the main part of the letter and contains the basic message.

Some common **closings** for personal letters include "Best wishes," "Love "Sincerely," and "Yours truly."

# Writing Business Letters

## Formatting Business Letters

Business letters follow one of several acceptable formats. In **block format,** each part of the letter begins at the left margin. A double space is used between paragraphs. In **modified block format,** some parts of the letter are indented to the center of the page. No matter which format is used, all letters in business format have a heading, an inside address, a salutation or greeting, a body, a closing, and a signature. These parts are shown and annotated on the model business letter below, formatted in modified block style.

## Model Business Letter

In this letter, Yolanda Dodson uses modified block format to request information.

Students for a Cleaner Planet
c/o Memorial High School
333 Veteran's Drive
Denver, CO 80211

January 25, 20—

Steven Wilson, Director
Resource Recovery Really Works
300 Oak Street
Denver, CO 80216

Dear Mr. Wilson:

Memorial High School would like to start a branch of your successful recycling program. We share your commitment to reclaiming as much reusable material as we can. Because your program has been successful in other neighborhoods, we're sure that it can work in our community. Our school includes grades 9–12 and has about 800 students.

Would you send us some information about your community recycling program? For example, we need to know what materials can be recycled and how we can implement the program.

At least fifty students have already expressed an interest in getting involved, so I know we'll have the people power to make the program work. Please help us get started.

Thank you in advance for your time and consideration.

Sincerely,

*Yolanda Dodson*

Yolanda Dodson

The **heading** shows the writer's address and organization (if any) and the date.

The **inside address** indicates where the letter will be sent.

A **salutation** is punctuated by a colon. When the specific addressee is not known, use a general greeting such as "To whom it may concern:"

The **body** of the letter states the writer's purpose. In this case, the writer requests information.

The **closing** "Sincerely" is common, but "Yours truly" or "Respectfully yours" are also acceptable. To end the letter, the writer types her name and provides a **signature.**

# Grammar, Usage, and Mechanics Handbook

## Parts of Speech

**Nouns** A **noun** is the name of a person, place, or thing. A **common noun** names any one of a class of people, places, or things. A **proper noun** names a specific person, place, or thing.

| ***Common Nouns*** | ***Proper Nouns*** |
|---|---|
| writer | Francisco Jiménez |

Use *apostrophes* with nouns to show ownership. Add an apostrophe and *s* to show the **possessive case** of most singular nouns. Add just an apostrophe to show the possessive case of plural nouns ending in *s* or *es*. Add an apostrophe and *s* to show the possessive case of plural nouns that do not end in *s* or *es*.

**Pronouns** A **pronoun** is a word that stands for a noun or for a word that takes the place of a noun. A **personal pronoun** refers to (1) the person speaking, (2) the person spoken to, or (3) the person, place, or thing spoken about.

| | ***Singular*** | ***Plural*** |
|---|---|---|
| ***First Person*** | I, me, my, mine | we, us, our, ours |
| ***Second Person*** | you, your, yours | you, your, yours |
| ***Third Person*** | he, him, his, she, her, hers, it, its | they, them, their, theirs |

A **demonstrative pronoun** directs attention to a specific person, place, or thing.

*These* are the juiciest pears I have ever tasted.

An **interrogative pronoun** is used to begin a question.

*Who* is the author of "Jeremiah's Song"?

An **indefinite pronoun** refers to a person, place, or thing, often without specifying which one.

*Many* of the players were tired.

*Everyone* bought something.

**Verbs** A **verb** is a word that expresses time while showing an action, a condition, or the fact that something exists. An **action verb** indicates the action of someone or something. A **linking verb** connects the subject of a sentence with a noun or a pronoun that renames or describes the subject. A **helping verb** can be added to another verb to make a single verb phrase.

**Adjectives** An **adjective** describes a noun or a pronoun or gives a noun or a pronoun a more specific meaning. Adjectives answer the questions *what kind, which one, how many,* or *how much.*

The articles *the, a,* and *an* are adjectives. *An* is used before a word beginning with a vowel sound.

A noun may sometimes be used as an adjective.

*family* home    *science* fiction

**Adverbs** An **adverb** modifies a verb, an adjective, or another adverb. Adverbs answer the questions *where, when, in what way,* or *to what extent.*

**Prepositions** A **preposition** relates a noun or a pronoun following it to another word in the sentence.

The ball rolled <u>under</u> the table.

**Conjunctions** A **conjunction** connects other words or groups of words. A **coordinating conjunction** connects similar kinds or groups of words. **Correlative conjunctions** are used in pairs to connect similar words or groups of words.

*both* Grandpa *and* Dad    *neither* they *nor* I

**Interjections** An **interjection** is a word that expresses feeling or emotion and functions independently of a sentence.

"Ah!" says he—

## Phrases, Clauses, and Sentences

**Sentences** A **sentence** is a group of words with two main parts: a complete subject and a complete predicate. Together, these parts express a complete thought.

We read that story last year.

A **fragment** is a group of words that does not express a complete thought.

"Not right away."

**Subject** The **subject** of a sentence is the word or group of words that tells whom or what the sentence is about. The simple subject is the essential noun, pronoun, or group of words acting as a noun that cannot be left out of the complete subject. A **complete subject** is the **simple subject** plus any modifiers. In the following example, the complete subject is underlined. The simple subject is italicized.

<u>Pony express *riders*</u> carried packages for miles.

A **compound subject** is two or more subjects that have the same verb and are joined by a conjunction.

*Neither the horse nor the driver* looked tired.

**Predicate** The **predicate** of a sentence is the verb or verb phrase that tells what the complete subject of the sentence does or is. The **simple predicate** is the essential verb or verb phrase that cannot be left out of the complete predicate. A **complete predicate** is the simple predicate plus any modifiers or complements. In the following example, the complete predicate is underlined. The simple predicate is italicized.

Pony express riders <u>*carried* packages for miles.</u>

A **compound predicate** is two or more verbs that have the same subject and are joined by a conjunction.

She *sneezed and coughed* throughout the trip.

**Complement** A **complement** is a word or group of words that completes the meaning of the predicate of a sentence. Five different kinds of complements can be found in English sentences: *direct objects, indirect objects, objective complements, predicate nominatives,* and *predicate adjectives.*

A **direct object** is a noun, pronoun, or group of words acting as a noun that receives the action of a transitive verb.

We watched the *liftoff.*

An **indirect object** is a noun, pronoun, or group of words that appears with a direct object and names the person or thing that something is given to or done for.

He sold the *family* a mirror.

An **objective complement** is an adjective or noun that appears with a direct object and describes or renames it.

I called Meg my *friend.*

A **subject complement** is a noun, pronoun, or adjective that appears with a linking verb and tells something about the subject. A subject complement may be a *predicate nominative* or a *predicate adjective.*

A **predicate nominative** is a noun or pronoun that appears with a linking verb and renames, or explains the subject.

Kiglo was the *leader.*

A **predicate adjective** is an adjective that appears with a linking verb and describes the subject of a sentence.

Roko became *tired.*

**Sentence Types** There are four types of sentences:

1. A **simple sentence** consists of a single independent clause.
2. A **compound sentence** consists of two or more independent clauses joined by a comma and a coordinating conjunction or by a semicolon.
3. A **complex sentence** consists of one independent clause and one or more subordinate clauses.
4. A **compound-complex sentence** consists of two or more independent clauses and one or more subordinate clauses.

There are four functions of sentences:

1. A **declarative sentence** states an idea and ends with a period.
2. An **interrogative sentence** asks a question and ends with a question mark.
3. An **imperative sentence** gives an order or a direction and ends with either a period or an exclamation mark.
4. An **exclamatory sentence** conveys a strong emotion and ends with an exclamation mark.

**Phrases** A phrase is a group of words, without a subject and a verb, that functions in a sentence as one part of speech.

A **prepositional phrase** is a group of words that includes a preposition and a noun or a pronoun that is the object of the preposition.

near the town with them

An **adjective phrase** is a prepositional phrase that modifies a noun or a pronoun by telling what kind or which one.

The house *on the corner* is new.

An **adverb phrase** is a prepositional phrase that modifies a verb, an adjective, or an adverb by pointing out where, when, in what manner, or to what extent.

Bring your saddle *to the barn.*

An **appositive phrase** is a noun or a pronoun with modifiers, placed next to a noun or a pronoun to add information and details.

The story, a *tale of adventure,* takes place in the Yukon.

A **participial phrase** is a participle modified by an adjective or an adverb phrase or accompanied by a complement. The entire phrase acts as an adjective.

*Running at top speed,* he soon caught up.

An **infinitive phrase** is an infinitive with modifiers, complements, or a subject, all acting together as a single part of speech. An infinitive is the verb form that starts with *to.*

I was happy *to sit down.*

**Clauses** A clause is a group of words with its own subject and verb. An **independent clause** can stand by itself as a complete sentence.

"I think it belongs to Rachel."

A **dependent clause** has a subject and a verb but cannot stand as a complete sentence; it can only be part of a sentence.

"Although it was late"

## Using Verbs, Pronouns, and Modifiers

**Principal Parts** A **verb** has four principal parts: the present, the present participle, the past, and the past participle.

**Regular verbs** form the past and past participle by adding *-ed* to the present form.

*Present:* walk *Past:* walked
*Present Participle:* (am) walking *Past Participle:* (have) walked

**Irregular verbs** form the past and past participle by changing form rather than by adding *-ed.*

*Present:* go *Past:* went
*Present Participle:* (am) going *Past Participle:* (have) gone

**Verb Tense** A **verb tense** tells whether the time of an action or condition is in the past, the present, or the future. Every verb has six tenses: *present, past, future, present perfect, past perfect,* and *future perfect.* The **present tense** shows actions that happen in the present. The **past tense** shows actions that have already happened. The **future tense** shows actions that will happen. The **present perfect tense** shows actions that begin in the past and continue to the present. The **past perfect tense** shows a past action or condition that ended before another past action. The **future perfect tense** shows a future action or condition that will have ended before another begins.

**Pronoun Case** The **case** of a pronoun is the form it takes to show its use in a sentence. There are three pronoun cases: *nominative, objective,* and *possessive.* The **nominative case** is used to name or rename the subject of the sentence. The nominative case pronouns are *I, you, he, she, it, we, you, they.*

*As the subject: She* is brave.

*Renaming the subject:* The leader is *she.*

The **objective case** is used as the direct object, indirect object, or object of a preposition. The objective case pronouns are *me, you, him, her, it, us, you, them.*

*As a direct object:* Tom called *me.*

*As an indirect object:* My friend gave *me* advice.

*As an object of a preposition:* She went without *me.*

The **possessive case** is used to show ownership. The possessive pronouns are *my, your, his, her, its, our, their, mine, yours, his, hers, its, ours, theirs.*

**Subject-Verb Agreement** To make a subject and a verb agree, make sure that both are singular or both are plural. Two or more singular subjects joined by *or* or *nor* must have a singular verb. When singular and plural subjects are joined by *or* or *nor,* the verb must agree with the closest subject.

*He is* at the door. They *drive* home.

Either *Joe* or *you are* going. Both *pets are* hungry.

**Pronoun-Antecedent Agreement** **Pronouns** must agree with their antecedents in number and gender. Use singular pronouns with singular antecedents and plural pronouns with plural antecedents. Many errors in pronoun-antecedent agreement occur when a plural pronoun is used to refer to a singular antecedent for which the gender is not specified.

*Incorrect:* Everyone did their best.

*Correct:* Everyone did his or her best.

The following indefinite pronouns are singular: *anybody, anyone, each, either, everybody, everyone, neither, nobody, no one, one, somebody, someone.* The following indefinite pronouns are plural: *both, few, many, several.* The following indefinite pronouns may be either singular or plural: *all, any, most, none, some.*

**Modifiers** The *comparative* and *superlative* degrees of most adjectives and adverbs of one or two syllables can be formed in either of two ways: Use *-er* or *more* to form a comparative degree and *-est* or *most* to form the superlative degree of most one- and two-syllable modifiers.

*More* and *most* can also be used to form the comparative and superlative degrees of most one- and two-syllable modifiers. These words should not be used when the result sounds awkward, as in "A greyhound is *more* fast than a beagle."

## Glossary of Common Usage

**accept, except:** *Accept* is a verb that means "to receive" or "to agree to." *Except* is a preposition that means "other than" or "leaving out." Do not confuse these two words.

Aaron sadly *accepted* his father's decision to sell Zlata.

Everyone *except* the fisherman had children.

**affect, effect:** *Affect* is normally a verb meaning "to influence" or "to bring about a change in." *Effect* is usually a noun, meaning "result."

**among, between:** *Among* is usually used with three or more items. *Between* is generally used with only two items.

**bad, badly:** Use the predicate adjective *bad* after linking verbs such as *feel, look,* and *seem.* Use *badly* whenever an adverb is required.

Mouse does not feel *bad* about tricking Coyote.

In the myth, Athene treats Arachne *badly.*

**beside, besides:** *Beside* means "at the side of" or "close to." *Besides* means "in addition to."

**can, may:** The verb *can* generally refers to the ability to act. The verb *may* generally refers to permission to act.

**different from, different than:** *Different from* is generally preferred over *different than.*

**farther, further:** Use *farther* when you refer to distance. Use *further* when you mean "to a greater degree or extent" or "additional."

**fewer, less:** Use *fewer* for things that can be counted. Use *less* for amounts or quantities that cannot be counted.

**good, well:** Use the predicate adjective *good* after linking verbs such as *feel, look, smell, taste,* and *seem.* Use *well* whenever you need an adverb.

**its, it's:** The word *its* with no apostrophe is a possessive pronoun. The word *it's* is a contraction for *it is.* Do not confuse the possessive pronoun *its* with the contraction *it's,* standing for "it is" or "it has."

**lay, lie:** Do not confuse these verbs. *Lay* is a transitive verb meaning "to set or put something down." Its principal parts are *lay, laying, laid, laid. Lie* is an intransitive verb meaning "to recline." Its principal parts are *lie, lying, lay, lain.*

**like, as:** *Like* is a preposition that usually means "similar to" or "in the same way as." *Like* should always be followed by an object. Do not use *like* before a subject and a verb. Use *as* or *that* instead.

**of, have:** Do not use *of* in place of *have* after auxiliary verbs like *would, could, should, may, might,* or *must.*

**raise, rise:** *Raise* is a transitive verb that usually takes a direct object. *Rise* is intransitive and never takes a direct object.

**set, sit:** *Set* is a transitive verb meaning "to put (something) in a certain place." Its principal parts are *set, setting, set, set. Sit* is an intransitive verb meaning "to be seated." Its principal parts are *sit, sitting, sat, sat.*

**than, then:** The conjunction *than* is used to connect the two parts of a comparison. Do not confuse *than* with the adverb *then,* which usually refers to time.

**that, which, who:** Use the relative pronoun *that* to refer to things or people. Use *which* only for things and *who* for people.

**when, where, why:** Do not use *when, where,* or *why* directly after a linking verb such as *is.* Reword the sentence.

*Faulty:* Suspense is *when* an author increases tension.

*Revised:* An author uses suspense to increase tension.

**who, whom:** Use *who* only as a subject in clauses and sentences and *whom* only as an object.

## Mechanics

### Capitalization

1. Capitalize the first word of a sentence.

   Young Roko glances down the valley.
2. Capitalize all proper nouns and adjectives.

   Mark Twain    Amazon River    Thanksgiving Day
3. Capitalize a person's title when it is followed by the person's name or when it is used in direct address.

   Doctor    General Khokhotov    Mrs. Price
4. Capitalize titles showing family relationships when they refer to a specific person, unless they are preceded by a possessive noun or pronoun.

   Granny-Liz    Margie's mother
5. Capitalize the first word and all other key words in the titles of books, periodicals, poems, stories, plays, paintings, and other works of art.

   from *Tom Sawyer*    "Grandpa and the Statue"
6. Capitalize the first word and all nouns in letter salutations and the first word in letter closings.

   Dear Willis,    Yours truly,

### Punctuation

#### End Marks

1. Use a **period** to end a declarative sentence, an imperative sentence, and most abbreviations.
2. Use a **question mark** to end a direct question or an incomplete question in which the rest of the question is understood.
3. Use an **exclamation mark** after a statement showing strong emotion, an urgent imperative sentence, or an interjection expressing strong emotion.

**Commas** Use commas:

1. before the conjunction to separate two independent clauses in a compound sentence.
2. to separate three or more words, phrases, or clauses in a series.
3. to separate adjectives of equal rank. Do not use commas to separate adjectives that must stay in a specific order.
4. after an introductory word, phrase, or clause.
5. to set off parenthetical and nonessential expressions.
6. with places and dates made up of two or more parts.
7. after items in addresses, after the salutation in a personal letter, after the closing in all letters, and in numbers of more than three digits.

**Semicolons** Use semicolons:

1. to join independent clauses that are not already joined by a conjunction.
2. to join independent clauses or items in a series that already contain commas.

**Colons** Use colons:

1. before a list of items following an independent clause.
2. in numbers giving the time, in salutations in business letters, and in labels used to signal important ideas.

**Quotation Marks**

1. A **direct quotation** represents a person's exact speech or thoughts and is enclosed in quotation marks.
2. An **indirect quotation** reports only the general meaning of what a person said or thought and does not require quotation marks.
3. Always place a comma or a period inside the final quotation mark of a direct quotation.
4. Place a question mark or an exclamation mark inside the final quotation mark if the end mark is part of the quotation; if it is not part of the quotation, place it outside the final quotation mark.

**Titles**

1. Underline or italicize the titles of long written works, movies, television and radio shows, lengthy works of music, paintings, and sculptures.
2. Use quotation marks around the titles of short written works, episodes in a series, songs, and titles of works mentioned as parts of collections.

**Hyphens** Use a **hyphen** with certain numbers, after certain prefixes, with two or more words used as one word, and with a compound modifier that comes before a noun.

**Apostrophes** Use apostrophes:

1. to show the possessive case of most singular nouns.
2. to show the possessive case of plural nouns ending in *s* and *es.*
3. to show the possessive case of plural nouns that do not end in *s* or *es.*
4. in a contraction to indicate the position of the missing letter or letters.

# Glossary

## PRONUNCIATION KEY

| Symbol | Sample Words | Symbol | Sample Words |
|---|---|---|---|
| a | at, tap, mat | ʊi | oil, toy, royal |
| ā | ate, rain, break | ʊu | out, now, sour |
| ä | car, father, heart | u | mud, ton, trouble |
| ch | chew, nature, such | ʉ | her, sir, word |
| e | end, feather, said | ’l | cattle, paddle, cuddle |
| ē | sea, steam, piece | ’n | sudden, hidden, sweeten |
| ə | ago, pencil, lemon | ŋ | ring, anger, pink |
| i | it, stick, gym | sh | shell, mission, fish |
| ī | nice, lie, sky | th | thin, nothing, both |
| ō | no, oat, low | *th* | then, mother, smooth |
| ô | all, law, taught | zh | vision, treasure, seizure |
| ʊʊ | look, would, pull | yʊʊ | cure, furious |
| o͞o | boot, drew, tune | yo͞o | cute, few, use |

Academic terms appear in blue type.

## A

**abode** (ə bōd) *n.* home; residence

**accusations** (ak′yo͞o zā′shənz) *n.* charges made against a person for doing something wrong

**acknowledge** (ak näl′ ij) *v.* recognize and admit

**adaptation** (ad′əp tā′shən) *n.* gradual change in behavior to adjust to accepted norms in society

**adequate** (ad′ i kwət) *adj.* sufficient; enough

**advocacy** (ad′və kə sē) *n.* support for a particular idea or mission

**affect** (ə fekt′) *v.* do something that produces a change in someone or something; influence

**aggressive** (ə gres′iv) *adj.* forceful, especially in a destructive or mean way

**ajar** (ə jär′) *adj.* slightly open

**analyze** (an′ə līz′) *v.* break into parts in order to study closely

**appearance** (ə pir′əns) *n.* how a person or thing looks or seems

**appreciate** (ə prē′shē āt′) *v.* be thankful for

**approximately** (ə präk′sə mit lē) *adv.* in a close, but not exact, way

**aptitude** (ap′ tə to͞od) *n.* talent; ability

**arid** (ar′id) *adj.* getting little rain, and therefore very dry

**assumption** (ə sump′shən) *n.* act of accepting something as true without proof

**assumptions** (ə sump′shənz) *n.* acts of accepting something as true without proof

**astonish** (ə stän′ ish) *v.* amaze

**attitude** (at′ə to͞od′) *n.* person's opinions and feelings about someone or something

**audible** (ô′ də bəl) *adj.* loud enough to be heard

**aversion** (ə vʉr′zhən) *n.* intense dislike

**awareness** (ə wer′ nəs) *n.* knowledge or understanding of a particular subject or situation

## B

**behavior** (bē hāv′yər) *n.* manner of conducting oneself

**bias** (bī′əs) *n.* slanted or prejudiced viewpoint

**bigots** (big′ əts) *n.* narrow-minded, prejudiced people

**blander** (bland′ ər) *adj.* more tasteless

**blunt** (blunt) *v.* lessen; make less forceful

**bound** (bound) *v.* tied

## C

**challenge** (chal′ənj) *n.* something that tests your skills and abilities

**characteristic** (kar′ək tər is′tik) *n.* trait; feature

**characterize** (kar′ək tər īz′) *v.* 1. be typical of someone or something; 2. describe someone or something in a particular way

**cite** (sīt) *v.* 1. mention something as proof or an example of something else; 2. refer to

**coax** (kōks) *v.* use gentle persuasion

**commemorated** (kə mem′ə rāt′ id) *v.* honored the memory of

**commissioned** (kə mish′ənd) *v.* appointed or hired to carry out a duty or task

**common** (käm′ən) *adj.* 1. ordinary; expected; 2. shared; public

**communal** (kə myoo͞n′ əl) *adj.* shared by all

**communicate** (kə myoo͞′ni kāt′) *v.* share ideas, thoughts or feelings; make known to others

**communication** (kə myoo͞′ni kā′shən) *n.* process of sharing information or expressing thoughts and feelings

**community** (kə myoo͞′nə tē) *n.* group of people who share an interest or who live near each other

**competition** (käm′pə tish′ən) *n.* event or game in which people or sides attempt to win

**complex** (käm pleks′) *adj.* 1. difficult to understand; 2. having many connected parts

**compose** (kəm pōz′) *v.* write or create a piece of music, art, or text

**compromise** (käm′prə mīz′) *n.* settling of differences in a way that allows both sides to feel satisfied

**compulsion** (kəm pul′ shən) *n.* driving, irresistible force

**conclude** (kən klo͞od′) *v.* finish; bring to a logical end

**conferred** (kən fʉrd′) *v.* met to discuss

**conflict** (kän flikt′) *n.* struggle between opposing forces

**consolation** (kän′ sə lā′ shən) *n.* something that comforts a disappointed person

**conspired** (kən spīrd′) *v.* planned together secretly

**contradiction** (kän′ trə dik′ shən) *n.* difference between two conflicting things that means they both cannot be true

**contraption** (kən trap′ shən) *n.* strange device or machine

**contrast** (kän′trast′) *v.* compare two things to show how they are different from each other

**contribute** (kən trib′yo͞ot) *v.* 1. add to; enrich; 2. provide

**conveyed** (kən vād′) *v.* made known; expressed

**convince** (kən vins′) *v.* cause to accept a point of view

**convincing** (kən vins′ iŋ) *adj.* persuasive

**coveted** (kuv′ it əd) *v.* wanted; desired

**cremated** (krē′māt′ əd) *v.* burned a dead body to ashes

**croon** (kro͞on) *v.* sing or hum quietly and soothingly

**crucial** (kro͞o′ shəl) *adj.* important; critical

**crystal** (kris′ təl) *adj.* made of clear, brilliant glass

**culminated** (kul′ mə nāt′ əd) *v.* reached its highest point, or climax

**culprit** (kul′ prit) *n.* guilty person

**culture** (kul′chər) *n.* customs of a group or community

**cunning** (kun′ iŋ) *adj.* sly; crafty

**cunningly** (kun′ iŋ lē) *adv.* cleverly

**curdled** (kʉrd′ ′ld) *adj.* rotten

**curiosity** (kyoor′ ē äs′ ə tē) *n.* desire to learn or know

**custom** (kus′təm) *n.* accepted practice

## D

**dabbling** (dab′ liŋ) *v.* wetting by dipping, splashing, or paddling in the water

**danger** (dān′jər) *n.* exposure to possible harm, injury, or loss

**debate** (dē bāt′) 1. *v.* discuss formally in front of others; 2. *n.* discussion or argument on a subject in which people express different opinions

**deceive** (dē sēv′) *v.* make someone believe something that is not true

**decipher** (dē sī′fər) *v.* make out the meaning of

**decreed** (di krēd′) *v.* officially ordered

**defiant** (dē fī′ ənt) *adj.* boldly resisting

**defies** (dē fīz′) *v.* boldly resists or opposes

**define** (dē fīn′) *v.* describe; explain

**definition** (def′ə nish′ən) *n.* sentence or phrase that states exactly what an idea, word, or phrase means

**describe** (di skrīb′) *v.* say what someone or something is like by giving details

**designated** (dez′ ig nāt′ əd) *v.* identified; pointed out

**desire** (di zīr′) *n.* wish or want

**desolate** (des′ ə lit) *adj.* lonely; solitary

**destitute** (des′ tə to͞ot′) *n.* people living in complete poverty

**deteriorates** (dē tir′ē ə rāts) *v.* gets worse

**determination** (dē tʉr′mi nā′shən) *n.* decision or conclusion

**devastated** (dev′ ə stāt′ əd) *v.* destroyed; completely upset

**devastating** (dev′ ə stāt′ iŋ) *adj.* destructive; overwhelming

**diagram** (dī′ə gram′) *n.* chart, drawing, or plan that makes something clearer to read and understand

**disagreement** (dis′ə grē′mənt) *n.* difference or conflict between people or groups

**disbanded** (dis band′ əd) *v.* broken up; dismissed

**discipline** (dis′ ə plin′) *n.* strict control

**discover** (di skuv′ər) *v.* find something hidden or previously unknown; find out

**dispute** (di spyo͞ot′) *n.* disagreement

**distinct** (di stiŋkt′) *adj.* separate and different

**diversity** (də vʉr′sə tē) *n.* variety, as of groups or cultures

**dolefully** (dōl′fəl lē) *adv.* with sadness and sorrow

**dominions** (də min′ yəns) *n.* governed countries or territories

**downy** (doʊ′ nē) *adj.* soft and fluffy

**duty** (do͞ot′ē) *n.* responsibility

## E

**effective** (e fek′tiv) *adj.* successful in producing the desired result

**eligible** (el′i jə bəl) *adj.* fit to be chosen; qualified

**emerged** (ē mʉrjd′) *v.* came out

**emphatic** (em fat′ ik) *adj.* expressing strong feeling

**endeavors** (en dev′ərz) *n.* attempts; efforts

**enhance** (en hans′) *v.* improve; make something better

**enrich** (en rich′) *v.* make better; improve in quality

**entertain** (ent′ər tān′) *v.* 1. amuse; 2. put on a performance

**environment** (en vī′rən mənt) *n.* 1. surroundings; 2. the natural world

**envying** (en′ vē iŋ) *v.* wanting something that someone else has

**epidemic** (ep′ ə dem′ ik) *n.* outbreak of a contagious disease

**equality** (ē kwôl′ ə tē) *n.* social state in which all people are treated the same

**ethnicity** (eth nis′ə tē) *n.* racial or cultural background

**evading** (ē vād′ iŋ) *v.* avoiding

**evaluate** (ē val′yo͞o āt′) *v.* judge or rate

**evaluations** (ē val′yo͞o ā′shənz) *n.* 1. acts of judging or rating something or someone; 2. judgments or interpretations

**evaporated** (ē vap′ ə rāt əd) *v.* changed from a liquid to a gas

**evidently** (ev′ ə dent′ lē) *adv.* clearly; obviously

**examine** (eg zam′ən) *v.* study in depth in order to find or check something

**exertion** (eg zʉr′ shən) *n.* physical work

**expectations** (ek′ spekt tā′ shənz) *n.* things looked forward to

**experiment** (ek sper′ə mənt) *n.* test to determine a result

**explain** (ek splān′) *v.* 1. describe; 2. make understandable

**explicit** (eks plis′it) *adj.* clearly stated; readily seen

**explore** (ek splôr′) *v.* 1. travel through an unfamiliar area to find out what it is like; 2. thoroughly discuss a topic

**express** (ek spres′) *v.* say or communicate a feeling

**exquisite** (eks′ kwiz it) *adj.* beautiful in a delicate way

## F

**facts** (fakts) *n.* true information about a topic

**family** (fam′ə lē) *n.* people related by blood or having a common ancestor

**fascinated** (fas′ ə nāt′ əd) *adj.* very interested

**fathom** (fa*th*′ əm) *n.* unit of length used to measure the depth of water

**feeble** (fē′ bəl) *adj.* weak

**feebleness** (fē′ bəl nəs) *n.* weakness

**feigned** (fānd) *v.* pretended or imitated

**fluent** (flo͞o′ ənt) *adj.* able to write or speak easily and smoothly

**flushed** (flusht) *v.* drove from hiding

**flustered** (flus′ tərd) *adj.* nervous; confused

**focus** (fō′kəs) *n.* direction; point of concentration

**forage** (fôr′ ij) *n.* food for domestic animals

**formal** (fôr′məl) *adj.* following established rules or customs

**formidable** (fôr′ mə də bəl) *adj.* impressive

**fosters** (fôs′tərz) *v.* promotes the growth or development of

**fragrant** (frā′ grənt) *adj.* sweet smelling

**fundamental** (fun′ də ment′ ′l) *adj.* basic; forming a foundation

**furor** (fyo͞or′ôr′) *n.* outburst of public anger or excitement

**furrowed** (fʉr′ōd) *v.* wrinkled

## G

**gauge** (gāj) *v.* estimate or judge

**globules** (gläb′ yo͞olz) *n.* drops of liquid

**granite** (gran′ it) *n.* hard, gray rock

**gratitude** (grat′ i to͞od′) *n.* thankful appreciation

**group** (gro͞op) *n.* collection or set, as of people

**groves** (grōvz) *n.* small groups of trees

**gumption** (gump′ shən) *n.* determination; initiative

## H

**habitats** (hab′ ə tats) *n.* places where specific animals or plants naturally live or grow

**haunches** (hônch′ əz) *n.* upper legs and hips of an animal

**hexagons** (hek′ sə gänz′) *n.* six-sided figures

**hoarding** (hôr′ diŋ) *n.* accumulation and storage of supplies

**hoed** (hōd) *v.* weeded or loosened soil with a metal hand tool

## I

**identify** (ī den′tə fī′) *v.* 1. recognize; 2. point out

**ignorant** (ig′ nə rənt) *adj.* not knowing facts or information

**ignore** (ig nôr′) *v.* pay no attention to

**illustrate** (il′ə strāt′) *v.* make something clear by providing examples

**image** (im′ij) *n.* picture; representation

**immensely** (i mens´ lē) *adv.* a great deal; very much

**impervious** (im pʉr´ vē əs) *adj.* not affected by something

**implored** (im plôrd´) *v.* begged

**imposters** (im päs´tərz) *n.* people or things pretending to be someone or something else

**impromptu** (im prämp´to͞o´) *adj.* unscheduled; unplanned

**incessantly** (in ses´ ənt lē) *adv.* without stopping

**individual** (in´də vij´o͞o əl) *n.* single person or thing

**inflicted** (in flikt´ əd) *v.* delivered something painful

**inform** (in fôrm´) *v.* tell; give information about

**information** (in´fər mā´shən) *n.* knowledge gained through study or experience

**inherent** (in hir´ ənt) *adj.* natural, basic, or inborn

**inquire** (in kwīr´) *v.* ask someone for information

**inquiry** (in´kwər ē) *n.* official process to find out why something happened

**insight** (in´sīt´) *n.* 1. ability to understand something clearly; 2. an understanding

**integration** (in´ tə grā´ shən) *n.* end of separation of cultural or racial groups

**intercedes** (in´tər sēdz´) *v.* makes a request on behalf of another

**interrogations** (in tər´ə gā´shənz) *n.* formal examinations that involve questioning the subject

**intervene** (in tər vēn´) *v.* come between in an effort to influence or help settle an action or argument

**interview** (in´tər vyo͞o´) *v.* ask a series of questions of a person in order to gain information

**intricate** (in´ tri kit) *adj.* complex; detailed

**investigate** (in ves´tə gāt´) *v.* examine thoroughly

**investigations** (in ves´tə gā´shənz) *n.* official attempts to find out the reasons for something, such as a crime or a problem

**investment** (in vest´mənt) *n.* act of devoting time or effort to a particular undertaking with the expectation of a worthwhile result

## J

**justifies** (jus´ tə fīz´) *v.* 1. excuses; 2. explains

## K

**knowledge** (näl´ij) *n.* result of learning; awareness

## L

**laborious** (lə bôr´ ē əs) *adj.* taking much work or effort

**learn** (lʉrn) *v.* gain knowledge or skills

**legal** (lē´gəl) *adj.* lawful

**legislation** (lej´ is lā´ shən) *n.* act of making laws; law-making

**listen** (lis´ən) *v.* pay attention to; heed

**literally** (lit´ər əl ē) *adv.* exactly

**loathed** (lōthd) *v.* hated

**luminous** (lo͞o´ mə nəs) *adj.* giving off light

## M

**maestro** (mīs´ trō) *n.* great musician

**malicious** (mə lish´ əs) *adj.* hateful; spiteful

**manned** (mand) *adj.* having human operators on board

**materials** (mə tir´ē əlz) *n.* things used for making or doing something

**maximize** (mak´ sə mīz´) *v.* make the most of

**meager** (mē´ gər) *adj.* 1. small in amount; 2. of poor quality

**media** (mē´dē ə) 1. *n. pl.* sources of information or expression, such as newspapers, television, and the Internet; 2. *adj.* relating to media

**meek** (mēk) *adj.* timid; not willing to argue

**minnow** (min ō) *n.* small fish

**misunderstanding** (mis´un dər stan´diŋ) *n.* state where words or a point of view fail to be communicated

**monarch** (man´ ərk) *n.* ruler, such as a king or queen

**morose** (mə rōs´) *adj.* gloomy; ill-tempered

**mortality** (môr tal´ ə tē) *n.* condition of being mortal, or having to die eventually

**mourning** (môr´niŋ) *v.* expressing grief, especially after someone dies

**muster** (mus´tər) *v.* gather together or summon

**mystery** (mis´ tə rē) *n.* something unexplained, unknown, or kept secret

## N

**negatives** (neg´ ə tivz) *n.* photographic images in which the light and dark areas are reversed

**nonchalantly** (nän´ shə länt´ lē) *adv.* seemingly uninterested

**nondescript** (nän´di skript´) *adj.* 1. hard to describe; 2. not interesting

**notions** (nō´shənz) *n.* general ideas

## O

**observe** (əb zʉrv´) *v.* watch someone or something carefully; notice

**obstacle** (äb´stə kəl) *n.* something in the way

**ominous** (äm´ ə nəs) *adj.* threatening

**opinion** (ə pin´ yən) *n.* belief based on what seems true or probable to one's own mind

**opposing** (ə pōz´ iŋ) *adj.* opposite; completely different

**opposition** (äp´ə zish´ən) *n.* person, group, or force that tries to prevent you from accomplishing something

**optimal** (äp´tə məl) *adj.* best or most favorable; optimum

**optimist** (äp´ tə mist) *n.* someone who takes the most hopeful view of matters

**outcome** (out´kum´) *n.* way a situation turns out; result or consequence

## P

**peeved** (pēvd) *adj.* irritated; annoyed

**perceive** (pər sēv´) *v.* see or view

**perception** (pər sep´shən) *n.* act of becoming aware of through one or more of the senses

**perceptions** (pər sep´shənz) *n.* observations, sensations, or mental images

**perilous** (per´ ə ləs) *adj.* dangerous

**perpetual** (pər pech´ o͞o əl) *adj.* constant; unending

**persistently** (pər sist´ ənt lē) *adv.* firmly and steadily

**perspective** (pər spek´tiv) *n.* point of view; viewpoint

**pertinent** (pʉrt´'n ənt) *adj.* connected or related to the topic

**pestering** (pes´ tər iŋ) *v.* annoying; bothering

**predict** (prē dikt´) *v.* say that something will happen before it happens

**presumptuous** (prē zump´ cho͞o əs) *adj.* 1. overconfident; 2. lacking respect

**process** (prä´ses´) *n.* method; series of actions taken to achieve a particular result

**produce** (prə do͞os´) *v.* make; create

**promote** (prə mōt´) *v.* encourage; contribute to the growth of

**prompted** (prämpt´id) *v.* urged into action

**psychologists** (sī käl´ ə jists) *n.* experts who study the human mind and behavior

**purpose** (pʉr´pəs) *n.* reason for doing something

## Q

**question** (kwes´chən) *v.* challenge the accuracy of; place in doubt

## R

**rash** (rash) *adj.* too hasty

**react** (rē akt´) *v.* respond to

**reaction** (rē ak´shən) *n.* response to an influence, action, or statement

**readapted** (rē ə dapt´ əd) *v.* gradually adjusted again

**realm** (relm) *n.* kingdom

**reassuring** (rē ə sho͝or´ iŋ) *adj.* having the effect of restoring confidence

**reflect** (ri flekt´) *v.* express or show

**refute** (ri fyo͞ot´) *v.* prove wrong

**regretted** (ri gret´ əd) *v.* felt sorry about

**relationship** (ri lā´shən ship´) *n.* connection

**relented** (ri lent´ əd) *v.* gave in

**reliable** (ri lī´ ə bəl) *adj.* dependable

**relished** (rel´isht) *v.* enjoyed; liked

**remote** (ri mōt´) *adj.* far away from anything else

**reproach** (ri prōach´) *n.* disapproval; criticism

**repulsive** (ri pul´siv) *adj.* causing intense dislike; disgusting

**resilient** (ri zil´ yənt) *adj.* able to spring back into shape

**resolution** (rez´ə lo͞o´shən) *n.* working out of a problem or conflict

**resources** (rē´ sôrs´ əz) *n.* natural features that enhance the quality of human life

**reveal** (ri vēl´) *v.* make known; show

**revived** (ri vīvd´) *v.* came back to life or consciousness

**riveted** (riv´ it id) *v.* anchored; completely absorbed by

**routed** (rout´ əd) *v.* completely defeated

## S

**saturation** (sach´ ə rā´ shən) *n.* state of being completely filled

**scorned** (skôrnd) *adj.* looked down upon

**scrutiny** (skro͞ot´'n ē) *n.* close, thorough inspection

**sensitive** (sen´ sə tiv) *adj.* easily hurt or affected

**sentimental** (sen tə ment´ əl) *adj.* emotional; showing tender feeling

**severe** (sə vir´) *adj.* harsh

**shed** (shed) *v.* cast off or lost

**shortsightedness** (shôrt´ sīt´ id nəs) *n.* condition of not considering the future effects of something

**shuffle** (shuf´ əl) *v.* walk with dragging feet

**significance** (sig nif´ə kəns) *n.* importance

**simultaneously** (sī´ məl tā´ nē əs lē) *adv.* at the same time

**slackening** (slak´ ən iŋ) *adj.* easing; becoming less active

**smattering** (smat´ ər iŋ) *n.* small number

**snare** (sner) *v.* catch; capture

**solemn** (säl´ əm) *adj.* serious; somber

**solve** (sälv) *v.* figure out an answer

**speak** (spēk) *v.* use oral language

**spectators** (spek´ tāt´ erz) *n.* people who watch

**spines** (spīnz) *n.* backbones

**spur** (spʉr) *v.* cause

**sputters** (sput´ ərz) *v.* makes hissing or spitting noises

**strategy** (strat´ə jē) *n.* method or plan

**strove** (strōv) *v.* struggled; made great efforts

**struggle** (strug´əl) *n.* fight

**subjected** (səb jekt´ id) *v.* caused one to experience

**subscribed** (səb skrīb´ əd) *v.* promised to give money in support of something

**successive** (sək ses´iv) *adj.* following, in order

**succumb** (sə kum´) *v.* give way to; submit to

**sufficient** (sə fish´ənt) *adj.* enough

**summoned** (sum´ ənd) *v.* called together

**supple** (sup´ əl) *adj.* able to bend easily; flexible

**swerve** (swʉrv) *n.* curving motion

**swindle** (swin´dəl) *n.* act of cheating or fraud

## T

**teach** (tēch) *v.* share information or knowledge

**team** (tēm) *n.* group with a common goal

**technology** (tek näl′ə jē) *n.* machines, equipment, and ways of doing things that are based on modern knowledge about science

**tentatively** (ten′ tə tiv lē) *adj.* hesitantly; with uncertainty

**theory** (thē′ə rē) *n.* explanatory idea not yet proved to be true

**tolerant** (täl′ ər ənt) *adj.* accepting; free from bigotry or prejudice

**torrent** (tôr′ ənt) *n.* flood

**tout** (tout) *v.* promote

**tradition** (trə dish′ən) *n.* customs, as of a social group or culture

**transfixed** (trans fikst′) *adj.* rooted to the spot

**translates** (trans′ lāts) *v.* expresses the same thing in another form

**translucent** (trans lo͞o′ sənt) *adj.* allowing some light through

**transmit** (trans mit′) *v.* send or give out

**transmitting** (trans mit′ tiŋ) *v.* sending or conveying from one thing to another

**trivialness** (triv′ē əl nes) *n.* state of having little importance

## U

**unanimous** (yo͞o nan′ ə məs) *adj.* based on complete agreement

**uncommonly** (un käm′ ən lē) *adv.* remarkably

**understand** (un′dər stand′) *v.* grasp or reach knowledge with respect to something

**understanding** (un′dər stan′diŋ) *n.* agreement

**unify** (yo͞o′nə fī′) *v.* bring together as one

**unique** (yo͞o nēk′) *adj.* one of a kind

**unscrupulous** (un′skro͞o′pyə ləs) *adj.* 1. not held back by ideas of right and wrong; 2. untrustworthy

**utter** (ut′ ər) *v.* speak

## V

**veranda** (və ran′ də) *n.* open porch, usually with a roof

**verge** (vʉrj) *n.* edge; brink

**viewpoint** (vyo͞o point′) *n.* particular way of thinking about a subject

**vital** (vīt′ ′l) *adj.* extremely important or necessary

**void** (void) *n.* emptiness

**vowed** (voud) *v.* promised solemnly

**vulnerable** (vul′ nər ə bəl) *adj.* open to attack

## W

**whimper** (hwim′ pər) *v.* make low, crying sounds

**withered** (with′ ərd) *adj.* dried up

**writhing** (rīth′ iŋ) *v.* squirming, often in response to pain

# Spanish Glossary

El vocabulario académico aparece en **azul**.

## A

**abode / domicilio** *s.* hogar; residencia

**accusations / acusaciones** *s.* cargos en contra de una persona por hacer algo incorrecto o ilegal

**acknowledge / reconocer** *v.* aceptar; admitir

**adaptation / adaptación** *s.* cambio gradual en el comportamiento para ajustarse a las normas aceptadas por la sociedad

**adequate / adecuado** *adj.* bastante; suficiente

**advocacy / defensa** *s.* apoyo para una idea o misión en particular

**affect / afectar** *v.* hacer algo que produce un cambio en alguien o algo; influenciar

**aggressive / agresivo** *adj.* violento, propenso a actuar en forma destructiva o grosera

**ajar / entreabierto** *adj.* abierto a medias

**analyze / analizar** *v.* separar las partes de un todo para examinarlo detenidamente

**appearance / apariencia** *s.* aspecto o parecer de una persona o cosa

**appreciate / apreciar** *v.* estar agradecido

**approximately / aproximadamente** *adv.* de una forma cercana o casi correcta mas no exacta

**aptitude / aptitud** *s.* talento; habilidad

**arid / árido** *adj.* muy seco; baldío

**assumption / suposición** *s.* creencia o aceptación de la existencia de algo sin tener pruebas

**assumptions / suposiciones** *s.* actos de aceptación de algo como una realidad sin tener pruebas

**astonish / asombrar** *v.* causar sorpresa grande y a veces repentina; maravillar; pasmar

**attitude / actitud** *s.* opiniones y sentimientos de una persona acerca de alguien o algo

**audible / audible** *adj.* lo suficientemente alto para que se pueda oír

**aversion / aversión** *s.* fuerte disgusto o repugnancia frente a alguien o algo

**awareness / conciencia** *s.* conocimiento adquirido por medio de la percepción o de información

## B

**behavior / comportamiento** *s.* la forma en la que uno se porta o actúa

**bias / parcialidad** *s.* tendencia a interpretar las cosas de manera sesgada o prejuiciosa

**bigots / intolerantes** *s.* personas de mentalidad cerrada, prejuiciosas

**blander / más insípido** *adj.* que tiene menos sabor

**blunt / suavizar** *v.* disminuir; hacer menos fuerte; reducir el filo

**bound / sujeto** *v.* atado

## C

**challenge / desafío** *s.* algo que pone a prueba las habilidades de una persona; reto

**characteristic / característica** *s.* rasgo; facción

**characterize / caracterizar** *v.* 1. ser típico de alguien o algo; 2. describir a alguien o a algo en una forma particular

**cite / citar** *v.* 1. mencionar algo como prueba o ejemplo de alguna otra cosa; 2. referirse a

**coax / convencer** *v.* persuadir de manera sutil

**commemorated / conmemoró** *v.* honró la memoria de

**commissioned / comisionó** *v.* designó o empleó para llevar a cabo una labor o un trabajo

**common / común** *adj.* 1. ordinario; frecuente; 2. compartido; público

**communal / comunal** *adj.* compartido por todos

**communicate / comunicar** *v.* compartir ideas, pensamientos o sentimientos, usualmente con palabras

**communication / comunicación** *s.* acto de compartir información o de expresar pensamientos y sentimientos

**community / comunidad** *s.* grupo de personas que tienen un interés en común o que viven cerca el uno del otro

**competition / competencia** *s.* evento o juego en que las personas o bandos pretenden ganar

**complex / complejo** *adj.* 1. difícil de entender; 2. que tiene muchas partes conectadas

**compose / componer** *v.* escribir o crear una pieza musical, una obra de arte o un texto

**compromise / solución** *s.* convenio satisfactorio entre dos partes

**compulsion / compulsión** *s.* impulso irresistible

**conclude / concluir** *v.* terminar; finalizar

**conferred / deliberó** *v.* se discutió

**conflict / conflicto** *s.* choque o lucha entre grupos opuestos

**consolation / consolación** *s.* algo que alivia la pena de una persona decepcionada

**conspired / conspiró** *v.* planeó de manera secreta

**contradiction / contradicción** *s.* diferencia entre dos cosas conflictivas que demuestra que sólo una es cierta

**contraption / artilugio** *s.* aparato o mecanismo extraño

**contrast / contrastar** *v.* comparar dos cosas para mostrar sus diferencias

**contribute / contribuir** *v.* 1. agregar; enriquecer; 2. proveer

**conveyed / comunicó** *v.* hizo saber; expresó

**convince / convencer** *v.* persuadir; incitar a aceptar un punto de vista

**convincing / convincente** *adj.* persuasivo

**coveted / codició** *v.* quiso; deseó

**cremated / cremado** *v.* quemar un cadáver hasta convertirlo en cenizas

**croon / canturrear** *v.* cantar o tararear suave y dulcemente

**crucial / crucial** *adj.* importante; crítico

**crystal / cristal** *adj.* hecho de vidrio claro y brillante

**culminated / culminó** *v.* alcanzó su punto más alto o clímax

**culprit / inculpado** *s.* persona culpable

**culture / cultura** *s.* conjunto de modos de vida y costumbres de un grupo o una comunidad

**cunning / astuto** *adj.* hábil; ingenioso

**cunningly / astutamente** *adv.* ingeniosamente

**curdled / cortado** *adj.* podrido

**curiosity / curiosidad** *s.* deseo de aprender o saber más sobre un tema

**custom / costumbre** *s.* lo que se hace comúnmente; práctica aceptada

## D

**dabbling / chapuzar** *v.* zambullirse, sumergirse o patalear en el agua

**danger / peligro** *s.* exposición a posible daño, lesión o pérdida

**debate / debatir** 1. *v.* discutir formalmente; 2. *s.* discusión o argumento sobre un tema en el que se expresan distintas opiniones

**deceive / engañar** *v.* hacer a alguien creer lo que no es cierto

**decipher / descifrar** *v.* encontrar el significado de

**decreed / decretó** *v.* creó un mandato oficial

**defiant / desafiante** *adj.* que resiste valientemente

**defies / desafía** *v.* se resiste o se opone valientemente o de manera abierta

**define / definir** *v.* determinar la naturaleza o establecer el significado de algo

**definition / definición** *s.* oración o frase que expresa el significado exacto de una palabra o frase

**describe / describir** *v.* decir cómo es algo o alguien al dar detalles acerca de éste

**designated / designó** *v.* señaló; marcó

**desire / deseo** *s.* acción de desear o querer

**desolate / desolado** *adj.* solo; solitario

**destitute / indigentes** *adj.* personas que viven en pobreza absoluta

**deteriorates / se deteriora** *v.* que se empeora

**determination / determinación** *s.* decisión o conclusión

**devastated / devastado** *v.* destruido; completamente disgustado

**devastating / devastador** *adj.* destructivo; arrollador

**diagram / diagrama** *s.* un cuadro, dibujo o plan que ayuda a que algo sea más fácil de entender

**disagreement / desacuerdo** *s.* diferencia o conflicto entre grupos o personas

**disbanded / desbandado** *v.* dividido; liquidado

**discipline / disciplina** *s.* entrenamiento; autocontrol o control estricto

**discover / descubrir** *v.* encontrar algo previamente desconocido; explorar

**dispute / disputa** *s.* desacuerdo

**distinct / distinto** *adj.* separado y diferente

**diversity / diversidad** *s.* variedad, como de grupos o culturas

**dolefully / tristemente** *adv.* de manera triste y penosa

**dominions / dominios** *s.* países o territorios gobernados

**downy / suave** *adj.* blando y esponjoso

**duty / deber** *s.* responsabilidad; obligación

## E

**effective / efectivo** *adj.* exitoso en producir los resultados deseados

**eligible / elegible** *adj.* apto para ser escogido; calificado

**emerged / emergió** *v.* apareció a la vista; se volvió visible

**emphatic / enfático** *adj.* que se siente o se hace con fuerza

**endeavors / esfuerzos** *s.* intentos; empeños

**enhance / mejorar** *v.* pasar algo a un estado mejor

**enrich / enriquecer** *v.* mejorar

**entertain / entretener** *v.* 1. divertir; 2. hacer una presentación

**environment / medio ambiente** *s.* 1. lo que nos rodea; 2. el mundo natural

**envying / envidiando** *v.* queriendo lo que otro posee

**epidemic / epidemia** *s.* proliferación de una enfermedad contagiosa

**equality / igualdad** *s.* estado de la sociedad en el que todas las personas se tratan de la misma manera

**ethnicity / etnicidad** *s.* origen cultural o racial

**evading / evadiendo** *v.* evitando

**evaluate / evaluar** *v.* juzgar; determinar el significado o valor de algo

**evaluations / evaluaciones** *s.* 1. actos de juzgar o calificar algo o alguien; 2. juicios o interpretaciones

**evaporated / evaporó** *v.* cambió de líquido a gas

**evidently / evidentemente** *adv.* claramente; obviamente

**examine / examinar** *v.* estudiar a fondo para hallar o verificar algo; observar detenidamente

**exertion / esfuerzo** *s.* trabajo físico

**expectations / expectativas** *s.* esperanzas de lo que viene

**experiment / experimento** *s.* prueba que determina un resultado

**explain / explicar** *v.* 1. describir; 2. esclarecer o aclarar

**explicit / explícito** *adj.* expresado claramente; visto de inmediato

**explore / explorar** *v.* 1. viajar por un área desconocida para descubrir cómo es; 2. discutir un tema detalladamente

**express / expresar** *v.* hablar de o comunicar un sentimiento

**exquisite / refinado** *adj.* hermoso y delicado

## F

**facts / hechos** *s.* la verdad o la realidad; información correcta acerca de un tema

**family / familia** *s.* personas de relación consanguínea o que tienen un antepasado en común

**fascinated / fascinado** *adj.* encantado; muy interesado

**fathom / braza** *s.* unidad de longitud para medir la profundidad del agua

**feeble / débil** *adj.* flojo; enclenque

**feebleness / debilidad** *s.* falta de fuerza

**feigned / fingió** *v.* pretendió; imitó

**fluent / fluido** *adj.* que escribe o habla con facilidad y soltura

**flushed / expulsó** *v.* obligó a salir de un lugar

**flustered / agitado** *adj.* nervioso; confuso

**focus / enfoque** *n.* punto central o tema de investigación

**forage / forraje** *s.* comida para animales domésticos

**formal / formal** *adj.* que sigue reglas o costumbres establecidas

**formidable / formidable** *adj.* imponente; impresionante

**fosters / fomenta** *v.* promueve el crecimiento o desarrollo de

**fragrant / fragante** *adj.* que emana un aroma dulce

**fundamental / fundamental** *adj.* básico; que forma una base

**furor / furor** *s.* explosión de ira o emoción pública

**furrowed / arrugado** *v.* hecho pliegues

## G

**gauge / medir** *v.* estimar o juzgar

**globules / glóbulos** *s.* gotas de un líquido

**granite / granito** *s.* piedra dura de color gris

**gratitude / gratitud** *s.* agradecimiento

**group / grupo** *s.* conjunto o agrupación, como de personas

**groves / arboledas** *s.* grupos pequeños de árboles

**gumption / arrojo** *s.* osadía o coraje; empuje

## H

**habitats / hábitats** *s.* lugares en los cuales ciertos animales o plantas viven o crecen de forma natural

**haunches / ancas** *s.* las patas posteriores de un animal

**hexagons / hexágonos** *s.* figuras de seis lados

**hoarding / acaparando** *v.* acumulando y almacenando provisiones como reservas

**hoed / limpió con la azada** *v.* cavó y removió tierra con una herramienta de metal

## I

**identify / identificar** *v.* 1. reconocer como existente; 2. señalar

**ignorant / ignorante** *adj.* que no sabe los hechos o que no tiene la información apropiada

**ignore / ignorar** *v.* hacer caso omiso; desconocer

**illustrate / ilustrar** *v.* aclarar algo al proveer un ejemplo

**image / imagen** *n.* retrato; representación

**immensely / inmensamente** *adv.* en grado extremo; muchísimo

**impervious / insensible** *adj.* que no es afectado por algo

**implored / implorado** *v.* suplicado

**imposters / impostores** *s.* personas o cosas que aparentan ser algo o alguien que no son

**impromptu / improvisado** *adj.* no planeado

**incessantly / incesantemente** *adv.* sin parar

**individual / individuo** *s.* una sola persona o cosa

**inflicted / infligió** *v.* causó sufrimiento o daño

**inform / informar** *v.* decir; dar información de algo

**information / información** *s.* conocimiento adquirido por medio del estudio o de la experiencia

**inherent / inherente** *adj.* natural, básico o innato

**inquire / preguntar** *v.* cuestionar con el fin de obtener información

**inquiry / indagación** *s.* proceso oficial con el fin de encontrar el porqué ocurrió algo

**insight / perspicacia** *s.* 1. habilidad de ver la verdad; 2. entendimiento claro

**integration / integración** *s.* fin de la separación de grupos culturales o raciales

**intercedes / intercede** *v.* actúa o pide por otra persona

**interrogations / interrogatorios** *s.* serie de preguntas formales dirigidas a un sujeto que tiene que contestarlas

**intervene / interviene** *v.* se interpone en una situación como influencia para ayudar a resolver una acción o argumento

**interview / entrevistar** *v.* hacer una serie de preguntas a una persona con el fin de obtener información

**intricate / intricado** *adj.* complejo; detallado

**investigate / investigar** *v.* examinar a fondo

**investigations / investigaciones** *s.* procesos oficiales para encontrar las razones por las cuales ocurrió algún suceso, como un crimen o problema

**investment / inversión** *s.* el acto de dedicar tiempo y esfuerzo a algo en particular con la expectativa de obtener un resultado que valga la pena

## J

**justifies / justifica** *v.* 1. da escusas; 2. explica

## K

**knowledge / conocimiento** *s.* el resultado del aprendizaje; acción de tener presente

## L

**laborious / laborioso** *adj.* que cuesta bastante trabajo o esfuerzo

**learn / aprender** *v.* obtener conocimiento o destrezas

**legal / legal** *adj.* conforme a las leyes

**legislation / legislación** *s.* ley

**listen / escuchar** *v.* prestar atención a; atender

**literally / literalmente** *adv.* exactamente

**loathed / abominado** *v.* odiado

**luminous / luminoso** *adj.* que despide luz

## M

**maestro / maestro** *s.* un gran músico

**malicious / malicioso** *adj.* que tiene mala intención; odioso

**manned / tripulado** *adj.* que tiene un operador humano abordo

**materials / materiales** *s.* cosas utilizadas para hacer algo

**maximize / maximizar** *v.* tomar el máximo provecho de algo

**meager / escaso** *adj.* precario; de poca cantidad

**media / medios de comunicación** *s.* conjunto de fuentes de información o expresión, tales como periódicos, televisión y la Internet

**meek / manso** *adj.* tímido; que no demuestra enfado

**minnow / pececillo** *s.* pez pequeño

**misunderstanding / malentendido** *s.* estado en el que palabras o un punto de vista no logra ser comunicado

**monarch / monarca** *s.* dominio por carácter hereditario, como el de un rey o una reina

**morose / lúgubre** *adj.* sombrío

**mortality / mortalidad** *s.* condición de ser mortal, o de tener que morir en algún momento

**mourning / luto** *s.* expresión de pena, especialmente después de que alguien muere

**muster / reunir** *v.* juntar las fuerzas; convocar

**mystery / misterio** *s.* algo inexplicable, desconocido o que se mantiene bajo secreto

## N

**negatives / negativos** *s.* imágenes fotográficas en las cuales la luz y las áreas oscuras se encuentran invertidas

**nonchalantly / con toda tranquilidad** *adv.* de manera despreocupada; con indiferencia

**nondescript / indefinido** *adj.* 1. difícil de describir; 2. no interesante; soso

**notions / nociones** *s.* ideas generales

## O

**observe / observar** *v.* ver algo o a alguien detalladamente; notar

**obstacle / obstáculo** *s.* algo que se interpone en el camino

**ominous / siniestro** *adj.* amenazante

**opinion / opinión** *s.* creencia basada en lo que parece ser cierto o probable según uno mismo

**opposing / opuesto** *adj.* contrario; completamente diferente

**opposition / oposición** *s.* persona, grupo o fuerza que trata de impedir el logro de algo

**optimal / óptimo** *adj.* mejor o más favorable

**optimist / optimista** *s.* alguien que tiende a ver las cosas de la manera más favorable

**outcome / resultado** *s.* la manera en que algo se resuelve; consecuencia

## P

**peeved / molesto** *adj.* irritado; fastidiado

**perceive / percibir** *v.* aceptar desde cierto punto de vista; ver

**perception / percepción** *s.* acto de darse cuenta de algo por medio de uno o más sentidos

**perceptions / percepciones** *s.* observaciones, sensaciones o imágenes mentales

**perilous / arriesgado** *adj.* peligroso

**perpetual / perpetuo** *adj.* constante; sin fin

**persistently / persistentemente** *adv.* de manera firme y constante

**perspective / perspectiva** *s.* punto de vista

**pertinent / pertinente** *adj.* conectado o relacionado con el tema

**pestering / molestando** *v.* fastidiando; irritando

**predict / predecir** *v.* decir que algo va a pasar antes de que suceda

**presumptuous / presumido** *adj.* 1. con exceso de confianza en sí mismo; 2. arrogante

**process / proceso** *s.* método; serie de acciones realizadas para lograr un resultado particular

**produce / producir** *v.* hacer; crear

**promote / promover** *v.* impulsar; contribuir al crecimiento de algo

**prompted / impulsó** *v.* llevó a la acción

**psychologists / psicólogos** *s.* expertos que estudian la mente y el comportamiento humanos

**purpose / propósito** *s.* razón por la cual se hace algo

## Q

**question / cuestionar** *v.* desafiar la verdad de algo; poner en duda

## R

**rash / imprudente** *adj.* muy precipitado

**react / reaccionar** *v.* responder; hacer algo al respecto

**reaction / reacción** *s.* respuesta a una influencia, acción o afirmación

**readapted / se adaptó de nuevo** *v.* se ajustó gradualmente otra vez

**realm / dominio** *s.* reino

**reassuring / tranquilizante** *adj.* que alivia, asegura o da confianza

**reflect / reflejar** *v.* expresar o mostrar

**refute / refutar** *v.* probar que alguien o algo está equivocado

**regretted / se arrepintió** *v.* sintió pesar por algo

**relationship / relación** *s.* conexión

**relented / cedió** *v.* se dejó convencer

**reliable / confiable** *adj.* del que se puede depender

**relished / se deleitó** *v.* gozó; disfrutó de

**remote / remoto** *adj.* muy lejos de todo lo demás

**reproach / reproche** *s.* acto de culpar; crítica

**repulsive / repulsivo** *adj.* que causa disgusto; que da asco

**resilient / resistente** *adj.* fuerte; que puede recobrar su estado original

**resolution / resolución** *s.* fin satisfactorio de un problema o conflicto

**resources / recursos** *s.* elementos naturales que mejoran la calidad de vida humana

**reveal / revelar** *v.* hacer saber; dar a conocer; demostrar

**revived / revivió** *v.* volvió a la vida o recobró conciencia

**riveted / cautivado** *v.* absorbido completamente por algo o alguien

**routed / derrotó** *v.* venció de manera decisiva

## S

**saturation / saturación** *s.* condición en la que se está completamente lleno

**scorned / desdeñado** *adj.* menospreciado

**scrutiny / escrutinio** *s.* inspección minuciosa

**sensitive / sensible** *adj.* que se hiere o afecta con facilidad

**sentimental / sentimental** *adj.* emotivo; que demuestra sentimientos tiernos

**severe / severo** *adj.* duro

**shed / mudó** *v.* perdió o cambió

**shortsightedness / falta de visión** *s.* carencia de proyección en el futuro; acto de no considerar los efectos futuros de una acción

**shuffle / arrastrar** *v.* caminar sin levantar los pies

**significance / significado** *s.* importancia

**simultaneously / simultáneamente** *adv.* al mismo tiempo

**slackening / aminorando** *v.* disminuyendo; volviéndose menos activo

**smattering / poquito** *s.* cantidad pequeña

**snare / apresar** *v.* atrapar; capturar

**solemn / solemne** *adj.* serio; sombrío

**solve / resolver** *v.* descifrar una respuesta

**speak / hablar** *v.* usar lenguaje oral; expresar con palabras

**spectators / espectadores** *s.* personas que miran con atención

**spines / espinazos** *s.* vértebras

**spur / estimular** *v.* causar

**sputters / chisporrotea** *v.* hace ruidos chispeantes o sibilantes

**strategy / estrategia** *s.* método o plan para alcanzar el éxito o lograr un objetivo

**strove / se esforzó** *v.* luchó; hizo un gran esfuerzo

**struggle / lucha** *s.* pelea

**subjected / sometió** *v.* forzó; causó

**subscribed / suscribió** *v.* prometió dar apoyo monetario a algo

**successive / sucesivo** *adj.* que sigue a otro; en orden

**succumb / sucumbir** *v.* ceder; someterse

**sufficient / suficiente** *adj.* cantidad satisfactoria

**summoned / convocó** *v.* citó o llamó a una reunión

**supple / ágil** *adj.* que usa su cuerpo con facilidad y soltura

**swerve / viraje** *s.* movimiento en curva

**swindle / estafa** *s.* acto de hacer trampa o fraude

## T

**teach / enseñar** *v.* compartir información o conocimiento

**team / equipo** *s.* grupo unido por una meta en común

**technology / tecnología** *s.* aplicación práctica de las ciencias en la industria; máquinas, equipo y procesos basados en el conocimiento moderno de la ciencia

**tentatively / tentativamente** *adv.* dudosamente; sin certeza y con vacilación

**theory / teoría** *s.* una idea explicativa que aún no ha sido comprobada

**tolerant / tolerante** *adj.* que acepta; libre de resistencia o prejuicios

**torrent / torrente** *s.* inundación

**tout / promover** *v.* promocionar; fomentar

**tradition / tradición** *s.* costumbre, como de un grupo social o cultura

**transfixed / embelesado** *adj.* fascinado

**translates / traduce** *v.* expresa la misma cosa en otra forma

**translucent / translúcido** *adj.* que permite pasar cierta cantidad de luz

**transmit / transmitir** *v.* enviar o repartir

**transmitting / transmitiendo** *v.* enviando o transfiriendo de una cosa a otra

**trivialness / trivialidad** *s.* estado de tener poca importancia

## U

**unanimous / unánime** *adj.* basado en un acuerdo total

**uncommonly / extraordinariamente** *adv.* fuera de lo común

**understand / entender** *v.* llegar a conocer y comprender algo

**understanding / entendimiento** *s.* acuerdo; fin de un conflicto

**unify / unificar** *v.* juntar para formar uno solo

**unique / único** *adj.* sin otro de su especie

**unscrupulous / inescrupuloso** *adj.* 1. que no actúa según lo que es o no es correcto; 2. que no genera confianza

**utter / pronunciar** *v.* articular; hablar

## V

**veranda / veranda** *s.* porche abierto, usualmente con techo

**verge / borde** *s.* orilla; límite

**viewpoint / punto de vista** *s.* pensamientos particulares con respecto a un tema

**vital / vital** *adj.* de extrema importancia o necesario

**void / vacío** *s.* espacio desocupado

**vowed / juró** *v.* prometió solemnemente

**vulnerable / vulnerable** *adj.* que puede ser atacado

## W

**whimper / lloriquear** *v.* emitir un llanto o lamento débil

**withered / marchitado** *adj.* que se ha secado

**writhing / retorciéndose** *v.* contorcionándo, usualmente a causa de dolor

# Index of Skills

## Literary Analysis

## Comprehension Skills

## Writing

### Applications



### Process

**Rubrics for Self-Assessment**



## Speaking and Listening

**Activities**



**Strategies**

## Research

### Activities

## Language Conventions



INDEX OF SKILLS

## Vocabulary



## Assessment

# Index of Authors and Titles

*The following authors and titles appear in the print and online versions of Pearson Literature.*

# Additional Selections: Author and Title Index

*The following authors and titles appear in the Online Literature Library.*

# Acknowledgments



Grateful acknowledgment is made to the following for copyrighted material: *English—Language Arts Content Standards for California Public Schools* reproduced by permission, California Department of Education, CD Press, 1430 N Street, Suite 3207, Sacramento, CA 95814.

**All Children's Hospital c/o Florida Suncoast Safe Kids Coalition** "2006 Safe Kids "Walk This Way" Program" from *http://www.allkids.org/body.cfm?xyzpdqabc=0&id=396&action=detail&ref=28.* Copyrgiht © 2007 All Children's Hospital. All rights reserved. Used by permission.

**Miriam Altshuler Literary Agency** "Treasure of Lemon Brown" by Walter Dean Myers from *Boy's Life Magazine, March 1983.* Copyright © 1983, by Walter Dean Myers. Used by permission of Miriam Altshuler Literary Agency, on behalf of Walter Dean Myers.

**American Broadcasting Music, Inc.** "Conjunction Junction" composed by Jack Sheldon and Bob Dorough. Copyright © 1973 American Broadcasting Music, Inc. Used by permission.

**Americas Magazine** "Mongoose on the Loose" reprinted from *Americas,* a bimonthly magazine published by the General Secretariat of the Organization of American States in English and Spanish. Content may not be copied without written permission. Used by permission.

**Arte Publico Press, Inc.** "Maestro" is used with permission from the publisher of *Borders* by Pat Mora. (Houston: Arte Publico Press - University of Houston © 1986). "Bailando" from *Chants* by Pat Mora. Used with permission from the publisher of *Chants* (Houston: Arte Publico Press - University of Houston copyright © 1985).

**Atheneum Books for Young Readers, an imprint of Simon & Schuster** "Papa's Parrot" from *Every Living Thing* by Cynthia Rylant. Text copyright © 1985 Cynthia Rylant. Used by permission of Atheneum Books for Young Readers, an imprint of Simon & Schuster Children's Publishing Division.

**Bantam Books, a division of Random House, Inc.** "The Eternal Frontier" from *Frontier* by Louis L'Amour, Photographs by David Muench, copyright © 1984 by Louis L'Amour Enterprises, Inc. Used by permission of Bantam Books, a division of Random House, Inc.

**Susan Bergholz Literary Services** "My First Free Summer" by Julia Alvarez, copyright © 2003 by Julia Alvarez. First published in *Better Homes and Gardens, August 2003.* Used by permission of Susan Bergholz Literary Services, New York, NY and Lamy, NM. All rights reserved.

**Brandt & Hochman Literary Agents, Inc.** "The Third Wish" from *Not What You Expected: A Collection of Short Stories* by Joan Aiken. Copyright © 1974 by Joan Aiken. Any electronic copying or redistribution of the text is expressly forbidden. Used by permission of Brandt & Hochman Literary Agents, Inc.

**Brooks Permissions** "Jim" Copyright © 1956 from *Bronzeville Boys and Girls* by Gwendolyn Brooks. Copyright © 1956 by Gwendolyn Brooks. Used by consent of Brooks Permissions.

**Curtis Brown Ltd.** "Two Haiku" ("O foolish ducklings…" and "After the moon sets…") first appeared in *Cricket Songs: Japanese Haiku,* published by Harcourt. Copyright © 1964 by Harry Behn. "Suzy and Leah" first published in *American Girl Magazine.* Copyright © 1993 by Jane Yolen. From *Dragonwings* by Laurence Yep from *Theatre For Young Audiences: Around The World In 21 Plays.* Copyright © 1992 by Laurence Yep. First appeared in *American Theatre Magazine.* Now appears in *Norton Anthology of Children's Literature.* Used by permission of Curtis Brown, Ltd. CAUTION: Professionals and amateurs are hereby warned that *Dragonwings,* being fully protected under the copyright Laws of the United States of America, the British Empire, including the Dominion of Canada, and all other countries of the Universal Copyright and Berne Conventions, are subject to royalty. All rights, including professional, amateur, motion picture, recitation, lecturing, public reading, radio and television broadcasting, and the rights of translation into foreign languages, are strictly reserved. All inquiries for *Dragonwings* should be addressed to Curtis Brown Ltd.

**CA Walk to School Headquarters** "Walk to School" from *www.cawalktoschool.com.* Copyright © 2006 California Center for Physical Activity.

**Canadian Broadcasting Corporation** "Charles Dickens's A Christmas Carol: A Radio Interview" from *http://www.victorianweb.org/authors/dickens/xmas/pva303.html.* Originally broadcast on the Canadian Broadcasting Corporation (The Great Northwest, Dec. 4, 2000). Copyright © Canadian Broadcasting Corporation. Used by courtesy of Canadian Broadcasting Corporation.

**Carnegie Hero Fund Commission** "The History of the Carnegie Hero Fund Commission." © The Carnegie Hero Commission. Reused with permission.

**Carus Publishing Company** "The Rhythms of Rap" by Kathiann M. Kowalski from *Odyssey's March 2002 issue: Music: Why Do We Love It?* Copyright © 2002, Cobblestone Publishing, 30 Grove Street, Suite C, Peterborough, NH 03458. All rights reserved. Used by permission of Carus Publishing Company.

**CBS News** "Win Some, Lose Some" by Charles Osgood. © 2001. Reprinted with permission of CBS News Archives.

**Chronicle Books** "The Travelers and the Bear" by Jerry Pinkney from *Aesop's Fables.* Copyright © 2000 by Jerry Pinkney.

**City of Melbourne** Stormwater Management Web Page from *http://www.melbourneflorida.org/stormwater/howyoucanhelp.htm.* Copyright City of Melbourne.

**City of Oceanside** City of Oceanside Clean Water Program from *www.oceansidecleanwaterprogram.org/kids.asp.* Copyright © City of Oceanside. Used by permission.

**ClearyWorks** "The Fox Outwits the Crow" by William Cleary from *www.clearyworks.com.* Used by permission of William Cleary, Burlington, Vermont.

**Cobblestone Publishing** "The Myth of the Outlaw" by Ruth M. Hamel. Copyright © 1996, *Cobblestone,* May96: Vol. 17, Issue 5. Carus Publishing. Used by permission.

**Code Entertainment** *The Monsters Are Due on Maple Street* by Rod Serling from *The Monsters Are Due on Maple Street.* Copyright © 1960 by Rod Serling; Copyright © 1988 by Carolyn Serling, Jodi Serling, and Anne Serling. Used by permission. CAUTION: Professionals and amateurs are hereby warned that *The Monsters Are Due on Maple Street,* being fully protected under the copyright laws of the United States of America, the British Commonwealth countries, including Canada, and the other countries of the Copyright Union, is subject to royalty. All rights, including professional, amateur, motion picture, recitation, lecturing, public reading, radio, television and cable broadcasting, and the rights of translation into foreign languages, are strictly reserved. All inquiries should be addressed to Code Entertainment.

**Don Congdon Associates, Inc.** "All Summer In A Day" by Ray Bradbury, published in *The Magazine of Fantasy and Science Fiction, March 1954.* Copyright © 1954, copyright © renewed 1982 by Ray Bradbury. From *No Gumption* by Russell Baker. Copyright © 1982 by Russell Baker. Used by permission of Don Congdon Associates, Inc.

**The Emma Courlander Trust** "All Stories Are Anansi's" from *The Hat-Shaking Dance And Other Ashanti Tales From Ghana* by Harold Courlander with Albert Kofi Prempeh Copyright © 1957, 1985 by Harold Courlander. Used by permission of The Emma Courlander Trust.

**Crystal Springs Uplands School** Crystal Springs Uplands School Theatre Contract from *http://www.csus.com/pageprint.cfm?p=1212.* Copyright © Crystal Springs Uplands School. Used by permission of the Crystal Springs Uplands School and John Hauer, Theater Manager and Production & Design Teacher.

**Dell Publishing, a division of Random House, Inc.** "The Luckiest Time of All" from *The Lucky Stone* by Lucille Clifton. Copyright © 1979 by Lucille Clifton. Used by permission of Dell Publishing, a division of Random House, Inc.

**Dial Books for Young Readers, a division of Penguin Young Readers Group** "The Three Century Woman" copyright © 1999 by Richard Peck, from *Past Present, Perfect Tense* by Richard Peck. Used by permission of Dial Books for Young Readers, a division of Penguin Young Readers Group, a member of Penguin Group (USA) Inc., 345 Hudson Street, New York, NY 10014. All rights reserved.

**Gregory Djanikian** "How I Learned English" by Gregory Djanikian from *Falling Deeply Into America,* Carnegie Mellon University, Copyright © 1989. Used by permission of the author.

**Dramatists Play Service Inc.** "Sorry, Wrong Number" by Lucille Fletcher. Copyright © renewed 1976, Lucille Fletcher. All rights reserved.

**Dutton Children's Books** From "The Tale of Mandarin Ducks" by Katherine Paterson, copyright © 1990 by Katherine Paterson, text. Used by permission of Dutton Children's Books, A Division of Penguin Young Readers Group, A Member of Penguin Group (USA) Inc. All rights reserved.

**Gulf Publishing** Look for the Differences (park sign) from *A Field Guide To Snakes Of California* by Philip R. Brown. Copyright © 1997.

**Farrar, Straus & Giroux, LLC** "Seal" from *Laughing Time: Collected Nonsense* by William Jay Smith. Copyright © 1990 by William Jay Smith. "Train Tune" from *The Blue Estuaries* by Louise Bogan. Copyright © 1968 by Louise Bogan. Copyright renewed © 1996 by Ruth Limmer. Used by permission of Farrar, Straus & Giroux, Inc.

**Joanna Farrell for the Estate of Juliet Piggott Wood** "Popocatepetl and Ixtlaccihuatl" by Juliet Piggott from *Mexican Folktales.* Used by permission of Mrs. J.S.E. Farrell.

**Food Security Learning Center** Food Security Learning Center from *www.worldhungeryear.org.* Copyright © 2007. All rights reserved. Used by permission.

**Freakonomics LLC** "Herd Mentality? The Freakonomics of Boarding a Bus" by Stephen J. Dubner. Copyright © 2007. Freakonomics LLC.

**Estate of Mona Gardner** "The Dinner Party" by Mona Gardner from *McDougal, Littell.* Copyright © 1942, 1970. Reprinted by permission.

**Georgia Department of Transportation** "Safe Routes to School: It's Happening in Metro Atlanta" from *http://www.atlantabike.org/srtsfrontpage.html.* Copyright © 2007. Used by permission of Georgia Department of Transportation, Atlanta Bicycle Campaign, and the Federal Highway Administration.

**Golden Books, an imprint of Random House Children's Book** "The Bride of Pluto"(retitled "Demeter and Persephone") from *The Golden Treasury of Myths and Legends* by Anne Terry White, illustrated by Alice and Martin Provensen, copyright © 1959, renewed copyright © 1987 by Random House, Inc. Used by permission of Golden Books, an imprint of Random House Children's Books, a division of Random House, Inc.

**June Hall Literary Agency c/o PFD** "One" from *When I Dance* by James Berry (Copyright © James Berry 1990) is reproduced by permission of PFD (www.pfd.co.uk) on behalf of James Berry.

**Harcourt, Inc.** Excerpt from "Seventh Grade" in *Baseball in April and Other Stories,* copyright © 1990 by Gary Soto. "Fog" from *Chicago Poems* by Carl Sandburg, copyright © 1916 by Holt, Rinehart and Winston and renewed copyright © 1944 by Carl Sandburg. This material may not be reproduced in any form or by any means without the prior written permission of the publisher. Used by permission of Harcourt, Inc.

**Harcourt Education Limited** "Tenochtitlan: Inside the Aztec Capital" from *The Aztecs: Worlds Of The Past* by Jacqueline Dineen. Used by permission of Harcourt Education.

**HarperCollins Publishers, Inc.** "Sarah Cynthia Sylvia Stout Would Not Take the Garbage Out" from *Where the Sidewalk Ends* by Shel Silverstein. Copyright © 2004 by Evil Eye Music, Inc. Used with permission from the Estate of Shel Silverstein and HarperCollins Children's Books. From *An American Childhood.* Copyright © 1987 by Annie Dillard. "How the Snake Got Poison" from *Mules and Men* by Zora Neale Hurston. Copyright © 1935 by Zora Neale Hurston. Copyright renewed © 1963 by John C. Hurston and Joel Hurston. Used by permission of HarperCollins Publishers.

**HarperTrophy, an Imprint of HarperCollins Publishers Inc.** From *Dragonwings* by Laurence Yep. Copyright © 1975 by Laurence Yep. Used by permission of HarperCollins Publishers.

**Harvard University Press** "I'm Nobody (#288)" by Emily Dickinson. Used by permission of the publishers and the Trustees of Amherst College from *The Poems Of Emily Dickinson,*

Thomas H. Johnson, ed., Cambridge, Mass.: The Belknap Press of Harvard University Press, Copyright © 1951, 1955, 1979, 1983 by the President and Fellows of Harvard College.

**Helmut Hirnschall** "I am a Native of North America" by Chief Dan George from *My Heart Soars.* Copyright © 1974 by Clarke Irwin. Used by permission.

**Edward D. Hoch** "Zoo" by Edward D. Hoch, copyright © 1958 by King Size Publications, Inc.; © renewed 1991 by Edward D. Hoch. Used by permission of the author.

**The Barbara Hogenson Agency, Inc.** "The Night the Bed Fell" from *My Life and Hard Times* by James Thurber. Copyright © 1933, 1961 by James Thurber. Used by arrangement with Rosemary Thurber and The Barbara Hogensen Agency, Inc. All rights reserved.

**Holiday House, Inc.** Copyright © 2006 by Russell Freedman From *Freedom Walkers: The Story of the Montgomery Bus Boycott.* All rights reserved. Used by permission of Holiday House, Inc.

**Meghan Holohan** "What Gives the Sunrise and Sunset Its Orange Glow" by Meghan Holohan from *www.gantdaily.com.* Used by permission of the author.

**Henry Holt and Company, Inc.** Excerpt from "My Dear Cousin Tovah" from *Letters From Rifka* by Karen Hesse. Copyright © 1992 by Karen Hesse. "Stopping by Woods on a Snowy Evening" from *The Poetry Of Robert Frost* edited by Edward Connery Lathem. Copyright © 1923, 1969 by Henry Holt and Company, copyright 1951 by Robert Frost. Used by permission of Henry Holt and Company, LLC. All rights reserved.

**Houghton Mifflin Harcourt** "Prayers of Steel" from *The Complete Poems of Carl Sandburg,* Revised and Expanded Edition, copyright © 1970, 1969 by Lilian Steichen Sandburg, Trustee, reprinted by permission of Houghton Mifflin Harcourt Publishing Company. The material may not be reproduced in any form or by any means without the prior written permission of the publisher.

**Hyperion Books for Children** "The Voyage" (including the Prologue) from *Tales From The Odyssey - Book Four: The Gray-Eyed Goddess* by Mary Pope Osborne. Copyright © 2003 by Mary Pope Osborne. Used by permission of Hyperion Books for Children. All rights reserved.

**Information Please®** "Fall of the Hindenburg" *www.infoplease.com.* Information Please® Database, Copyright © Pearson Education, Inc. All rights reserved. Used by permission.

**Jacksonville Zoo and Gardens** "Jacksonville Zoo & Gardens Leading the Charge in Northeast Florida to Save the Frogs!" from *http://www.jaxzoo.org/about/amphibianconservationpr.asp.* All content copyright © 2008 Jacksonville Zoo and Gardens. Special appreciation to Jacksonville Zoo & Gardens, Jacksonville, FL, for information on the frog crisis.

**Japan Publications, Inc.** "On sweet plum blossoms," "Has spring come indeed?" and "Temple bells die out" by Bashō from *One Hundred Famous Haiku* by Daniel C. Buchanan. Copyright © 1973. Used by permission of Japan Publications, Inc.

**Stanleigh Jones** "He-y, Come on O-ut!" by Shinichi Hoshi translated by Stanleigh Jones from *The Best Japanese Science Fiction Stories.* Reprinted with the permission of Stanleigh Jones.

**The Estate of Barbara Jordan** "All Together Now" by Barbara Jordan from *Sesame Street Parents.* Used by permission of Hilgers Bell & Richards Attorneys at Law for the Estate of Barbara Jordan.

**The Kansas City Star** "The Wrong Orbit: Senator Has No Legitimate Business Blasting Into Space" *Kansas City Star* Editorial from *The Kansas City Star, 1/20/98.* Used with permission of *The Kansas City Star* © Copyright 2007 *The Kansas City Star.* All rights reserved. Format differs from original publication. Not an endorsement.

**Kinseido Publishing Co., Ltd.** "Conversational Ballgames" by Nancy M. Sakamoto from *Polite Fictions: Why Japanese And Americans Seem Rude To Each Other.* Used by permission.

**Alfred A. Knopf, Inc.** "Mother to Son" from *The Collected Poems of Langston Hughes* by Langston Hughes, edited by Arnold Rampersad with David Roessel, Associate Editor. Copyright © 1994 by The Estate of Langston Hughes. Used by permission of Alfred A. Knopf, a division of Random House, Inc.

**Alfred A. Knopf Children's Books** "The People Could Fly" from *The People Could Fly: American Black Folktales* by Virginia Hamilton, copyright © 1985 by Virginia Hamilton, illustrations copyright © 1985 by Leo and Diane Dillon. Used by permission of Alfred A. Knopf, an imprint of Random House Children's Books, a division of Random House, Inc.

**Barbara S. Kouts Literary Agency** "The Bear Boy" by Joseph Bruchac from *Flying with the Eagle, Racing the Great Bear.* Copyright © 1993 by Joseph Bruchac. Used with permission.

**Samantha Larson** "Everest 2007" by Samantha Larson from *www.samanthalarson.blogspot.com.* Copyright © 2006 SamanthaLarson.com. Used by permission.

**Little, Brown and Company, Inc.** "The Real Story of a Cowboy's Life" (The Grandest Enterprise Under God 1865–1874) from *The West: An Illustrated History* by Geoffrey Ward. Little Brown and Company. Copyright © 1996 by The West Book Project, Inc. Used by permission.

**Gina Maccoby Literary Agency** "mk" from *Open Your Eyes* by Jean Fritz. Copyright © 2003 by Jean Fritz. Used by permission of The Gina Maccoby Literary Agency.

**Naomi Long Madgett** "Life" by Naomi Long Madgett from *One and the Many,* copyright © 1956; *Remembrances of Spring: Collected Early Poems,* copyright © 1993. Used by permission of the author.

**Dennis Martin** Chart: "Maslow's Theory of Motivation and Human Needs" by Abraham Maslow. Reprinted by permission of Dennis C. Martin, Retired Los Angeles County Public Reference Librarian and Idea Curator Webmaster and Creator of the Alphabetical Brain Vocabulary at: *www.self-lib.com*

**Meriwether Publishing Ltd.** "My Head is Full of Starshine" from *Acting Natural* by Peg Kehret, copyright © 1991 Meriwether Publishing Ltd. Used by permission.

**Eve Merriam c/o Marian Reiner** "Onomatopoeia" from *It Doesn't Always Have To Rhyme* by Eve Merriam. Copyright © 1964, 1992 Eve Merriam. Used by permission of Marian Reiner Literary Agency.

**Edna St. Vincent Millay Society** "The Courage That My Mother Had" by Edna St. Vincent Millay, from *Collected Poems,*

HarperCollins. Copyright © 1954, 1982 by Norma Millay Ellis. All rights reserved. Used by permission of Elizabeth Barnett, literary executor.

**William Morris Agency** *A Christmas Carol: Scrooge and Marley* by Israel Horovitz. Copyright © 1994 by Fountain Pen, LLC. Used by permission of William Morris Agency, LLC on behalf of the Author. All rights reserved. CAUTION: Professionals and amateurs are hereby warned that *A Christmas Carol: Scrooge and Marley* is subject to a royalty. It is fully protected under the copyright laws of the United States of America and of all countries covered by the International Copyright Union (including the Dominion of Canada and the rest of the British Commonwealth), the Berne Convention, the Pan-American Copyright Convention and the Universal Copyright Convention as well as all countries with which the United States has reciprocal copyright relations. All rights, including professional/amateur stage rights, motion picture, recitation, lecturing, public reading, radio broadcasting, television, video or sound recording, all other forms of mechanical or electronic reproduction, such as CD-ROM, CD-I, information storage and retrieval systems and photocopying, and the rights of translation into foreign languages, are strictly reserved. Particular emphasis is laid upon the matter of readings, permission for which must be secured from the Author's agent in writing. Inquiries concerning rights should be addressed to: William Morris Agency, LLC, 1325 Avenue of the Americas, New York, NY 10019, Attn: Eric Lupfer

**William Morrow & Company, Inc., a division of HarperCollins** "Winter" from *Cotton Candy On A Rainy Day* by Nikki Giovanni. Copyright © 1978 by Nikki Giovanni. Used by permission of William Morrow & Company, Inc., a division of HarperCollins Publishers, Inc.

**Naomi Shihab Nye** "The Rider" by Naomi Shihab Nye from *Invisible.* Used by permission.

**Harold Ober Associates, Inc.** "Stolen Day" by Sherwood Anderson from *This Week Magazine.* Copyright © 1941 by Sherwood Anderson. Copyright renewed © 1968 by Eleanor Copenhaver Anderson. Used by permission of Harold Ober Associates Incorporated.

**ODYSSEY Magazine (Cobblestone Publishing)** "A Special Gift—The Legacy of 'Snowflake' Bentley" by Barbara Eaglesham from *Odyssey's December 2002 Issue: Chilly Science: Ice and Snow,* Copyright © 2002, Carus Publishing Company. Published by Cobblestone Publishing, 30 Grove Street, Suite C, Peterborough, NH 03458. All rights reserved. Used by permission of the publisher.

**The Ohio State University** "Intrinsic Motivation Doesn't Exist, Researcher Says" by Jeff Grabmeier. Copyright ©. The Ohio State University Department of Research Communications.

**Ama B. Patterson** "Martin Luther King" by Raymond Richard Patterson. Used by permission of the Estate of Raymond R. Patterson.

**Pearson Education** "Joseph R. McCarthy" from *Prentice Hall United States History,* in *Prentice Hall United States History,* pp. 873–875. © Pearson Education, Inc., or it's affiliates. Used with permission. All rights reserved.

**People Weekly** "Picks & Pans: A Christmas Carol (TNT)" by Terry Kelleher from *People Weekly, December 6th, 1999, Vol.52. People Weekly* Copyright © 1999 All Rights Reserved *Time Inc.* Used by permission.

**Perseus Books** "Alligator" by Bailey White from *Mama Makes Up Her Mind And Other Dangers Of Southern Living.* Copyright © 1993 by Bailey White. Used by permission of Da Capo Press, a member of Perseus Books Group. All rights reserved.

**Piñata Books, an imprint of Arte Publico Press** "The Desert Is My Mother" is used with permission from the publisher of *My Own True Name* by Pat Mora. (Houston: Arte Publico Press - University of Houston copyright © 1985).

**Psychology Today** "Forget Fun, Embrace Enjoyment—Making the Emotion of Sport Fit a Lifetime of Competition in the Sporting Life" by Adam Naylor. Copyright © 2012, *Psychology Today.* Used by permission.

**G. P. Putnam's Sons, a division of Penguin Group (USA) Inc.** "Two Kinds" from *The Joy Luck Club* by Amy Tan, copyright © 1989 by Amy Tan. Used by permission of G.P. Putnam's Sons, a division of Penguin Group (USA) Inc.

**Random House, Inc.** "Melting Pot" from *Living Out Loud* by Anna Quindlen, copyright © 1987 by Anna Quindlen. Used by permission of Random House, Inc.

**Marian Reiner, Literary Agent** "Weather" from *Catch a Little Rhyme* by Eve Merriam. Copyright © 1966 by Eve Merriam. Copyright renewed © 1994 by Dee Michel and Guy Michel. Used by permission of Marian Reiner.

**Wendy Rose** "Loo-Wit" by Wendy Rose from *The Halfbreed Chronicles and Other Poems.* Copyright © 1985 by Wendy Rose. Used by permission.

**Salem Witch Museum** "The Salem Witch Trials of 1692" Copyright. Used with permission of the Salem Witch Museum, Salem, Massachusetts. *http://www.salemwitchmuseum.com/education*

**Santa Rosa Plateau Ecological Reserve** Rattlesnakes (park sign) from *http://www.californiaherps.com/images/signs/knowyoursnakessignmt306.jpg.*

**Scholastic Inc.** "The Great Fire" by Jim Murphy from *Scholastic Hardcover.* Copyright © 1995 by Jim Murphy. All rights reserved. Published by Scholastic Inc.

**Scribner, a division of Simon & Schuster** "Rattlesnake Hunt" from *Cross Creek* by Marjorie Kinnan Rawlings. Copyright © 1942 by Marjorie Kinnan Rawlings: copyright renewed © 1970 by Norton Baskin and Charles Scribner's Sons. From *Angela's Ashes* by Frank McCourt. Copyright © 1996 by Frank McCourt. Used by permission of Scribner, an imprint of Simon & Schuster Adult Publishing Group. All rights reserved.

**Seaside Music Theater** "Costume Rental Policy" from *www.seasidemusictheater.org.* Copyright © 2006 Seaside Music Theater. All rights reserved. Used by Permission.

**Simon & Schuster, Inc.** "A Day's Wait" from *Winner Take Nothing* by Ernest Hemingway. Copyright © 1933 Charles Scribner's Sons. Copyright renewed © 1961 by Mary Hemingway.

**Simon & Schuster Books for Young Readers** "The Fox and the Crow" from *The Fables of Aesop Selected, Told Anew and Their History Traced* by Joseph Jacobs. Copyright © 1964 Macmillan Publishing Company. Used by the permission of Simon & Schuster Books for Young Readers, an imprint of Simon & Schuster Children's Publishing Division.

**John Sousanis** "Toned-down 'Christmas Carol' has more spirit" by John Sousanis, from *The Oakland Press, November 29, 2000, Vol. 156, No. 280.* Copyright © 2000 The Oakland Press. Used by permission of John Sousanis.

**Star Tribune** "Veteran Returns, Becomes Symbol" (Original title "Astronaut Glenn: He Can Inspire America Again") from *Minneapolis Star Tribune, January 19, 1998.* Copyright © 1998 *Star Tribune,* Minneapolis, MN. Used by Permission.

**The Statue of Liberty-Ellis Island Foundation, Inc.** "Byron Yee: Discovering a Paper Son" from *http://www.ellisisland.org/immexp/wseix_3_3.asp?* Copyright © 2000 by The Statue of Liberty-Ellis Island Foundation, Inc. *www.ellisisland.org.* Used by permission.

**Tech Media Network** "Follow the Leader: Democracy in Herd Mentality" by Michael Schirber. Copyright © 2005. Used with permission of the TechMedia Network.

**Piri Thomas** "Amigo Brothers" by Piri Thomas from *Stories from El Barrio.* Used by permission of the author.

**TrueCompetition.Org** "Get More From Competition" by Christopher J. Funk and David Shields, Ph.D. Copyright © 2010. *TrueCompetition.org.* Used with permission.

**The University of Georgia** "On the Boardwalk" by Amanda E. Swennes from *Outreach,* Winter 2007. Copyright © 2007 by the University of Georgia. Used by permission. All rights reserved.

**The University of Georgia Press** "Volar: To Fly" from *The Latin Deli: Prose and Poetry.* Copyright by Judith Ortiz Cofer. Used by permission of the author and The University of Georgia Press.

**University of Notre Dame Press** From *Barrio Boy* by Ernesto Galarza. Copyright © 1971 by University of Notre Dame Press. Used by permission of the University of Notre Dame Press. All rights reserved.

**The Vagabond School of the Drama** "The Flat Rock Playhouse Apprentice Showcase ad Apprentice Application Form" from www.flatrockplayhouse.org. Used by permission.

**Viking Penguin, Inc.** From *What Makes a Rembrandt a Rembrandt?* by Richard Mühlberger. Copyright © 1993 by The Metropolitan Museum of Art. "The Other Frog Prince" by Jon Scieszka and Lane Smith from *The Stinky Cheese Man & Other Fairly Stupid Tales.* Text Copyright © Jon Scieszka, 1992. Illustration © Lane Smith, 1992. "Grasshopper Logic" from *Squids Will Be Squids: Fresh Morals, Beastly Fables by Jon Scieszka,* copyright © 1998 Jon Scieszka, text. Illustrations by Lane Smith © 1998. "Duckbilled Platypus vs. BeefSnakStik®" from *Squids Will Be Squids: Fresh Morals, Beastly Fables* by Jon Scieszka, copyright © 1998 Jon Scieszka, text. Illustrations by Lane Smith © 1998. "Sun and Moon in a Box (Zuni)" from *American Indian Trickster Tales* by Richard Erdoes and Alfonso Ortiz, copyright © 1998 by Richard Erdoes & The Estate of Alfonso Ortiz. Used by permission of Viking Penguin, a division of Penguin Young Readers Group, A member of Penguin Group (USA) Inc., 345 Hudson Street, New York, NY 10014. All rights reserved.

**The Washington Post** From *The Washington Post, 8/30/2011,* "Video game competitiveness, not violence, spurs aggression, study suggests" by Jennifer LaRue Huget. Copyright © 2011. *The Washington Post.* All rights reserved. Used by permission.

**WGBH Educational Foundation** "Harriet Tubman" by the WGBH Educational Foundation. Copyright. Used by permission of the WGBH Educational Foundation.

**The Wylie Agency, Inc.** From *Grandpa and the Statue* by Arthur Miller. Copyright © 1945 by Arthur Miller. Used with permission of The Wylie Agency. CAUTION: Professionals and amateurs are hereby warned that *Grandpa and the Statue,* being fully protected under the copyright Laws of the United States of America, the British Empire, including the Dominion of Canada, and all other countries of the Universal Copyright and Berne Conventions, are subject to royalty. All rights, including professional, amateur, motion picture, recitation, lecturing, public readin g, radio and television broadcasting, and the rights of translation into foreign languages, are strictly reserved. All inquiries for *Grandpa and the Statue* should be addressed to The Wylie Agency, Inc.

**Laurence Yep** "Ribbons" by Laurence Yep from *American Girl magazine, Jan/Feb 1992.* Used by permission of the author.

**The Young Authors Foundation, Inc.** "Zoos: Joys or Jails?" by Rachel F. from *www.teenink.com.* Copyright © 2003 by Teen Ink, The 21st Century and The Young Authors Foundation, Inc. All rights reserved. Used by permission.

**Robert Zimmerman** "Life Without Gravity" by Robert Zimmerman from *Muse Magazine, April 2002.* © 2002 Carus Publishing Company. All rights reserved. Used by permission, author Zimmerman owns the rights.

**Zoological Society of San Diego** "Kid Territory: Why Do We Need Zoos?" from *http://www.sandiegozoo.org/kids/readaboutit_why_zoos.html.* Copyright © Zoological Society of San Diego. Used by permission of the Zoological Society of San Diego.

# Credits

**Photos Credits**

Photo locators denoted as follows: Top (T), Center (C), Bottom (B), Left (L), Right (R), Background (Bkgd)

**Cover** Mikhail P./Shutterstock

18 ©Images/Corbis; 24 Underwood & Underwood/Corbis; 26 Ingram Publishing/Fotosearch; 27 Image 1/CORBIS; 27 Paolo Koch/Photo Researchers, Inc.; 29 ©Michael Nicholson/CORBIS; 30 Paolo Koch/Photo Researchers, Inc.; 32 Joel Simon/Getty Images; 34 © Punchstock/Getty; 35 Joel Simon/Getty Images; 36 R. Dev/Photo Researchers, Inc.; 40 Gallo Images/CORBIS; 42 Mark Smith/Photo Researchers, Inc; 46 Marc Brasz/CORBIS; 48 Simon Marcus/CORBIS; 52 ©Tomasz Markowski/Shutterstock; 53 (R) Lawrence Manning/CORBIS, (Inset) Photo by CBS Photo Archive/Getty Images; 56 Charles E. Rotkin/CORBIS; 57 © Oleksiy Maksymenko/Alamy; 59 Rubberball/Superstock; 60 Newmann/CORBIS; 61 John Molloy/Getty Images; 68 Pearson Education, Inc. 69 ©Svetlana Larina/Shutterstock; 70 ©Svetlana Larina/Shutterstock; 72©Tatsiana_S/Shutterstock; 75 ©Tatsiana_S/Shutterstock; 76 ©Potapov Alexander/Shutterstock; 77 ©Svetlana Larina/Shutterstock; 79 Courtesy of the Library of Congress; 80 Prentice Hall; 82 © Alinari Archives/CORBIS; 83 ©Bert de Ruiter/Alamy; 84 ©Bettmann/CORBIS; 86 Topham/The Image Works; 86 ©3 song photography/Shutterstock; 88 ©ivy photo/Shutterstock; 89 ©Tad Denson/Shutterstock; 90 © Ryan Pyle/Corbis; 91 (R) Stockbyte,(L) Shubroto Chattopadhyay/CORBIS; 92 Alex Mares-Manton/Getty; 98 ©Mikael Damkier/Shutterstock; 100 ©clearviewstock/Fotolia; 102–104 My Life and Hard Times Copyright ©1933 by James Thurber. Copyright © renewed 1961 by James Thurber. Reprinted by arrangement with Rosemary A. Thurber and The Barbara Hogenson Agency.; 106 ©Mikael Damkier/Shutterstock; 110 © Punchstock; 112 Louis Fox/Getty Images; 113 ©Mikael Damkier/Shutterstock; 132 J&L Images/Photodisc/Getty Images; 134 (T) Nice One Productions/CORBIS,(B) Matthias Haker Photography/Flickr/Getty Images; 136 Nice One Productions/CORBIS; 137 Hans Neleman/Getty Images; 140 ©David Madison, 2013; 148 ©EtiAmmos/Shutterstock; 152 ©Denis Kuvaev/Shutterstock; 153 Adam Naylor; 156 ©Andi Berger/Shutterstock; 158 ©Karim Kadim/AP Photo; 160 ©Berit Roald/AFP/Getty Images/Newscom; 161 Gary Gershoff/WireImage/Getty Images; 172 ©Alex White/Fotolia; 181 Album/Art Resource, NY; 181 Pearson Education, Inc.; 186 ©Bruce Rolff/Shutterstock; 194 ©Alan Uster/Shutterstock; 195 N.A.S.A./JF Kennedy Library; 198 NASA/Photo Researchers, Inc.; 202 Bettmann/CORBIS; 204 ©WorldFoto/Alamy; 206 Stephen Dunn/Staff/Getty Images; 212 ©Tim Sharp/AP Photo; 214 Terry Ashe/Time Life Pictures/Getty Images; 215 ©Lightspring/Shutterstock; 216 Dirk Anschutz/Stone/Getty Images; 220 AP/Wide World Photos; 222 © Dorling Kindersley; 224 ©Eric Isselée/Fotolia; 225 Judith Miller/Dorling Kindersley/Morning Star Gallery; 226 Jerry Young/© Dorling Kindersley; 227 Peter Arnold/Getty; 232 ©BestPhotoPlus/Shutterstock; 234 Stockbyte/Getty Images, Inc; 236 Cusp/SuperStock; 239 Francis G. Mayer/Corbis; 240 ©BestPhotoPlus/Shutterstock; 241 ©Adam Gryko/Shutterstock; 242 ©BestPhotoPlus/Shutterstock; 245 ©BestPhotoPlus/Shutterstock; 264 Forest Woodward/Vetta/Getty Images; 266 © H. Armstrong Roberts/CORBIS; 273 Yvonne Hemsey/Getty Images; 278 ©chrisbrignell/Shutterstock; 281 Dominic DiSaia/Blend Images/SuperStock; 284 ©Robin Heal/Shutterstock; 287 (BL) Getty Images, (R) ©mangojuicy/Shutterstock; 290 (L) Snow Crystals by W.A. Bentley and W.J. Humphreys, Dover Publications, (Border) ©Scott Camazine/Photo Researchers, Inc.; (Bkgd) ©Dudarev Mikhail/Shutterstock; 292 (Bkgd) ©Dudarev Mikhail/Shutterstock, (Border) ©Scott Camazine/Photo Researchers, Inc.; 296 ©Transia_art/Shutterstock; 296 ©Digital-Clipart/Shutterstock; 299 ©Digital-Clipart/Shutterstock; 308 Library of Congress; 310 ©Images/Corbis; 318 Cheron Bayna; 322 ©rolffimages/Fotolia; 330 (BCL) Oscar/CORBIS, (TCL) HANDOUT/KRT/Newscom, (T)(c) Jan Cobb, (B) Snark/Art Resource; 331 Ken Canning/E+/Getty Images; 332 Corey Hochachka/DesignPics/IPNStock; 334 Phillip Colla/Oceanlight; 336 ©ori-artiste/Shutterstock; 342 Time Life Pictures/Getty Images; 343 Steve Allen/Jupiter Images; 344 (T) The Newark Museum/Art Resource, NY, (Bkgd) ©Alexpi/Shutterstock; 345 ©David Pinzer Photography/Image Source/Corbis; 346 (C) istockphoto, (Bkgd) ©Radoslaw Lecyk/Shutterstock; 352 (T) G. Paul Bishop, (TCL) ©Georgios Kollidas/Fotolia, (B) 352 ©Jeff Albertson/CORBIS; 354–355 ©Gary Bell/Corbis; 356–357 ©1974, renewed 202 EVIL EYE, LLC. Reprinted with permission from the Estate of Shel Silverstein and Harper Collins Children's Books.; 358 C Squared Studios/Getty Images; 364 (TCL) Bettmann/CORBIS, (BCL) Bettmann/CORBIS, (T) Time Life Pictures/Getty Images, (B) © Nancy Crampton; 365 Martin Zwick/age fotostock/SuperStock; 366 ©Vlue/Shutterstock; 368 The Granger Collection, New York; 370 ©Andrey_Popov/Shutterstock; 374 (CL) Bettmann/CORBIS, (CR) Library of Congress, (L) ©Steven Sum/Shutterstosck, (R) ©Leonid Tit/Fotolia; 376 ©Leonid Tit/Fotolia; 380 Seth Joel/Photographer's Choice RF/Getty Images; 398 ©Fine Art Photographic Library/CORBIS; 400 ©ollirg/Fotolia; 405 Time Life Pictures/Getty Images; 411 ©Bettmann/CORBIS; 412 ©St Petersburg Times/ZUMAPRESS/Newscom; 416 ©adoc-photos/Corbis; 420 The Granger Collection; 421 Thomas Northcut/Getty Images; 423 Seth Resnick/Corbis; 426 ©Kar/Shutterstock; 429 Bettmann/Corbis; 432 ©North Wind Picture Archives/Alamy; 436 ©Glasshouse Images/Alamy; 442 AP Photo/Craig Line; 444–445 ©photo-bank.kiev.ua/Shutterstock; 453 Boston Productions/Prentice Hall; 460 Lou Jones/Lonely Planet Images/Getty Images; 466 © Steve Azzara/Sygma/Corbis; 468 ©Dorling Kindersley Ltd; 469 ©Dorling Kindersley Ltd; 469 ©Dorling Kindersley Ltd; 470, 471, 472, 475 ©Dorling Kindersley Ltd; 476 Mary Evans Picture Library; 479 ©Dorling Kindersley Ltd; 481, 483, 486, 489, 491, 493, 494, 502, 503, 505, 509, 511 ©Dorling Kindersley Ltd; 512 David Toase/Getty Images; 515 ©Dorling Kindersley Ltd; 518 ©Dorling Kindersley Ltd; 519 ©Dorling Kindersley Ltd; 523 ©Dorling Kindersley Ltd; 524 ©Dorling Kindersley Ltd; 528 (CL)Renown/The Kobal Collection/Art Resource, NY, 528 Photofest; 531 ©Dorling Kindersley Ltd; 534 Michal Daniel; 539 Ralph A. Clevenger/CORBIS; 540 Buddy Mays/CORBIS; 541 David W. Hamilton/Getty Images, Inc; 550 ©Dorling Kindersley Ltd; 562 ©Associated Press; 564 (BL) ©CBS/Landov, (Bkgd) William Whitehurst/Corbis; 569, 572, 580, 581, 582 ©CBS/Landov; 583 Bettmann/CORBIS; 588 (Bkgd) ©koka55/Shutterstock,Tom Grill/Photographer's Choice RF/Getty Images 590 ©koka55/Shutterstock; 593 Punchstock; 595 (B) AP/Wide World Photos, (T) ©William Silver/Shutterstock; 598 ©Bettmann/CORBIS; 600 ©Bettmann/CORBIS; 604 ©Peabody Essex Museum, Salem, Massachusetts, USA/The Bridgeman Art Library; 609 ©Angelo Merendino/Corbis; 611 ©Orjan F. Ellingvag/Dagens Naringsliv/Corbis; 614 ©Steven Sum/Shutterstosck; 617 ©Frank Parker/age fotostock/SuperStock; 620 Jose Luis Magana/AP Images; 626 ASSOCIATED PRESS; 628 Anthony Pappone/Flickr/Getty Images; 636 Prentice Hall; 640 ©Martin Puddy/Corbis; 648 ©Christie's Images/The Bridgeman Art Library; 652 Leeds Museums and Galleries (City Art Gallery) U.K.; 653 (TL) The Granger Collection; 653 (BL) Andrea Jemolo/CORBIS, (BR) Massimo Listri/Corbis; (BC) Mimmo Jodice/Corbis, (CR) Andrea Jemolo/Corbis, (BCL)©espion/Fotolia; 660 ©Daniel Prudek/Shutterstock; 662 Private Collection/Bridgeman Art Library; 663 Werner Forman/Corbis; 664 The Art Archive/Museo Franz Mayer Mexico/Gianni Dagli Orti/The Picture Desk/Art Resource-NY; 665 Museum fur Volkerkunde, Vienna, Austria/The Bridgeman Art Library; 666 Charles & Josette Lenara/CORBIS; 667 Biblioteca Nacional de Mexico, Mexico/Giraudon/The Bridgeman Art Library; 668 Ullses Ruiz/epa/Corbis; 684 Book Cover illustrated by Leo and Diane Dillon, ©1985 by Knopf Children, from THE PEOPLE COULD FLY AMERICAN BLACK FOLKTALES by Virginia Hamilton, illustrated by Leo and Diane Dillon. Used by permission of Alfred A. Knopf, an imprint of Random House Children's Books, a division of Random House, Inc. Any third party use of this material, outside

of this publication, is prohibited.; 686 ©Robert Adrian Hillman/ Shutterstock; 694 bpk, Berlin/Dietmar Katz/Art Resource, NY; 698 Samantha Larson; 700 Samantha Larson; 701 Samantha Larson; 703 Samantha Larson; 705 Samantha Larson; 707 (BR) ©Daniel Prudek/ Shutterstock, (TR)bpk, Berlin/Dietmar Katz/Art Resource, NY; 726 ©Bettmann/CORBIS; 728 (Bkgd) ©Rafael Martin-Gaitero/Shutterstock, (B) ©kaktuzoid/Shutterstock; 731 Ramon Espinosa/Associated Press; 737 (L) Gregory Djanikian, (R) Duomo/Corbis; 740 Reprinted by permission of The Gina Maccoby Literary Agency. Copyright©1982 by Jean Fritz; 741 Doug Landreth/Corbis; 742 Hulton-Deutsch Collection/Corbis; 744 Hulton-Deutsch Collection/Corbis; 746 Reprinted by permission of The Gina Maccoby Literary Agency. Copyright©1982 by Jean Fritz; 749 Reprinted by permission of The Gina Maccoby Literary Agency. Copyright©1982 by Jean Fritz; 752 Time Life Pictures/National Archives/ Time Life Pictures/Getty Images; 756 Reed Kaestner/Corbis; 759 Courtesy of the Library of Congress; 760 The Granger Collection, New York; 761 Sophie Bassouls/CORBIS Sygma; 764 ©Franz Marc Frei/LOOK/ Photoshot; 766 Jeremy Horner/CORBIS; 776 Pearson Education, Inc.

## Staff Credits

Dori Amtmann, Tricia Battipede, Rachel Beckman, Nancy Bolsover, Laura Brancky, Odette Calderon, Pam Carey, Kelly Casanova, Geoff Cassar, Jessica Cohn, Kyle Cooper, Sarah Cunningham, Anthony DeSacia, Kim Doster, Irene Ehrmann, Andy Ekedahl, Sandy Engleman, Samantha Fahy, Janet Fauser, Amy Fleming, Pam Gallo, Mark Gangi, Nicole Gee, Susan Graef, Leslie Griffin, Elaine Goldman, Brian Hawkes, Steve Hernacki, Martha Heller, Amanda House, Rick Hickox, Patricia Isaza, Etta Jacobs, Blair Jones, Jim Kelly, Nathan Kinney, Sarah Kraus, Gregory Lynch, Nancy Mace, Jim McPherson, Charles Morris, Pa Moua, Elizabeth Nielsen, Kim Ortell, Kathleen Pagliaro, Jennie Rakos, Sheila Ramsay, Karen Randazzo, Julianne Regnier, Christopher Richardson, Melissa Schreiner, Hillary Schwei, Jeff Shagawat, Susan Sheehan, Charlene Smith, DeAnn Smith, Sheila Smith, Cynthia Summers, Morgan Taylor, Brian Thomas, Lucia Tirondola, Karen Tully, Merle Uuesoo, Kristen Varina, Jackie Westbrook, Jessica White